QUANTITATIVE APTITUDE

QUANTITATIVE APTITUDE

for

COMPETITIVE EXAMINATIONS

Highly recommended for:

- IBPS PO / SBI PO / Specialist Officers' Exam / RBI
- UPSC Exams: Civil Services / NDA / CDS Forest & Engineering Services etc.
- LIC / GIC AAO & ADO Exam
- SSC Exam for Asstt. Grade / CPO-SI / CBI / Income Tax Inspectors
- Railway Recruitment Board Exam
- CTET and STET
- CLAT
- MAT / CAT / IIFT / IGNOU / GRE / Hotel Management
- Campus Selection Tests etc.

Dipak Kumar Yugnirmal

Publisher

UNICORN BOOKS

F-2/16, Ansari Road, Daryaganj, New Delhi-110002
☎ 011-23275434, 23262683, 23250704 • *Fax:* 011-23257790
E-mail: info@unicornbooks.in • *Website:* www.unicornbooks.in

Branch : Mumbai
23-25, Zaoba Wadi, Thakurdwar, Mumbai-400002
☎ 022-22010941, 022-22053387
E-mail: rapidex@bom5.vsnl.net.in

ISBN 978-81-7806-373-7

Edition: 2016

Printed at : Param Offsetters, Okhla, New Delhi-110020

Preface

This book of Quantitative Aptitude has been written especially for the aspirants of almost all competitive exams like Bank PO, SBI-PO, IBPS, RBI Exam, Bank Specialist officers' Exam, UPSC, Railway Recruitment Boards Exams, SSC Combined Preliminary Exam, IGNOU, NDA, NIFT, Hotel Management, Sub-Inspector of Police, CBI, CPO Exam, Bank Clerk, TET, Campus Recruitment Tests and all management exams including CAT, MAT, GMAT etc.

For developing a practical, concise and yet a comprehensive book emphasis has been given to the trends of previous years' exams and the needs and requirements of the students/aspirants in a balanced manner.

Unlike most other books, this book covers a wide range of topics without complicating them.

Each chapter starts with the basic and essential description of the mathematical theorems and formulae followed by a section of solved examples. Then comes the part 'Exercises' - starting with simpler problems and then moving on to difficult ones - which tests the student's knowledge and understanding of the subject and at the same time develops it further. Each exercise contains Multiple Choice Questions and their Answers. Many difficult problems are also provided with Explanatory notes to help the students master their skills.

Not only will this book prepare a student for any quantitative aptitude section of a competitive exam, but it's great for job placement tests as well. It is one of the best reference guides that will help an aspirant get his elementary mathematics right.

Lastly, I request all my readers to let me know the errors and deficiencies which, in-spite of my best efforts, might have crept in; and also to send me their suggestions so that I can improve upon the content of this book further.

Dipak Kumar Yugnirmal

CONTENTS

SECTION-I

ARITHMETICAL ABILITY

1. NUMBER SYSTEM

Quantitative aptitude deals mainly with the different topics in Arithmetic, which is the Science providing relations of numbers to one another. It includes all the methods that are applicable to numbers.

Numbers are expressed by means of figures 1, 2, 3, 4, 5, 6, 7, 8, 9 and 0 — called digits. Out of these 0 is called insignificant digit whereas the others are called significant digits.

We also have Binary Number System. It uses only 0 and 1. There are other Number Systems too.

Every digit in a number has a **face value** and a **place value.** The **face value** of a digit equals the value of the digit itself, irrespective of its place in the numeral.

For determining the **place value** of the digit in a given number we begin from the extreme right as Unit's place, Ten's place, Hundred's place, Thousand's place and so on. It has been illustrated with an example given below :

The number 5394728316 may be represented as:

Billion	*Ten Crore's*	*Crone's*	*Ten Lac's (million)*	*Lac's*	*Ten Thousand's*	*Thousand's*	*Hundred's*	*Ten's*	*Unit's*
10^9	10^8	10^7	10^6	10^5	10^4	10^3	10^2	10^1	10^0
5	3	9	4	7	2	8	3	1	6

CLASSIFICATION OF NUMBERS

Natural Numbers: These are also called counting numbers as these are the numbers we use for counting purposes. The set of natural numbers is represented by

N: {1, 2, 3, 4....}.

Whole Numbers: These include all natural numbers plus zero. So, we can denote the set of whole numbers by W: {0, 1, 2, 3....}.

Integers: These include all whole numbers along with negative numbers. The set is represented by

I: {.... –5, –4, –3, –2, –1, 0, 1, 2, 3, ...}

Thus, we see that whole numbers consist of positive integers and zero. Similarly, natural numbers consist of positive integers.

Even Numbers: A number which is completely divisible by 2 is called an even number. In other words; such numbers have 2 as one of their factors. For example

: ...., –4, –2, 0, 2, 4, 6, 8, ...

Here $-4 = \mathbf{2}(-2)$, $8 = \mathbf{2} \times 4$, $30 = \mathbf{2} \times 3 \times 5$

Other examples of even numbers are 2, 4, 6, 8, 10..... (A number is said to be a factor or sub-multiple of another when it divides the other exactly)

For example, 2 and 3 are factors of 6.

Odd Numbers: These numbers are not completely divisible by 2. In other words, a number which is not even is an odd number.

For example, ... –3, –1, 1, 3, 5, 7, 9......

It may be noted that zero is an exception to this even-odd classification.

Cyclic Numbers: A cyclic number is such an integer of *n* digits which on being multiplied by some integer gives a product containing the same n digits as in the original number and these digits are in the same cyclic order in the product.

For example, 142857 is a cyclic number, as

1 × 142857 = 142857	4 × 142857 = 571428
2 × 142857 = 285714	5 × 142857 = 714285
3 × 142857 = 428571	6 × 142857 = 857142

It is clear that in each product the digits of given number 142857 appear in the cyclic order.

Fractions: A fraction is a number which represents a ratio or division of two integers. It is expressed in the form $\frac{p}{q}$ where '*p*' and '*q*' are integers. '*p*' is called the numerator and '*q*' is called the denominator.

A fraction cannot have zero ($q \neq 0$) as its denominator since division by zero is not defined.

Zero divided by any non-zero integer is always zero.

A fraction with 1 as the denominator is the same as the whole number which is its numerator.

For example, $\frac{8}{1}$ is 8; $\frac{0}{1}$ is 0.

Equivalent Fractions: Two fractions are said to be equivalent if they represent the same ratio or number. So, if we multiply or divide the numerator and denominator of a fraction by the same non-zero integer, the result obtained will be equivalent to the original fraction.

For example, $\frac{2}{7} = \frac{3\times 2}{3\times 7} = \frac{6}{21}$; $\quad \frac{15}{25} = \frac{\frac{15}{5}}{\frac{25}{5}} = \frac{3}{5}$

Real Number: Any measurement carried out in the physical world gives some meaningful figure or value or number. This number is called **Real Number.** It consists of two groups:

(*i*) Rational Number: A rational number can always be represented by a fraction of the form $\frac{p}{q}$, where p and q are integers and q is not equal to zero ($q \neq 0$). All integers and fractions are rational numbers.

For example, $2\left(=\frac{2}{1}\right), \frac{2}{3}, \frac{4}{5}, \frac{6}{13}$ etc.

(*ii*) Irrational Number: An irrational number can't be expressed in the form of $\frac{p}{q}$, where $q \neq 0$.

For example, $\sqrt{3}, \sqrt{2}$. It gives only an approximate answer in the form of a fraction or decimal number. The digits after the decimal point are non-ending. The same holds true for $\pi = 3.14$....... which again is irrational. Alternatively, we can say that an infinite non-recurring decimal number is an irrational number.

Prime Number: A prime number is a number which has no factor besides itself and unity, i.e; it is divisible only by itself and 1 but not by any other number.

For example: 2, 3, 5, 7, 11, 17, 19, 23, 29, 31, 37, 41, 43, 47, 53, 59, 61, 67, 71, 73, 79, 83, 89, 97, 101, 103, 107.

Note: (*i*) '2' is the only even number which is prime.

(*ii*) All prime numbers other than 2 are odd numbers but all odd numbers are not prime numbers. For example, 9 is an odd number but it is not a prime number as it is divisible by 3.

(*iii*) The largest prime number known so far is $2^{2281} - 1$ which is of about 700 digits.

Composite Number: A composite number is one which has other factors besides itself and unity. Thus, it is a non-prime number. For example, 4, 6, 9, 14, 15 etc.

Note: (*i*) '1' is neither prime nor composite.

(*ii*) A composite number may be even or odd.

The number of ways in which a number N can be expressed as product of two factors which are relatively prime to each other is $\mathbf{2^{m-1}}$, where m is the number of different prime factors of N.

For example, $540 = 2^2 \times 3^3 \times 5 \quad (= 4 \times 27 \times 5)$

$\therefore$ $m = 3(i.e., 2, 3, 5)$

$\therefore$ No. of ways $= 2^{3-1} = 4$

i.e., 20×27, 4×135, 108×5, 540×1.

Consecutive Integers: These are series of numbers differing by 1 in ascending or descending order.

For example, 12, 13, 14, 15.....

Similarly, examples of consecutive even numbers are

4, 6, 8, 10 .... 22, 24, 26, 28 ..... and so on.

Examples of consecutive prime numbers are

7, 11, 13, 17....

DIVISIBILITY

Divisibility by 2

Rule: Any number, the last digit of which is either even or 0, is divisible by 2.

For example: 12,86,130,568926 and 5983450 are divisible by 2 but 13,133 and 596351 are not divisible by 2.

Divisibility by 3

Rule: If the sum of the digits of a number is divisible by 3, the number is also divisible by 3.

For example: 123 : 1 + 2 + 3 = 6 is divisible by 3; hence 123 is also divisible by 3.

Divisibility by 4

Rule: If the last two digits of a number is divisible by 4, the number is divisible by 4. The number having two or more zeros at the end is also divisible by 4.

For example: 526428 : 28 is divisible by 4, therefore, the number is divisible by 4.

Note: The same rule is applicable to check the divisibility by 25. That is, a number is divisible by 25 if its last two digits are either zeros or divisible by 25.

Divisibility by 5

Rule: If a number ends in 5 or 0, the number is divisible by 5.

For example: 1345 : As its last digit is 5, it is divisible by 5.

Divisibility by 6

Rule: If a number is divisible by both 3 and 2, the number is also divisible by 6. So, for a number to be divisible by 6,

1. The number should end with an even digit or 0 and
2. The sum of its digits should be divisible by 3.

For example: 63924: The first condition is fulfilled as the last digit (4) is an even number and also the sum of digits (6 + 3 + 9 + 2 + 4 =) 24 is divisible by 3; therefore, the number is divisible by 6.

Divisibility by 7

First of all we recall the osculator for 7. for your convenience, as $7 \times 3 = 21$ (one more than $\underline{2} \times 10$), our negative osculator is 2. This osculator '2' is our key-digit. This and only this digit is used to check the divisibility of any number by 7. See how it works:

1. Is 112 divisible by 7?

Sol. Step I. $\underline{11}\ \underline{2}$: $11 - 2 \times 2 = 7$

As 7 is divisible by 7, the number 112 is also divisible by 7.

2. Is 2961 divisible by 7?

Sol. Step I: $\underline{296}\ \underline{1}$: $296 - 1 \times 2 = 294$

Step II: $\underline{29}\ \underline{4}$: $29 - 4 \times 2 = 21$

As 21 is divisible by 7, the number is also divisible by 7.

Divisibility by 8

Rule: If the last three digits of a number is divisible by 8, the number is also divisible by 8. Also, if the last three digits of a number are zeros, the number is divisible by 8.

For example: 135923120 : as 120 is divisible by 8, the number is also divisible by 8.

Note: The same rule is applicable to check the divisibility by 125.

Divisibility by 9

Rule: If the sum of all the digits of a number is divisible by 9, the number is also divisible by 9.

For example: 39681 : 3 + 9 + 6 + 8 + 1 = 27 is divisible by 9, hence the number is also divisible by 9.

Divisibility by 10

Rule: Any number which ends with zero is divisible by 10. There is no need to discuss this rule.

Divisibility by 11

Rule: If the sums of digits at odd and even places are equal or differ by a number divisible by 11, then the number is also divisible by 11.

1. 3245682 : $S_1 = 3 + 4 + 6 + 2 = 15$ and $S_2 = 2 + 5 + 8 = 15$

As $S_1 = S_2$, the number is divisible by 11.

Divisibility by 12

Rule: Any number which is divisible by both 4 and 3, is also divisible by 12.

To check the divisibility by 12, we

1. first divide the last two-digit number by 4. If it is not divisible by 4, the number is not divisible by 12. If it is divisible by 4 then
2. check whether the number is divisible by 3 or not.

1. 135792 : 92 is divisible by 4 and also (1 + 3 + 5 + 7 + 9 + 2 =) 27 is divisible by 3; hence the number is divisible by 12.

Divisibility by 13

Osculator for 13 is 4. But this time our osculator is not negative (as in case of 7). It is 'one-more' osculator. So, the working will be different now. This can be seen in the following examples.

1. Is 143 divisible by 13?

Sol. $\underline{14}\ \underline{3}$: $14 + 3 \times 4 = 26$

Since 26 is divisible by 13, the number 143 is also divisible by 13.

or,

This working may further be simplified as :

Step I: 1 4 3

16 [4 × 3 (from 14$\underline{3}$) + 4 (from 1$\underline{4}$3)]

Step II: 26/16 [4 × 6 (from 1 $\underline{6}$) + 1 (from $\underline{1}$6) + 1 (from $\underline{1}$43) = 26]

As 26 is divisible by 13, the number is also divisible by 13.

Note: The working of second method is also very systematic. At the same time it is more acceptable because it has less writing work.

Divisibility by 14

Any number which is divisible by both 2 and 7, in also divisible by 14. That is, the number's last digit should be even and at the same time the number should be divisible by 7.

Divisibility by 15

Any number which is divisible by both 3 and 5 is also divisible by 15.

Divisibility by 16

Any number whose last 4 digit number is divisible by 16 is also divisible by 16.

Divisibility by 17

Negative osculator for 17 is 5 (see note). The working for this is the same as in the case of 7.

1. Check the divisibility of 1904 by 17.

Sol. $\underline{190}\ \underline{4}$: 190 – 5 × 4 = 170

Since 170 is divisible by 17, the given number is also divisible by 17.

Note: Students are suggested not to go up to the last calculation. Whenever you find the number divisible by the given number on right side of your calculation, stop further calculation and conclude the result.

Divisibility by 18

Rule: Any number which is divisible by 9 and has its last digit (unit-digit) even (or zero), is divisible by 18.

For example: 926568 : Digit-sum is multiple of nine (i.e., divisible by 9) and unit-digit (8) is even, hence the number is divisible by 18.

Divisibility by 19

If you recall, the 'one-more' osculator for 19 is 2. The method is similar to that of 13, which is well known to you. Let us take an example.

For example: 146264

Sol. 1 4 9 2 6 4
19/9/12/11/14
Thus, our number is divisible by 19.

Note: You must have understood the working (see the case of 13).

SOLVED EXAMPLE

1. In a three digit number the digit in the unit's place is twice the digit in the ten's place and 1.5 times the digit in the hundred's place. If the sum of all the three digits of the number is 13, what is the number?

(*a*) 364 (*b*) 436 (*c*) 238 (*d*) 634

Sol. (*b*) Let the ten's digit be x.

$\therefore$ Unit's digit = $2x$

and hundred's digits = $\frac{2x}{1.5}$

According to the question,

$$x + 2x + \frac{2x}{1.5} = 13 \quad \Rightarrow \quad 6.5x = 13 \times 1.5$$

$$\Rightarrow x = \frac{13 \times 1.5}{6.5} = 3$$

∴ Unit's digit = 6 and hundred's digit $= \frac{6}{1.5} = 4$

∴ Number = 436

2. Two numbers are less than the third number by 50% and 54% respectively. By how much percent is the second number less than the first number?

(*a*) 13 (*b*) 10 (*c*) 12 (*d*) None of these

Sol. (*d*) Let the third number be 100.

∴ First number = 50 and

Second number = 100 – 54 = 46

Decrease = 50 – 46 = 4

∴ Required percentage $= \frac{4}{50} \times 100 = 8$

3. If $(28)^3$ is subtracted from the square of a number, the answer so obtained is 1457. What is the number?

(*a*) 127 (*b*) 136 (*c*) 142 (*d*) 153

Sol. (*d*) Let the number be x.

According to the question,

$x^2 - (28)^3 = 1457$

$\Rightarrow x^2 - 21952 = 1457 \Rightarrow x^2 = 21952 + 1457 = 23409$

$\Rightarrow x = \sqrt{23409} = 153$

4. The difference between a number and $\frac{2}{5}$th of the number is 30. The number is

(*a*) 57 (*b*) 50 (*c*) 75 (*d*) None of these

Sol. (*b*) Let the number be x.

According to the question,

$$x - \frac{2x}{5} = 30 \Rightarrow \frac{3x}{5} = 30 \Rightarrow x = \frac{30 \times 5}{3} = 50$$

5. What is the greater of two numbers whose product is 1092 and the sum of the two numbers exceeds their difference by 42?

(*a*) 48 (*b*) 44 (*c*) 52 (*d*) 54

Sol. (*c*) Let the numbers be x and y respectively.

According to the question,

$x + y - (x - y) = 42$

$\Rightarrow 2y = 42$

$\Rightarrow y = \frac{42}{2} = 21 \qquad \therefore x = \frac{1092}{21} = 52$

6. The difference between 58% of a number and 39% of the same number is 247. What is 62% of that number?

(*a*) 1300 (*b*) 806 (*c*) 754 (*d*) 1,170

Sol. (*b*) Let the number be x.

According to the question,

$(58 - 39)\%$ of $x = 247$

$\Rightarrow \quad x \times \frac{19}{100} = 247 \qquad \Rightarrow x = \frac{247 \times 100}{19} = 1300$

$\therefore \quad 62\%$ of $1300 = 1300 \times \frac{62}{100} = 806$

7. If the sum of four consecutive even numbers is 228, which is the smallest of the numbers?

(*a*) 52 (*b*) 54 (*c*) 56 (*d*) 48

Sol. (*b*) According to the question,

$x + x + 2 + x + 4 + x + 6 = 228$

$\Rightarrow \quad 4x + 12 = 228 \Rightarrow 4x = 228 - 12 = 216$

$\therefore \quad x = \frac{216}{4} = 54$

$\therefore$ The smallest even number = 54.

8. The total number of integers between 200 and 400, each of which either begins with 3 or ends with 3 or both, is

(*a*) 10 (*b*) 100 (*c*) 110 (*d*) 120

Sol. (*c*) When 3 lies at hundreds place

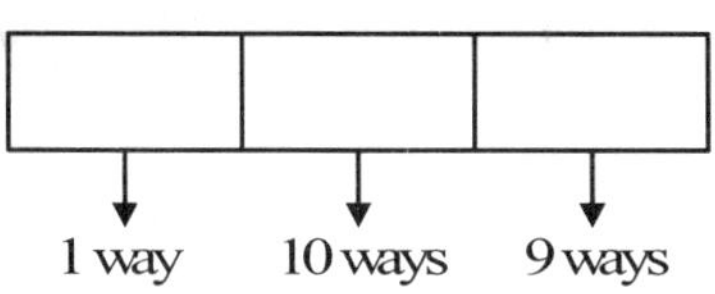

$\therefore$ Total integers $= 10 \times 9 = 90$

When 3 lies at units place

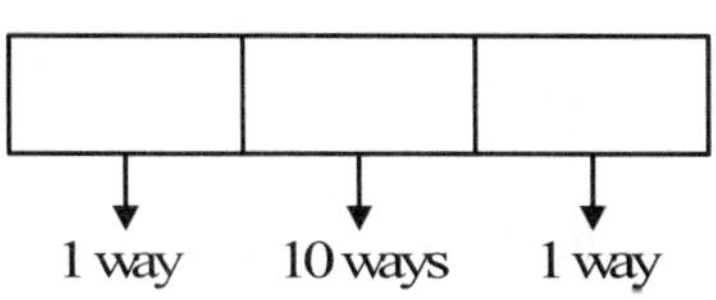

Total integers = 10

When 3 lies at unit's and hundred's place

Total integers = 10

$\therefore$ Total integers $= 90 + 10 + 10 = 110$

9. If a and b are two distinct natural numbers, which one of the following is true?

(a) $\sqrt{a+b} > \sqrt{a} + \sqrt{b}$ (b) $\sqrt{a+b} = \sqrt{a} + \sqrt{b}$

(c) $\sqrt{a+b} < \sqrt{a} + \sqrt{b}$ (d) $ab = 1$

Sol. (c) $\left(\sqrt{a+b}\right)^2 = a+b$

$\left(\sqrt{a}+\sqrt{b}\right)^2 = a+b+2\sqrt{ab}$

Here, $a + b < a + b + 2\sqrt{ab}$

Clearly, $\sqrt{a+b} < \sqrt{a} + \sqrt{b}$

EXERCISE

1. 7589 – ? = 3434

(a) 4242 (b) 4155 (c) 1123 (d) 11023

2. 3251 + 587 + 369 – ? = 3007

(a) 1250 (b) 1300 (c) 1375 (d) 1200

3. 4300731 – ? = 2535618

(a) 1865113 (b) 1775123 (c) 1765113 (d) 1675123

4. $9\frac{3}{4} + 7\frac{2}{17} - 9\frac{1}{15} = ?$

(a) $7\frac{719}{1020}$ (b) $9\frac{817}{1020}$ (c) $9\frac{719}{1020}$ (d) $7\frac{817}{1020}$

5. –84 × 29 + 365 = ?

(a) 2436 (b) 2801 (c) –2801 (d) –2071

6. 4500 × ? = 3375

(a) $\frac{2}{5}$ (b) $\frac{3}{4}$ (c) $\frac{1}{4}$ (d) $\frac{3}{5}$

7. $(1000)^9 + 10^{24} = ?$

(a) 10000 (b) 1000 (c) 100 (d) 10

8. (800 ÷ 64) × (1296 ÷ 36) = ?

(a) 420 (b) 460 (c) 500 (d) none of these

9. $(12)^3 \times 6^4 \div 432 = ?$

(a) 5184 (b) 5060 (c) 5148 (d) none of these

10. 217 × 217 + 183 × 183 = ?

(a) 79698 (b) 80578 (c) 80698 (d) 81268

11. What is the unit digit in 7^{105} ?

(a) 2 (b) 3 (c) 4 (d) 7

12. What is the unit digit in the product $(3^{65} \times 6^{59} \times 7^{71})$?
(*a*) 1 (*b*) 2 (*c*) 4 (*d*) 6

13. On dividing a number by 56, we get 29 as remainder. On dividing the same number by 8, what will be the remainder?
(*a*) 4 (*b*) 5 (*c*) 6 (*d*) 7

14. On dividing a number by 5, we get 3 as remainder. What will be the remainder when the square of this number is divided by 5?
(*a*) 0 (*b*) 1 (*c*) 2 (*d*) 4

15. How many of the following numbers are divisible by 132?
264, 396, 462, 792, 968, 2178, 5184, 6336
(*a*) 4 (*b*) 5 (*c*) 6 (*d*) 7

16. On dividing a number by 357, we get 39 as remainder. On dividing the same number by 17, what will be the remainder?
(*a*) 0 (*b*) 3 (*c*) 5 (*d*) 11

17. Which one of the following numbers is exactly divisible by 11?
(*a*) 235641 (*b*) 245642 (*c*) 315624 (*d*) 415624

18. On dividing a number by 68, we get 269 as dividend and 0 as remainder. On dividing the same number by 67, what will be the remainder?
(*a*) 0 (*b*) 1 (*c*) 2 (*d*) 3

19. In a division sum, the remainder is 0. A student mistook the divisor by 12 instead of 21 and obtained 35 as quotient. What is the correct quotient?
(*a*) 0 (*b*) 12 (*c*) 13 (*d*) 20

20. On dividing 2272 as well as 875 by 3-digit number N, we get the same remainder. The sum of the digits of N is:
(*a*) 10 (*b*) 11 (*c*) 12 (*d*) 13

21. The difference of two numbers is 1365. On dividing the larger number by the smaller, we get 6 as quotient and 15 as remainder. What is the smaller number?
(*a*) 240 (*b*) 270 (*c*) 295 (*d*) 360

22. The difference between a positive proper fraction and its reciprocal is $\frac{9}{20}$. The fraction is:
(*a*) $\frac{3}{5}$ (*b*) $\frac{3}{10}$ (*c*) $\frac{4}{5}$ (*d*) $\frac{5}{4}$

23. The sum of the two numbers is 12 and their product is 35. What is the sum of the reciprocals of these numbers?
(*a*) $\frac{12}{35}$ (*b*) $\frac{1}{35}$ (*c*) $\frac{35}{8}$ (*d*) $\frac{7}{32}$

24. What will be the remainder when 17^{200} is divided by 18?
(*a*) 17 (*b*) 16 (*c*) 1 (*d*) 2

25. A number when divided successively by 4 and 5 leaves remainders 1 and 4 respectively. When it is successively divided by 5 and 4, then the respective remainders will be
(*a*) 1, 2 (*b*) 2, 3 (*c*) 3, 2 (*d*) 4, 1

26. On multiplying a number by 7, the product is a number each of whose digits is 3. The smallest such number is:
(*a*) 47619 (*b*) 47719 (*c*) 48619 (*d*) 47649

27. If n is a natural number, then $(6n^2 + 6n)$ is always divisible by:
(*a*) 6 only (*b*) 6 and 12 both (*c*) 12 only (*d*) by 18 only

28. The difference of the squares of two consecutive even integers is divisible by which of the following integers?
(*a*) 3 (*b*) 4 (*c*) 6 (*d*) 7

29. It is being given that $(2^{32} + 1)$ is completely divisible by a whole number. Which of the following numbers is completely divisible by this number?
(*a*) $(2^{16} + 1)$ (*b*) $(2^{16} - 1)$ (*c*) 7×2^{33} (*d*) $(2^{96} + 1)$

30. A number when divided by 296 leaves 75 as remainder. When the same number is divided by 37, the remainder will be:
(*a*) 1 (*b*) 2 (*c*) 8 (*d*) 11

ANSWERS

1	2	3	4	5	6	7	8	9	10
(*b*)	(*d*)	(*c*)	(*d*)	(*d*)	(*b*)	(*b*)	(*d*)	(*a*)	(*b*)
11	**12**	**13**	**14**	**15**	**16**	**17**	**18**	**19**	**20**
(*c*)	(*c*)	(*b*)	(*d*)	(*a*)	(*c*)	(*d*)	(*b*)	(*d*)	(*a*)
21	**22**	**23**	**24**	**25**	**26**	**27**	**28**	**29**	**30**
(*b*)	(*c*)	(*a*)	(*c*)	(*b*)	(*a*)	(*b*)	(*b*)	(*a*)	(*a*)

SOME SELECTED EXPLANATORY ANSWERS

2.
$$\begin{array}{r} 3251 \\ +\ 587 \\ +\ 369 \\ \hline 4207 \\ \hline \end{array}$$

Let $4207 - x = 3007$
Then, $x = 4207 - 3007 = 1200.$

4. Given sum $= 9+\frac{3}{4}+7+\frac{2}{17}-9-\frac{1}{15}$

$$= (9 + 7 - 9) + \frac{3}{4} + \frac{2}{17} - \frac{1}{15}$$

$$= 7 + \frac{765 + 120 - 68}{1020} = 7\frac{817}{1020}$$

6. $4500 \times x = 3375$ $\quad x = \frac{3375}{4500} = \frac{3}{4}$

```
45) 3375 (75
    315
     225
     225
      ×
```

7. $\frac{(1000)^9}{10^{24}} = \frac{(10^3)^9}{10^{24}} = \frac{10^{27}}{10^{24}} = 10^{(27-24)} = 10^3 = 1000.$

9. $\frac{(12)^3 \times 6^4}{432} = \frac{(12)^3 \times 6^4}{12 \times 6^2} = (12)^2 \times 6^2 = (72)^2 = 5184.$

10. $(217)^2 + (183)^2 = (200 + 17)^2 + (200 - 17)^2$
$= 2[(200)^2 + (17)^2]$ $\quad [(a + b)^2 + (a - b)^2 = 2(a^2 + b^2)]$
$= 2[40000 + 289] = (2 \times 40289) = 80578.$

11. Unit digit in 7^{105} = Unit digit in $[(7^4)^{26} \times 7]$
But, unit digit in $(7^4)^{26} = 1$.
$\therefore$ Unit digit in $7^{105} = (1 \times 7) = 7$.

13. Let x be the number & y be the quotient. Then,
$x = 56 \times y + 29 = (8 \times 7y) + (8 \times 3) + 5 = 8 \times (7y + 3) + 5.$
$\therefore$ Required remainder = 5.

14. Suppose that the number is x and on dividing x by 5, we get k as quotient and 3 as remainder.
$\therefore$ $x = 5k + 3 \Rightarrow x^2 = (5k + 3)^2 = (25k^2 + 30k + 9)$
$= 5(5k^2 + 6k + 1) + 4$
$\therefore$ On dividing x^2 by 5, we get 4 as reminder.

15. A number is divisible by the divisor, if it has all factors of divisor.
$132 = 11 \times 3 \times 4$.
Clearly, 968 is not divisible by 3
None of 462 and 2178 is divisible by 4.
And, 5184 is not divisible by 11.
Each one of the remaining four numbers is divisible by each one of 4, 3 and 11. So, there are 4 such numbers.

17. $(4 + 5 + 2) - (1 + 6 + 3) = 1$, not divisible by 11.
$(2 + 6 + 4) - (4 + 5 + 2) = 1$, not divisible by 11.
$(4 + 6 + 1) - (2 + 5 + 3) = 1$, not divisible by 11.
$(4 + 6 + 1) - (2 + 5 + 4) = 0$, So, 415624 is divisible by 11.

21. Let the smaller number be x. then larger number $= (x + 1365)$
$\therefore\ x + 1365 = 6x + 15 \Rightarrow 5x = 1350 \Rightarrow x = 270.$
$\therefore$ Smaller number = 270.

22. Let the required fraction be x. Then, $\frac{1}{x} - x = \frac{9}{20}$

$$\therefore\ \frac{1-x^2}{x} = \frac{9}{20} \Rightarrow 20 - 20x^2 = 9x \Rightarrow 20x^2 + 9x - 20 = 0$$

$$\Rightarrow\ 20x^2 + 25x - 16x - 20 = 0 \Rightarrow 5x(4x + 5) - 4(4x + 5) = 0$$

$$\Rightarrow\ (4x + 5)(5x - 4) = 0 \Rightarrow x = \frac{4}{5}.$$

23. Let the numbers be a and b. Then, $a + b = 12$ and $ab = 35$.

$$\therefore\ \frac{a+b}{ab} = \frac{12}{35} \Rightarrow \left(\frac{1}{b} + \frac{1}{a}\right) = \frac{12}{35}$$

$\therefore$ Sum of reciprocals of given numbers $= \frac{12}{35}$.

28. Let the two consecutive even integers be $2x$ and $(2x + 2)$. Then,
$(2x + 2)^2 - (2x)^2 = (2x + 2 + 2x)(2x + 2 - 2x)$
$= 2(4x + 2) = 4(2x + 1)$, which is divisible by 4.

30. Suppose that the number is x.
then from question,
$x = 296q + 75 = (37 \times 8q + 37 \times 2) + 1$
$= 37 \times (8q + 2) + 1$
Thus, when the number is divided by 37, the remainder is 1.

~~~~~~
~~~~~~

2. HCF AND LCM

A number is said to be *multiple* of another when it is exactly divisible by the other. Similarly, we can define common multiple as the number which is exactly divisible by numbers for whom it is common. For example, 10 is a common multiple for 2 as well as 5. The numbers 20, 30, 40 etc. are other common multiples of 2 and 5.

For 2 and 3, common multiples are 6, 12, 18 and so on.

For 4 and 6, common multiples are 12, 24, 36 and so on.

LEAST COMMON MULTIPLE (LCM)

LCM of two or more numbers is the smallest number which is common multiple of the given numbers. In other words, LCM of given numbers is the smallest number which is exactly divisible by each of them.

For example, the LCM for

3 and 7 is 21

3 and 5 is 15

4 and 6 is 12

We can find LCM by two methods.

(1) Facterization Method (2) Common division method.

HIGHEST COMMON FACTOR (HCF)

HCF of any given set of numbers is the greatest (highest) factor common to them. It is also known as Greatest Common Factor (GCF) or Greatest Common Measure (GCM) or Highest Common Divisor (HCD).

HCF too can be found by two methods.

(1) Facterization method (2) Division method.

SOLVED EXAMPLE

1. Find the HCF of 126, 396 and 5400.

Sol. I. $126 = 2 \times 3 \times 3 \times 7 = \mathbf{2 \times 3^2} \times 7$

$396 = 2 \times 2 \times 3 \times 3 \times 11 = \mathbf{2^2 \times 3^2} \times 11$

$5400 = 2 \times 2 \times 2 \times 3 \times 3 \times 3 \times 5 \times 5 = \mathbf{2^3 \times 3^3} \times 5^2$

II. The factors common to all the given numbers are 2 and 3 and their lowest powers are 1 (2^1) and 2 (3^2) respectively. Only the product of 2 and 3^2 can divide all the given numbers.

HCF = 2×3^2 = **18 Ans.**

Note: 2 × 3 = 6 is also a factor common to all the numbers i.e., all given numbers are divisible by 6 but it is less than 18 and hence is not the Highest Common Factor (HCF).

2. Find the LCM of $3\frac{1}{4}, \frac{3}{4}, 9\frac{3}{5}$ and $4\frac{6}{9}$.

Sol. $4\frac{6}{9} = \frac{14}{3}$; $9\frac{3}{5} = \frac{48}{5}$; $3\frac{1}{4} = \frac{13}{4}$ and $\frac{3}{4}$

LCM of Numerators 14, 48, 13 and 3 :

2	14, 48, 13, 3
3	7, 24, 13, 3
	7, 8, 13, 1

LCM = 2 × 3 × 7 × 8 × 13 = 4368

HCF of Denominators 3, 5, 4, 4:

We clearly see that there is no factor which is common to all. Hence, HCF will be 1.

$$\text{LCM} = \frac{\text{LCM of Numerators}}{\text{HCF of Denominators}} = \frac{4368}{1}$$

∴ Required LCM = **4368 Ans.**

3. Find the HCF of $3\frac{24}{46}$ and $4\frac{18}{92}$.

Sol. $3\frac{24}{46} = 3\frac{12}{23} = \frac{81}{23}$; $4\frac{18}{92} = 4\frac{9}{46} = \frac{193}{46}$

HCF of numerators 81 and 193 is 1.

LCM of denominators 23 and 46 is 46.

$$\therefore \text{ Required HCF} = \frac{\text{HCF of Numerators}}{\text{LCM of Denominators}} = \frac{\mathbf{1}}{\mathbf{46}} \textbf{ Ans.}$$

EXERCISE

1. 252 can be expressed as a product of primes as:

(*a*) 2 × 2 × 3 × 3 × 7 (*b*) 2 × 2 × 2 × 3 × 7

(*c*) 3 × 3 × 3 × 3 × 7 (*d*) 2 × 3 × 3 × 3 × 7

2. Which of the following fractions is the largest ?

(a) $\frac{7}{8}$ (b) $\frac{13}{16}$ (c) $\frac{31}{40}$ (d) $\frac{63}{80}$

3. The smallest fraction, which each of $\frac{6}{7}, \frac{5}{14}, \frac{10}{21}$ will divide exactly, is :

(a) $\frac{30}{7}$ (b) $\frac{30}{98}$ (c) $\frac{60}{147}$ (d) $\frac{50}{294}$

4. H.C.F. of $4 \times 27 \times 3125$, $8 \times 9 \times 25 \times 7$ & $16 \times 81 \times 5 \times 11 \times 49$ is:

(a) 180 (b) 360 (c) 540 (d) 1260

5. Find the highest common factor of 36 and 84.

(a) 4 (b) 6 (c) 12 (d) 18

6. The smallest number which when diminished by 7, is divisible by 12, 16, 18, 21 and 28 is :

(a) 1008 (b) 1015 (c) 1022 (d) 1032

7. The L.C.M. of 22, 54, 108, 135 and 198 is:

(a) 330 (b) 1980 (c) 5940 (d) 11880

8. The G.C.D. of 1.08, 0.36 and 0.9 is:

(a) 0.03 (b) 0.9 (c) 0.18 (d) 0.108

9. H.C.F. of 3240, 3600 and a third number is 36 and their L.C.M. is $2^4 \times 3^5 \times 5^2 \times 7^2$. The third number is:

(a) $2^2 \times 3^5 \times 7^2$ (b) $2^2 \times 5^3 \times 7^2$ (c) $2^5 \times 5^2 \times 7^2$ (d) $2^3 \times 5^2 \times 7^2$

10. Three numbers are in the raio 1 : 2 : 3 and their H.C.F. is 12. The numbers are :

(a) 4, 8, 12 (b) 5, 10, 15 (c) 10, 20, 30 (d) 12, 24, 36

11. The ratio of two numbers is 3 : 4 and their H.C.F. is 4. Their L.C.M. is:

(a) 12 (b) 16 (c) 24 (d) 48

12. The sum of two numbers is 528 and their H.C.F. is 33. The number of pairs of numbers satisfying the above conditions is:

(a) 4 (b) 6 (c) 8 (d) 12

13. The product of two numbers is 4107. If the H.C.F. of these numbers is 37, then the greater number is:

(a) 101 (b) 107 (c) 111 (d) 185

14. The least multiple of 7, which leaves a remainder of 4, when divided by 6, 9, 15 and 18 is:

(a) 74 (b) 94 (c) 184 (d) 364

15. Three numbers which are co-prime to each other are such that the product of the first two is 551 and that of the last two is 1073. The sum of the three numbers is :

(*a*) 75 (*b*) 81 (*c*) 85 (*d*) 89

16. The L.C.M. of two numbers is 48. The numbers are in the ratio 2 : 3. The sum of the numbers is :

(*a*) 28 (*b*) 32 (*c*) 40 (*d*) 64

17. Three numbers are in the ratio of 3 : 4 : 5 and their L.C.M. is 2400. Their H.C.P. is :

(*a*) 40 (*b*) 80 (*c*) 120 (*d*) 200

18. The H.C.F. of two numbers is 11 and their L.C.M. is 7700. If one of the numbers is 275, then the other is :

(*a*) 279 (*b*) 283 (*c*) 308 (*d*) 318

19. The least number which when divided by 5, 6, 7 and 8 leaves a remainder 3, but when divided by 9 leaves no remainder, is :

(*a*) 1677 (*b*) 1683 (*c*) 2523 (*d*) 3363

20. The L.C.M. of two numbers is 495 and their H.C.F. is 5. If the sum of the numbers is 10, then their difference is :

(*a*) 10 (*b*) 46 (*c*) 70 (*d*) 90

21. If the sum of two numbers is 55 and the H.C.F. and L.C.M. of these numbers are 5 and 120 respectively, then the sum of the reciprocals of the numbers is equal to :

(*a*) $\frac{55}{601}$ (*b*) $\frac{601}{55}$ (*c*) $\frac{11}{120}$ (*d*) $\frac{120}{11}$

22. Product of two co-prime numbers is 117. Their L.C.M. should be :

(*a*) 1 (*b*) 117

(*c*) equal to their H.C.F. (*d*) cannot be calculated

23. The H.C.F. of two numbers is 8. Which one of the following can never be their L.C.M. ?

(*a*) 24 (*b*) 48 (*c*) 56 (*d*) 60

24. The H.C.F. of two numbers is 23 and the other two factors of their L.C.M. are 13 and 14. The larger of the two numbers is :

(*a*) 276 (*b*) 299 (*c*) 322 (*d*) 345

25. The H.C.F. and L.C.M. of two numbers are 11 and 385 respectively. If one number lies between 75 and 125, then that number is :

(*a*) 77 (*b*) 88 (*c*) 99 (*d*) 110

26. The least number, which when divided by 48, 60, 72, 108 and 140 leaves 38, 50, 62, 98 and 130 as remainders respectively, is :
(*a*) 11115 (*b*) 15110 (*c*) 15120 (*d*) 15210

27. L.C.M. of two prime numbers x and y $(x > y)$ is 161. The value of $3y - x$ is :
(*a*) −2 (*b*) −1 (*c*) 1 (*d*) 2

28. The greatest possible length which can be used to measure exactly the lengths 7 m, 3 m 85 cm, 12 m 95 cm is :
(*a*) 15 cm (*b*) 25 cm (*c*) 35 cm (*d*) 42 cm

29. The maximum number of students among them 1001 pens and 910 pencils can be distributed in such a way that each student gets the same number of pens and same number of pencils is :
(*a*) 91 (*b*) 910 (*c*) 1001 (*d*) 1911

30. A rectangular courtyard 3.78 metres long and 5.25 metres wide is to be paved exactly with square tiles, all of the same size. What is the largest size of the tile which could be used for the purpose ?
(*a*) 14 cms (*b*) 21 cms (*c*) 42 cms (*d*) None of these

31. Find the greatest number that will divide 43, 91 and 183 so as to leave the same remainder in each case.
(*a*) 4 (*b*) 7 (*c*) 9 (*d*) 13

32. Let N be the greatest number that will divide 1305, 4665 and 6905, leaving the same remainder in each case. Then sum of the digits in N is :
(*a*) 4 (*b*) 5 (*c*) 6 (*d*) 8

33. The greatest number which on dividing 1657 and 2037 leaves remainders 6 and 5 respectively, is :
(*a*) 123 (*b*) 127 (*c*) 235 (*d*) 305

34. A, B and C start at the same time in the same direction to run around a circular stadium. A completes a round in 252 seconds, B in 308 seconds and C in 198 seconds, all starting at the same point. After what time will they meet again at the starting point?
(*a*) 26 minutes 18 seconds (*b*) 42 minutes 36 seconds
(*c*) 45 minutes (*d*) 46 minutes 12 seconds

35. What will be the least number which when doubled will be exactly divisible by 12,18, 21 and 30?
(*a*) 196 (*b*) 630 (*c*) 1260 (*d*) 2520

36. The least number, which when divided by 12, 15, 20 and 54 leaves in each case a remainder of 8, is :
(*a*) 504 (*b*) 536 (*c*) 544 (*d*) 548

37. The least number which should be added to 2497 so that the sum is exactly divisible by 5, 6, 4 and 3 is :

(*a*) 3 (*b*) 13 (*c*) 23 (*d*) 33

ANSWERS

1	2	3	4	5	6	7	8	9	10
(*a*)	(*a*)	(*a*)	(*a*)	(*c*)	(*b*)	(*c*)	(*c*)	(*a*)	(*d*)
11	**12**	**13**	**14**	**15**	**16**	**17**	**18**	**19**	**20**
(*d*)	(*a*)	(*c*)	(*d*)	(*c*)	(*c*)	(*a*)	(*c*)	(*b*)	(*a*)
21	**22**	**23**	**24**	**25**	**26**	**27**	**28**	**29**	**30**
(*c*)	(*b*)	(*d*)	(*c*)	(*a*)	(*b*)	(*a*)	(*c*)	(*a*)	(*b*)
31	**32**	**33**	**34**	**35**	**36**	**37**			
(*a*)	(*a*)	(*b*)	(*d*)	(*b*)	(*d*)	(*c*)			

SOME SELECTED EXPLANATORY ANSWERS

2. L.C.M. of 8, 16, 40 and 80 = 80.

$\frac{7}{8}=\frac{70}{80};\ \frac{13}{16}=\frac{65}{80};\ \frac{31}{40}=\frac{62}{80}.$

Since, $\frac{70}{80}>\frac{65}{80}>\frac{63}{80}>\frac{62}{80}$, so $\frac{7}{8}>\frac{13}{16}>\frac{63}{80}>\frac{31}{40}$.

So, $\frac{7}{8}$ is the largest.

3. Required frection = L.C.M. of $\frac{6}{7},\ \frac{5}{14},\ \frac{10}{21}=\frac{\text{L.C.M. of 6, 5, 10}}{\text{H.C.F. of 7, 14, 21}}=\frac{30}{7}$.

4. $4 \times 27 \times 3125 = 2^2 \times 3^3 \times 5^5$; $8 \times 9 \times 25 \times 7 = 2^3 \times 3^2 \times 5^2 \times 7$; $16 \times 81 \times 5 \times 11 \times 49 = 2^4 \times 3^4 \times 5 \times 7^2 \times 11$.

$\therefore$ H.C.F. = $2^2 \times 3^2 \times 5 = 180$.

5. $36 = 2^2 \times 3^2$; $84 = 2^2 \times 3 \times 7$.

$\therefore$ H.C.F. = $2^2 \times 3 = 12$.

6. Required number = (L.C.M. of 12, 16, 18, 21, 28) + 7 = 1008 + 7 = 1015.

8. Given numbers are 1.08, 0.36 and 0.90. H.C.F. of 108, 36 and 90 is 18.

$\therefore$ H.C.F. of given numbers = 0.18.

9. $3240 = 2^3 \times 3^4 \times 5$; $3600 = 2^4 \times 3^2 \times 5^2$; $36 = 2^2 \times 3^2$.

We know that H.C.F. is the product of lowest powers of common factors, so the third number must have $(2^2 \times 3^2)$ as its factor.

Since L.C.M. is the product of highest powers of common prime factors, so the third number must have 3^5 and 7^2 as its factors.

$\therefore$ Third number = $2^2 \times 3^5 \times 7^2$.

10. Let the required numbers be x, $2x$ and $3x$. Then, their H.C.F. = x So, $x = 12$.

$\therefore$ The numbers are 12, 24 and 36.

12. As the H.C.F. of two numbers is 33.

Suppose that the two numbers are $33x + 33y$.

then, $33x + 33y = 528$

$\Rightarrow \quad x + y = 16.$

Now, co-primes with sum 16 are (1, 15), (3, 13), (5, 11) and (7, 9).

$\therefore$ Required numbers are $(33 \times 1, 33 \times 15)$, $(33 \times 3, 33 \times 13)$, $(33 \times 5, 33 \times 11)$, $(33 \times 7, 33 \times 9)$.

The number of such pairs is 4.

13. Suppose that the numbers are $37a$ and $37b$. Then, $37a \times 37b = 4107$ $\Rightarrow ab = 3$.

Now, co-primes with product 3 are (1, 3).

So, the required numbers are $(37 \times 1, 37 \times 3)$ *i.e.*, (1, 111).

$\therefore$ Greater number = 111.

14. L.C.M. of 6, 9, 15 and 18 is 90.

Let required number be $90k + 4$, which is a multiple of 7.

Least value of k for which $(90k + 4)$ is divisible by 7 is $k = 4$.

$\therefore$ Required number = $90 \times 4 + 4 = 364$.

15. Since the numbers are co-prime, they contain only 1 as the common factor.

Also, the given two products have the middle number in common.

So, middle number = H.C.F. or 551 and 1073 = 29;

First number = $\left(\frac{551}{29}\right) = 19$; Third number = $\left(\frac{1073}{29}\right) = 37$.

$\therefore$ Required sum = $(19 + 29 + 37) = 85$.

18. Other number = $\left(\frac{11 \times 7700}{275}\right) = 308$.

19. L.C.M. of 5, 6, 7, 8 = 840.

$\therefore$ Required number is of the form $840k + 3$.

Least value of k for which $(840k + 3)$ is divisible by 9 is $k = 2$.

$\therefore$ Required number = $(840 \times 2 + 3) = 1683$.

22. H.C.F. of co-prime numbers is 1. So, L.C.M. = $\frac{117}{1} = 117$.

23. H.C.F. of two numbers divides their L.C.M. exactly. Clearly, 8 is not a factor of 60.

24. Clearly, the numbers are (23 × 13) and (23 × 14).
∴ Larger number = (23 × 14) = 322.

25. As the H.C.F. of two numbers is 11
Suppose that the two such numbers are $11x$ and $11y$
Then, $11x \times 11y = 4235 \Rightarrow xy = 35$.
Now, co-primes with product 35 are (1, 35) and (5, 7).
So, the numbers are (11 × 1, 11 × 35) and (11 × 5, 11 × 7).
Since one number lies between 75 and 125; the suitable pair is (55, 77).
Hence, required number = 77.

26. Here (48 – 38) = 10, (60 – 50) = 10, (72 – 62) = 10, (108 – 98) = 10 & (140 – 130) = 10.
∴ Required number = (L.C.M. of 48, 60, 72, 108, 140) – 10
= 15120 – 10 = 15110.

27. H.C.F. of two prime numbers is 1. Product of numbers = (1 × 161) = 161.
Let the numbers be a and b. Then, $ab = 161$.
Now, co-primes with product 161 are (1, 161) and (7, 23).
Since x and y are prime numbers and $x > y$, we have $x = 23$ and $y = 7$.
∴ $3y - x = (3 \times 7) - 23 = -2$.

31. Required number = H.C.F. of (91 – 43), (183 – 91) and (183 – 43)
= H.C.F. of 48, 92 and 140 = 4.

32. N= H.C.F. of (4665 – 1305), (6905 – 4665) and (6905 – 1305)
= H.C.F. of 3360, 2240 and 5600 = 1120.
Sum of digits in N = (1 + 1 + 2 + 0) = 4.

33. Required number = H.C.F. of (1657 – 6) and (2037 – 5)
= H.C.F. of 1651 and 2032 = 127.

34. L.C.M. of 252, 308 amd 198 = 2772.
So, A, B and C will again meet at the starting point in 2772 sec. *i.e.,* 46 min. 12 sec.

35. L.C.M. of 12, 18, 21, 30
= 2 × 3 × 2 × 3 × 7 × 5 = 1260.
∴ Required number = (1260 ÷ 2) = 630.

2	12 – 18 – 21 – 30
3	6 – 9 – 21 – 15
	2 – 3 – 7 – 5

36. Required number = (L.C.M. of 12, 15, 20, 54) + 8 = 540 + 8 = 548.

37. L.C.M. of 5, 6, 4 and 3 = 60. On dividing 2497 by 60, the remainder is 37.
∴ Number to be added = (60 – 37) = 23.

~~~~~~
~~~~~~

3. DECIMAL FRACTIONS

Fractions in which the denominators are power of 10 are called decimal fractions.

For example: $\frac{1}{10}, \frac{7}{10}, \frac{9}{1000}$ etc.

Comparison of Fractions: Suppose some fractions are to be arranged in ascending or descending order of magnitude. Then, convert each one of the given fractions in the decimal form, and arrange them accordingly.

Suppose, we have to arrange the fractions $\frac{3}{5}, \frac{6}{7}$ and $\frac{7}{9}$ in descending order.

Now, $\frac{3}{5} = 0.6,\ \frac{6}{7} = 0.857,\ \frac{7}{9} = 0.777\ ......$

Since $0.857 > 0.777 ...... > 0.6$, so $\frac{6}{7} > \frac{7}{9} > \frac{3}{5}$.

Recurring Decimal: If in a decimal fraction, a figure or a set of figures is repeated continuously, then such a number is called a ***recurring decimal.***

In a recurring decimal, if a single figure is repeated, then it is expressed by putting a dot on it. If a set of figures is repeated, it is expressed by putting a bar on the set.

Thus, $\frac{1}{3} = 0.333 .... = 0.\dot{3};\ \frac{22}{7} = 3.142857142857 ..... = 3.\overline{142857}$.

Pure Recurring Decimal: A decimal fraction in which all the figures after the decimal point are repeated, is called a pure recurring decimal.

Converting a Pure Recurring Decimal Into Vulgar Fraction: Write the repeated figures only once in the numerator and take as many nines in the denominator as is the number of repeating figures.

Thus, $0.\dot{5} = \frac{5}{9};\ 0.\overline{53} = \frac{53}{99};\ 0.\overline{067} = \frac{67}{999}$; etc.

Mixed Recurring Decimal: A decimal fraction in which some figures do not repeat and some of them are repeated, is called a mixed recurring decimal.

e.g., $0.17333 = 0.17\overline{3}$.

Converting a Mixed Recurring Decimal Into Vulgar fraction: In the numerator, take the difference between the number formed by all the digits after decimal point (taking repeated digits only once) and that formed by the digits which are not repeated. In the denominator, take the number formed by as many nines as there are repeating digits followed by as many zeros as is the number of non-repeating digits.

$$\text{Thus, } 0.16 = \frac{16-1}{90} = \frac{15}{90} = \frac{1}{6};\ 0.22\overline{73} = \frac{2273-22}{9900} = \frac{2251}{9900}.$$

3. Some Basic Formulae:

1. $(a + b)(a - b) = (a^2 - b^2)$.
2. $(a + b)^2 = (a^2 + b^2 + 2ab)$.
3. $(a - b)^2 = (a^2 + b^2 - 2ab)$.
4. $(a + b + c)^2 = a^2 + b^2 + c^2 + 2(ab + bc + ca)$.
5. $(a^3 + b^3) = (a + b)(a^2 - ab + b^2)$
6. $(a^3 - b^3) = (a - b)(a^2 + ab + b^2)$.
7. $(a^3 + b^3 + c^3 - 3abc) = (a + b + c)(a^2 + b^2 + c^2 - ab - bc - ac)$.
8. When $a + b + c = 0$, then $a^3 + b^3 + c^3 = 3abc$.

APPROXIMATION AND CONTRACTION

Rule: Increase the last figure by 1 if the succeeding figure be 5 or greater than 5.

For Example: (*i*) The approximate value of 0.3689 up to three decimal places is 0.369.

(*ii*) The approsimate value of 0.3684 up to three decimal places is 0368.

(*iii*) The approximate value of 0.3685 up to three decimal places is 0.369.

(*iv*) The approximate value of 0.3689 up to two decimal places is 0.37.

(*v*) The approximate value of 0.3468 up to one decimal place is 0.3

Note: Decimals which are correct at one, two, three ... places are said to be correct to the nearest tenth, hundredth, thousandth, ... respectively.

CONTRACTED ADDITION

Set down the decimals under one another. Then add in the usual way, taking care that the last figure retained be increased by 1 if the succeeding figure be 5 or greater than 5.

SOLVED EXAMPLE

1. Find $324.\overline{786} + 10.19\overline{3}$.

Sol.

324.78	678	67
10.19	333	33
334.98	012	00

Thus, ans = $334.98\overline{012}$

Verification: $324.\overline{786} = 324 + \dfrac{786}{999}$

$$10.19\overline{3} = 10 + \frac{193-19}{900} = 10 + \frac{174}{900}$$

$$324.\overline{786} + 10.19\overline{3} = 324 + 10 + \frac{786}{999} + \frac{174}{900}$$

$$= 334 + \frac{786 \times 900 + 174 \times 999}{999 \times 900}$$

$$= 334 + \frac{78600 + 174 \times 111}{99900} = 334 + \frac{97914}{99900}$$

$$= 334\frac{98012 - 98}{99900} = 334.98\overline{012}.$$

2. Find $324.\overline{786} - 10.19\overline{3}$.

Sol.

324.78	678	67
10.19	333	33
314.59	345	34

Thus, ans = $314.59\overline{345}$

Verification: $324.\overline{786} - 10.19\overline{3} = 324 + \dfrac{786}{999} - \left(10 + \dfrac{174}{900}\right)$

$$= 314 + \frac{786 \times 900 - 174 \times 999}{999 \times 900} = 314 + \frac{786 \times 100 - 174 \times 111}{99900}$$

$$= 314 + \frac{59286}{99900} = 314\frac{59345 - 59}{99900} = 314.59\overline{345}.$$

3. Find $17.\overline{83} + 0.00\overline{7} + 310.020\overline{2}$

Sol.

17.838	38	38
0.007	77	77
310.020	22	22
327.866	38	37

Thus, ans = $327.866\overline{38}$

4. Find $17.10\overline{86} - 7.984\overline{9}$

Sol.

17.108	68	68
7.984	99	99
9.123	68	69

Thus, ans = $9.123\overline{68}$.

5. $17.2\overline{6} \div 2 = 17\frac{26-2}{90} \div 2 = 17\frac{24}{90} \times \frac{1}{2} = 17\frac{4}{15} \times \frac{1}{2}$

$= \frac{259}{30} = \frac{240+19}{30} = 8 + \frac{19}{30}$

$= 8 + \frac{57}{90} = 8 + \frac{63-6}{90} = 8 + 0.6\overline{3} = 8.6\overline{3}$

Another way of calculation is

$$17.2\overline{6} \div 2 = 8 + \frac{19}{30} = 8 + \frac{6.33...}{10} = 8 + 0.633\ ...$$

$$= 8 + 0.6\overline{3} = 8.6\overline{3}$$

Second Method:

```
2) 17.266...(8.633...
   16
   12
   12
    06
     6
    06
```

Thus, ans = $8.6\overline{3}$

6. $36.3\overline{43} \div 7 = 36.34343 \ldots \div 7$

Sol.

```
7) 36.34343...(5.19
   35
   ---
    13
     7
   ----
     64
     63
   ----
      13
```

The process of division repeats so our quotient becomes 5.1919....

i.e. $5.\overline{19}$.

7. Find the sum of 320.4321, 29.042934, .0085279 and .3412 correct to 3 decimal places.

Sol.

```
   320.4321
    29.04293
      .00852
      .3412
  ----------
   349.82475
```

Ans = 349.825

Remark: If you are asked to get the answer correct to three decimal places, then use not more than 5 (two more) decimal places during calculation.

EXERCISE

1. Which of the following has fractions in ascending order?

(*a*) $\frac{1}{3}, \frac{2}{5}, \frac{4}{7}, \frac{3}{5}, \frac{5}{6}, \frac{6}{7}$ (*b*) $\frac{1}{3}, \frac{2}{5}, \frac{3}{5}, \frac{4}{7}, \frac{5}{6}, \frac{6}{7}$

(*c*) $\frac{1}{3}, \frac{2}{5}, \frac{3}{5}, \frac{5}{6}, \frac{4}{7}, \frac{6}{7}$ (*d*) $\frac{2}{5}, \frac{3}{5}, \frac{1}{3}, \frac{4}{7}, \frac{5}{6}, \frac{6}{7}$

2. If $47.2506 = 4A + \frac{7}{B} + 2C + \frac{5}{D} + 6E$, then the value of 5A + 3B + 6C + D + 3E is :

(*a*) 53.6003 (*b*) 53.603 (*c*) 153.6003 (*d*) 213.003

3. 337.62 + 8.591 + 34.4 = ?

(*a*) 370.611 (*b*) 380.511 (*c*) 380.611 (*d*) 426.97

4. 617 + 6.017 + 0617 + 6.0017 = ?

(*a*) 6.2963 (*b*) 62.965 (*c*) 629.6357 (*d*) None of these

5. 792.02 + 101.32 – 306.76 = ?
(*a*) 586.58 (*b*) 893.34 (*c*) 997.11 (*d*) 1200.10

6. 12.1212 + 17.0005 –9.1102 = ?
(*a*) 20.0015 (*b*) 20.0105 (*c*) 20.0115 (*d*) 20.1015

7. 3889 + 12.952 – ? = 3854.002
(*a*) 47.095 (*b*) 47.752 (*c*) 47.932 (*d*) 47.95

8. 138.009 + 341.981 – 146.305 = 123.6 + ?
(*a*) 120.085 (*b*) 120.85 (*c*) 220.085 (*d*) None of these

9. 832.58 – 242.31 = 779.84 – ?
(*a*) 179.57 (*b*) 199.57 (*c*) 295.05 (*d*) None of these

10. What will come in place of question mark in the following equation?
54. (?) 3 + 543 + 5.43 = 603.26
(*a*) 5 (*b*) 6 (*c*) 8 (*d*) None of these

11. Which of the following are in descending order of their value?
(*a*) $\frac{5}{9}, \frac{7}{11}, \frac{8}{15}, \frac{11}{17}$ (*b*) $\frac{5}{9}, \frac{7}{15}, \frac{11}{17}, \frac{8}{15}$
(*c*) $\frac{11}{17}, \frac{7}{11}, \frac{8}{15}, \frac{5}{9}$ (*d*) $\frac{11}{17}, \frac{7}{11}, \frac{5}{9}, \frac{8}{15}$

12. What is the difference between the biggest and the smallest fraction among $\frac{2}{3}, \frac{3}{4}, \frac{4}{5}$ and $\frac{5}{6}$?
(*a*) $\frac{1}{6}$ (*b*) $\frac{1}{12}$ (*c*) $\frac{1}{20}$ (*d*) $\frac{1}{30}$

13. Which of the following fractions is greater than $\frac{3}{4}$ and less than $\frac{5}{6}$?
(*a*) $\frac{1}{2}$ (*b*) $\frac{2}{3}$ (*c*) $\frac{4}{5}$ (*d*) $\frac{9}{10}$

14. When 0.232323 .... is convert3ed into a fraction, then the result is:
(*a*) $\frac{1}{5}$ (*b*) $\frac{2}{9}$ (*c*) $\frac{23}{99}$ (*d*) $\frac{23}{100}$

15. The rational number for the rational number for the recurring decimal 0.125125 ... is
(*a*) $\frac{63}{487}$ (*b*) $\frac{119}{993}$ (*c*) $\frac{125}{999}$ (*d*) None of these

16. When $0.\overline{47}$ is converted into a fraction, the result is:

(*a*) $\frac{46}{90}$ (*b*) $\frac{46}{99}$ (*c*) $\frac{47}{90}$ (*d*) $\frac{47}{99}$

17. The least among the following is:

(*a*) 0.2 (*b*) $1 \div 0.2$ (*c*) $0.\overline{2}$ (*d*) $(0.2)^2$

18. $\frac{.009}{?} = .01$

(*a*) .0009 (*b*) .09 (*c*) .9 (*d*) 9

19. The value of $0.5\overline{7}$ is:

(*a*) $\frac{57}{10}$ (*b*) $\frac{57}{99}$ (*c*) $\frac{26}{45}$ (*d*) $\frac{52}{9}$

20. The value of $2.1\overline{36}$ is :

(*a*) $\frac{47}{220}$ (*b*) $\frac{68}{495}$ (*c*) $2\frac{3}{22}$ (*d*) None of these

21. $\frac{(0.1667)(0.8333)(0.3333)}{(0.2222)(0.6667)(0.1250)}$ is approximately equal to:

(*a*) 2 (*b*) 2.40 (*c*) 2.43 (*d*) 2.50

22. The value of $\frac{3.157 \times 4126 \times 3.194}{63.972 \times 2835.121}$ is closest to:

(*a*) 0.002 (*b*) 0.02 (*c*) 0.2 (*d*) 2

23. The value of $\frac{489.1375 \times 0.1483 \times 1.956}{0.0873 \times 92.581 \times 99.749}$ is closest to:

(*a*) 0.006 (*b*) 0.06 (*c*) 0.6 (*d*) 6

24. $(0.2 \times 0.2 + 0.01)(0.1 \times 0.1 + 0.02)^{-1}$ is equal to:

(*a*) $\frac{5}{3}$ (*b*) $\frac{9}{5}$ (*c*) $\frac{41}{4}$ (*d*) $\frac{41}{12}$

25. If $2994 \div 14.5 = 172$, then $29.94 \div 1.45 = ?$

(*a*) 0.172 (*b*) 1.72 (*c*) 17.2 (*d*) 172

26. If $1^3 + 2^3 + ... + 9^3 = 2025$, then the value of $(0.11)^3 + (0.22)^3 + ... + (0.99)^3$ is is close to :

(*a*) 0.2695 (*b*) 0.3695 (*c*) 2.695 (*d*) 3.695

27. Find the value of the following expression upto four places of decimals.

$$\left[1+\frac{1}{1\times 2}+\frac{1}{1\times 2\times 4}+\frac{1}{1\times 2\times 4\times 8}+\frac{1}{1\times 2\times 4\times 8\times 16}\right]$$

(*a*) 1.6414 (*b*) 1.6414 (*c*) 1.6416 (*d*) 1.6428

28. The correct expression of $6.4\overline{6}$ in the fractional form is:

(*a*) $\frac{646}{99}$ (*b*) $\frac{64640}{1000}$ (*c*) $\frac{640}{100}$ (*d*) $\frac{640}{99}$

29. Let F = $0.841\overline{81}$. When F is written as a fraction in lowest terms, the denominator exceeds the numerator by :

(*a*) 13 (*b*) 14 (*c*) 29 (*d*) 87

30. The value of $\frac{(0.96)^3-(0.1)^3}{(0.96)^2+0.096+(0.1)^2}$ is:

(*a*) 0.86 (*b*) 0.95 (*c*) 0.97 (*d*) 1.06

31. The value of $\frac{(67.542)^2-(32.458)^2}{75.458-40.374}$:

(*a*) 1 (*b*) 10 (*c*) 100 (*d*) None of these

32. The price of commodity X increases by 40 paise every year, while the price of commodity Y increases by 15 paise every year. If in 2001, the price of commodity X was ₹ 4.20 and that of Y was ₹ 6.30, in which year commodity X will cost 40 paise more than the commodity Y?

(*a*) 2010 (*b*) 2011 (*c*) 2012 (*d*) 2013

33. A tailor has 37.5 metres of cloth and he has to make 8 pieces out of a metre of cloth. How many pieces can he make out of this cloth?

(*a*) 320 (*b*) 360 (*c*) 400 (*d*) None of these

34. 4.036 divided by 0.04 gives:

(*a*) 1.009 (*b*) 10.09 (*c*) 100.9 (*d*) None of these

35. Consider the following quotients:

1. 368.39 divided by 17
2. 170.50 divided by 62
3. 875.65 divided by 83

Their correct sequence in decreasing order is:

(*a*) 1, 3, 2 (*b*) 2, 1, 3 (*c*) 2, 3, 1 (*d*) 3, 1, 2

36. How many digits will be there to the right of the decimal point in the product of 95.75 and .02554?

(*a*) 5 (*b*) 6 (*c*) 7 (*d*) None of these

37. Which of the following is equal to 3.14×10^6?
(*a*) 314 (*b*) 3140 (*c*) 3140000 (*d*) None of these

ANSWERS

1	**2**	**3**	**4**	**5**	**6**	**7**	**8**	**9**	**10**
(*a*)	(*c*)	(*c*)	(*c*)	(*a*)	(*c*)	(*d*)	(*d*)	(*d*)	(*c*)
11	**12**	**13**	**14**	**15**	**16**	**17**	**18**	**19**	**20**
(*d*)	(*a*)	(*c*)	(*c*)	(*c*)	(*d*)	(*d*)	(*c*)	(*c*)	(*c*)
21	**22**	**23**	**24**	**25**	**26**	**27**	**28**	**29**	**30**
(*d*)	(*c*)	(*b*)	(*a*)	(*c*)	(*c*)	(*c*)	(*d*)	(*d*)	(*a*)
31	**32**	**33**	**34**	**35**	**36**	**37**			
(*c*)	(*b*)	(*d*)	(*c*)	(*a*)	(*b*)	(*c*)			

SOME SELECTED EXPLANATORY ANSWERS

1. Converting each of the given fractions into decimal form, we get:

$\frac{1}{3} = 0.033$, $\frac{2}{5} = 0.4$, $\frac{4}{7} = 0.57$, $\frac{3}{5} = 0.6$, $\frac{5}{6} = 0.82$, $\frac{6}{7} = 0.857$.

Clearly, $0.33 < 0.4 < 0.57 < 0.6 < 0.82 < 0.857$.

So, $\frac{1}{3} < \frac{2}{5} < \frac{4}{7} < \frac{3}{5} < \frac{5}{6} < \frac{6}{7}$.

2. $4A + \frac{7}{B} + 2C + \frac{5}{D} + 6E = 47.2506$

$\Rightarrow 4A + \frac{7}{B} + 2C + \frac{5}{D} + 6E = 40 + 7 + 0.2 + 0.05 + 0.0006$

Comparing the terms on both sides, we get:

$4A = 40$, $\frac{7}{B} = 7$, $2C = 0.2$, $\frac{5}{D} = 0.05$, $6E = 0.0006$

or $A = 10$, $B = 1$, $C = 0.1$, $D = 100$, $E = 0.0001$.

$\therefore 5A + 5B + 6C + D + 3E$
$= (5 \times 10) + (3 \times 1) + (6 \times 0.1) + 100 + (3 \times 0.0001)$
$= 50 + 3 + 0.6 + 100 + 0.0003 = 153.6003$.

3.
$$\begin{array}{r} 337.62 \\ +\ 8.591 \\ \hline 380.611 \\ \hline \end{array}$$

4.
$$\begin{array}{r} 617.00 \\ 6.017 \\ 0.617 \\ +\ 6.0017 \\ \hline 629.6357 \\ \hline \end{array}$$

6. Given expression = (12.1212 + 17.0005) – 9.1102
= (29.1217 – 9.1102) = 20.0115.

7. Let 3889 + 12.952 – x = 3854.002.
The, x = (3889 + 12.952) – 3854.002 = 3901.952 – 3854.002 = 47.95.

8. Let 138.009 + 341.981 – 146.305 = 123.6 + x.
Then, x = (138.009 + 341.981) – (146.305 + 123.6)
= 479.99 – 269.905 = 210.085

9. Let 832.58 – 242.32 = 779.84 – x.
Then, x = (779.84 + 242.31) – 832.58 = 1022.15 – 832.58 = 189.57.

10. Let x + 543 + 5.43 = 603.26.
Then, x = 603.26 – (543 + 5.43) = 603.26 – 548.43 = 54.83.
∴ Missing digit = 8.

11. Converting each of the given fractions into decimal form, we get:

$\frac{5}{9} = 0.55, \ \frac{7}{11} = 0.63, \ \frac{8}{15} = 0.533, \ \frac{11}{17} = 0.647.$

Clearly, 0.647 > 0.63 > 0.55 > 0.533. So, $\frac{11}{17} > \frac{7}{11} > \frac{5}{9} > \frac{8}{15}$.

12. Converting each of the given fractions into decimal form, we get:

$\frac{2}{3} = 0.66, \ \frac{3}{4} = 0.75, \ \frac{4}{5} = 0.8, \ \frac{5}{6} = 0.833.$

Since 0.833 > 0.8 > 0.75 > 0.66, so $\frac{5}{6} > \frac{4}{5} > \frac{3}{4} > \frac{2}{3}$.

∴ Required difference = $\left(\frac{5}{6} - \frac{2}{3}\right) = \frac{1}{6}$.

13. $\frac{3}{4} = 0.75, \ \frac{5}{6} = 0.833, \ \frac{1}{2} = 0.5, \ \frac{2}{3} \ 0.66, \ \frac{4}{5} = 0.8, \ \frac{9}{10} = 0.9.$
Clearly, 0.8 lies between 0.75 and 0.833.

∴ $\frac{4}{5}$ lies between $\frac{3}{4}$ and $\frac{5}{6}$.

14. 0.232323..... = $0.\overline{23} = \frac{23}{99}$.

15. 0.125125.... = $0.\overline{125} = \frac{125}{999}$.

16. $0.\overline{47} = \frac{47}{99}.$

17. $1 + 0.2 = \frac{1}{0.2} = \frac{10}{2} = 5;\ \ 0.\overline{2} = 0.222.....; (0.2)^2 = 0.04.$

$0.04 < 0.2 < 0.22 .... < 5.$

Since 0.04 is the least, so $(0.2)^2$ is the least.

18. Let $\frac{.009}{x} = .01$. Then, $x = \frac{.009}{.01} = \frac{.9}{1} = .9.$

19. $0.5\overline{7} = \frac{57-5}{90} = \frac{52}{90} = \frac{26}{45}.$

20. $2.1\overline{36} = 2 + 0.1\overline{36} = 2 + \frac{136-1}{990} = 2 + \frac{3}{22} = 2\frac{3}{22}.$

21. Given expression $= \frac{(0.3333)}{(0.2222)} \times \frac{(0.1667)(0.8333)}{(0.6667)(0.1250)} = \frac{3333}{2222} \times \frac{\frac{1}{6} \times \frac{5}{6}}{\frac{2}{3} \times \frac{125}{1000}}$

$= \left(\frac{3}{2} \times \frac{1}{6} \times \frac{5}{6} \times \frac{3}{2} \times 8\right) = \frac{5}{2} = 2.50.$

22. $\frac{3.157 \times 4126 \times 3.198}{63.972 \times 2835.121} \approx \frac{3.5 \times 4126 \times 3.2}{64 \times 2835} = \frac{32 \times 4126 \times 32}{64 \times 2835} \times \frac{1}{100}$

$= \frac{66016}{2835} \times \frac{1}{100} = \frac{23.28}{100} = 0.23 \approx 0.2.$

23. $\frac{489.1375 \times 0.0483 \times 1.956}{0.0873 \times 92.581 \times 99.749} \approx \frac{489 \times 0.05 \times 2}{0.09 \times 93 \times 100} = \frac{489}{9 \times 93 \times 10}$

$= \frac{163}{279} \times \frac{1}{10} = \frac{0.58}{10} = 0.058 \approx 0.06.$

25. $\frac{29.94}{1.45} = \frac{299.4}{14.5} = \left(\frac{2994}{14.5} \times \frac{1}{10}\right) = \frac{172}{10} = 17.2.$

26. $(0.11)^3 + (0.22)^3 + ... + (0.99)^3 = (0.11)^3(1^3 + 2^3 + ... + 9^3)$

$= 0.001331 \times 2025 = 2.6953275 \approx 2.695.$

28. $6.\overline{46} = 6 + 0.\overline{46} = 6 + \frac{46}{99} = \frac{594+46}{99} = \frac{640}{99}.$

29. $0.84\overline{181} = \dfrac{84181-841}{99000} = \dfrac{83340}{99000} = \dfrac{463}{550}.$

$\therefore$ Required difference = (550 – 463) = 84.

31. Given expression $= \dfrac{(67.542)^2-(32.458)^2}{(67.542+7.196)-(32.458+7.916)}$

$= \dfrac{(67.542)^2-(32.458)^2}{67.542-32.458} = (67.542 + 32.458) = 100.$

32. Suppose commodity X will cost 40 paise more than Y after z years. Then,
$(4.20 + 0.40z) - (6.30 + 0.15z) = 0.40$

$\Leftrightarrow 0.25z = 0.40 + 2.10 \;\Leftrightarrow\; z = \dfrac{2.50}{0.25} = \dfrac{250}{25} = 10.$

$\therefore$ X will cost 40 paise more than Y 10 years after 2001 *i.e.,* in 2011.

33. Length of each piece $= \left(\dfrac{1}{8}\right)$m = 0.125 m.

$\therefore$ Required number of pieces $= \left(\dfrac{37.5}{0.125}\right) = \left(\dfrac{375\times100}{125}\right) = 300.$

34. $\dfrac{4.036}{0.04} = \dfrac{403.6}{4} = 100.9.$

35. 1. 36839 ÷ 17 = 2167. Dividend contains 2 places of decimal.
$\therefore$ 368.39 ÷ 17 = 21.67.

2. 17050 ÷ 62 = 275. Dividend contains 2 places of decimal.
$\therefore$ 170.50 ÷ 62 = 275.

3. 87565 ÷ 83 = 1055. Divident contains 2 places of decimal.
$\therefore$ 875.65 ÷ 83 = 10.55.

Since 21.67 > 10.55 > 2.75, the desired order is 1, 3, 2.

36. Sum of digits right to decimal places = 7.
Since the last digit to the extreme right will be zero (5 × 4 = 20), so thre will be 6 significant digis to the right of the decimal point.

37. $3.14 \times 10^6 = 3.140000 \times 1000000 = 3140000.$

~~~~~~
~~~~~~

4. SIMPLIFICATION

Simplification means expressing in a simpler form. In order to simplify an expression we use the operations in the following order which is easily remembered as "BODMAS" *i.e.*, (*i*) Bracket (*ii*) of (*iii*) Division (*iv*) Multiplication (*v*) Addition (*vi*) Subtraction. 'Of' means multiplication but is operated even before division.

Brackets are of four types and they are operated in the following order,

Bar or line, ( ), { } and [ ]

Thus, the complete order of operation will be

____, (), { }, [ ], of, ÷, ×, +, –.

Order of + and – can be interchanged or they can be operated simultaneously too.

SOLVED EXAMPLE

1. Simplify $200 \div 2\,5 \times 4 + 12 - 3$.

Sol. $8 \times 4 + 12 - 3 = 32 + 12 - 3 = 41$.

2. Find the value of $64 + 16 \div 2 - 6$ of $7 + 3 \times 2$.

Sol. $64 + 16 \div 2 - 42 + 3 \times 2 = 64 + 8 - 42 + 3 \times 2$

$= 64 + 8 - 42 + 6 = 78 - 42 = 36$.

3. Find the value of $10 - \left[6 - \left\{7 - \left(6 - \overline{8 - 5}\right)\right\}\right]$

Sol. $10 - [6 - \{7 - (6 - 3)\}] = 10 - [6 - \{7 - 3\}]$

$= 10 - [6 - 4] = 10 - 2 = 8$.

4. Evaluate $0.5 \times 0.5 + 1.5 \div 0.5$.

Sol. $0.5 \times 0.5 + 3 = 0.25 + 3 = 3.25$.

5. Simplify $2 + [2 + 25 \div \{2 + 24 \div (2 + 2 \times 3)\}]$.

Sol. $2 + [2 + 25 \div (2 + 24 \div 8\}] = 2 + [2 + 25 \div \{2 + 3\}]$

$= 2 + [2 + 25 \div 5] = 2 + [2 + 5] = 2 + 7 = 9$.

6. Solve $4\frac{2}{3} + 7\frac{1}{3} \times 1\frac{1}{2} + \frac{1}{2} - 3\frac{1}{3}$

Sol. $\frac{14}{3} + \frac{22}{3} \times \frac{3}{2} + \frac{1}{2} - \frac{10}{3} = \frac{14}{3} + \frac{22}{3} \times 3 - \frac{10}{3}$

$= \frac{14}{3} + 22 - \frac{10}{3} = 22 + \frac{4}{3} = 22 + 1\frac{1}{3} = 23\frac{1}{3}$.

EXERCISE

1. $(8 \div 88) \times 8888088 = ?$

(*a*) 808008 (*b*) 808080 (*c*) 808088 (*d*) 8008008

2. The value of $1001 \div 11$ of 13 is:

(*a*) 7 (*b*) 91 (*c*) 143 (*d*) 169

3. $(-5)(4)(2)\left(-\frac{1}{2}\right)\left(\frac{3}{4}\right) = ?$

(*a*) –30 (*b*) –15 (*c*) 15 (*d*) 30

4. What mathematical operation should come at the place of '?' in the equation: $2 ? 6 - 12 \div 4 + 2 = 11$.

(*a*) + (*b*) – (*c*) × (*d*) ÷

5. Which of the following will come in place of both the question marks in the following equation?

$$\frac{128 \div 16 \times ? - 7 \times 2}{7^2 - 8 \times 6 + ?^2} = 1$$

(*a*) 3 (*b*) 14 (*c*) 16 (*d*) 17

6. Simplify: $18 - [5 - \{6 + 2(7 - \overline{8 - 5})\}]$.

(*a*) 13 (*b*) 15 (*c*) 27 (*d*) 32

7. Evaluate: $\frac{8 - [5 - (-3 + 2)] \div 2}{|5 - 3| - |5 - 8| \div 3}$.

(*a*) 2 (*b*) 3 (*c*) 4 (*d*) 5

8. $1\frac{3}{4} + 5\frac{1}{3} + 3\frac{2}{5} = ?$

(*a*) $9\frac{2}{5}$ (*b*) $9\frac{29}{60}$ (*c*) $10\frac{2}{5}$ (*d*) $10\frac{29}{60}$

9. $\frac{-\frac{1}{2} - \frac{2}{3} + \frac{4}{5} - \frac{1}{3} + \frac{1}{5} + \frac{3}{4}}{\frac{1}{2} + \frac{2}{3} - \frac{4}{3} + \frac{1}{3} - \frac{1}{5} - \frac{4}{5}}$ is simplified to:

(*a*) $-\frac{3}{10}$ (*b*) $\frac{-10}{3}$ (*c*) –2 (*d*) 1

10. $\frac{3}{5}$ of $\frac{4}{7}$ of $\frac{5}{9}$ of $\frac{21}{24}$ of 504 = ?

(*a*) 63 (*b*) 69 (*c*) 84 (*d*) 109

11. Supply the two missing figures in order indicate by x and y in the given equation, the fractions being in their lowest therms,

$$5\frac{1}{x} \times y\frac{3}{4} = 20$$

(*a*) 3, 1 (*b*) 3, 3 (*c*) 4, 1 (*d*) 5, 3

12. By how much is three-fifth of 350 greater than four-seventh of 210?

(*a*) 95 (*b*) 110 (*c*) 90 (*d*) 210

13. Two-fifth of one-fourth of three-seventh of a number is 15. What is half of that number?

(*a*) 94 (*b*) 96 (*c*) 188 (*d*) 175

14. If $a * b = \frac{ab}{a+b}$, find the value of $3 * (3 * -1)$.

(*a*) –3 (*b*) –1.5 (*c*) –1 (*d*) $\frac{2}{3}$

15. If $a * b * c$ mean $\frac{a+b}{c}$ for all numbers except 0, then $(a * b * c) * a * b$ is equal to:

(*a*) 0 (*b*) 1 (*c*) $\frac{a+b+c}{ab}$ (*d*) $\frac{a+b+ac}{bc}$

16. 7 is added to a certain number; the sum is multiplied by 5; the product is divided by 9 and 3 is subtracted from the quotient. The remainder left is 12. The number is:

(*a*) 20 (*b*) 30 (*c*) 40 (*d*) 60

17. A student was asked to solve the fraction $\dfrac{\frac{7}{3}+1\frac{1}{2} \text{ of } \frac{5}{3}}{2+1\frac{2}{3}}$ and his answer was $\frac{1}{4}$. By hou much was his answer wrong?

(*a*) 1 (*b*) $\frac{1}{55}$ (*c*) $\frac{1}{220}$ (*d*) None of these

18. Simplify: $\dfrac{\frac{1}{3}+\frac{3}{4}\left(\frac{2}{5}-\frac{1}{3}\right)}{1\frac{2}{3} \text{ of } \frac{3}{4}-\frac{1}{4} \text{ of } \frac{4}{5}}$

(*a*) $\frac{1}{63}$ (*b*) $\frac{23}{40}$ (*c*) $\frac{23}{55}$ (*d*) $\frac{23}{63}$

19. If $(a - b)$ is 6 more than $(c + b)$ and $(a + b)$ is 3 less than $(c - d)$, then $(a - c)$ is :

(*a*) 0.5 (*b*) 1 (*c*) 1.5 (*d*) None of these

20. If $(a + b + 2c + 3d)(a - b - 2c + 3d) = (a - b + 2c - 3d)(a + b - 2c - 3d)$, then $2bc$ is equal to:

(*a*) $\frac{3}{2}$ (*b*) $\frac{3a}{2d}$ (*c*) $3ad$ (*d*) a^2d^2

21. The value of $\dfrac{1}{2+\dfrac{1}{2+\dfrac{1}{2-\frac{1}{2}}}}$ is:

(*a*) $\frac{3}{8}$ (*b*) $\frac{19}{8}$ (*c*) $\frac{8}{3}$ (*d*) $\frac{8}{19}$

22. If $\dfrac{2+\dfrac{1}{3\frac{4}{5}}}{2+\dfrac{1}{3+\dfrac{1}{1+\frac{1}{4}}}} = x$, then the value of x is :

(*a*) $\frac{1}{7}$ (*b*) $\frac{3}{7}$ (*c*) 1 (*d*) $\frac{8}{7}$

23. If $\dfrac{37}{13} = 2+\dfrac{1}{x+\dfrac{1}{y+\frac{1}{z}}}$, where x, y, z are natural numbers, then x, y, z are:

(*a*) 1, 2, 5 (*b*) 1, 5, 2 (*c*) 5, 2, 11 (*d*) 11, 2, 5

24. Which of the following values of x and y satisfy the following equations I and II ?

I. $3x + y = 19$ II. $x - y = 9$

(*a*) –7, –2 (*b*) –7, 2 (*c*) 7, –2 (*d*) 7, 2

25. The value of $\frac{3}{1^2 \cdot 2^2} + \frac{5}{2^2 \cdot 3^2} + \frac{7}{3^2 \cdot 4^2} + \frac{9}{4^2 \cdot 5^2} + \frac{11}{5^2 \cdot 6^2} + \frac{13}{6^2 \cdot 7^2} + \frac{15}{7^2 \cdot 8^2} + \frac{17}{8^2 \cdot 9^2} + \frac{19}{9^2 \cdot 10^2}$ is :

(*a*) $\frac{1}{100}$ (*b*) $\frac{99}{100}$ (*c*) 1 (*d*) $\frac{101}{100}$

26. Income of a company doubles after every one year. If the initial income was ₹ 4 lakhs, what would be the income after 5 years?

(*a*) ₹ 1.24 crores (*b*) ₹ 1.28 crores
(*c*) ₹ 1.25 crores (*d*) ₹ 2.56 crores

27. On sports day, if 30 children were made to stand in a column, then 26 columns could be formed. If 24 children were made to stand in a column, then how many columns could be formed?

(*a*) 20 (*b*) 22 (*c*) 29 (*d*) 45

28. A light was seen at intervals of 13 seconds. It was seen for the first time at-1 hr. 54 min 50 sees. a.m. and the last time at 3 hrs. 17 min. 49 sees. a.m. How many times was the light seen?

(*a*) 360 (*b*) 375 (*c*) 378 (*d*) 384

29. A man earns ₹ 20 on the first day and spends ₹ 15 on the next day. He again earns ₹ 20 on the third day and spends ₹ 15 on the fourth day. If he continues to save like this, how soon will he have ₹ 60 in hand?

(*a*) On 17th day (*b*) On 27th day
(*c*) On 30th day (*d*) On 40th day

30. It costs ₹ x each to make the first thousand copies of a compact disc and ₹ y to make each subsequent copy. If z is greater than 2000, how much will it cost to make z copies of the compact disc?

(*a*) $zx - zy$ (*b*) $1000\,x + yz$
(*c*) $1000\,(x - y) + yz$ (*d*) $1000\,(z - y) + xz$

31. The total monthly salary of 4 men and 2 women is ₹ 46,000. If a woman earns ₹ 500 more than a man, what is the monthly salary of a woman?

(*a*) ₹ 6500 (*b*) ₹ 7500 (*c*) ₹ 8000 (*d*) None of these

32. Nitesh got two and a half times as many marks in English as in History. If his total marks in the two subjects are 140, the marks obtained by him in English are:

(*a*) 40 (*b*) 75 (*c*) 90 (*d*) 100

33. Water boils at 212°F or 100°C and melts at 32°F or 0°C. If the temperature of a particular day is 35°C, it is equivalent to :

(*a*) 85°F (*b*) 90°F (*c*) 95°F (*d*) 99°F

34. There are two examination rooms A and B. If 10 students are sent from A to B, then the number of students in each room is the same. If 20 candidates are sent from B to A, then the number of students in A is double the number of students in B. The number of students in room A is:

(*a*) 20 (*b*) 80 (*c*) 100 (*d*) 200

35. The price of 2 sarees and 4 shirts is ₹ 1600. With the same money one can buy 1 saree and 6 shirts. If one wants to buy 12 shirts, how much shall be have to pay?

(*a*) ₹ 1200 (*b*) ₹ 2400

(*c*) ₹ 4800 (*d*) Cannot be determine

36. One-third of Panas's savings in National Savings Certificate is equal to one-half of his savings in Public Provident Fund. If he has ₹ 1,50,000 as total savings, how much has he saved in Public Provident Fund?

(*a*) ₹ 30,000 (*b*) ₹ 50,000 (*c*) ₹ 60,000 (*d*) ₹ 90,000

37. The fluid contained in a bucket can fill four large bottles or seven small bottles. A full large bottle is used to fill an empty small bottle. What fraction of the fluid is left over in the large bottle when the small one is full?

(*a*) $\frac{2}{7}$ (*b*) $\frac{3}{7}$ (*c*) $\frac{5}{7}$ (*d*) $\frac{6}{7}$

38. Peter gave one-fourth of the amount he had to Michael. Michael in turn gave half of what he received from Peter to Sam. If the difference between the remaining amount with Peter and the amount received by Sam is ₹ 500, how much money did Michael receive from Peter?

(*a*) ₹ 100 (*b*) ₹ 200 (*c*) ₹ 400

(*d*) Data inadequate

39. An institute organised a fete and $\frac{1}{5}$ of the girls and $\frac{1}{8}$ of the boys participated in the same. What fraction of the total number of students took part in the fete?

(*a*) $\frac{2}{13}$ (*b*) $\frac{13}{40}$ (*c*) Data inadequate (*d*) None of these

40. At an International Dinner, $\frac{1}{5}$ of the people attending were French men. If the number of French women at the dinner was $\frac{2}{3}$ greater than the number of French men, and there were no other French people at the dinner, then what fraction of the people at the dinner were not French?

(*a*) $\frac{1}{5}$ (*b*) $\frac{2}{5}$ (*c*) $\frac{2}{3}$ (*d*) $\frac{7}{15}$

41. One-third of the boys and one-half of the girls of a college participated in a social work project. If the number of participating students is 300 out of which 100 are boys, what is the total number of students in the college?

(*a*) 500 (*b*) 600 (*c*) 700 (*d*) 800

42. A fires 5 shots to B's 3 but A kills only once in 3 shots while B kills one in 2 shots. When B has missed 27 times, A has killed:

(*a*) 30 birds (*b*) 60 birds (*c*) 72 birds (*d*) 90 birds

43. N number of persons decided to raise ₹ 3 lakhs by equal contributions from each. Had they contributed ₹ 50 each extra, the contribution would have been ₹ 3.25 lakhs. How many persons are there?

(*a*) 400 (*b*) 450 (*c*) 600 (*d*) None of these

44. In a regular week, there are 5 working days and for each day, the working hours are 8. A man gets ₹ 2.40 per hour For regular work and ₹ 3.20 per hours for overtime. If he earns ₹ 432 in 4 weeks, then how many hours does he work for?

(*a*) 160 (*b*) 175 (*c*) 180 (*d*) 195

45. A sum of ₹ 312 was divided among 100 boys and girls in such a way that each boy gets ₹ 3.60 and each girl ₹ 2.40. The number of girls is:

(*a*) 35 (*b*) 40 (*c*) 60 (*d*) 65

46. In an examination, a student scores 4 marks for every correct answer and loses 1 mark for every wrong answer. If he attempts in all 60 questions and secures 130 marks, the number of questions he attempts correctly, is:

(*a*) 35 (*b*) 38 (*c*) 40 (*d*) 42

47. A man has ₹ 480 in the denominations of one-rupee notes, five-rupee notes and ten-rupee notes. The number of notes of each denomination is equal. What is the total number of notes that he has?

(*a*) 45 (*b*) 60 (*c*) 75 (*d*) 90

48. On Children's Day, sweets were to be equally distributed among 175 children in a school. Actually on the Children's Day, 35 children were absent and therefore each child got 4 sweets extra. Total how many sweets were available for distribution?
(*a*) 2400 (*b*) 2480 (*c*) 2680 (*d*) None of these

ANSWERS

1	2	3	4	5	6	7	8	9	10
(*a*)	(*a*)	(*c*)	(*c*)	(*a*)	(*c*)	(*d*)	(*d*)	(*a*)	(*c*)
11	**12**	**13**	**14**	**15**	**16**	**17**	**18**	**19**	**20**
(*b*)	(*c*)	(*d*)	(*a*)	(*d*)	(*a*)	(*d*)	(*d*)	(*c*)	(*c*)
21	**22**	**23**	**24**	**25**	**26**	**27**	**28**	**29**	**30**
(*d*)	(*c*)	(*b*)	(*c*)	(*b*)	(*b*)	(*a*)	(*d*)	(*a*)	(*c*)
31	**32**	**33**	**34**	**35**	**36**	**37**	**38**	**39**	**40**
(*c*)	(*d*)	(*c*)	(*c*)	(*b*)	(*c*)	(*b*)	(*b*)	(*a*)	(*d*)
41	**42**	**43**	**44**	**45**	**46**	**47**	**48**		
(*c*)	(*a*)	(*d*)	(*b*)	(*b*)	(*b*)	(*d*)	(*d*)		

SOME SELECTED EXPLANATORY ANSWERS

1. $\frac{8}{88} \times 8888088 = \frac{1}{11} \times 8888088 = 808008.$

2. $1001 \div 143 = 7.$

3. $\left(5 \times 4 \times 2 \times \frac{1}{2} \times \frac{3}{4}\right) = 15.$

5. Let $\frac{128 \div 16 \times x - 7 \times 2}{7^2 - 8 \times 6 + x^2} = 1.$

Then, $8x - 7 \times 2 = 49 - 48 + x^2 \Leftrightarrow 8x - 14 = 1 + x^2$
$\Leftrightarrow x^2 - 8x + 15 = 0$
$\Leftrightarrow (x - 3)(x - 5) = 0$
$\Leftrightarrow x = 3$ or $x = 5$.

6. $18 - [5 - \{6 + 2(7 - 3)\}] = 18 - [5 - \{6 + 2 \times 4\}]$
$= 18 - [5 - \{6 + 8\}] = 18 - [5 - 14]$
$= 18 - [-9] = 18 + 9 = 27.$

8. $\frac{7}{4} + \frac{16}{3} + \frac{17}{5} = \frac{105 + 320 + 204}{60} = \frac{629}{60} = 10\frac{29}{60}.$

9. $$\frac{\left(-\frac{2}{3}-\frac{1}{3}\right)+\left(\frac{4}{5}+\frac{1}{5}\right)+\left(\frac{3}{4}-\frac{1}{2}\right)}{\left(\frac{2}{3}-\frac{4}{3}+\frac{1}{3}\right)-\left(\frac{1}{5}+\frac{4}{5}\right)+\frac{1}{2}}$$

$$=\frac{-1+1+\frac{1}{4}}{-\frac{1}{3}-1+\frac{1}{2}}=\frac{\frac{1}{4}}{\frac{-2-6+3}{6}}=\frac{\frac{1}{4}}{-\frac{5}{6}}=\frac{1}{4}\times\left(-\frac{6}{5}\right)=\frac{-3}{10}.$$

10. $\left(\frac{3}{5}\times\frac{4}{7}\times\frac{5}{9}\times\frac{21}{24}\times 504\right) = 84.$

12. $\frac{3}{5}$ of 350 – $\frac{4}{7}$ of 210 = 210 – 120 = 90.

13. Let the required number is x.

Then, from question $\frac{2}{5}$ of $\frac{1}{4}$ of $\frac{3}{7}$ of $x = 15$

$\Leftrightarrow x = \left(15\times\frac{7}{3}\times 4\times\frac{5}{2}\right) = 350 \Leftrightarrow \frac{1}{2}x = 175.$

14. $(3 * -1) = \frac{3\times(-1)}{3+(-1)}=\frac{-3}{2}$. So, $3 * (3 * -1)$

$$= 3 * \left(\frac{-3}{2}\right)=\frac{3\times\left(\frac{-3}{2}\right)}{3+\left(\frac{-3}{2}\right)}=\frac{-9}{2}\times\frac{2}{3}=-3.$$

15. $(a * b * c) * a * b = \left(\frac{a+b}{c}\right)*a*b=\frac{\left(\frac{a+b}{c}\right)+a}{b}=\frac{a+b+ac}{bc}.$

16. Let the required number is x. Then, from question,

$\frac{5(x+7)}{9} - 3 = 12 \Leftrightarrow 5(x + 7) - 27 = 108 \Leftrightarrow 5x + 35 = 135$

$\Leftrightarrow 5x = 100 \Leftrightarrow x = 20.$

17. $\dfrac{\dfrac{7}{3}+1\dfrac{1}{2}\text{ of }\dfrac{5}{3}}{2+1\dfrac{2}{3}}=\dfrac{\dfrac{7}{3}+\dfrac{3}{2}\text{ of }\dfrac{5}{3}}{2+\dfrac{5}{3}}=\dfrac{\dfrac{7}{3}+\dfrac{5}{2}}{\dfrac{11}{3}}=\dfrac{29}{6}\times\dfrac{3}{11}=\dfrac{29}{22}.$

$\therefore$ Required answer $=\dfrac{29}{22}-\dfrac{1}{4}=\dfrac{58-11}{44}=\dfrac{47}{44}=1\dfrac{3}{44}.$

18. $\dfrac{\dfrac{1}{3}+\dfrac{3}{4}\left(\dfrac{6-5}{15}\right)}{\dfrac{5}{3}\text{ of }\dfrac{3}{4}-\dfrac{1}{5}}=\dfrac{\dfrac{1}{3}+\dfrac{3}{4}\times\dfrac{1}{15}}{\dfrac{5}{4}-\dfrac{1}{5}}=\dfrac{\dfrac{1}{3}+\dfrac{1}{20}}{\dfrac{25-4}{20}}=\dfrac{23}{60}\times\dfrac{20}{21}=\dfrac{23}{63}.$

19. $(a-b)-(c+d)=6$ and $(c-d)-(a+b)=3$
$\Rightarrow (a-b)-(c+d)=6$ and $(c-a)-(b+d)=3$
$\Rightarrow (b+d)=(a-c)-6$ and $(b+d)=(c-a)-3$

$\Rightarrow (a-c)-6=(c-a)-3 \Rightarrow 2(a-c)=3 \Rightarrow (a-c)=\dfrac{3}{2}=1.5.$

20. $(a+b+2c+3d)(a-b-2c+3d)=(a-b+2c-3d)(a+b-2c-3d)$
$\Rightarrow [(a+b)+(2c+3d)][(a-b)-(2c-3d)]$
$\quad = [(a-b)+(2c-3d)][(a+b)-(2c+3d)]$
$\Rightarrow (a+b)(a-b)-(a+b)(2c-3d)+(a-b)+(2c-3d)-(2c+3d)(2c-3d)$
$\quad = (a-b)(a+b)-(a-b)(2c+3d)+(a+b)+(2c-3d)-(2c+3d)(2c-3d)$

$\Rightarrow (a+b)(2c-3d)=(a-b)(2c+3d)$
$\Rightarrow 2ac-3ad+2bc-3bd=2ac+3ad-2bc-3bd$
$\Rightarrow 4bc=6ad \Rightarrow 2bc=3ad.$

21. $\dfrac{1}{2+\dfrac{1}{2+\dfrac{1}{(3/2)}}}+\dfrac{1}{2+\dfrac{1}{2+\dfrac{2}{3}}}=\dfrac{1}{2+\dfrac{1}{(8/3)}}=\dfrac{1}{2+\dfrac{3}{8}}=\dfrac{1}{(19/8)}=\dfrac{8}{19}.$

22. $x=\dfrac{2+\dfrac{1}{(19/5)}}{2+\dfrac{1}{3+\dfrac{1}{(5/4)}}}=\dfrac{2+\dfrac{5}{19}}{2+\dfrac{1}{3+\dfrac{4}{5}}}=\dfrac{2+\dfrac{5}{19}}{2+\dfrac{1}{(19/5)}}=\dfrac{2+\dfrac{5}{19}}{2+\dfrac{5}{19}}=1.$

23. $2+\cfrac{1}{x+\cfrac{1}{y+\cfrac{1}{z}}}=\frac{37}{13}=2\frac{11}{13}=2+\frac{11}{13}\Rightarrow\cfrac{1}{x+\cfrac{1}{y+\cfrac{1}{z}}}=\frac{11}{13}\Rightarrow x+\cfrac{1}{y+\cfrac{1}{z}}=\frac{13}{11}$

$\Rightarrow x+\cfrac{1}{y+\cfrac{1}{z}}=1+\frac{2}{11}\Rightarrow x=1, y+\frac{1}{z}=\frac{11}{2}=5\frac{1}{2}=5+\frac{1}{2}\Rightarrow x=1, y=5, z=2.$

24. Adding (*i*) and (*ii*), we get : $4x = 28$ or $x = 7$.
Putting $x = 7$ in (*ii*), we get: $y = -2$.

25. Given exp. $=\left(\frac{1}{1^2}-\frac{1}{2^2}\right)+\left(\frac{1}{2^2}-\frac{1}{3^2}\right)+\left(\frac{1}{3^2}-\frac{1}{4^2}\right)+\left(\frac{1}{4^2}-\frac{1}{5^2}\right)+\ldots..$

$+\left(\frac{1}{9^2}-\frac{1}{10^2}\right)$

$=\left(\frac{1}{1^2}-\frac{1}{10^2}\right)=\left(1-\frac{1}{100}\right)=\frac{99}{100}.$

27. Total number of children = $(30 \times 16) = 480$.

$\therefore$ Number of columns of 24 children each = $\left(\frac{480}{24}\right) = 20$.

28.

Hrs.	Min.	Sec.
3	17	49
(–) 1	54	50
1	22	59

Total time = $(1 \times 60 + 22)$ min. + 59 sec. $(82 \times 60 + 59)$ sec. 4979 sec.

$\therefore$ Number of times the light is seen = $\left(\frac{4979}{13}+1\right)=384$.

29. Money saved in 2 days = ₹ (20 – 15) = ₹ 5.

Money saved in 1 days = ₹ $\frac{5}{2}$

Money saved in 16 days = ₹ $\left(\frac{5}{2}\times 16\right)$ = ₹ 40.

On 17th day, money in hand = ₹ (40 + 20) = ₹ 60.

30. Required cost = ₹ $[1000 \times x + (z - 1000) \times y]$ = ₹ $(1000x + zy - 1000y)$
= ₹ $[1000 (x - y) + yz]$.

31. Suppose that the monthly salary of man is ₹ P.
Then, monthly salary of a woman = ₹ (P + 500).
$\therefore$ 4P + 2 (P + 500) = 46000 $\Leftrightarrow$ 6P = 45000 $\Leftrightarrow$ P = 7500.
Monthly salary of a woman = P + 500 = ₹ 8000.

32. Suppose that marks in History = x. Then, marks in English = $\frac{5}{2}x$.

$$\therefore x + \frac{5}{2}x = 140 \Leftrightarrow \frac{7}{2}x = 140 \Leftrightarrow x = \left(\frac{140 \times 2}{7}\right) = 40.$$

Hence, marks in English = $\frac{5}{2}x = \left(\frac{5}{2} \times 40\right) = 100$.

33. Let F and C denote the temperatures in Fahrenheit and Celsius respectively.

Then, $\frac{F-32}{212-32} = \frac{C-0}{100-0} \Leftrightarrow \frac{F-32}{180} = \frac{C}{100}$.

If C = 35, then F = $\left(\frac{35}{100} \times 180\right) + 32 = 63 + 32 = 95$.

34. Let the number of students in rooms A and B be x and y respectively. Then,
$x - 10 = y + 10 \Rightarrow x - y = 20$ ...(*i*)
and $x + 20 = 2 (y - 20) \Rightarrow x - 2y = -60$ ...(*ii*)
Solving (*i*) and (*ii*), we get : $x = 100$, $y = 80$.

35. Let the price of a saree and a shirt be ₹ x and ₹ y respectively.
Then, $2x + 4y = 1600$ ...(*i*) and $x + 6y = 1600$ ...(*ii*)
Solving (*i*) and (*ii*), We get: $x = 400$, $y = 200$.
$\therefore$ Cost of 12 shirts = ₹ (12 × 200) = ₹ 2400.

36. Suppose that the savings in N.S.C. is ₹ x then saving in P.P.F. is ₹ $(150000 - x)$ Then, from question, $\frac{1}{3}x = \frac{1}{2}(150000 - x)$

$$\Leftrightarrow \frac{x}{3} = \frac{x}{2} = 75000 \Leftrightarrow \frac{5x}{6} = 75000 \Leftrightarrow x = \left(\frac{750000 \times 6}{5}\right) = 90000.$$

$\therefore$ Savings in Public Provident Fund = ₹ (150000 – 90000) = ₹ 60000.

37. Suppose that the capacity of the bucket is P litres. Then,

Capacity of 1 large bottle = $\frac{P}{4}$; Capacity of 1 small bottle = $\frac{P}{7}$.

Fluid left in large bottle = $\left(\frac{P}{4}-\frac{P}{7}\right)=\frac{3P}{28}$.

$\therefore$ Required fraction = $\left(\frac{3P/28}{P/4}\right)=\left(\frac{3P}{28}\times\frac{4}{P}\right)=\frac{3}{7}$.

38. Suppose initially Peter and had ₹ x. Then,

Amount received by Michael = ₹ $\left(\frac{x}{4}\right)$.

Amount remaining with Peter + ₹$\left(x-\frac{x}{4}\right)$ = ₹ $\left(\frac{3x}{4}\right)$

Amount received by Sam = ₹ $\left(\frac{1}{2}\times\frac{x}{4}\right)$ = ₹ $\left(\frac{x}{8}\right)$.

$\therefore\ \frac{3x}{4}-\frac{x}{8}=500 \Leftrightarrow 5x=4000 \Leftrightarrow x=800.$

Hence, amount received by Miehael = $(x/4)$ = ₹ 200.

39. Out of 5 girls, 1 took part in fete. Out of 8 boys, 1 took part in fete.

$\therefore$ Out of 13 students, 2 took part in fete.

Hence, $\frac{2}{13}$ of the total number took part in fete.

40. French men = $\frac{1}{5}$; French women = $\left(\frac{1}{5}+\frac{2}{3}\times\frac{1}{5}\right)=\frac{5}{15}=\frac{1}{3}$.

French people = $\left(\frac{1}{5}+\frac{1}{3}\right)=\frac{8}{15}$. $\therefore$ Not-French = $\left(1-\frac{8}{15}\right)=\frac{7}{15}$.

41. Number of boys who participate = 100.

$\therefore\ \frac{1}{3}$ of boys = 100 or total number of boys = 300.

Number of girls who participate = 200.

$\therefore\ \frac{1}{2}$ of girls = 200 or total number of girls = 400.

Hence, total number of students = (300 + 400) = 700.

42. Let the total number of shots be x. Then,

Shots fired by A = $\frac{5}{8}x$; Shots fired by B = $\frac{3}{8}x$.

Killing shots by A = $\frac{1}{3}$ of $\frac{5}{8}x=\frac{5x}{24}$; Shots missed by B = $\frac{1}{2}$ of $\frac{3}{8}x=\frac{3}{16}x$.

$\therefore \quad \frac{3x}{16} = 27$ or $x = \left(\frac{27 \times 16}{3}\right) = 144.$

Birds killed by A $= \frac{5x}{24} = \left(\frac{5}{24} \times 144\right) = 30.$

44. Suppose the man works overtime for x hours.
Now, working hours in 4 weeks $= (5 \times 8 \times 4) = 160.$
$\therefore$ $160 \times 2.40 + x \times 3.20 = 432 \Leftrightarrow 3.20x = 432 - 384 = 48 \Leftrightarrow x = 15.$
Hence, total hours of work $= (160 + 15) = 175.$

45. Suppose that the number of boys $= x$. Then, number of girls $= (100 - x)$.
$\therefore$ $3.60x + 2.40\ (100 - x) = 312 \Leftrightarrow 1.20x = 312 - 240 = 72 \Leftrightarrow x = 60.$
Hence, number of girls $= (100 - x) = 40.$

46. Let the number of correct answers be x. Number of incorrect answers $= (60 - x)$.
$\therefore$ $4x - (60 - x) = 130 \Leftrightarrow 5x = 190 \Leftrightarrow x = 38.$

47. Let number of notes of each denomination be x.
Then, $x + 5x + 10x = 480 \Leftrightarrow 16x = 480 \Leftrightarrow x = 30.$
Hence, total number of notes $= 3x = 90.$

48. Suppose that the total number of sweets is x. Then,
$\frac{x}{140} - \frac{x}{175} = 4 \Leftrightarrow 5x - 4x = 4 \times 700 \Leftrightarrow x = 2800.$

~~~~~~
~~~~~~

5. SQUARE ROOTS AND CUBE ROOTS

SQUARE ROOTS

Square root is opposite of Square. Square root of a given number may be defined as the number whose square is equal to the given number. In other words, square root of a given number is the number when multiplied by itself, gives the product equal to the given number.

For example, $\sqrt{4} = 2$ and $2 \times 2 = 4$.

$\sqrt{9} = 3$ and $3 \times 3 = 9$

There are two methods of finding square root of a number.

Method A: By Factorisation

This method is generally used where the given number is a perfect square or when the number can be written as product of such factors whose square roots are known.

I. Write the given number as product of prime factors.

II. Take the product of prime factors, choosing one for every pair.

Method B: By Division

It is the most general method of finding square roots and is applicable to all cases.

I. Mark off groups of two-digits, starting from right. The extreme group may be either single digit or a pair.

II. Start division process from the extreme left group.

III. For the second stage add the quotient to the divisor. The divisor of this stage will be equal to this sum with the quotient for this stage suffixed to it. The next dividend is always obtained by annexing the next pair of digits (of the dividend) to the remainder of the previous stage.

IV. For the next stage again add the divisor and the quotient of the previous stage. The divisor for this stage will be formed in the same manner as explained for the second stage in Step III.

V. Continue Step IV till all the groups get exhausted. In case a remainder is left, annex two zeros to it and put a decimal point in the quotient.

At every stage after this we will annex two zeros to the remainder.

Continue to the number of decimal places required in the result.

The quotient is equal to the square root of the given number.

SQUARE ROOTS OF DECIMALS

First make 2-digit groups separately for the portions on the left and right of decimal point. For the portion of left, the procedure as same as given above in Method II (point I). For the portion on the right of decimal point, you should annex zero to complete the pair (if needed).

After forming the pairs as above, ignore the decimal point and find the square root by division method explained above. In the result the number of decimal places is half of the number of decimal places in the given number.

CUBE ROOTS

Cube root of a number x is the number whose cube is x. It is denoted by $\sqrt[3]{x}$ or $x^{\frac{1}{3}}$.

To Find Cube Root by Factorisation: Express the given number as product of prime factors. Then take the product of prime numbers, choosing one out of three of each type.

Remember:

If the cube ends in 1, then its cube root ends in 1
If the cube ends in 2, then its cube root ends in 8
If the cube ends in 3, then its cube root ends in 7
If the cube ends in 4, then its cube root ends in 4
If the cube ends in 5, then its cube root ends in 5
If the cube ends in 6, then its cube root ends in 6
If the cube ends in 7, then its cube root ends in 3
If the cube ends in 8, then its cube root ends in 2
If the cube ends in 9, then its cube root ends in 9
If the cube ends in 0, then its cube root ends in 0

We observe that 1,4,6,9 and 0 repeat themselves and 2, 3, 7 and 8 have complement of 10 i.e., 8, 7, 3 and 2 respectively.

Thus, while determining the cube root of a number consisting of more than 3 digits, we can find the extreme right digit (R) of the cube roots.

Now in the given number, form groups of three consecutive digits, starting from the extreme right. The last group (extreme left) may consist of less than three digits. The number of such 3-digit groups equals the number of digits in the cube root.

The first digit (i.e., extreme left) digit of the cube root (L) is the greatest digit satisfying $L^3 \leq$ last group.

Thus we can easily find the extreme left digit (*L*), the extreme right digit (*R*) and the number of digits in the cube root.

Cube Roots of Exact Cubes consisting of upto 6-digits.

If the number consists of upto 3-digits, its cube root will be less than 10 and can be easily found from the above table of cubes.

For numbers consisting of 4,5 or 6-digits, the cube root will consist of 2-digits. These two digits can be easily found using the above method for extreme left and extreme right digits.

Cube Roots of Exact Cubes having 7, 8 or 9 digits.

In such numbers, we will get three 3-digit groups and hence their cube roots will consist of 3-digits. Let us denote the middle digit by M.

L and R will be written as before. Procedure to find M is illustrated in the examples given below.

CUBE ROOT OF DECIMALS

First make 3 digit groups separately for the portions on the left and right of the decimal point. You can annex zeros, if needed, for the portion on the right of the decimal point, in order to convert it into true 3-digit groups. For the portion on the left the procedure is same as discussed above. Annexing of zeros will not be required if the given number is an exact cube.

Thereafter, ignore the decimal point and find the cube root. Finally, put the decimal point such that the number of decimal places in the cube root is one-third of the number of decimal places in the given number.

Surds: Any root of a rational number which cannot be easily calculated is called a surd. Surds are irrational numbers and can't be exactly obtained.

For example, $\sqrt{2}, \sqrt{6}, \sqrt{8}, \sqrt[3]{4}, \sqrt[4]{5}, \pi$, etc.

A surd consisting wholly of an irrational number is called a pure surd.

For example, $\sqrt{2}, \sqrt[3]{7}, \sqrt{6}$ etc.

A surd consisting of the product of a rational number and an irrational number is called a mixed surd.

For example, $3\sqrt{2}, 2\sqrt{3}, 4\sqrt[4]{5}$ etc.

A mixed surd can be converted into a pure surd but its converse is not always true.

For example, $$3\sqrt{2} = (3^2)^{\frac{1}{2}}\sqrt{2} = \sqrt{9}.\sqrt{2} = \sqrt{18}$$

$$2\sqrt{2} = (2^2)^{\frac{1}{2}}\sqrt{2} = \sqrt{4}.\sqrt{2} = \sqrt{8}$$

$$2\sqrt[4]{5} = \left(2^4\right)^{\frac{1}{4}} \sqrt[4]{5} = \sqrt[4]{16}.\sqrt[4]{5} = \sqrt[4]{80}$$

$$\sqrt{32} = \sqrt{16 \times 2} = 4\sqrt{2}$$

$$\sqrt[3]{54} = \sqrt[3]{27 \times 2} = 3\sqrt[3]{2}$$

$$\sqrt[4]{48} = \sqrt[4]{16 \times 3} = 2\sqrt[4]{3}$$

But $\sqrt{6}, \sqrt[3]{12}, \sqrt[4]{54}$ etc. can't be expressed as mixed surds.

Order of Surds: $a^{\frac{1}{n}}$ is called the surd of nth order.

For example, $\sqrt{5}$ is a surd of 2nd order.

$$\left(\sqrt{5} = 5^{\frac{1}{2}}\right)$$

$(16)^{\frac{1}{7}}$ is a surd of 7th order.

We can also change the order of surds in the following way:

$$3^{\frac{1}{2}} = 3^{\frac{2}{4}} = \left(3^2\right)^{\frac{1}{4}} = 9^{\frac{1}{4}}.$$

Comparing the Magnitudes of Surds: For comparing Surds, convert each of them into forms having the same order and then compare their bases.

ADDITION AND SUBTRACTION OF SURDS

Similar surds can be added and subtracted but dissimilar surds can't be added and subtracted.

For example, $2\sqrt{3} + 5\sqrt{3} = 7\sqrt{3}$

$$4\left(5^{\frac{1}{6}}\right) + 8\left(5^{\frac{1}{6}}\right) = 12\left(5^{\frac{1}{6}}\right)$$

But we can't add $2\sqrt{3}$ and $5\sqrt{2}$

or, $2\sqrt{3}$ and $5\sqrt[3]{3}$

MULTIPLICATION OF SURDS

$$a^{\frac{1}{n}} \times b^{\frac{1}{n}} \times c^{\frac{1}{n}} \times .... = (a \times b \times c \times .....)^{\frac{1}{n}}$$

$$a^{\frac{1}{m}} \times a^{\frac{1}{n}} \times a^{\frac{1}{p}} \times .... = a^{\frac{1}{m}+\frac{1}{n}+\frac{1}{p}+....}$$

SOLVED EXAMPLE

1. Find me value of $\sqrt{1764}$.

Sol.

$$1764 = 2 \times 2 \times 3 \times 3 \times 7 \times 7$$

$$\sqrt{1764} = 2 \times 3 \times 7 = 42$$

2. Find the value of $\sqrt{48}$.

Sol.

$$48 = 2 \times 2 \times 2 \times 2 \times 3$$

$$\sqrt{48} = 2 \times 2 \times \sqrt{3} = 4\sqrt{3}$$

(We know that, $\sqrt{3} = 1.732$)

$$= 4 \times 1.732 = 6.928.$$

3. Find the value of $\sqrt{142884}$.

Sol.

Divisor ↓	3 7 8 ← Quotient
3	$\overline{14}\ \overline{28}\ \overline{84}$ ← Dividend
3	9
67	5 28
7	4 69
748	59 84
8	59 84
	× ×

4. $\sqrt[3]{27} = ?$

Sol. $27 = 3 \times 3 \times 3$

So, $\sqrt[3]{27} = 3$

5. $\sqrt[3]{216} = ?$

Sol. $216 = 2 \times 2 \times 2 \times 3 \times 3 \times 3$

So, $\sqrt[3]{216} = 2 \times 3 = 6$

6. $\sqrt[3]{54} = ?$

Sol. $\sqrt[3]{54} = \sqrt[3]{3 \times 3 \times 3 \times 2} = 3\sqrt[3]{2}$

Note: 54 is not an exact cube while 27 is an exact cube.

Now, we will discuss a short-cut method of finding cube roots of exact cubes which can be easily applied to numbers consisting of upto six digits. For using this method, the cubes of 1 to 9 must be remembered by heart.

7. Find cube roots of 2197.

Sol. We start with making 3-digit groups, starting from extreme right.

$\overline{2}\,\overline{197}$ 2 lies between 1^3 and 2^3, i.e., more than 1^3 but less than 2^3.

So, L = 1

197 ends in 7. So, R = 3, Answer is 13.

8. Find the cube root of 1860667.

Sol. First make 3-digit groups, starting from extreme right.

$\overline{1}\,\overline{860}\,\overline{867}$

L = 1; R = 3 since 867 ends in 7.

Subtract R^3 from the given number. Delete the unit's digit in the balance obtained.

$$R^3 = 3^3 = 27$$

$$\begin{array}{r} 1\ \ 860\ \ 867 \\ 27 \\ \hline 1\ \ 860\ \ 840 \\ \hline \end{array}$$

Deleting extreme right digit 0 we get 186084.

Middle digit of the cube root is obtained by writing $3R^2M$ and comparing it with the number obtained above (i.e.; 186084)

$$3R^2M = 3 \times 3^2M = 27M$$

27M is contained in 186084.

Since the last digit in 186084 is 4. This is possible only when M = 2.

So, answer is 123.

9. Find the cube root of 30.371328.

Sol. $\overline{30}.\overline{371}\,\overline{328}$

L = 3 as 30 lies between 3^3 and 4^3

R = 2 since 328 ends in 8.

$R^3 = 8$

$$\begin{array}{r} 30\ \ 371\ \ 328 \\ 8 \\ \hline 30\ \ 371\ \ 320 \\ \hline \end{array}$$

$$3R^2M = 3 \times 2^2M = 12M$$

So, M = 1

Cube root of 30.371328 will be 3.12.

Since the given number has six decimal places, its cube root will have 1/3rd of 6 i.e. two decimal places.

10. Compare $3^{\frac{1}{2}}$, $5^{\frac{1}{3}}$ and $4^{\frac{1}{6}}$.

Sol. Take LCM of root indices i.e., orders of the Surds LCM of 2, 3 and 6 is 6.

Express each surd into 6th order

$$3^{\frac{1}{2}} = 3^{\frac{3}{6}} = (3^3)^{\frac{1}{6}} = (27)^{\frac{1}{6}}$$

$$5^{\frac{1}{3}} = 5^{\frac{2}{6}} = (5^2)^{\frac{1}{6}} = (25)^{\frac{1}{6}}$$

$$4^{\frac{1}{6}} = 4^{\frac{1}{6}}$$

Now, $\quad 27 > 25 > 4$

So, $\quad (27)^{\frac{1}{6}} > (25)^{\frac{1}{6}} > 4^{\frac{1}{6}}$

or, $\quad 3^{\frac{1}{2}} > 5^{\frac{1}{3}} > 4^{\frac{1}{6}}$

11. Find the value of (*i*) $\sqrt{2} \times \sqrt{3} \times \sqrt{4}$

(*ii*) $5^{\frac{1}{6}} \times 2^{\frac{1}{6}} \times 3^{\frac{1}{6}}$

Sol. (*i*) $\sqrt{2} \times \sqrt{3} \times \sqrt{4} = \sqrt{2 \times 3 \times 4} = \sqrt{24} = \sqrt[2]{6}$

(*ii*) $5^{\frac{1}{6}} \times 2^{\frac{1}{6}} \times 3^{\frac{1}{6}} = (5 \times 2 \times 3)^{\frac{1}{6}} = (30)^{\frac{1}{6}}$

EXERCISE

1. If $x * y = x + y + \sqrt{xy}$, the value of $6 * 24$ is:

(*a*) 41 (*b*) 42 (*c*) 43 (*d*) 44

2. The value of $\sqrt{10+\sqrt{25+\sqrt{108+\sqrt{154+\sqrt{225}}}}}$ is :

(*a*) 4 (*b*) 6 (*c*) 8 (*d*) 10

3. Evaluate : $\sqrt{41-\sqrt{21+\sqrt{19-\sqrt{9}}}}$.

(*a*) 3 (*b*) 5 (*c*) 6 (*d*) 6.4

4. How many two-digit numbers satisfy satisfy this property: The last digit (unit's digit) of the square of the two-digit number is 8?
(*a*) 1 (*b*) 2 (*c*) 3 (*d*) None of these

5. $28\sqrt{?}+1426=\frac{3}{4}$ of 2872
(*a*) 576 (*b*) 676 (*c*) 1296 (*d*) 1444

6. If $\sqrt{1369+\sqrt{.0615+x}} = 37.25$, then x is equal to:
(*a*) 10^{-1} (*b*) 10^{-2} (*c*) 10^{-3} (*d*) None of these

7. If $\sqrt{(x-1)(y+2)} = 7$, x and y being positive whole numbers, then the values of x and y respectively are:
(*a*) 8, 5 (*b*) 15, 12 (*c*) 22, 19 (*d*) None of these

8. The approximate value of $\frac{3\sqrt{12}}{2\sqrt{28}} \div \frac{2\sqrt{21}}{\sqrt{98}}$ is :
(*a*) 1.0605 (*b*) 1.0727 (*c*) 1.6007 (*d*) 1.6026

9. The value of $\sqrt{\frac{(0.03)^2+(0.21)^2+(0.065)^2}{(0.003)^2+(0.021)^2+(0.0065)^2}}$ is:
(*a*) 0.1 (*b*) 10 (*c*) 10^2 (*d*) 10^3

10. If $3a = 4b = 6c$ and $a + b + c = 27\sqrt{29}$, then $\sqrt{a^2+b^2+c^2}$ is:
(*a*) $3\sqrt{29}$ (*b*) 81 (*c*) 87 (*d*) None of these

11. The value of $\frac{1+\sqrt{0.01}}{1-\sqrt{0.1}}$ is close to:
(*a*) 0.6 (*b*) 1.1 (*c*) 1.6 (*d*) 1.7

12. If $\sqrt{5} = 2.236$, then the value of $\frac{\sqrt{5}}{2}-\frac{10}{\sqrt{5}}+\sqrt{125}$ is equal to:
(*a*) 5.59 (*b*) 7.826 (*c*) 8.944 (*d*) 10.062

13. The least perfect square, which is divisible by each of 21, 36 and 66, is:
(*a*) 213444 (*b*) 214344 (*c*) 214434 (*d*) 231444

14. Find the smallest number by which 5808 should be multiplied so that the product becomes a perfect square.
(*a*) 2 (*b*) 3 (*c*) 7 (*d*) 11

15. What is the least number which should be subtracted from 0.000326 to make it a perfect squate?
(*a*) 0.000002 (*b*) 0.000004 (*c*) 0.02 (*d*) 0.04

16. Given $\sqrt{5} = 2.2361$, $\sqrt{3} = 1.7321$ then $\dfrac{1}{\sqrt{5}-\sqrt{3}}$ is equal to:
(*a*) 1.98 (*b*) 1.984 (*c*) 1.9841 (*d*) 2

17. $\dfrac{1}{(\sqrt{9}-\sqrt{8})}-\dfrac{1}{(\sqrt{8}-\sqrt{7})}+\dfrac{1}{(\sqrt{7}-\sqrt{6})}-\dfrac{1}{(\sqrt{6}-\sqrt{5})}+\dfrac{1}{(\sqrt{5}-\sqrt{4})}$ is equal to:
(*a*) 0 (*b*) $\dfrac{1}{3}$ (*c*) 1 (*d*) 5

18. $\left[\dfrac{3\sqrt{2}}{\sqrt{6}-\sqrt{3}}-\dfrac{4\sqrt{3}}{\sqrt{6}-\sqrt{2}}-\dfrac{6}{\sqrt{8}-\sqrt{12}}\right]=?$
(*a*) $\sqrt{3}-\sqrt{2}$ (*b*) $\sqrt{3}+\sqrt{2}$ (*c*) $5\sqrt{3}$ (*d*) 1

19. If $\sqrt{2} = 1.414$, the square root of $\dfrac{\sqrt{2}-1}{\sqrt{2}+1}$ is nearest to:
(*a*) 0.172 (*b*) 0.414 (*c*) 0.586 (*d*) 1.414

20. $\dfrac{3+\sqrt{6}}{5\sqrt{3}-2\sqrt{12}-\sqrt{32}+\sqrt{50}}=?$
(*a*) $\sqrt{3}$ (*b*) $3\sqrt{2}$ (*c*) 6 (*d*) None of these

21. The value of $\dfrac{1}{(216)^{-\frac{2}{3}}}+\dfrac{1}{(256)^{-\frac{3}{4}}}+\dfrac{1}{(32)^{-\frac{1}{5}}}$ is :
(*a*) 102 (*b*) 105 (*c*) 107 (*d*) 109

22. The value of $[(10)^{150} \div (10)^{146}]$ is :
(*a*) 1000 (*b*) 10000 (*c*) 100000 (*d*) 10^6

23. $(256)^{0.16} \times (256)^{0.09} = ?$
(*a*) 4 (*b*) 16 (*c*) 64 (*d*) 256.25

24. $(18)^{3.5} \div (27)^{3.5} \times 6^{3.5} = 2^{?}$:
(*a*) 3.5 (*b*) 4.5 (*c*) 6 (*d*) 7

25. The value of $\dfrac{(243)^{0.13}\times(243)^{0.07}}{(7)^{0.25}\times(49)^{0.075}\times(343)^{0.2}}$ is :
(*a*) $\dfrac{3}{7}$ (*b*) $\dfrac{7}{3}$ (*c*) $1\dfrac{3}{7}$ (*d*) $2\dfrac{2}{7}$

26. If $\left(\frac{a}{b}\right)^{x-1} = \left(\frac{b}{a}\right)^{x-3}$, then the value of x is :

(a) $\frac{1}{2}$ (b) 1 (c) 2 (d) $\frac{7}{2}$

27. If $x = 3+2\sqrt{2}$, then the value of $\left(\sqrt{x} - \frac{1}{\sqrt{x}}\right)$ is :

(a) 1 (b) 2 (c) $2\sqrt{2}$ (d) $3\sqrt{3}$

28. If m and n are whole numbers such tha $m^n = 121$, then the value of $(m-1)^{n+1}$ is:

(a) 1 (b) 10 (c) 121 (d) 1000

29. $\frac{1}{1+a^{(n-m)}} + \frac{1}{1+a^{(m-n)}} = ?$

(a) 0 (b) $\frac{1}{2}$ (c) 1 (d) a^{m+n}

30. $\frac{1}{1+x^{(b-a)}+x^{(c-a)}} + \frac{1}{1+x^{(a-b)}+x^{(c-b)}} + \frac{1}{1+x^{(b-c)}+x^{(a-c)}} = ?$

(a) 0 (b) 1 (c) x^{a-b-c} (d) None of these

31. $\left(\frac{x^b}{x^c}\right)^{(b+c-a)} \left(\frac{x^c}{x^a}\right)^{(c+a-b)} \left(\frac{x^a}{x^b}\right)^{(a+b-c)} = ?$

(a) x^{abc} (b) 1 (c) $x^{ab+bc+ca}$ (d) x^{a+b+c}

32. If $3^{(x-y)} = 27$ and $3^{(x+y)} = 243$, then x is equal to:

(a) 0 (b) 2 (c) 4 (d) 6

ANSWERS

1	2	3	4	5	6	7	8	9	10
(b)	(a)	(c)	(d)	(b)	(c)	(a)	(a)	(b)	(c)
11	**12**	**13**	**14**	**15**	**16**	**17**	**18**	**19**	**20**
(c)	(b)	(a)	(b)	(a)	(c)	(d)	(c)	(b)	(a)
21	**22**	**23**	**24**	**25**	**26**	**27**	**28**	**29**	**30**
(a)	(b)	(a)	(d)	(a)	(c)	(b)	(d)	(c)	(b)
31	**32**								
(b)	(c)								

SOME SELECTED EXPLANATORY ANSWERS

1. $6*24 = 6 + 24 + \sqrt{6\times 24} = 30+\sqrt{144} = 30+12 = 42.$

2. From question $= \sqrt{10+\sqrt{25+\sqrt{108+\sqrt{154+15}}}} = \sqrt{10+\sqrt{25+\sqrt{108+\sqrt{169}}}}$

$= \sqrt{10+\sqrt{25+\sqrt{108+13}}} = \sqrt{10+\sqrt{25+\sqrt{121}}}$

$= \sqrt{10+\sqrt{25+11}} = \sqrt{10+\sqrt{36}} = \sqrt{10+6} = \sqrt{16} = 4.$

3. From question $= \sqrt{41-\sqrt{21+\sqrt{19-3}}} = \sqrt{41-\sqrt{21+\sqrt{16}}} = \sqrt{41-\sqrt{21+4}}$

$= \sqrt{41-\sqrt{25}} = \sqrt{41-5} = \sqrt{36} = 6.$

5. Let $28\sqrt{x}+1426 = 3\times 718.$

Then, $28\sqrt{x} = 2154-1426 \Leftrightarrow 28\sqrt{x} = 728 \Leftrightarrow \sqrt{x} = 26$
$\Leftrightarrow x = (26)^2 = 676.$

6. $37+\sqrt{.0615+x} = 37.25 \Leftrightarrow \sqrt{0615+x} = 0.25$

$\Leftrightarrow .0615 + x = (0.25)^2 = 0.0625 \Leftrightarrow x = .001 = \frac{1}{10^3} = 10^{-3}$

7. $\sqrt{(x-1)(y+2)} = 7 \Rightarrow (x-1)(y+2) = (7)^2 \Rightarrow (x-1) = 7$ and $(y+2) = 7$
$\Rightarrow x = 8$ and $y = 5.$

8. From question: $\frac{3\sqrt{12}}{2\sqrt{28}}\times\frac{\sqrt{98}}{2\sqrt{21}}\times\frac{3\sqrt{4\times 3}}{2\sqrt{4\times 7}}\times\frac{\sqrt{49\times 2}}{2\sqrt{21}} = \frac{6\sqrt{3}}{4\sqrt{7}}\times\frac{7\sqrt{2}}{2\sqrt{21}}$

$= \frac{21\sqrt{6}}{4\sqrt{7\times 21}} = \frac{21\sqrt{6}}{28\sqrt{3}} = \frac{21\sqrt{2}}{28} = \frac{3\sqrt{2}}{4}$

9. From question: $\sqrt{\dfrac{(0.03)^2+(0.21)^2+(0.065)^2}{\left(\frac{0.03}{10}\right)^2+\left(\frac{0.21}{10}\right)^2+\left(\frac{0.065}{10}\right)^2}}$

$= \sqrt{\dfrac{100[(0.03)^2+(0.21)^2+(0.065)^2]}{(0.03)^2+(0.21)^2+(0.065)^2}} = \sqrt{100} = 10.$

10. $4b = 6c \Rightarrow b = \frac{3}{2}c$ and $3a = 4b \Rightarrow a = \frac{4}{3}b = \frac{4}{3}\left(\frac{3}{2}c\right) = 2c.$

$$a + b + c = 27\sqrt{29} \Rightarrow 2c + \frac{3}{2}c + c = 27\sqrt{29} \Rightarrow \frac{9}{2}c = 27\sqrt{29}$$

$$\Rightarrow c = 6\sqrt{29}.$$

11. $$\frac{1+\sqrt{0.01}}{1-\sqrt{0.1}} = \frac{1+0.1}{1-0.316} = \frac{1.1}{0.684}$$

$$= \frac{1100}{684} = 1.6.$$

13. L.C.M. of 21, 36, 66 = 2772. Now, $2772 = 2 \times 2 \times 3 \times 3 \times 7 \times 11$.
To make it a perfect square, it must be multiplied by 7×11.
So, required number = $2^2 \times 3^2 \times 7^2 \times 11^2 = 213444$.

14. $5808 = 2 \times 2 \times 2 \times 2 \times 3 \times 11 \times 11 = 2^2 \times 2^2 \times 3 \times 11^2$
To make it a perfect square, it must be multiplied by 3.

15. $0.000326 = \frac{326}{10^6}$.

$$\begin{array}{r|l} 1 & \overline{3}\,\overline{26}\ (18 \\ & 1 \\ \hline 28 & 226 \\ & 224 \\ \hline & 2 \end{array}$$

$\therefore$ Required number to be subtracted = $\frac{2}{10^6} = 0.000002.$

16. $$\frac{1}{(\sqrt{5}-\sqrt{3})} = \frac{1}{(\sqrt{5}-\sqrt{3})} \times \frac{(\sqrt{5}+\sqrt{3})}{(\sqrt{5}+\sqrt{3})} = \frac{(\sqrt{5}+\sqrt{3})}{(5-3)}$$

$$= \frac{(2.2361+1.7321)}{2} = \frac{3.9682}{2} = 1.9841.$$

17. From question = $$\frac{1}{(\sqrt{9}-\sqrt{8})} \times \frac{(\sqrt{9}+\sqrt{8})}{(\sqrt{9}+\sqrt{8})} - \frac{1}{(\sqrt{8}-\sqrt{7})} \times \frac{(\sqrt{8}+\sqrt{7})}{(\sqrt{8}+\sqrt{7})} +$$

$$\frac{1}{(\sqrt{7}-\sqrt{6})} \times \frac{(\sqrt{7}+\sqrt{6})}{(\sqrt{7}+\sqrt{6})} - \frac{1}{(\sqrt{6}-\sqrt{5})} \times \frac{(\sqrt{6}+\sqrt{5})}{(\sqrt{6}+\sqrt{5})} +$$

$$\frac{1}{(\sqrt{5}-\sqrt{4})} \times \frac{(\sqrt{5}+\sqrt{4})}{(\sqrt{5}+\sqrt{4})}$$

$$= \frac{(\sqrt{9}+\sqrt{8})}{(9-8)} - \frac{(\sqrt{8}+\sqrt{7})}{(8-7)} + \frac{(\sqrt{7}+\sqrt{6})}{(7-6)} - \frac{(\sqrt{6}+\sqrt{5})}{(6-5)} + \frac{(\sqrt{5}+\sqrt{4})}{(5-4)}$$

$$= (\sqrt{9}+\sqrt{8})-(\sqrt{8}+\sqrt{7})+(\sqrt{7}+\sqrt{6})-(\sqrt{6}+\sqrt{5})+(\sqrt{5}+\sqrt{4})$$

$$= (\sqrt{9}+\sqrt{4}) = 3 + 2 = 5.$$

19. $\frac{\sqrt{2}-1}{\sqrt{2}+1} = \frac{(\sqrt{2}-1)}{(\sqrt{2}+1)} \times \frac{(\sqrt{2}-1)}{(\sqrt{2}-1)} = (\sqrt{2}-1)^2.$

$\therefore \sqrt{\frac{\sqrt{2}-1}{\sqrt{2}+1}} = (\sqrt{2}-1) = (1.414 - 1) = 0.414.$

20. From question $= \frac{3+\sqrt{6}}{5\sqrt{3}-4\sqrt{3}-4\sqrt{2}+5\sqrt{2}} = \frac{(3+\sqrt{6})}{(\sqrt{3}+\sqrt{2})}$

$$= \frac{(3+\sqrt{6})}{(\sqrt{3}+\sqrt{2})} \times \frac{(\sqrt{3}-\sqrt{2})}{(\sqrt{3}-\sqrt{2})} = \frac{3\sqrt{3}-3\sqrt{2}+3\sqrt{2}-2\sqrt{3}}{(3-2)} = \sqrt{3}.$$

21. $\frac{1}{(216)^{-\frac{2}{3}}} + \frac{1}{(256)^{-\frac{3}{4}}} + \frac{1}{(32)^{-\frac{1}{5}}} = \frac{1}{(6^3)^{-\frac{2}{3}}} + \frac{1}{(4^4)^{\left(-\frac{3}{4}\right)}} + \frac{1}{(2^5)^{-\frac{1}{5}}}$

$$= \frac{1}{6^{3\times\frac{(-2)}{3}}} + \frac{1}{4^{4\times\frac{(-3)}{4}}} + \frac{1}{2^{5\times\frac{(-1)}{5}}} = \frac{1}{6^{-2}} + \frac{1}{4^{-3}} + \frac{1}{2^{-1}}$$

$$= (6^2 + 4^3 + 2^1) = (36 + 64 + 2) = 102.$$

22. $(10)^{150} \div (10)^{146} = \frac{(10)^{150}}{(10)^{146}} = (10)^{(150-146)} = 10^4 = 10000.$

23. $(256)^{0.16} \times (256)^{0.09} = (256)^{(0.16+0.09)} = (256)^{0.25} = (256)^{\left(\frac{25}{100}\right)}$

$$= (256)^{\frac{1}{4}} = (4^4)^{\frac{1}{4}} = 4^{\left(4\times\frac{1}{4}\right)} = 4^1 = 4$$

24. $(18)^{3.5} \div (27)^{3.5} \times 6^{3.5} = 2^x$

$\Leftrightarrow (18)^{3.5} \times \frac{1}{(27)^{3.5}} \times 6^{3.5} = 2^x \Leftrightarrow (3^2 \times 2)^{3.5} \times \frac{1}{(3^3)^{3.5}} \times (2 \times 3)^{3.5} = 2^x$

$\Leftrightarrow 3^{(2\times 3.5)} \times 2^{3.5} \times \frac{1}{3^{(3\times 3.5)}} \times 2^{3.5} \times 3^{3.5} = 2^x$

$\Leftrightarrow 3^7 \times 2^{3.5} \times \frac{1}{3^{10.5}} \times 2^{3.5} \times 3^{3.5} = 2^x \quad \Leftrightarrow 2^7 = 2^x \Leftrightarrow x = 7.$

25. $$\frac{(243)^{0.13}\times(243)^{0.07}}{7^{0.25}\times(49)^{0.075}\times(343)^{0.2}}=\frac{(243)^{(0.13+0.07)}}{7^{0.25}\times(7^2)^{0.075}\times(7^3)^{0.2}}$$

$$=\frac{(243)^{0.2}}{7^{0.25}\times 7^{(2\times0.075)}\times 7^{(3\times0.2)}}=\frac{(3^5)^{0.2}}{7^{0.25}\times 7^{0.15}\times 7^{0.6}}=\frac{3^{(5\times0.2)}}{7^{(0.25+0.15+0.6)}}=\frac{3^1}{7^1}=\frac{3}{7}.$$

26. $$\left(\frac{a}{b}\right)^{x-1}=\left(\frac{b}{a}\right)^{x-3}\Leftrightarrow\left(\frac{a}{b}\right)^{x-1}=\left(\frac{a}{b}\right)^{-(x-3)}=\left(\frac{a}{b}\right)^{(3-x)}$$

$$\Leftrightarrow x-1=3-x\Leftrightarrow 2x=4\Leftrightarrow x=2.$$

27. $$\left(\sqrt{x}-\frac{1}{\sqrt{x}}\right)^2=x+\frac{1}{x}-2=(3+2\sqrt{2})+\frac{1}{(3+2\sqrt{2})}-2$$

$$=(3+2\sqrt{2})+\frac{1}{(3+2\sqrt{2})}\times\frac{(3-2\sqrt{2})}{(3-2\sqrt{2})}-2$$

$$=(3+2\sqrt{2})+(3-2\sqrt{2})-2=4.$$

28. We know that $11^2 = 121$. Putting $m = 11$ and $n = 2$, we get:

$(m-1)^{n+1}=(11-1)^{(2+1)}=10^3=1000.$

29. $$\frac{1}{1+a^{(n-m)}}+\frac{1}{1+a^{(m-n)}}=\frac{1}{\left(1+\frac{a^n}{a^m}\right)}+\frac{1}{\left(1+\frac{a^m}{a^n}\right)}$$

$$=\frac{a^m}{(a^m+a^n)}+\frac{a^n}{(a^m+a^n)}=\frac{(a^m+a^n)}{(a^m+a^n)}=1.$$

30. From question: $$\frac{1}{\left(1+\frac{x^b}{x^a}+\frac{x^c}{x^a}\right)}+\frac{1}{\left(1+\frac{x^a}{x^b}+\frac{x^c}{x^b}\right)}+\frac{1}{\left(1+\frac{x^b}{x^c}+\frac{x^a}{x^c}\right)}$$

$$=\frac{x^a}{(x^a+x^b+x^c)}+\frac{x^b}{(x^a+x^b+x^c)}+\frac{x^c}{(x^a+x^b+x^c)}$$

$$=\frac{(x^a+x^b+x^c)}{(x^a+x^b+x^c)}=1.$$

31. From question: $x^{(b-c)(b+c-a)}.x^{(c-a)(c+a-b)}.x^{(a-b)(a+b-c)}$

$$=x^{(b-c)(b+c)-a(b-c)}.x^{(c-a)(c+a)-b(c-a)}.x^{(a-b)(a+b)-c(a-b)}$$

$$=x^{(b^2-c^2+c^2-a^2+a^2-b^2)}.x^{-a(a-c)-b(c-a)-c(a-b)}$$

$$=(x^0\times x^0)=(1\times1)=1.$$

6. AVERAGE

An average, or more accurately an arithmetic mean is, in crude terms, the sum of n different data divided by n.

For example, if a batsman scores 35, 45 and 37 runs in first, second and third innings respectively, then his average runs in 3 innings is equal to

$\frac{35 + 45 + 37}{3} = 39$ runs.

Therefore, the two mostly used formula in this chapter are:

$$\text{Average} = \frac{\text{Total of data}}{\text{No. of data}}$$

$$\text{And, Total} = \text{Average} \times \text{No. of data}$$

AVERAGE RELATED TO SPEED

If a person travels a distance at a speed of x km/hr and the same distance at a speed of y km/hr, then the average speed during the whole journey is given by $\frac{2xy}{x + y}$ km/hr.

or

If half of the journey is travelled at a speed of x km/hr and the next half at a speed of y km/hr, then average speed during the whole journey is $\frac{2xy}{x + y}$ km/hr.

or,

If a man goes to a certain place at a speed of x km/hr and returns to the original place at a speed of y km/hr, then the average speed during up-and-down journey is $\frac{2xy}{x + y}$ km/hr.

Note: In all the above three cases the two parts of the journey are equal; hence the last two may be considered as a special case of the first. That's why all the three lead to the same result.

If a person travels three equal distances at a speed of x km/hr, y km/hr and z km/hr respectively, then the average speed during the whole journey is

$\frac{3xyz}{xy + yz + xz}$ km/hr.

SOLVED EXAMPLE

1. In a class, 5 students got their respective marks as 140, 220, 310, 240 and 430. Find their average marks.

Sol. Average marks $= \dfrac{140 + 220 + 310 + 240 + 430}{5}$

$$= \frac{1340}{5} = 268 \text{ marks.}$$

2. Sachin scored 60, 110, 80 and 140 runs in four matches. What is his average score in the four matches?

Sol. Average score $= \dfrac{60 + 110 + 80 + 140}{4} = \dfrac{390}{4}$

$= 97.5$ runs.

3. Calculate the mean of the following frequency distribution of marks:

Marks (x_n)	*No. of students* (f_n)
10	4
20	3
40	6
50	8
60	11
70	15
80	10
90	5

$$\bar{x} = \frac{(10 \times 4) + (20 \times 3) + (40 \times 6) + (50 \times 8) + (60 \times 11) + (70 \times 15) + (80 \times 10) + (90 \times 5)}{4 + 3 + 6 + 8 + 11 + 15 + 10 + 5}$$

$$= \frac{40 + 60 + 240 + 400 + 660 + 1050 + 800 + 450}{62} = \frac{3700}{62}$$

$= 59.68$ (approx.)

4. A train runs 25 miles at a speed of 30 m.p.h. next 50 miles at 40 m.p.h., then for next 6 minutes at 10 m.p.h. and finally completes the remaining 24 miles at a speed of 24 m.p.h. What is the average speed in miles per hour?

Sol. Here time taken during different ntervals is treated as weights.
Time taken to cover 25 miles at 30 m.p.h.

$$= \frac{60}{30} \times 25 = 50 \text{ minutes}$$

Time taken to cover 50 miles at 40 m.p.h.

$$= \frac{60}{40} \times 50 = 75 \text{ minutes}$$

Distance covered in 6 minutes at 10 m.p.h.

$$= \frac{10}{60} \times 6 = 1 \text{ mile.}$$

Time taken to cover 24 miles at 24 miles at 24 m.p.h. = 60 minutes

Speed in m.p.h. (x)	*Time taken (t)*
30	50
40	75
10	6
24	60

Weighted Average Speed

$$\bar{x} = \frac{(30 \times 50) + (40 \times 75) + (10 \times 6) + (24 \times 60)}{50 + 75 + 6 + 60}$$

$$= \frac{1500 + 3000 + 60 + 1440}{191} = \frac{6000}{191}$$

$= 31.41$ m.p.h.

We can carry out the calculation in the tabular form itself.

x	*t*	*t.x*
30	50	1500
40	75	3000
10	6	60
24	60	1440
Total	$\Sigma t = 191$	$\Sigma tx = 6000$

$$\bar{x} = \frac{6000}{191} = 31.41.$$

5. Find the Geometric mean of 2, 9 and 12.

Sol. G.M. $= \sqrt[3]{2 \times 9 \times 12} = \sqrt[3]{216} = 6.$

6. Find the harmonic mean of 2, 4, 5 and 10.

Sol. $$\text{H.M.} = \frac{1}{\frac{1}{4}\left[\frac{1}{2}+\frac{1}{4}+\frac{1}{5}+\frac{1}{10}\right]}$$

$$= \frac{4}{\left(\frac{10+5+4+2}{20}\right)} = \frac{4}{\frac{21}{20}} = \frac{80}{21}.$$

EXERCISE

1. If the mean of a, b, c is M and $ab + bc + ca = 0$, then the mean of a^2, b^2, c^2 is :

(*a*) M^2 (*b*) $3M^2$ (*c*) $6M^2$ (*d*) $9M^2$

2. The average of the two-digit numbers, which remain the same when the digits interchange their positions, is:

(*a*) 33 (*b*) 44 (*c*) 55 (*d*) 66

3. The average of 20 numbers is zero. Of them at the most, how many may be greater than zero?

(*a*) 0 (*b*) 1 (*c*) 10 (*d*) 19

4. Sanjeev was asked to find the arithmetic mean of the numbers 3, 11, 7, 9, 15, 13, 8, 19, 17, 21, 14 and x. He found the mean to be 12. What should be the number in place of x?

(*a*) 3 (*b*) 7 (*c*) 17 (*d*) 31

5. Yugnirmal obtained 76, 65, 82, 67 and 85 marks (out of 100) in English, Mathematics, Physics, Chemistry and Biology. What are his average marks?

(*a*) 65 (*b*) 69 (*c*) 75 (*d*) 76

6. The average age of 35 students in a class is 16 years. The average age of 21 students is 14. What is the average age of remaining 14 students?

(*a*) 15 years (*b*) 17 years (*c*) 18 years (*d*) 19 years

7. The average of five consecutive odd numbers is 61. What is the difference between the highest and lowest numbers?

(*a*) 2 (*b*) 5

(*c*) 8 (*d*) Cannot be determined

8. The average score of a cricketer for ten matches is 38.9 runs. If the average for the first six matches is 42, then find the average for the last four matches.

(*a*) 33.25 (*b*) 33.5 (*c*) 34.25 (*d*) 35

9. A car owner buys petrol at ₹ 7.50, ₹ 8 and ₹ 8.50 per litre for three successive years. What approximately is the average cost per litre of petrol if he spends ₹ 4000 each year?

(*a*) ₹ 7.98 (*b*) ₹ 8 (*c*) ₹ 8.50 (*d*) ₹ 9

10. Out of 9 persons, 8 persons spent ₹ 30 each for, their meals. The ninth one spent ₹ 20 more than the average expenditure of all the nine. The total money spent by all of them was:

(*a*) ₹ 260 (*b*) ₹ 290 (*c*) ₹ 292.50 (*d*) ₹ 400.50

11. A library has an average of 510 visitors on Sundays and 240 on other days. The average number of visitors per day in a month of 30 days beginning with a Sunday is:

(*a*) 250 (*b*) 276 (*c*) 280 (*d*) 285

12. A family consists of grandparents, parents and three grandchildren. The average age of the grandparents is 67 .years, that of the parents is 35 years and that of the grandchildren is 6 years. What is the average age of the family?

(*a*) $28\frac{4}{7}$ years (*b*) $31\frac{5}{7}$ years (*c*) $32\frac{1}{7}$ years (*d*) None of these

13. The average annual income (in ₹) of certain agricultural workers is S and that of other workers is T. The number of agricultural workers is 11 times that of other workers. Then the average monthly income (in ₹) of all the workers is :

(*a*) $\frac{S+T}{2}$ (*b*) $\frac{S+11T}{2}$ (*c*) $\frac{1}{11S}+T$ (*d*) $\frac{11S+T}{12}$

14. 16 children are to be divided into two groups A and B of 10 and 6 children. The average percent marks obtained by the children pf group A is 75 and the average percent marks of all the 16 children is 76. What is the average percent marks of children of group B?

(*a*) $77\frac{1}{3}$ (*b*) $77\frac{2}{3}$ (*c*) $78\frac{1}{3}$ (*d*) $78\frac{2}{3}$

15. In the first 10 overs of a cricket game, the run rate was only 3.2. What should be the run rate in the remaining 40 overs to reach the target of 282 runs?

(*a*) 6.25 (*b*) 6.5 (*c*) 6.75 (*d*) 7

16. The average of 8 numbers is 20. The average of first two numbers is $15\frac{1}{2}$ and that of the next three is $21\frac{1}{3}$. If the sixth number be less than the seventh and eighth numbers by 4 and 7 respectively, then the eighth number is:
(*a*) 18 (*b*) 22 (*c*) 25 (*d*) 27

17. Of the four numbers, the first is twice the second, the second is one-third of the third and the third is 5 times the fourth. The average of the numbers is 24.75. The largest of these numbers is:
(*a*) 9 (*b*) 25 (*c*) 30 (*d*) None of these

18. The average of six numbers is 3.95. The average of two of them is 3.4, while the average of the other two is 3.85. What is the average of the-remaining two numbers?
(*a*) 4.5 (*b*) 4.6 (*c*) 4.7 (*d*) 4.8

19. The average price of 10 books is ₹ 12 while the average price of 8 of these books is ₹ 11.75. Of the remaining two books, if the price of one book is 60% more than the price of the other, what is the price of each of these two books?
(*a*) ₹ 5, ₹ 7.50 (*b*) ₹ 8, ₹ 12 (*c*) ₹ 10, ₹ 16 (*d*) ₹ 12, ₹ 14

20. Of the three numbers, the average of the first and the second is greater than the average of the second and the third by 15. What is the difference between the first and the third of the three numbers?
(*a*) 15 (*b*) 45 (*c*) 60 (*d*) None of these

21. A company produces on an average 4000 items per month for the first 3 months. How many items it must produce on an average per month over the next 9 months, to average 4375 items per month over the whole?
(*a*) 4500 (*b*) 4600 (*c*) 4680 (*d*) 4710

22. A grocer has a sale of ₹ 6435, ₹ 6927, ₹ 6855, ₹ 7230 and ₹ 6562 for 5 consecutive months. How much sale must he have in the sixth month so that he gets an average sale of ₹ 6500?
(*a*) ₹ 4991 (*b*) ₹ 5991 (*c*) ₹ 6001 (*d*) ₹ 6991

23. In Panas's opinion, his weight is greater than 65 kg but less than 72 kg. His brother does not agree with Panas and he thinks that Panas's weight is greater than 60 kg bat less than 70 kg. His mother's view is that his weight cannot be greater than 68 kg. If all of them are correct in their estimation, what is the average of different probable weights of Panas?

(*a*) 67 kg (*b*) 68 kg
(*c*) Data inadequate (*d*) None of these

24. The average age of students of a class is 15.8 years. The average age of boys in the class is 16.4 years and that of the girls is 15.4 years. The ratio of the number of boys to the number of girls in the class is:
(*a*) 1 : 2 (*b*) 2 : 3 (*c*) 3 : 4 (*d*) 3 : 5

25. A certain factory employed 600 men and 400 women and the average wage was ₹ 25.50 per day. If a woman got ₹ 5 less than a man, then what are their daily wages?
(*a*) Man : ₹ 25; Woman : ₹ 20
(*b*) Man : ₹ 27.50, Woman : ₹ 22.50
(*c*) Man : ₹ 30, Woman : ₹ 25
(*d*) Man ; ₹ 32.50, Woman : ₹ 27.50

26. The average age of husband, wife and their child 3 years ago was 27 years and that of wife and the child 5 years ago was 20 years. The present age of the husband is:
(*a*) 35 years (*b*) 40 years (*c*) 50 years (*d*) None of these

27. The average age of a husband and his wife was 23 years at the time of their marriage. After five years they have a one-year old child. The average age of the family now is:
(*a*) 19 years (*b*) 23 years (*c*) 28.5 years (*d*) 29.3 years

28. The average weight of 3 men A, B and C is 84 kg. Another man D joins the group and the average now becomes 80 kg. If another man E, whose weight is 3 kg more than that of D, replaces A, then the average weight of B, C, D and E becomes 79 kg. The weight of A is:
(*a*) 70 kg (*b*) 72 kg (*c*) 75 kg (*d*) 80 kg

29. A cricketer has a certain average for 10 innings. In the eleventh inning, he scored 108 runs, thereby increasing his average by 6 runs. His new average is :
(*a*) 48 runs (*b*) 52 runs (*c*) 55 runs (*d*) 60 runs

30. The average monthly salary of 20 employees in an organisation is ₹ 1500. If the manager's salary is added, then the average salary increases by ₹ 100. What is the manager's monthly salary?
(*a*) ₹ 2000 (*b*) ₹ 2400 (*c*) ₹ 3600 (*d*) ₹ 4800

31. The average monthly income of P and Q is ₹ 5050. The average monthly income of Q and R is ₹ 6250 and the average monthly income of P and R is ₹ 5200. The monthly income of P is:
(*a*) ₹ 3500 (*b*) ₹ 4000 (*c*) ₹ 4050 (*d*) ₹ 5000

32. The average age of 36 students in a group is 14 years. When teacher's age is included to it, the average increases by one. What is the teacher's age in years?

(*a*) 31 (*b*) 36
(*c*) 51 (*d*) Cannot be determined

33. The average weight of 45 students in a class is 52 kg, Five of them whose average weight is 48 kg leave the class and other 5 students whose average weight is 54 kg join the class. What is the new average weight (in kg) of the, class?

(*a*) $52\frac{1}{3}$ (*b*) $52\frac{1}{2}$ (*c*) $52\frac{2}{3}$ (*d*) None of these

34. The average weight of 8 persons increases by 2.5 kg when a new person comes in place of one of them weighing 65 kg. What might be the weight of the new person?

(*a*) 76 kg (*b*) 76.5 kg
(*c*) 85 kg (*d*) Data inadequate

35. The average weight of three boys A, B and C is $54\frac{1}{3}$ kg, while the average weight of three boys B, D and E is 53 kg. What is the average weight of A, B, C, D and E?

(*a*) 52.4 kg (*b*) 53.2 kg
(*c*) 53.8 kg (*d*) Data inadequate

36. The average temperature of the town in the first four days of a month was 58 degrees. The average for the second, third, fourth and fifth days was 60 degrees. If the temperatures of the first and fifth days were in the ratio 7 : 8, then what is the temperature on the fifth day?

(*a*) 64 degrees (*b*) 62 degrees (*c*) 56 degrees (*d*) None of these

ANSWERS

1	2	3	4	5	6	7	8	9	10
(*b*)	(*c*)	(*d*)	(*b*)	(*c*)	(*d*)	(*c*)	(*c*)	(*a*)	(*c*)
11	**12**	**13**	**14**	**15**	**16**	**17**	**18**	**19**	**20**
(*d*)	(*b*)	(*d*)	(*b*)	(*a*)	(*c*)	(*d*)	(*b*)	(*c*)	(*d*)
21	**22**	**23**	**24**	**25**	**26**	**27**	**28**	**29**	**30**
(*a*)	(*a*)	(*d*)	(*b*)	(*b*)	(*b*)	(*a*)	(*c*)	(*a*)	(*c*)
31	**32**	**33**	**34**	**35**	**36**				
(*b*)	(*c*)	(*c*)	(*c*)	(*d*)	(*a*)				

SOME SELECTED EXPLANATORY ANSWERS

1. We have: $\left(\frac{a+b+c}{3}\right) = \text{M}$ or $(a + b + c) = 3\text{M}$.

Now, $(a + b + c)^2 = (3\text{M})^2 = 9\text{M}^2$

$\Leftrightarrow a^2 + b^2 + c^2 + 2(ab + bc + ca) = 9\text{M}^2$

$\Leftrightarrow a^2 + b^2 + c^2 = 9\text{M}^2$. $\quad [\because (ab + bc + ca) = 0]$

$\therefore$ Required mean $= \left(\frac{a^2+b^2+c^2}{3}\right) = \frac{9\text{M}^2}{3} = 3\text{M}^2$.

2. Average $= \left(\frac{11+22+33+44+55+66+77+88+99}{9}\right)$

$= \left[\frac{(11+99)+(22+88)+(33+77)+(44+66)+55}{9}\right]$

$= \left(\frac{4\times 110+55}{9}\right) = \frac{495}{9} = 55$.

3. Average of 20 numbers = 0.

$\therefore$ Sum of 20 numbers $= (0 \times 20) = 0$.

It is quite possible that 19 of these numbers may be positive and if their sum is a, then 20th number is $(-a)$.

4. From question,

We have $\left(\frac{3+11+7+9+15+13+8+19+17+21+14+x}{12}\right) = 12$

or $137 + x = 144$ or $x = 144 - 137 = 7$.

5. Required Average $= \left(\frac{76+65+82+67+85}{5}\right) = \left(\frac{375}{5}\right) = 75$.

6. Sum of the ages of 14 students $= (16 \times 35) - (14 \times 21) = 560 - 294 = 266$.

$\therefore$ Required average $= \left(\frac{266}{14}\right) = 19$ years.

7. Suppose that the numbers are x, $x + 2$, $x + 4$, $x + 6$ and $x + 8$.

Then, $\frac{x+(x+2)+(x+4)+(x+6)+(x+8)}{5} = 61$

or $5x + 20 = 305$ or $x = 57$.

So, required difference $= (57 + 8) - 57 = 8$.

8. Required average $= \dfrac{(38.9 \times 10) - (42 \times 6)}{4} = \dfrac{137}{4} = 34.25.$

9. Total quantity of petrol consumed in 3 years $= \left(\dfrac{4000}{7.50} + \dfrac{4000}{8} + \dfrac{4000}{8.50}\right)$ litres

$$= 4000\left(\frac{2}{15} + \frac{1}{8} + \frac{2}{17}\right) = \left(\frac{76700}{51}\right) \text{ litres.}$$

Total amount spent = ₹ (3 × 4000) = ₹ 12000.

$\therefore$ Average cost = ₹$\left(\dfrac{12000 \times 51}{76700}\right) =$ ₹$\dfrac{6120}{767} =$ ₹ 7.98.

10. Suppose that the average expenditure is ₹ x. Then,
$9x = 8 \times 30 + (x + 20)$ or $9x = x + 260$ or $8x = 260$ or $x = 32.50$.
$\therefore$ Total money spent $= 9x =$ ₹ (9 × 32.50) = ₹ 292.50.

11. Since the month begins with a Sunday, so there will be five Sundays in the month.

$\therefore$ Required average $= \left(\dfrac{510 \times 5 + 240 \times 25}{30}\right) = \dfrac{8550}{30} = 285.$

12. Required average $= \left(\dfrac{67 \times 2 + 35 \times 2 + 6 \times 3}{2 + 2 + 3}\right)$

$$= \left(\frac{134 + 70 + 14}{7}\right) = \frac{222}{7} = 31\frac{5}{7} \text{ years.}$$

13. Supose that the number of other workers is x.
Then, number of agricultural wokers $= 11x$.
Total number of workers $= 12x$.

$\therefore$ Average monthly income $= \dfrac{\text{S} \times 11x + \text{T} \times x}{12x} = \dfrac{11\text{S} + \text{T}}{12}.$

14. Required average $= \dfrac{(76 \times 16) - (75 \times 10)}{6} = \left(\dfrac{1216 - 750}{6}\right)$

$$= \frac{466}{6} = \frac{233}{3} = 77\frac{2}{3}.$$

15. Required run rate $= \dfrac{282 - (3.2 \times 10)}{40} = \dfrac{250}{40} = 6.25.$

16. Let the eighth number be x. Then, sixth number = $(x - 7)$.
Seventh number = $(x - 7) + 4 = (x - 3)$.

So, $\left(2 \times 15\frac{1}{2}\right) + \left(3 \times 21\frac{1}{3}\right) + (x - 7) + (x - 3) + x = 8 \times 20$

$\Leftrightarrow 31 + 64 + (3x - 10) = 160 \Leftrightarrow 3x = 75 \Leftrightarrow x = 25.$

17. Let the fourth number be x.

Then, third number = $5x$, second number = $\frac{5x}{3}$ and first number = $\frac{10x}{3}$.

$x + 5x + \frac{5x}{3} + \frac{10x}{3} = (24.75 \times 4)$ or $11x = 99$ or $x = 9$.

So, the numbers are 9, 45, 15 and 30.
∴ Largest number = 45.

18. Sum of the remaining two numbers $= (3.95 \times 6) - [(3.4 \times 2) + (3.85 \times 2)]$
$= 23.70 - (6.8 + 7.7)$
$= 23.70 - 14.5 = 9.20.$

∴ Required average $= \left(\frac{9.2}{2}\right) = 4.6$

19. Total price of the two books = ₹ $[(12 \times 10) - (11.75 \times 8)]$
= ₹ $(120 - 94)$ = ₹ 26.
Let the price of one book be ₹ x
Then, the price of other book = ₹ $(x + 60\% \text{ of } x)$
= ₹ $\left(x + \frac{3}{5}x\right)$ = ₹ $\left(\frac{8x}{5}\right)$.

So, $x + \frac{8x}{5} = 26 \Leftrightarrow 13x = 130 \Leftrightarrow x = 10.$

∴ The prices of the two books are ₹ 10 and ₹ 16.

20. Let the numbers be x, y and z.

Then, $\left(\frac{x + y}{2}\right) - \left(\frac{y + z}{2}\right) = 15$ or $(x + y) - (y + z) = 30$ or $x - z = 30$.

21. Required average $= \frac{(4375 \times 12) - (4000 \times 3)}{9} = \frac{52500 - 12000}{9}$

$= \frac{40500}{9} = 45000.$

22. Total sale for 5 months = ₹ (6435 + 6927 + 6855 + 7230 + 6562)
= ₹ 34009.

∴ Required sale = ₹ [(6500 × 6) – 34009]
= ₹ (39000 – 34009) = ₹ 4991.

24. Let the ration be k : 1. Then,

$k \times 16.4 + 1 \times 15.4 = (k + 1) \times 15.8$

$\Leftrightarrow$ $(16.4 - 15.8)\, k = (15.8 - 15.4)$ $\Leftrightarrow$ $k = \frac{0.4}{0.6} = \frac{2}{3}.$

∴ Required ratio = $\frac{2}{3} : 1 = 2 : 3.$

25. Let the daily wage of a man be ₹ x.
Then, daily wage of a woman = ₹ $(x - 5)$.
Now, $600x + 400\,(x - 5) = 25.50 \times (600 + 400)$
$\Leftrightarrow$ $1000x = 27500$ $\Leftrightarrow$ $x = 27.50.$
∴ Man's daily wasges = ₹ 27.50; Woman's daily wages
= $(x - 5)$ = ₹ 22.50.

26. Sum of the present ages of husband, wife and child
= (27 × 3 + 3 × 3) years = 50 years.
Sum of the present ages of wife and child
= (20 × 2 + 5 × 2) years = 50 years.
∴ Husband's present age = (90 – 50) years = 40 years.

27. Sum of the present ages of husband, wife and child
= (23 × 21 + 5 × 2) + 1 = 57 years.

∴ Required average = $\left(\frac{57}{3}\right)$ = 19 years.

28. Suppose that A, B, C, D and E represent their respective weights. Then,
A + B + C = (84 × 3) = 252 kg, A + B + C + D = (80 × 4) = 320 kg.
∴ D = (320 – 252) kg 68 kg, E = (68 + 3) kg = 71 kg.
B + C + D + E = (79 × 4) = 316 kg.
Now, (A + B + C + D) – (B + C + D + E) = (320 – 316) kg = 4 kg.
∴ A – E = 4 $\Rightarrow$ A = (4 + E) = 75 kg.

29. Let average for 10 innings be x. Then,

$\frac{10x + 108}{11} = x + 6 \Rightarrow 11x + 66 = 10x + 108 \Rightarrow x = 42.$

∴ New average = $(x + 6)$ = 48 runs.

30. From question Manager's salary = ₹ (16000 × 21 – 1500 × 20) = ₹ 3600.

31. Let P, Q and R represent their respective monthly incomes. Then, we have:

$P + Q = (5050 \times 2) = 10100$ ...(*i*)

$Q + R = (6250 \times 2) = 12500$ ...(*ii*)

$P + R = (5200 \times 2) = 10400$ ...(*iii*)

Adding (*i*), (*ii*) and (*iii*), we get : $2(P + Q + R) = 33000$

or $P + Q + R = 16500$ ...(*iv*)

Subtracting (*ii*) from (*iv*), we get $P = 4000$.

$\therefore$ P's monthly income = ₹ 4000.

32. From question Age of the teacher = $(37 \times 15 - 36 \times 14)$ years = 51 years.

33. Sum of the weights of the students after replacement

$= [(52 \times 45) - (48 \times 5) + (54 \times 5)]$ kg = 2370 kg.

$\therefore$ New average = $\left(\frac{2370}{45}\right)$ kg = $53\frac{2}{3}$ kg.

34. Total weight increased = (8×2.5) kg = 20 kg.

Weight of new person = $(65 + 20)$ kg = 85 kg.

35. Total weight of $(A + B + C) = \left(54\frac{1}{3} \times 3\right)$ kg = 163 kg.

Tatal weight of $(B + D + E) = (53 \times 3)$kg = 159 kg.

Adding both, we get: $A + 2B + C + D + E = (163 + 159)$ kg = 322 kg.

So, to find the average weight of five we should have know B's weight, which is not given. So, the data is inadequate.

~~~~~~
~~~~~~

7. PROBLEMS ON NUMBERS

In this chapter, questions involving a set of numbers are put in the form of a puzzle. You have to analyse the given conditions, assume the unknown numbers and form equations accordingly, which on solving yield the unknown numbers.

SOLVED EXAMPLE

1. A number it as much greater than 36 as is less than 86. Find the number.

Sol. Let the number be x.

Then, $x - 36 = 86 - x \Leftrightarrow 2x = 86 + 36 = 122 \Leftrightarrow x = 61$.

Hence, the required number is 61.

2. Find a number such that when 15 is subtracted from 7 times that number, the result is 10 more than twice the number.

Sol. Let the number be x. Then, $7x - 15 = 2x + 10 \Leftrightarrow 5x = 25 \Leftrightarrow x = 5$. Hence, the required number is 5.

3. The sum of two numbers is 184. If one-third of the one exceeds one-seventh of the other by 8, find the smaller number.

Sol. Let the numbers be x and $(184 - x)$. Then,

$$\frac{x}{3} - \frac{(184 - x)}{7} = 8 \Leftrightarrow 7x - 3(184 - x) = 168 \Leftrightarrow 10x = 720 \Leftrightarrow x = 72.$$

So, the numbers are 72 and 112. Hence, smaller number = 72.

EXERCISE

1. The difference between a number and its three-fifth is 50. What is the number?

(*a*) 75 (*b*) 100 (*c*) 125 (*d*) None of these

2. If a number is decreased by 4 and divided by 6, the result is 8. What would be the result if 2 is subtracted from the number and then it is divided by 5?

(*a*) $9\frac{2}{3}$ (*b*) 10 (*c*) $10\frac{1}{5}$ (*d*) $11\frac{1}{5}$

3. If the digit in the unit's place of a two-digit number is halved and the digit in the ten's place is doubled, the number thus obtained is equal to the number obtained by interchanging the digits. Which of the following is definitely true?

(*a*) Sum of the digits is a two-digit number.
(*b*) Digit in the unit's place is twice the digit in the ten's place.
(*c*) Digits in the unit's place and the ten's place are equal.
(*d*) Digit in the unit's place is half of the digit in the ten's place.

4. If 50 is subtracted from two-third of a number, the result is equal to sum of 40 and one-fourth of that number. What is the number?
(*a*) 174 (*b*) 216 (*c*) 246 (*d*) 336

5. The difference between a two-digit number and the number obtained by interchanging the two digits is 63. Which is the smaller of the two numbers?
(*a*) 29 (*b*) 70
(*c*) 92 (*d*) Cannot be determined

6. A certain number of two digits is three times the sum of its digits and if 45 be added to it, the digits are reversed. The number is:
(*a*) 23 (*b*) 27 (*c*) 32 (*d*) 72

7. The sum of three numbers is 264. If the first number be twice the second and third number be one-third of the first, then the second number is:
(*a*) 48 (*b*) 54 (*c*) 72 (*d*) 84

8. The sum of the digits of a two-digit number is $\frac{1}{5}$ of the difference between the number and the number obtained by interchanging the positions of the digits. What is definitely the difference between the digits of that number?
(*a*) 5 (*b*) 7
(*c*) 9 (*d*) Cannot be determined

9. The product of two number is 192 and the sum of these two numbers is 28. What is the smaller of these two numbers?
(*a*) 12 (*b*) 14 (*c*) 16 (*d*) 18

10. The difference between two positive integers is 3. If the sum of their squares is 369, then the sum of the numbers is:
(*a*) 25 (*b*) 27 (*c*) 33 (*d*) 81

11. In a two-digit number, the digit in the unit's place is more than twice the digit in ten's place by 1. If the digits in the unit's place and the ten's place are interchanged, difference between the newly formed number and the original number is less than the original number by 1. What is the original number?
(*a*) 25 (*b*) 37 (*c*) 49 (*d*) 52

12. In a two-digit number, the digit in the unit's place is four times the digit in ten's place and sum of the digits is equal to 10. What is the number?
(*a*) 14 (*b*) 41 (*c*) 82 (*d*) None of these

13. A number consists of two digits such that the, digit in the ten's place is less by 2 than the digit in the unit's place. Three times the number added to $\frac{6}{7}$ times the number obtained by reversing the digits equals 108. The sum of the digits in the number is :

(*a*) 6 (*b*) 7 (*c*) 8 (*d*) 9

14. The sum of the digits of a two-digit number is 15 and the difference between the digits is 3. What is the two-digit number?

(*a*) 69 (*b*) 78
(*c*) 96 (*d*) Cannot be determined

15. In a two-digit number, if it is known that its unit's digit exceeds its ten's digit by 2 and that the product of the given number and the sum of its digits is equal to 144, then the number is:

(*a*) 24 (*b*) 26 (*c*) 42 (*d*) 46

16. The difference between a two-digit number and the number obtained by interchanging the positions of its digits is 36. What is the difference between the two digits of that number ?

(*a*) 3 (*b*) 4
(*c*) 9 (*d*) Cannot be determined

17. Find a positive number which when increased by 17 is equal to 60 times the reciprocal of the number.

(*a*) 3 (*b*) 10 (*c*) 17 (*d*) 20

18. One-fifth of a number is equal to $\frac{5}{8}$ of another number. If 35 is added to the first number, it becomes four times of the second number. The second number is:

(*a*) 25 (*b*) 40 (*c*) 70 (*d*) 125

19. If the sum of one-half and one-fifth of a number exceeds one-third of that number by $7\frac{1}{3}$, the number is :

(*a*) 15 (*b*) 18 (*c*) 20 (*d*) 30

20. A number of two digits has 3 for its unit's digit, and the sum of digits is $\frac{1}{7}$ of the number itself. The number is

(*a*) 43 (*b*) 53 (*c*) 63 (*d*) 73

21. If the numerator of a fraction is increased by 2 and the denominator is increased by 3, the fraction becomes $\frac{7}{9}$ and if both the numerator as well as the denominator are decreased by 1, the fraction becomes $\frac{4}{5}$. What is the original fraction?

(*a*) $\frac{5}{6}$ (*b*) $\frac{9}{11}$ (*c*) $\frac{13}{16}$ (*d*) $\frac{17}{21}$

22. The sum of three consecutive odd numbers is 20 more than the first of these numbers. What is the middle number?

(*a*) 7 (*b*) 9
(*c*) 11 (*d*) Data inadequate

23. If $2\frac{1}{2}$ is added to a number and the sum multiplied by $4\frac{1}{2}$ and 3 is added to the product and then dividing the sum by $1\frac{1}{5}$, the quotient becomes 25. What is the number?

(*a*) $2\frac{1}{2}$ (*b*) $3\frac{1}{2}$ (*c*) $4\frac{1}{2}$ (*d*) $5\frac{1}{2}$

24. A two-digit number is such that the product of the digits is 8. When 18 is added to the number, then the digits are reversed. The number is:

(*a*) 18 (*b*) 24 (*c*) 42 (*d*) 81

25. The denominator of a fraction is 3 more than the numerator. If the numerator as well as the denominator is increased by 4, the fraction becomes $\frac{4}{5}$. What was the original fraction?

(*a*) $\frac{8}{11}$ (*b*) $\frac{5}{8}$ (*c*) $\frac{10}{13}$ (*d*) $\frac{7}{10}$

26. The numerator and denominator of a fraction are in the ratio of 2 : 3. If 6 is subtracted from the numerator, the result is a fraction that has a value $\frac{2}{3}$ of the original fraction. The numerator of the original fraction is:

(*a*) 6 (*b*) 18 (*c*) 27 (*d*) 36

27. The digit in the unit's place of a number is equal to the digit in the ten's place of half of that number and the digit in the tea's place of that number is less than the digit in unit's place of half of the number by 1. If the sum of the digits of the number is 7, then what is the number?

(a) 34 (b) 52
(c) 162 (d) Cannot be determined

28. The sum of four numbers is 64. If you add 3 to the first number, 8 is subtracted from the second number, the third is multiplied by 3 and the fourth is divided by 3, then all the results are equal. What is the difference between the largest and the smallest of the original numbers?
(a) 21 (b) 27 (c) 32 (d) None of these

29. The sum of the squares of three numbers is 138, while the sum of their products taken two at a time is 131. Their sum is:
(a) 20 (b) 30 (c) 40 (d) None of these

ANSWERS

1	2	3	4	5	6	7	8	9	10
(c)	(b)	(b)	(b)	(d)	(b)	(c)	(d)	(a)	(b)
11	**12**	**13**	**14**	**15**	**16**	**17**	**18**	**19**	**20**
(b)	(d)	(a)	(d)	(a)	(b)	(a)	(b)	(c)	(c)
21	**22**	**23**	**24**	**25**	**26**	**27**	**28**	**29**	
(a)	(b)	(b)	(b)	(a)	(b)	(b)	(c)	(a)	

SOME SELECTED EXPLANATORY ANSWERS

2. Suppose the required number is x.

Then, $\frac{x-4}{6} = 8 \Leftrightarrow x - 4 = 48 \Leftrightarrow x = 52.$

$\therefore \quad \frac{x-2}{5} = \frac{52-2}{5} = \frac{50}{5} = 10.$

3. Let the ten's digit be x and unit's digit be y.

Then, $10 \times 2x + \frac{1}{2}y = 10y + x \Leftrightarrow 20x - x = 10y - \frac{y}{2}$

$\Leftrightarrow \; 19x = \frac{19}{2}y \quad \Leftrightarrow y = 2x.$

Thus, the unit's digit is twice the ten's digit.

4. Suppose that the required number is P.

Then, $\frac{2}{3}P - 50 = \frac{1}{4}P + 40 \Leftrightarrow \frac{2}{3}P - \frac{1}{4}P = 90 \Leftrightarrow \frac{5P}{12} = 90$

$\Leftrightarrow \; P = \left(\frac{90 \times 12}{5}\right) = 216.$

5. Let the ten's digit be x and unit's digit be y.
Then, $(10x + y) - (10y + x) = 63 \Leftrightarrow 9(x - y) = 63 \Leftrightarrow x - y = 7$.
Thus, none of the numbers can be determined.

6. Let the ten's digit be x and unit's digit be y.
Then, $10x + y = 3(x + y) \quad \Leftrightarrow \quad 7x - 2y = 0$ ...(*i*)
$10x + y + 45 = 10y + x \quad \Leftrightarrow \quad y - x = 5$ ... (*ii*)
Solving (*i*) and (*ii*), we get : $x = 2$ and $y = 7$.
$\therefore$ Required number = 27.

7. Let the second number be x. Then, first number = $2x$ and third number = $\frac{2x}{3}$.

$$\therefore\ 2x + x + \frac{2x}{3} = 264 \Leftrightarrow \frac{11x}{3} = 264 \Leftrightarrow x = \left(\frac{264 \times 3}{11}\right) = 72.$$

8. Let the ten's digit be x and unit's digit be y.

Then, $x + y = \frac{1}{5}[(10x + y) - (10y + x)] \Leftrightarrow 5x + 5y = 9x - 9y \Leftrightarrow 4x = 14y$.

Thus, the value of $(x - y)$ cannot be determined from the given data.

10. Suppose the required number is x. Then from question,
$x^2 + (x + 3)^2 = 369 \Leftrightarrow x^2 + x^2 + 9 + 6x = 369$
$\Leftrightarrow 2x^2 + 6x - 360 = 0 \Leftrightarrow x^2 + 3x - 180 = 0$
$\Leftrightarrow (x + 15)(x - 12) = 0 \Leftrightarrow x = 12$
So, the numbers are 12 and 15.
$\therefore$ Required sum = $(12 + 15) = 27$.

11. Let the ten's digit be x. Then, unit's digit = $2x + 1$.
$[10x + (2x + 1)] - [\{10(2x + 1) + x\} - \{10x + (2x + 1)\}] = 1$
$\Leftrightarrow (12x + 1) - (9x + 9) = 1 \Leftrightarrow 3x = 9 \Leftrightarrow x = 3$.
So, ten's digit = 3 and unit's digit = 7. Hence, original number = 37.

12. Let the ten's digits be a. Then, unit's digit = $4a$.
$\therefore\ a + 4a = 10 \Leftrightarrow 5a = 10 \Leftrightarrow a = 2$.
So, ten's digit = 2, unit's digit = 8.
Hence, the required number is 28.

13. Let the unit's digit be x. Then, ten's digit = $(x - 2)$.

$$\therefore\ 3[10(x - 2) + x] + \frac{6}{7}[10x + (x - 2)] = 108$$

$\Leftrightarrow 231x - 420 + 66x - 12 = 756 \Leftrightarrow 297x = 1188 \Leftrightarrow x = 4$.
Hence, sum of the digits = $x + (x - 2) = 2x - 2 = 6$.

15. Let the ten's digit be x. Then, unit's digit $= x + 2$.
Number $= 10x + (x + 2) = 11x + 2$; Sum of digits $= x + (x + 2) = 2x + 2$.
$\therefore (11x + 2)(2x + 2) = 144 \Leftrightarrow 22x^2 + 26x - 140 = 0$
$\Leftrightarrow 11x^2 + 13x - 70 = 0$
$\Leftrightarrow (x - 2)(11x + 35) = 0 \Leftrightarrow x = 2.$
Hence, required number $= 11x + 2 = 24$.

16. Let the ten's digit be x and unit's digit be y.
Then, $(10x + y) - (10y + x) = 36 \Leftrightarrow 9(x - y) = 36 \Leftrightarrow x - y = 4.$

18. Suppose the two numbers be a and b. Then, $\frac{1}{5}a = \frac{5}{8}b \Leftrightarrow b = \frac{8}{25}a.$

Now, $a + 35 = 4b \Leftrightarrow a + 35 = \frac{32}{25}a \Leftrightarrow \frac{7}{25}a = 35$

$\Leftrightarrow a = \left(\frac{35 \times 25}{7}\right) = 125.$

$\therefore$ Second number $= b = \frac{8}{25}a = \left(\frac{8}{25} \times 125\right) = 40.$

19. Suppose the required number is x.
Then, $\left(\frac{1}{2}x + \frac{1}{5}x\right) - \frac{1}{3}x = \frac{22}{3} \Leftrightarrow \frac{11x}{30} = \frac{22}{3} \Leftrightarrow \frac{11x}{30} = \frac{22}{3}$

$\Leftrightarrow \quad x = \left(\frac{22 \times 30}{3 \times 11}\right) = 20.$

20. Let the ten's digit be x. Then, number $= 10x + 3$ and sum of digits $= (x + 3)$.

So, $(x + 3) = \frac{1}{7}(10x + 3) \Leftrightarrow 7x + 21 = 10x + 3 \Leftrightarrow 3x = 18 \Leftrightarrow x = 6.$
Hence, the number is 63.

21. Let the fraction be $\frac{x}{y}\cdot$ Then,
$\frac{x+2}{y+3} = \frac{7}{9} \Leftrightarrow 9x - 7y = 3$ ...(i) and $\frac{x-1}{y-1} = \frac{4}{5} \Leftrightarrow 5x - 4y = 1$ ...(ii)

22. Suppose the three numbers are x, $x + 2$ and $x + 4$.
The, $x + (x + 2) + (x + 4) = x + 20 \Leftrightarrow 2x = 14 \Leftrightarrow x = 7.$
$\therefore$ Middle number $= x + 2 = 9.$

23. Suppose the required number is x,

From question, $\frac{4\frac{1}{2}\left(x + 2\frac{1}{2}\right) + 3}{1\frac{1}{5}} = 25 \Leftrightarrow \frac{\frac{9}{2}\left(x + \frac{5}{2}\right) + 3}{\frac{6}{5}} = 25$

$\Leftrightarrow \frac{9x}{2} + \frac{45}{4} + 3 = 25 \times \frac{6}{5} = 30 \Leftrightarrow \frac{9x}{2} = 30 - \frac{57}{4} \Leftrightarrow \frac{9x}{2} = \frac{63}{4}$

$\Leftrightarrow x = \left(\frac{63}{4} \times \frac{2}{9}\right) = \frac{7}{2} = 3\frac{1}{2}.$

24. Let the ten's and unit's digit be x and $\frac{8}{x}$ respectively.

Then, $\left(10x + \frac{8}{x}\right) + 18 = 10 \times \frac{8}{x} + x \quad \Leftrightarrow \quad 10x^2 + 8 + 18x = 80 + x^2$

$\Leftrightarrow \; 9x^2 + 18x - 72 = 0 \;\; \Leftrightarrow \;\; x^2 + 2x - 8 = 0$

$\Leftrightarrow (x + 4)(x - 2) = 0 \;\; \Leftrightarrow \;\; x = 2.$

So, ten's digit = 2 and unit's digit = 4. Hence, required number = 24.

25. Suppose the numerator be x. Then, denominator = $x + 3$.

From question, $\frac{x+4}{(x+3)+4} = \frac{4}{5} \Leftrightarrow 5(x + 4) - 4(x + 7) \Leftrightarrow x = 8.$

Hence, the fraction is $\frac{8}{11}$.

26. Let the fraction be $\frac{2x}{3x}$. Then, $\frac{2x-6}{3x} = \frac{2}{3} \times \frac{2x}{3x} \Leftrightarrow \frac{2x-6}{3x} = \frac{4x}{9x}$

$\Leftrightarrow 18x^2 - 54x - 12x^2 \Leftrightarrow 6x^2 = 54x \Leftrightarrow x = 9.$

Hence, numerator of the original fraction = $2x$ = 18.

27. Let the ten's digit be x and unit's digit be y. Then, $\frac{10x + y}{2} = 10y + (x + 1)$

$\Leftrightarrow 10x + y = 20y + 2x + 2 \Leftrightarrow 8x - 19y = 2$ ...(i) and $x + y = 7$ ...(*ii*)

Solving, (*i*) and (*ii*), we get : $x = 5$, $y = 2$. Hence, required number = 52.

28. Suppose the four numbers be a, b, c and d. Let $a + 3 = b - 3 = 3c = \frac{d}{3} = x.$

Then, $a = x - 3$, $b = x + 3$, $c = \frac{x}{3}$ and $d = 3x$.

$a + b + c + d = 64 \quad \Rightarrow (x - 3) + (x + 3) + \frac{x}{3} + 3x = 64$

$\Rightarrow 5x + \frac{x}{3} = 64 \;\Rightarrow 16x = 192 \;\Rightarrow x = 12.$

Thus, the numbers are 9, 15, 4 and 36.

$\therefore$ Required difference = (36 – 4) = 32.

29. Let the three numbers are A, B and C.

Then, $A^2 + B^2 + C^2 = 138$ and $(AB + BC + CA) = 131$.

$(A + B + C)^2 = A^2 + B^2 + C^2 = 2(AB + BC + CA) = 138 + 2 \times 131 = 400$

$\Rightarrow \; (A + B + C) = \sqrt{400} = 20.$

~~~~~~
~~~~~~

8. PROBLEMS ON AGES

To solve the problems based on ages, students are required to have the knowledge of linear equations. This method needs some basic concepts as well as some more time than it deserves. Sometimes it is easier to solve the problems by taking the given choices in account. But this hit-and-trial method proves costly sometimes, when we reach our solution much later. We have tried to evaluate some easier as well as quicker methods to solve these type of questions. Although we are not able to cover each type of questions in this section, our attempt is to minimise your difficulties.

- t_1 yrs earlier the father's age was x times that of his son. At present the father's age is y times that of his son. What are the present ages of the son and the father ?

$$\text{Son's age} = \frac{t_1(x-1)}{x-y}$$

- The present age of the father is y times the age of his son. t_2 yrs hence, the father's age become z time the age of his son. What are the present ages of the father and his son?

$$\text{Son's age} = \frac{(z-1)t_2}{y-z}$$

- t_1 yrs earlier the age of the father was x times the age of his son. t_2 yrs hence, the age of the father becomes z times the age of his son. What are the present ages of the son and the father?

$$\text{Son's age} = \frac{t_2(z-1)+t_1(x-1)}{(x-z)}$$

DIRECT FORMULA

Father : Son

Present age = $x : y$

After T yrs = $a : b$

$$\text{Then Son's age} = y \times \frac{\text{T}(a-b)}{\text{difference of cross product}}$$

$$\text{and, Father's age} = x \times \frac{\text{T}(a-b)}{\text{difference of cross product}}$$

Note : 1. While evaluating the difference of cross-product always take the +ve sign.

2. Both the above direct formulas look similar. The only difference you can find is in the denominators. But it has been simplified as "difference of cross-products" to make it easier to remember. So with the help of one formula only you can solve both the questions.

SOLVED EXAMPLE

1. The age of father 3 years ago was 8 times the age of his son. Presently the father's age is 5 times that of the son. Find their present ages.

Sol. Let the present age of son be x years.

Then, the present age of father = $5x$ years.

3 years ago,

$$\text{Son's age} = (x - 3) \text{ years}$$
$$\text{Father's age} = (5x - 3) \text{ years}$$

But 3 years ago the father's age was 8 times that of his son. Therefore, we can write

$$8(x - 3) = 5x - 3$$

or, $$8x - 24 = 5x - 3$$

or, $$3x = 21$$

or, $$x = 7 \text{ years}$$

and $$5x = 35 \text{ years}$$

We get the present age of son = 7 years

and the present age of father = 35 years.

Note: We could also state the above problem as below:

3 years ago the ratio of ages of father to son was 8:1. At present the ratio of their ages is 5:1. Find their present ages.

In other words 8 times can be expressed as 8 : 1 or $\frac{8}{1}$.

2. The age of A, t_1 years ago was n_1 times the age of B. At present A's age is n_2 times that of B. Find their present ages.

Sol. Let the present age of B be x years.

Then, the present age of A = n_2x years.

t_1 years ago,

$$n_1 (x - t_1) = n_2 x - t_1$$

or, $$n_1x - n_1t_1 = n_2x - t_1$$

or, $$(n_1 - n_2)x = (n_1 - 1)t_1$$

or, $$x = \left(\frac{n_1 - 1}{n_1 - n_2}\right)t_1$$

So, $$\text{B's present age} = \left(\frac{n_1 - 1}{n_1 - n_2}\right)t_1$$

$$\text{A's present age} = \left(\frac{n_1 - 1}{n_1 - n_2}\right)n_2\, t_1$$

3. Verify Ex. 1 using the results derived in Ex. 2.

Sol. Here, take A as father and B as his son.

$n_1 = 8$; $n_2 = 5$; $t_1 = 3$ years

$$\text{Son's present age} = \left(\frac{n_1 - 1}{n_1 - n_2}\right)t_1$$

$$= \frac{8-1}{8-5} \times 3 = \frac{7}{3} \times 3$$

Son's present age = 7 years.

Father's present age = 7 × 5 = 35 years.

4. The ratio on Ram's present age to Mohan's present age is 5 : 6. 8 years hence this ratio changes to 7:8. Find their present ages.

Sol. Let Mohan's present age be $6x$ years.

Then, Ram's present age = $5x$ years.

8 years hence,

$$\frac{5x+8}{6x+8} = \frac{7}{8}$$

or, $40x + 64 = 42x + 56$

or, $2x = 8$

or, $x = 4$

∴ Mohan's present age = $6x$ = 24 years.

and Ram's present age = $5x$ = 20 years.

EXERCISE

1. Present ages of X and Y are in the ratio 5 : 6 respectively. Seven years hence this ratio will become 6 : 7 respectively What is X's present age in years?

(*a*) 35 (*b*) 42

(*c*) 49 (*d*) Cannot be determined

2. At present, the ratio betw:en the ages of Panas and Dipak is 4 :3. After 6 years, Panas's age will be 26 years. What is the age of Dipak at present?

(*a*) 12 years (*b*) 15 years (*c*) $19\frac{1}{2}$ years (*d*) 21 years

3. Yugnirmal is younger than Rahul by 4 years. If their ages are in the respective ratio of 7 : 9, how old is Yugnirmal?
(*a*) 16 years (*b*) 18 years (*c*) 28 years (*d*) None of these

4. The ratio between the present ages of P and Q is 5 : 7 respectively. If the difference between Q's present age and P's age after 6 years is 2, what is the total of P's and Q's present ages?
(*a*) 48 years (*b*) 52 years
(*c*) 56 years (*d*) Cannot be determined

5. The ratio between the present ages of P and Q is 6 : 7. If Q is 4 years old that P, what will be the ratio of the ages of P and Q after 4 years?
(*a*) 3:4 (*b*) 3:5 (*c*) 4 : 3 (*d*) None of these

6. Six years ago, the ratio of the ages of Kunal and Sagar was 6 : 5. Four years hence, the ratio of their ages will be 11 : 10. What is Sagar's age at present?
(*a*) 16 years (*b*) 18 years
(*c*) 20 years (*d*) Cannot be determined

7. Present ages of Sameer and Anand are in the ratio of 5 : 4 respectively. Three years hence, the ratio of their ages will become 11 : 9 respectively. What is Anand's present age in years?
(*a*) 24 (*b*) 27
(*c*) 40 (*d*) Cannot be determined

8. The ratio between the school ages of Neelam and Shaan is 5 : 6 respectively If the ratio between the one-third age of Neelam and half of Shaan's age is 5 : 9, then what is the school age of Shaan?
(*a*) 25 years (*b*) 30 years
(*c*) 36 years (*d*) Cannot be determined

9. The ratio between the present ages of A and B is 5 : 3 respectively. The ratio between A's age 4 years ago and B's age 4 years hence is 1 : 1. What is the ratio between A's age 4 years hence and B's age 4 years ago?
(*a*) 1 : 3 (*b*) 2 : 1 (*c*) 3 : 1 (*d*) 4 : 1

10. Eighteen years ago, a father was three times as old as his son. Now the father is only twice as old as his son. Then the sum of the present ages of the son and the father is:
(*a*) 54 (*b*) 72 (*c*) 105 (*d*) 108

11. A person's present age is two-fifth of the age of his mother. After 8 years, he will be one-half of the age of his mother. How old is the mother at present?
(*a*) 32 years (*b*) 36 years (*c*) 40 years (*d*) 48 years

12. Panas's grandfather was 8 times older to her 16 years ago. He would be 3 times of her age 8 years from now. Eight years ago, what was the ratio of Panas's age to that of her grandfather?

(*a*) 1 : 2 (*b*) 1 : 5 (*c*) 3 : 8 (*d*) None of these

13. The age of father 10 years ago was thrice the age of his son. Ten years hence, father's age will be twice that of his son. The ratio of their present ages is:

(*a*) 5 : 2 (*b*) 7 : 3 (*c*) 9 : 2 (*d*) 13 : 4

14. The sum of the present ages of a father and his son is 60 years. Six years ago, father's age was five times the age of the son. After 6 years, son's age will be:

(*a*) 12 years (*b*) 14 years (*c*) 18 years (*d*) 20 years

15. Q is as much younger than R as he is older than T. If the sum of the ages of R and T is 50 years, what is definitely the difference between R and Q's age?

(*a*) 1 year (*b*) 2 years (*c*) 25 years (*c*) Data inadequate

16. Krishna got married 8 years ago. His present age is $\frac{6}{5}$ times his age at the time of his marriage. Krishna's sister was 10 years younger to him at the time of his marriage. The age of Krishna's sister is :

(*a*) 32 years (*b*) 36 years (*c*) 38 years (*d*) 40 years

17. Father is aged three times more than his son Ronit. After 8 years, he would be two and a half times of Ronit's age. After further 8 years, how many times would he be of Ronit's age?

(*a*) 2 times (*b*) $2\frac{1}{2}$ times (*c*) $2\frac{3}{4}$ times (*d*) 3 times

18. A father said to his son, "I was as old as you are at present at the time of your birth." If father's age is 38 years now, then son's age five years back was:

(*a*) 14 years (*b*) 19 years (*c*) 33 years (*d*) 38 years

19. Ayesha's father was 38 years of age when she was born while her mother was 36 years old when her brother four years younger to her was born. What is the difference between the ages of her parents?

(*a*) 2 years (*b*) 4 years (*c*) 6 years (*d*) 8 years

20. A person was asked to state his age in years. His reply was, "Take my age three years hence, multiply it by 3 and then subtract three times my age three years ago and you will know how old I am." What was the age of the person?

(*a*) 18 years (*b*) 20 years (*c*) 24 years (*d*) 32 years

ANSWERS

1	2	3	4	5	6	7	8	9	10
(*a*)	(*b*)	(*d*)	(*a*)	(*d*)	(*a*)	(*a*)	(*d*)	(*c*)	(*d*)
11	**12**	**13**	**14**	**15**	**16**	**17**	**18**	**19**	**20**
(*c*)	(*d*)	(*b*)	(*d*)	(*d*)	(*c*)	(*a*)	(*b*)	(*c*)	(*a*)

SOME SELECTED EXPLANATORY ANSWERS

1. Suppose that the present ages of X and Y are $5x$ years and $6x$ years respectively.

Then, $\frac{5x+7}{6x+7} = \frac{6}{7} \Leftrightarrow 7(5x + 7) = 6(6x + 7) \Leftrightarrow x = 7.$

$\therefore$ X's present age = $5x$ = 35 years.

2. Let the present ages of Panas and Deepak be x years and $3x$ years respectively. Then,

$4x + 6 = 26 \Leftrightarrow 4x = 20 \Leftrightarrow x = 5.$

$\therefore$ Deepak's age = $3x$ = 15 yeans.

3. Let Rahul's age be x years. Then, Yugnirmal age = $(x - 7)$ years.

$\therefore \frac{x-7}{x} = \frac{7}{9} \Leftrightarrow 9x - 63 = 7x \Leftrightarrow 2x = 63 \Leftrightarrow x = 31.5.$

Hence, Yugnirmal age $(x - 7)$ = 24.5 years.

4. Suppose that the present ages of P and Q are $5x$ years and $7x$ years respectively.

Then, $7x - (5x + 6) = 2 \Leftrightarrow 2x = 8 \Leftrightarrow x = 4.$

$\therefore$ Required sum = $5x + 7x = 12x$ = 48 years.

5. Let P's age and Q's age be $6x$ years and $7x$ years respectively.

Then, $7x - 6x = 4 \Leftrightarrow x = 4.$

$\therefore$ Required ratio = $(6x + 4) : (7x + 4) = 28 : 32 = 7 : 8.$

6. Let the ages of Kunal and Sagar 6 years ago be $6x$ and $5x$ years respectively.

Then, $\frac{(6x+6)+4}{(5x+6)+4} = \frac{11}{10} \Leftrightarrow 10(6x + 10) = 11(5x + 10)$

$\Leftrightarrow 5x = 10 \Leftrightarrow x = 2.$

$\therefore$ Sagar's present age = $(5x + 6)$ = 16 years.

7. Suppose that the present ages of Sameer and Anand are $5x$ years and $4x$ years respectively.

Then, $\frac{5x+3}{4x+3} = \frac{11}{9} \Leftrightarrow 9(5x + 3) = 11(4x + 3) \Leftrightarrow x = 6.$

$\therefore$ Anand's present age = $4x$ = 24 years.

8. Let the school ages of Neelam and Shaan be $5x$ and $6x$ years respectively. According to the question

$$\frac{\frac{1}{3}\times 5x}{\frac{1}{2}\times 6x} = \frac{5}{9} \Leftrightarrow \left(\frac{1}{3}\times 9\times 5x\right) = \left(\frac{1}{5}\times 6x\right) \Leftrightarrow 15 = 15.$$

Thus, Shaan's age cannot be determined.

9. Let the present ages of A and B be $5x$ and $3x$ years respectively.

Then, $\frac{5x-4}{3x-4} = \frac{1}{1} \Leftrightarrow 5x - 4 = 3x + 4 \Leftrightarrow 2x = 8 \Leftrightarrow x = 4.$

$\therefore$ Required ratio $= (5x + 4) : (3x - 4) = 24 : 8 = 3 : 1.$

10. Let the present ages of the son and father be x and $2x$ years respectively. Then, $(2x - 18) = 3(x - 18) \Leftrightarrow x = 36.$

$\therefore$ Required sum $= (2x + x) = 3x = 108$ years.

11. Let the mother's present age be x years. Then the person's present age = $\left(\frac{2}{5}x\right)$ years.

$$\therefore \left(\frac{2}{5}x + 8\right) = \frac{1}{2}(x + 8) \Leftrightarrow 2(2x + 40) = 5(x + 8) \Leftrightarrow x = 40.$$

12. 16 years ago, let T = x years and G = $8x$ years.

After 8 years from now, T = $(x + 16 + 8)$ years and G = $(8x + 16 + 8)$ years.

$\therefore 8x + 24 = 3(x + 24) \Leftrightarrow 5x = 48.$

8 years ago, $\frac{T}{G} = \frac{x+8}{8x+8} = \frac{\frac{48}{5}+8}{8\times\frac{48}{5}+8} = \frac{88}{424} = \frac{11}{53}.$

14. Suppose that the present ages of son and father are x and $(60 - x)$ years respectively.

Then, $(60 - x) - 6 = 5(x - 6) \Leftrightarrow 54 - x = 5x - 30 \Leftrightarrow 6x = 84 \Leftrightarrow x = 14.$

$\therefore$ Son's age after 6 years $= (x + 6) = 20$ years.

16. Let Krishna's present age be x years. Then, his age at the time of marriage $= (x - 8)$ years.

$\therefore x = \frac{6}{5}(x - 8) \Leftrightarrow 5x = 6x - 48 \Leftrightarrow x = 48.$

Krishna's sister's age at the time of his marriage $= (x - 8) - 10 = (x - 18)$
$= 30$ years.

$\therefore$ Krishna's sister's present age $= (30 + 8)$ years $= 38$ years.

17. Suppose Ronit's present age be x years. Then, father's present age = $(x + 3x)$ years = $4x$ years.

$\therefore$ $(4x + 8) = \frac{5}{2}(x + 8) \Leftrightarrow 8x + 16 = 5x + 40 \Leftrightarrow 3x = 24 \Leftrightarrow x = 8.$

Hence, required ratio = $\frac{(4x + 16)}{(x + 16)} = \frac{48}{24} = 2.$

18. Let the son's present age be x years.

Then, $(38 - x) = x \Leftrightarrow 2x = 38 \Leftrightarrow x = 19.$

$\therefore$ Son's age 5 years back = (19 – 5) years = 14 years.

19. Mother's age when Ayesha's brother was born = 36 years.

Father's age when Ayesha's brother was born = (38 + 4) years = 42 years.

$\therefore$ Required difference = (42 – 36) years = 6 years.

20. Suppose the present age of the person is x years.

Then, $3(x + 3) - 3(x - 3) = x \Leftrightarrow (3x + 9) - (3x - 9) = x \Leftrightarrow x = 18.$

~~~~~~
~~~~~~

9. PERCENTAGE

Percentage is a method of expressing fractions or parts of any quantity into an equivalent form. Percentage is expressed in terms of hundredths i.e., the term per cent means for every hundred. A fraction whose denominator is 100 is called a percentage and the numerator of such a fraction is called the rate percent. It is denoted by the symbol %.

So, 100% means 100 hundredths of $\frac{100}{100} = 1$

50% means 50 hundredths or $\frac{50}{100} = \frac{1}{2}$

In other words, the rate percent is the quantity for every hundred.

For example, 12% means 12 for every hundred

i.e., $$12\% = \frac{12}{100} = \frac{3}{25}$$

When we say that Ram spends 25% of his income on food, it means for every ₹ 100 earned Ram spends ₹ 25 on his food. If his income is ₹ 400 i.e.; 100 +100 + 100 + 100, he spends on his food ₹ (25+ 25+ 25 + 25) = ₹ 100. Here we have taken one ₹ 25 for every ₹ 100 earned. Alternatively, this can be calculated as

$$25\% \text{ of ₹ } 400 = \frac{25}{100} \times \text{₹ } 400$$

(Here 'of' has been replaced by multiplication sign)

$$= \frac{1}{4} \times \text{₹ } 400 = \text{₹ } 100$$

(***Note:*** $\frac{1}{4}$ is the fractional equivalent of the fate percent 25%)

What we have done here is that we have operated $25\% = \frac{1}{4}$ on ₹ 400.

In order to save time it is advisable to remember the fractional or decimal equivalent of commonly used rate percent.

Percentage-Decimal Conversion: As defined earlier, percentage can be expressed as a fraction with numerator equal to rate percent and denominator as 100. Its decimal equivalent can be easily written by putting in die rate percent a decimal point after leaving two extreme right digits.

For example, $125\% = 1.25$

$25\% = 0.25$

$5\% = 0.05$ and so on.

In order to, convert a decimal into a percentage we need to multiply the decimal number by 100. This is equivalent to moving the decimal point by two digits to its right.

For example, $0.145 = 14.5\%$

$0.54 = 54\%$

$03 = 30\%$

$0.03 = 3\%$ and so on.

Percentage-Fraction Conversion: A fraction is converted into its percentage form by first changing the fraction into a decimal number and then changing the decimal into a percentage. Some cases where denominator is submultiple or multiple of 100, we reduce the denominator to 100 by multiplying with a suitable factor both its numerator and denominator;

For example, $\frac{2}{5} = 0.4 = 0.4 \times 100\% = 40\%$

Alternatively, $\frac{2}{5} = \frac{2 \times 20}{5 \times 20} = \frac{40}{100} = 40\%$

$$\frac{20}{400} = \frac{\frac{20}{4}}{\frac{400}{4}} = \frac{5}{100} = 5\%$$

To convert a percentage into a fraction, we write the rate percent in the numerator and put 100 in the denominator. We then reduce it to its lowest terms.

For example, $45\% = \frac{45}{100} = \frac{9}{20}$

$125\% = \frac{125}{100} = \frac{5}{4}$ or $1\frac{1}{4}$

$33\% = \frac{33}{100}$ and so on.

Note: $133\frac{1}{3}\% = \frac{400}{3}\% = \frac{400}{3 \times 100} = \frac{4}{3}$ or $1\frac{1}{3}$

Use of fractional or decimal equivalent of percentage makes calculation easier and saves time.

For example, $20\% \text{ of } 46 = \frac{20}{100} \times 46 = \frac{920}{100} = 9.2$

Alternatively, $20\% = \frac{20}{100} = \frac{1}{5}$

So, $20\% \text{ of } 46 = \frac{1}{5} \times 46 = 9.2$

But in some special cases it is preferable not to reduce fraction to its lowest terms.

For example, 4% of 700

$$4\% = \frac{4}{100} = \frac{1}{25} \text{ and}$$

$$4\% \text{ of } 700 = \frac{1}{25} \times 700 = 28$$

But if we had retained 4% as $\frac{4}{100}$, then $4\% \text{ of } 700 = \frac{4}{100} \times 700$

$$= 4 \times 7 = 28$$

In general, it is advantageous to reduce the fraction to its lowest terms. We give below the fractional equivalents of some of the commonly used percentages. Try to remember these through practice.

$1\% = \frac{1}{100}$	$2\% = \frac{1}{50}$	$3\frac{1}{8}\% = \frac{1}{32}$	$4\% = \frac{1}{25}$
$5\% = \frac{1}{20}$	$6\frac{1}{4}\% = \frac{1}{16}$	$8\% = \frac{2}{25}$	$8\frac{1}{3}\% = \frac{1}{12}$
$10\% = \frac{1}{10}$	$12\% = \frac{3}{25}$	$12\frac{1}{2}\% = \frac{1}{8}$	$13\frac{1}{3}\% = \frac{2}{15}$
$14\frac{2}{3}\% = \frac{1}{7}$	$15\% = \frac{3}{20}$	$16\% = \frac{4}{25}$	$16\frac{2}{3}\% = \frac{1}{6}$
$20\% = \frac{1}{5}$	$25\% = \frac{1}{4}$	$33\frac{1}{3}\% = \frac{1}{3}$	$37\frac{1}{2}\% = \frac{3}{8}$
$40\% = \frac{2}{5}$	$50\% = \frac{1}{2}$	$60\% = \frac{3}{5}$	$62\frac{1}{2}\% = \frac{5}{8}$

$66\frac{2}{3}\% = \frac{2}{3}$	$75\% = \frac{3}{4}$	$80\% = \frac{4}{5}$	$83\frac{1}{3}\% = \frac{5}{6}$
$87\frac{1}{2}\% = \frac{7}{8}$	$100\% = 1$	$120\% = \frac{6}{5}$	$125\% = \frac{5}{4}$
$133\frac{1}{3}\% = \frac{4}{3}$	$150\% = \frac{3}{2}$	$175\% = \frac{7}{4}$	$200\% = 2$

Sometimes it is much easier to use decimal equivalent of percentage in calculations.

For example, 25% of 400

$$0.25 \times 400 = 100$$

So, through enough practice you will get an idea of which equivalent form of percentage is to be used where in order to simplify calculations and save time.

SOLVED EXAMPLE

1. *Evaluate:*

(*i*) 28% of 450 + 45% of 280

(*ii*) $16\frac{2}{3}\%$ of 600 gm – $33\frac{1}{3}\%$ of 180 gm

Sol. (*i*) 28% of 450 + 45% of 280 $= \left(\frac{28}{100} \times 450 + \frac{45}{100} \times 280\right)$

$$= (126 + 126) = 252.$$

(*ii*) $16\frac{2}{3}\%$ of 600 gm – $33\frac{1}{3}\%$ of 180 gm

$$= \left[\left(\frac{50}{3} \times \frac{1}{100} \times 600\right) - \left(\frac{100}{3} \times \frac{1}{100} \times 180\right)\right] \text{gm}$$

$$= (100 - 60) \text{ gm} = 40 \text{ gm}.$$

2. (*i*) 2 is what percent of 50?

(*ii*) $\frac{1}{2}$ is what percent of $\frac{1}{3}$?

(*iii*) What percent of 7 is 84?

(*iv*) What percent of 2 metric tonnes is 40 quintals?

(*v*) What percent of 6.5 litres is 130 ml?

Sol. (*i*) Required percentage $= \left(\frac{2}{50} \times 100\right)\% = 4\%$.

(*ii*) Required percentage $= \left(\frac{1}{2} \times \frac{3}{1} \times 100\right)\% = 150\%$.

(*iii*) Required percentage $= \left(\frac{84}{7} \times 100\right)\% = 1200\%$.

(*iv*) 1 metric tonne = 10 quintals.

$\therefore$ Required percentage $= \left(\frac{40}{2 \times 10} \times 100\right)\% = 200\%$.

(*v*) Required percentage $= \left(\frac{130}{6.5 \times 1000} \times 100\right)\% = 2\%$.

3. If the sales tax be reduced from $3\frac{1}{2}\%$ to $3\frac{1}{3}\%$, then what difference does it make to a person who purchases an article with marked price ₹ 8400?

Sol. Required difference $= \left(3\frac{1}{2}\% \text{ or ₹ } 8400\right) - \left(3\frac{1}{3}\% \text{ or ₹ } 8400\right)$

$$= \left(\frac{7}{2} - \frac{10}{3}\right)\% \text{ of ₹ } 8400 = \frac{1}{6}\% \text{ or ₹ } 8400$$

$$= ₹ \left(\frac{1}{6} \times \frac{1}{100} \times 8400\right) = ₹ 14.$$

4. In an election between two candidates, 75% of the voters cast their votes, out of which 2% of the votes were declared invalied. A candidate got 9261 votes which were 75% of the total valid votes. Find the total number of votes enrolled in that election.

Sol. Let the total number of votes enrolled be x. Then,

Number of votes cast = 75% of x. Valid votes = 98% of (75% of x).

$\therefore$ Votes got by the candidate = 75% of [98% of (75% of x)] = 9261

$$\Leftrightarrow \left(\frac{75}{100} \times \frac{98}{100} \times \frac{75}{100} \times x\right) = 9261$$

$$\Leftrightarrow x = \left(\frac{9361 \times 100 \times 100 \times 100}{75 \times 98 \times 75}\right) = 16800.$$

5. During one year, the population of a town increased by 5% and during the next year, the population decreased by 5%. If the total populatin is 9975 at the end of the second year, then what was the population size in the beginning of the first year?

Sol. Population in the beginning of the first year

$$= \frac{9975}{\left(1+\frac{5}{100}\right)\left(1-\frac{5}{100}\right)} = \left(9975 \times \frac{20}{21} \times \frac{20}{19}\right) = 10000.$$

EXERCISE

1. What percent of a day is 3 hours ?

(*a*) $12\frac{1}{2}\%$ (*b*) $16\frac{2}{3}\%$ (*c*) $18\frac{2}{3}\%$ (*d*) $22\frac{1}{2}\%$

2. 40% of 1640 + ? = 35% of 980 + 150% of 850

(*a*) 372 (*b*) 842 (*c*) 962 (*d*) 1062

3. What percent of ₹ 2650 is ₹ 1987.50?

(*a*) 60% (*b*) 75% (*c*) 80% (*d*) 90%

4. 60% of 264 is the same as:

(*a*) 10% of 44 (*b*) 15% of 1056 (*c*) 30% of 132 (*d*) None of these

5. 88% of 370 + 24% of 210 – ? =118

(*a*) 256 (*b*) 258 (*c*) 268 (*d*) 358

6. The ratio 5 : 4 expressed as a percent equals :

(*a*) 12.5% (*b*) 40% (*c*) 80% (*d*) 125%

7. What is 15 percent of ₹ 34?

(*a*) ₹ 3.40 (*b*) ₹ 3.75 (*c*) ₹ 4.50 (*d*) ₹ 5.10

8. The difference between a number and its two-fifth is 510. What is 10% of that number?

(*a*) 12.75 (*b*) 85 (*c*) 204 (*d*) None of these

9. The sum of two numbers is $\frac{28}{25}$ of the first number. The second number is what percent of the first?

(*a*) 12% (*b*) 14% (*c*) 16% (*d*) 18%

10. In a competitive examination in State A, 6% candidates got selected from the total appeared candidates. State B had an equal number of candidates appeared and 7% candidates got selected with 80 more candidates got selected than A. What was the number of candidates appeared from each State?

(*a*) 7600 (*b*) 8000 (*c*) 8400 (*d*) Data inadequate

11. If ₹ 2800 is $\frac{2}{7}$ percent of the value of a house, the worth of the house (in ₹) is:
(*a*) 8,00,000 (*b*) 9,80,000 (*c*) 10,00,000 (*d*) 12,00,000

12. Two-fifth of one-third of three-seventh of a number is 15. What is 40 percent of that number?
(*a*) 72 (*b*) 84 (*c*) 136 (*d*) None of these

13. It costs Re. 1, to photocopy a sheet of paper. However, 2% discount is allowed on all photocopies done after first 1000 sheets. How much will it cost to copy 6000 sheets of paper?
(*a*) ₹ 3920 (*b*) ₹ 3980 (*c*) ₹ 4900 (*d*) ₹ 4920

14. A number, when 35 is subtracted from it, reduces to its 80 percent. What is four-fifth of that number?
(*a*) 70 (*b*) 90 (*c*) 120 (*d*) 140

15. The sum of two numbers is 2490. If 6.5% of one number is equal to 8.5% of the other, then the numbers are:
(*a*) 989, 1501 (*b*) 1011, 1479 (*c*) 1401, 1089 (*d*) 1411, 1079

16. A housewife saved ₹ 2.50 in buying an item on sale. If she spent ₹ 25 for the item, approximately how much percent she saved in the transaction?
(*a*) 8% (*b*) 9% (*c*) 10% (*d*) 11%

17. If 25% of a number is subtracted from a second number, the second number reduces to its five-sixth. What is the ratio of the first number to the second number?
(*a*) 1 : 3 (*b*) 2 : 3 (*c*) 3 : 2 (*d*) Data inadequate

18. When any number is divided by 12, then dividend becomes $\frac{1}{4}$th of the other number. By how much percent first number is greater than the second number?
(*a*) 150 (*b*) 200 (*c*) 300 (*d*) Data inadequate

19. Two numbers A and B are such that the sum of 5% of A and 4% of B is two-third of the sum of 6% of A and 8% of B. Find the ratio of A : B.
(*a*) 2:3 (*b*) 1 : 1 (*c*) 3 : 4 (*d*) 4 : 3

20. Three candidates contested an election and received 1136, 7636 and 11628 votes respectively. What percentage of the total votes did the winning candidate get?
(*a*) 57% (*b*) 60% (*c*) 65% (*d*) 90%

21. Mukesh buys goods worth ₹ 6650. He gets a rebate of 6% on it. After getting the rebate, he pays sales tax @ 10%. Find the amount he will have to pay for the goods.

(*a*) ₹ 6876.10 (*b*) ₹ 6999.20 (*c*) ₹ 6654 (*d*) ₹ 7000

22. The price of a car is ₹ 3,25,000. It was insured to 85% of its price. The car was damaged completely in an accident and the insurance company paid 90% of the insurance. What was the difference between the price of the car and the amount received?
(*a*) ₹ 32,500 (*b*) ₹ 48,750 (*c*) ₹ 76,375 (*d*) ₹ 81,250

23. A student secures 90%, 60% and 54% marks in test papers with 100, 150 and 200 respectively as maximum marks. The percentage of his aggregate is:
(*a*) 64 (*b*) 68 (*c*) 70 (*d*) None of these

24. A batsman scored 110 runs which included 3 boundaries and 8 sixes. What percent of his total score did he make by running between the wickets?
(*a*) 45% (*b*) $45\frac{5}{11}\%$ (*c*) $54\frac{6}{11}\%$ (*d*) 55%

25. In an examination, 35% of the students passed and 455 failed. How many students appeared for the examination?
(*a*) 490 (*b*) 700 (*c*) 845 (*d*) 1300

26. In an election a candidate who gets 84% of the votes is elected by a majority of 476 votes. What is the total number of votes polled ?
(*a*) 672 (*b*) 700 (*c*) 749 (*d*) 848

27. In an examination, 5% of the applicants were found ineligible and 85% of the eligible candidates belonged to the general category. If 4275 eligible candidates belonged to other categories, then how many candidates applied for the examination?
(*a*) 30,000 (*b*) 35,000 (*c*) 37,000 (*d*) None of these

28. 10% of the voters did not cast their vote in an election between two candidates. 10% of the votes polled were found invalid. The successful candidate got 54% of the valid votes and won by a majority of 1620 votes. The number of voters enrolled on the voters' list was :
(*a*) 25000 (*b*) 33000 (*c*) 35000 (*d*) 40000

29. 8% of the people eligible to vote are between 18 and 21 years of age. In an election, 85% of those eligible to vote, who were between 18 and 21, actually voted. In that election, the number of persons between 18 and 21, who actually voted, was what percent of those eligible to vote?
(*a*) 4.2 (*b*) 6.4 (*c*) 6.8 (*d*) 8

30. Two tailors X and Y are paid a total of ₹ 550 per week by their employer. If X is paid 120 percent of the sum paid to Y, how much is Y paid per week?
(*a*) ₹ 200 (*b*) ₹ 250 (*c*) ₹ 300 (*d*) None of these

31. Gauri went to the stationers and bought things worth ₹ 25, out of which 30 paise went on sales tax on taxable purchases. If the tax rate was 6%, then what was the cost of the tax free items?
(*a*) ₹ 15 (*b*) ₹ 15.70 (*c*) ₹ 19.70 (*d*) ₹ 20

32. In a certain school, 20% of students are below 8 years of age. The number of students above 8 years of age is $\frac{2}{3}$ of the number of students of 8 years age which is 48. What is the total number of students in the school?
(*a*) 72 (*b*) 80 (*c*) 120 (*d*) None of these

33. In an election between two candidates, one got 55% of the total valid votes, 20% of the votes were invalid. If the total number of votes was 7500, the number of valid votes that the other candidate got, was:
(*a*) 2700 (*b*) 2900 (*c*) 3000 (*d*) 3100

34. Two students appeared at an examination. One of them secured 9 marks more than the other and his marks were 56% of the sum of their marks. The marks obtained by them are :
(*a*) 39, 30 (*b*) 41, 32 (*c*) 42, 33 (*d*) 43, 34

35. If x is 80% of y, then what percent of $2x$ is y?
(*a*) 40% (*b*) $62\frac{1}{2}\%$ (*c*) $66\frac{2}{3}\%$ (*d*) 80%

36. If A = x% of y and B = y% of x, then which of the following is true?
(*a*) A is smaller than B.
(*b*) A is greater than B.
(*c*) Reletionship between A and B cannot be determined.
(*d*) If x is smaller than y, then A is greater than B.

Directions (Questions 37 to 41) : *A survey of magazine reading habits of the people living in five cities P, Q, R, S and T is summarised in a table given below. The Column I in the table gives percentage of magazine-readers in each city who read only one magazine a week. The Column II gives the total number of magazine-readers who read two or more magazines a week. Bead the table and then answer these questions:*

City	I	II
P	75	6000
Q	80	3500
R	60	3000
S	55	2700
T	25	4200

37. The city with the lowest number of magazine-readers is :

(*a*) Q (*b*) R (*c*) S (*d*) T

38. Which city has the highest number of magazine-readers who read only one magazine a week?

(*a*) P (*b*) Q (*c*) R (*d*) S

39. The highest number of magazine-readers in any given city is:

(*a*) 17500 (*b*) 18000 (*c*) 24000 (*d*) 30000

40. How many magazine-readers in city Q read only one magazine a week?

(*a*) 14000 (*b*) 18000 (*c*) 12500 (*d*) 16500

41. The total number of all the magazine-readers in the five cities who read only one magazine a week is:

(*a*) 19400 (*b*) 24000 (*c*) 41200 (*d*) 42000

42. The production of a company has ups and downs every year. The production increases for two consecutive years consistently by 15% and in the third year it decreases by 10%. Again in the next two years it increases by 15% each year and decreases by 10% in the third year. If we start counting from the year 1998, approximately what will be the effect on production of the company in 2002?

(*a*) 27% increase (*b*) 32% increase
(*c*) 37% increase (*d*) 42% increase

43. Out of 450 students of a school, 325 play football, 175 play cricket and 50 neither play football nor cricket. How many students play both football and cricket?

(*a*) 50 (*b*) 75 (*c*) 100 (*d*) 225

44. In the month of January, the Railway Police caught 4000 ticketless travellers. In February, the number rose by 5%. However, due to constant vigil by the Police and the Railway staff, the number reduced by 5% in March and in April it further reduced by 10%. The total number of ticketless travellers caught in the month of April was:

(*a*) 3125 (*b*) 3255 (*c*) 3575 (*d*) 3591

45. Aman gave 40% of the amount he had to Rohan. Rohan in turn gave one-fourth of what he received from Aman to Sahil. After paying ₹ 200 to the taxi driver out of the amount he got from Rohan, Sahil now has ₹ 600 left with him. How much amount did Aman have?

(*a*) ₹ 4000 (*b*) ₹ 8000 (*c*) ₹ 12,000 (*d*) Data inadequate

46. Yugnirmal spends 24% of his monthly income on food and 15% on the education of his children. Of the remaining salary, he spends 25% on entertainment and 20% on conveyance. He is now left with ₹ 10,736. What is the monthly Salary of Yugnirmal?

(*a*) ₹ 27,600 (*b*) ₹ 28,000 (*c*) ₹ 31,200 (*d*) ₹ 32,000

47. 405 sweets were distributed equally among children in such a way that the number of sweets received by each child is 20% of the total number of children. How many sweets did each child receive?

(*a*) 9 (*b*) 15 (*c*) 18 (*d*) 45

48. The sum of the number of boys and girls in a school is 150. If the number of boys is x, then the number of girls becomes x% of the total number of students. The number of boys is :

(*a*) 40 (*b*) 50 (*c*) 60 (*d*) 90

49. A salesman is allowed $5\frac{1}{2}$% discount on the total sales made by him plus a bonus of $\frac{1}{2}$% on the sales over ₹ 10,000. If his total earnings were ₹ 1990, then his total sales (in ₹) were :

(*a*) 30,000 (*b*) 32,000 (*c*) 34,000 (*d*) 35,000

50. In an examination, there are three papers and a candidate has to get 35% of the total to pass. In one paper, he gets 62 out of 150 and in the second 35 out of 150. How much must he get, out of 180, in.the third paper to just qualify for a pass?

(*a*) 60.5 (*b*) 68 (*c*) 70 (*d*) 71

51. In a History examination, the average for the entire class was 80 marks. If 10% of the students score 95 marks and 20% scored 90 marks, what was the average marks of the remaining students of the class?

(*a*) 65.5 (*b*) 72.5 (*c*) 75 (*d*) 85

52. In a recent survey, 40% houses contained two or more people. Of those houses containing only one person, 25% were having only a male. What is the percentage of all houses, which contain exactly one female and no males?

(*a*) 15 (*b*) 40 (*c*) 75 (*d*) None of these

53. $37\frac{1}{2}$% of the candidates in an examination were girls, 75% of the boys and $62\frac{1}{2}$% of the girls passed and 342 girls faild. The number of boys failed was:

(*a*) 350 (*b*) 360 (*c*) 370 (*d*) 380

54. The price of an article was increased by r%. Later the new price was decreased by r%. If the latest price is Re. 1, then the original price was:

(*a*) ₹ 1 (*b*) ₹ $\left(\frac{1-r^2}{100}\right)$ (*c*) ₹ $\frac{\sqrt{1-r^2}}{100}$ (*d*) ₹ $\left(\frac{10000}{10000-r^2}\right)$

55. Petrer could save 10% of his income. Two years later when his income is increased by 20%, he could save the same amount only as before. By how much precent has his expenditure increased?

(*a*) 22% (*b*) $22\frac{2}{9}\%$ (*c*) $23\frac{1}{3}\%$ (*d*) 24%

56. An empty fuel tank of a car was filled with A type petrol. When the tank was half-empty, it was filled with B type petrol. Again when the tank was half-empty, it was filled with A type petrol. When the tank was half-empty again, it was filled with B type petrol. What is the percentage of A type petrol at present in the tank?

(*a*) 33.5% (*b*) 37.5% (*c*) 40% (*d*) 50%

57. A number is increased by 20% and then again by 20%. By what percent should the increased number be reduced so as to get back the original number?

(*a*) $19\frac{11}{31}\%$ (*b*) $30\frac{5}{9}\%$ (*c*) 40% (*d*) 44%

58. The price of tea being increased by 20%, a man reduces his consumption by 20%. By how much percent will his expenses for tea be decreased?

(*a*) 2% (*b*) 4% (*c*) 6% (*d*) 8%

59. The price of wheat falls by 16%. By what percentage a person can increase the consumption of wheat so that his overall budget does not change?

(*a*) 16% (*b*) 18% (*c*) 18.5% (*d*) 19%

60. If inflation increases at a rate of 8% p.a., what will a ₹ 20 article cost at the end of two years?

(*a*) Between ₹ 20 and ₹ 21 (*b*) Between ₹ 21 and ₹ 22
(*c*) Between ₹ 22 and ₹ 23 (*d*) Between ₹ 23 and ₹ 24

61. The value of a machine depreciates at the rate of 10% every year. It was purchased 3 years ago. If its present value is ₹ 8748, its purchase price was:

(*a*) ₹ 10,000 (*b*) ₹ 11,372 (*c*) ₹ 12,000 (*d*) ₹ 12,500

62. From the salary of an officer, 10% is deducted as house rent, 20% of the rest, he spends on conveyance, 20% of the rest he pays as income tax and 10% of the balance, he spends on clothes. Then, he is left with ₹ 15,552. Find his total salary.

(*a*) ₹ 25,000 (*b*) ₹ 30,000 (*c*) ₹ 35,000 (*d*) ₹ 40,000

63. In some quantity of ghee, 60% is pure ghee and 40% is vanaspati. If 10 kg of pure ghee is added, then the strength of vanaspati ghee becomes 20%. The original quantity was:
(*a*) 10 kg (*b*) 15 kg (*c*) 20 kg (*d*) 25 kg

64. Rakesh spends 40% of his salary on food, 20% on house rent, 10% on entertainment and 10% *on* conveyance. If his savings at the end of a month are ₹ 1500, then his monthly salary is:
(*a*) ₹ 6000 (*b*) ₹ 7500 (*c*) ₹ 8000 (*d*) ₹ 10,000

65. The total population of a village is 5000. The number of males and females increases by 10% and 15% respectively and consequently the population of the village becomes 5600. What was the number of males in the village?
(*a*) 2000 (*b*) 2500 (*c*) 3000 (*d*) 4000

66. Amit's monthly income is 30% more than that of Raunaq. Raunaq's monthly income is 20% less than that of Deepak. If the difference between the monthly incomes of Amit and Deepak is ₹ 800, what is the monthly income of Raunaq?
(*a*) ₹ 12,000 (*b*) ₹ 16,000 (*c*) ₹ 20,000 (*d*) Data inadequate

67. In an examination in which full marks were 800, A gets 20% more than B, B gets 20% more than C, and C gets 15% less than D. If A got 5,76, what percentage of full marks did D get (approximately)?
(*a*) 45.7 (*b*) 51.2 (*c*) 58.8 (*d*) 61.7

68. In an examination, the percentage of students qualified to the number of students appeared from school A is 70%. In school B, the number, of students appeared is 20% more than the students appeared from school A and the number of students qualified from school B is 50% more than the students qualified from school A. What is the percentage of students qualified to the number of students appeared from school B?
(*a*) 30% (*b*) 70% (*c*) 78.5% (*d*) 87.5%

69. One type of liquid contains 20% water and the second type pf liquid contains 35% of water. A glass is filled with 10 parts of first liquid and 4 parts of second liquid. The percentage of water in the new mixture in the glass is:
(*a*) 20% (*b*) $24\frac{2}{7}\%$ (*c*) 37% (*d*) 40%

70. The population of a variety of tiny bush in an experimental field increased by 10% in the first year, increased by 8% in the second year but decreased by 10% in the third year. If the present number of bushes in the experimental field is 26730, then the number of bushes in the beginning was :
(*a*) 25000 (*b*) 27000 (*c*) 28000 (*d*) 24600

71. Mr. X, a businessman had the income in the year 2000, such that he earned a profit of 20% on his investment in the business. In the year 2001, his investment was less by ₹ 5000 but still had the same income (Income = Investment + Profit) as that in 2000. Thus, the percent profit earned in 2001 increased by 6%. What was his investment in 2000?
(*a*) ₹ 1,02,000 (*b*) ₹ 1,05,000 (*c*) ₹ 1,50,500 (*d*) None of these

72. In an examination, 34% of the students failed in Mathematics and 42%, failed in English. If 20% of the students failed in both the subjects, then the percentage of students who passed in both the subjects was:
(*a*) 44 (*b*) 50 (*c*) 54 (*d*) 56

73. A spider climbed $62\frac{1}{2}\%$ of the height of the pole in one hour and in the next hour it covered $12\frac{1}{2}\%$ of the remaining height. If the height of the pole is 192 m, then distance climbed in second hour is:
(*a*) 3 m (*b*) 5 m (*c*) 7 m (*d*) 9 m

74. In an examination, 65% students passed, in Civics and 60% in History, 40% passed in both of these subjects. If 90 students failed in History and Civics both, then what is the total number of students?
(*a*) 600 (*b*) 650 (*c*) 700 (*d*) 750

ANSWERS

1	2	3	4	5	6	7	8	9	10
(*a*)	(*c*)	(*b*)	(*b*)	(*b*)	(*d*)	(*d*)	(*b*)	(*a*)	(*b*)
11	**12**	**13**	**14**	**15**	**16**	**17**	**18**	**19**	**20**
(*b*)	(*d*)	(*d*)	(*d*)	(*d*)	(*b*)	(*b*)	(*b*)	(*d*)	(*a*)
21	**22**	**23**	**24**	**25**	**26**	**27**	**28**	**29**	**30**
(*a*)	(*c*)	(*a*)	(*b*)	(*b*)	(*b*)	(*a*)	(*a*)	(*c*)	(*b*)
31	**32**	**33**	**34**	**35**	**36**	**37**	**38**	**39**	**40**
(*c*)	(*d*)	(*a*)	(*c*)	(*b*)	(*d*)	(*d*)	(*a*)	(*c*)	(*a*)
41	**42**	**43**	**44**	**45**	**46**	**47**	**48**	**49**	**50**
(*c*)	(*c*)	(*c*)	(*d*)	(*b*)	(*d*)	(*a*)	(*c*)	(*c*)	(*d*)
51	**52**	**53**	**54**	**55**	**56**	**57**	**58**	**59**	**60**
(*c*)	(*d*)	(*d*)	(*d*)	(*b*)	(*b*)	(*b*)	(*b*)	(*d*)	(*d*)
61	**62**	**63**	**64**	**65**	**66**	**67**	**68**	**69**	**70**
(*c*)	(*b*)	(*a*)	(*b*)	(*c*)	(*b*)	(*c*)	(*d*)	(*b*)	(*a*)
71	**72**	**73**	**74**						
(*b*)	(*a*)	(*d*)	(*a*)						

SOME SELECTED EXPLANATORY ANSWERS

1. Required percentage $= \left(\frac{3}{24} \times 100\right)\% = \frac{25}{2}\% = 12\frac{1}{2}\%.$

2. Let 40% of 1640 + x = 35% of 980 + 150% or 850

Then, x = 35% of 980 + 150% of 850 – 40% of 1640

$= \left(\frac{35}{100} \times 980 + \frac{150}{100} \times 850\right) - \left(\frac{40}{100} \times 1640\right) = (343 + 1275 - 656)$

$= (1618 - 656) = 962.$

3. Required percentage $= \left(\frac{1987.50}{2650} \times 100\right)\% = \left(\frac{19875}{265} \times \frac{1}{100} \times 100\right)\% = 75\%.$

4. 60% of 264 $= \left(\frac{60}{100} \times 264\right) = 158.40$; 10% of 44 $= \left(\frac{10}{100} \times 44\right) = 4.40$;

15% of 1056 $= \left(\frac{15}{100} \times 1056\right) = 158.40$;

30% of 132 $= \left(\frac{30}{100} \times 132\right) = 39.60.$

$\therefore$ 60% or 264 = 15% of 1056.

5. Let 88% of 370 + 24% of 210 – x = 118.

Then, $x = \left(\frac{88}{100} \times 370\right) + \left(\frac{24}{100} \times 210\right) - 118$

$= 325.60 + 50.40 - 118 = 376 - 118 = 258.$

6. $5 : 4 = \frac{5}{4} = \left(\frac{5}{4} \times 100\right)\% = 125\%.$

7. 15% of ₹ 34 = ₹$\left(\frac{15}{100} \times 34\right)$ = ₹ 5.10.

8. Suppose that the number be P. Then, $P - \frac{2}{5}P = 510 \Leftrightarrow \frac{3}{5}P = 510$

$\Leftrightarrow P = \left(\frac{510 \times 5}{3}\right) = 850. \quad \therefore$ 10% of 850 = 85.

9. Suppose the two numbers are x and y. Then, $x + y = \frac{28}{25}x \Leftrightarrow y = \frac{28}{25}x - x$

$\Leftrightarrow y = \frac{3}{25}x \Leftrightarrow \frac{y}{x} = \left(\frac{3}{25} \times 100\right)\% = 12\%.$

10. Let the number of candidates appeared from each state be x.
Then, 7% of x – 6% of x = 80 $\Leftrightarrow$ $x = 80 \times 100 = 8000$.

11. Suppose the worth of the house is ₹ x.

Then, $\frac{2}{7}\%$ of $x = 2800 \Leftrightarrow \left(\frac{2}{7} \times \frac{1}{100} \times x\right) = 2800$

$$\Leftrightarrow x = \left(\frac{2800 \times 100 \times 7}{2}\right) = 9{,}80{,}000.$$

12. Suppose that the number is x. Then, $\frac{2}{5}$ of $\frac{1}{3}$ of $\frac{3}{7}$ of $x = 15$

$$\Leftrightarrow x = \left(15 \times \frac{7}{3} \times 3 \times \frac{5}{2}\right) = \frac{525}{2}.$$

$$\therefore 40\% \text{ of } \frac{525}{2} = \left(\frac{40}{100} \times \frac{525}{2}\right) = 105.$$

13. Total cost = ₹ [1 × 1000 + (100 – 2)% of 1 × 4000]
= (1000 + 0.98 × 4000) = ₹ (1000 + 3920) = ₹ 4920.

14. Suppose that the number is k.

Then, $l - 35 = \frac{80}{100}k \Leftrightarrow k - \frac{80}{100}k = 35$

$$\Leftrightarrow k = \frac{35 \times 100}{20} = 175 \Leftrightarrow \frac{4}{5}k = 140.$$

15. Suppose that the numbers are x and y. Then, 6.5% of x = 8.5% of y

$$\Leftrightarrow x = \frac{85}{65}y = \frac{17}{13}y.$$

Now, $x + y = 2490 \Rightarrow \frac{17}{13}y + y = 2490 \Rightarrow \frac{30}{13}y = 2490$

$$\Rightarrow y = \left(\frac{2490 \times 13}{30}\right) = 1079.$$

$\therefore$ One number = y = 1079, other number = $\frac{17}{13}y = 1411$.

16. Actual price = ₹ (25 + 2.50) = ₹ 27.50.

$$\therefore \quad \text{Saving} = \left(\frac{2.50}{27.50} \times 100\right)\% = \frac{100}{11}\% = 9\frac{1}{11}\% \approx 9\%.$$

17. Suppose the two numbers are x and y. Then, y – 25% of $x = \frac{5}{6}y$

$\Leftrightarrow y - \frac{5}{6}y = \frac{25}{100}x \Leftrightarrow \frac{y}{6} = \frac{x}{4} \Leftrightarrow \frac{x}{y} = \frac{4}{6} = \frac{2}{3}.$

18. Suppose the two numbers be x and y. Then, $\frac{x}{12} = \frac{y}{4} \Leftrightarrow x = 3y.$

Hence, required percentage $= \left(\frac{x-y}{y} \times 100\right)\% = \left(\frac{2y}{y} \times 100\right)\% = 200\%.$

19. 5% of A + 4% of B $= \frac{2}{3}$ (6% of A + 8% of B)

$\Leftrightarrow \frac{5}{100}A + \frac{4}{100}B = \frac{2}{3}\left(\frac{6}{100}A + \frac{8}{100}B\right)$

$\Leftrightarrow \frac{1}{20}A + \frac{1}{25}B = \frac{1}{25}A + \frac{4}{75}B \Leftrightarrow \left(\frac{1}{20} - \frac{1}{25}\right)A = \left(\frac{4}{75} - \frac{1}{25}\right)B$

$\Leftrightarrow \frac{1}{100}A = \frac{1}{75}B \Leftrightarrow \frac{A}{B} = \frac{100}{75} = \frac{4}{3}.$

20. Here, total number of votes polled = (1136 + 7636 + 11628) = 20400.

$\therefore$ Required percentage $= \left(\frac{11628}{20400} \times 400\right)\% = 57\%.$

21. Rebate = 6% of ₹ 6650 = ₹$\left(\frac{6}{100} \times 6650\right)$ = ₹ 399.

Sales tax = 10% of ₹ (6650 – 399) = ₹ $\left(\frac{10}{100} \times 6251\right)$ = ₹ 625.10.

$\therefore$ Final amount = ₹ (6251 + 625.10) = ₹ 6876.10.

22. From question, Amount paid to car owner = 90% of 85% of ₹ 3,25,000

= ₹ $\left(\frac{90}{100} \times \frac{85}{100} \times 325000\right)$ = ₹ 2,48,625.

Hence, Required difference = ₹ (325000 – 248625) = ₹ 76,375.

23. Total marks secured = (90% of 100 + 60% of 150 + 54% of 200)

$= \left(\frac{90}{100} \times 100 + \frac{60}{100} \times 150 + \frac{54}{100} \times 200\right)$

= (90 + 90 + 108) = 288.

Total maximum marks = (100 + 150 + 200) = 450.

$\therefore$ Aggregate percentage $= \left(\frac{288}{450} \times 100\right)\% = 64\%.$

24. Number of runs made by running $= 110 - (3 \times 4 + 8 \times 6) = 50.$

$\therefore$ Required percentage $= \left(\frac{50}{110} \times 100\right)\% = 45\frac{5}{11}\%.$

25. Suppose the number of students appeared be x.

Then, 65% of $x = 455 \Leftrightarrow \frac{65}{100}x = 455 \Leftrightarrow x = \left(\frac{455 \times 100}{65}\right) = 700.$

26. Let the total number of votes polled be x.
Then, votes polled by other candidate $= (100 - 84)\%$ of $x = 16\%$ of x.

$\therefore$ 84% of $x -$ 16% of $x = 476 \Leftrightarrow \frac{68}{100}x = 476 \Leftrightarrow x = \left(\frac{476 \times 100}{68}\right) = 700.$

27. Let the total number of application be x.
Number of eligible candidates = 95% of x.
Eligible candidates of other categories = 15% of (95% of x)

$$= \left(\frac{15}{100} \times \frac{95}{100} \times x\right) = \frac{57}{400}x.$$

$\therefore \frac{57}{400}x = 4275 \Leftrightarrow x = \left(\frac{4275 \times 400}{57}\right) = 30000.$

28. Let the total number of voters be x. Then, Votes polled = 90% of x.
Valid votes = 90% of (90% of x).
$\therefore$ 54% of [90% of (90% of x)] – 46% of [90% of (90% of (90% of x)] = 1620
$\Leftrightarrow$ 8% of [90% of (90% of x)] = 1620

$\Leftrightarrow \frac{8}{100} \times \frac{90}{100} \times \frac{90}{100} \times x = 1620 \Leftrightarrow x = \left(\frac{1620 \times 100 \times 100 \times 100}{8 \times 90 \times 90}\right) = 25000.$

30. Let the sum paid to Y per week be ₹ z. Then, z + 120% of $z = 550$

$\Leftrightarrow z + \frac{120}{100}z = 550 \Leftrightarrow \frac{11}{5}z = 550 \Leftrightarrow z = \left(\frac{550 \times 5}{11}\right) = 250.$

31. Let the amount of taxable purchases be ₹ x.

Then, 6% of $x = \frac{30}{100} \Leftrightarrow x = \left(\frac{30}{100} \times \frac{100}{6}\right) = 5.$

$\therefore$ Cost of tax free items = ₹ [25 – (5 + 0.30)] = ₹ 19.70.

32. Suppose the number of students inthe school x. Then,
Number of students of or above 8 years = (100 – 20)% of x = 80% of x.

$\therefore$ 80% of $x = 48 + \frac{2}{3}$ of $48 \Leftrightarrow \frac{80}{100}x = 80 \Leftrightarrow x = 100.$

33. Number of valid votes = 80% of 7500 = 6000.
Valid votes polled by other candidate = 45% of 6000

$$= \left(\frac{45}{100} \times 6000\right) = 2700.$$

34. Let their marks be $(x + 9)$ and x.

Then, $x + 9 = \frac{56}{100}(x + 9 + x) \Leftrightarrow 25(x + 9) = 14(2x + 9)$

$\Leftrightarrow 3x = 99 \Leftrightarrow x = 33.$

So, their marks are 42 and 33.

35. $x = 80\%$ of $y \Leftrightarrow x = \frac{80}{100}y \Leftrightarrow \frac{y}{x} = \frac{5}{4} \Leftrightarrow \frac{y}{2x} = \frac{5}{8}.$

Hence, required percentage $= \left(\frac{y}{2x} \times 100\right)\% = \left(\frac{5}{8} \times 100\right)\% = 62\frac{1}{2}\%.$

36. $x\%$ of $y = \left(\frac{x}{100} \times y\right) = \left(\frac{y}{100} \times x\right) = y\%$ of $x \Rightarrow$ A = B.

37. Solution 37-41

Let the number of magazine-readers in city P be x.

Then, (100 – 75)% of $x = 6000 \Leftrightarrow \frac{25}{100}x = 6000$

$\Leftrightarrow x = \left(\frac{6000 \times 100}{25}\right) = 24000.$

Number of readers in P, reading only one magazine a week

= (24000 – 6000) = 18000.

Similarly, we can find these values in other cases. Thus, we have the fallowing table :

City	No. of magazine-readers	No. of readers reading only one magazine a week
P	24000	18000
Q	17500	14000
R	7500	4500
S	6000	3300
T	5600	1400

37. The lowest number of magazine-readers is 5600 and this is in the case of city T.

38. The highest number of magazine-readers who read only one magazine a week is 18000 and this is in the case of city P.

39. The highest number of magazine-readers is 24000.

40. Number of magazine-readers in city Q reading only one magazine a week = 14000.

41. Total number of magazine-readers reading only one magazine a week = (18000 + 14000 + 4500 + 3300 + 1400) = 41200.

42. Suppose that the production in 1998 are 100 units. Then,

$$\text{Production in 2002} = 100 \times \left(1 + \frac{15}{100}\right)^2 \left(1 - \frac{10}{100}\right)\left(1 + \frac{15}{100}\right)$$

$$= \left(100 \times \frac{23}{20} \times \frac{23}{20} \times \frac{9}{10} \times \frac{23}{20}\right) = 136.88.$$

$\therefore$ Increase in production = (136.88 – 100)% = 36.88% = 37%.

43. From question $n(A) = 325$, $n(B)$

$$= 175,\ n(A \cup B) = 450 - 50 = 400.$$

$$\text{Required number} = n(A \cap B) = n(A) + n(B) - n(A \cup B)$$

$$= 325 + 175 - 400 = 100.$$

44. Number of ticketless travellers in April

$$= 4000 \times \left(1 + \frac{5}{100}\right)\left(1 - \frac{5}{100}\right)\left(1 - \frac{10}{100}\right) = \left(4000 \times \frac{21}{20} \times \frac{19}{20} \times \frac{9}{10}\right) = 3591.$$

45. Let the amount with Aman be ₹ x.

Then, amount received by Sahil = $\frac{1}{4}$ of 40% of ₹ x = 10% of ₹ x.

$\therefore$ 10% of x = 600 + 200 $\Leftrightarrow$ $\frac{10}{100}x = 800$ $\Leftrightarrow$ $x = 800 \times 10 = 8000$.

46. Suppose that the monthly salary of Yugnirmal is ₹ x.

Then, [100 – (25 + 20)]% of [100 – (24 + 15)]% of x = 10736

$$\Leftrightarrow \frac{55}{100} \times \frac{61}{100} \times x = 10736 \Leftrightarrow x = \left(\frac{10736 \times 100 \times 100}{55 \times 61}\right) = 32000.$$

47. Let the total number of children be x.

Then, $x \times$ (20% of x) = 405 $\Leftrightarrow$ $\frac{1}{5}x^2 = 405 \Leftrightarrow x^2 = 2025$ $\Leftrightarrow$ $x = 45$.

$\therefore$ Number of sweets received by each child = 20% of 45 = 9.

48. We have : $x + x\%$ of $150 = 150$

$$\Leftrightarrow x + \frac{x}{100} \times 150 = 150 \Leftrightarrow \frac{5}{2}x = 150 \Leftrightarrow x = \left(\frac{150 \times 2}{5}\right) = 60.$$

49. Let the total sales be ₹ x. Then, $5\frac{1}{2}\%$ of $x + \frac{1}{2}\%$ of $(x - 10000) = 1990$

$$\Leftrightarrow \frac{11}{2} \times \frac{1}{100} \times x + \frac{1}{2} \times \frac{1}{100} \times (x - 10000) = 1990$$

$$\Leftrightarrow 12x - 10000 = 398000 \Leftrightarrow 12x = 408000 \Leftrightarrow x = 34000.$$

50. Let the marks required be x. Then, $(62 + 35 + x) = 35\%$ of $(150 + 150 + 180)$

$$\Leftrightarrow 97 + x = \frac{35}{100} \times 480 \Leftrightarrow x = 168 - 97 = 71.$$

51. Let the number of students in the class be 100 and let the required average be x.

Then, $(10 \times 95) + (20 \times 90) + (70 \times x) = (100 \times 80)$

$$\Leftrightarrow 70x = 8000 - (950 + 1800) = 5250 \Leftrightarrow x = 75.$$

52. Let the total number of houses be x. Then,

$\therefore$ Number of houses having one female only

$$= (100 - 25)\% \text{ of } (100 - 40)\% \text{ of } x = \left(\frac{75}{100} \times \frac{60}{100} \times x\right) = \frac{9}{20}x.$$

$$\therefore \text{Required percentage} = \left(\frac{9x}{20} \times \frac{1}{x} \times 100\right)\% = 45\%.$$

53. Let the total number of candidates be x.

Then, $\left(100 - 62\frac{1}{2}\right)\%$ of $37\frac{1}{2}\%$ of $x = 342$

$$\Leftrightarrow \frac{75}{2} \times \frac{1}{100} \times \frac{75}{2} \times \frac{1}{100} \times x = 342 \Leftrightarrow \frac{9x}{64} = 342 \Leftrightarrow x = \left(\frac{342 \times 64}{9}\right) = 2432.$$

Number of boys failed $= (100 - 75)\%$ of $\left(100 - 37\frac{1}{2}\right)\%$ of 2432

$$= \left(\frac{25}{100} \times \frac{125}{2} \times \frac{1}{100} \times 2432\right) = 380.$$

54. Let the original price be ₹ x.

$\therefore (100 - r)\%$ of $(100 + r)\%$ of $x = 1$

$$\Rightarrow \frac{(100 - r)}{100} \times \frac{(100 + r)}{100} \times x = 1 \Rightarrow x = \frac{100 \times 100}{(100 - r)(100 + r)} = \frac{10000}{(10000 - r^2)}.$$

57. Let original number = 100.

New number = 120% of 120% of 100 = $\left(\frac{120}{100} \times \frac{120}{100} \times 100\right) = 144.$

Decrease on 144 = 44. Decrease on 100 = $\left(\frac{44}{144} \times 100\right)\% = 30\frac{5}{9}\%.$

58. Let original consumption = 100 units and original price = ₹ 100 per unit.
Original expenditure = ₹ (100 × 100) = ₹ 10000.
New expenditure = ₹ (120 × 80) = ₹ 9600.

$\therefore$ Decrease in expenditure = $\left(\frac{400}{10000} \times 100\right)\% = 4\%.$

59. Increase in consumption = $\left[\frac{R}{(100 - R)} \times 100\right]\% = \left(\frac{16}{84} \times 100\right)\% = \frac{400}{21}\%$

$= 19.04\% = 19\%.$

60. Cost after 2 years = ₹ $\left[20 \times \left(1 + \frac{8}{100}\right)^2\right]$ = ₹ $\left(20 \times \frac{27}{25} \times \frac{27}{25}\right)$ = ₹ 23.33.

61. Purchase price = ₹ $\left[\frac{8748}{\left(1 - \frac{10}{100}\right)^3}\right]$ = ₹ $\left(8748 \times \frac{10}{9} \times \frac{10}{9} \times \frac{10}{9}\right)$ = ₹ 12000.

62. Let the total salary be ₹ x.
Then, (100 – 10)% of (100 – 20)% of (100 – 20)% of (100 – 10)% of x = 15552

$\Leftrightarrow \left(\frac{90}{100} \times \frac{80}{100} \times \frac{80}{100} \times \frac{90}{100} \times x\right) = 15552$

$\Leftrightarrow x = \left(\frac{15552 \times 10000}{64 \times 81}\right) = 30000.$

63. Suppose that the original quantity was x kg.

Vanaspati ghee in x kg = $\left(\frac{40}{100}x\right)$ kg = $\left(\frac{2x}{5}\right)$ kg.

Now, $\frac{\frac{2x}{5}}{x + 10} = \frac{20}{100} \Leftrightarrow \frac{2x}{5x + 50} = \frac{1}{5} \Leftrightarrow 5x = 50 \Leftrightarrow x = 10.$

64. Saving = [100 – (40 + 20 + 10 + 10)]% = 20%. Let the monthly salary be ₹ x

Then, 20% of x = 1500 ⇔ $\frac{20}{100}x = 1500$ ⇔ $x = 1500 \times 5 = 7500$.

65. Let the number of males be x. Then, number of females = $(5000 - x)$.

∴ 10% of x + 15% of $(5000 - x) = (5600 - 5000)$

$$\Leftrightarrow \frac{10}{100}x + \frac{15}{100}(5000 - x) = 600 \Leftrightarrow 10x + 75000 - 15x = 60000$$

$$\Leftrightarrow 5x = 15000 \Leftrightarrow x = 3000.$$

66. Let Deepak's monthly income = ₹ 100. Then, Raunaq's monthly income = ₹ 80. Amit's monthly income = ₹ $\left(\frac{130}{100} \times 80\right)$ = ₹ 104.

If difference between Amit's and Deepak's income is ₹ 4, then Raunaq's income = ₹ 80.

If difference is ₹ 800, Raunaq's income = ₹$\left(\frac{80}{4} \times 800\right)$ = ₹ 16000.

67. A = $\frac{120}{100}$ B, B = $\frac{120}{100}$ C and C = $\frac{85}{100}$ D.

∴ B = $\frac{5}{6}$ A, C = $\frac{5}{6}$ B and D = $\frac{20}{17}$ C.

$$B = \frac{5}{6} \times 576 = 480;\ C = \frac{5}{6} \times 480 = 400;\ D = \frac{20}{17} \times 400 = \frac{8000}{17}.$$

So, required percentage = $\left(\frac{8000}{17} \times \frac{1}{800} \times 100\right)\%$ = 58.82%.

69. Required percentage = $\left(\frac{20\% \text{ of } 10 + 35\% \text{ of } 4}{10 + 4} \times 100\right)\%$

$$= \left(\frac{3.4}{14} \times 100\right)\% = 24\frac{2}{7}\%.$$

70. Number of bushes in the beginning

$$= \frac{26730}{\left(1 + \frac{10}{100}\right)\left(1 + \frac{8}{100}\right)\left(1 - \frac{10}{100}\right)} = \left(26730 \times \frac{10}{11} \times \frac{25}{27} \times \frac{10}{9}\right) = 25000.$$

71. Suppose that Mr. X investment in the year 2000 be ₹ P.

Then, income in 2000 = ₹ [P + 20% of P] = ₹ $\frac{120}{100}$P.

Income in 2001 = ₹ $\left[\frac{126}{100}(P - 5000)\right]$

$$\therefore \frac{120}{100}P = \frac{126}{100}(P - 5000) \Leftrightarrow 120P = 126(P - 5000)$$

$$\Leftrightarrow 6P = 630000 \Leftrightarrow P = 105000$$

73. Height climbed in second hour = $12\frac{1}{2}\%$ of $\left(100 - 62\frac{1}{2}\right)\%$ of 192 m

$$= \left(\frac{25}{2} \times \frac{1}{100} \times \frac{75}{2} \times \frac{1}{100} \times 192\right) \text{ m} = 9 \text{ m}.$$

74. Suppose that the total number of students are k
Number passed in one or both is given by:
$n(A \cup B) = n(A) + n(B) - n(A \cap B) = 65\%$ of k + 60% of k – 40% of k

$$= \left(\frac{65}{100}k + \frac{60}{100}k - \frac{40}{100}k\right) = \frac{85}{100}k = \frac{17}{20}k.$$

Failed in both = $\left(k - \frac{17}{20}k\right) = \frac{3k}{20}$.

$$\therefore \frac{3k}{20} = 90 \Leftrightarrow k = \left(\frac{90 \times 20}{3}\right) = 600.$$

~~~~~~
~~~~~~

10. PROFIT AND LOSS

In this chapter, the use of "Rule of Fraction" is dominant. We should understand this rule very well because it is going to be used in almost all the questions.

THE RULE OF FRACTION SAYS

If our required value is greater than the supplied value we should multiply the value with a fraction which is more than one. And if our required value is less than the supplied value we should multiply the supplied value with a fraction which is less than one.

1. If there is a gain of $x\%$, the calculating figures would be 100 and $(100 + x)$.
2. If there is a loss of $y\%$, the calculating figures would be 100 and $(100 - y)$.
3. If thre required value is more than the supplied value, our multiplying fractions should be $\frac{100 + x}{100}$ or $\frac{100}{100 - y}$ (both are greater than 1).
4. If the required value is less than the supplied value, our multiplying fractions should be $\frac{100}{100 + x}$ or $\frac{100 - y}{100}$ (both are less than 1).

Profit = Selling Price (SP) – Cost Price (CP)

Loss = Cost Price (CP) – Selling Price (SP)

TO FIND THE GAIN OR LOSS PER CENT

The profit or loss is generally reckoned as so much percent on the cost.

$$\text{Gain or loss per cent} = \frac{\text{Loss or gain}}{\text{CP}} \times 100$$

Direct formula:

$$\%\ \text{gain} = \frac{\text{Error}}{\text{True value} - \text{Error}} \times 100$$

$$\text{or,}\ \ \%\ \text{gain} = \frac{\text{True weight} - \text{False weight}}{\text{False weight}} \times 100$$

If the shopkeeper sells his goods at $x\%$ loss on cost price but uses y gm instead of z gm, then his% profit or loss is $[100 - x]\frac{z}{y} - 100$ as the sign is +ve or –ve.

Case I: If a seller uses 'X' gm in place of one kg (1000 gm) to sell his goods and bears a loss of $x\%$ on cost price then his actual gain or loss percentage is $(100 - x)\left[\dfrac{100}{X}\right] - 100$ according as the sign is +ve or –ve.

Case II: If a seller uses 'X' gm in place of one kg (1000 gm) to sell his goods and gains a profit of $x\%$ on cost price, then his actual gain or loss percentage is $(100 + x)\left[\dfrac{100}{X}\right] - 100$ according as the sign is +ve or –ve.

Combining the two cases, we have

Gain or loss% $= (100 \pm x)\left[\dfrac{100}{X}\right] - 100$ according as the sign is +ve or –ve.

When there are two successive profits of $x\%$ and $y\%$ then the resultant profit percent is given by

$$\left(x + y + \frac{xy}{100}\right)$$

When there is a profit of $x\%$ and loss of $y\%$ in a transaction, then the resultant profit or loss percent is given by

$$\left(x - y - \frac{xy}{100}\right)$$

according to the + ve and the –ve signs respectively.

When cost price and selling price are reduced by the same amount (say A) then

$$\text{Cost price} = \frac{[\text{Initial profit \%} + \text{Increase in profit \%}] \times A}{\text{Increase in profit \%}}$$

"An article is sold at P% profit. If its CP is lowered by ₹ c and at the same time its SP is also lowered by ₹ s, the percentage of profit increases by $p\%$ the cost price of the article."

$$= \frac{c(P + p) - 100(s - c)}{p}$$

If cost price of x articles is equal to the selling price of y articles, the profit percentage $= \dfrac{x - y}{y} \times 100\%$.

If x part is sold at m% profit, y part is sold at n% profit, z part is sold at p% profit and ₹ P is earned as overall profit then the value of total consignment

$$= \frac{P \times 100}{xm + ny + pz}$$

A man purchases a certain number of articles at x a rupee and the same number at y a rupee. He mixes them together and sells them at z a rupee. Then his gain or loss %

$$= \left[\frac{2xy}{z(x+y)} - 1\right] \times 100$$ according as the sign is +ve or – ve.

If a trademan marks his goods at x% above his cost price and allows purchasers a discount of y% for cash, then there is $\left(x - y - \frac{xy}{100}\right)$% profit or loss according to + ve or –ve sign respectively.

Note: x = marked percentage above CP
y = discount in percent
z = profit in percent
Then there exists a relationship;

$$z = x - y - \frac{xy}{100}.$$

SOLVED EXAMPLE

1. By selling 33 metres of cloth, one gains the selling price of 11 metres. Find the gain percent.

Sol. (S.P. of 33 m) – (C.P. of 33 m) = Gain = S.P. of 11 m.
∴ S.P. of 22 m = C.P. of 33 m.
Let C.P. of each metre be Re. 1. Then, C.P. of 22 m = ₹ 22, S.P. of 22 m = ₹ 33.
∴ Gain % = $\left(\frac{11}{22} \times 100\right)\% = 50\%$.

2. A tradesman sold an article at a loss of 20%. If the selling price had been increased by ₹ 100, there would have been a gain of 5%. What was the cost price of the article?

Sol. Let C.P. be ₹ x. Then, (105% of x) – (80% of x) = 100 or 25% of x = 100
∴ $\frac{x}{4} = 100$ or $x = 400$.
So, C.P. = ₹ 400.

3. A man bought a horse and a carriage for ₹ 3000. He sold the horse at a gain of 20% and the carriage at a loss of 10%, thereby gaining 2% on the whole. Find the cost of the horse.

Sol. Let the C.P. of the horse be ₹ x. Then, C.P. of the carriage = ₹ $(3000 - x)$.

$\therefore$ 20% of x – 10% of $(3000 - x)$ = 2% of 3000

$$\Rightarrow \frac{x}{5} - \frac{(3000 - x)}{10} = 60 \Rightarrow 2x - 3000 + x = 600$$

$$\Rightarrow 3x = 3600 \Rightarrow x = 1200.$$

Hence, C.P. of the horse = ₹ 1200.

4. When a producer allows 36% commission on the retail price of his product, he earns a profit of 8.8%, What would be his profit percent if the commission is reduced by 24%?

Sol. Let retail price = ₹ 100. Then, commission = ₹ 36.

$\therefore$ S.P. = ₹ (100 – 36) = ₹ 64.

But, profit = 8.8%.

$$\therefore \text{C.P.} = ₹ \left(\frac{100}{108.8} \times 64\right) = ₹ \frac{1000}{17}.$$

New commission = ₹ 12. New S.P. = ₹ (100 – 12) = ₹ 88.

$$\text{Gain} = ₹ \left(88 - \frac{1000}{17}\right) = ₹ \frac{496}{17}.$$

$$\therefore \text{Gain \%} = \left(\frac{496}{17} \times \frac{17}{1000} \times 100\right)\% = 49.6\%.$$

EXERCISE

1. A shopkeeper sells one transistor for ₹ 840 at a gain of 20% and another for ₹ 960 at a loss of 4%. His total gain or loss percent is:

(*a*) $5\frac{15}{17}\%$ loss (*b*) $5\frac{15}{17}\%$ gain (*c*) $6\frac{2}{3}\%$ gain (*d*) None of these

2. If selling price is doubled, the profit triples. Find the profit percent :

(*a*) $66\frac{2}{3}$ (*b*) 100 (*c*) $105\frac{1}{3}$ (*d*) 120

3. The cost price of 20 articles is the same as the selling price of x articles. If the profit is 25%, then the value of x is:

(*a*) 15 (*b*) 16 (*c*) 18 (*d*) 25

4. A man buys a cycle for ₹ 1400 and sells it at a loss of 15%. What is the selling price of the cycle?
(*a*) ₹ 1090 (*b*) ₹ 1160 (*c*) ₹ 1190 (*d*) ₹ 1202

5. The profit earned by selling an article for ₹ 832 is equal to the loss incurred when the same article is sold for ₹ 448. What should be the sale price for making 50% profit?
(*a*) ₹ 920 (*b*) ₹ 960 (*c*) ₹ 1060 (*d*) ₹ 1200

6. A shopkeeper professes to sell his goods at cost price but uses a weight of 800 gm instead of kilogram weight. Thus, he makes a profit of:
(*a*) 20% (*b*) $16\frac{2}{3}\%$ (*c*) 25% (*d*) None of these

7. Arvind mixes three varieties of groundnuts costing ₹ 50, ₹ 20 and ₹ 30 per kg in the ratio 2 : 4 : 3 in terms of weight, and sells the mixture at ₹ 33 per kg. What percentage of profit does he make?
(*a*) 8% (*b*) 9% (*c*) 10% (*d*) None of these

8. If a man reduces the selling price of a fan from ₹ 400 to ₹ 380, his loss increases by 2%. The cost price of the fan is:
(*a*) ₹ 480 (*b*) ₹ 500 (*c*) ₹ 600 (*d*) None of these

9. When a plot is sold for ₹ 18,700, the owner loses 15%. At what price must the plot be sold in order to gain 15%?
(*a*) ₹ 21,000 (*b*) ₹ 22,500 (*c*) ₹ 25,300 (*d*) ₹ 25,800

10. A fruitseller sells mangoes at the rate of ₹ 9 per kg and thereby loses 20%. At what price per kg, he should have sold them to make a profit of 5%?
(*a*) ₹ 11.81 (*b*) ₹ 12 (*c*) ₹ 12.25 (*d*) ₹ 12.31

11. A man pays ₹ 6.40 for on item. He adds water and sells the mixture at ₹ 8 per litre, thereby making 37.5% profit. The proportion of water to item received by the customers is :
(*a*) 1 : 10 (*b*) 1 : 12 (*c*) 1 : 15 (*d*) 1 : 20

12. A shopkeeper purchased 70 kg of potatoes for ₹ 420 and sold the whole lot at the rate of ₹ 6.50 per kg. What will be his gain percent?
(*a*) $4\frac{1}{6}\%$ (*b*) $6\frac{1}{4}\%$ (*c*) $8\frac{1}{3}\%$ (*d*) 20%

13. The ratio between the sale price and the cost price of an article is 7 : 5. What is the ratio between the profit and the cost price of that article?
(*a*) 2 : 7 (*b*) 5 : 2 (*c*) 7 : 2 (*d*) None of these

14. Panas buys an old scooter for ₹ 4700 and spends ₹ 800 on its repairs. If he sells the scooter for ₹ 5800, his gain percent is :

(*a*) $4\frac{4}{7}\%$ (*b*) $5\frac{5}{11}\%$ (*c*) 10% (*d*) 12%

15. In a certain store, the profit is 320% of the cost. If the cost increases by 25% but the selling price remains constant, approximately what percentage of the selling price is the profit?

(*a*) 30% (*b*) 70% (*c*) 100% (*d*) 250%

16. Sanjeev purchased a machine for ₹ 80,000 and spent ₹ 5000 on repair and ₹ 1000 on transport and sold it with 25% profit. At what price did he sell the machine?

(*a*) ₹ 1,05,100 (*b*) ₹ 1,06,250 (*c*) ₹ 1,07,500 (*d*) ₹ 1,17,500

17. The percentage profit earned by selling an article for ₹ 1920 is equal to the percentage loss incurred by selling the same article far ₹ 1280. At what price should the article be sold to make 25% profit?

(*a*) ₹ 2000 (*b*) ₹ 2200 (*c*) ₹ 2400 (*d*) None of these

18. Arun purchased 30 kg of wheat at the rate of ₹ 11.50 per kg and 20 kg of wheat at the rate of ₹ 14.25 per kg. He mixed the two and sold the mixture. Approximately what price per kg should he sell the mixture to make 30% profit?

(*a*) ₹ 14.80 (*b*) ₹ 15.40 (*c*) ₹ 15.60 (*d*) ₹ 16.30

19. If on selling 12 notebooks, a seller makes a profit equal to the selling price of 4 notebooks, what is his percent profit?

(*a*) $16\frac{2}{3}$ (*b*) 25 (*c*) 50 (*d*) None of these

20. A man buys 2 dozen bananas at ₹ 16 per dozen. After selling 18 bananas at the rate of ₹ 12 per dozen, the shopkeeper reduced the rate to ₹ 4 per dozen. The percent loss is:

(*a*) 25.2% (*b*) 32.4% (*c*) 36.5% (*d*) 37.5%

21. Dipak bought apples at the rate of 8 for ₹ 34 and sold them at the rate of 12 for ₹ 57. How many apples should be sold to earn net profit of ₹ 45?

(*a*) 90 (*b*) 100 (*c*) 135 (*d*) 150

22. Dinesh bought some fruits at the rate of 16 for ₹ 24 and sold them at the rate of 8 for ₹ 18. What is the profit percent?

(*a*) 25% (*b*) 40% (*c*) 50% (*d*) 60%

23. A man purchased a box full of pencils at the rate of 7 for ₹ 9 and sold all of them at the rate of 8 for ₹ 11. In this transaction, he gained ₹ 10. How many pencils did the box contain?
(*a*) 100 (*b*) 112 (*c*) 114 (*d*) 115

24. The marked price of a watch was ₹ 720. A man bought the same for ₹ 550.80 after getting two successive discounts, the first being 10%. What was the second discount rate?
(*a*) 12% (*b*) 14% (*c*) 15% (*d*) 18%

25. Gopal purchased 20 dozens of toys at the rate of ₹ 375 per dozen. He sold each one of them at the rate of ₹ 33. What was his percentage profit?
(*a*) 3.5 (*b*) 4.5 (*c*) 5.6 (*d*) 6.5

26. Ganesh purchased 30 kg of rice at the rate of ₹ 17.50 per kg and another 30 kg rice at a certain rate. He mixed the two and sold the entire quantity at the rate of ₹ 18.60 per kg and made 20% overall profit. At what price per kg did he purchase the lot of another 30 kg rice?
(*a*) ₹ 12.50 (*b*) ₹ 13.50 (*c*) ₹ 14.50 (*d*) ₹ 15.50

27. Sanjeev bought a scooter for a certain sum of money. He spent 10% of the cost on repairs and sold the scooter for a profit of ₹ 1100. How much did he spend on repairs if he made a profit of 20%?
(*a*) ₹ 400 (*b*) ₹ 440 (*c*) ₹ 500 (*d*) ₹ 550

28. A property dealer sells a house for ₹ 6,30,000 and in the bargain makes a profit of 5%. Had he sold it for ₹ 5,00,000, then what percentage of loss or gain he would have made?
(*a*) $2\frac{1}{4}$% gain (*b*) 10% loss (*c*) $12\frac{1}{4}$% loss (*d*) $16\frac{2}{3}$% loss

29. A manufacturer undertakes to supply 2000 pieces of a particular component at ₹ 25 per piece. According to his estimates, even if 5% fail to pass the quality tests, then he will make a profit of 25%. However, as it turned out, 50% of the components were rejected. What is the loss to the manufacturer?
(*a*) ₹ 12,000 (*b*) ₹ 13,300 (*c*) ₹ 14,000 (*d*) ₹ 15,000

30. Applied to a bill for ₹ 1,00,000, the difference between a discount of 40% and two successive discounts of 36% and 4% is:
(*a*) Nil (*b*) ₹ 1440 (*c*) ₹ 2500 (*d*) ₹ 1960

31. Ritik bought a microwave oven and paid 10% less than the original price. He sold it with 30% profit on the price he had paid. What percentage of profit did Ritik earn on the original price?
(*a*) 17% (*b*) 20% (*c*) 27% (*d*) 32%

32. A dishonest dealer professes to sell his goods at cost price. But he uses a false weight and thus gains $6\frac{18}{47}\%$. For a kg, he uses a weight of :

(*a*) 940 gms (*b*) 947 gms (*c*) 953 gms (*d*) 960 gms

33. By mixing two brands of tea and selling the mixture at the rate of ₹ 177 par kg, a shopkeeper makes a profit of 18%. If to every 2 kg of one brand costing ₹ 200 per kg, 3 kg of the other brand is added, then how much per kg does the other brand cost?

(*a*) ₹ 110 (*b*) ₹ 120 (*c*) ₹ 140 (*d*) None of these

34. Albert buys 4 horses and 9 cows for ₹ 13,400, If he sells the horses at 10% profit and the cows at 20% profit, then he earns a total profit of ₹ 1880. The cost of a horse is :

(*a*) ₹ 1000 (*b*) ₹ 2000 (*c*) ₹ 2500 (*d*) ₹ 3000

35. A cloth merchant sold half of his cloth at 20% profit, half of the remaining at 20% loss and the rest was sold at the cost price. In the total transaction, his gain or loss will be:

(*a*) Neither loss nor gain (*b*) 5% loss

(*c*) 5% gain (*d*) 10% gain

36. A person purchases 90 clocks and sells 40 clocks at a gain of 10% and 50 clocks at a gain of 20%. If he sold all of them at a uniform profit of 15%, then he would have got ₹ 40 less. The cost price of each clock is:

(*a*) ₹ 50 (*b*) ₹ 60 (*c*) ₹ 80 (*d*) ₹ 90

37. A shopkeeper sells two watches for ₹ 308 each. On one he gets 12% profit and on the other 12% loss. His profit or loss in the entire transaction was:

(*a*) Neither profit, nor loss (*b*) $1\frac{11}{25}\%$ loss

(*c*) $1\frac{11}{25}\%$ profit (*d*) $3\frac{2}{25}\%$ loss

38. Pankaj sells an article at a loss of $12\frac{1}{2}\%$. Had he sold it for ₹ 51.80 more, he would have earned a profit of 6%. The cost price of the article is:

(*a*) ₹ 280 (*b*) ₹ 300 (*c*) ₹ 380 (*d*) ₹ 400

39. Girish sold sarees at ₹ 266 each after giving 5% discount on labelled price. Had he not given the discount, he would have earned a profit of 12% on the cost price. What was the cost price of each saree?

(*a*) ₹ 240 (*b*) ₹ 260 (*c*) ₹ 280 (*d*) None of these

40. A pair of articles was bought for ₹ 37.40 at a discount of 15%. What must be the marked price of each of the articles?

(*a*) ₹ 11 (*b*) ₹ 22 (*c*) ₹ 33 (*d*) ₹ 44

41. A trader marked the price of his commodity so as to include a profit of 25%. He allowed discount of 16% on the marked price. His actual profit was:

(*a*) 5% (*b*) 9% (*c*) 16% (*d*) 25%

42. A fan is listed at ₹ 1500 and a discount of 20% is offered on the list price. What additional discount must be offered to the customer to bring the net price to ₹ 1104?

(*a*) 8% (*b*) 10% (*c*) 12% (*d*) 15%

43. The price of a VCR is marked at ₹ 12,000. If successive discounts of 15%, 10% and 5% be allowed, then at what price does a customer buy it?

(*a*) ₹ 8400 (*b*) ₹ 8721 (*c*) ₹ 8856 (*d*) None of these

44. A shopkeeper expects a gain of $22\frac{1}{2}\%$ on his cost price. If in a week, his sale was of ₹ 392, what was his profit?

(*a*) ₹ 18.20 (*b*) ₹ 70 (*c*) ₹ 72 (*d*) ₹ 88.25

45. The difference between a discount of 35% arid two successive discounts of 20% on a certain bill was ₹ 22. Find the amount of the bill.

(*a*) ₹ 200 (*b*) ₹ 1100 (*c*) ₹ 2200 (*d*) Data inadequate

46. A trader mixes 26 kg of rice at ₹ 20 per kg with 30 kg of rice of other variety at ₹ 36 per kg and sells the mixture at ₹ 30 per kg. His profit percent is :

(*a*) No profit, no loss (*b*) 5%
(*c*) 8% (*d*) 10%

47. A shopkeeper purchased 150 identical pieces of calculators at the rate of ₹ 250 each. He spent an amount of ₹ 2500 on transport and packing. He fixed the labelled price of each calculator at ₹ 320. However, he decided to give a discount of 5% on the labelled price. What is the percentage profit earned by him?

(*a*) 14% (*b*) 15% (*c*) 16% (*d*) 20%

48. Satyam sold an article offering a discount of 5% and earned a profit of 23.5%. What would have been the percentage of profit earned if no discount was offered?

(*a*) 24.5 (*b*) 28.5 (*c*) 30 (*d*) data inadequate

49. A shopkeeper sold a T.V. set for ₹ 17,940 with a discount of 8% and earned a profit of 19.6%. What would have been the percentage of profit earned if no discount was offered ?

(*a*) 24.8% (*b*) 25% (*c*) 26.4% (*d*) None of these

50. Kunal bought a suitcase with 15% discount on the labelled price. He sold the suitcase for ₹ 2880 with 20% profit on the labelled price. At what price did he buy the suitcase?

(*a*) ₹ 2040 (*b*) ₹ 2400 (*c*) ₹ 2604 (*d*) ₹ 2640

51. A trader marked his goods at 20% above the cost price. He sold half the stock at the marked price, one quarter at a discount of 20% on the marked price and the rest at a discount of 40% on the marked price. His total gain is:

(*a*) 2% (*b*) 4.5% (*c*) 13.5% (*d*) 15%

52. By selling an article at $\frac{2}{5}$ of the marked price, there is a loss of 25%. The ratio of the marked price and the cost price of the article is:

(*a*) 2 : 5 (*b*) 5 : 2 (*c*) 8 : 15 (*d*) 15 : 8

53. At what percent above the cost price must a shopkeeper mark his goods so that he gains 20% even after giving a discount of 10% on the marked price?

(*a*) 25% (*b*) 30% (*c*) $33\frac{1}{3}\%$ (*d*) $37\frac{1}{2}\%$

54. By selling an umbrella for ₹ 300, a shopkeeper gains 20%. During a clearance sale, the shopkeeper allows a discount of 10% op the marked price. His gain percent during the sale is:

(*a*) 7 (*b*) 7.5 (*c*) 8 (*d*) 9

55. The labelled price of a cupboard is ₹ 6500. The shopkeeper sold it by giving 5% discount on the labelled price and earned a profit of 15%. What approximately is the cost price of the cupboard?

(*a*) ₹ 5000 (*b*) ₹ 5350 (*c*) ₹ 5600 (*d*) ₹ 5800

56. A trader marked the selling price of an article at 10% above the cost price. At the time of selling, he allows certain discount and suffers a loss of 1%. He allowed a discount of:

(*a*) 9% (*b*) 10% (*c*) 10.5% (*d*) 11%

57. At what price should a shopkeeper mark a radio that costs him ₹ 1200 in order that he may offer a discount of 20% on the marked price and still make a profit of 25%?

(*a*) ₹ 1675 (*b*) ₹ 1875 (*c*) ₹ 1900 (*d*) ₹ 2025

58. Rashmi sells 25 articles at ₹ 45 per article after giving 10% discount and earns 50% profit. If the discount is not given, the profit gained is:

(*a*) 60% (*b*) $60\frac{2}{3}\%$ (*c*) 66% (*d*) $66\frac{2}{3}\%$

59. Garima purchased a briefcase with an additional 10% discount, on the reduced price after deducting 20% on the labelled price. If the labelled price was ₹ 1400, at what price did she purchase the briefcase?
(a) ₹ 980 (b) ₹ 1008 (c) ₹ 1056 (d) ₹ 1120

60. Nishant gives 12% additional discount on the discounted price, after giving an initial discount of 20% on the labelled price of a radio. If the final sale price of the radio is ₹ 704, then what is its labelled price?
(a) ₹ 844.80 (b) ₹ 929.28 (c) ₹ 1000 (d) ₹ 1044.80

ANSWERS

1	2	3	4	5	6	7	8	9	10
(b)	(b)	(b)	(c)	(b)	(c)	(c)	(d)	(c)	(a)
11	**12**	**13**	**14**	**15**	**16**	**17**	**18**	**19**	**20**
(a)	(c)	(d)	(b)	(b)	(c)	(a)	(d)	(c)	(d)
21	**22**	**23**	**24**	**25**	**26**	**27**	**28**	**29**	**30**
(a)	(c)	(b)	(b)	(c)	(b)	(c)	(d)	(b)	(b)
31	**32**	**33**	**34**	**35**	**36**	**37**	**38**	**39**	**40**
(a)	(a)	(d)	(b)	(c)	(c)	(b)	(a)	(d)	(b)
41	**42**	**43**	**44**	**45**	**46**	**47**	**48**	**49**	**50**
(a)	(a)	(b)	(c)	(c)	(b)	(a)	(c)	(d)	(a)
51	**52**	**53**	**54**	**55**	**56**	**57**	**58**	**59**	**60**
(a)	(d)	(c)	(c)	(b)	(b)	(b)	(d)	(b)	(c)

SOME SELECTED EXPLANATORY ANSWERS

1. C.P. of 1st transistor = ₹ $\left(\frac{100}{120} \times 840\right)$ = ₹ 700

C.P. of 2nd transistor = ₹ $\left(\frac{100}{96} \times 960\right)$ = ₹ 1000.

2. Suppose C.P. is ₹ x and S.P. is ₹ y.
Then, $3(y - x) = (2y - x) \Rightarrow y = 2x$
Profit – ₹ $(y - x)$ = ₹ $(2x - x)$ = ₹ x

$\therefore$ Profit% = $\left(\frac{x}{x} \times 100\right)\%$ = 100%.

3. Let C.P. of each article be Re. 1
$\therefore$ C.P. of x articles = ₹ x;
S.P. of x articles = ₹ 20.

$\therefore$ Profit percent $= \dfrac{20 - x}{x} \times 100 = 25 \Rightarrow 2000 - 100x = 25x$

$\Rightarrow 125x = 2000 \Rightarrow x = 16.$

4. S.P. = 85% of ₹ 1400 = ₹ $\left(\dfrac{85}{100} \times 1400\right)$ = ₹ 1190.

5. Let C.P. = ₹ x. Then, $832 - x = x - 448 \Rightarrow 2x = 1280 \Rightarrow x = 640$

$\therefore$ Required S.P. = 150% of ₹ 640 = ₹$\left(\dfrac{150}{100} \times 640\right)$ = ₹ 960.

7. Suppose he bought 2 kg, 4 kg and 3 kg of the three varieties
C.P. of 9 kg = ₹ (2 × 50 + 4 × 20 + 3 × 30) = ₹ 270
S.P. of 9 kg = ₹ (9 × 33) = ₹ 297
Profit = 297 – 270 = 27

$\therefore$ Profig% $= \left(\dfrac{27}{270} \times 100\right)\% = 10\%.$

8. Suppose that the C.P. is ₹ x. Then, 2% of x = (400 – 380) = 20

$\Rightarrow \dfrac{x}{50} = 20 \Rightarrow x = 1000.$

9. From question 85 : 18700 = 115 : x or $x = \left(\dfrac{18700 \times 115}{85}\right) = 25300$

Hence, S.P. = ₹ 25,300.

11. Cost Price of the mixture = ₹ $\left(\dfrac{100}{137.5} \times 8\right)$ = ₹ $\dfrac{64}{11}$

there,

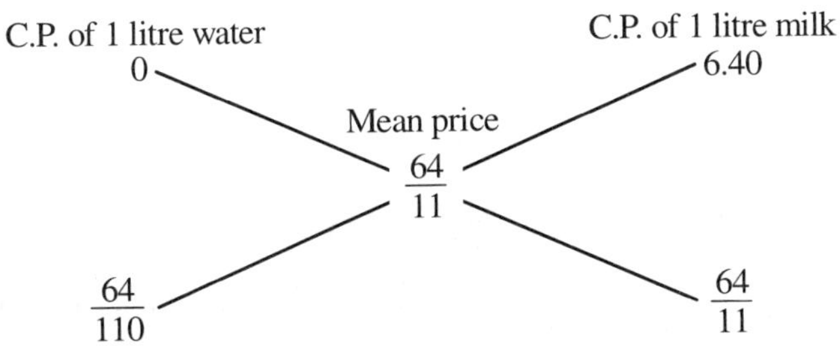

Hence, required ratio $= \dfrac{64}{110} : \dfrac{64}{11} = 1 : 10.$

12. C.P. of 1 kg = ₹ $\left(\frac{420}{70}\right)$ = ₹ 6.

S.P. of 1 kkg = ₹ 6.50

Gain = 6.5 – 6 = 0.5

∴ Gain% = $\left(\frac{0.50}{6} \times 100\right)\% = \frac{25}{3}\% = 8\frac{1}{3}\%$.

13. Let C.P. = ₹ $5x$ and S.P. = ₹ $7x$

Then, Gain = ₹ $2x$

∴ Required ratio = $2x : 5x = 2 : 5$.

14. C.P. of the article = ₹ (4700 + 800) = ₹ 5500;

S.P. = ₹ 5800

Gain = 5800 – 550 = 300

Gain% = $\left(\frac{300}{5500} \times 100\right)\% = 5\frac{5}{11}\%$.

15. Suppose the C.P. = ₹ 100. Then, Profit = ₹ 320, S.P. = ₹ 420

Again, New C.P. = 125% of ₹ 100 = ₹ 125; New S.P. = ₹ 420

Profit = ₹ (420 – 125) = ₹ 295

∴ Required percentage = $\left(\frac{295}{420} \times 100\right)\% = \frac{1475}{21}\% \approx 70\%$.

16. C.P. = ₹ (80000 + 5000 + 1000) = ₹ 86000 and Profit = 25% (given)

∴ S.P. = 125% of ₹ 86000 = ₹ $\left(\frac{125}{100} \times 86000\right)$ = ₹ 107500.

17. Suppose that the C.P. us ₹ x

Then, $\frac{1920 - x}{x} \times 100 = \frac{x - 1280}{x} \times 100$

$\Rightarrow$ $1920 - x = x - 1280$

$\Rightarrow$ $2x = 3200 \Rightarrow x = 1600$

∴ Required S.P. = 125% of ₹ 1600 = ₹ $\left(\frac{125}{100} \times 1600\right)$ = ₹ 2000.

18. C.P. of 50 kg wheat = ₹ (30 × 11.50 + 20 × 14.25) = ₹ (345 + 285) = ₹ 630.

S.P. of 50 kg wheat = 130% of ₹ 630 = ₹ $\left(\frac{130}{100} \times 630\right)$ = ₹ 819.

∴ S.P. per kg = ₹ $\left(\frac{819}{50}\right)$ = ₹ 16.38 ≈ ₹ 1630.

20. C.P. = ₹ (16 × 2) = 32. S.P. = ₹ (12 × 1.5 + 4 × 0.5) = ₹ (18 + 2) = ₹ 20.

$\therefore$ Loss% = $\left(\frac{12}{32} \times 100\right)\%$ = 37.5%.

22. Cost price of 1 fruit = ₹ $\frac{24}{16}$ = ₹ $\frac{3}{2}$

Selling price of 1 fruit = ₹ $\frac{18}{8}$ = ₹ $\frac{9}{4}$

Profit = $\frac{9}{4} - \frac{3}{2} = \frac{3}{4}$

$\therefore$ Profit% = $\frac{\frac{3}{4}}{\frac{3}{2}} \times 100 = \frac{2}{4} \times 100$ = 50%.

23. Suppose, number of pencils bought = L.C.M. of 7 and 8 = 56.

C.P. of 56 pencils = ₹ $\left(\frac{9}{7} \times 56\right)$ = ₹ 72. S.P. of 56 pencils

= ₹ $\left(\frac{11}{8} \times 56\right)$ = ₹ 77

Now, ₹ 5 are gained on 56 pencils.

So, ₹ 10 are gained on $\left(\frac{56}{5} \times 10\right)$ = 112 pencils.

24. Let the second discount rate be x%.
Then, (100 – x)% of 90% of 720 = 550.80

$\Rightarrow \frac{(100 - x)}{100} \times \frac{90}{100} \times 720 = 550.80$

$= \left(\frac{55080}{9 \times 72}\right) = 85 \Rightarrow x = 15$

$\therefore$ Second discount rate = 15%.

25. C.P. of 1 toy = ₹ $\left(\frac{375}{12}\right)$ = ₹ 31.25

S.P. of 1 toy = ₹ 33

Profit = 33 – 31.25 – 1.75

$\therefore$ Profit% = $\left(\frac{1.75}{31.25} \times 100\right)\% = \frac{28}{5}\%$ = 5.6%.

27. Suppose the C.P. is ₹ x. Then, 20% of x = 1100

$$\frac{20}{100} \times x = 1100$$

$$\Rightarrow \quad x = 5500$$

C.P. = ₹ 5500 and Expenditure on repairs = 10%

$$\text{Actual price} = ₹ \left(\frac{100}{110} \times 5500\right) = ₹\ 5000$$

∴ Expenditure on repairs = ₹ (5500 – 5000) = ₹ 500.

28. $$\text{C.P.} = ₹ \left(\frac{100}{105} \times 630000\right) = ₹\ 600000$$

$$\therefore \text{ Required loss\%} = \left(\frac{100000}{600000} \times 100\right)\% = 16\frac{2}{3}\%.$$

29. $$\text{Total cost incurred} = ₹\left[\frac{100}{125} \times 25 \times (95\% \text{ of } 2000)\right]$$

$$= ₹\left(\frac{100}{125} \times 25 \times 1900\right) = ₹\ 38000$$

Loss to the manufacturer = ₹ [38000 – (25 × 1000)] = ₹ 13000.

30. S.P. in 1st case = 60% of ₹ 100000 = ₹ 60000

S.P. in 2nd case = 96% of 64% of ₹ 100000

$$= ₹\left(\frac{96}{100} \times \frac{64}{100} \times 100000\right) = ₹\ 61440$$

∴ Difference = ₹ (61440 – 60000) = ₹ 1440.

31. Suppose that the original price is ₹ 100.

Then C.P. = ₹ 90, and S.P. = 130% of ₹ 90 = $₹\left(\frac{130}{100} \times 90\right)$ = ₹ 117.

∴ Required percentage = (117 – 100)% = 17%.

32. Let error = x gms. Then, $\frac{x}{1000 - x} \times 100 = 6\frac{18}{47}$

$$\Leftrightarrow \frac{100x}{1000 - x} = \frac{300}{47}$$

$\Leftrightarrow$ $47x = 3\ (1000 - x)$ $\Leftrightarrow$ $50x = 3000$ $\Leftrightarrow$ $x = 60$

∴ Weight used = (1000 – 60) = 940 gms.

33. Suppose the cost of the other brand is ₹ x per kg
then, C.P. of 5 kg = ₹ $(2 \times 200 + 3 \times x)$ = ₹ $(400 + 3x)$
and S.P. of 5 kg = ₹ (5×177) = ₹ 885

$$\therefore \quad \frac{885 - (400 + 3x)}{400 + 3x} \times 100 = 18 \Leftrightarrow \frac{485 - 3x}{400 + 3x} = \frac{9}{50}$$

$$\Rightarrow 24250 - 150x = 3600 + 27x \Leftrightarrow 177x = 20650$$

$$\Leftrightarrow x = \left(\frac{350}{3}\right) = 116\frac{2}{3}.$$

So, cost of the other brand = ₹ 116.66.

35. Suppose that the C.P. of total stocks is ₹ x

Then C.P. of $\frac{1}{2}$ stock = ₹$\frac{x}{2}$ and C.P. of $\frac{1}{4}$ stock = ₹$\frac{x}{4}$

$$\text{Total S.P.} = ₹\left[\left(120\% \text{ of } \frac{x}{2}\right) + \left(80\% \text{ of } \frac{x}{4}\right) + \frac{x}{4}\right]$$

$$= ₹\left(\frac{3x}{5} + \frac{x}{5} + \frac{x}{4}\right) = ₹\frac{21x}{20}$$

$$\text{Gain} = ₹\left(\frac{21x}{20} - x\right) = ₹\frac{x}{20}$$

$$\therefore \text{Gain\%} = \left(\frac{x}{20} \times \frac{1}{x} \times 100\right)\% = 5\%.$$

36. Suppose that the C.P. of each clock is ₹ x. Then, C.P. of 90 clocks = ₹ $90x$.
$\therefore$ From question [(110% of $40x$) + (120% of $50x$)] – (115% of $90x$) = 40
$\Rightarrow 44x + 60x - 103.5x = 40$
$\Rightarrow 0.5x = 40 \Rightarrow x = 80.$

37. $\text{Loss\%} = \left(\frac{\text{Common Loss and Gain\%}}{10}\right)^2\% = \left(\frac{12}{10}\right)^2\% = \frac{36}{25}\% = 1\frac{11}{25}\%.$

38. Suppose that the C.P. is ₹ x. Then, $(106\% \text{ of } x) - \left(87\frac{1}{2}\% \text{ of } x\right) = 51.80$

$$\Rightarrow 18\frac{1}{2}\% \text{ of } x = 51.80 \Rightarrow x = \left(\frac{51.80 \times 100 \times 2}{37}\right) = 280.$$

39. S.P. of 1 saree = ₹ 266. Let the labelled price of each saree be ₹ x

Then, $\frac{95}{100}x = 266 \Rightarrow x = ₹\left(\frac{266 \times 100}{95}\right) = ₹\ 280$

Now, S.P. = ₹ 280, Profit = 12%

$\therefore$ C.P. of 1 saree = ₹ $\left(\frac{100}{112} \times 280\right)$ = ₹ 250.

40. From question, S.P. of each article = ₹ $\left(\frac{37.40}{2}\right)$ = ₹ 18.70

Suppose that the market price is ₹ x

Then, 85% of $x = 18.70 \Rightarrow x = \left(\frac{18.70 \times 100}{85}\right) = 22.$

41. Suppose that the C.P. is ₹ 100. Then, marked price = ₹ 125

S.P. = 84% or ₹ 125 = ₹ $\left(\frac{84}{100} \times 125\right)$ = ₹ 105

$\therefore$ Profit% = (105 – 100)% = 5%.

42. S.P. after 1st discount = ₹ $\left(\frac{80}{100} \times 1500\right)$ = ₹ 1200

Net S.P. = ₹ 1104

Discount on ₹ 1200 = ₹ 96

$\therefore$ Required discount = $\left(\frac{96}{1200} \times 100\right)\%$ = 8%.

43. Actual price = 95% of 90% of 85% of ₹ 12000

= ₹ $\left(\frac{95}{100} \times \frac{90}{100} \times \frac{85}{100} \times 12000\right)$ = ₹ 8721.

44. C.P. = ₹ $\left(\frac{100}{122.50} \times 392\right)$ = ₹ $\left(\frac{1000}{1225} \times 392\right)$ = ₹ 320

$\therefore$ Profit = ₹ (392 – 320) = ₹ 72.

45. Let the amount of the bill be ₹ x

Then, (65% of x) – (80% of 80% of x) = 22

$$\Rightarrow \left(\frac{65}{100} \times x\right) - \left(\frac{80}{100} \times \frac{80}{100} \times x\right) = 22$$

$$\Rightarrow \frac{65}{100}x - \frac{64}{100}x = 22 \Rightarrow \frac{x}{100} = 22 \Rightarrow x = 2200.$$

46. C.P. of 56 kg rice = ₹ (26 × 20 + 30 × 36) = ₹ (520 + 1080) = ₹ 1600.
S.P. of 56 kg rice = ₹ (56 × 30) = ₹ 1680.

$$\therefore \text{ Gain} = \left(\frac{80}{1600} \times 100\right)\% = 5\%.$$

47. Cost of each calculator = ₹ $\left(250 + \frac{2500}{150}\right)$ = ₹ $266\frac{2}{3}$

S.P. of each calculator = ₹ $\left(\frac{95}{100} \times 320\right)$ = ₹ 304

$$\therefore \text{ Profit\%} = \left(\frac{112}{3} \times \frac{3}{800} \times 100\right)\% = 14\%.$$

48. Let C.P. be ₹ 100. Then, S.P. = ₹ 123.50

Let marked price be ₹ x. Then, $\frac{95}{100}x = 123.50 \Rightarrow x =$ ₹ $\left(\frac{12350}{95}\right)$ = ₹ 130

Now, S.P. = ₹ 130, C.P. = ₹ 100

∴ Profit% = 30%.

49. S.P. = ₹ 17940. Let marked price be ₹ x

Then, $\frac{92}{100}x = 17940 \Rightarrow x =$ ₹ $\left(17940 \times \frac{100}{92}\right)$ = ₹ 19500

C.P. = ₹ $\left(\frac{100}{119.6} \times 17940\right)$ = ₹ $\left(\frac{1000}{1196} \times 17940\right)$ = ₹ 15000

Now C.P. = ₹ 15000. S.P. = ₹ 19500

$$\therefore \text{ Required profit\%} = \left(\frac{4500}{15000} \times 100\right)\% = 30\%.$$

50. Let the labelled price be ₹ x. Then, 120% of x = 2880

$$\Rightarrow x = \left(\frac{2880 \times 100}{120}\right) = 2400$$

∴ C.P. = 85% of ₹ 2400 = ₹ $\left(\frac{85}{100} \times 2400\right)$ = ₹ 2040.

51. Let C.P. of whole stock = ₹ 100. Then, Marked Price of whole stock = ₹ 120

M.P. of $\frac{1}{2}$ stock = ₹ 60, M.P. of $\frac{1}{4}$ stock = ₹ 30

∴ Total S.P. = ₹ [60 + (80% of 30) + (60% of 30)]
= ₹ (60 + 24 + 18) = ₹ 102

Hence, gain% = (102 – 100)% = 2%.

52. Let cost price = ₹ 100

Then, $\frac{2}{5}$ of (Marked Price) = 75 ⇒ Marked Price = ₹ $\left(\frac{75 \times 5}{2}\right)$ = ₹ $\frac{375}{2}$

∴ Required ratio = $\frac{375}{2}$: 100 = 375 : 200 = 15 : 8.

53. Let C.P. = ₹ 100. Then, S.P. = ₹ 120
Again, suppose that market price is ₹ x. Then, 90% of x = 120

$\Rightarrow x = \left(\frac{120 \times 100}{90}\right) = 133\frac{1}{3}$

∴ Marked price = $33\frac{1}{3}\%$ above C.P.

54. Marked price = ₹ 300. C.P. = ₹ $\left(\frac{100}{120} \times 300\right)$ = ₹ 250

Sale price = 90% of ₹ 300 = ₹ 270

∴ Required gain% = $\left(\frac{20}{250} \times 100\right)\%$ = 8%.

55. S.P. = 95% of ₹ 6500 = ₹ $\left(\frac{95}{100} \times 6500\right)$ = ₹ 6175

Profit = 15%

∴ C.P. = ₹ $\left(\frac{110}{115} \times 6175\right)$ = ₹ 5369.56 ≈ ₹ 5350.

56. Let C.P. = ₹ 100. Then, Marked Price = ₹ 110, S.P. = ₹ 99

∴ Discount% = $\left(\frac{11}{110} \times 100\right)\%$ = 10%.

57. C.P. = ₹ 1200. S.P. = 125% of ₹ 1200 = ₹ $\left(\frac{125}{100} \times 1200\right)$ = ₹ 1500

Let marked price be ₹ x. Then, 80% of x = 1500

$\Rightarrow x = \left(\frac{1500 \times 100}{80}\right) = 1875$

$\therefore$ Marked price = ₹ 1875.

58. S.P. of 1 article = ₹ 45. Let marked price of each article be ₹ x

Then, $\frac{90}{100}x = 45 \Rightarrow x =$ ₹ $\left(\frac{45 \times 100}{90}\right)$ = ₹ 50

C.P. = ₹ $\left(\frac{100}{150} \times 45\right)$ = ₹ 30

Now, C.P. = ₹ 30, S.P. = ₹ 50

$\therefore$ Required profit% $= \left(\frac{20}{30} \times 100\right)\% = 66\frac{2}{3}\%$.

59. C.P. = 90% of 80% of ₹ 1400 = ₹ $\left(\frac{90}{100} \times \frac{80}{100} \times 1400\right)$ = ₹ 1008.

60. Let the labelled price be ₹ x

88% of 80% of $x = 704 \Rightarrow x = \left(\frac{704 \times 100 \times 100}{88 \times 80}\right) = 1000.$

~~~~~~
~~~~~~

11. RATIO AND PROPORTION

The number of times one quantity contains another quantity of the same kind is called the **ratio** *of the two quantities.*

Clearly, the ratio of two quantities is equivalent to the fraction that one quantity is of the other.

Observe carefully that the two quantities must be of the same kind. There can be a ratio between ₹ 20 and ₹ 30, but there can be no ratio between ₹ 20 and 30 mangoes.

The ratio 2 to 3 is written as 2 : 3 or $\frac{2}{3}$. 2 and 3 are called the **terms of the ratio.** 2 is the first term and 3 is the second term.

The first term of a ratio is called the **antecedent** and the second the **consequent.**

In the ratio 2 : 3, 2 is the antecedent and 3 is the consequent.

Note: The word 'antecedent' literally means 'that which goes before'.

The word 'consequent' literally means 'that which goes after'.

Since the quotient obtained on dividing one concrete quantity by another of the same kind is an abstract number, the ratio between two concrete quantities of the same kind is an **abstract number.** Thus, the ratio between ₹ 5 and ₹ 7 is 5 : 7.

Since a fraction is not altered by multiplying or dividing both its numerator and denominator by the same number, a ratio which is also a fraction is not altered by multiplying or dividing both its terms by the same number.

Thus 3 : 5 is the same as 6 : 10, and 15 : 20 is the same as 3 : 4.

COMPOUND RATIO

Ratios are **compounded** *by multiplying together the antecedents for a new antecedent, and the consequents for a new consequent.*

Ex.: Find the ratio compounded of the four ratios :

4 : 3, 9 : 13, 26 : 5 and 2 : 15

Sol. The required ratio = $\frac{4 \times 9 \times 26 \times 2}{3 \times 13 \times 5 \times 15} = \frac{16}{25}$

Note: When the ratio 4 : 3 is compounded with itself the resulting ratio is $4^2 : 3^2$. It is called the **duplicate ratio** of 4 : 3.

Similarly, $4^3 : 3^3$ is the **triplicate ratio** of 4 : 3.

$\sqrt{4} : \sqrt{3}$ is called the **subduplicate ratio** of 4 : 3.

$a^{1/3} : b^{1/3}$ is **subtriplicate ratio of** a and b.

INVERSE RATIO

If 2 : 3 be the given ratio, then $\frac{1}{2} : \frac{1}{3}$ or 3 : 2 is called its **inverse** or **reciprocal ratio.**

If the antecedent = the consequent, the ratio is called the **ratio of equality,** such as 3:3.

If the antecedent > the consequent, the ratio is called the **ratio of greater inequality,** as 4:3.

If the antecedent < the consequent, the ratio is called the **ratio of less inequality,** as 3 : 4.

PROPORTION

Consider the two ratios:

1st ratio	2nd ratio
6 : 18	8 : 24

Since 6 is one-third of 18, and 8 is one-third of 24, the two ratios are equal. The equality of ratios is called **proportion.**

The numbers 6, 18, 8 and 24 are said to be in **proportion.**

The proportion may be written as

6 : 18 : : 8 : 24 (6 is to 18 as 8 is to 24)

or, 6 : 18 = 8 : 24 or, $\frac{6}{18} = \frac{8}{24}$.

The numbers 6, 18, 8 and 24 are called the **terms. 6 is** the **first term,** 18 the **second,** 8 the **third,** and 24 the **fourth.** The first and fourth terms, i.e., 6 and 24 are called the **extremes** (end terms), and the second and the third terms, i.e., 18 and 8 are called the **means** (middle terms). 24 is called the **fourth** proportional.

1. *If four quantities be in* **proportion,** *the product of the extremes is equal to the product of the means.*

   Let the four quantities 3, 4, 9 and 12 be in proportion.

   We have $\frac{3}{4} = \frac{9}{12}$

Multiply each ratio by 4 × 12

$\therefore \quad \frac{3}{4} \times 4 \times 12 = \frac{9}{12} \times 4 \times 12$

$\therefore \quad 3 \times 12 = 4 \times 9$

2. *Three quantities of the same kind are said to be in* **continued proportion** *when the ratio of the first to the second is equal to the ratio of the second to the third.*

The second quantity is called the **mean proportional** *between the first and the third; and the third quantity is called the* **third proportional** *to the first and second.*

Thus, 9, 6 and 4 are in continued proportion for 9 : 6 : : 6 : 4.

Hence, 6 is the mean proportional between 9 and 4, and 4 is the third proportional to 9 and 6.

SOLVED EXAMPLE

1. If $a : b = 5 : 9$ and $b : c = 4 : 7$, find $a : b : c$.

Sol. $a : b = 5 : 9$ and $b : c = 4 : 7 = \left(4 \times \frac{9}{4}\right) : \left(7 \times \frac{9}{4}\right) = 9 : \frac{63}{4}$

$\Rightarrow \quad a : b : c = 5 : 9 : \frac{63}{4} = 20 : 36 : 63.$

2. If $x : y = 3 : 4$, find $(4x + 5y) : (5x - 2y)$.

Sol. $\frac{x}{y} = \frac{3}{4} \Rightarrow \frac{4x + 5y}{5x - 2y} = \frac{4\left(\frac{x}{y}\right) + 5}{5\left(\frac{x}{y}\right) - 2} = \frac{\left(4 \times \frac{3}{4} + 5\right)}{\left(5 \times \frac{3}{4} - 2\right)} = \frac{(3 + 5)}{\left(\frac{7}{4}\right)} = \frac{32}{7}.$

3. Divide ₹ 672 in the ratio 5 : 3.

Sol. Sum of ratio terms = (5 + 3) = 8.

$\therefore$ First part = ₹ $\left(672 \times \frac{5}{8}\right)$ = ₹ 420; Second part = ₹ $\left(672 \times \frac{3}{8}\right)$ = ₹ 252.

EXERCISE

1. A fraction which bears the same ratio to $\frac{1}{27}$ that $\frac{3}{11}$ dees to $\frac{5}{9}$, is equal to :

(*a*) $\frac{1}{55}$ (*b*) $\frac{1}{11}$ (*c*) $\frac{3}{11}$ (*d*) 55

2. If ₹ 782 be divided into three parts, proportional to $\frac{1}{2} : \frac{2}{3} : \frac{3}{4}$, then the first part is :
(*a*) ₹ 182 (*b*) ₹ 190 (*c*) ₹ 196 (*d*) ₹ 204

3. Two numbers are in the ratio 1 : 2. If 7 is added to both, their ratio changes to 3 : 5. The greater number is:
(*a*) 24 (*b*) 26 (*c*) 28 (*d*) 32

4. The sum of three numbers is 98. If the ratio of the first to the second is 2 : 3 and that of the second to the third is 5 : 8, then the second number is:
(*a*) 20 (*b*) 30 (*c*) 48 (*d*) 58

5. If $x : y = 5 : 2$, then $(8x + 9y) : (8x + 2y)$ is:
(*a*) 22 : 29 (*b*) 26 : 61 (*c*) 29: 22 (*d*) 61 : 26

6. If 10% of x = 25% of y, then $x : y$ is equal to:
(*a*) 1 : 2 (*b*) 2 : 4 (*c*) 5 : 1 (*d*) 10 : 1

7. If A : B = 2 : 3, B : C = 4 : 5 and C : D = 6 : 7, then A : B : C : D is:
(*a*) 16 : 22 : 30 : 35 (*b*) 16 : 24 : 15 : 35
(*c*) 16 : 24 : 30 : 35 (*d*) 18 : 24 : 36 : 35

8. If $0.75 : x :: 5 : 8$, then x is equal to:
(*a*) 1.12 (*b*) 1.20 (*c*) 1.25 (*d*) 1.30

9. The fourth proportional to 5, 8, 15 is :
(*a*) 18 (*b*) 24 (*c*) 19 (*d*) 20

10. x varies inversely as square of y. Given that $y = 2$ for $x = 1$. The value of x for $y = 6$ will be equal to:
(*a*) 3 (*b*) 9 (*c*) $\frac{1}{3}$ (*d*) $\frac{1}{9}$

11. If ₹ 510 be divided among A, B, C in such a way that A gets $\frac{2}{3}$ of what B gets and B gets $\frac{1}{4}$ of what C gets, then their shares are respectively:
(*a*) ₹ 120, ₹ 240, ₹ 150 (*b*) ₹ 60, ₹ 90, ₹ 360
(*c*) ₹ 150, ₹ 300, ₹ 60 (*d*) None of these

12. Two numbers are in the ratio 3 . 5. If 9 is subtracted from each, the new numbers are in the ratio 12 : 23. The smaller number is :
(*a*) 27 (*b*) 33 (*c*) 49 (*d*) 55

13. If A : B : C = 2 : 3 : 4, then $\frac{A}{B} : \frac{B}{C} : \frac{C}{A}$ is equal to :
(*a*) 4 : 9 : 16 (*b*) 8 : 9 : 12 (*c*) 8 : 9 : 16 (*d*) 8 : 9 : 24

14. A sum of ₹ 1300 is divided amongst P, Q, R and S such that
$\frac{\text{P's share}}{\text{Q's share}} = \frac{\text{Q's share}}{\text{R's share}} = \frac{\text{R's share}}{\text{S's share}} = \frac{2}{3}$. Then, P's share is :
(*a*) ₹ 140 (*b*) ₹ 160 (*c*) ₹ 240 (*d*) ₹ 320

15. If 40% of a number is equal to two-third of another number, what is the ratio of first number to the second number?
(*a*) 2 : 5 (*b*) 3 : 7 (*c*) 5 : 3 (*d*) 7 : 3

16. In a mixture of 60 litres, the ratio of milk and water is 2 : 1. If this ratio is to be 1 : 2, then the quantity of water to be further added is:
(*a*) 20 litres (*b*) 30 litres (*c*) 40 litres (*d*) 60 litres

17. The ratio of the number of boys and girls in a college is 7 : 8. If the percentage increase in the number of boys and girls be 20% and 10% respectively, what will be the new ratio?
(*a*) 8 : 9 (*b*) 17 : 18
(*c*) 21 : 22 (*d*) Cannot be determined

18. A sum of money is to be distributed among A, B, C, D in the proportion of 5 : 2 : 4 : 3. If C gets ₹ 1000 more than D, what is B's share?
(*a*) ₹ 500 (*b*) ₹ 1500 (*c*) ₹ 2000 (*d*) None of these

19. A and B together have ₹ 1210. If $\frac{4}{15}$ of A's amount is equal to $\frac{2}{5}$ of B's amount, how much amount does B have?
(*a*) ₹ 460 (*b*) ₹ 484 (*c*) ₹ 550 (*d*) ₹ 664

20. Ratio of the earnings of A and B is 4 : 7. If the earnings of A increase by 50% and those of B decrease by 25%, the new ratio of their earnings becomes 8 : 7. What are A's earnings?
(*a*) ₹ 21,000 (*b*) ₹ 26,000
(*c*) ₹ 28,000 (*d*) Data inadequate

21. Seats for Mathematics, Physics and Biology in a school are in the ratio 5 : 7 : 8. There is a proposal to increase these seats by 40%, 50% and 75% respectively. What will be the ratio of increased seats?
(*a*) 2 : 3 : 4 (*b*) 6 : 7 : 8 (*c*) 6 : 8 : 9 (*d*) None of these

22. In a bag, there are coins of 25 p, 10 p and 5 p in the ratio of 1 : 2 : 3. If there are ₹ 30 in all, how many 5 p coins are there?
(*a*) 50 (*b*) 100 (*c*) 150 (*d*) 200

23. An amount of ₹ 2430 is divided among A, B and C such that if their shares be reduced by ₹ 5, ₹ 10 and ₹ 15 respectively, the remainders shall be in the ratio of 3 : 4 : 5. Then, B's share was :

(*a*) ₹ 605 (*b*) ₹ 790 (*c*) ₹ 800 (*d*) ₹ 810

24. Salaries of Ravi and Sumit are in the ratio 2 : 3. If the salary of each is increased by ₹ 4000, the new ratio becomes 40 : 57. What is Sumit's present salary?

(*a*) ₹ 17,000 (*b*) ₹ 20,000 (*c*) ₹ 25,500 (*d*) None of these

25. The salaries of A, B, C are in the ratio 2 : 3 : 5. If the increments of 15%, 10% and 20% are allowed respectively in their salaries, then what will be the new ratio of their salaries?

(*a*) 3 : 3 : 10 (*b*) 10 : 11 : 20
(*c*) 23 : 33 : 60 (*d*) Cannot be determined

ANSWERS

1	2	3	4	5	6	7	8	9	10
(*a*)	(*d*)	(*c*)	(*b*)	(*c*)	(*b*)	(*c*)	(*b*)	(*b*)	(*d*)
11	**12**	**13**	**14**	**15**	**16**	**17**	**18**	**19**	**20**
(*b*)	(*b*)	(*d*)	(*b*)	(*c*)	(*d*)	(*c*)	(*c*)	(*b*)	(*d*)
21	**22**	**23**	**24**	**25**					
(*a*)	(*c*)	(*d*)	(*d*)	(*c*)					

SOME SELECTED EXPLANATORY ANSWERS

1. Let $x : \frac{1}{27} :: \frac{3}{11} : \frac{5}{9}$. Then, $x \times \frac{5}{9} = \frac{1}{27} \times \frac{3}{11}$

$\Leftrightarrow \quad x = \left(\frac{1}{27} \times \frac{3}{11} \times \frac{9}{5}\right) = \frac{1}{55}$.

2. From question, Given ratio $= \frac{1}{2} : \frac{2}{3} : \frac{3}{4} = 6 : 8 : 9$.

$\therefore$ 1st part $= ₹\left(782 \times \frac{6}{23}\right) = ₹\ 204$.

3. Suppose that the numbers are x and $2x$ Then, $\frac{x+7}{2x+7} = \frac{3}{5}$

$\Leftrightarrow \quad 5(x + 7) = 3(2x + 7) \quad \Leftrightarrow \quad x = 14.$

$\therefore$ Gretest number = 28.

4. Let the three parts be A, B, C. Then,

$A : B = 2 : 3$ and $B : C = 5 : 8 = \left(5 \times \frac{3}{5}\right) : \left(8 \times \frac{3}{5}\right) = 3 : \frac{24}{5}$

$\Rightarrow \quad A : B : C = 2 : 3 : \frac{24}{5} = 10 : 15 : 24 \quad \Rightarrow \quad B = \left(98 \times \frac{15}{49}\right) = 30.$

5. Let $x = 5k$ and $y = 2k$. Then, $\frac{8x + 9y}{8x + 2y} = \frac{(8 \times 5k) + (9 \times 2k)}{(8 \times 5k) + (2 \times 2k)} = \frac{58k}{44k} = \frac{29}{22}.$

$\Rightarrow \quad (8x + 9y) : (8x + 2y) = 29 : 22.$

6. 10% of x = 20% of $y \Leftrightarrow \frac{10x}{100} = \frac{20y}{100} \Leftrightarrow \frac{x}{y} = \frac{20}{10} = \frac{2}{1}.$

7. $A : B = 2 : 3$, $B : C = 4 : 5 = \left(4 \times \frac{3}{4}\right) : \left(5 \times \frac{3}{4}\right) = 3 : \frac{15}{4}$

and $C : D = 6 : 7 = \left(6 \times \frac{15}{24}\right) : \left(7 \times \frac{15}{24}\right) = \frac{15}{4} : \frac{35}{8}$

$\Rightarrow \quad A : B : C : D = 2 : 3 : \frac{15}{4} : \frac{35}{8} = 16 : 24 : 30 : 35.$

8. $(x \times 5) = (0.75 \times 8) \Rightarrow x = \frac{6}{5} = 1.20.$

9. Suppose that the fourth proportional is x.

Then, $5 : 8 :: 15 : x \Leftrightarrow 5x = (8 \times 15) \Leftrightarrow x = \frac{(8 \times 15)}{5} = 24.$

10. From question, $x = \frac{k}{y^2}$, where k is a constant.

Now, For $y = 2$ and $x = 1$

$1 = \frac{k}{(2)^2} \Rightarrow k = 4.$

$\therefore \quad x = \frac{4}{y^2} \quad \Rightarrow \quad x = \frac{4}{6^2}$, when $y = 6 \quad \Rightarrow \quad x = \frac{4}{36} = \frac{1}{9}.$

11. $\left(A = \frac{2}{3}B \text{ and } B = \frac{1}{4}C\right) \Leftrightarrow \frac{A}{B} = \frac{2}{3}$ and $\frac{B}{C} = \frac{1}{4}$

$\Rightarrow \quad A : B = 2 : 3$ and $B : C = 1 : 4 = 3 : 12 \Rightarrow A : B : C = 2 : 3 : 12.$

$\therefore$ A's share = ₹ $\left(510 \times \frac{2}{17}\right)$ = ₹ 60; B's share = ₹ $\left(510 \times \frac{3}{17}\right)$ = ₹ 90;

C's share = ₹ $\left(510 \times \frac{12}{17}\right)$ = ₹ 360.

12. Suppose that the numbers are $3x$ and $5x$. Then, $\frac{3x-9}{5x-9} = \frac{12}{23}$

$\Leftrightarrow$ $23(3x - 9) = 12(5x - 9)$ $\Leftrightarrow$ $9x = 99$ $\Leftrightarrow$ $x = 11$.

$\therefore$ The smaller number = $(3 \times 11) = 33$.

13. Suppose that the A= $2x$, B = $3x$ and C = $4x$

Then, $\frac{A}{B} = \frac{2x}{3x} = \frac{2}{3}, \frac{B}{C} = \frac{3x}{4x} = \frac{3}{4}$

and $\frac{C}{A} = \frac{4x}{2x} = \frac{2}{1}$ $\Rightarrow$ $\frac{A}{B} : \frac{B}{C} : \frac{C}{A} = \frac{2}{3} : \frac{3}{4} : \frac{2}{1}$ = 8 : 9 : 24.

14. Let P = $2x$ and Q = $3x$. Then, $\frac{Q}{R} = \frac{2}{3}$ $\Rightarrow$ $R = \frac{3}{2}Q = \left(\frac{3}{2} \times 3x\right) = \frac{9x}{2}$.

Also, $\frac{R}{S} = \frac{2}{3}$ $\Rightarrow$ $S = \frac{3}{2}R = \left(\frac{3}{2} \times \frac{9x}{2}\right) = \frac{27x}{4}$.

Thus, P = $2x$, Q = $3x$, R = $\frac{9x}{2}$ and S = $\frac{27x}{4}$.

Now, P + Q + R + S = 1300 $\Leftrightarrow$ $\left(2x + 3x + \frac{9x}{2} + \frac{27x}{4}\right) = 1300$

$\Leftrightarrow$ $(8x + 12x + 18x + 27x) = 5200$

$\Leftrightarrow$ $65x = 5200$ $\Leftrightarrow$ $x = \frac{5200}{65} = 80$.

$\therefore$ P's share = ₹(2×80) = ₹ 160.

15. Let 40% of $x = \frac{2}{3}y$.

Then, $\frac{40x}{100} = \frac{2y}{3}$ $\Leftrightarrow$ $\frac{2x}{5} = \frac{2y}{3}$ $\Leftrightarrow$ $\frac{x}{y} = \left(\frac{2}{3} \times \frac{5}{2}\right) = \frac{5}{3}$.

$\therefore$ $x : y = 5 : 3$.

16. Initially Milk : Water = 2 : 1. Quantity of milk in the mixture

= $\left(60 \times \frac{2}{3}\right)$ litres = 40 litres.

Quantity of water in it = (60 – 40) litres = 20 litres.
So, Required ratio = 1 : 2.
Let quantity of water to be added further be x litres.

Then, milk : water = $\dfrac{40}{(20 + x)}$.

Now, $\dfrac{40}{(20+x)} = \dfrac{1}{2} \Leftrightarrow 20 + x = 80 \Leftrightarrow x = 60.$

Quantity of water to be further added = 60 litres.

17. Initially number of boys : girls = $7x : 8x$. Their increased number is (120% of $7x$) and (110% of $8x$)

i.e. $\left(\dfrac{120}{100} \times 7x\right)$ and $\left(\dfrac{110}{100} \times 8x\right)$ *i.e.* $\dfrac{42x}{5}$ and $\dfrac{44x}{5}$.

$\therefore$ Required ratio = $\dfrac{42x}{5} : \dfrac{44x}{5} = 21 : 22.$

18. Suppose that the shares of A, B, C and D be ₹ $5x$, ₹ $2x$, ₹ $4x$ and ₹ $3x$ respectively.
Then, $4x - 3x = 1000 \Leftrightarrow x = 1000.$
$\therefore$ B's share = ₹ $2x$ = ₹ (2×1000) = ₹ 2000.

19. $\dfrac{4}{15}\text{A} = \dfrac{2}{5}\text{B} \Leftrightarrow \text{A} = \left(\dfrac{2}{5} \times \dfrac{15}{4}\right)\text{B} \Leftrightarrow \text{A} = \dfrac{3}{2}\text{B}$

$\Leftrightarrow \dfrac{\text{A}}{\text{B}} = \dfrac{3}{2} \Leftrightarrow \text{A : B} = 3 : 2$

$\therefore$ B's share = ₹ $\left(1210 \times \dfrac{2}{5}\right)$ = ₹ 484.

20. Suppose that original earnings of A and B be ₹ $4x$ and ₹ $7x$.

New earnings of A = 150% of ₹ $4x$ = ₹ $\left(\dfrac{150}{100} \times 4x\right)$ = ₹ $6x$.

New earnings of B = 75% of ₹ $7x$ = ₹ $\left(\dfrac{75}{100} \times 7x\right)$ = ₹ $\dfrac{21x}{4}$.

$\therefore 6x : \dfrac{21x}{4} = 8 : 7 \Leftrightarrow \dfrac{6x \times 4}{21x} = \dfrac{8}{7}.$

This does not give x. So, the given data is inadequate.

21. From question, set for Mathematics, Physics and Biology be $5x$, $7x$ and $8x$ respectively.

Number of increased seats are (140% of $5x$), (150% of $7x$) and (175% of $8x$)

i.e. $\left(\frac{140}{100}\times 5x\right)$, $\left(\frac{150}{100}\times 7x\right)$ and $\left(\frac{175}{100}\times 8x\right)$ *i.e.* $7x$, $\frac{21x}{2}$ and $14x$.

$\therefore$ Required ratio $= 7x : \frac{21x}{2} : 14x = 14x : 21x : 28x = 2 : 3 : 4.$

22. Let the number of 25 p, 10 p and 5 p coins be x, $2x$ and $3x$ respectively.

Then, sum of their values = ₹$\left(\frac{25x}{100}+\frac{10\times 2x}{100}+\frac{5\times 3x}{100}\right)$ = ₹$\frac{60x}{100}$.

$\therefore \quad \frac{60x}{100} = 30 \Leftrightarrow x = \frac{30\times 100}{60} = 50.$

Hence, the number of 5 p coins = (3 × 50) = 150.

23. Remainder = ₹ [2430 – (5 + 10 + 15)] = ₹ 2400.

$\therefore$ B's share = ₹ $\left[\left(2400\times\frac{4}{12}\right)+10\right]$ = ₹ 810.

24. Let the original salaries of Ravi and Sumit be ₹ $2x$ and ₹ $3x$ respectively.

Then, $\frac{2x+4000}{3x+4000} = \frac{40}{57} \Leftrightarrow 57(2x + 4000) = 40(3x + 4000)$

$\Leftrightarrow 6x = 68000 \Leftrightarrow 3x = 34000.$

Sumit's present salary = $(3x + 4000)$ = ₹(34000 + 4000) = ₹ 38,000.

25. Let A = $2k$, B = $3k$ and C = $5k$.

A's new salary $= \frac{115}{100}$ of $2k = \left(\frac{115}{100}\times 2k\right) = \frac{23}{10}k$

B's new salary $= \frac{110}{100}$ of $3k = \left(\frac{110}{100}\times 3k\right) = \frac{33}{10}k$

C's new salary $= \frac{120}{100}$ of $5k = \left(\frac{120}{100}\times 5k\right) = 6k.$

$\therefore$ New raito $= \frac{23k}{10} : \frac{33k}{10} : 6k = 23 : 33 : 60.$

~~~~~~
~~~~~~

12. PARTNERSHIP

Partnership : When two or more than two persons run a business jointly, they are called ***partners*** and the deal is known as ***partnership***.

Ratio of Division of Gains :

(*i*) *When investments of all the partners are for the same time,* the gain or loss is distributed among the partners in the ratio of their investments.

Suppose A and B invest ₹ x and ₹ y respectively for a year in a business, then at the end of the year :

(A's share of profit) : (B's share of profit) = $x : y$.

(*ii*) *When investments are for different time periods,* then equivalent capitals are calculated for a unit of time by taking (capital × number of units of time). Now, gain or loss is divided in the ratio of these capitals.

Suppose A invests ₹ x for p months and B invests ₹ y for q months, then

(A's share of profit) : (B's share of profit) = $xp : yq$.

Working and Sleeping Partners : A partner who manages the business is known, as a ***working partner*** and the one who simply invests the money is a ***sleeping partner***.

SOLVED EXAMPLE

1. A, B and C started a business by investing ₹ 1,20,000, ₹ 1,35,000 and ₹ 1,50,000 respectively. Find the share of each, out of an annual profit of ₹ 56,700.

Sol. Ratio of shares of A, B and C = Ratio of their investments
= 120000 : 135000 : 150000
= 8 : 9 : 10.

$\therefore$ A's share = ₹ $\left(56700 \times \frac{8}{27}\right)$ = ₹ 16800.

B's share = ₹ $\left(56700 \times \frac{9}{27}\right)$ = ₹ 18900.

C's share = ₹ $\left(56700 \times \frac{10}{27}\right)$ = ₹ 21000.

2. A, B and C enter into partnership. A invests 3 times as much as B invests and B invests two-third of what C invests. At the end of the year, the profit earned is ₹ 6600. What is the share of B?

Sol. Let C's capital = ₹ x. Then, B's capital = ₹$\frac{2}{3}x$.

$$\text{A's capital} = ₹\left(3 \times \frac{2}{3}x\right) = ₹\ 2x.$$

$$\therefore \quad \text{Ratio of their capitals} = 2x\ \frac{2}{3}x : x = 6 : 2 : 3.$$

$$\text{Hence, B's share} = ₹\left(6600 \times \frac{2}{11}\right) = ₹\ 1200.$$

3. A invested ₹ 76,000 in a business. After few months, B joined him with ₹ 57,000. At the end of the year, the total profit was divided between them in the ratio 2 : 1. After how many months did B join?

Sol. Suppose B joined after x months. Then, B's money was invested for $(12 - x)$ months.

$$\therefore \quad \frac{76000 \times 12}{57000 \times (12 - x)} = \frac{2}{1} \Leftrightarrow 912000 = 114000\ (12 - x)$$

$$\Leftrightarrow 114\ (12 - x) = 912$$

$$\Leftrightarrow (12 - x) = 8 \quad \Leftrightarrow \quad x = 4.$$

Hence, B joined after 4 months.

EXERCISE

1. A and B started a business investing ₹ 85,000 and ₹ 15,000 respectively. In what ratio the profit earned after 2 years be divided between A and B respectively?
(*a*) 3 : 4 (*b*) 3 : 5 (*c*) 15 : 23 (*d*) None of these

2. A, B and C enter into a partnership and their shares are in the ratio $\frac{1}{2} : \frac{1}{3} : \frac{1}{4}$. After 2 months, A withdraws half of his capital and after 10 months, a profit of ₹ 378 is divided among them. What is B's share?
(*a*) ₹ 129 (*b*) ₹ 144 (*c*) ₹ 156 (*d*) ₹ 168

3. P and Q are partners in a business. P contributes $\frac{1}{4}$ of the capital for 15 months and Q received $\frac{2}{3}$ of the profit. For how long Q's money was used?
(*a*) 6 months (*b*) 9 months (*c*) 10 months (*d*) 1 year

4. Shekhar started a business investing ₹ 25,000 in 1999. In 2000, he invested an additional amount of ₹ 10,000 and Rajeev joined him with an amount of ₹ 35,000. In 2001, Shekhar invested another additional amount of ₹ 10,000 and Jatin joined them with an amount of ₹ 35,000. What will be Rajeev's share in the profit of ₹ 1,50,000 earned at the end of 3 years from the start of the business in 1999?
(*a*) ₹ 45,000 (*b*) ₹ 50,000 (*c*) ₹ 70,000 (*d*) ₹ 75,000

5. A and B entered into partnership with capitals in the ratio 4 : 5. After 3 months, A withdrew $\frac{1}{4}$ of his capital and B withdrew $\frac{1}{5}$ of his capital. The gain at the end of 10 months was ₹ 760. A's share in this profit is:
(*a*) ₹ 330 (*b*) ₹ 360 (*c*) ₹ 380 (*d*) ₹ 430

6. In a business, A and C invested amounts in the ratio 2 : 1, whereas the ratio between amounts invested by A and B was 3 : 2. If ₹ 1,57,300 was their profit, how much amount did B receive?
(*a*) ₹ 24,200 (*b*) ₹ 36,300 (*c*) ₹ 48,400 (*d*) ₹ 72,600

7. Arun, Kamal and Vinay invested ₹ 8000, ₹ 4000 and ₹ 8000 respectively in a business. Arun left after six months. If after eight months, there was a gain of ₹ 4005, then what will be the share of Kamal?
(*a*) ₹ 890 (*b*) ₹ 1335 (*c*) ₹ 1602 (*d*) ₹ 1780

8. A, B and C enter into a partnership. They invest ₹ 40,000, ₹ 80,000 and ₹ 1,20,000 respectively. At the end of the first year, B withdraws ₹ 40,000, while at the end of the second year, C withdraws ₹ 80,000. In what ratio will the profit be shared at the end of 3 years?
(*a*) 2 : 3 : 5 (*b*) 3 : 4 : 7 (*c*) 4 : 5 : 9 (*d*) None of these

9. Kittu started a software business by investing ₹ 50,000. After six months, Nanda joinet her with a capital of ₹ 80,000. After 3 years, they earned a profit of ₹ 24,500. What was Kittu's share in the profit?
(*a*) ₹ 9423 (*b*) ₹ 10,250 (*c*) ₹ 12,500 (*d*) None of these

10. A and B start a business with investments of ₹ 5000 and ₹ 4500 respectively. After 4 months, A takes out half of his capital. After two more months, B takes out one-third of his capital while C joins them with a capital of ₹ 7000. At the end of a year, they earn a profit of ₹ 5080. Find the share of each member in the profit.
(*a*) A – ₹ 1400, B – ₹ 1900, C – ₹ 1780
(*b*) A – ₹ 1600, B – ₹ 1800, C – ₹ 1680
(*c*) A – ₹ 1800, B – ₹ 1500, C – ₹ 1780
(*d*) A – ₹ 1680, B – ₹ 1600, C – ₹ 1800

11. A, B and C rent a pasture. A puts 10 oxen for 7 months, B puts 12 oxen for 5 months and C puts 15 oxen for 3 months for grazing. If the rent of the pasture is ₹ 175, how much must C pay as his share of rent?
(*a*) ₹ 45 (*b*) ₹ 50 (*c*) ₹ 55 (*d*) ₹ 60

12. Two friends P and Q started a business investing in the ratio of 5 : 6. R joined them after six months investing an amount equal to that of Q's. At the end of the year, 20% profit was earned which was equal to ₹ 98,000. What was the amount invested by R?
(*a*) ₹ 1,05,000 (*b*) ₹ 1,75,000 (*c*) ₹ 2,10,000 (*d*) None of these

13. A and B started a partnership business investing some amount in the ratio of 3 : 5. C joined them after six months with an amount equal to that of B. In what proportion should the profit at the end of one year be distributed among A, B and C?
(*a*) 3 : 5 : 2 (*b*) 3 : 5 : 5 (*c*) 6 : 10 : 5 (*d*) None of these

14. P, Q and R enter into a partnership investing ₹ 35,000, ₹ 45,000 and ₹ 55,000 respectively. The respective shares of P, Q and R in an annual profit of ₹ 40,500 are:
(*a*) ₹ 10,500, ₹ 13,500, ₹ 16,500
(*b*) ₹ 11,500, ₹ 13,000, ₹ 16,000
(*c*) ₹ 11,-OOG, ₹ 14,000, ₹ 15,500
(*d*) ₹ 11,500, ₹ 12,500, ₹ 16,500

15. A, B and C enter into a partnership in the ratio $\frac{7}{2} : \frac{4}{3} : \frac{6}{5}$. After 4 months, A increases his share by 50%. If the total profit at the end of one year be ₹ 21,600, then B's share in the profit is:
(*a*) ₹ 2100 (*b*) ₹ 2400 (*c*) ₹ 3600 (*d*) ₹ 4000

16. A starts business with ₹ 3500 and after 5 months, B joins with A as his partner. After a year, the profit is divided in the ratio 2:3. What is B's contribution in the capital?
(*a*) ₹ 7500 (*b*) ₹ 8000 (*c*) ₹ 8500 (*d*) ₹ 9000

17. Three partners shared the profit in a business in the ratio 5 : 7 : 8. They had partnered for 14 months, 8 months and 7 months respectively. What was the ratio of their investments?
(*a*) 5 : 7 : 8 (*b*) 28 : 49 : 64 (*c*) 38 : 28 : 21 (*d*) None of these

18. A began a business with ₹ 85,000. He was joined afterwards by B with ₹ 42,500. For how much period does B join, if the profits at the end of the year are divided in the ratio of 3 : 1?
(*a*) 4 months (*b*) 5 months (*c*) 6 months (*d*) 8 months.

19. A and B started a business in partnership investing ₹ 20,000 and ₹ 15,000 respectively. After six months, C joined them with ₹ 20,000. What will be B's share in the total profit of ₹ 25,000.earned at the end of 2 years from the starting of the business?

(*a*) ₹ 7500 (*b*) ₹ 9000 (*c*) ₹ 9500 (*d*) None of these

20. Aman started a business investing ₹ 70,000. Rakhi joined him after six months with an amount of ₹ 1,05,000 and Sagar joined them with ₹ 1.4 lakhs after another six months. The amount of profit earned should be distributed in what ratio among Aman, Rakhi and Sagar respectively, 3 years after Aman started the business?

(*a*) 7 : 6 : 10 (*b*) 12 : 15 : 16 (*c*) 42 : 45 : 56 (*d*) None of these

21. A, B and C jointly thought of engaging themselves in a business venture. It was agreed that A would invest ₹ 6500 for 6 months, B, ₹ 8400 for 5 months and C, ₹ 10,000 for 3 months. A wants to be the working member for which he was to receive 5% of the profits. The .profit earned was ₹ 7400. Calculate the share of B in the profit.

(*a*) ₹ 1900 (*b*) ₹ 2660 (*c*) ₹ 2800 (*d*) ₹ 2840

22. Birendra started a business investing ₹ 9000. After five months, Sameer joined with a capital of ₹ 8000. If at the end of the year, they earn a profit of ₹ 6970, then what will be the share of Sameer in the profit?

(*a*) ₹ 1883.78 (*b*) ₹ 2380 (*c*) ₹ 3690 (*d*) ₹ 5864

ANSWERS

1	2	3	4	5	6	7	8	9	10
(*d*)	(*b*)	(*c*)	(*b*)	(*a*)	(*c*)	(*a*)	(*b*)	(*d*)	(*b*)
11	**12**	**13**	**14**	**15**	**16**	**17**	**18**	**19**	**20**
(*a*)	(*c*)	(*c*)	(*a*)	(*d*)	(*d*)	(*d*)	(*d*)	(*a*)	(*b*)
21	**22**								
(*b*)	(*b*)								

SOME SELECTED EXPLANATORY ANSWERS

1. A : B = 85000 : 15000 = 85 : 15 = 17 : 3.

2. Ratio of intitial investments = $\frac{1}{2} : \frac{1}{3} : \frac{1}{4} = 6 : 4 : 3$.

Let their initial investments be $6x$, $2x$ and $3x$ respectively.

$A : B : C = (6x \times 2 + 3x \times 10) : (4x \times 12) : (3x \times 12)$

$= 42 : 48 : 36 = 7 : 8 : 6.$

$\therefore$ B's share = ₹$\left(378 \times \frac{8}{21}\right)$ = ₹ 144.

3. Let the total profit be ₹ z. Then,

Q's share = ₹ $\frac{2z}{3}$, A's share = ₹ $\left(z - \frac{2z}{3}\right)$ = ₹ $\frac{z}{3}$.

$\therefore$ P : Q = $\frac{z}{3} : \frac{2z}{3}$ = 1 : 2.

Let the total capital be ₹ x and suppose Q's money was used for x months.

Then, $\dfrac{\frac{1}{4}x \times 15}{\frac{3}{4}x \times y} = \frac{1}{2} \Leftrightarrow y = \left(\frac{15 \times 2}{3}\right) = 10.$

Thus, Q's money was used for 10 months.

4. Shekhar : Rajeev : Jatin
= (25000 × 12 + 35000 × 12 + 45000 × 12) : (35000 × 12)
= 1260000 : 840000 : 420000 = 3 : 2 : 1.

$\therefore$ Rajeev's share = ₹ $\left(150000 \times \frac{2}{6}\right)$ = ₹ 50000.

5. $A : B = \left[4x \times 3 + \left(4x - \frac{1}{4} \times 4x\right) \times 7\right] : \left[5x \times 3 + \left(5x - \frac{1}{5} \times 5x\right) \times 7\right]$

$= (12x + 21x) : (15x + 28x) = 33x : 43x = 33 : 43.$

$\therefore$ A's share = ₹$\left(760 \times \frac{33}{76}\right)$ = ₹ 330.

6. A : B = 3 : 2 ⇒ B : A = 2 : 3 = 4 : 6 and A : C = 2 : 1 = 6 : 3.
So, B : A : C = 4 : 6 : 3 or A : B : C = 6 : 4 : 3.

$\therefore$ B's share = ₹$\left(157300 \times \frac{4}{13}\right)$ = ₹ 48400.

7. Arun : Kamal : Vinay = (8000 × 6) : (4000 × 8) : (8000 × 8)
= 48 : 32 : 64 = 3 : 2 : 4.

$\therefore$ Kamal's shart = ₹$\left(4005 \times \frac{2}{9}\right)$ = ₹ 890.

8. A : B : C = (40000 × 36) : (80000 × 12 + 40000 × 24) :
(120000 × 24 + 40000 × 12)
= 144 : 192 : 336 = 3 : 4 : 7.

9. Kittu : Nanda = (50000 × 36) : (80000 × 30) = 3 : 4.

$\therefore$ Simran's share = ₹ $\left(24500 \times \frac{3}{7}\right)$ = ₹105000.

10. A : B : C = (5000 × 4 + 2500 × 8) : (4500 × 6 + 3000 × 6) : (7000 × 6)
= 40000 : 45000 : 42000 = 40 : 45 : 42

$\therefore$ A's share = ₹$\left(5080 \times \frac{40}{127}\right)$ = ₹ 1600;

B's share = ₹$\left(5080 \times \frac{45}{127}\right)$ = ₹ 1800;

C's share = ₹$\left(5080 \times \frac{42}{127}\right)$ = ₹ 1680.

11. A : B : C = 10 × 7 : 12 × 5 : 15 × 3 = 70 : 60 : 45 = 14 : 12 : 9.

$\therefore$ C's rent = ₹$\left(175 \times \frac{9}{35}\right)$ = ₹ 45.

12. Let the total profit be ₹ *z*.

Then, 20% of x = 98000 $\Rightarrow$ $x = \left(\frac{98000 \times 100}{20}\right)$ = 490000.

Let the capitals os P, Q and R be ₹ 5x, ₹ 6x and ₹ 6x respectively. Then,
(5x × 12) + (6x × 12) + (6x × 6) = 490000 × 12

$\Leftrightarrow$ 168x = 490000 × 12 $\Leftrightarrow$ $x = \left(\frac{490000 \times 12}{168}\right)$ = 35000.

$\therefore$ R's investment = 6x = ₹ (6 × 35000) = ₹ 210000.

13. Let the initial investments of A and B be 3x and 5x.
A : B : C = (3x × 12) : (5x × 12) : (5x × 6) = 36 : 60 : 30 = 6 : 10 : 5.

14. P : Q : R = 35000 : 45000 : 55000 = 7 : 9 : 11.

P's share = ₹ $\left(40500 \times \frac{7}{27}\right)$ = ₹ 10500.

Q's share = ₹ $\left(40500 \times \frac{9}{27}\right)$ = ₹ 13500.

R's share = ₹ $\left(40500 \times \frac{11}{27}\right)$ = ₹ 16500.

15. Ratio of initial investments = $\frac{7}{2} : \frac{4}{3} : \frac{6}{5}$ = 105 : 40 : 36.

Let the initial investments be 105x, 40x and 36x.

$\therefore \quad A : B : C = \left(105x \times 4 + \frac{150}{100} \times 105x \times 8\right) : (40x \times 12) : (36x \times 12)$

$= 1680x : 480x : 432x = 35 : 10 : 9.$

Hence, B's share = ₹ $\left(21600 \times \frac{10}{54}\right)$ = ₹ 4000.

16. Let B's capital ₹ x. Then, $\frac{3500 \times 12}{7x} = \frac{2}{3} \Leftrightarrow 14x = 126000 \Leftrightarrow x = 9000.$

17. Let their investments be ₹ x for 14 months; ₹ y for 8 months and ₹ z for 7 months respectively.

Then, $14x : 8y : 7z = 5 : 7 : 8.$

Now, $\frac{14x}{8y} = \frac{5}{7} \Leftrightarrow 70x = 40y \Leftrightarrow y = \frac{7}{4}x.$

And, $\frac{14x}{7z} = \frac{5}{8} \Leftrightarrow 112x = 35z \Leftrightarrow z = \frac{112}{35}x = \frac{16}{5}x.$

$\therefore \quad x : y : z = x : \frac{7}{4}x : \frac{16}{5}x = 20 : 35 : 64.$

18. Suppose B joined for x months.

Then, $\frac{85000 \times 12}{42500 \times x} = \frac{3}{1}$ or $x = \frac{85000 \times 12}{42500 \times 3} = 8$. So, B joined for 8 months.

19. A : B : C = (20000 × 24) : (15000 × 24) : (20000 × 18) = 4 : 3 : 3.

$\therefore$ B's share = ₹ $\left(25000 \times \frac{3}{10}\right)$ = ₹ 7500.

20. Aman : Rakhi : Sagar = (70000 × 36) : (105000 × 30) : (140000 × 24)
= 12 : 15 : 16.

21. For managing, A receives = 5% of ₹ 7400 = ₹ 370.

Balance = ₹ (7400 – 370) = ₹ 7030.

Ratio of their investments = (6500 × 6) : (8400 × 5) : (10000 × 3)
= 39000 : 42000 : 30000 = 13 : 14 : 10.

$\therefore$ B's share = ₹ $\left(7030 \times \frac{14}{37}\right)$ = ₹ 2660.

22. Birendra : Sameer = (9000 × 12) : (8000 × 7) = 108 : 56 = 27 : 14.

$\therefore$ Sameer's share = ₹ $\left(6970 \times \frac{14}{11}\right)$ = ₹ 2380.

~~~~~~
~~~~~~

13. CHAIN RULE

Direct Proportion: *Two quantities are said to be directly proportional, if on the increase (or decrease) of the one, the other increases (or decreases) to the same extent*

Ex. 1. ***Cost is directly proportional to the number of articles.***
(More Articles, More Cost)

Ex. 2. ***Work done is directly proportional to the number of men working on it.***
(More Men, More Work)

Indirect Proportion : *Two quantities are said to be indirectly proportional, if on the increase of the one, the other decreases to the same extent and vice-versa.*

Ex. 1. ***The time taken by a car in covering a certain distance is inversely proportional to the speed of the car.***
(More speed, Less is the time taken to cover a distance)

Ex. 2. ***Time taken to finish a work is inversely proportional to the number of persons working at it.***
(More persons, Less is the time taken to finish a job)

Remark : In solving questions by chain rule, we compare every item with the term to be found out.

SOLVED EXAMPLE

1. If 15 toys cost ₹ 234, what do 35 toys, cost?

Sol. Let the required cost be ₹ x. Then,

More toys, More cost ***(Direct Proportion)***

$\therefore$ $15 : 35 :: 234 : x \Leftrightarrow (15 \times x) = (35 \times 234)$

$$\Leftrightarrow x = \left(\frac{35 \times 234}{15}\right) = 546.$$

Hence, the cost of 35 toys is ₹ 546.

2. If the wages of 6 men for 15 days-be ₹ 2100, then find the wages of 9 men for 12 days.

Sol. Let the required wages be ₹ x

More men, More wages ***(Direct Proportion)***
Less days, Less wages ***(Direct Proportion)***

$$\left.\begin{array}{l}\text{Men } 6 : 9 \\ \text{Days } 15 : 12\end{array}\right\} :: 2100 : x$$

$\therefore \quad (6 \times 15 \times x) = (9 \times 12 \times 2100) \quad \Leftrightarrow \quad x = \left(\frac{9 \times 12 \times 2100}{6 \times 15}\right) = 2520.$

Hence, the required wages are ₹ 2520.

3. If 9 engines consume 24 metric tonnes of coal, when each if working 8 hours a day, how much coal will be required for 8 engines, each running 13 hours a day, it being given that 3 engines of former type consume as much as 4 engines of latter type?

Sol. Let 3 engines of former type consume 1 unit in 1 hour.
Then, 4 engines of latter type consume 1 unit in 1 hour.

$\therefore$ 1 engine of former type consumes $\frac{1}{3}$ unit in 1 hour.

1 engine of latter type consumes $\frac{1}{4}$ unit in 1 hour.

Let the required consumption of coal be x units.

Less engines, Less coal consumed ***(Direct Proportion)***
More working hours. More coal consumed ***(Direct Proportion)***
Less rate of consumption, Less coal consumed ***(Direct Proportion)***

$$\left.\begin{array}{ll}\text{Number of engines} & 9 : 8 \\ \text{Working hours} & 8 : 13 \\ \text{Rate of consumption} & \frac{1}{3} : \frac{1}{4}\end{array}\right\} :: 24 : x$$

$\therefore \quad \left(9 \times 8 \times \frac{1}{3} \times x\right) = \left(8 \times 13 \times \frac{1}{4} \times 24\right) \Leftrightarrow 24x = 624 \Leftrightarrow x = 26.$

Hence, the required consumption of coal = 26 metric tonnes.

EXERCISE

1. If 7 spiders make 7 webs in 7 days, then 1 spider will make 1 web in how many days?

(*a*) 1 (*b*) $\frac{7}{2}$ (*c*) 7 (*d*) 49

2. Running at the same constant rate, 6 identical machines can produce a total of 270 bottles per minute. At this rate, how many bottles could 10 such machines produce in 4 minutes?

(*a*) 648 (*b*) 1800 (*c*) 2700 (*d*) 10800

3 10 men, working 6 hours a day can complete a work in 18 days. How many hours a day must 15 men work to complete the same work in 12 days ?

(*a*) 6 (*b*) 10 (*c*) 12 (*d*) 15

4. 4 mat-weavers can weave 4 mats in 4 days. At the same rate, how many mats would be woven by 8 mat-weavers in 8 days?
(a) 4 (b) 8 (c) 12 (d) 16

5. 3 pumps, working 8 hours a day, can empty a tank in 2 days. How many hours a day must 4 pumps work to empty the tank in 1 day?
(a) 9 (b) 10 (c) 11 (d) 12

6. Panas completes $\frac{5}{8}$ of a job in 10 days. At this rate, how many more days will it take him to finish the job?
(a) 5 (b) 6 (c) 7 (d) $7\frac{1}{2}$

7. If the cost of x metres of wire is ₹ d, then what is the cost of y metres of wire at the same rate?
(a) ₹ (yd) (b) ₹ $\left(\frac{yd}{x}\right)$ (c) ₹ (xd) (d) ₹ $\left(\frac{xy}{d}\right)$

8. A fort had provision of food for 150 men for 45 days. After 10 days, 25 men left the fort. The number of days for which the remaining food will last, is :
(a) $29\frac{1}{5}$ (b) $37\frac{1}{4}$ (c) 42 (d) 54

9. A wheel that has 6 cogs is meshed with a larger wheel of 14 cogs. When the smaller wheel has made 21 revolutions, then the number of revolutions made by the larger wheel is:
(a) 4 (b) 9 (c) 12 (d) 49

10. In a camp, there is a meal for, 120 men or 200 children. If 150 children have taken the meal, how many men will be catered to with the remaining meal?
(a) 20 (b) 30 (c) 40 (d) 50

11. An industrial loom weaves 0.128 metres of cloth every second. Approximately, how many seconds will it take for the loom to weave 25 metres of cloth?
(a) 178 (b) 195 (c) 204 (d) 488

12. If the price of 6 toys is ₹ 264.37, what will be the approximate price of 5 toys?
(a) ₹ 140 (b) ₹ 100 (c) ₹ 200 (d) ₹ 220

13. In a dairy farm, 40 cows eat 40 bags of husk in 40 days. In how many days one cow will eat one bag of husk?
(a) 1 (b) $\frac{1}{40}$ (c) 40 (d) 80

14. If a quarter kg of potato costs 60 paise, how many paise will 200 gm cost?
(*a*) 48 paise (*b*) 54 paise (*c*) 56 paise (*d*) 72 paise

15. 39 persons can repair a road in 12 days, working 5 hours a day. In how many days will 30 persons, working 6 hours a day, complete the work?
(*a*) 10 (*b*) 13 (*c*) 14 (*d*) None of these

16. A flagstaff 17.5 m high casts a shadow of length 40.25 m. The height of the building, which casts a shadow of length 28.75 m under similar conditions will be:
(*a*) 10 m (*b*) 12.5 m (*c*) 17.5 m (*d*) 21.25 m

17. If 8 men can reap 80 hectares in 24 days, then how many hectares can 36 men reap in 30 days?
(*a*) 350 (*b*) 400 (*c*) 425 (*d*) 450

18. 36 men can complete a piece of work in 18 days. In how many days will 27 men complete the same work?
(*a*) 12 (*b*) 18 (*b*) 22 (*d*) 24

19. A contractor undertook to do a certain piece of work, in 9 days. He employed certain number of men, but 6 of them being absent from the very first day, the rest could finish the work in 15 days. The number of men originally employed were :
(*a*) 12 (*b*) 15 (*c*) 18 (*d*) 24

20. A contractor employed 30 men to do a piece of work in 38 days. After 25 days, he employed 5 men more and the work was finished one day earlier. How many days he would have been behind, if he had not employed additional men?
(*a*) 1 (*b*) $1\frac{1}{4}$ (*c*) $1\frac{3}{4}$ (*d*) None of these

ANSWERS

1	2	3	4	5	6	7	8	9	10
(*c*)	(*b*)	(*a*)	(*d*)	(*d*)	(*b*)	(*b*)	(*c*)	(*b*)	(*b*)
11	**12**	**13**	**14**	**15**	**16**	**17**	**18**	**19**	**20**
(*b*)	(*d*)	(*c*)	(*a*)	(*b*)	(*b*)	(*d*)	(*d*)	(*b*)	(*a*)

SOME SELECTED EXPLANATORY ANSWERS

1. Suppose that the required number of days be *d*.

$$\therefore \left.\begin{array}{ll}\text{Spiders} & 1 : 7 \\ \text{Webs} & 7 : 1\end{array}\right\} : : 7 : d$$

$$\therefore \quad 1 \times 7 \times d = 7 \times 1 \times 7 \quad \Leftrightarrow \quad d = 7.$$

2. Suppose that the required number of bottles is x.

$$\left.\begin{array}{ll}\text{Machines} & 6:10\\ \text{Time (in Minutes)} & 1:4\end{array}\right\} :: 270 : x$$

$\therefore\ 6 \times 1 \times x = 10 \times 4 \times 270 \Leftrightarrow x = \dfrac{10 \times 4 \times 270}{6} \Leftrightarrow x = 1800.$

3. Let the required number of hours per day be x.

$$\left.\begin{array}{ll}\text{Men} & 15:10\\ \text{Days} & 12:18\end{array}\right\} :: 6 : x$$

$\therefore\ 15 \times 12 \times x = 10 \times 18 \times 6 \Leftrightarrow x = \dfrac{10 \times 18 \times 6}{15 \times 12} \Leftrightarrow x = 6.$

4. Suppose that the required number of mats be x.

$$\left.\begin{array}{ll}\text{Weavers} & 4:8\\ \text{Days} & 4:8\end{array}\right\} :: 4 : x$$

$\therefore\ 4 \times 4 \times x = 8 \times 8 \times 4 \Leftrightarrow x = \dfrac{(8 \times 8 \times 4)}{(4 \times 4)} = 16.$

6. Work finished $= \dfrac{5}{8}$. Remaining work $= \left(1 - \dfrac{5}{8}\right) = \dfrac{3}{8}$.

Suppose that the required number of days to finish the work is x.

Then, $\dfrac{5}{8} : \dfrac{3}{8} :: 10 : x \Leftrightarrow \dfrac{5}{8} \times x = \dfrac{3}{8} \times 10 \Leftrightarrow x = \left(\dfrac{3}{8} \times 10 \times \dfrac{8}{5}\right) = 6.$

7. From question, Cost of x metres = ₹ d

Cost of 1 metre = ₹$\left(\dfrac{d}{x}\right)$

$\therefore$ Cost of 1 metre = ₹ $\dfrac{d}{x}$

$\therefore$ Cost of y metres = ₹ $\left(\dfrac{d}{x} \times y\right)$ = ₹ $\left(\dfrac{yd}{x}\right)$.

8. **Initially:** 150 men had food for 35 days (given)

Suppose 125 men had food for x days

Again,

$\therefore\ 125 : 150 :: 35 : x \Leftrightarrow 125 \times x = 150 \times 35$

$\Leftrightarrow x = \dfrac{150 \times 35}{125} \Leftrightarrow x = 42$

Hence, the remaining food will last for 42 days.

9. Suppose that the required number of revolutions made by larger wheel is x.

$\therefore\ 14 : 6 :: 21 : x \Leftrightarrow 14 \times x = 6 \times 21 \Leftrightarrow x = \left(\dfrac{6 \times 21}{14}\right) = 9.$

11. Suppose that the required time is t seconds.

$\therefore\ 0.128 : 25 :: 1 : t$

$$\Leftrightarrow 0.128 \times t = 25 \times 1 \Leftrightarrow t = \frac{25}{0.128} = \frac{25 \times 1000}{128} \Leftrightarrow t = 195.31.$$

$\therefore$ Required time $\approx$ 195 sec.

12. Price of 6 toys is ₹ 264.37

$\therefore$ Price of 5 toys is $\frac{264.37}{6} \times 5$ = ₹ 220 (Approx)

13. Let the required number of days be x.

$$\left.\begin{matrix}\text{Cows} & 1 : 40 \\ \text{Bags} & 40 : 1\end{matrix}\right\} :: 40 : x$$

$\therefore\ 1 \times 40 \times x = 40 \times 1 \times 40 \Leftrightarrow x = 40.$

15. Suppose that the required number of days be x.

$$\left.\begin{matrix}\text{Persons} & 30 : 39 \\ \text{Working hrs/day} & 6 : 5\end{matrix}\right\} :: 12 : x$$

$$\therefore\ 30 \times 6 \times x = 39 \times 5 \times 12 \Leftrightarrow x = \frac{39 \times 5 \times 12}{30 \times 6} \Leftrightarrow x = 13.$$

16. Let the height of the building be x metres.

$\therefore\ 40.25 : 28.75 :: 17.5 : x \Leftrightarrow 40.25 \times x = 28.75 \times 17.5$

$$\Leftrightarrow x = \frac{(28.75 \times 17.5)}{40.25} \Leftrightarrow x = 12.5.$$

17. Let the required number of hectares be x.

$$\left.\begin{matrix}\text{Men} & 8 : 36 \\ \text{Days} & 24 : 30\end{matrix}\right\} :: 80 : x$$

$$\therefore\ 8 \times 24 \times x = 36 \times 30 \times 80 \Leftrightarrow x = \frac{(36 \times 30 \times 80)}{(8 \times 24)} \Leftrightarrow x = 450.$$

18. Let the required number of days be x.

$\therefore\ 27 : 36 :: 18 : x \Leftrightarrow 27 \times x = 36 \times 18$

$$\Leftrightarrow x = \frac{36 \times 18}{27} \Leftrightarrow x = 24.$$

19. Suppose there be x men at the beginning.

$\therefore\ 15 : 9 :: x : (x - 6) \Leftrightarrow 15(x - 6) = 9x \Leftrightarrow 6x = 90 \Leftrightarrow x = 15.$

20. After 25 days, 35 men complete the work in 12 days.

Thus, 35 men can finish the remaining work in 12 days.

$\therefore$ 30 men can do it in $\frac{(12 \times 35)}{30}$ = 14 days, which is **1 day behind.**

~~~~~~
~~~~~~

14. TIME AND WORK

If 'M_1' persons can do 'W_1' works in 'D_1' days and 'M_2' persons can do 'W_2' works in 'D_2' days then we have a very general formula in the relationship of

$\mathbf{M_1D_1W_2 = M_2D_2W_1}$.

The above relationship can be taken as a very basic and all-in-one formula. We also derive.

1. *More men less days* and conversely *more days less men.*
2. *More men more work* and conversely *more work more men.*
3. *More days more work work* and conversely *more work more days.*

If we include the working hours (say T_1 and T_2) for the two groups. then the relationship is

$$\mathbf{M_1D_1T_1W_2 = M_2D_2T_2W_1}$$

Again, if the efficiency (say E1 and E2) of the persons in two groups is different then the relationship is

$$\mathbf{M_1D_1T_1E_1W_2 = M_2D_2T_2E_2W_1}$$

SOLVED EXAMPLE

1. Worker A takes 8 hours to do a job. Worker B takes 10 hours to do the same job. How long should it take both A and B, working together but independently, to do the same job?

Sol. A's 1 hour's work $= \frac{1}{8}$, B's 1 hour's work $= \frac{1}{10}$.

(A' + B)'s 1 hour's work $= \left(\frac{1}{8} + \frac{1}{10}\right) = \frac{9}{40}$.

$\therefore$ Both A and B will finish the work in $\frac{40}{9} = 4\frac{4}{9}$ days.

2. A and B together can complete a piece of work in 4 days. If A alone can complete the same work in 12 days, in how many days can B alone complete that work?

Sol. (A + B)'s 1 day's work $= \frac{1}{4}$, A's 1 day's work $= \frac{1}{12}$.

$\therefore$ B's 1 day's work $= \left(\frac{1}{4} - \frac{1}{12}\right) = \frac{1}{6}$.

Hence, B alone can complete the work in 6 days.

3. A is twice as good a workman as B and together they finish a piece of work in 18 days. In how many days will A alone finish the work?

Sol. (A's 1 day's work) : (B's 1 day's work) = 2 : 1.

$$\text{(A + B)'s 1 day's work} = \frac{1}{18}.$$

Divide $\frac{1}{18}$ in the ratio 2 : 1.

$$\therefore \quad \text{A's 1 day's work} = \left(\frac{1}{18} \times \frac{2}{3}\right) = \frac{1}{27}.$$

Hence, A alone can finish the work in 27 days.

EXERCISE

1. A and B can together finish a work in 30 days. They worked together for 20 days and then B left. After another 20 days, A finished the remaining work. In how many days A alone can finish the job?
   (*a*) 40 (*b*) 50 (*c*) 54 (*d*) 60
2. A, B and C are employed to do a piece of work for ₹ 529. A and B together are supposed to do $\frac{19}{23}$ of the work and B and C together $\frac{8}{23}$ of the work. What amount should A be paid?
   (*a*) ₹ 315 (*b*) ₹ 345 (*c*) ₹ 355 (*d*) ₹ 375
3. A tyre has two punctures. The first puncture alone would have made the tyre flat in 9 minutes and the second alone would have done it in 6 minutes. If air leaks out at a constant rate, how long does it take both the punctures together to make it flat?
   (*a*) $1\frac{1}{2}$ minutes (*b*) $3\frac{1}{2}$ minutes (*c*) $3\frac{3}{5}$ minutes (*d*) $4\frac{1}{4}$ minutes
4. Kim can do a work in 3 days while David can do the same work in 2 days. Both of them finish the work together and get ₹ 150. What is the share of Kim?
   (*a*) ₹ 30 (*b*) ₹ 60 (*c*) ₹ 70 (*d*) ₹ 75
5. A man can do a job in 15 days. His fattier takes 20 days and his son finishes it in 25 days. How long will they take to complete the job if they all work together?
   (*a*) Less than 6 days (*b*) Exactly 6 days
   (*c*) Approximately 6.4 days (*d*) More than 10 days

6. Sakshi can do a piece of work in 20 days. Tanya is 25% more efficient than Sakshi. The number of days taken by Tanya to do the same piece of work is:

(*a*) 15 (*b*) 16 (*c*) 18 (*d*) 25

7. A and B can do. a work in 12 days, B and C in 15 days, C and A in 20 days. If A, B and C work together, they will complete the work in:

(*a*) 5 days (*b*) $7\frac{5}{6}$ days (*c*) 10 days (*d*) $15\frac{2}{3}$ days

8. Ronald and Elan are working on an assignment. Ronald takes 6 hours to type 32 pages on a computer, while Elan takes 5 hours to type 40 pages. How much time will they take, working together on two different computers to type an assignment of 110 pages?

(*a*) 7 hours 30 minutes (*b*) 8 hours
(*c*) 8 hours 15 minutes (*d*) 8 hours 25 minutes

9. A and B can do a work in 8 days, B and C can do the same work in 12 days. A, B and C together can finish it in 6 days. A and C together will do it in:

(*a*) 4 days (*b*) 6 days (*c*) 8 days (*d*) 12 days

10. A takes twice as much time as B or thrice as much time as C to finish a piece of work. Working together, they can finish the work in 2 days. B can do the work alone in:

(*a*) 4 days (*b*) 6 days (*c*) 8 days (*d*) 12 days

11. P can complete a work in 12 days working 8 hours a day. Q can complete the same work in 8 days working 10 hours a day. If both P and Q work together, working 8 hours a day, in how many days can they complete the work?

(*a*) $5\frac{5}{11}$ (*b*) $5\frac{6}{11}$ (*c*) $6\frac{5}{11}$ (*d*) $6\frac{6}{11}$

12. A can do a piece of work in 4 hours; B and C together can do it in 3 hours, while A and C together can do it in 2 hours. How long will B alone take to do it?

(*a*) 8 hours (*b*) 10 hours (*c*) 12 hours (*d*) 24 hours

13. A can do a certain work in the same time in which B and C together can do it. If A and B together could do it in 10 days and C alone in 50 days, then B alone could do it in:

(*a*) 15 days (*b*) 20 days (*c*) 25 days (*d*) 30 days

14. A works twice as fast as B. If B can complete a work in 12 days independently, the number of days in which A and B can together finish the work is:

(*a*) 4 days (*b*) 6 days (*c*) 8 days (*d*) 18 days

15. A is thrice as good a workman as B and therefore is able to finish a job in 60 days less than B. Working together, they can do it in:

(*a*) 20 days (*b*) $22\frac{1}{2}$ days (*c*) 25 days (*d*) 30 days

16. A man can do a piece of work in 5 days, but with the help of his son, he can do it in 3 days. In what time can the son do it alone?

(*a*) $6\frac{1}{2}$ days (*b*) 7 days (*c*) $7\frac{1}{2}$ days (*d*) 8 days

17. A is 30% more efficient than B. How much time will they, working together, take to complete a job which A alone could have done in 23 days?

(*a*) 11 days (*b*) 13 days (*c*) $20\frac{3}{17}$ days (*d*) None of these

18. A can do a work in 15 days and B in 20 days. If they work on it together for 4 days, then the fraction of the work that is left is:

(*a*) $\frac{1}{4}$ (*b*) $\frac{1}{10}$ (*c*) $\frac{7}{15}$ (*d*) $\frac{8}{15}$

19. Twenty-four men can complete a work in sixteen days. Thirty-two women can complete the same work, in twenty-four days. Sixteen men and sixteen women started working and worked for twelve days. How many more men are to be added to complete the remaining work in 2 days?

(*a*) 16 (*b*) 24 (*c*) 36 (*d*) 48

20. A man, a woman and a boy can complete a job in 3, 4 and 12 days respectively. How many boys must assist 1 man and 1 woman to complete the job in $\frac{1}{4}$ of a day?

(*a*) 1 (*b*) 4 (*c*) 19 (*d*) 41

21. 10 women can complete a work in 7 days and 10 children take 14 days to complete the work. How many days will 5 women and 10 children take to complete the work?

(*a*) 3 (*b*) 5

(*c*) 7 (*d*) Cannot be determined

22. 10 men can complete a piece of work in 15 days and 15 women can complete the same work in 12 days. If all the 10 men and 15 women work together, in how many days will the work get completed?

(*a*) 6 (*b*) $6\frac{1}{3}$ (*c*) $6\frac{2}{3}$ (*d*) $7\frac{2}{3}$

23. A and B can do a piece of work in 30 days, while B and C can do the same work in 24 days and C and A in 20 days. They all work together for 10 days when, B and C leave. How many days more will A take to finish the work?

(*a*) 18 days (*b*) 24 days (*c*) 30 days (*d*) 36 days

24. If 6 men and 8 boys can do a piece of work in 10 days while 26 men and 48 boys can do the same in 2 days, the time taken by 15 men and 20 boys in doing the same type of work will be :

(*a*) 4 days (*b*) 5 days (*c*) 6 days (*d*) 7 days

25. A does a work in 10 days and B does the same work in 15 days. In how many days they together will do the same work?

(*a*) 5 days (*b*) 6. days (*c*) 8 days (*d*) None of these

26. A, B and C can do a piece of work in 20, 30 and 60 days respectively. In how many days can A do the work if he is assisted by B and C on every third day?

(*a*) 12 days (*b*) 15 days (*c*) 16 days (*d*) 18 days

27. A does $\frac{4}{5}$ of a work in 20 days. He then calls in B and they together finish the remaining work in 3 days. How long B alone would take to do the whole work?

(*a*) 23 days (*b*) 37 days (*c*) $37\frac{1}{2}$ days (*d*) 40 days

28. If 12 men and 16 boys can do a piece of work in 5 days; 13 men and 24 boys can do it in 4 days, then the ratio of the daily work done by a man to that of a boy is :

(*a*) 2 : 1 (*b*) 3 : 1 (*c*) 3 : 2 (*d*) 5 : 4

29. A and B can do a piece of work in 45 days and 40 days respectively. They began to do the work together but A leaves after some days and then B completed the remaining work in 23 days. The number of days after which A left the work was :

(*a*) 6 (*b*) 8 (*c*) 9 (*d*) 12

30. Twenty women can do a work in sixteen days. Sixteen men can complete the same work in fifteen days. What is the ratio between the capacity of a man and a woman?

(*a*) 3 : 4 (*b*) 4 : 3
(*c*) 5 : 3 (*d*) Data inadequate

31. A can finish a work in 18 days and B can do the same work in half the time taken by A. Then, working together, what part of the same work they can finish in a day ?

(*a*) $\frac{1}{6}$ (*b*) $\frac{1}{9}$ (*c*) $\frac{2}{5}$ (*d*) $\frac{3}{7}$

32. A, B and C can complete a piece of work in 24, 6 and 12 days respectively. Working together, they will complete the same work in:

(*a*) $\frac{1}{24}$ day (*b*) $\frac{7}{24}$ day (*c*) $3\frac{3}{7}$ days (*d*) 4 days

33. A alone can do a piece of work in 6 days and B alone in 8 days. A and B undertook to do it for ₹ 3200. With the help of C, they completed the work in 3 days. How much is to be paid to C?

(*a*) ₹ 375 (*b*) ₹ 400 (*c*) ₹ 600 (*d*) ₹ 800

34. A and B together can complete a work in 12 days, A alone can complete it in 20 days. If B does the work only for half a day daily, then in how many days A and B together will complete the work?

(*a*) 10 days (*b*) 11 days (*c*) 15 days (*d*) 20 days

35. A alone can complete a work in 16 days and B alone in 12 days. Starting with A, they work on alternate days. The total work will be completed in:

(*a*) 12 days (*b*) 13 days (*c*) $13\frac{5}{7}$ days (*d*) $13\frac{3}{4}$ days

36. X can do a piece of work in 40 days. He works at it for 8 days and then Y finished it in 16 days. How long will they together take to complete the work?

(*a*) $13\frac{1}{3}$ days (*b*) 15 days (*c*) 20 days (*d*) 56 days

37. A can do a piece of work in 14 days which B can do in 31 days. They begin together but 3 days before the completion of the work, A leaves off. The total number of days to complete the work is:

(*a*) $6\frac{3}{5}$ (*b*) $8\frac{1}{2}$ (*c*) $10\frac{1}{5}$ (*d*) $13\frac{1}{2}$

38. A machine P can print one lakh books in 8 hours, machine Q can print the same number of books in 10 hours while machine R can print them in 12 hours. All the machines are started at 9 a.m. while machine P is closed at 11 a.m. and the remaining two machines complete the work. Approximately at what time will the work be finished?

(*a*) 11: 30 a.m. (*b*) 12 noon (*c*) 12:30 p.m. (*d*) 1 p.m.

39. 12 men can complete a piece of work in 4 days, while 15 women can complete the same work in 4 days. 6 men start working on the job and after working for 2 days, all of them stopped working. How many women should be put on the job to complete the remaining work, if it is to be completed in 3 days?

(*a*) 15 (*b*) 18 (*c*) 22 (*d*) Data inadequate

40. Three men, four women and six children can complete a work in seven days. A woman does double the work a man does and a child does half the work a man does. How many women alone can complete this work in 7 days?

(*a*) 7 (*d*) 8

(*c*) 12 (*d*) Cannot be determined

41. A and B can complete a work in 15 days and 10 days respectively. They started doing the work together but after 2 days B had to leave and A alone completed the remaining work. The whole work was completed in:

(*a*) 8 days (*b*) 10 days (*c*) 12 days (*d*) 15 days

42. 10 men and 15 women together can complete a work in 6 days. It takes 100 days for one man alone to complete the same work. How many days will be required for one woman alone to complete the same work?

(*a*) 90 (*b*) 125 (*c*) 145 (*d*) None of these

43. 12 men complete a work in 9 days. After they have worked for 6 days, 6 more men join them. How many days will they take to complete the remaining work?

(*a*) 2 days (*b*) 3 days (*c*) 4 days (*d*) 5 days

44. A can finish a work in 24 days, B in 9 days and C in 12 days. B and C start the work but are forced to leave after 3 days. The remaining work was done by A in:

(*a*) 5 days (*b*) 6 days (*c*) 10 days (*d*) $10\frac{1}{2}$ days

45. A can finish a work in 18 days and B can do the same work in 15 days. B worked for 10 days and left the job. In how many days, A alone can finish the remaining work?

(*a*) 5 (*b*) $5\frac{1}{2}$ (*c*) 6 (*d*) 8

46. A and B together can do a piece of work in 30 days. A having worked for 16 days, B finishes the remaining work alone in 44 days. In how many days shall B finish the whole work alone?

(*a*) 30 days (*b*) 40 days (*c*) 60 days (*d*) 70 days

47. X and Y can do a piece of work in 20 days and 12 days respectively. X started the work alone and then after 4 days Y joined him till the completion of the work. How long did the work last?

(*a*) 6 days (*b*) 10 days (*c*) 15 days (*d*) 20 days

ANSWERS

1	2	3	4	5	6	7	8	9	10
(*d*)	(*b*)	(*c*)	(*b*)	(*c*)	(*b*)	(*c*)	(*c*)	(*c*)	(*b*)
11	**12**	**13**	**14**	**15**	**16**	**17**	**18**	**19**	**20**
(*a*)	(*c*)	(*c*)	(*a*)	(*b*)	(*c*)	(*b*)	(*d*)	(*b*)	(*d*)
21	**22**	**23**	**24**	**25**	**26**	**27**	**28**	**29**	**30**
(*c*)	(*c*)	(*a*)	(*a*)	(*b*)	(*b*)	(*c*)	(*a*)	(*c*)	(*b*)
31	**32**	**33**	**34**	**35**	**36**	**37**	**38**	**39**	**40**
(*a*)	(*c*)	(*b*)	(*c*)	(*d*)	(*a*)	(*c*)	(*d*)	(*a*)	(*a*)
41	**42**	**43**	**44**	**45**	**46**	**47**			
(*c*)	(*d*)	(*a*)	(*c*)	(*c*)	(*c*)	(*b*)			

SOME SELECTED EXPLANATORY ANSWERS

1. (A + B)'s 20 days' work = $\left(\frac{1}{30} \times 20\right) = \frac{2}{3}$. Remaining work = $\left(1 - \frac{2}{3}\right) = \frac{1}{3}$.

Now, $\frac{1}{3}$ work is done by A in 20 days.

Whole work will be done by A in (20 × 3) = 60 days.

2. Work done by A = $\left(1 - \frac{8}{23}\right) = \frac{15}{23}$.

$\therefore$ A : (B + C) = $\frac{15}{23} : \frac{8}{23}$ = 15 : 8.

So, A's share = ₹ $\left(\frac{15}{23} \times 529\right)$ = ₹ 345.

3. 1 minute's work of both the punctures = $\left(\frac{1}{9} + \frac{1}{6}\right) = \frac{5}{18}$.

So, both the punctures will make the tyre flat in $\frac{18}{5} = 3\frac{3}{5}$ min.

4. Kim's wages : David's wages = Kim's 1 day's work : David's 1 day's work

$$= \frac{1}{3} \cdot \frac{1}{2} = 2 : 3.$$

$$\therefore \quad \text{Kim's share} = ₹ \left(\frac{2}{5} \times 150\right) = ₹ 60.$$

5. 1 day's work of the three persons $= \left(\frac{1}{15} + \frac{1}{20} + \frac{1}{25}\right) = \frac{47}{300}$.

So, all the three together will complete the work in $\frac{300}{47}$ 6.4 days.

6. Ratio of times taken by Sakshi and Tanya = 125 : 100 = 5 : 4.
Suppose Tanya takes x days to do the work.

$5 : 4 : : 20 : x \Rightarrow x = \left(\frac{4 \times 20}{5}\right) \Rightarrow x = 16$ days.

Hence, Tanya takes 16 days to complete the work.

7. (A + B)'s 1 day's work $= \frac{1}{12}$; (B + C)'s 1 day's work $= \frac{1}{15}$; (A + C)'s 1 day's work $= \frac{1}{20}$.

Adding, we get : 2(A + B + C)'s 1 day's work $= \left(\frac{1}{12} + \frac{1}{15} + \frac{1}{20}\right) = \frac{12}{60} = \frac{1}{5}$.

$\therefore$ (A + B + C)'s 1 day's work $= \frac{1}{10}$.

So, A, B and C together can complete the work in 10 days.

8. Number of pages typed by Ronald in 1 hour $= \frac{32}{6} = \frac{16}{3}$.

Number of pages typed by Elan in 1 hour $= \frac{40}{5} = 8$.

Number of pages typed by both in 1 hour $= \left(\frac{16}{3} + 8\right) = \frac{40}{3}$.

$\therefore$ Time taken by both to type 110 pages $= \left(110 \times \frac{3}{40}\right)$ hrs

$$= 8\frac{1}{4} \text{ hrs} = 8 \text{ hrs } 15, \text{ min.}$$

9. (A + B + C)'s 1 day's work = $\frac{1}{6}$; (A + B)'s 1 day's work = $\frac{1}{8}$;

(B + C)'s 1 day's work = $\frac{1}{12}$.

$\therefore$ (A + C)'s 1 day's work = $\left(2 \times \frac{1}{6}\right) - \left(\frac{1}{8} + \frac{1}{12}\right) = \left(\frac{1}{3} - \frac{5}{24}\right) = \frac{3}{24} = \frac{1}{8}$.

So, A and C together will do the work in 8 days.

10. Suppose A, B and C take x, $\frac{x}{2}$ and $\frac{x}{3}$ hours respectively to finish the work.

Then, $\left(\frac{1}{x} + \frac{2}{x} + \frac{3}{x}\right) = \frac{1}{2} \Rightarrow \frac{6}{x} = \frac{1}{2} \Rightarrow x = 12.$

So, B takes 6 hours to finish the work.

11. P can complete the work in (12 × 8) hrs. = 96 hrs.
Q can complete the work in (8 × 10) hrs. = 80 hrs.

$\therefore$ P's 1 hour's work = $\frac{1}{96}$ and Q's 1 hour's work = $\frac{1}{80}$.

(P + Q)'s 1 hour's work = $\left(\frac{1}{96} + \frac{1}{80}\right) = \frac{11}{480}$.

So, both P and Q will finish the work in $\left(\frac{11}{480}\right)$ hrs.

$\therefore$ Number of days of 8 hours each = $\left(\frac{480}{11} \times \frac{1}{8}\right) = \frac{60}{11}$ days = $5\frac{5}{11}$ days.

12. A's 1 hour's work = $\frac{1}{4}$; (B + C)'s 1 hour's work = $\frac{1}{3}$; (A + C)'s 1 hour's work = $\frac{1}{2}$.

(A + B + C)'s 1 hour's work = $\left(\frac{1}{4} + \frac{1}{3}\right) = \frac{7}{12}$.

B's 1 hour's work = $\left(\frac{7}{12} - \frac{1}{2}\right) = \frac{1}{12}$.

$\therefore$ B alone will take 12 hours to do the work.

13. (A + B)'s 1 day's work = $\frac{1}{10}$; C's 1 day's work = $\frac{1}{50}$.

(A + B + C)'s 1 day's work = $\left(\frac{1}{10} + \frac{1}{50}\right) = \frac{6}{50} = \frac{3}{25}$ ...(*i*)

Also, A's 1 day's work = (B + C)'s 1 day's work ...(*ii*)

From (*i*) and (*ii*), we get : 2 × (A's 1 day's work) = $\frac{3}{25}$.

$\Rightarrow$ A's 1 day's work = $\frac{3}{50}$.

$\therefore$ B's 1 day's work = $\left(\frac{1}{10} - \frac{3}{50}\right) = \frac{2}{50} = \frac{1}{25}$.

So, B alone could do the work in 25 days.

14. Ratio of rates of working of A and B = 2 : 1. So, ratio of times taken = 1 : 2.

$\therefore$ A's 1 day's work = $\frac{1}{6}$; B's 1 day's work = $\frac{1}{12}$.

(A + B)'s 1 day's work = $\left(\frac{1}{6} + \frac{1}{12}\right) = \frac{3}{12} = \frac{1}{4}$.

So, A and B together can finish the work in 4 days.

15. Ratio of times taken by A and B = 1 : 3.
If difference of time is 2 days, B takes 3 days.

If difference of time is 60 days, B takes $\left(\frac{3}{2} \times 60\right)$ = 90 days.

So, A takes 30 days to do the work.

A's 1 day's work = $\frac{1}{30}$, B's 1 day's work = $\frac{1}{90}$.

(A + B)'s 1 day's work = $\left(\frac{1}{30} + \frac{1}{90}\right) = \frac{4}{90} = \frac{2}{45}$.

$\therefore$ A and B together can do the work in $\frac{45}{2} = 22\frac{1}{2}$ days.

16. Son's 1 day's work = $\left(\frac{1}{3} - \frac{1}{5}\right) = \frac{2}{15}$.

$\therefore$ The son alone can do the work in $\frac{15}{2} = 7\frac{1}{2}$ days.

17. Ratio of times taken by A and B = 100 : 130 = 10 : 13.
Suppose B takes x days to do the work.

Then, 10 : 13 : : 23 : x $\Rightarrow x = \left(\frac{23 \times 13}{10}\right) \Rightarrow x = \frac{299}{10}$.

A's 1 day's work $= \frac{1}{23}$; B's 1 days work $= \frac{10}{299}$.

(A + B)'s 1 day's work $= \left(\frac{1}{23} + \frac{10}{299}\right) = \frac{23}{299} = \frac{1}{13}$.

$\therefore$ A and B together can complete the job in 13 days.

18. A's 1 day's work $= \frac{1}{15}$; B's 1 day's work $= \frac{1}{20}$.

(A + B)'s 1 day's work $= \left(\frac{1}{15} + \frac{1}{20}\right) = \frac{7}{60}$.

(A + B)'s 4 days' work $= \left(\frac{7}{60} \times 4\right) = \frac{7}{15}$.

$\therefore$ Remaining work $= \left(1 - \frac{7}{15}\right) = \frac{8}{15}$.

19. 1 man's 1 day's work $= \frac{1}{384}$; 1 woman's 1 day's work $= \frac{1}{768}$.

Work done in 12 days $= 12\left(\frac{16}{384} + \frac{1}{768}\right) = \left(12 \times \frac{3}{48}\right) = \frac{3}{4}$.

Remaining work $= \left(1 - \frac{3}{4}\right) = \frac{1}{4}$.

20. (1 man + 1 woman)'s 1 day's work $= \left(\frac{1}{3} + \frac{1}{4}\right) = \frac{7}{12}$.

Work done by 1 man and 1 woman in $\frac{1}{4}$ day $= \left(\frac{7}{12} \times \frac{1}{4}\right) = \frac{7}{48}$.

Remaining work $= \left(1 - \frac{7}{48}\right) = \frac{41}{48}$.

Work done by 1 boy in $\frac{1}{4}$ day $= \left(\frac{1}{12} \times \frac{1}{4}\right) = \frac{1}{48}$.

$\therefore$ Number of boys required $= \left(\frac{41}{48} \times 48\right) = 41$.

21. 1 woman's 1 day's work $= \frac{1}{70}$; 1 child's 1 day's work $= \frac{1}{140}$.

(5 women + 10 children)'s 1 day's work $= \left(\frac{5}{70} + \frac{10}{140}\right) = \left(\frac{1}{14} + \frac{1}{14}\right) = \frac{1}{7}$.

$\therefore$ 5 women and 10 children will complete the work in 7 days.

22. 10 men's 1 day's work $= \frac{1}{15}$; 15 women's 1 day's work $= \frac{1}{12}$.

(10 men + 15 momen)'s 1 day's work $= \left(\frac{1}{15} + \frac{1}{12}\right) = \frac{9}{60} = \frac{3}{20}$.

$\therefore$ (10 men and 15 women will complete the work in $\frac{3}{20} = 6\frac{2}{3}$ days.

23. 2(A + B + C)'s 1 day's work $= \left(\frac{1}{30} + \frac{1}{24} + \frac{1}{20}\right) = \frac{15}{120} = \frac{1}{8}$.

$\Rightarrow$ (A + B + C)'s 1 day's work $= \frac{1}{16}$.

Work done by A, B and C in 10 days $= \frac{10}{16} = \frac{5}{8}$.

Remaining work $= \left(1 - \frac{5}{8}\right) = \frac{3}{8}$.

A's 1 day's work $\left(\frac{1}{16} - \frac{1}{24}\right) = \frac{1}{48}$.

Now, $\frac{1}{48}$ work is done by A in 1 day.

So, $\frac{3}{8}$ work will be done by A in $\left(48 \times \frac{3}{8}\right) = 18$ days.

24. Let 1 man's 1 day's work = x and 1 boy's 1 day's work = y.

Then, $6x + 8y = \frac{1}{10}$ and $26x + 48y = \frac{1}{2}$.

25. A's 1 day's work $= \frac{1}{10}$ and B's 1 day's work $= \frac{1}{15}$.

$\therefore$ (A + B)'s 1 day's work $= \left(\frac{1}{10} + \frac{1}{15}\right) = \frac{1}{6}$.

So, both together will finish the work in 6 days.

26. A's 2 days' work $= \left(\frac{1}{20} \times 2\right) = \frac{1}{10}$.

(A + B + C)'s. 1 day's work $= \left(\frac{1}{20} + \frac{1}{30} + \frac{1}{60}\right) = \frac{6}{60} = \frac{1}{10}$.

Work done in 3 days $= \left(\frac{1}{10} + \frac{1}{10}\right) = \frac{1}{5}$.

Now, $\frac{1}{5}$ work is done in 3 days.

$\therefore$ Whole work will be done in $(3 \times 5) = 15$ days.

27. Whole work is done by A in $\left(20 \times \frac{5}{4}\right) = 25$ days.

Now, $\left(1 - \frac{4}{5}\right)$ *i.e.*, $\frac{1}{5}$ work is done by A and B in 3 days.

Whole work will be done by A and B in $(3 \times 5) = 15$ days.

A's 1 day's work $= \frac{1}{25}$, (A + B)'s 1 day's work $= \frac{1}{15}$.

$\therefore$ B's 1 day's work $= \left(\frac{1}{15} - \frac{1}{25}\right) = \frac{4}{150} = \frac{2}{75}$.

So, B alone would do the work in $\frac{75}{2} = 37\frac{1}{2}$ days.

28. Let 1 man's 1 day's work $= x$ and 1 boy's 1 day's work $= y$.

Then, $12x + 16y = \frac{1}{5}$ and $13x + 24y = \frac{1}{4}$.

Solving these two equations, we get : $x = \frac{1}{100}$ and $y = \frac{1}{200}$.

$\therefore$ Required ratio $= x : y = \frac{1}{100} : \frac{1}{200} = 2 : 1$.

29. (A+B)'s 1 day's work $= \left(\frac{1}{45} + \frac{1}{40}\right) = \frac{17}{360}$.

Work done by B in 23 days $= \left(\frac{1}{45} + \frac{1}{40}\right) = \frac{17}{360}$.

Remaining work $= \left(1 - \frac{23}{40}\right) = \frac{17}{40}$.

Now, $\frac{17}{360}$ work was done by (A + B) in 1 day.

$\frac{17}{360}$ work was done by (A + B) in $\left(1 \times \frac{360}{17} \times \frac{17}{40}\right) = 9$ days.

$\therefore$ A left after 9 days.

30. (20×16) women can complete the work in 1 day.

$\therefore$ 1 woman's 1 day's work $= \frac{1}{320}$.

(16 × 15) men can complete the work in 1 day.

$\therefore$ 1 man'.s 1 day's work = $\frac{1}{240}$.

So, required ratio = $\frac{1}{240} : \frac{1}{320} = 4 : 3$.

31. A's 1 day's work = $\frac{1}{18}$ and B's 1 day's work = $\frac{1}{9}$.

$\therefore$ (A + B)'s 1 day's work = $\left(\frac{1}{18} + \frac{1}{9}\right) = \frac{1}{6}$.

32. (A + B + C)'s 1 day's work = $\left(\frac{1}{24} + \frac{1}{6} + \frac{1}{12}\right) = \frac{7}{24}$.

So, A, B and C together will complete the job in $\frac{24}{7} = 3\frac{3}{7}$ days.

33. C's 1 days work = $\frac{1}{3} - \left(\frac{1}{6} + \frac{1}{8}\right) = \frac{1}{3} - \frac{7}{24} = \frac{1}{24}$.

A's wages : B's wages : C's wages = $\frac{1}{6} : \frac{1}{8} : \frac{1}{24} = 4 : 3 : 1$.

$\therefore$ C's share = ₹ $\left(\frac{1}{8} \times 3200\right)$ = ₹ 400.

34. B's 1 day's work = $\left(\frac{1}{12} - \frac{1}{20}\right) = \frac{6}{20} = \frac{1}{30}$.

Now, (A + B)'s 1 day's work = $\left(\frac{1}{20} + \frac{1}{60}\right) = \frac{4}{60} = \frac{1}{15}$.

[$\because$ B works for half day only]

So, A and B together will complete the work in 15 days.

35. (A + B) 2 days' work = $\left(\frac{1}{16} + \frac{1}{12}\right) = \frac{7}{48}$.

Work done in 6 pairs of days = $\left(\frac{7}{48} \times 6\right) = \frac{7}{8}$.

Remaining work = $\left(1 - \frac{7}{8}\right) = \frac{1}{8}$.

Work done by A on 13th day = $\frac{1}{16}$. Remaining work = $\left(\frac{1}{8} - \frac{1}{16}\right) = \frac{1}{16}$.

On 14th day, it is B's turn.

$\frac{1}{12}$ work is done by B in 1 day. $\frac{1}{16}$ work is done by B in $\left(12 \times \frac{1}{16}\right) = \frac{3}{4}$ day.

$\therefore$ Total time taken = $13\frac{3}{4}$ days.

36. Work done by X in 8 days = $\left(\frac{1}{40} \times 8\right) = \frac{1}{5}$. Remaining work = $\left(1 - \frac{1}{5}\right) = \frac{4}{5}$.

Now, $\frac{4}{5}$ work is done by Y in 16 days.

Whole work will be done by Y in $\left(16 \times \frac{5}{4}\right)$ = 20 days.

$\therefore$ X's 1 day's work = $\frac{1}{40}$, Ys 1 day's work = $\frac{1}{20}$.

(X + Y)'s 1 day's work = $\left(\frac{1}{40} + \frac{1}{20}\right) = \frac{3}{40}$.

Hence, X and Y will together complete the work in = $\frac{40}{3} = 13\frac{1}{3}$ days.

37. B's 3 days' work = $\left(\frac{1}{21} \times 3\right) = \frac{1}{7}$. Remaining work = $\left(1 - \frac{1}{7}\right) = \frac{6}{7}$.

(A + B)'s 1 day's work = $\left(\frac{1}{14} + \frac{1}{21}\right) = \frac{5}{42}$.

Now, $\frac{5}{42}$ work is done by A and B in 1 day.

$\therefore$ $\frac{6}{7}$ work is done by A and B in $\left(\frac{42}{5} \times \frac{6}{7}\right) = \frac{36}{5}$ days.

Hence, total time taken = $\left(3 + \frac{36}{5}\right)$ days = $10\frac{1}{5}$ days.

38. (P + Q + R)'s 1 hour's work = $\left(\frac{1}{8} + \frac{1}{10} + \frac{1}{12}\right) = \frac{37}{120}$.

Work done by P, Q and R in 2 hours = $\left(\frac{37}{120} \times 2\right) = \frac{37}{60}$.

Remaining work = $\left(1 - \frac{37}{60}\right) = \frac{23}{60}$.

(Q + R)'s 1 hour's work = $\left(\frac{1}{10} + \frac{1}{12}\right) = \frac{11}{60}$.

Now, $\frac{11}{60}$ work is done by Q and R in 1 hour.

So, $\frac{23}{60}$ work will be done by Q and R in $\left(\frac{60}{11} \times \frac{23}{60}\right) = \frac{23}{11}$ hours $\approx$ 2 hours.

So, the work will be finished approximately 2 hours after 11 a.m., *i.e.*, around 1 p.m.

39. 1 man's 1 day's work $= \frac{1}{48}$; 1 woman's 1 day's work $= \frac{1}{60}$.

6 men's 2 days' work $= \left(\frac{6}{48} \times 2\right) = \frac{1}{4}$. Remaining work $= \left(1 - \frac{1}{4}\right) = \frac{3}{4}$.

Now, $\frac{1}{60}$ work is done in 1 day by 1 woman.

So, $\frac{3}{4}$ work will be done in 3 days by $\left(60 \times \frac{3}{4} \times \frac{1}{3}\right)$ = 15 women.

40. Let 1 woman's 1 day's work = x.

Then, 1 man's 1 day's work $= \frac{x}{2}$ and 1 child's 1 day's work $= \frac{x}{4}$.

So, $\left(\frac{3x}{2} + 4x + \frac{6x}{4}\right) = \frac{1}{7} \Rightarrow \frac{28x}{4} = \frac{1}{7} \Rightarrow x = \left(\frac{1}{7} \times \frac{4}{28}\right) = \frac{1}{49}$.

$\therefore$ 1 woman alone can complete the work in 49 days.

So, to complete the work in 7 days, number of women required $= \left(\frac{49}{7}\right) = 7$.

41. (A + B)'s 1 day's work $= \left(\frac{1}{15} + \frac{1}{10}\right) = \frac{1}{6}$.

Work done by A and B in 2 days $= \left(\frac{1}{6} \times 2\right) = \frac{1}{3}$.

Remaining work $= \left(1 - \frac{1}{3}\right) = \frac{2}{3}$.

Now, $\frac{1}{15}$ work is done by A in 1 day.

$\therefore$ $\frac{2}{3}$ work will be done by A in $\left(15 \times \frac{2}{3}\right)$ = 10 days.

Hence, total time taken = (10 + 2) = 12 days.

42. 1 man's 1 day's work = $\frac{1}{100}$. (10 men + 15 women)'s 1 day's work = $\frac{1}{6}$.

15 women's 1 day's work = $\left(\frac{1}{6}-\frac{10}{100}\right)=\left(\frac{1}{6}-\frac{1}{10}\right)=\frac{1}{15}$.

1 woman's 1 day's work = $\frac{1}{225}$.

$\therefore$ 1 woman alone can complete the work in 225 days.

43. 1 man's 1 day's work = $\frac{1}{108}$.

12 men's 6 days' work = $\left(\frac{1}{9}\times 6\right)=\frac{2}{3}$. Remaining work = $\left(1-\frac{2}{3}\right)=\frac{1}{3}$.

18 men's 1 day's work = $\left(\frac{1}{108}\times 18\right)=\frac{1}{6}$.

$\frac{1}{6}$ work is done by them in 1 day.

$\therefore$ $\frac{1}{3}$ work is dbne by thcm in $\left(6\times\frac{1}{3}\right)$ = 2 days.

44. (B + C)'s 1 day's work = $\left(\frac{1}{9}+\frac{1}{12}\right)=\frac{7}{36}$.

Work done by B and C in 3 days = $\left(\frac{7}{36}\times 3\right)=\frac{7}{12}$.

Remaining work = $\left(1-\frac{7}{12}\right)=\frac{5}{12}$.

Now, $\frac{1}{24}$ work is done by A in 1 day.

So, $\frac{5}{12}$ work is xlofle by A in $\left(24\times\frac{5}{12}\right)$ = 10 days.

45. B's 10 days' work = $\left(\frac{1}{15}\times 10\right)=\frac{2}{3}$. Remaining work = $\left(1-\frac{2}{3}\right)=\frac{1}{3}$.

Now, $\frac{1}{18}$ work is done by A in 1 day.

$\therefore$ $\frac{1}{3}$ work is done by A in $\left(18\times\frac{1}{3}\right)$ = 6 days.

46. Let A's 1 day's work = x and B's 1 day's work = y.

Then, $x + y = \frac{1}{30}$ and $16x + 44y = 1$.

Solving these two equations, we get : $x = \frac{1}{60}$ and $y = \frac{1}{60}$.

$\therefore$ B's 1 day's work = $\frac{1}{60}$.

Hence, B alone shall finish the whole work in 60 days.

47. Work done by X in 4 days = $\left(\frac{1}{20} \times 4\right) = \frac{1}{5}$.

Remaining work = $\left(1 - \frac{1}{5}\right) = \frac{4}{5}$.

(X + Y)'s 1 day's work = $\left(\frac{1}{20} + \frac{1}{12}\right) = \frac{8}{60} = \frac{2}{15}$.

Now, $\frac{2}{15}$ work is done by X and Y in 1 day.

So, $\frac{4}{5}$ work will be done by X and Y in $\left(\frac{15}{2} \times \frac{4}{5}\right)$ = 6 days.

Hence, total time taken = (6 + 4) days = 10 days.

~~~~~~
~~~~~~

15. PIPES AND CISTERNS

Pipes and Cisterns problems are almost the same as those of Time and Work problems. Thus, if a pipe fills a tank in 6 hrs, then the pipe fills $\frac{1}{6}$th of the tank in 1 hour. The only difference with Pipes and Cisterns problems is that there are outlets as well as inlets. Thus, there are agents (the outlets) which perform negative work too. The rest of the process is almost similar.

Inlet: A pipe connected with a tank (or a cistern or a reservoir) is called an inlet, if it fills it.

Outlet: A pipe connected with a tank is called an **outlet,** if it empties it.

FORMULAE:

(*i*) If a pipe can fill a tank in x hours, then the part filled in 1 hour $= \frac{1}{x}$.

(*ii*) If a pipe can empty a tank in y hours, then the part of the full tank emptied in 1 hour $= \frac{1}{y}$.

(*iii*) If a pipe can fill a tank in x hours and another pipe can empty the full tank in y hours, then the net part filled in 1 hour, when both the pipes are opened $= \left(\frac{1}{x} - \frac{1}{y}\right)$.

$\therefore$ time taken to fill the tank, when both the pipes are opened $= \frac{xy}{y - x}$

(*iv*) If a pipe can fill a tank in x hrs and another can fill the same tank in y hrs, then the net part filled in 1 hr, when both the pipes are opened $= \left(\frac{1}{x} + \frac{1}{y}\right)$.

$\therefore$ time taken to fill the tank $= \frac{xy}{y + x}$

(*v*) If a pipe fills a tank in x hrs and another fills the same tank in y hrs, but a third one empties the full tank in z hrs, and all of them are opened together, the net part filled in 1 hr $= \left[\frac{1}{x} + \frac{1}{y} - \frac{1}{z}\right]$

$\therefore$ time taken to fill the tank $= \frac{xyz}{yz + xz - xy}$ hrs.

(*vi*) A pipe can fill a tank in x hrs. Due to a leak in the bottom it is filled in y hrs. If the tank is full, the time taken by the leak to empty the tank $= \frac{xy}{y-x}$ hrs.

SOLVED EXAMPLE

1. Pipe A can fill a tank in 20 hours while pipe B alone can fill it in 30 hours and pipe C can empty the full tank in 40 hours. If all the pipes are opened together, how much time will be needed to make the tank full?

Sol. Net part filled in 1 hour $= \left(\frac{1}{20} + \frac{1}{30} - \frac{1}{40}\right) = \frac{7}{120}$.

$\therefore$ The tank will be full in $\frac{120}{7}$ *i.e.*, $17\frac{1}{7}$ hours.

2. Two pipes A and B can fill a tank in 24 minutes and 32 minutes respectively. If both the pipes are opened simultaneously, after how much time should B be closed so that the tank is full in 18 minutes?

Sol. Let B be closed after x munutes. Then, part filled by (A + B) in x min. + part filled by A in $(18 - x)$ min. = 1.

$$\therefore \quad x\left(\frac{1}{24} + \frac{1}{32}\right) + (18 - x) \times \frac{1}{24} = 1$$

or $\frac{7x}{96} + \frac{18 - x}{24} = 1$ or $7x + 4(18 - x) = 96$

or, $3x = 24 \quad \therefore \quad x = 8$.

So, B should be closed after 8 min.

3. Three pipes A, B and C can fill a cistern in 6 hrs. After working together for 2 hours, C is closed and A and B fill the cistern in 8 hrs. Then find the time in which the cistern can be filled by pipe C.

Sol. A + B + C can fill in 1 hr $= \frac{1}{6}$ of cistern.

A + B + C can fill in 2 hrs $= \frac{2}{6} = \frac{1}{3}$ of cistern.

Unfilled part $= \left(1 - \frac{1}{3} = \right)\frac{2}{3}$ is filled by A + B in 8 hrs.

$\therefore$ (A + B) can fill the cistern in $\frac{8 \times 3}{2} = 12$ hrs.

And we have (A + B + C) can fill the cistern in 6 hrs.

$\therefore$ C = (A + B + C) – (A + B) can fill the cistern in $\dfrac{12 \times 6}{12 - 6} = 12$ hrs.

EXERCISE

1. Pipe A can fill a tank in 5 hours, pipe B in 10 hours and pipe C in 30 hours. If all the pipes are open, in how many hours will the tank be filled?
(*a*) 1.5 hours (*b*) 2.5 hours (*c*) 3 hours (*d*) 3.5 hours

2. Two pipes A and B together can fill a cistern in 4 hours. Had they been opened separately, then B would have taken 6 hours more than A to fill the cistern. How much time will be taken by A to fill the cistern separately?
(*a*) 1 hr (*b*) 2 hrs (*c*) 6 hrs (*d*) 8 hrs

3. Two pipes A and B can separately fill a cistern in 60 minutes and 75 minutes respectively. There is a third pipe in the bottom of the cistern to empty it, If all the three pipes are simultaneously opened, then the cistern is full in 50 minutes. In how much time the third pipe alone can empty the cistern?
(*a*) 90 min (*b*) 100 min (*c*) 110 min (*d*) 120 min

4. Two pipes can fill a tank in 20 and 24 minutes respectively and a waste pipe can empty 3 gallons per minute. All the three pipes working together can fill the tank in 15 minutes. The capacity of the tank is :
(*a*) 60 gallons (*b*) 100 gallons (*c*) 120 gallons (*d*) 180 gallons

5. Three taps A, B and C can fill a tank in 12, 15 and 20 hours respectively. If A is open all the time and B and C are open for one hour each alternately, the tank will be full in:
(*a*) 6 hrs (*b*) $6\frac{2}{3}$ hrs (*c*) 7 hrs (*d*) $7\frac{1}{2}$ hrs

6. Pipes A and B can fill a tank in 5 and 6 hours respectively. Pipe C can empty it in 12 hours. If all the three pipes are opened together, then the tank will be filled in:
(*a*) $1\frac{13}{17}$ hours (*b*) $2\frac{8}{11}$ hours (*c*) $3\frac{9}{17}$ hours (*d*) $4\frac{1}{2}$ hours

7. Two pipes A and B can fill a tank in 15 minutes and 20 minutes respectively. Both the pipes are opened together but after 4 minutes, pipe A is turned off. What is the total time required to fill the tank?
(*a*) 10 min 20 sec (*b*) 11 min 45 sec
(*c*) 12 min-30 sec (*d*) None of these

8. A tap can fill a tank in 6 hours. After half the tank is filled, three more similar taps are opened. What is the total time taken to fill the tank, completely?

(*a*) 3 hrs 15 min (*b*) 3 hrs 45 min
(*c*) 4 hrs (*d*) 4 hrs 15 min

9. A large tanker can be filled by two pipes A and B in 60 minutes and 40 minutes respectively. How many minutes will it take to fill the tanker from empty state if B is used for half the time and A and B fill it together for the other half?

(*a*) 15 min (*b*) 20 min (*c*) 27.5 min (*d*) 30 min

10. Two pipes A and B can fill a tank in 20 and 30 minutes respectively. If both the pipes are used together, then how long will it take to fill the tank?

(*a*) 12 min (*b*) 15 min (*c*) 25 min (*d*) 50 min

11. Two pipes A and B can fill a cistern in $37\frac{1}{2}$ minutes and 45 minutes respectively. Both pipes are opened. The cistern will be filled in just half an hour, if the pipe B is turned off after :

(*a*) 5 min (*b*) 9 min (*c*) 10 min (*d*) 15 min

12. A tank is filled in 5 hours by three pipes A, B and C. The pipe C is twice as fast as B and B is twice as fast as A. How much time will pipe A alone take to fill the tank?

(*a*) 20 hrs (*b*) 25 hrs (*c*) 35 hrs (*d*) None of these

13. Three pipes A, B and C can fill a tank in 6 hours. After working at it together for 2 hours, C is closed and A and B can fill the remaining part in 7 hours. The number of hours taken by C alone to fill the tank is:

(*a*) 10 hours (*b*) 12 hours (*c*) 14 hours (*d*) 16 hours

14. A pump can fill a tank with water in 2 hours. Because of a leak, it took $2\frac{1}{3}$ hours to fill the tank. The leak can drain all the water of the tank in:

(*a*) $4\frac{1}{3}$ hrs (*b*) 7 hrs (*c*) 8 hrs (*d*) None of these

15. Three pipes A, B and C can fill a tank from empty to full in 30 minutes, 20 minutes and 10 minutes respectively. When the tank is empty, all the three pipes are opened. A, B and C discharge chemical solutions P, Q and R respectively. What is the proportion of solution R in the liquid in the tank after 3 minutes?

(*a*) $\frac{5}{11}$ (*b*) $\frac{6}{11}$ (*c*) $\frac{7}{11}$ (*d*) $\frac{8}{11}$

16. A cistern can be filled by a tap in 4 hours while it car be emptied by another tap in 9 hours. If both the taps are opened simultaneously then after how much time will the cistern get filled?

(*a*) 4.5 hrs (*b*) 5 hrs (*c*) 6.5 hrs (*d*) 7.2 hrs

17. A water tank is two-fifth full. Pipe A can fill a tank in 10 minutes and pipe B can empty it in 6 minutes. If both the pipes are open, how long will it take to empty or fill the tank completely?

(*a*) 6 min. to empty (*b*) 6 min. to fill
(*c*) 9 min. to empty (*d*) 9 min. to fill

18. A tank is filled by three pipes with uniform flow. The first two pipes operating simultaneously fill the tank in the same time during which the tank is filled by the third pipe alone. The second pipe fills the tank 5 hours faster than the first pipe and 4 hours slower than the third pipe. The time required by the first pipe is:

(*a*) 6 hrs (*b*) 10 hrs (*c*) 15 hrs (*d*) 30 hrs

19. One pipe can fill a tank three times as fast as another pipe. If together the two pipes can fill the tank in 36 minutes, then the slower pipe alone will be able to fill the tank in:

(*a*) 8.1 min (*b*) 108 min (*c*) 144 min (*d*) 192 min

ANSWERS

1	2	3	4	5	6	7	8	9	10
(*c*)	(*c*)	(*b*)	(*c*)	(*c*)	(*c*)	(*d*)	(*b*)	(*d*)	(*a*)
11	**12**	**13**	**14**	**15**	**16**	**17**	**18**	**19**	
(*c*)	(*c*)	(*b*)	(*d*)	(*b*)	(*d*)	(*a*)	(*c*)	(*c*)	

SOME SELECTED EXPLANATORY ANSWERS

1. Part filled by (A + B + C) in 1 hour $= \left(\frac{1}{5}+\frac{1}{10}+\frac{1}{30}\right)=\frac{1}{3}$.

$\therefore$ All the three pipes together will fill the-tank in 3 hours.

2. Suppose that the pipe A alone is fill the tank in x hrs the cistern be filled by pipe A alone in x hours.

Then, pipe B will fill it in $(x + 6)$ hours.

$$\therefore \frac{1}{x}+\frac{1}{(x+6)}=\frac{1}{4} \Leftrightarrow \frac{x+6+x}{x(x+6)}=\frac{1}{4}$$

$$\Leftrightarrow x^2-2x-24=0 \Leftrightarrow (x-6)(x+4)=0$$

$$\Leftrightarrow x=6.$$

3. Work done by the third pipe in 1 min.

$$= \frac{1}{50} - \left(\frac{1}{60} + \frac{1}{75}\right) = \left(\frac{1}{50} - \frac{3}{100}\right) = -\frac{1}{100}.$$

$\therefore$ The third pipe alone can empty the cistern in 100 min.

4. Work done by the waste pipe in 1 minute

$$= \frac{1}{15} - \left(\frac{1}{20} + \frac{1}{24}\right) = \left(\frac{1}{15} - \frac{11}{120}\right) = -\frac{1}{40}.$$

$\therefore$ Volume of $\frac{1}{40}$ part = 3 gallons.

Volume of whole = (3 × 40) gallons = 120 gallons.

5. (A + B)'s 1 hour's work = $\left(\frac{1}{12} + \frac{1}{15}\right) = \frac{9}{60} = \frac{3}{20}.$

(A + C)'s 1 hour's work = $\left(\frac{1}{12} + \frac{1}{20}\right) = \frac{8}{60} = \frac{2}{15}.$

Part filled in 2 hrs = $\left(\frac{3}{20} + \frac{2}{15}\right) = \frac{17}{60};$

Part filled in 6 hrs = $\left(3 \times \frac{17}{60}\right) = \frac{17}{20}.$

Remaining part = $\left(1 - \frac{17}{20}\right) = \frac{3}{20}.$

Now, it is the turn of A and B and $\frac{3}{20}$ part is filled by A and B in 1 hour.

$\therefore$ Total time taken to fill the tank = (6 + 1) hrs = 7 hrs.

6. Part filled in 1 hour = $\left(\frac{1}{5} + \frac{1}{6} - \frac{1}{12}\right) = \frac{17}{60}.$

$\therefore$ The tank will be full in $\frac{60}{17}$ hrs *i.e.,* $3\frac{9}{17}$ hrs.

7. Part filled by together by together in 4 minutes = $4\left(\frac{1}{15} + \frac{1}{20}\right) = \frac{7}{15}.$

Remaining part = $\left(1 - \frac{7}{15}\right) = \frac{8}{15}.$

Part filled by B in 1 minute = $\frac{1}{20}$.

$\frac{1}{20} : \frac{8}{15} :: 1 : x$ or $x = \left(\frac{8}{15} \times 1 \times 20\right) = 10\frac{2}{3}$ min. = 10 min. 40 sec.

$\therefore$ The tank will be full in (4 min. + 10 min. 40 sec) = 14 min. 40 sec.

8. Time taken by one tap to fill half the tank = 3 hrs.

Part filled by the four taps in 1 hour = $\left(4 \times \frac{1}{6}\right) = \frac{2}{3}$.

From question, half tank is filled by first tap

So, Remaining part = $\left(1 - \frac{1}{2}\right) = \frac{1}{2}$.

$\therefore \frac{2}{3} : \frac{1}{2} :: 1 : x$ or $x = \left(\frac{1}{2} \times 1 \div \frac{3}{2}\right) = \frac{3}{4}$ hrs *i.e.*, 45 mins.

So, total time taken to fill full tank = 3 hrs 45 min.

9. Part filled by (A + B) in 1 minute = $\left(\frac{1}{60} + \frac{1}{40}\right) = \frac{1}{24}$.

Suppose the tank is filled in t minutes.

Then, $\frac{t}{2}\left(\frac{1}{24} + \frac{1}{40}\right) = 1 \Leftrightarrow \frac{t}{2} \times \frac{1}{15} = 1$

t = 30 min

Hence, the tank is filled in 30 mints.

10. Part filled by A in 1 min. = $\frac{1}{20}$;

Part filled by B in 1 min. = $\frac{1}{30}$.

Part filled by A and B together in 1 min. = $\left(\frac{1}{20} + \frac{1}{30}\right) = \frac{1}{12}$.

$\therefore$ Both the pipes can fill the tank in 12 minutes.

11. Part filled in 1 hours = $\frac{1}{6}$

Part filled in 2 hours = $\frac{2}{6} = \frac{1}{3}$,

Remaining part = $\left(1-\frac{1}{3}\right)=\frac{2}{3}$.

$\therefore$ (A + B)'s 7 hour's work = $\frac{2}{3}$; (A + B)'s 1 hour's work = $\frac{2}{21}$.

$\therefore$ C's 1 hour's work = [(A + B + C)'s 1 hour's work – (A + B)'s 1 hour's work]

$$=\left(\frac{1}{6}-\frac{2}{21}\right)=\frac{1}{14}.$$

$\therefore$ C alone can fill the tank in 14 hours.

12. Let the pipe A alone takes t hours to fill the tank.

Then, pipes B and C will take $\frac{t}{2}$ and $\frac{t}{4}$ hours respectively to fill the tank.
According to the question,

$$\therefore \quad \frac{1}{t}+\frac{2}{t}+\frac{4}{t}=\frac{1}{5} \quad \Leftrightarrow \quad \frac{7}{t}=\frac{1}{5} \quad \Leftrightarrow \quad t = 35 \text{ hrs.}$$

13. Suppose that the pipe B is turned off after x minutes. Then,
Part filled by pipe (A + B) in x min.
+ Part filled by pipe A in $(30 - x)$ min. = 1.

$$\therefore \quad x\left(\frac{2}{75}+\frac{1}{45}\right)+(30-x)\frac{2}{75}=1$$ {here, from question (A + B) fill $37\frac{1}{2}=\frac{75}{2}$ Part in 1 mints}

$$\Leftrightarrow \frac{11x}{225}+\frac{(60-2x)}{75}-1 \quad \Leftrightarrow \quad 11x+180-6x=225 \quad \Leftrightarrow x = 9 \text{ mints.}$$

14. Portion of the tank empty by the leak in 1 hour = $\left(\frac{1}{2}-\frac{3}{7}\right)=\frac{1}{14}$.

$\therefore$ Leak will empty the tank in 14 hrs.

15. Part filled by (A + B + C) in 3 minutes

$$=3\left(\frac{1}{30}+\frac{1}{20}+\frac{1}{10}\right)=\left(3\times\frac{11}{60}\right)=\frac{11}{20}.$$

Part filled by C in 3 minutes = $\frac{3}{10}$.

Hence, Required ratio = $\left(\frac{3}{10}\times\frac{20}{11}\right)=\frac{6}{11}$.

16. Part filled in 1 hour = $\left(\frac{1}{4}-\frac{1}{9}\right)=\frac{5}{36}$.

$\therefore$ The cistern will be filled in $\frac{36}{5}$ hrs *i.e.,* 7.2 hrs.

17. From question, pipe B is faster than pipe A and so, the tank will be emptied.

Part to be emptied = $\frac{2}{5}$.

Part emptied by (A + B) in 1 minute = $\left(\frac{1}{6}-\frac{1}{10}\right)=\frac{1}{15}$.

$\therefore \quad \frac{1}{15}:\frac{2}{5}::1:x \quad$ or $\quad x=\left(\frac{2}{5}\times 1\div\frac{1}{15}\right)$ = 6 min.

So, the tank will be emptied in 6 min.

19. Suppose that the slower pipe alone fill the tank in t minutes.

Then, faster pipe will fill it in $\frac{t}{3}$ minutes.

$\therefore \quad \frac{1}{t}+\frac{3}{t}=\frac{1}{36} \quad \Leftrightarrow \quad \frac{4}{t}=\frac{1}{36} \quad \Leftrightarrow \quad t = 144$ min.

~~~~~~
~~~~~~

16. TIME AND DISTANCE

Formulae

(*i*) Speed = $\frac{\text{Distance}}{\text{Time}}$ (*ii*) Time = $\frac{\text{Distance}}{\text{Speed}}$

(*iii*) Distance = Speed × Time

(*iv*) If the speed of a body is changed in the ratio $a : b$, then the ratio of the time taken changes in the ratio $b : a$.

(*v*) x km/hr = $\left(x \times \frac{5}{18}\right)$ m/sec.

(*vi*) x metres/sec = $\left(x \times \frac{18}{5}\right)$ km/hr.

If a certain distance is covered at x km/hr and the same further distance is covered at y km/hr then the average speed during the whole journey is $\frac{2xy}{x+y}$ km/hr.

Direct formula

1. Required distance

$$= \frac{\text{Product of two speeds}}{\text{Difference of two speeds}} \times \text{Difference between arrival times.}$$

2. Required distance = Total time taken × $\frac{\text{Product of the two speeds}}{\text{Addition of the two speeds}}$

3. Distance = $\frac{2 \times \text{Time} \times S_1 \times S_2}{S_1 + S_2}$

   Where S_1 = Speed during first half and
   S_2 = Speed during second half of journey

4. Meeting point's distance from starting point

$$= \frac{S_1 \times S_2 \times \text{Difference in time}}{\text{Difference in speed}}$$

   where S_1 and S_2 are the speeds of the first and the second trains respectively.

5. When the ratio of speeds of A and B is $a : b$, then in this case:

   Distance travelled by A = 2 × Distance of two points $\left(\frac{a}{a+b}\right)$

and distance travelled by B = 2 × Distance of two points $\left(\frac{b}{a+b}\right)$

If two persons A and B start at the same time in opposite directions from two points and after passing each other they complete the journeys in '*a*' and '*b*' hrs respectively, then A's speed : B's speed = $\sqrt{b} : \sqrt{a}$

6. Speed and time taken are inversely proportional.
Therefore, $S_1T_1 = S_2T_2 = S_3T_3$ .....
Where S_1, S_2 S_3 .... are the speeds
and T_1, T_2, T_3 ..... are the time taken to travel the same distance.

SOLVED EXAMPLE

1. A man covers a certain distance between his house and office on scooter. Having an average speed of 30 km/hr, he is late by 10 min. However, with a speed of 40 km/hr, he reaches his office 5 min earlier. Find the distance between his house and office.

Sol. Let the distance between office and house is *x* km.

Time taken to cover *x* km at 30 km/hr = $\frac{x}{30}$ hrs.

Time taken to cover *x* km at 40 km/hr = $\frac{x}{40}$ hrs.

Difference between the time taken = 15 min = $\frac{1}{4}$ hr.

∴ $\frac{x}{30} - \frac{x}{40} = \frac{1}{4}$ or $4x - 3x = 30$ or $x = 30$

Hence, the required distance is 30 km.

2. A boy goes to school at a speed of 3 km/hr and returns to the village at a speed of 2 km/hr. If he takes 5 hrs in all, what is the distance between the village and the school?

Sol. Let the distance between village and school *x* km.

Then time taken during the first journey = $\frac{x}{3}$ hr.

and time taken during the second journey = $\frac{x}{2}$ hr.

∴ $\frac{x}{3} + \frac{x}{2} = 5 \Leftrightarrow \frac{2x + 3x}{6} = 5 \Leftrightarrow 5x = 30.$

∴ $x = 6$

∴ required distance = 6 km.

3. Walking $\frac{3}{4}$ of his usual speed, a person is 10 min late to his office. Find his usual time to cover the distance.

Sol. Let the usual time be x min.

Time taken at $\frac{3}{4}$ of the usual speed = $\frac{4x}{3}$ min

$\therefore \quad \frac{4}{3}x - x = 10 \Rightarrow \frac{x}{3} = 10 \Rightarrow x = 30$ min.

4. Two runners cover the same distance at the rate of 15 km and 16 km per hour respectively. Find the distance travelled when one takes 16 minutes longer than the other.

Sol. Let the distance be x km.

Time taken by the first runner = $\frac{x}{15}$ hrs

Time take by the second runner = $\frac{x}{16}$ hrs

Now, $\frac{x}{15} - \frac{x}{16} = \frac{16}{60}$

or, $\frac{x(16-15)}{15 \times 16} = \frac{16}{60}$

$\therefore \quad x = \frac{16}{60} \times 15 \times 16 = 64$ km

5. A man rode out a certain distance by train at the rate of 25 km an hour and walked back at the rate of 4 km per hour. The whole journey took 5 hours and 48 minutes. What distance did he ride?

Sol. Let the distance be x km.

Then time spent in journey by train = $\frac{x}{25}$ hrs.

And time spent in journey by walking = $\frac{x}{4}$ hrs.

Therefore, $\frac{x}{25} + \frac{x}{4} = 5$ hrs 48 minutes.

or, $\frac{29x}{100} = 5\frac{48}{60} = \frac{29}{5} \quad \therefore x = \frac{100}{5} = 20$ km

EXERCISE

1. A car is running at a speed of 108 kmph. What distance will it cover in 15 seconds?
   (*a*) 45 metres (*b*) 55 metres (*c*) 450 metres (*d*) None of these
2. The ratio between the speeds of two trains is 7 : 8. If the second train runs 4000 kms in 4 hours, then the speed of the first train is:
   (*a*) 70 km/hr (*b*) 75 km/hr (*c*) 84 km/hr (*d*) 87.5 km/hr
3. A car moves at the speed of 80 km/hr. What is the speed of the car in metres per second?
   (*a*) 8 m/sec (*b*) $20\frac{1}{9}$ m/sec (*c*) $22\frac{2}{9}$ m/sec (*d*) None of these
4. Sound is said to travel in air at about 1100 feet per second. A man hears the axe striking the tree, $\frac{11}{5}$ seconds after he sees it strike the tree. How far is the man from the wood chopper?
   (*a*) 2197 ft (*b*) 2420 ft (*c*) 2500 ft (*d*) 2629 ft
5. An express train travelled at an average speed of 100 km/hr, stopping for 3 minutes after every 75 km. How long did it take to reach its destination 600 km from the starting point?
   (*a*) 6 hrs 21 min (*b*) 6 hrs 24 min
   (*c*) 6 hrs 27 min (*d*) 6 hrs 30 min
6. Pavan crosses a 600 m long street in 5 minutes. What is his speed in km per hour?
   (*a*) 3.6 (*b*) 7.2 (*c*) 8.4 (*d*) None of these
7. An athlete runs 200 metres race in 24 seconds. His speed is:
   (*a*) 20 km/hr (*b*) 24 km/hr (*c*) 28.5 km/hr (*d*) 30 km/hr
8. A train travels at an average of 50 miles per hour for $2\frac{1}{2}$ hours and then travels at a speed of 70 miles per hour for $1\frac{1}{2}$ hours. How far did the train travel in the entire 4 hours?
   (*a*) 120 miles (*b*) 150 miles (*c*) 200 miles (*d*) 230 miles
9. One of the two buses completes a journey of 300 km in $7\frac{1}{2}$ hours and the other a journey of 450 km in 9 hours. The ratio of their average speeds is:
   (*a*) 2 : 3 (*b*) 3 : 4 (*c*) 4 : 5 (*d*) 8 : 9

10. A motor car starts with the speed of 70 km/hr with its speed increasing every two hours by 10 kmph. In how many hours will it cover 345 kms?

(*a*) $2\frac{1}{4}$ hrs (*b*) 4 hrs 5 min (*c*) $4\frac{1}{2}$ hrs (*d*) None of these

11. A car travels the first one-third of a certain distance with a speed of 10 km/hr, the next one-third distance with a speed of 20 km/hr, and the last one-third distance with a speed of 60 km/hr, The average speed of the car for the whole journey is:

(*a*) 18 km/hr (*b*) 24 km/hr (*c*) 30 km/hr (*d*) 36 km/hr

12. Anna left for city A from city B at 5.20 a.m. She travelled at the speed of 80 km/hr for 2 hours 15 minutes. After that the speed was reduced to 60 km/hr. If the distance between two cities is 350 kms, at what time did Anna reach city A?

(*a*) 9.20 a.m. (*b*) 9.25 a.m. (*c*) 9.35 a.m. (*d*) None of these

13. The distance between two cities A and B is 330 km. A train starts from A at 8 a.m. and travels towards B at 60 km /hr. Another train starts from B at 9 a.m. and travels towards A at 75 km/hr. At what time do they meet?

(*a*) 10 a.m. (*b*) 10.30 a.m. (*c*) 11 a.m. (*d*) 11.30 a.m.

14. A person has to cover a distance of 6 km in 45 minutes. If he covers one-half of the distance in two-thirds of the total time; to cover the remaining distance in the remaining time, his speed (in km/hr) must be:

(*a*) 6 km/hr (*b*) 8 km/hr (*c*) 12 km/hr (*d*) 15 km/hr

15. Two cars P and Q start at the same time from A and B which are 120 km apart. If the two cars travel in opposite directions, they meet after one hour and if they travel in same direction (from A towards B), then P meets Q after 6 hours. What is the speed of car P?

(*a*) 60 kmph (*b*) 70 kmph (*c*) 120 kmph (*d*) None of these

16. Panas travels 600 km by train at 80 km/hr, 800 km by ship at 40 km/hr, 500 km by aeroplane at 400 km/hr and 100 km by car at 50 km/hr What is the average speed for the entire distance?

(*a*) 60 km/hr (*b*) $60\frac{5}{123}$ km/hr (*c*) 62 km/hr (*d*) None of these

17. A and B walk around a circular track. They start at 8 a.m. from the same point in the opposite directions. A and B walk at a speed of 2 rounds per hour and 3 rounds per hour respectively. How many times shall they cross each other before 9.30 a.m.?

(*a*) 5 (*b*) 6 (*c*) 7 (*d*) 8

18. A person travels from P to Q at a speed of 40 kmph and returns by increasing his speed by 50%. What is his average speed for both the trips?

(*a*) 36 kmph (*b*) 45 kmph (*c*) 48 kmph (*d*) 50 kmph

19. Satyam goes to his school from his house at a speed of 3 km/hr and returns at a speed of 2 km/hr. If he takes 5 hours in going and coming, the distance between his house and school is:

(*a*) 5 km (*b*) 5.5 km (*c*) 6 km (*d*) 6.5 km

20. Pavikay on tour travels first 160 km at 64 km/hr and the next 160 km at 80 km/hr. The average speed for the first 320 km of the tour is :

(*a*) 35.55 km/hr (*b*) 36 km/hr
(*c*) 71.11 km/hr (*d*) 71 km/hr

21. A farmer travelled a distance of 61 km in 9 hours. He travelled partly on foot @ 4 km/hr and partly on bicycle @ 9 km/hr. The distance travelled on foot is:

(*a*) 14 km (*b*) 15 km (*c*) 16 km (*d*) 17 km

22. The speed of a car increases by 2 kms after every one hour. If the distance travelled in the first one hour was 35 kms, what was the total distance travelled in 12 hours?

(*a*) 456 kms (*b*) 482 kms (*c*) 552 kms (*d*) None of these

23. In covering a certain distance, the speeds of A and B are in the ratio of 3 : 4. A takes 30 minutes more than B to reach the destination. The time taken by A to reach the destination is:

(*a*) 1 hour (*b*) $1\frac{1}{2}$ hours (*c*) 2 hours (*d*) $2\frac{1}{2}$ hours

24. A train can travel 50% faster than a car. Both start from point A at the same time and reach point B 75 kms away from A at the same time. On the way, however, the train lost about 12.5 minutes while stopping at the stations. The speed of the car is :

(*a*) 100 kmph (*b*) 110 kmph (*c*) 120 kmph (*d*) 130 kmph

25. A train when moves at an average speed of 40 kmph, reaches its destination on time. When its average speed becomes 35 kmph, then it reaches its destination 15 minutes late. Find the length of journey.

(*a*) 30 km (*b*) 40 km (*c*) 70 km (*d*) 80 km

26. Yugnirmal is travelling on his cycle and has calculated to reach point A at 2 P.M. if he travels at 10 kmph; he will reach there at 12 noon if he travels at 15 kmph. At what speed must he travel to reach A at 1 P.M.?

(*a*) 8 kmph (*b*) 11 kmph (*c*) 12 kmph (*d*) 14 kmph

27. A walks around a circular field at the rate of one round per hour while B runs around it at the rate of six rounds per hour. They start in the same direction from the same point at 7.30 a.m. They shall first cross each other at :

(*a*) 7.42 a.m. (*b*) 7.48 a.m. (*c*) 8.10 a.m. (*d*) 8.30 a.m.

28. The jogging track in a sports complex is 726 metres in circumference. Deepak and his wife start from the same point and walk in opposite directions at 4.5 km/hr and 3.75 km/hr respectively. They will meet for the first time in:

(*a*) 4.9 min (*b*) 5.28 min (*c*) 5.5 min (*d*) 6 min

29. It takes eight hours for a 600 km journey, if 120 km is done by train and the rest by car. It takes 20 minutes more, if 200 km is done by train and the rest by cat. The ratio of the speed of the train to that of the car is:

(*a*) 2 : 3 (*b*) 3 : 2 (*c*) 3 : 4 (*d*) 4 : 3

30. In a flight of 600 km, an aircraft was slowed down due to bad weather. Its average speed for the trip was reduced by 200 km/hr and the time of flight increased by 30 minutes. The duration of the flight is:

(*a*) 1 hour (*b*) 2 hours (*c*) 3 hours (*d*) 4 hours

31. A salesman travels a distance of 50 km in 2 hours and 30 minutes. Flow much faster, in kilometres per hour, on an average, must he travel to make such a trip in $\frac{5}{6}$ hour less time?

(*a*) 10 (*b*) 20 (*c*) 30 (*d*) None of these

32. With a uniform speed a car covers the distance in 8 hours. Had the speed been increased by 4 km /hr, the same distance could have been covered in $7\frac{1}{2}$ hours. What is the distance covered?

(*a*) 420 km (*b*) 480 km (*c*) 640 km (*d*) None of these

33. A is faster than B. A and B each walk 24 km. The sum of their speeds is 7 km/hr and the sum of times taken by them is 14 hours. Then, A's speed is equal to:

(*a*) 3 km/hr (*b*) 4 km/hr (*c*) 5 km/hr (*d*) 7 km/hr

34. A can complete a journey in 10 hours. He travels first half of the journey at the rate of 21 km/hr and second half at the rate of 24 km/hr. Find the total journey in km

(*a*) 220 km (*b*) 224 km (*c*) 230 km (*d*) 234 fern

ANSWERS

1	2	3	4	5	6	7	8	9	10
(*c*)	(*d*)	(*c*)	(*b*)	(*a*)	(*d*)	(*d*)	(*d*)	(*c*)	(*c*)
11	**12**	**13**	**14**	**15**	**16**	**17**	**18**	**19**	**20**
(*a*)	(*d*)	(*c*)	(*c*)	(*b*)	(*d*)	(*c*)	(*c*)	(*c*)	(*c*)
21	**22**	**23**	**24**	**25**	**26**	**27**	**28**	**29**	**30**
(*c*)	(*c*)	(*c*)	(*c*)	(*c*)	(*c*)	(*a*)	(*b*)	(*c*)	(*a*)
31	**32**	**33**	**34**						
(*a*)	(*b*)	(*b*)	(*b*)						

SOME SELECTED EXPLANATORY ANSWERS

1. Speed = 108 kmph = $\left(108 \times \frac{5}{18}\right)$ m/sec = 30 m/sec.

$\therefore$ Distance covered in 15 sec. = (30 × 15) m = 450 m.

2. Let the speeds of two trains be $7x$ and $8x$ km/hr.

Then, $8x = \frac{400}{4} = 100 \Rightarrow x = \left(\frac{100}{8}\right) = 12.5$.

$\therefore$ Speed of first train = (7 × 12.5) km/hr = 87.5 km/hr.

3. Speed = $\left(80 \times \frac{5}{18}\right)$ m/sec = $\frac{200}{9}$ m/sec = $22\frac{2}{9}$ m/sec.

4. Distance = $\left(1100 \times \frac{11}{5}\right)$ feet = 2420 feet.

5. Time taken to cover 600 km with speed 100 kmph = $\left(\frac{600}{100}\right)$ hrs = 6 hrs.

Number of stoppages = $\frac{600}{75} - 1 = 7$.

Total time of stoppage = (3 × 7) min = 21 min.
Hence, total time taken = 6 hrs 21 min.

6. Speed = $\left(\frac{600}{5 \times 60}\right)$ m/sec = 2 m/sec = $\left(2 \times \frac{18}{5}\right)$ km/hr = 7.2 km/hr.

7. Speed = $\frac{200}{24}$ m/sec = $\frac{25}{3}$ m/sec = $\left(\frac{25}{3} \times \frac{18}{5}\right)$ km/hr = 30 km/hr.

8. Total distance travelled by the train = $\left[\left(50 \times \frac{5}{2}\right) + \left(70 \times \frac{3}{2}\right)\right]$ miles

$= (125 + 105)$ miles $= 230$ miles.

9. Ratio of speeds of the two buses = $\left(300 \times \frac{2}{15}\right) : \left(\frac{450}{9.}\right) = 40 : 50 = 4 : 5.$

11. Suppose the total distance travelled is x km and the average speed of the car the whole journey be y km/hr.

Then, $\frac{(x/3)}{10} + \frac{(x/3)}{20} + \frac{(x/3)}{60} = \frac{x}{y} \Leftrightarrow \frac{x}{30} + \frac{x}{60} + \frac{x}{180} = \frac{x}{y}$

$\Leftrightarrow \frac{1}{18} y = 1 \Leftrightarrow y = 18$ km/hr.

12. Distance covered in 2 hrs 15 min *i.e.,* $2\frac{1}{4}$ hrs = $\left(80 \times \frac{9}{4}\right)$ hrs = 180 hrs.

Time taken to cover remaining distance = $\left(\frac{350 - 180}{60}\right)$ hrs = $\frac{17}{6}$ hrs

$= 2\frac{5}{6}$ hrs = 2 hrs 50 min.

Total time taken = (2 hrs 15 min + 2 hrs 50 min) = 5 hrs 5 min.
So, Anna reached city A at 10.25 a.m.

13. Suppose they meet x hrs after 8 a.m. Then,
(Distance moved by first in x hrs) + (Distance moved by second in $(x - 1)$ hrs) = 330

$\therefore \quad 60x + 75(x - 1) = 330 \Rightarrow x = 3.$

So, They meet at (8 + 3), *i.e.,* 11 a.m.

14. Remaining distance = 3 km and Remaining time = $\left(\frac{1}{3} \times 45\right)$ min

$= 15$ min $= \frac{1}{4}$ hour.

$\therefore$ Required speed = (3×4) km/hr = 12 km/hr.

16. Total distance travelled = (600 + 800 + 500 + 100) km = 2000 km.

Total time taken = $\left(\frac{600}{80} + \frac{800}{40} + \frac{500}{400} + \frac{100}{50}\right)$ hrs = $\frac{123}{4}$ hrs.

$$\therefore \quad \text{Average speed} = \left(2000 \times \frac{4}{123}\right) \text{ km/hr} = \left(\frac{8000}{123}\right) \text{ km/hr}$$

$$= 65\frac{5}{123} \text{ km/hr.}$$

17. Relative speed = (2 + 3) = 5 rounds per hour.
So, they cross each other 5 times in an hour and 2 times in half an hour.
Hence, they cross each other 7 times before 9.30 a.m.

18. Speed on return trip = 150% of 40 = 60 kmph.

$$\therefore \quad \text{Average speed} = \left(\frac{2 \times 40 \times 60}{40 + 60}\right) \text{ km/hr} = \left(\frac{4800}{100}\right) \text{ km/hr} = 48 \text{ km/hr.}$$

19. Average speed $= \left(\frac{2 \times 3 \times 2}{3 + 2}\right) \text{ km/hr} = \frac{12}{5} \text{ km/hr.}$

Distance travelled $= \left(\frac{12}{5} \times 5\right) \text{ km} = 12 \text{ km.}$

$\therefore$ Distance between house and school $= \left(\frac{12}{2}\right) \text{ km} = 6 \text{ km.}$

20. Total time taken $= \left(\frac{160}{64} + \frac{160}{80}\right) \text{ hrs} = \frac{9}{2} \text{ hrs.}$

$\therefore$ Average speed $= \left(320 \div \frac{9}{2}\right) \text{ km/hr} = 71.11 \text{ km/hr.}$

21. Suppose that the distance travelled on foot is x km.
Then, distance travelled on bicycle = $(61 - x)$ km.

So, $\frac{x}{4} + \frac{(61 - x)}{9} = 9$

$$\Leftrightarrow \quad 9x + 4(61 - x) = 9 \times 36$$
$$\Leftrightarrow \quad 5x = 80 \Leftrightarrow \quad x = 16 \text{ km.}$$

22. Total distance travelled in 12 hours = (35 + 37 + 39 + ... upto 12 terms).
This is an A.P.
First term a = 35 common difference, d = 2 and number of term, n = 12

$$\therefore \quad \text{Required distance} = \frac{12}{2}[2 \times 35 + (12 - 1) \times 2]$$
$$= 6(70 + 22) = 552 \text{ km.}$$

23. Ratio of speeds = 3 : 4 and Ratio of times taken = 4 : 3.
Suppose A takes $4x$ hrs and B takes $3x$ hrs to reach the destination. Then,

$$4x - 3x = \frac{30}{60} = \frac{1}{2} \text{ or } x = \frac{1}{2}.$$

$\therefore$ Time taken by A = $4x$ hrs = $\left(4 \times \frac{1}{2}\right)$ hrs = 2 hrs.

24. Suppose that the speed of the car is x kmph.

Then, speed of the train = $\frac{150}{100} x = \left(\frac{3}{2} x\right)$ kmph.

$$\therefore \quad \frac{75}{x} - \frac{75}{\frac{3}{2}x} = \frac{125}{10 \times 60} \Leftrightarrow \frac{75}{x} - \frac{50}{x} = \frac{5}{24}$$

$$\Leftrightarrow x = \left(\frac{25 \times 24}{5}\right) = 120 \text{ kmph.}$$

25. Difference between timings = 15 min = $\frac{1}{4}$ hr (given)

Suppose that the length of journey is x km.

Then, $\frac{x}{35} - \frac{x}{40} = \frac{1}{4} \Leftrightarrow 8x - 7x = 70 \Leftrightarrow x = 70$ km.

28. Clearly, the two will meet when they are 726 m apart.
To be (4.5 + 3.75) = 8.25 km apart, they take 1 hour.

To be 726 m apart, they take $\left(\frac{100}{825} \times \frac{726}{1000}\right)$ hrs = $\left(\frac{242}{2750} \times 60\right)$ min

= 5.28 min

30. Suppose that the duration of the flight is x hours. Then,

$$\frac{600}{x} - \frac{600}{x + \frac{1}{2}} = 200$$

$$\Leftrightarrow \quad \frac{600}{x} - \frac{1200}{2x+1} = 200$$

or, $3(2x + 1) - 6(x) = x(2x + 1)$

or, $x(2x + 1) = 3$

$\Leftrightarrow 2x^2 + x - 3 = 0 \quad \Leftrightarrow (2x + 3)(x - 1) = 0$

$\Leftrightarrow x = 1$ hr.

31. Time required = (2 hrs 30 min – 50 min) = 1 hr 40 min = $1\frac{2}{3}$ hrs = $\frac{5}{3}$ hrs

$\therefore$ Required speed = $\left(50 \div \frac{5}{3}\right)$ km/hr = 30 km/hr.

Original speed = $\left(50 \div \frac{5}{2}\right)$ km/hr = 20 km/hr.

$\therefore$ Difference in speed = (30 – 20) km/hr = 10 km/hr.

32. Suppose that the distance is x km. Then,

$$\frac{x}{7\frac{1}{2}} - \frac{x}{8} = 4 \Leftrightarrow \frac{2x}{15} - \frac{x}{8} = 4 \Leftrightarrow x = 480 \text{ km.}$$

33. Let A's speed = x km/hr. Then, B's speed = $(7 - x)$ km/hr.

So, $\frac{24}{x} + \frac{24}{(7-x)} = 14 \Leftrightarrow 24(7-x) + 24x = 14x(7-x)$

$\Leftrightarrow 14x^2 - 98x + 168 = 0 \Leftrightarrow x^2 - 7x + 12 = 0$

$\Leftrightarrow (x-3)(x-4) = 0 \Leftrightarrow x = 3$ or $x = 4$.

Since, A is faster than B, so A's speed = 4 km/hr and B's speed = 3 km/hr.

34. Suppose that the total distance is x km. Then,

$$\frac{\frac{1}{2}x}{21} + \frac{\frac{1}{2}x}{24} = 10 \Rightarrow \frac{x}{21} + \frac{x}{24} = 20$$

$$\Rightarrow 15x = 168 \times 20 \Rightarrow x = \left(\frac{168 \times 20}{15}\right) = 224 \text{ km.}$$

~~~~~~
~~~~~~

17. PROBLEMS ON TRAINS

This chapter is the same as the previous chapter (Time & Distance). The only difference is that the length of the moving object (train) is also considered in this chapter.

Some important things to be noticed in this chapter are:

1. When two trains are moving in **opposite** directions their speeds should be **added** to find the relative speed.
2. When they are moving in the **same** direction the relative speed is the **difference** of their speeds.
3. When a train passes a platform it should travel the length equal to the sum of the lengths of **train & platform both.**

SOLVED EXAMPLE

Trains passing a telegraph post or a stationary man

1. How many seconds will a train 100 metres long running at the rate of 36 km an hour take to pass a certain telegraph post?

Sol. In passing the post the train must travel its own length.

$$\text{Now, } 36 \text{ km/hr} = 36 \times \frac{5}{18} = 10 \text{ m/sec.}$$

$$\therefore \quad \text{required time} = \frac{100}{10} = 10 \text{ seconds.}$$

Trains crossing a bridge or passing a railway station

2. How long does a train 110 metres long running at the rate of 36 km/hr take to cross a bridge 132 metres in length?

Sol. In crossing the bridge the train must travel its own length plus the length of the bridge.

$$\text{Now, } 36 \text{ km/hr} = 36 \times \frac{5}{18} = 10 \text{ m/sec.}$$

$$\text{Length to covere} = 110 + 132 = 242 \text{ m}$$

$$\therefore \quad \text{required time} = \frac{242}{10} = 24.2 \text{ seconds.}$$

Trains running in opposite direction

3. Two trains 121 metres and 99 metres in length respectively are running in opposite directions, one at the rate of 40 km and the other at the rate of 32 km an hour. In what time will they be completely clear of each other from the moment they meet ?

Sol. As the two trains are moving in opposite directions their relative speed = 40 + 32 = 72 km/hr, *i.e.* they are approaching each other at 72 km/hr or 20 m/sec.

Total length 121 + 99

$\therefore$ the required time $= \dfrac{\text{Total length}}{\text{Relative speed}} = \dfrac{121 + 99}{20} = 11$ sees.

Train running in the same direction

4. In Ex 3 if the trains were running in the same direction, in what time will they be clear of each other?

Sol. Relative speed $= 40 - 32 = 8$ km/hr $= \dfrac{20}{9}$ m/sec

Total length = 121 + 99 = 220 m.

$\therefore$ required time $= \dfrac{\text{Total length}}{\text{Relative speed}} = \dfrac{220}{20} \times 9 = 99$ sec.

EXERCISE

1. Two trains, one from Howrah to Patna and the other from Patna to Howrah, start simultaneously. After they meet, the trains reach their destinations after 9 hours and 16 hours respectively. The ratio of their speeds is:
   (*a*) 2 : 3 (*b*) 4 : 3 (*c*) 6:7 (*d*) 9 : 16
2. A jogger running at 9 kmph alongside a railway track is 240 metres ahead of the engine of a 120 metre long train running at 45 kmph in the same direction. In how much time will the train pass the jogger?
   (*a*) 3.6 sec (*b*) 18 sec (*c*) 36 sec (*d*) 72 sec
3. How many seconds will a 500 metre long train take to cross a man walking with a speed of 3 km/hr in the direction of the moving train if the speed of the train is 63 km/hr?
   (*a*) 25 (*b*) 30 (*c*) 40 (*d*) 45
4. A train 280 m long, running with a speed of 63 km/hr will cross a pole in?
   (*a*) 15 sec (*b*) 16 sec (*c*) 18 sec (*d*) 20 sec
5. Two trains 140 m and 160 m long run at the speed of 60 km/hr and 40 km/hr respectively in opposite directions on parallel tracks. The time (in seconds) which they take to cross each other, is:
   (*a*) 9 sec (*b*) 9.6 sec (*c*) 10 sec (*d*) 10.8 sec

6. In what time will a train 100 metres long cross an electric pole, if its speed be 144 km/hr?
(*a*) 2.5 seconds (*b*) 4.85 seconds (*c*) 8 seconds (*d*) 12.5 seconds

7. How long does a train 110 metres long running at the speed of 72 km/hr take to cross a bridge 132 metres in length?
(*a*) 9.8 sec (*b*) 12.1 sec (*c*) 13.42 sec (*d*) 14.3 sec

8. Two goods train each 500 m long, are running in opposite directions on parallel tracks. Their speeds are 45 km/hr and 30 km/hr respectively. Find the time taken by the slower train to pass the driver of the faster one.
(*a*) 12 sec (*b*) 24 sec (*c*) 48 sec (*d*) 60 sec

9. A train passes a station platform in 36 seconds and a man standing on the platform in 20 seconds. If the speed of the train is 54 km/hr, what is the length of the platform?
(*a*) 120 m (*b*) 240 m (*c*) 300 m (*d*) None of these

10. The length of the bridge which a train 130 metres long and travelling at 45 km/hr can cross in 30 seconds, is:
(*a*) 200 m (*b*) 225 m (*c*) 245 m (*d*) 250 m

11. Two trains running in opposite directions cross a man standing on the platform in 27 seconds and 17 seconds respectively and they cross each other in 23 seconds. The ratio of their speeds is :
(*a*) 1 : 3 (*b*) 3 : 2 (*c*) 3 : 4 (*d*) None of these

12. A train running at the speed of 60 km/hr crosses a pole in 9 seconds. What is the length of the train?
(*a*) 120 metres (*b*) 180 metres (*c*) 324 metres (*d*) None of these

13. Two trains of equal lengths take 10 seconds and 15 seconds respectively to cross a telegraph post. If the length of each train be 120 metres, in what time (in seconds) will they cross each other travelling in opposite direction?
(*a*) 10 (*b*) 12 (*c*) 15 (*d*) 20

14. A train 125 m long passes a man, running at 5 kmph in the same direction in which the train is going, in 10 seconds. The speed of the train is:
(*a*) 45 km/hr (*b*) 50 km/hr (*c*) 54 km/hr (*d*) 55 km/hr

15. A 300 metre long train crosses a platform in 39 seconds while it crosses a signal pole in 18 seconds. What is the length of the platform?
(*a*) 320 m (*b*) 350 m (*c*) 650 m (*d*) Data inadequate

16. A train covers a distance of 12 km in 10 minutes. If it takes 6 seconds to pass a telegraph post, then the length of the train is:
(*a*) 90 m (*b*) 100 m (*c*) 120 m (*d*) 140 m

17. Two trains, each 100 m long, moving in opposite directions, cross each other in 8 seconds. If one is moving twice as fast the other, then the speed of the faster train is:
(*a*) 30 km/hr (*b*) 45 km/hr (*c*) 60 km/hr (*d*) 75 km/hr

18. Two trains are running in opposite directions with the same speed. If the length of each train is 120 metres and they cross each other in 12 seconds, then the speed of each train (in km/hr) is:
(*a*) 10 (*b*) 18 (*c*) 36 (*d*) 72

19. Two trains are moving in opposite directions @ 60 km/hr and 90 km/hr. Their lengths are 1.10 km and 0.9 km respectively. The time taken by the slower train to cross the faster train in seconds is:
(*a*) 36 sec (*b*) 45 sec (*c*) 48 sec (*d*) 49 sec

20. Two trains are running at 40 km/hr and 20 km/hr respectively in the same direction. Fast train completely passes a man sitting in the slower train in 5 seconds. What is the length of the fast train?
(*a*) 23 m (*b*) $23\frac{2}{9}$ m (*c*) 27 m (*d*) $27\frac{7}{9}$ m

21. A 270 metres long train running at the speed of 120 kmph crosses another train running in opposite direction at the speed of 80 kmph in 9 seconds. What is the length of the other train?
(*a*) 230 m (*b*) 240 m (*c*) 260 m (*d*) 320 m

22. A train 110 metres long is running with a speed of 60 kmph. In what time will it pass a man who is running at 6 kmph in the direction opposite to that in which the train is going?
(*a*) 5 sec (*b*) 6 sec (*c*) 7 sec (*d*) 10 sec

23. Two trains of equal length are running on parallel lines in the same direction at 46 km/hr and36 km/hr. The fester train passes the slower train in 36 seconds. The length of each train is:
(*a*) 50 m (*b*) 72 m (*c*) 80 m (*d*) 82 m

ANSWERS

1	2	3	4	5	6	7	8	9	10
(*b*)	(*c*)	(*b*)	(*b*)	(*d*)	(*a*)	(*b*)	(*c*)	(*b*)	(*c*)
11	**12**	**13**	**14**	**15**	**16**	**17**	**18**	**19**	**20**
(*b*)	(*d*)	(*b*)	(*b*)	(*b*)	(*c*)	(*c*)	(*c*)	(*c*)	(*d*)
21	**22**	**23**							
(*a*)	(*b*)	(*a*)							

SOME SELECTED EXPLANATORY ANSWERS

1. Suppose that two trains are P and Q

Speed of the train $\alpha \frac{1}{\text{time}}$ taken to cover the distance

$\therefore$ P's speed : Q's speed = $\sqrt{16} : \sqrt{9} = 4 : 3$.

2. Speed of train relative to jogger = (45 – 9) km/hr = 36 km/hr

$$= \left(36 \times \frac{5}{18}\right) \text{ m/sec} = 10 \text{ m/sec}$$

Distance to be covered = (240 + 120) m = 360 m.

$$\therefore \quad \text{Time taken} = \left(\frac{360}{10}\right) \text{ sec} = 36 \text{ sec.}$$

3. Speed of train relative to man = (63 – 3) km/hr = 60 km/hr

$$= \left(60 \times \frac{5}{18}\right) \text{ m/sec} = \frac{50}{3} \text{ m/sec.}$$

$$\therefore \text{ Time taken to pass the man} = \left(500 \times \frac{3}{50}\right) \text{ sec} = 30 \text{ sec.}$$

4. Speed = $\left(63 \times \frac{5}{18}\right)$ m/sec = $\frac{35}{2}$ m/sec.

Time taken = $\left(280 \times \frac{2}{35}\right)$ sec = 16 sec.

6. Speed = $\left(144 \times \frac{5}{18}\right)$ m/sec = 40 m/sec.

Time taken = $\left(\frac{100}{40}\right)$ sec = 2.5 sec.

7. Speed = $\left(72 \times \frac{5}{18}\right)$ m/sec = 20 m/sec.

Total distance covered = (110 + 132) m = 242 m.

$$\therefore \quad \text{Required time} = \left(\frac{242}{20}\right) \text{ sec} = 12.1 \text{ sec.}$$

8. Relative speed = (45 + 30) km/hr

$$= \left(75 \times \frac{5}{18}\right) \text{ m/sec} = \left(\frac{125}{6}\right) \text{ m/sec.}$$

Distance covered = (500 + 500) m = 1000 m.

$$\text{Required time} = \left(1000 \times \frac{6}{125}\right) \text{ sec} = 48 \text{ sec.}$$

9. Speed $= \left(54 \times \frac{5}{18}\right)$ m/sec = 15 m/sec.

Length of the train = (15 × 20) m = 300 m

Let the length of the platform be x metres

then from question $x + 300 = 15 \times 6$

$x + 300 = 540$

∴ $x = 240$

Length of plateform = 240 m.

10. Speed $= \left(45 \times \frac{5}{18}\right)$ m/sec $= \left(\frac{25}{2}\right)$ m/sec; Time = 30 sec.

Suppose that the length of bridge is l metres.

Then, $\frac{130 + l}{30} = \frac{25}{2} \Leftrightarrow 2(130 + l) = 750 \Leftrightarrow l = 245$ m.

11. Suppose that the speeds of the two trains are x m/sec and y m/sec respectively. Then,

length of the first train = $27x$ metres, and length of the second train = $17y$ metres.

$$\frac{27x + 17y}{x + y} = 23 \Leftrightarrow 27x + 17y$$

$$= 23x + 23y \Leftrightarrow 4x = 6y \Leftrightarrow \frac{x}{y} = \frac{3}{2}.$$

12. Seed – $\left(60 \times \frac{5}{18}\right)$ m/sec $= \left(\frac{50}{3}\right)$ m/sec.

Length of the train = (Speed × Time) $= \left(\frac{50}{3} \times 9\right)$ m = 150 m.

14. Speed of the train relative to man $= \left(\frac{125}{10}\right)$ m/sec $= \left(\frac{25}{2}\right)$ m/sec.

$$= \left(\frac{25}{2} \times \frac{18}{5}\right) \text{ km/hr} = 45 \text{ km/hr}.$$

Suppose that the speed of the train is x kmph.

Then, relative speed $= (x - 5)$, kmph.

$\therefore \quad x - 5 = 45$ or $x = 50$ kmph.

15. Speed $= \left(\frac{300}{18}\right)$ m/sec $= \frac{50}{3}$ m/sec.

Suppose that the length of the platform is d metres.

Then, $\frac{d + 300}{39} = \frac{50}{3} \Leftrightarrow 3(d + 300) = 1950 \quad \Leftrightarrow \quad d = 350$ m.

16. Speed $= \left(\frac{12}{10} \times 60\right)$ km/hr $= \left(72 \times \frac{5}{18}\right)$ m/sec $= 20$ m/sec.

Length of the train = (Speed × Time) = (20×6) m = 120 m.

17. Let the speed of the slower train be x m/sec.

Then, speed of the faster train $= 2x$ m/sec.

Relative speed $= (x + 2x)$ m/sec $= 3x$ m/sec.

$\therefore \quad \frac{(100 + 100)}{8} = 3x \Leftrightarrow 24x = 200 \Leftrightarrow x = \frac{25}{3}.$

So, speed of the faster train $= \frac{50}{3}$ m/sec

$$= \left(\frac{50}{3} \times \frac{18}{5}\right) \text{ km/hr} = 60 \text{ km/hr}.$$

18. Let the speed of each train be x m/sec.

Then, relative speed of the two trains $= 2x$ m / sec.

So $\quad 2x = \frac{(120 + 120)}{12}$

$\Leftrightarrow \quad 2x = 20 \; x = 10$

$\therefore \quad$ Speed of each train = 10 m/sec

$$= \left(10 \times \frac{18}{5}\right) \text{ km/hr} = 36 \text{ km/hr}.$$

19. Relative speed $= (60 + 90)$ km/hr

$$= \left(150 \times \frac{5}{18}\right) \text{ m/sec} = \left(\frac{125}{3}\right) \text{ m/sec}$$

Distance covered = (1.10 + 0.9) km = 2 km = 2000 m

Required time = $\left(2000 \times \frac{3}{125}\right)$ sec = 48 sec.

20. Relative speed = (40 – 20) km/hr

$= \left(20 \times \frac{5}{18}\right) \text{ m/sec} = \left(\frac{50}{9}\right) \text{ m/sec.}$

Length of faster train = $\left(\frac{50}{9} \times 5\right) \text{ m} = \frac{250}{9} \text{ m} = 27\frac{7}{9} \text{ m.}$

21. Relative speed = (120 + 80) km/hr

$= \left(200 \times \frac{5}{18}\right) \text{ m/sec} = \left(\frac{500}{9}\right) \text{ m/sec.}$

Suppose that the length of the other train is l metres.

Then, $\frac{l + 270}{9} = \frac{500}{9} = l + 270 = 500 \Leftrightarrow l = 230.$

22. Speed of train relative to man = (60 + 6) km/hr = 66 km/hr

$= \left(66 \times \frac{5}{18}\right) \text{ m/sec} = \left(\frac{55}{3}\right) \text{ m/sec.}$

$\therefore$ Time taken to pass the man = $\left(110 \times \frac{3}{55}\right)$ sec = 6 sec.

~~~~~~
~~~~~~

18. BOATS AND STREAMS

Normally by speed of the boat or swimmer we mean the speed of the boat (or swimmer) in still water. If the boat (or the swimmer) moves against the stream then it is called upstream and if it moves with the stream, it is called downstream.

If the speed of the boat (or the swimmer) is x and if the speed of the stream is y then, while upstream the effective speed of the boat $= x - y$ and while downstream the effective speed of the boat $= x + y$.

If x km per hour be the man's rate in still water, and y km per hour the rate of the current. Then

$x + y$ = man's rate with current

$x - y$ = man's rate against current.

Adding and subtracting and then dividing by 2.

$x = \frac{1}{2}$(man's rate with current + his rate against current)

$y = \frac{1}{2}$ (man's rate with current - his rate against current)

Hence we have the following two facts:

(*i*) A man's rate in still water ifs half the sum of his rates with and against the current.

(*ii*) The rate of the current is half the difference between the rates of the man with and against the current.

SOLVED EXAMPLE

1. A man can row upstream at 10 km/hr and down stream at 16 km/hr. Find the man's rate in still water and the rate of the current.

Sol. Rate in still water $= \frac{1}{2}(10 + 16) = 13$ km/hr

Rate of current $= \frac{1}{2}(16 - 10) = 3$ km/hr

2. A man swims down stream 30 km and upstream 18 km, taking 3 hrs each time. What is the velocity of current?

Sol. Man's rate down stream = $\frac{30}{3}$ km/hr = km/hr

Man's rate upstream = $\frac{30}{3}$ km/hr = 6 km/hr

$\therefore$ Velocity of stream = $\frac{(10-6)}{2}$ = 2 km/hr

3. There is a road beside a river. Two friends started from a place A, moved to a temple situated at another place B and then returned to A again. One of them moves on a cycle at a speed of 12 km/hr, while the other sails on a boat at a speed of 10 km/hr. If the river flows, at the speed of 4 km/hr, which of the two friends will return to place A first?

Sol. Clearly, the cyclist moves both ways at a speed of 12 km/hr.
So, average speed of the cyclist = 12 km/hr.
The boat sailor moves downstream @ (10 + 4) *i.e.,* 14 km/hr and upstream @ (10 – 4) *i.e.*, 6 km/hr.

So, average speed of the boat sailor = $\left(\frac{2 \times 14 \times 6}{14 + 6}\right)$ km/hr.

$= \frac{42}{5}$ km/hr = 8.4 km/hr.

Since the average speed of the cyclist is greater, he will return to A first.

4. A man can row $7\frac{1}{2}$ kmph in still water. If in a river running at 1.5 km an hour, it takes him 50 minutes to row to a place and back, how far off is the place?

Sol. Speed downstream = (7.5 + 1.5) kmph = 9 kmph;
Speed upstream = (7.5 – 1.5) kmph = 6 kmph,
Let the required distance be x km. Then,

$$\frac{x}{9} + \frac{x}{6} = \frac{50}{60} \Leftrightarrow 2x + 3x = \left(\frac{5}{6} \times 18\right)$$

$$\Leftrightarrow 5x = 15 \Leftrightarrow x = 3.$$

Hence, the required distance is 3 km.

5. A man can row 40 km upstream and 55 km downstream in 13 hours. Also, he can row 30 km upstream and 44 km downstream in 10 hours. Find the speed of the man in still water and the speed of the current.

Sol. Let rate upstream = x km/hr and rate downstream = y km/hr.

Then, $\frac{40}{x} + \frac{55}{y} = 13$ ... (*i*) and $\frac{30}{x} + \frac{44}{y} = 10$ ...(*ii*)

Multiplying (*ii*) by 4 and (*i*) by 3 and subtracting, we get:

$\frac{11}{y} = 1$ or $y = 11$.

Substituting $y = 11$ in (*i*), we get : $x = 5$.

Rate of man in still water = $\frac{1}{2}(11 + 5)$ kmph = 8 kmph.

Rate of current = $\frac{1}{2}(11 - 5)$ kmph = 3 kmph.

EXERCISE

1. A motorboat, whose speed is 15 km /hr in still water goes 30 km downstream and conies back in a total of 4 hours 30 minutes. The speed of the stream is:

(*a*) 3.5 km/hr (*b*) 5 km/hr (*c*) 7 km/hr (*d*) 8 km/hr

2. Rakhi can row at 5 kmph in still water. If the velocity of current is 1 kmph and it takes him 1 hour to row to a place and come back, how far is the place?

(*a*) 2.4 km (*b*) 2.5 km (*c*) 3 km (*d*) 3.6 km

3. A boat can travel with a speed of 13 km/hr in still water. If the speed of the stream is, 4 km/hr, find the time taken by the boat to go 68 km downstream.

(*a*) 2 hours (*b*) 3 hours (*c*) 4 hours (d) 5 hours

4. A boat takes 90 minutes less to travel 36 miles downstream than to travel the same distance upstream. If the speed of the boat in still water is 10 mph, the speed of the stream is:

(*a*) 2 mph (*b*) 2.5 mph (*c*) 3 mph (*d*) 4 mph

5. In one hour, a boat goes 11 km along the' stream and 5 km against the stream. The speed of the boat in still water (in km/hr) is:

(*a*) 3 km/hr (*b*) 5 km/hr (*c*) 8 km/hr (*d*) 9 km/hr

6. A man can row three-quarters of a kilometre against the stream in $11\frac{1}{4}$ minutes. The speed of the man in still water is :

(*a*) 2 km/hr (*b*) 3 km/hr (*c*) 4 km/hr (*d*) 5 km/hr

7. A boat running downstream covers a distance of 16 km in 2 hours while for covering the same distance upstream, it takes 4 hours. What is the speed of the boat in still water?

(*a*) 4 km/hr (*b*) 6 km/hr (*c*) 8 km/hr (*d*) Data inadequate

8. A boat running upstream takes 8 hours 48 minutes to cover a certain distance, while it takes 4 hours to cover the same distance running downstream. What is the ratio between the speed of the boat and speed of the water current respectively?

(*a*) 2 : 1 (*b*) 3: 2 (*c*) 8 : 3 (*d*) None of these

9. A boatman goes 2 km against the current of the stream in 1 hour and goes 1 km along the current in 10 minutes. How long will it take to go 5 km in stationary water?

(*a*) 40 minutes (*b*) 1 hour (*c*) 1 hr 15 min (*d*) 1 hr 30 min

10. A man's speed with the current is 15 km/hr and the speed of the current is 2.5 km/hr. The man's speed against the current is:

(*a*) 8.5 km/hr (*b*) 9 km/hr (*c*) 10 km/hr (*d*) 12.5 km/hr

11. A boat covers a certain distance downstream in 1 hour, while it comes back in $1\frac{1}{2}$ hours. If the speed of the stream be 3 kmph, what is the speed of the boat in still water?

(*a*) 12 kmph (*b*) 13 kmph (*c*) 14 kmph (*d*) 15 kmph

12. At his usual rowing rate, Panas can travel 12 miles downstream in a certain river in 6 hours less than it takes him to travel the same distance upstream. But if he could double his usual rowing rate for his 24-mile round trip, the downstream 12 miles would then take only one hour less than the upstream 12 miles. What is the speed of the current in miles per hour?

(*a*) $1\frac{1}{3}$ (*b*) $1\frac{2}{3}$ (*c*) $2\frac{1}{3}$ (*d*) $2\frac{2}{3}$

ANSWERS

1	2	3	4	5	6	7	8	9	10
(*b*)	(*a*)	(*c*)	(*a*)	(*c*)	(*d*)	(*b*)	(*c*)	(*c*)	(*c*)
11	**12**								
(*d*)	(*d*)								

SOME SELECTED EXPLANATORY ANSWERS

1. Suppose that the speed of the stream is x km/hr. Then,
Speed downstream = $(15 + x)$ km/hr, Speed upstream = $(15 - x)$ km/hr.

$\therefore \quad \dfrac{30}{(15+x)} + \dfrac{30}{(15-x)} = 4\dfrac{1}{2} \Leftrightarrow \dfrac{900}{225-x^2} = \dfrac{9}{2} \Leftrightarrow 9x^2 = 225$

$\Leftrightarrow x^2 = 25 \quad \Leftrightarrow x = 5$ km/hr.

2. Speed downstream = (5 + 1), kmph = 6 kmph;

Upstream speed = (5 – 1) kmph = 4 kmph.

Let the required distance be x km.

Then, $\dfrac{x}{6} + \dfrac{x}{4} = 1 \Leftrightarrow 2x + 3x = 12$

$\Leftrightarrow x = 2.4$ km.

4. Let the speed of the stream is x mph. Then,

Speed downstream = $(10 + x)$ mph,

Speed upstream = $(10 - x)$ mph.

$\therefore \quad \dfrac{36}{(10-x)} - \dfrac{36}{(10+x)} = \dfrac{90}{60} \Leftrightarrow 72x \times 60 = 90\ (100 - x^2)$

$\Leftrightarrow x^2 + 48x + 100 = 0$

$\Leftrightarrow (x + 50)(x - 2) = 0 \Leftrightarrow x = 2$ mph.

5. Speed of boat in still water = $\dfrac{1}{2}(11 + 5)$ kmph = 8 kmph.

6. Upstream speed = $\left(\dfrac{750}{450}\right)$ m/sec = $\dfrac{10}{9}$ m/sec;

Downstream speed = $\left(\dfrac{750}{450}\right)$ m/sec = $\dfrac{5}{3}$ m/sec.

$\therefore$ Rate in still water = $\dfrac{1}{2}\left(\dfrac{10}{9} + \dfrac{5}{3}\right)$ m/sec = $\dfrac{25}{18}$ m/sec = $\left(\dfrac{25}{18} \times \dfrac{18}{5}\right)$ km/hr

= 5 km/hr.

7. Downstream speed = $\left(\dfrac{16}{2}\right)$ kmph = 8 kmph;

Upstream speed = $\left(\dfrac{16}{4}\right)$ kmph = 4 kmph

$\therefore$ Speed in still water = $\dfrac{1}{2}(8 + 4)$ kmph = 6 kmph.

8. Suppose that the man' upstream speed is x kmph and that downstream speed is y kinph. Then, Distance covered upstream in 8 hrs 48 min. = Distance covered downstream in 4 hrs

$$\Rightarrow \left(x \times 8\frac{4}{5}\right) = (y \times 4) \Rightarrow \frac{44}{5}x = 4y \Rightarrow y = \frac{11}{5}x.$$

So, Required ratio $= \left(\frac{y+x}{2}\right) : \left(\frac{y-x}{2}\right) = \left(\frac{16x}{5} \times \frac{1}{2}\right) : \left(\frac{6x}{5} \times \frac{1}{2}\right)$

$= \frac{8}{5} : \frac{3}{5} = 8 : 3$

9. Rate downstream $= \left(\frac{1}{10} \times 60\right)$ km/hr = 6 km/hr;

Rate upstream = 2 km/hr.

Speed in still water $= \frac{1}{2}(6 + 2)$ km/hr = 4 km/hr.

$\therefore$ Required time $= \left(\frac{5}{4}\right)$ hrs $= 1\frac{1}{4}$ hrs = 1 hr 15 min

11. Suppose that the speed of the boat in still water be u kmph. Then, Speed downstream = $(u + 3)$ kmph, Speed upstream = $(u - 3)$ kmph.

$$\therefore (u + 3) \times 1 = (u - 3) \times \frac{3}{2} \Leftrightarrow 2u + 6 = 3u - 9$$

$$\Leftrightarrow u = 15 \text{ kmph.}$$

12. Suppose that the speed in still water is x mph and the speed of the current is y mph. Then, Speed upstream = $(x - y)$; Speed downstream = $(x + y)$

$$\therefore \frac{12}{(x-y)} - \frac{12}{(x+y)} = 6 \Leftrightarrow 6(x^2 - y^2) = 24y$$

$$\Leftrightarrow x^2 - y^2 = 4y$$

$$\Leftrightarrow x^2 = (4y + y^2) \quad ...(i)$$

And, $\frac{12}{(2x-y)} - \frac{12}{(2x+y)} = 1 \Leftrightarrow 4x^2 - y^2 = 24y$

$$\Leftrightarrow x^2 = \frac{24y + y^2}{4} \quad ...(ii)$$

From (i) and (ii), we have:

$$4y + y^2 = \frac{24y + y^2}{4} \Leftrightarrow 16y + 4y^2 = 24y + y^2 \Leftrightarrow 3y^2 = 8y$$

$$\Leftrightarrow y = \frac{8}{3}.$$

$\therefore$ Speed of the current $= \frac{8}{3}$ mph $= 2\frac{2}{3}$ mph.

~~~~~~
~~~~~~

19. ALLIGATION OR MIXTURE

Alligation is the rule that enables us

(*i*) to find the mean or average value of mixture when the prices of two or more ingredients which may be mixed together and the proportion in which they are mixed are given (this is **Alligation Medial**); and

(*ii*) to find the proportion in which the ingredients at given prices must be mixed to produce a mixture at a given price. This is **Alligation alternate.**

Note : (1) the word *Alligation* literally means *linking*. The rule takes its name from the lines or links used in working out question on mixture.

(2) Alligation method is applied for **percentage value, ratio, rate, prices, speed** etc and not for absolute values. That is, whenever per cent, per hour, per kg, per km etc are being compared, we can use Alligation.

Rule of Alligation: If the grandients are mixed in a ratio, then

$$\frac{\text{Quantity of cheaper}}{\text{Quantity of dearer}} = \frac{\text{CD of dearer} - \text{Mean price}}{\text{Mean price} - \text{CP of cheaper}}$$

We represent it as under:

CP of unit quantity of cheaper (c)   CP of unit quantity of dearer (d)

Mean price
(m)

(d – m)   (m – c)

Then, (cheaper quantity) : (dearer quantity) = (d – m) : (m – c)

SOLVED EXAMPLE

1. In what proportion must rice at ₹ 3.10 per kg be mixed with rice at ₹ 3.60 per kg, so that the mixture be worth ₹ 3.25 a kg?

Sol. C.P. of 1 kg. cheaper price (310 paise)   C.P. of 1 kg. dearer price (360 paise)

Mean price
(325 paise)

35   15

By the alligation rule: $\dfrac{\text{(Quantity of cheaper rice)}}{\text{(Quantity of dearer rice)}} = \dfrac{35}{15} = \dfrac{7}{3}.$

$\therefore$ They must be mixed in the ratio 7 : 3.

2. How many kg. of salt at 42 P per kg. must a man mix with 25 kg. of salt at 24 P per kg. so that he may, on selling the mixture at 40 P per kg, gain 25% on the outlay?

Sol. Cost price of mixture = $40 \times \dfrac{100}{125}$ P = 32 P per kg.

.... (By the rule of fraction)

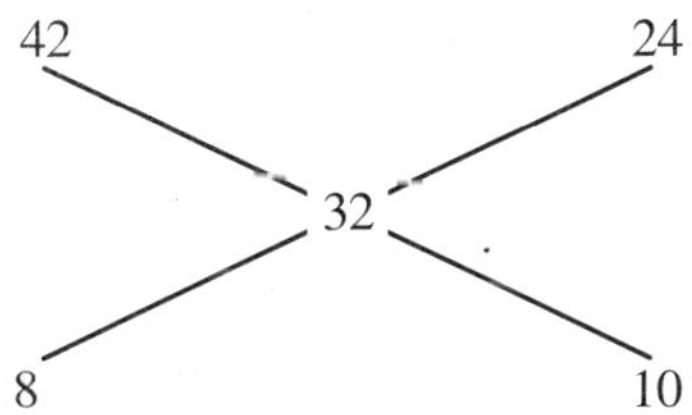

Ratio = 4 : 5

Thus for every 5 kg. of salt at 24 P, 4 kg. of salt at 42 P is used.

$\therefore$ the required no. of kg = $25 \times \dfrac{4}{5} = 20.$

3. A mixture of a certain quantity of milk with 16 litres of water is worth 90 P per litre. If pure milk be worth ₹ 1.08 per litre how much milk is there in the mixture?

Sol. The mean value is 90 P and the price of water is 0 P.

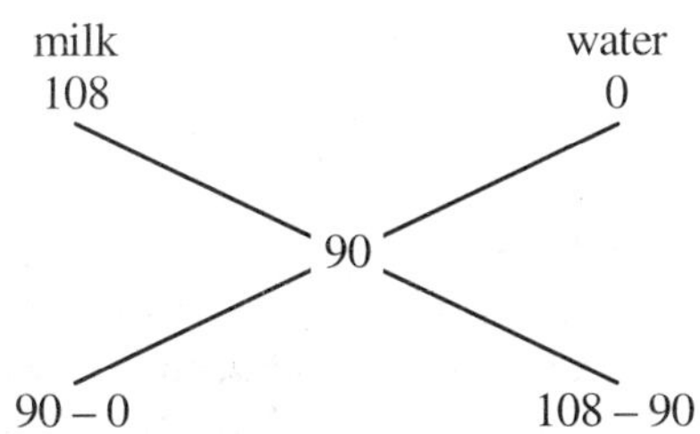

By the Alligation Rule, milk and water are in the ratio of 5 : 1.

$\therefore$ quantity of milk in the mixture = 5 × 16 = 80 litres.

EXERCISE

1. Two vessels A and B contain milk and water mixed in the ratio 8 : 5 and 5 : 2 respectively. The ratio in which these two mixtures be mixed to get a new mixture containing $69\frac{3}{13}\%$ milk, is:

(*a*) 2 : 7 (*b*) 3 : 5 (*c*) 5 : 2 (*d*) 5 : 7

2. In what ratio must water be mixed with milk to gain $16\frac{2}{3}\%$ on selling the mixture at cost price?

(*a*) 1 : 6 (*b*) 6 : 1 (*c*) 2 : 3 (*d*) 4 : 3

3. In what ratio must a grocer mix two varieties of pulses costing ₹ 15 and ₹ 20 per kg respectively so as to get a mixture worth ₹ 16.50 per kg?

(*a*) 3 : 7 (*b*) 5 : 7 (*c*) 7 : 3 (*d*) 7 : 5

4. In what ratio must a grocer mix two varieties of tea worth ₹ 60 a kg and ₹ 65 a kg so that by selling the mixture at ₹ 68.20 a kg he may gain 10%?

(*a*) 3 : 2 (*b*) 3 : 4 (*c*) 3 : 5 (*d*) 4 : 5

5. Find the ratio in which tea at ₹ 7.20 a kg be mixed with tea at ₹ 5.70 a kg to produce a mixture worth ₹ 6.30 a kg.

(*a*) 1 : 3 (*b*) 2 : 3 (*c*) 3 : 4 (*d*) 4 : 5

6. The cost of Type 1 seed is ₹ 15 per kg and Type 2 seed is ₹ 20 per kg. If both Type 1 and Type 2 are mixed in the ratio of 2 : 3, then the price per kg of the mixed variety of seed is:

(*a*) ₹ 18 (*b*) ₹ 18.50 (*c*) ₹ 19 (*d*) ₹ 19.50

7. A jar full of whisky contains 40% alcohol. A part of this whisky is replaced by another containing 19% alcohol and now the percentage of alcohol was found to be 26%. The quantity of whisky replaced is:

(*a*) $\frac{1}{3}$ (*b*) $\frac{2}{3}$ (*c*) $\frac{2}{5}$ (*d*) $\frac{3}{5}$

8. One quality of wheat at ₹ 9.30 per kg is mixed with another quality at a certain rate in the ratio 8 : 7. If the mixture so formed be worth ₹ 10 per kg, what is the rate per kg of the second quality of wheat?

(*a*) ₹ 10.30 (*b*) ₹ 10.60 (*c*) ₹ 10.80 (*d*) ₹ 11

9. Tea worth ₹ 126 per kg and ₹ 135 per kg are mixed with a third variety in the ratio 1 : 1 : 2, If the mixture is worth ₹ 153 per kg, the price of the third variety per kg will be :

(*a*) ₹ 169.50 (*b*) ₹ 170 (*c*) ₹ 175.50 (*d*) ₹ 180

10. 8 litres are drawn from a Jarr full of wine and is then filled with water. This operation is performed three more times. The ratio of the quantity of wine now left in cask to that of the water is 16 : 81. How much wine did the cask hold originally?

(*a*) 18 litres (*b*) 24 litres (*c*) 32 litres (*d*) 42 litres

11. A vessel is filled with liquid, 3 parts of which are water and 5 parts syrup. How much of the mixture must be drawn off and replaced with water so that the mixture may be half water and half syrup?

(*a*) $\frac{1}{3}$ (*b*) $\frac{1}{4}$ (*c*) $\frac{1}{5}$ (*d*) $\frac{1}{7}$

ANSWERS

1	2	3	4	5	6	7	8	9	10
(*a*)	(*a*)	(*c*)	(*a*)	(*b*)	(*a*)	(*b*)	(*c*)	(*c*)	(*b*)
11									
(*c*)									

SOME SELECTED EXPLANATORY ANSWERS

1. Let cost of 1 litre milk be Re. 1.

Milk in 1 litre mix. in A = $\frac{8}{10}$ litre, C.P. of 1 litre mix. in A = Re. $\frac{8}{13}$.

Milk in 1 litre mix. in B = $\frac{7}{5}$ litre, C.P. of 1 litre mix. in B = Re. $\frac{5}{7}$.

Milk in 1 litre of final mix. = $\left(\frac{900}{13} \times \frac{1}{100} \times 1\right) = \frac{9}{13}$ litre, Mean price

$$= \text{Re. } \frac{9}{13}.$$

By the rule of alligation, we have:

C.P. of 1 litre mixture in A C.P. of 1 litre mixture in B

$\frac{8}{13}$ $\frac{5}{7}$

Mean price

$\frac{9}{13}$

$\frac{2}{91}$ $\frac{1}{13}$

$\therefore$ Required ratio = $\frac{2}{91} : \frac{1}{13} = 2 : 7.$

2. Suppose that the cost price of 1 litre of milk is ₹ 1

S.P. of 1 litre of mixture = Re. 1,

$$\text{Gain} = \frac{50}{3}\%$$

$\therefore$ C.P. of 1 litre of mixture $= \left(100 \times \frac{3}{350} \times 1\right)$

$$= \text{Re. } \frac{6}{7}.$$

By the rule of alligation, we have:

C.P. of 1 litre of water — 0

C.P. of 1 litre of milk — Re. 1

Mean price — Re. $\frac{6}{7}$

$\frac{1}{7}$ — $\frac{6}{7}$

$\therefore$ Ratio of water and milk $= \frac{1}{7} : \frac{6}{7} = 1 : 6.$

3. By the rule of alligation:

Cost of 1 kg pulses of 1st kind — ₹ 15

Cost of 1 kg pulses of 2nd kind — ₹ 20

Mean price — ₹ 16.50

3.50 — 1.50

$\therefore$ Required rate = 3.50 : 1.50

= 35 : 15 = 7 : 3.

4. S.P. of 1 kg of the mixture = ₹ 68.20, Gain = 10%.

C.P. of a kg of the mixture = ₹ $\left(\frac{100}{110} \times 68.20\right)$ = ₹ 62.

By the rule of alligation, we have:

Cost of 1 kg tea of 1st kind ₹ 60 — Cost of 1 kg tea of 2nd kind ₹ 65

Mean price ₹ 62

3 — 2

Hence, Required ratio = 3 : 2.

5. By the rule of alligation :

Cost of 1 kg tea 1st kind $720p$ — Cost of 1 kg tea of 2nd kind $570p$

Mean price $630p$

60 — 90

$\therefore$ Required ratio = 60 : 90 = 2 : 3.

6. Suppose that the price of 1 kg mixture is ₹ x.

Cost of 1 kg of Type 1 seed ₹ 15 — Cost of 1 kg of Type 2 seed ₹ 20

Mean price ₹ x

$(20 - x)$ — $(x - 15)$

$$\therefore \quad \frac{(20 - x)}{(x - 15)} = \frac{2}{3}$$

$$\Rightarrow \quad 60 \quad 3x = 2x - 30$$

$$\Rightarrow \quad 5x = 90 \Rightarrow x = 18.$$

Hence, price of the mixture is ₹ 18 per kg.

7. By the rule of alligation, we have:

Strength of first jar — 40% Strength of 2nd jar — 19%

Mean strength 26%

(26 – 19) (40 – 26)

So, ratio of 1st and 2nd quantities = 7 : 14
= 1 : 2.

$\therefore$ Required quantity replaced $= \frac{2}{3}$.

8. Let the rate of the second quality be ₹ x per kg.
By the rule of alligation, we have :

C.P. of 1 kg wheat of 1st kind — 930 p C.P. of 1 kg wheat of 2nd kind — $(100\,x)\,p$

Mean price 1000 p

$(100\,x - 1000)\,p$ 70 p

$$\therefore \quad \frac{100x - 1000}{70} = \frac{8}{7}$$

$$\Rightarrow \quad 700x - 7000 = 560$$

$$\Rightarrow \quad 700x = 7560 \Rightarrow x = ₹\ 10.80.$$

9. Since first and second varieties are mixed in equal proportions, so their average price $= ₹\left(\frac{126 + 135}{2}\right) = ₹\ 130.50.$

So, the mixture is formed by mixing two varietie, one at ₹ 130.50 per kg and the other at say, ₹ x per kg in the ratio 2 : 2, *i.e.*, 1 : 1. We have to find x.

By the rule of alligation, we have:

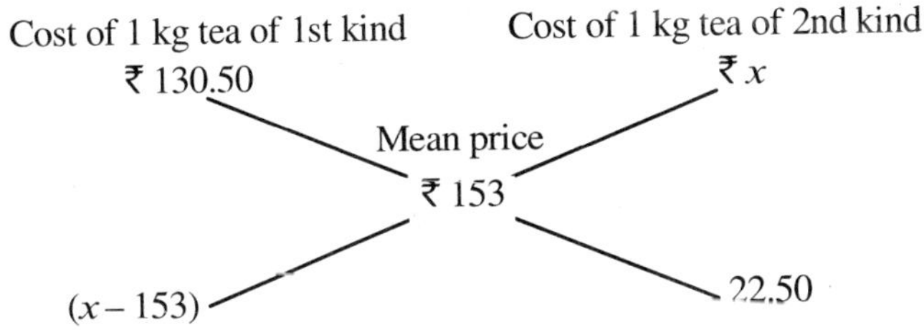

$\therefore \quad \dfrac{x - 153}{22.50} = 1 \Rightarrow x - 153 = 22.50 \Rightarrow x = 175.50.$

Hence, price of the third variety = ₹ 175.50 per kg.

10. Suppose that the quantity of the wine in the Jarr originally is x litres.

Then, quantity of wine left in the Jarr after 4 opertions = $\left[x\left(1 - \dfrac{8}{x}\right)^4\right]$ litres.

$$\therefore \quad \frac{x\left(1 - \frac{8}{x}\right)^4}{x} = \frac{16}{81}$$

$$\Rightarrow \left(1 - \frac{8}{x}\right)^4 = \left(\frac{2}{3}\right)^4 \Rightarrow \left(\frac{x - 8}{x}\right) = \frac{2}{3}$$

$\Rightarrow \quad 3x - 24 = 2x \Rightarrow x = 24.$

~~~~~~
~~~~~~

20. SIMPLE INTEREST

Interest is the money paid by the borrower to the lender for the use of money lent.

The sum lent is called the **principal. Interest** is usually calculated at the rate of so many rupees for every ₹ 100 of the money lent for a year. This is called the **rate** per cent **per annum.**

'Per annum' means for a year. The words 'per annum' are sometimes omitted. Thus 6 p.c. means that ₹ 6 is the interest on ₹ 100 in one year.

The sum of the principal and interest is called the **amount.**

The interest is usually paid **yearly, half-yearly** or **quarterly** as agreed upon.

Interest is of two kinds, **Simple** and **Compound.** When interest is calculated on the original principal for any length of time it is called **simple interest. Compound interest** is defined in the next chapter.

To find Simple Interest (SI) multiply the principal by the number of years and by the rate per cent and divide the result by 100.

This may be remembered in the symbolic form

$$SI = \frac{p \times t \times r}{100}$$

Where I = interest, p = principal, t = number of years, r = rate %

Interest for a number of days

When the time is given in days or in years and days, 365 days are reckoned to a year. But when the time is given in months and days, 12 months are reckoned to a year and 30 days to the month. The day on which the money is paid back should be included but not the day on which it is borrowed, *i.e.*, in counting, the first day is omitted.

To find principal

Since $I = \frac{\text{P t r}}{100}$. $\quad\therefore\quad \boxed{P = \frac{100\,I}{Pr}}$

To find rate %

Since $I = \frac{\text{Prt}}{100}$ $\quad\therefore\quad \boxed{r = \frac{100\,I}{P\,t}}$

To find Time

Since $I = \frac{Prt}{100}$. $\therefore$ $\boxed{t = \frac{100\,I}{P\,r}}$

The annul payment that will discharge a debt of ₹ A due in t years at the rate of interest $r\%$ per annum is $\dfrac{100A}{100t + \dfrac{rt(1t-1)}{2}}$.

Directs formula

Two equal amounts of money are deposited at $r_1\%$ and $r_2\%$ for t_1 and t_2 yrs resspectively. If the difference between their interest is I_d then Sum = $\dfrac{I_d \times 100}{r_1t_1 - r_2t_2}$.

SOLVED EXAMPLE

1. Find the simple interest on ₹ 400 for 5 years at 6 per cent.

Sol. $SI = \frac{400 \times 5 \times 6}{100} = ₹\ 120.$

2. Find the simple interest on ₹ 306.25 from March 3rd to July 27th at $3\frac{3}{4}\%$ per annum.

Sol. Interest $= ₹\ 306\frac{1}{4} \times \frac{146}{365} \times \frac{15}{4} \times \frac{1}{100}$

$= ₹\ \frac{1225}{4} \times \frac{2}{5} \times \frac{15}{4} \times \frac{1}{100} = ₹\ \frac{147}{32}$

$= ₹\ 4.59$ nerly.

3. What sum of money will produce ₹ 143 interest in $3\frac{1}{4}$ years at $2\frac{1}{2}$ p.c. simple interest?

Sol. Let the required sum be ₹ P. Then

$₹\ P = ₹\ \dfrac{100 \times 143}{3\frac{1}{4} \times 2\frac{1}{2}} = ₹\ \dfrac{100 \times 143 \times 4 \times 2}{13 \times 5} = ₹\ 1760.$

4. A sum of ₹ 468.75 was lent out at simple interest and at the end of 1 year 8 months the total amount was ₹ 500. Find the rate of interest per cent per annum.

Sol. Here P = ₹ 468.75, $t = 1\frac{2}{3}$ or $\frac{5}{3}$ years.

I = ₹ (500 – 468.75) = ₹ 31.25.

$\therefore$ rate p.c. = $\dfrac{100 \times 31.25}{468.75 \times \frac{5}{3}} = 100 \times \dfrac{3125}{46875} \times \dfrac{3}{5} = 4.$

5. A lent ₹ 600 to B for 2 years, and ₹ 150 to C for 4 years and received altogether from both ₹ 90 as interest. Find the rate of interest, simple interest being calculated.

Sol. ₹ 600 for 2 years = ₹ 1200 for 1 year

and ₹ 150 for 4 years = ₹ 600 for 1 year.

Int. = ₹ 90.

$\therefore$ Rate = $\dfrac{90 \times 100}{1800 \times 1} = 5\%.$

6. In what time will ₹ 8500 amount to ₹ 15767.50 at $4\frac{1}{2}$ per cen per annum?

Sol. Here interest = ₹ 15767.50 – ₹ 8500 = ₹ 7267.50.

$\therefore$ $t = \dfrac{7267.50 \times 100}{8500 \times 4.5}$ = 19 years.

7. A sum of money doubles itself in 10 years at simple interest. What is the rate of interest?

Sol. Let the sum be ₹ 100.

After 10 years it becomes ₹ 200.

$\therefore$ Interest = 200 – 100 = 100

Then, rate = $\dfrac{100\,I}{P\,t} = \dfrac{100 \times 100}{100 \times 10} = 10\%.$

EXERCISE

1. A sum of money at simple interest amounts to ₹ 815 in 3 years and to ₹ 854 in 4 years. The sum is:

(*a*) ₹ 650 (*b*) ₹ 690 (*c*) ₹ 698 (*d*) ₹ 700

2. What will be the ratio of simple interest earned by certain amount at the same rate of interest for 6 years and that for 9 years?

(*a*) 1 : 3 (*b*) 1:4 (*c*) 2 : 3 (*d*) Data inadequate

3. At what rate percent per annum will the simple interest on a sum of money be $\frac{2}{5}$ of the amount in 10 years?

(*a*) 4% (*b*) $5\frac{2}{3}\%$ (*c*) 6% (*d*) $6\frac{2}{3}\%$

4. An automobile financier claims to be lending money at simple interest, but he includes the interest every six months for calculating the principal. If he is charging an interest of 10%, the effective rate of interest becomes :

(*a*) 10% (*b*) 10.25% (*c*) 10.5% (*d*) None of these

5. A sum of money lent out at simple interest amounts to ₹ 720 after 2 years and to ₹ 1020 after a further period of 5 years. The sum is:

(*a*) ₹ 500 (*b*) ₹ 600 (*c*) ₹ 700 (*d*) ₹ 710

6. A sum of ₹ 12,500 amounts to ₹ 15,500 in 4 years at the rate of simple interest. What is the rate of interest?

(*a*) 3% (*b*) 4% (*c*) 5% (*d*) 6%

7. In how many years, ₹ 150 will produce the same interest @ 8% as ₹ 800 produce in 3 years @ $4\frac{1}{2}\%$?

(*a*) 6 (*b*) 8 (*c*) 9 (*d*) 12

8. A sum fetched a total simple interest of ₹ 4016.25 at the rate of 9 p.c.p.a. in 5 years. What is the sum?

(*a*) ₹ 4462.50 (*b*) ₹ 8032.50 (*c*) ₹ 8900 (*d*) ₹ 8925

9. How much time will it take for Panas amount of ₹ 450 to yield ₹ 81 as interest at 4.5% per annum of simple interest?

(*a*) 3.5 years (*b*) 4 years (*c*) 4.5 years (*d*) 5 years

10. What is the present worth of ₹ 132 due in 2 years at 5% simple interest per annum ?

(*a*) ₹ 112 (*b*) ₹ 118.80 (*c*) ₹ 120 (*d*) ₹ 122

11. ₹ 800 becomes ₹ 956 in 3 years at a certain rate of simple interest. If the rate of interest is increased by 4%, what amount will ₹ 800 become in 3 years ?

(*a*) ₹ 1020.80 (*b*) ₹ 1025 (*c*) ₹ 1052 (*d*) Data inadequate

12. Jyotish took a loan from a bank at the rate of 12% p.a. simple interest. After 3 years he had to pay ₹ 5400 interest only for the period. The principal amount borrowed by him was :

(*a*) ₹ 2000 (*b*) ₹ 10,000 (*c*) ₹ 15,000 (*d*) ₹ 20,000

13. Reena took a loan of ₹ 1200 with simple interest for as many years as the rate of interest. If she paid ₹ 432 as interest at the end of the loan period, what was the rate of interest?

(*a*) 3.6 (*b*) 6
(*c*) 18 (*d*) Cannot be determined

14. Janak borrows ₹ 5000 for 2 years at 4% p.a. simple interest. He immediately lends it to another person at $6\frac{1}{4}\%$ p.a. for 2 years. Find his gain in the transaction per year.

(*a*) ₹ 112.50 (*b*) ₹ 125 (*c*) ₹ 150 (*d*) ₹ 167.50

15. A certain amount earns simple interest of ₹ 1750 after 7 years. Had the interest been 2% more, how much more interest would it have earned?

(*a*) ₹ 35 (*b*) ₹ 245
(*c*) ₹ 350 (*d*) Cannot be determined

16. A sum of money amounts to ₹ 9800 after 5 years and ₹ 12005 after 8 years at the same rate of simple interest. The rate of interest per annum is:

(*a*) 5% (*b*) 8% (*c*) 12% (*d*) 15%

17. A sum invested at 5% simple interest per annum grows to ₹ 504 in 4 years. The same amount at 10% simple interest per annum in $2\frac{1}{2}\%$ years will grow to:

(*a*) ₹ 420, (*b*) ₹ 450 (*c*) ₹ 525 (*d*) ₹ 550

18. Mr. Ganesh borrowed some money at the rate of 6% p.a. for the first three years, 9% p.a. for the next five years and 13% p.a. for the period beyond eight years. If the total interest paid by him at the end of eleven years is ₹ 8160, how much money did he borrow?

(*a*) ₹ 8000 (*b*) ₹ 10,000 (*c*) ₹ 12,000 (*d*) None of these

19. Simple interest on a certain amount is $\frac{9}{16}$ of the principal. If the numbers representing the rate of interest in percent and time in years be equal, then time, for which the principal is lent out, is:

(*a*) $2\frac{1}{2}$ years (*b*) $6\frac{1}{2}$ years (*c*) 7 years (*d*) $7\frac{1}{2}$ years

20. An amount of ₹ 1,00,000 is invested in two types of shares. The first yields an interest of 9% p.a. and the second, 11% p.a. If the total interest at the end of one year is $9\frac{3}{4}\%$, then the amount invested in each share was :

(*a*) ₹ 52,500; ₹ 47,500 (*b*) ₹ 62,500; ₹ 37,500
(*c*) ₹ 72,500; ₹ 27,500 (*d*) ₹ 82,500; ₹ 17,500

21. Divide ₹ 2379 into 3 parts so that their amounts after 2, 3 and 4 years respectively may be equal, the rate of interest being 5% per annum at simple interest. The first part is:
(*a*) ₹ 759 (*b*) ₹ 792 (*c*) ₹ 818 (*d*) ₹ 828

22. A sum of ₹ 725 is lent in the beginning of a year at a certain rate of interest. After 8 months, a sum of ₹ 362.50 more is lent but at the rate twice the former. At the end of the year, ₹ 33.50 is earned as interest from both the loans. What was the original rate of interest ?
(*a*) 3.6% (*b*) 4.5% (*c*) 5% (*d*) None of these

23. The difference between the simple interest received from two different sources on ₹ 1500 for 3 years is ₹ 13.50. The difference between their rates of interest is:
(*a*) 0.1% (*b*) 0.2% (*c*) 0.3% (*d*) 0.4%

24. Mr. Panas invested in all ₹ 2600 at 4%, 6% and 8% per annum simple interest. At the end of the year, he got the same interest in all the three cases. The money invested at 4% is:
(*a*) ₹ 200 (*b*) ₹ 600 (*c*) ₹ 800 (*d*) ₹ 1200

25. If the annual rate of simple interest increases from 10% to $12\frac{1}{2}\%$, a man's yearly income increases by ₹ 1250. His principal (in ₹) is :
(*a*) 45,000 (*b*) 50,000 (*c*) 60,000 (*d*) 65,000

26. Mr. Thomas invested an amount of ₹ 13,900 divided in two different schemes A and B at the simple interest rate of 14% p.a. and 11% p.a. respectively. If the total amount of simple interest earned in 2 years be ₹ 3508, what was the amount invested in Scheme B?
(*a*) ₹ 6400 (*b*) ₹ 6500 (*c*) ₹ 7200 (*d*) ₹ 7500

27. The price of a T.V. set worth ₹ 20,000 is to be paid in 20 instalments of ₹ 1000 each. If the rate of interest be 6% per annum, and the first instalment be paid at the time of purchase, then, the value of the last instalment covering the interest as well will be :
(*a*) ₹ 1050 (*b*) ₹ 2050 (*c*) ₹ 3000 (*d*) None of these

28. A moneylender finds that due to a fall in the annual rate of interest from 8% to $7\frac{3}{4}\%$, his yearly income diminishes by ₹ 61.50. His capital is:
(*a*) ₹ 22,400 (*b*) ₹ 23,800 (*c*) ₹ 24,600 (*d*) ₹ 26,000

29. A lends ₹ 2500 to B and a certain sum to C at the same time at 7% p.a. simple interest. If after 4 years, A altogether receives ₹ 1120 as interest from B and C, then the sum lent to C is:
(*a*) ₹ 700 (*b*) ₹ 1500 (*c*) ₹ 4000 (*d*) ₹ 6500

30. Peter invested an amount of ₹ 12,000 at the rate of 10 p.c.p.a. simple interest and another amount at the rate of 20 p.c.p.a. simple interest. The total interest earned at the end of one year on the total amount invested became 14 p.c.p.a. Find the total amount invested.
(*a*) ₹ 20,000 (*b*) ₹ 22,000 (*c*) ₹ 24,000 (*d*) ₹ 25,000

31. A lent ₹ 5000 to B for 2 years and ₹ 3000 to C for 4 years on simple interest at the same rate of interest and received ₹ 2200 in all from both of them as interest. The rate of interest per annum is:
(*a*) 5% (*b*) 7% (*c*) $7\frac{1}{8}\%$ (*d*) 10%

ANSWERS

1	2	3	4	5	6	7	8	9	10
(*c*)	(*c*)	(*a*)	(*b*)	(*b*)	(*d*)	(*c*)	(*d*)	(*b*)	(*c*)
11	**12**	**13**	**14**	**15**	**16**	**17**	**18**	**19**	**20**
(*c*)	(*c*)	(*b*)	(*a*)	(*d*)	(*c*)	(*c*)	(*a*)	(*d*)	(*b*)
21	**22**	**23**	**24**	**25**	**26**	**27**	**28**	**29**	**30**
(*d*)	(*d*)	(*c*)	(*d*)	(*b*)	(*a*)	(*d*)	(*c*)	(*b*)	(*a*)
31									
(*d*)									

SOME SELECTED EXPLANATORY ANSWERS

1. S.I. for 1 year = ₹ (854 – 815) = ₹ 39.
S.I. for 3 years = ₹ (39 × 3) = ₹ 117.
∴ Principle = ₹ (815 – 117) = ₹ 698.

2. Suppose that the principal is P and rate of interet is R%.

$$\therefore \text{ Required ratio} = \left[\frac{\frac{(P \times R \times 6)}{100}}{\frac{(P \times R \times 9)}{100}}\right] = \frac{6PR}{9PR} = \frac{6}{9} = 2 : 3.$$

3. Let sum = x. Then, S.I. = $\frac{2x}{5}$ and Time = 10 years (given).

Hence, Rate = $\left(\frac{100 \times 2x}{x \times 5 \times 10}\right)\%$ = 4%.

4. Let the sum is ₹ 100. Then,

S.I. for first 6 months = ₹ $\left(\frac{100 \times 10 \times 1}{100 \times 2}\right)$ = ₹ 5.

S.I. for last 6 months = ₹ $\left(\frac{105 \times 10 \times 1}{100 \times 2}\right)$ = ₹ 5.25.

So, amount at the end of 1 year = ₹ (100 + 5 + 5.25) = ₹ 110.25.

∴ Effective rate = (110.25 – 100) = 10.25%.

5. S.I. for 5 years = ₹ (1020 – 720) = ₹ 300.

S.I. for 2 years = ₹ $\left(\frac{300}{5} \times 2\right)$ = ₹ 120.

∴ Principal – ₹ (720 – 120) = ₹ 600.

6. S.I. = ₹ (15500 – 12500) = ₹ 3000.

Rate = $\left(\frac{100 \times 3000}{12500 \times 4}\right)\%$ = 6%.

7. Principle = ₹ 800, Rate R = $4\frac{1}{2}\% = \frac{9}{2}\%$, Time T = 3 years.

then, S.I. = ₹ $\left(800 \times \frac{9}{2} \times \frac{3}{100}\right)$ = ₹ 108.

Now, P = ₹ 150, S.I. = ₹ 108, R = 8%.

∴ Time = $\left(\frac{100 \times 108}{150 \times 8}\right)$ years = 9 years.

8. Principal = ₹$\left(\frac{100 \times 4016.25}{9 \times 5}\right)$ = ₹ $\left(\frac{401625}{45}\right)$ = ₹ 8925.

9. Required time = $\left(\frac{100 \times 81}{450 \times 4.5}\right)$ years = 4 years.

10. Suppose that the present worth is ₹ x. Then, S.I. = ₹ $(132 - x)$.

so, from question $\left(\dfrac{x \times 5 \times 2}{100}\right) = 132 - x$

$\Leftrightarrow \quad 10x = 13200 - 100x$

$\Leftrightarrow \quad 110x = 13200 \quad \Leftrightarrow \quad x = 120.$

11. S.I. = ₹ (956 – 800) = ₹ 156.

and, Rate = $\left(\dfrac{100 \times 156}{800 \times 3}\right)\% = 6\dfrac{1}{2}\%.$

New rate = $\left(6\dfrac{1}{2} + 4\right)\% = 10\dfrac{1}{2}\%.$

and, New S.I. = ₹ $\left(800 \times \dfrac{21}{2} \times \dfrac{3}{100}\right)$ = ₹ 252.

$\therefore$ New amount = ₹ (800 + 252) = ₹ 1052.

13. Let rate = R% and time = R years. Then,

$\left(\dfrac{1200 \times R \times R}{100}\right) = 432$

$\Leftrightarrow \quad 12R^2 = 432 \quad \Leftrightarrow \quad R^2 = 36 \quad \Leftrightarrow \quad R = 6.$

14. Gain in 2 yrs. = ₹ $\left[\left(5000 \times \dfrac{25}{4} \times \dfrac{2}{100}\right) - \left(\dfrac{5000 \times 4 \times 2}{100}\right)\right]$

= ₹ (625 – 400) = ₹ 225.

$\therefore$ Gain in 1 year = ₹ $\left(\dfrac{225}{2}\right)$ = ₹ 112.50.

16. S.I. for 3 years = ₹ (12005 – 9800) = ₹ 2205.

S.I. for 5 years = ₹ $\left(\dfrac{2205}{3} \times 5\right)$ = ₹ 3675.

$\therefore$ Principal = ₹ (9800 – 3675) = ₹ 6125.

Hence, rate = $\left(\dfrac{100 \times 3675}{6125 \times 5}\right)\% = 12\%.$

17. Suppose that the sum is ₹ x, Then S.I. = ₹ $(504 - x)$.

$\therefore \quad \left(\dfrac{x \times 5 \times 4}{100}\right) = 504 - x \quad \Leftrightarrow \quad 20x = 50400 - 100x$

$\Leftrightarrow \quad 120x = 50400 \quad \Leftrightarrow \quad x = 420.$

Now, P = ₹ 420, R = 10%, T = $\frac{5}{2}$ years.

S.I. = ₹ $\left(\frac{420 \times 10}{100} \times \frac{5}{2}\right)$ = ₹ 105.

$\therefore$ Amount = ₹ (420 + 105) = ₹ 525.

19. Let sum = x. Then, S.I. = $\frac{9}{16}x$.

again, suppose that rate = R% and time = R years.

$$\therefore \quad \left(\frac{x \times R \times R}{100}\right) = \frac{9x}{16} \quad \Leftrightarrow \quad R^2 = \frac{900}{16}$$

$$\Leftrightarrow \quad R = \frac{30}{4} = 7\frac{1}{2}.$$

Hence, time = $7\frac{1}{2}$ years.

20. Let the sum invested at 9% is ₹ x and that invested at 11% is ₹ (100000 – x).

$$\text{Then, } \left(\frac{x \times 9 \times 1}{100}\right) + \left[\frac{(100000 - x) \times 11 \times 1}{100}\right] = \left(100000 \times \frac{39}{4} \times \frac{1}{100}\right)$$

$$\frac{9x + 1100000 - 11x}{100} = \frac{39000}{4} = 9750$$

$$2x = (1100000 - 975000) = 125000 \quad \Leftrightarrow \quad x = 62500$$

$\therefore$ Sum invested at 9% = ₹ 62500.

Sum invested at 11% = ₹ (100000 – 62500) = ₹ 37500.

21. Let the parts be x, y and [2379 – (x + y)].

$$x + \left(x \times 2 \times \frac{5}{100}\right) = y + \left(y \times 3 \times \frac{5}{100}\right) = z + \left(z \times 4 \times \frac{5}{100}\right)$$

$$\Rightarrow \quad \frac{11x}{10} = \frac{23y}{20} = \frac{6z}{5} = k \quad \Rightarrow \quad x = \frac{10k}{11}, \; y = \frac{20k}{23}, \; z = \frac{5k}{6}$$

But $x + y + z = 2379$

$$\Rightarrow \quad \frac{10k}{10} + \frac{20k}{23} + \frac{5k}{6} = 2379$$

$$\Rightarrow \quad 1380k + 1320k + 1265\,k = 2379 \times 11 \times 23 \times 6$$

$$\Rightarrow \quad k = \frac{2379 \times 11 \times 23 \times 6}{3965} = \frac{3 \times 11 \times 23 \times 6}{5}$$

$\therefore \quad x = \left(\frac{10}{11} \times \frac{3 \times 11 \times 23 \times 6}{5}\right) = 828.$

Hence, the first part is ₹ 828.

22. Suppose that the original rate is R%. Then, new rate = (2R)%.

$$\therefore \quad \left(\frac{725 \times R \times 1}{100}\right) + \left(\frac{362.50 \times 2R \times 1}{100 \times 3}\right) = 33.50$$

$(2125 + 725)\ R = 33.50 \times 100 \times 3 = 10050$

$R = \frac{10050}{2900} = 3.46$

$\therefore$ Original rate = 3.46%.

23. $\left(\frac{1500 \times R_1 \times 3}{100}\right) - \left(\frac{1500 \times R_2 \times 3}{100}\right) = 13.50$

$\Leftrightarrow \quad 4500\ (R_1 - R_2) = 1350$

$\Leftrightarrow \quad R_1 - R_2 = \frac{1350}{4500} = 0.3\%.$

24. Let the parts be x, y and $[2600 - (x + y)]$. Then,

$$\frac{x \times 4 \times 1}{100} = \frac{y \times 6 \times 1}{100} = \frac{[2600 - (x + y)] \times 8 \times 1}{100}$$

$\therefore \quad \frac{y}{x} = \frac{4}{6} = \frac{2}{3}$ or $y = \frac{2}{3}x.$

So, $\frac{x \times 4 \times 1}{100} = \frac{\left(2600 - \frac{5}{3}x\right) \times 8}{100}$

$\Leftrightarrow \quad 4x = \frac{(7800 - 5x) \times 8}{3} \quad \Leftrightarrow \quad 52x = (7800 \times 8)$

$\Leftrightarrow \quad x = \left(\frac{7800 \times 8}{52}\right) = 1200.$

$\therefore$ Money invested at 4% = ₹ 1200.

25. Suppose that the sum is ₹ x. Then, $\left(x \times \frac{25}{2} \times \frac{1}{100}\right) - \left(\frac{x \times 10 \times 1}{100}\right) = 1250$

$\Leftrightarrow \quad 25x - 20x = 250000$

$\Leftrightarrow \quad 5x = 250000 \quad \Leftrightarrow \quad x = 50000.$

28. Suppose that the capital is ₹ x. Then, $\left(\frac{x \times 8 \times 1}{100}\right) - \left(x \times \frac{31}{4} \times \frac{1}{100}\right) = 61.50$

$\Leftrightarrow \quad 32x - 31x = 6150 \times 4 \quad \Leftrightarrow \quad x = 24600.$

29. Suppose that the sum lent to C is ₹ p.

Then, $\left(\frac{2500 \times 7 \times 4}{100}\right) + \left(\frac{p \times 7 \times 4}{100}\right) = 1120$

$\Leftrightarrow \quad \frac{7}{25}p = (1120 - 700) \quad \Rightarrow p = \left(\frac{420 \times 25}{7}\right) = 1500.$

30. Let the second amount is ₹ x. Then

$\left(\frac{12000 \times 10 \times 1}{100}\right) + \left(\frac{x \times 20 \times 1}{100}\right) = \left[\frac{(12000 + x) \times 14 \times 1}{100}\right]$

$\Leftrightarrow \quad 12000 + 20x = 168000 + 14x \quad \Leftrightarrow \quad 6x = 48000 \quad \Leftrightarrow \quad x = 8000.$

$\therefore$ Total investment = ₹ (12000 + 8000) = ₹ 20000.

31. Let the rate is R% p.a.

Then, $\left(\frac{5000 \times R \times 2}{100}\right) + \left(\frac{3000 \times R \times 4}{100}\right) = 2200$

$\Leftrightarrow \quad 100R + 120R = 2200 \quad \Leftrightarrow \quad R = \left(\frac{2200}{220}\right) = 10.$

$\therefore$ Rate = 10%.

~~~~~~
~~~~~~

21. COMPOUND INTEREST

Money is said to be lent at Compound Interest (CI) when at the end of a year or other fixed period the interest that has become due is not paid to the lender, but is added to the sum lent, and the amount thus obtained becomes the principal for the next period. The process is repeated until the amount for the last period has been found. The difference between the original principal and the final amount is called **Compound Interest** (CI).

Important Formulae

Let Principal = ₹ P, Time = t yrs and Rate = $r\%$ per annum

Case I: When interest is compounded annually:

$$\text{Amount} = P\left[1+\frac{r}{100}\right]^t$$

Case II: When interest is compounded half-yearly.

$$\text{Amount} = P\left[1+\frac{\frac{r}{2}}{100}\right]^{2t} = P\left[1+\frac{r}{200}\right]^{2t}$$

Case III: When interest is compounded quarterly :

$$\text{Amount} = P\left[1+\frac{\frac{r}{4}}{100}\right]^{4t} = P\left[1+\frac{r}{400}\right]^{4t}$$

Case IV: When rate of interest is $r_1\%$, $r_2\%$ and $r_3\%$ for 1st year, 2nd year and 3rd year respectively,

$$\text{then Amount} = P\left[1+\frac{r_1}{100}\right]\times\left[1+\frac{r_2}{100}\right]\times\left[1+\frac{r_3}{100}\right]$$

The above-mentioned formulae are not new for you. We think that all of you know their uses. When dealing with the above formulae, some mathematical calculations become lengthy and take more time. To simplify the calculations and save the valuable time we are giving some extra informations.

The problems are generally asked upto the period of 3 years and the rates of interest are 10%, 5% and 4%. We have the basic formula:

$$\text{Amount} = \text{Principal}\left(1+\frac{\text{rate}}{100}\right)^{\text{time}}$$

If the principal is Re 1, the amount for first, second and third years will be

$\left(1+\frac{r}{100}\right), \left(1+\frac{r}{100}\right)^2$ and $\left(1+\frac{r}{100}\right)^3$ respectively.

And if the rate of interest is 10%, 5% and 4%, these values will be

$$\left(\frac{11}{10}\right), \left(\frac{11}{10}\right)^2, \left(\frac{11}{10}\right)^3$$

$$\left(\frac{21}{20}\right), \left(\frac{21}{20}\right)^2, \left(\frac{21}{20}\right)^3$$

$$\left(\frac{26}{25}\right), \left(\frac{26}{25}\right)^2, \left(\frac{26}{25}\right)^3$$

The above informations can be put in the tabular form as given below:

Principal = Re 1, then CI:

Time	1 Year	2 Years	3 Years
r	$\left(1+\frac{r}{100}\right)$	$\left(1+\frac{r}{100}\right)^2$	$\left(1+\frac{r}{100}\right)^3$
10	$\frac{11}{10}$	$\frac{121}{100}$	$\frac{1331}{1000}$
5	$\frac{21}{20}$	$\frac{441}{400}$	$\frac{9261}{8000}$
4	$\frac{26}{25}$	$\frac{676}{625}$	$\frac{17576}{15625}$

The above table should be remembered.

When Diference Between SI and CI is give

Theorem: *When difference between the compound interest and simple interest on a certain sum of money for 2 years at r% rate is ₹x, then the sum is given by:*

$$\text{Sum} = \frac{\text{Difference} \times 100 \times 100}{\text{Rate} \times \text{Rate}} = \frac{x(100)^2}{r^2} = x\left(\frac{100}{r}\right)^2$$

And when sum is given and difference between SI and CI is asked, then

$$\text{Difference} = \text{Sum}\left(\frac{r}{100}\right)^2$$

Theorem: *If the diffrence between CI and SI on a certain sum for 3 years at r% is ₹ x, the sum will be* $\frac{\text{Difference} \times (100)^3}{r^2(300+r)}$ *and if the sum is given and the difference is asked, then*

$$\text{Difference} = \frac{Sr^2(300+r)}{(100)^3}$$

SOLVED EXAMPLE

1. ₹ 7500 is borrowed at CI at the rate of 4% per annum. What will be the amount to be paid after 2 yrs?

Sol. As the rate of interest is 4% per annum and the time is 2 yrs, our concerned fraction would be $\frac{676}{625}$. From the above table, you know that Re 1 becomes ₹ $\frac{676}{625}$ at 4% per annum after 2 yrs. So after 2 yrs ₹ 7500 will produce $7500 \times \frac{676}{625}$ = ₹ 8112.

2. In what time will ₹ 390625 amount to ₹ 456976 at 4% compound interest ?

Sol. $\therefore \quad P\left(1+\frac{r}{100}\right)^t = A$

$\therefore \quad 390625\left(1+\frac{4}{100}\right)^t = 456976$

$\therefore \quad \left(1+\frac{1}{25}\right)^t = \frac{456976}{390625} \qquad \therefore \left(\frac{26}{25}\right)^t = \left(\frac{26}{25}\right)^4$

$\therefore \quad t = 4 \qquad \therefore$ the required time is 4 years.

3. At what rate per cent compounded yearly will ₹ 80,000 amount to ₹ 88,200 in 2 yrs?

Sol. We have $80{,}000\left(1+\frac{r}{100}\right)^2 = 88{,}200$

or, $\left(1+\frac{r}{100}\right)^2 = \frac{88{,}200}{80{,}000} = \frac{441}{400} = \left(\frac{21}{20}\right)^2$

or, $1+\frac{r}{100} = \frac{21}{20} \qquad \therefore r = 5\%.$

4. The compound interest on a certain sum for 2 yrs is ₹ 40.80 and simple interest is ₹ 40.00. Find the rate of interest per annum and the sum.

Sol. A little reflection will show that the difference between the simple and compound interests for 2 yrs is the interest on the first year's interest.

$$\text{First year's SI} = ₹\ \frac{40}{2} = ₹\ 20$$

CI – SI = ₹ 40.8 – ₹ 40 = Re 0.80

Interest on ₹ 20 for 1 year = Re 0.80

$$\therefore \quad \text{Interest on ₹ 100 for 1 yr} = ₹\ \frac{80 \times 100}{100 \times 20} = ₹\ 4$$

$\therefore$ rate = 4%

$\therefore$ Now, principal P is given by

$$P = \frac{100 \times I}{tr} = \frac{100 \times 40}{2 \times 4} = ₹\ 500$$

Quicker Method (Direct Formula) [For 2 yrs only]:

$$\text{Rate} = \frac{\text{Difference in CI and SI}}{\text{SI}} \times 100$$

$$\text{Thus, in this case, rate} = \frac{2 \times 0.8}{40} \times 100 = 4\%$$

$$\text{And Sum} = \frac{40 \times 100}{4 \times 2} = ₹\ 500.$$

5. What sum of money at compound interest will amount to ₹ 2249.52 in 3 years, if the rate of interest is 3% for the first year, 4% for the second year, and 5% for the third year?

Sol. The general formula for such question is:

$$A = P\left(1 + \frac{r_1}{100}\right)\left(1 + \frac{r_2}{100}\right)\left(1 + \frac{r_3}{100}\right)\ldots$$

where A = Amount, P = Principal and r_1, r_2, r_3 are the rates of interest for different years.

In the above case:

$$2249.52 = P\left(1 + \frac{3}{100}\right)\left(1 + \frac{4}{100}\right)\left(1 + \frac{5}{100}\right)$$

or, $\quad 2249.52 = P(1.03)\ (1.04)\ (1.05)$

$$\therefore \quad P = \frac{2249.52}{1.03 \times 1.04 \times 1.05} = ₹\ 2000$$

Direct formula: By the rule of fraction:

$$\text{Principal} = 2249.52\left(\frac{100}{103}\right)\left(\frac{100}{104}\right)\left(\frac{100}{105}\right) = ₹\ 2000.$$

6. A man borrows ₹ 3000 at 10% compound rate of interest. At the end of each year he pays back ₹ 1000. How much amount should he pay at the end of the third year to clear all his dues?

Sol. The general formula for the above question may be written as: If a man borrows ₹ P at r% compound interest and pays back ₹ A at the end of each year, then at the end of the nth year he should pay ₹

$$P\left[1 + \frac{r}{100}\right]^n$$

$$A\left[\left(1+\frac{r}{100}\right)^{n-1} + \left(1+\frac{r}{100}\right)^{n-2} + ... + \left(1+\frac{r}{100}\right)^{1}\right]$$

In the above case:

$$3000\left[1+\frac{10}{100}\right]^3 - 1000\left[\left(1+\frac{10}{100}\right)^2 + \left(1+\frac{10}{100}\right)^1\right]$$

$$= 3000\left(\frac{11}{10} \times \frac{11}{10} \times \frac{11}{10}\right) - 1000\left[\left(\frac{11}{10}\right)^2 + \frac{11}{10}\right]$$

$$= 3993 - \left\{1000 \times \frac{121}{100} + 1000 \times \frac{11}{10}\right\}$$

$$= 3993 - 1210 - 1100 = ₹\ 1683.$$

EXERCISE

1. The difference between the simple interest on a certain stun at the rate of 10% per annum; for 2 years and compound interest which is compounded every 6 months is ₹ 124.05. What is the principal sum?

(*a*) ₹ 6000 (*b*) ₹ 8000 (*c*) ₹ 10,000 (*d*) ₹ 12,000

2. The difference between simple and compound interests compounded annually on a certain sum of money for 2 years at 4% per annum is Re. 1. The sum (in ₹) is:

(*a*) 625 (*b*) 630 (*c*) 640 (*d*) 650

3. The compound interest on ₹ 30,000 at 7% per annum is ₹ 4347. The period (in years) is :

(*a*) 2 (*b*) $2\frac{1}{2}$ (*c*) 3 (*d*) 4

4. In how many years will a sum of ₹ 800 at 10% per annum compounded semi-annually become ₹ 926.10?

(*a*) $1\frac{1}{3}$ (*b*) $1\frac{1}{2}$ (*c*) $2\frac{1}{3}$ (*d*) $2\frac{1}{2}$

5. The principal that amounts to ₹ 4913 in 3 years at $6\frac{1}{4}\%$ per annum compound interest compounded annually, is :

(*a*) ₹ 3096 (*b*) ₹ 4076 (*c*) ₹ 4085 (*d*) ₹ 4096

6. Panas invested ₹ 15,000 @ 10% per annum for one year. If the interest is compounded half-yearly, then the amount received by Panas at the end of the year will be:

(*a*) ₹ 16,500 (*b*) ₹ 16,525.50 (*c*) ₹ 16,537.50 (*d*) None of these

7. Mr. Sanjeev saves ₹ 200 at the end of each year and lends the money at 5% compound interest. How much will it become at the end of 3 years?

(*a*) ₹ 565.25 (*b*) ₹ 635 (*c*) ₹ 662.02 (*d*) ₹ 666.50

8. The effective annual rate of interest corresponding to a nominal rate of 6% per annum payable half-yearly is:

(*a*) 6.06% (*b*) 6.07% (*c*) 6.08% (*d*) 6.09%

9. The compound interest on a certain sum for 2 years at 10% per annum is ₹ 525. The simple interest on the same sum for double the time at half the fate percent per annum is :

(*a*) ₹ 400 (*b*) ₹ 500 (*c*) ₹ 600 (*d*) ₹ 800

10. What annual payment will discharge a debt of ₹ 1025 due in 2 years at the rate of 5% compound interest?

(*a*) ₹ 550 (*b*) ₹ 551.25 (*c*) ₹ 560 (*d*) ₹ 560.75

11. A bank offers 5% compound interest calculated on half-yearly basis. A customer deposits ₹ 1600 each on 1st January and 1st July of a year. At the end of the year, the amount he would have gained by way of interest is

(*a*) ₹ 120 (*b*) ₹ 121 (*c*) ₹ 122 (*d*) ₹ 123

12. What will be the difference between simple and compound interest @ 10% per annum on a sum of ₹ 1000 after 4 years?

(*a*) ₹ 31 (*b*) ₹ 32.10 (*c*) ₹ 40.40 (*d*) ₹ 64.10

13. If the simple interest on a sum of money for 2 years at 5% per annum is ₹ 50, what is the compound interest on the same sum at the same rate and for the same time?
(*a*) ₹ 51.25 (*b*) ₹ 52 (*c*) ₹ 54.25 (*d*) ₹ 60

14. The difference between simple interest and compound interest on ₹ 1200 for one year at 10% per-annum reckoned half-yearly is:
(*a*) ₹ 2.50 (*b*) ₹ 3 (*c*) ₹ 3.75 (*d*) ₹ 4

15. If the compound interest on a sum for 2 years at $12\frac{1}{2}\%$ per annum is ₹ 510, the simple interest on the same sum at the same rate for the same period of time is :
(*a*) ₹ 400 (*b*) ₹ 450 (*c*) ₹ 460 (*d*) ₹ 480

16. Mr. Yugnirmal invested an amount of ₹ 8000 in a fixed deposit scheme for 2 years at compound interest rate 5 p.c.p.a. How much amount will Mr. Yugnirmal get on maturity of the fixed deposit?
(*a*) ₹ 8600 (*b*) ₹ 8620 (*c*) ₹ 8800 (*d*) None of these

17. What will be the compound interest on a sum of ₹ 25,000 after 3 years at the rate of 12 p.c.p.a.?
(*a*) ₹ 9000.30 (*b*) ₹ 9720 (*c*) ₹ 10123.20 (*d*) ₹ 10483.20

18. A sum of money placed at compound interest doubles itself in 5 years. It will amount to eight times itself at the same rate of interest in:
(*a*) 7 years (*b*) 10 years (*c*) 15 years (*d*) 20 years

19. A sum of money invested at compound interest amounts to ₹ 800 in 3 years and to ₹ 840 in 4 years. The rate of interest per annum is :
(*a*) $2\frac{1}{2}\%$ (*b*) 4% (*c*) 5% (*d*) $6\frac{2}{3}\%$

20. There is 60% increase in an amount in 6 years at simple interest. What will be the compound interest of ₹ 12,000 after 3 years at the same rate?
(*a*) ₹ 2160 (*b*) ₹ 3120 (*c*) ₹ 3972 (*d*) None of these

21. Mr. Dua invested money in two schemes A and B offering compound interest @ 8 p.c.p.a. and 9 p.c.p.a. respectively. If the total amount of interest accrued through two schemes together in two years was ₹ 4818.30 and the total amount invested was ₹ 27,000, what was the amount invested in Scheme A?
(*a*) ₹ 12,000 (*b*) ₹ 13,500
(*c*) ₹ 15,000 (*d*) Cannot be determined

22. The difference between compound interest and simple interest on an amount of ₹ 15,000 for 2 years is ₹ 96. What is the rate of interest per annum?
(*a*) 8 (*b*) 10 (*c*) 12 (*d*) None of these

23. A sum of money is borrowed and paid back in two annual instalments of ₹ 882 each allowing 5% compound interest. The sum borrowed was:
(*a*) ₹ 1620 (*b*) ₹ 1640 (*c*) ₹ 1680 (*d*) ₹ 1700

24. The least number of complete years in which a sum of money put out at 20% compound interest will be more than doubled is:
(*a*) 3 (*b*) 4 (*c*) 5 (*d*) 6

25. On a sum of money, the simple interest for 2 years is ₹ 660, while the compound interest is ₹ 696.30, the rate of interest being the same in both the cases. The rate of interest is :
(*a*) 10% (*b*) 10.5% (*c*) 12% (*d*) None of these

ANSWERS

1	2	3	4	5	6	7	8	9	10
(*b*)	(*a*)	(*a*)	(*b*)	(*d*)	(*c*)	(*c*)	(*d*)	(*b*)	(*b*)
11	**12**	**13**	**14**	**15**	**16**	**17**	**18**	**19**	**20**
(*b*)	(*d*)	(*a*)	(*b*)	(*d*)	(*d*)	(*c*)	(*c*)	(*c*)	(*c*)
21	**22**	**23**	**24**	**25**					
(*a*)	(*a*)	(*b*)	(*b*)	(*d*)					

SOME SELECTED EXPLANATORY ANSWERS

1. Suppose that the sum is Z, then from question,

$$Z\left[\left(1+\frac{5}{100}\right)^4-1\right]-\frac{Z\times 10\times 2}{100}=124.05$$

$$\Rightarrow Z\left[\left(\frac{21}{20}\right)^4-1-\frac{1}{5}\right]=124.05 \Rightarrow Z\left[\frac{194481}{160000}-\frac{6}{5}\right]=\frac{12405}{100}$$

$$\Rightarrow Z\left[\frac{194481-192000}{160000}\right]=\frac{12405}{100} \Rightarrow Z=\left(\frac{12405}{100}\times\frac{160000}{2481}\right)=8000.$$

2. Let the sum be ₹ x. Then,

$$\text{C.I.}=\left[x\left(1+\frac{4}{100}\right)^2-x\right]=\left(\frac{676}{625}x-x\right)=\frac{51}{625}x.$$

$$\text{S.I.} = \left(\frac{x \times 4 \times 2}{100}\right) = \frac{2x}{25}.$$

$$\therefore \quad \frac{51x}{625} - \frac{2x}{25} = 1 \text{ or } x = 625.$$

3. Amount = ₹ (30000 + 4347) = ₹ 34347.

Let the time be n year.

Then,

$$30000\left(1 + \frac{7}{100}\right)^n = 34347 \Leftrightarrow \left(\frac{107}{100}\right)^n = \frac{34347}{30000} = \frac{11449}{10000} = \left(\frac{107}{100}\right)^2.$$

$\therefore \quad n = 2$ years.

4. Suppose that the time is n years. Then,

$$800 \times \left(1 + \frac{5}{100}\right)^{2n} = 926.10 \text{ or } \left(1 + \frac{5}{100}\right)^{2n} = \frac{9261}{8000}$$

$$\text{or} \quad \left(\frac{21}{20}\right)^{2n} = \left(\frac{21}{20}\right)^3 \quad \text{or} \quad 2n = 3 \text{ or } n = \frac{3}{2}.$$

$$\therefore \quad n = 1\frac{1}{2} \text{ years.}$$

5. $$\text{Principal} = ₹\left[\frac{4913}{\left(1 + \frac{25}{4 \times 100}\right)^3}\right] = ₹\left(4913 \times \frac{16}{17} \times \frac{16}{17} \times \frac{16}{17}\right) = ₹\ 4096.$$

6. P = ₹ 15000 R = 10% p.a. = 5%per half-year; T = 1 year = 2 half-years.

$$\therefore \quad \text{Amount} = ₹\left[15000 \times \left(1 + \frac{5}{100}\right)^2\right] = ₹\left(15000 \times \frac{21}{20} \times \frac{21}{20}\right)$$

$$= ₹\ 16537.50.$$

7. $$\text{Amount} = ₹\left[200\left(1 + \frac{5}{100}\right)^3 + 200\left(1 + \frac{5}{100}\right)^2 + 200\left(1 + \frac{5}{100}\right)\right]$$

$$= ₹\left[200 \times \frac{21}{20} \times \frac{21}{20} \times \frac{21}{20} + 200 \times \frac{21}{20} \times \frac{21}{20} + 200 \times \frac{21}{20}\right]$$

$$= ₹\left[200 \times \frac{21}{20}\left(\frac{21}{20} \times \frac{21}{20} + \frac{21}{20} + 1\right)\right] = ₹\ 662.02.$$

8. Amount of ₹ 100 for1 year when compounded half-yearly

$$= ₹\left[100 \times \left(1 + \frac{3}{100}\right)^2\right] = ₹\ 106.09.$$

$\therefore$ Effective rate = (106.09 – 100)% = 6.09%.

9. Suppose that the Sum is ₹ Z, then from question,

$$\left[Z\left(1 + \frac{10}{100}\right)^2 - Z\right] = 525 \Leftrightarrow Z\left[\left(\frac{11}{10}\right)^2 - 1\right]$$

$$= 525 \Leftrightarrow Z = \left(\frac{525 \times 100}{21}\right) = 2500.$$

$\therefore$ Sum = ₹ 2500.

$$\text{So, S.I.} = ₹\left(\frac{2500 \times 5 \times 4}{100}\right) = ₹\ 500.$$

10. Suppose that the each instalment is ₹ x. Then,

$$\frac{x}{\left(1 + \frac{5}{100}\right)} + \frac{x}{\left(1 + \frac{5}{100}\right)^2} = 1025 \Leftrightarrow \frac{20x}{21} + \frac{400x}{441} = 1025$$

$$\Leftrightarrow 820\,x = 1025 \times 441 \Leftrightarrow x = \left(\frac{1025 \times 441}{820}\right) = 551.25.$$

So, value of each instalment = ₹ 551.25.

11. $$\text{Amount} = ₹\left[1600 \times \left(1 + \frac{5}{2 \times 100}\right)^2 + 1600 \times \left(1 + \frac{5}{2 \times 100}\right)\right]$$

$$= ₹\left[1600 \times \frac{41}{40} \times \frac{41}{40} + 1600 \times \frac{41}{40}\right]$$

$$= ₹\left[1600 \times \frac{41}{40}\left(\frac{41}{40} + 1\right)\right] = ₹\left(\frac{1600 \times 41 \times 81}{40 \times 40}\right) = ₹\ 3321.$$

$\therefore$ C.I. = ₹ (3321 – 3200) = ₹ 121.

12. $$\text{S.I.} = ₹\left(\frac{1000 \times 10 \times 4}{100}\right) = ₹\ 400.$$

$$\text{C.I.} = ₹\left[1000 \times \left(1 + \frac{10}{100}\right)^4 - 1000\right] = ₹\ 464.10.$$

$\therefore$ Difference = ₹ (464.10 – 400) = ₹ 64.10.

13. Sum = ₹$\left(\frac{50 \times 100}{2 \times 5}\right)$ = ₹ 500.

Amount = ₹ $\left[500 \times \left(1 + \frac{5}{100}\right)^2\right]$ = ₹ $\left(500 \times \frac{21}{20} \times \frac{21}{20}\right)$ = ₹ 551.25.

∴ C.I. = ₹ (551.25 – 500) = ₹ 51.25.

14. S.I. = ₹ $\left(\frac{1200 \times 10 \times 1}{100}\right)$ = ₹ 120.

C.I. = ₹ $\left[1200 \times \left(1 + \frac{5}{100}\right)^2 - 1200\right]$ = ₹ 123.

∴ Difference = ₹ (123 – 120) = ₹ 3.

15. Let the sum is ₹ P. Then,

$$\left[P\left(1 + \frac{25}{2 \times 100}\right)^2 - P\right] = 510 \text{ or } P\left[\left(\frac{9}{8}\right)^2 - 1\right] = 510 \text{ or } P = \left(\frac{510 \times 64}{17}\right) = 1920.$$

∴ Sum = ₹ 1920.

So, S.I. = ₹$\left(\frac{1920 \times 25 \times 2}{2 \times 100}\right)$ = ₹ 480.

16. Amount = ₹$\left[8000 \times \left(1 + \frac{5}{100}\right)^2\right]$ = ₹ $\left(8000 \times \frac{21}{20} \times \frac{21}{20}\right)$ = ₹ 8820.

17. Amount = ₹$\left[25000 \times \left(1 + \frac{12}{100}\right)^3\right]$ = ₹ $\left(25000 \times \frac{28}{25} \times \frac{28}{25} \times \frac{28}{25}\right)$

= ₹ 35123.20.

∴ C.I. = ₹ (35123.20 – 25000) = ₹ 10123.20.

18. $P\left(1 + \frac{R}{100}\right)^5 = 2P \Rightarrow \left(1 + \frac{R}{100}\right)^5 = 2$ ...(*i*)

Again from question,

$$P\left(1 + \frac{R}{100}\right)^n = 8P \Rightarrow \left(1 + \frac{R}{100}\right)^n = 8 = 2^3 = \left\{\left(1 + \frac{R}{100}\right)^5\right\}^3$$

[*using* (*i*)]

$$\Rightarrow \quad \left(1+\frac{R}{100}\right)^n = \left(1+\frac{R}{100}\right)^{15} \Rightarrow n = 15.$$

$\therefore$ Required time =15 years.

20. Let P = ₹ 100. Then, S.I. ₹ 60 and T = 6 years.

$$\therefore \quad R = \frac{100 \times 60}{100 \times 6} = 10\% \text{ p.a.}$$

Now, P = ₹ 12000, T = 3 years and R = 10% p.a.

$$\therefore \quad \text{C.I.} = ₹\left[12000 \times \left\{\left(1+\frac{10}{100}\right)^3 - 1\right\}\right] = ₹\left(12000 \times \frac{331}{1000}\right) = ₹\ 3972.$$

21. Let the investment in scheme A is ₹ x.
Then, investment in scheme B = ₹ $(27000 - x)$.

$$\therefore \quad \left[x \times \left\{\left(1+\frac{8}{100}\right)^2 - 1\right\} + (27000 - x)\left\{\left(1+\frac{9}{100}\right)^2 - 1\right\}\right] = 4818.30.$$

$$\Leftrightarrow \quad \left(x \times \frac{104}{625}\right) + \frac{1881\,(27000 - x)}{10000} = \frac{481830}{100}$$

$\Leftrightarrow$ $1664x + 1881\ (27000 - x) = 48183000$

$\Leftrightarrow$ $(1881x - 1664x) = (50787000 - 48183000)$

$$\Leftrightarrow \quad 217x = 2604000 \quad \Leftrightarrow \quad x = \frac{2604000}{217} = 12000.$$

$$\textbf{22.} \quad \left[15000 \times \left(1+\frac{R}{100}\right)^2 - 15000\right] - \left(\frac{15000 \times R \times 2}{100}\right) = 96$$

$$\Leftrightarrow \quad 15000\left[\left(1+\frac{R}{100}\right)^2 - 1 - \frac{2R}{100}\right] = 96$$

$$\Leftrightarrow \quad 15000\left[\frac{(100+R)^2 - 10000 - 200\,R}{10000}\right] = 96$$

On solving for R^2

$$\Leftrightarrow \quad R^2 = \frac{96 \times 2}{3} = 64 \quad \Leftrightarrow \quad R = 8.$$

$\therefore$ Rate = 8%.

23. Principal

= (P.W. of ₹ 882 due 1 year hence) + (P.W. or ₹ 882 due 2 years hence)

$$= \left[\frac{882}{\left(1+\frac{5}{100}\right)} + \frac{882}{\left(1+\frac{5}{100}\right)^2}\right] = \left(\frac{882 \times 20}{21} + \frac{882 \times 400}{441}\right) = ₹\ 1640.$$

24. $P\left(1+\frac{20}{100}\right)^n > 2P$ or $\left(\frac{6}{5}\right)^n > 2$

Now, $\left(\frac{6}{5} \times \frac{6}{5} \times \frac{6}{5} \times \frac{6}{5}\right) > 2.$ So, $n = 4$ years.

~~~~~~
~~~~~~

22. WORK AND WAGE

The wage earned by a worker is directly proportional to the amount of work he does. As discussed in the previous chapter, the amount of work done by a person depends on his efficiency and time spent. Efficiency is inversely proportional to the time taken to do the work. Thus, wages are distributed in direct proportion to the amount of work done by individual workers.

Total wage earned by a group of persons is given by (assuming equal efficiency for each person),

Total wage = One person's one day's wage × Number of persons × Number of days.

SOLVED EXAMPLE

1. A can do a work in 10 days while B can do it in 8 days. Both of them work together to do the work. If the total amount paid for the work is ₹ 180, how much is A's share in it?

Sol. A's daily work $= \dfrac{1}{10}$

B's daily work $= \dfrac{1}{8}$

When working together, the total amount of work done by each of them will be in the same ratio as their daily work. And hence the ratio of their wages will be also in the ratio of their daily work.

∴ Ratio of their wages,

$$\text{A's : B's} = \frac{1}{10} : \frac{1}{8} = 8 : 10 \text{ or } 4 : 5$$

$$\therefore \quad \text{A's share} = \left(\frac{4}{4+5}\right) \times ₹\ 180 = ₹\ 80.$$

2. A can do a certain piece of work in d_1 days and B in d_2 days. Both of them Work together to do the work. If the total amount paid for the work is ₹ M, how much would each get?

Sol. A's daily work $= \dfrac{1}{d_1}$

B's daily work $= \dfrac{1}{d_2}$

The amount of work done by them will be in the same ratio as their daily work because both of them work together for the same time period. And hence, the ratio of their wages wilt also be me same as ratio of their daily works.

A's share: B's share = $\frac{1}{d_1} : \frac{1}{d_2} = d_2 : d_1$.

3. Verify the results of Ex. (1) using the formula derived in Ex. (2).

Sol. A's share = ₹ $\left(\frac{d_2}{d_1 + d_2}\right)$M

Here, d_1 = 10 days, d_2 = 8 days, M = ₹ 180

∴ A's share = $\left(\frac{8}{10+8}\right) \times 180$ = ₹ 80.

4. A, B and C can do a work in 8, 12 and 20 days respectively. They finish the work together and earn ₹ 620. What is the share of each?

Sol. A's share: B's share: C's share = $\frac{1}{8} : \frac{1}{12} : \frac{1}{20}$

Multiplying each ratio by the LCM of their denominators it becomes

$= \frac{120}{8} : \frac{120}{12} : \frac{120}{20} = 15 : 10 : 6$

∴ A's share = $\left(\frac{15}{15+10+6}\right) \times$ ₹ 620

$= \frac{15}{31} \times 620$ = ₹ 300

B's share = $\left(\frac{10}{15+10+6}\right) \times 620$ = ₹ 200

C's share = ₹ 620 – (300 + 200) = ₹ 120.

5. Verify the results of Ex. (4) using the relations derived in example 2.

Sol. Here, d_1 = 8 days, d_2 = 12 days and d_3 = 20 days

A's share : B's share : C's share

$= d_2d_3 : d_1d_3 : d_1d_2$

= (12 × 20) : (8 × 20) : (8 × 12) = 240 : 160 : 96

= (16 × 15) : (16 × 10) : (16 × 6) = 15 : 10 : 6.

EXERCISE

1. Samiara, Mahira and Kiara rented a set of DVDs at a rent of ₹ 578. If they used it for 8 hours, 12 hours and 14 hours respectively, what is Kiara's share of rent to be paid?
(*a*) ₹ 238 (*b*) ₹ 204 (*c*) ₹ 192 (*d*) ₹ 215

2. A daily-wage labourer was engaged for a certain number of days for ₹ 5,750; but being absent on some of those days he was paid only ₹ 5,000. What was his maximum possible daily wage?
(*a*) ₹ 125 (*b*) ₹ 250 (*c*) ₹ 375 (*d*) ₹ 500

3. A man and a boy received ₹ 800 as wages for 5 days for the work they did together. The man's efficiency in the work was three times that of the boy. What are the daily wages of the boy?
(*a*) ₹ 76 (*b*) ₹ 56 (*c*) ₹ 44 (*d*) ₹ 40

4. A can do a work in 12 days and B in 16 days. If both of them work together to do the work and get ₹ 2100, find the share of each.
(*a*) 800, 1700 (*b*) 900, 1600 (*c*) 1600, 900 (*d*) None of these

5. Ram can do a work in 9 days arid Shyam in 15 days. If both work together to complete the work, in what ratio should the total earnings be shared?
(*a*) 3 : 5 (*b*) 5 : 3 (*c*) 2 : 3 (*d*) None of these

6. A can do a work in 20 days. After 5 days he is joined by B and they together finish the work in next 10 days. If the total amount paid for the work is ₹ 1600, find the share of each.
(*a*) ₹ 375 (*b*) ₹ 387 (*c*) ₹ 400 (*d*) None of these

7. A, B and C undertake to do a work for ₹ 660. A and B together do $\frac{5}{8}$ of the work and the remaining work is done by C alone. How much should C get?
(*a*) ₹ 177 (*b*) ₹ 180 (*c*) ₹ 210 (*d*) None of these

8. A, B and C contract to do a work for ₹ 4200. A can do the work in 6 days, B in 10 days and C in 12 days. If they work together to do die work, what is the share of each?

	A	B	C		A	B	C
(*a*)	1000	1200	2000	(*b*)	1100	1100	2000
(*c*)	1000	2000	1200	(*d*)	2000	1200	1000

9. A can do a work in 15 days. A and B together do the same work in 10 days. If they are paid ₹ 1500 for the work, how should the money be divided between A and B?
(*a*) 1000, 500 (*b*) 500, 1000 (*c*) 750, 750 (*d*) None of these

10. A and B undertake to do a work together for ₹ 600. A alone can do it in 15 days B in 20 days. But with the assistance of C they finish it in 5 days. How is the money to be divided among them?

	A	B	C		A	B	C
(*a*)	200	200	200	(*b*)	200	250	150
(*c*)	200	150	250	(*d*)	150	200	250

11. A, B and C together earn ₹ 375 in 5 days. A and B together earn ₹ 450 in 10 days. A and C together earn ₹ 200 in 4 days. Find the daily earning of each.

	A	B	C		A	B	C
(*a*)	25	30	20	(*b*)	20	25	30
(*c*)	30	25	20	(*d*)	30	20	25

12. Wage of 10 women for 5 days is ₹ 1250. The daily wage of a man is twice that of a woman. How many men must work for 8 days to earn ₹ 1600?
(*a*) 7 (*b*) 6 (*c*) 5 (*d*) 4

13. 5 men and 6 women can earn ₹ 2160 in 4 days. 8 men and 10 women can earn ₹ 4400 in 5 days. In how many days can 4 men and 9 women earn ₹ 1800?
(*a*) 3 (*b*) 4 (*c*) 5 (*d*) 6

14. 2 men and 1 woman can complete a piece of work in 14 days while 4 women and 2 men can do the same work in 8 days. If a man gets ₹ 60 per day, what should be the wages per day of a woman?
(*a*) ₹ 30 (*b*) ₹ 35 (*c*) ₹ 40 (*d*) ₹ 50

15. A, B and C undertake to do a job for ₹ 1110. A can do the job in 12 days, B in 15 days and C in 18 days. What does C get?
(*a*) ₹ 300 (*b*) ₹ 275 (*c*) ₹ 335 (*d*) ₹ 339

16. A can complete a job in 12 days, while B can complete the job in 15 days. Both of them worked for 5 days, and the rest of the work was finished by C, If their total earning was 720. Find the wages of B?
(*a*) ₹ 95 (*b*) ₹ 100 (*c*) ₹ 104 (*d*) ₹ 240

17. A, B and C undertake to complete a piece of work for ₹ 2574. A works for 8 days, B for 9 days and C for 12 days to complete the work. If their daily wages are in the ratio of 3 : 5 : 4, what does C get?
(*a*) ₹ 987 (*b*) ₹ 1035 (*c*) ₹ 1100 (*d*) None of these

18. A, B and C undertake to complete a piece of work for ₹ 1440. A alone can complete the work in 8 days, B in 12 days and C in 16 days. They complete the work with the help of D in 3 days. What does D get?
(*a*) ₹ 265 (*b*) ₹ 270 (*c*) ₹ 300 (*d*) None of these

ANSWERS

1	2	3	4	5	6	7	8	9	10
(*a*)	(*b*)	(*d*)	(*c*)	(*b*)	(*c*)	(*b*)	(*d*)	(*a*)	(*c*)
11	**12**	**13**	**14**	**15**	**16**	**17**	**18**		
(*b*)	(*d*)	(*a*)	(*c*)	(*a*)	(*d*)	(*d*)	(*b*)		

SOME SELECTED EXPLANATORY ANSWERS

1. Ratio of rent's sharing = 8 : 12 : 14 = 4 : 6 : 7
Total rent = ₹ 578

Share of Kiara = $\frac{7}{17} \times 578$ = ₹ 238.

2. It is required to find the highest common factor of 5750 and 5000, because his daily wage is their common factor.
Hence, the daily wage is ₹ 250.

3. Man : boy = 3 : 1

$\therefore$ Boy's share = $\frac{1}{4} \times 800$ = ₹ 200

$\therefore$ The daily wage of boy = ₹$\left(\frac{200}{5}\right)$ = ₹ 40.

4. A's shares ₹ 1600, B's share = ₹900

5. A's share : B's share = 5 : 3

6. A works for total (5 + 10) = 15 days

A's work for 15 days = $\frac{15}{20} = \frac{3}{4}$

$\therefore$ B's share of work = $1 - \frac{3}{4} = \frac{1}{4}$

A's share : B's share = $\frac{3}{4} : \frac{1}{4}$ = 3 : 1

A's share = $\left(\frac{3}{3+1}\right)$ × ₹ 1600 = ₹ 1200

B's share = ₹ (1600 – 1200) = ₹ 400.

8. A's share = ₹ 2000, B's share = ₹ 1200,
C's share = ₹ 1000

14. (2 men and 1 woman)'s one day's work = $\frac{1}{14}$

In other words, 2 × 14 men and 1 × 14 women can complete the work in one day. ...(*i*)

(4 women and 2 men)'s one day's work = $\frac{1}{8}$

In other words, 4 × 8 women and 2 × 8 men can complete the work in one day. ...(*ii*)

Now, from equations (i) and (*ii*),

28 men and 14 women = 16 men and 32 women

12 men = 18 women

18 women will get = ₹ 12 × 60 per day.

1 woman will get = ₹ $\frac{12 \times 60}{18}$ = ₹ 40 per day.

15. A's one day work = $\frac{1}{11}$

B's one day work = $\frac{1}{15}$

C's one day work = $\frac{1}{18}$

Ratio of their one day's work

$= \frac{1}{12} : \frac{1}{15} : \frac{1}{18} = 15 : 12 : 10$

∴ The amount C gets = $\frac{1110 \times 10}{37}$ = ₹ 300

~~~~~~
~~~~~~

23. PROBABILITY

IMPORTANT FACTS AND FORMULAE

Probability is a measurement of uncertainty. In this chapter chances of the happening of events are considered.

1. **Experiment:** An operation which can produce some well-defined outcomes is called an experiment.

2. **Random Experiment:** An experiment in which all possible outcomes are known and the exact output cannot be predicted in advance, is called a random experiment.

   Examples of Performing a Random Experiment :

   (*i*) Rolling an unbiased dice.
   (*ii*) Tossing a fair coin.
   (*iii*) Drawing a card from a pack of well-shuffled cards.
   (*iv*) Picking up a ball of certain colour from a bag containing balls of different colours.

   Details:

   (*i*) When we throw a coin. Then either a Head (H) or a Tail (T) appears.
   (*ii*) A dice is a solid cube, having 6 faces, marked 1, 2, 3, 4, 5, 6 respectively. When we throw a die, the outcome is the number that appears on its upper face.
   (*iii*) A pack of cards has 52 cards.
   It has 13 cards of each suit, namely **Spades, Clubs, Hearts** and **Diamonds**.
   Cards of spades and clubs are **black cards**.
   Cards of hearts and diamonds are **red cards**.
   There are 4 honours of each suit.
   These are **Aces, Kings, Queens** and **Jacks**.
   These are called **face cards**.

3. **Sample Space:** When we perform an experiment, then the set S of all possible outcomes is called the **Sample Space**.

   Examples of Sample Spaces:

   (*i*) In tossing a coin, S = {H, T}.
   (*ii*) If two coins are tossed, then S = {HH, HT, TH, TT}.
   (*iii*) In rolling a dice, we have, S = {1, 2, 3, 4, 5, 6}.

4. Event: Any subset of a sample space is called an event.

5. Probability of Occurrence of an Event :

Let S be the sample space and let E be an event.

Then, $E \subseteq S$.

$$\therefore \qquad P(E) = \frac{n(E)}{n(S)}.$$

6. Results on Probability :

(*i*) $P(S) = 1$ (*ii*) $0 \leq P(E) \leq 1$ (*iii*) $P(\phi) = 0$

(*iv*) For any events A and B, we have :
$P(A \cup B) = P(A) + P(B) - P(A \cap B)$

(*v*) If $\bar{A}$ denotes (not-A), then $P(\bar{A}) = 1 - P(A)$.

Mutually Exclusive Events: Two or more events are said to be *mutually exclusive* if the happening of any one of them excludes the happening of all others in a single (*i.e.* same) experiment. Thus in the throw of a single dice the events 5 and 6 are mutually exclusive because if the events 5 happens no other event is possible in the same experiment. Here *one and only one* of the events can take place at a time, excluding all others.

Equally Likely Cases: Two or more events are said to be *equally likely* if the chances of their happening are equal, *i.e.* there is no preference of any one event to the other. Thus in a throw of an unbiased dice, the coming up of 1, 2, 3, 4, 5 or 6 is equally likely. In the throw of an unbiased coin, the coming up of head or tail is equally likely.

Independent and Dependent Events: An event is said to be *independent* if its happening is not affected by the happening of other events and if it does not affect the happening of other events. Thus in the throw of a dice repeatedly, coming up of 5 on the first throw is independent of coming up of 5 again in the second throw.

SOLVED EXAMPLE

1. A natural number is randomly selected and divided by 5. Find the probability that the remainder is an odd number.

Sol. Division of any natural number by 5 will give remainder 0, 1, 2, 3 or 4. Out of these total five only 1 and 3 are odd numbers.

$\therefore$ Probability that the remainder is an odd number $= \frac{2}{5}$.

2. In a throw of a coin, find the probability of getting a head.

Sol. Here S = {H, T} and E = {H}

$$\therefore \quad P(E) = \frac{n(E)}{n(S)} = \frac{1}{2}.$$

3. Two unbiased coins are tossed. What is the probability of getting at most one head?

Sol. Here, S = {HH, HT, TH, T T}.

Let E = event of getting at most one head.

∴ E = {TT, HT, TH).

$$\therefore \quad P(E) = \frac{n(E)}{n(S)} = \frac{3}{4}.$$

4. An unbiased die is tossed. Find the probability of getting a multiple of 3.

Sol. Here, S = {1, 2, 3, 4, 5, 6}.

Let E be the event of getting a multiple of 3.

Then, E = {3, 6}.

$$\therefore \quad P(E) = \frac{n(E)}{n(S)} = \frac{2}{6} = \frac{1}{3}.$$

5. In a simultaneous throw of a pair of dice, find the probability of getting a total more than 7.

Sol. Here, $n(S) = (6 \times 6) = 36$.

Let E = Event of getting a total more than 7

= {(2, 6), (3, 5), (3, 6), (4, 4), (4, 5), (4, 6), (5, 3), (5, 4), (5, 5), (5, 6), (6, 2), (6, 3), (6, 4), (6, 5), (6, 6)}.

$$\therefore \quad P(E) = \frac{n(E)}{n(S)} = \frac{15}{36} = \frac{5}{12}.$$

6. A bag contains 6 white and 4 black balls. Two balls are drawn at random. Find the probability that they are of the same colour.

Sol. Let S be the sample space. Then,

n (S) = Number of ways of drawing 2 balls out of (6 + 4)

$$= {}^{10}C_2 = \frac{(10 \times 9)}{(2 \times 1)} = 45.$$

Let E = Event of getting both balls of the same colour. Then,

$n(E)$ = Number of ways of drawing (2 balls out of 6) or (2 balls out of 4)

$$= ({}^6C_2 + {}^4C_2) = \frac{(6 \times 5)}{(2 \times 1)} + \frac{(4 \times 3)}{(2 \times 1)} = (15 + 6) = 21.$$

$$\therefore \; P(E) = \frac{n(E)}{n(S)} = \frac{21}{45} = \frac{7}{15}.$$

7. Two dice are thrown together. What is the probability that the sum of the numbers on the two faces is divisible by 4 or 6?

Sol. Clearly, $n(S) = 6 \times 6 = 36$.

Let E be the event that the sum of the numbers on the two faces is divisible by 4 or 6. Then

$$E = \{(1, 3), (1, 5), (2, 2), (2, 4), (2, 6), (3, 1), (3, 3), (3, 5), (4, 2), (4, 4), (5, 1), (5, 3), (6, 2), (6, 6)\}$$

$\therefore \quad n(E) = 14.$

Hence, $P(E) = \frac{n(E)}{n(S)} = \frac{14}{36} = \frac{7}{18}.$

EXERCISE

Directions (Qs. 1-2): *Study the following information carefully to answer the following questions:*

A basket contains 3 blue, 2 green and 5 red balls.

1. If four balls are picked at random, what is the probability that two are green and two are blue?

(*a*) $\frac{1}{18}$ (*b*) $\frac{1}{70}$ (*c*) $\frac{3}{5}$ (*d*) None of these

2. If three balls are picked up at random, what is the probability that at least one is red?

(*a*) $\frac{1}{2}$ (*b*) $\frac{7}{12}$ (*c*) $\frac{11}{12}$ (*d*) $\frac{1}{5}$

3. In a box, there are 10 black and 5 red balls. If one ball is picked up randomly, what is the probability that it is a black ball?

(*a*) $\frac{1}{2}$ (*b*) $\frac{1}{3}$ (*c*) $\frac{2}{3}$ (*d*) $\frac{4}{5}$

4. One-third of 12 mangoes got rotten. If 4 mangoes are taken out randomly, what is the probability that no mango is rotten?

(*a*) $\frac{14}{99}$ (*b*) $\frac{2}{3}$ (*c*) $\frac{16}{99}$ (*d*) None of these

5. In a box, there are 3 red and 7 black caps. One cap is picked up randomly. What is the probability that it is not a red cap?

(*a*) $\frac{3}{10}$ (*b*) $\frac{2}{5}$ (*c*) $\frac{9}{10}$ (*d*) None of these

6. A bag contains 2 red, 3 green and 2 blue balls. 2 balls are to be drawn randomly. What is the probability that the balls drawn contain no blue ball?

(*a*) $\frac{5}{7}$ (*b*) $\frac{10}{21}$ (*c*) $\frac{2}{7}$ (*d*) $\frac{11}{21}$

7. In a box there are 8 red, 7 blue and 6 green balls. One ball is picked up randomly. What is the probability that it is neither red nor green?

(*a*) $\frac{7}{19}$ (*b*) $\frac{2}{3}$ (*c*) $\frac{3}{4}$ (*d*) None of these

8. Two cards are drawn at random from a pack of 52 cards. The probability that the drawn cards are both aces, is

(*a*) $\frac{2}{445}$ (*b*) $\frac{1}{218}$ (*c*) $\frac{4}{1569}$ (*d*) $\frac{1}{221}$

9. A box contains 4 black balls, 3 red balls and 5 green balls. 2 balls are drawn from the box at random.What is the probability that both the balls are of the same colour?

(*a*) $\frac{47}{68}$ (*b*) $\frac{1}{6}$ (*c*) $\frac{19}{66}$ (*d*) $\frac{2}{11}$

10. Find the probability of getting a number less than 5 in a single throw of a die.

(*a*) $\frac{2}{3}$ (*b*) $\frac{1}{4}$ (*c*) $\frac{1}{3}$ (*d*) None of these

11. A card is drawn from a pack of 52 cards. Find the probability that it is
(*i*) a red suit (*ii*) a heart (*iii*) an honour card
(*iv*) an ace (*v*) a digit-card

12. Four departments send a delegation for a seminar. Each delegation consists of 6 men and 6 women. The group leaders from the two departments are men and from the other two are women. Find the probability of choosing either a woman or one of the leaders as the chairman of the meeting.

(*a*) $\frac{3}{10}$ (*b*) $\frac{8}{13}$ (*c*) $\frac{5}{14}$ (*d*) None of these

13. In a class there are 10 boys and 5 girls. A group of 3 students is to be selected to represent the class. Find the probability that it has 2 boys and 1 girl.

(*a*) $\frac{37}{87}$ (*b*) $\frac{45}{91}$ (*c*) $\frac{23}{59}$ (*d*) None of these

14. The probability of an event is $\frac{2}{5}$. Find the odds against the event.

(*a*) 3 : 2 (*b*) 2 : 3 (*c*) 4 : 9 (*d*) None of these

15. If the odds in favour of winning a race by three horses are respectively 2 : 5, 3 : 7 and 4 : 9, find the probability that one of these horses will win.

(*a*) $\frac{513}{817}$ (*b*) $\frac{147}{346}$ (*c*) $\frac{536}{847}$ (*d*) None of these

16. A man can kill a bird once in three shots. On the basis of this assumption he fires three shots. What is the chance that a bird is killed?

(*a*) $\frac{5}{9}$ (*b*) $\frac{19}{27}$ (*c*) $\frac{7}{18}$ (*d*) None of these

17. A palace has total 18 gates of which 2 are permanently closed. To check visitors security men stand on 12 gates. What is the probability that a man can enter the palace unchecked?

(*a*) $\frac{4}{7}$ (*b*) $\frac{2}{3}$ (*c*) $\frac{1}{4}$ (*d*) None of these

ANSWERS

1	2	3	4	5	6	7	8	9	10
(*b*)	(*c*)	(*c*)	(*a*)	(*d*)	(*b*)	(*d*)	(*d*)	(*c*)	(*a*)
11	**12**	**13**	**14**	**15**	**16**	**17**			
(-)	(*d*)	(*b*)	(*a*)	(*d*)	(*b*)	(*c*)			

SOME SELECTED EXPLANATORY ANSWERS

1. Number of ways of picking 4 balls out of 10 balls = $^{10}C_4$

$$= \frac{10 \times 9 \times 8 \times 7}{1 \times 2 \times 3 \times 4} = 210$$

Favourable number of cases = $^2C_2 \times {}^3C_2 = 3$

$\therefore$ Required Probability = $\frac{3}{210} = \frac{1}{70}$.

2. Total number of balls = 3 + 2 + 5 = 10 balls.

No. of ways of selecting three balls none of them are red

$$= {}^{(10-5)}C_3 = {}^5C_3$$

No. of ways of selecting 3 balls out of 10 balls = ${}^{10}C_3$

Hence, probability $= \dfrac{{}^5C_3}{{}^{10}C_3} = \dfrac{1}{12}$

Hence, required probability $= 1 - \dfrac{1}{12} = \dfrac{11}{12}$.

3. Required Probability $= \dfrac{{}^{10}C_1}{{}^{15}C_1} \approx \dfrac{10}{15} = \dfrac{2}{3}$.

4. From question,

No. of rotten mangoes $= 12 \times \dfrac{1}{3} = 4$

Out of 12 mangoes 4 can be chosen in ${}^{12}C_4$ ways.

So, exhaustive number of case = ${}^{12}C_4$

$$= \frac{12 \times 11 \times 10 \times 9}{1 \times 2 \times 3 \times 4} = 495$$

No rotten mangoes means all unrotten mangoes. The number of ways of selecting all four unrotten mangoes out of 8 is ${}^8C_4$.

$\therefore$ Favourable number of cases

$$= {}^8C_4 = \frac{8 \times 7 \times 6 \times 5}{1 \times 2 \times 3 \times 4} = 70$$

So, required probability

$$= \frac{\text{Favourable number of cases}}{\text{Exhaustive number of cases}} = \frac{70}{495} = \frac{14}{99}.$$

5. Total number of caps = 3 + 7 = 10

$\therefore$ Exhaustive number of cases = ${}^{10}C_1 = 10$

Cap drawn is not of red colour.

$\therefore$ Favourable number of cases = ${}^7C_1 = 7$

$\because$ Required probability $= \dfrac{7}{10}$.

6. Total number of balls = 2 + 3 + 2 = 7

$\therefore$ Exhaustive number of cases $n(S) = {}^7C_2 = \dfrac{7 \times 6}{2} = 21$

Now, the drawn balls must not be blue.

∴ 2 balls can be selected from 2 red + 3 green = 5 balls in ${}^5C_2$ ways.

∴ Favourable number of cases $n(E) = {}^5C_2 = \frac{5 \times 4}{2} = 10$

∴ Required Probability $= \frac{n(E)}{n(S)} = \frac{10}{21}$.

7. There are 21 balls in the box out of which 1 ball can be picked in ${}^{21}C_1$ ways

So, exhaustive number of cases $= {}^{21}C_1 = 21$

Neither red nor green ball means blue ball. The number of ways of selecting 1 blue ball out of 7 is ${}^7C_1$.

∴ Required probability $= \frac{7}{21} = \frac{1}{3}$.

8. Total number ways of drawing 2 cards out of 52 cards

$$= {}^{52}C_2 = \frac{52 \times 51}{2} = 26 \times 51$$

Number of ways 2 aces can be drawn out of total 4 aces

$$= {}^4C_2 = \frac{4 \times 3}{2} = 6$$

∴ Hence required probability

$$= \frac{{}^4C_2}{{}^{52}C_2} = \frac{6}{26 \times 51} = \frac{1}{13 \times 17} = \frac{1}{221}.$$

9. Total balls = 4 + 3 + 5 = 12

Out of 12, we are drawing 2 balls at random

The 2 balls can be drawn in ${}^{12}C_2$ ways.

Then probably for both ball are of same colour.

$$= \frac{{}^4C_2 + {}^3C_2 + {}^5C_2}{{}^{12}C_2} = \frac{3 + 6 + 10}{6 \times 11} = \frac{19}{66}.$$

10. Outcome less than 5 in a throw of a dia. = {1, 2, 3, 4}

∴ $n(E) = 4$

and $n(S) = 6$

Hence, required probability $= \frac{4}{6} = \frac{2}{3}$.

11. (*i*) $\frac{1}{2}$ (*ii*) $\frac{1}{4}$ (*iii*) $\frac{4}{13}$ (*iv*) $\frac{1}{13}$ (*v*) $\frac{9}{13}$

12. $\frac{13}{24}$

13. 2 boys selected out of 10 boys in ${}^{10}C_2$ ways and 1 girl to be selected out of 5 girls in ${}^{5}C_1$ ways

No. of ways of selecting 3 child out of 15 childs = ${}^{15}C_3$

Hence, required probability = $\frac{{}^{10}C_2 \times {}^{5}C_1}{{}^{15}C_3} = \frac{45}{91}$.

14. 3 : 2

15. $\frac{813}{910}$.

16. $\frac{19}{27}$ Odds against = 220 : 1.

17. Out of the total 18 gates 2 are permanently closed

$\therefore$ A man can enter from any one of the remaining 18 – 2 = 16 gates. On 12 gates there are security men to check the visitors.

$\therefore$ No. of gates which are open but don't have security men

$= 16 - 12 = 4$

$\therefore$ Chances favourable to the man entering the palace unchecked = 4

Total possible ways of entering the palace = 16

$\therefore$ Probability that a man can enter the palace unchecked = $\frac{4}{16} = \frac{1}{4}$.

~~~~~~
~~~~~~

24. GEOMETRY: LINES, TRIANGLES, QUADRILATERALS AND CIRCLES

LINES AND ANGLES

AXIOMS/POSTULATES: The basic facts which are taken for granted, without proof, are called axioms.

The postulates are:

- Space contains at least two distinct points.
- A line contains infinitely many points and contains at least two distinct points.
- A plane is a set of many points and contains at least three non-collinear points.
- If two distinct plane intersect, then their intersection is a straight line.
- Halves of equals are equal.
- Through a given point, there pass an infinite number of lines.
- Given two distinct points P and Q, there is one and only one line that contains both the points.
- Three or more than three points are said to be collinear, then there is a line which contains them all.
- Two lines can intersect at the most at one point.
- Two lines having a common point are known as intersecting point.
- Two lines which are both parallel to the same line are parallel to each other.
- Point is represented by a dot on which length, breadth and height cannot be measured.

Line Segment: The straight path between two points P and Q is called a line segment PQ.

- P and Q are end points of line segment.
- It has a definite length.
- Distance between P and Q is length of the line segment PQ.

Ray: A ray extends indefinitely in one direction. This is exhibited by an arrow *i.e.,* PQ.

- P is called initial point.
- It has no definite length.

- It cannot be drawn but can simply be represented on the plane of a paper.

Line: A line segment $\overline{PQ}$ when extended indefinitely to both the directions is called line $\overline{PQ}$.

- Line has no end points.
- Line has no definite length.
- Line cannot be drawn.
- Line is a set of infinite points.

Intersecting Lines : Two lines having a common point are called intersecting lines. This-common point is point of intersection *i.e.*, 'O'.

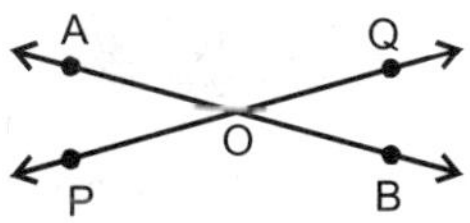

Concurrent Lines: Three or more lines intersecting at the same point are said to be concurrent.

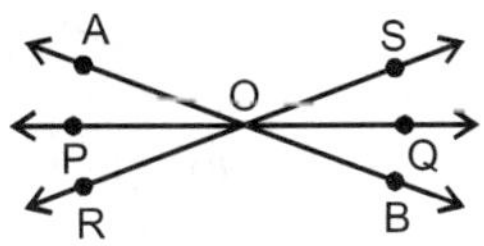

Parallel Lines: Two lines l and m in a plane are said to be parallel. If they have no common point and we write $l \parallel m$.

Angles: A figure consisting of two rays with end points is called an angle.

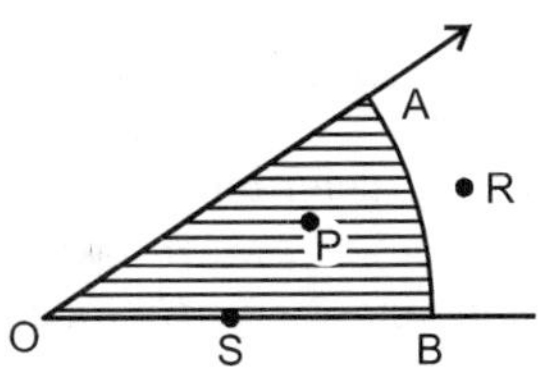

- P is a point in the interior of ∠AOB.
- S is a point on ∠AOB.

- R is a point in the exterior of ∠AOB.

An Angle of 360°: If a ray OP starting from its original position OP, rotates about OQ, in the anticlockwise direction and after making a complete revolution it comes back to its original position we say it has rotated through 360 degree written as 360°.

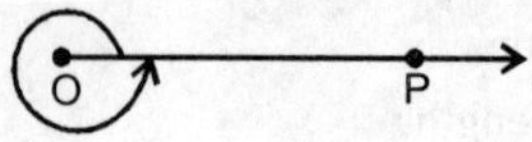

- 1° = 60 minutes, written as 60′
- 1′ = 60 seconds, written as 60″
- If the sum of two angles is 90°, then they are complementary to each other.
- If the sum of two angles is 180°, they are supplementary to each other.

EXERCISE

1. Lines *l* and *m* intersect at O, forming angles as shown in figure. If $x = 45°$, then values of *y, z* and *u* are respectively:
(*a*) 45°, 135°, 135°
(*b*) 135°, 135°, 45°
(*c*) 135°, 45°, 135°
(*d*) 115°, 45°, 115°

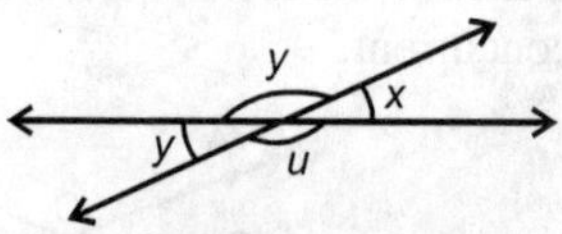

2. An angles which is greater than 180° but less than 360° is called:
(*a*) a reflex angle (*b*) a right angle
(*c*) an adjacent angle (*d*) none of these

3. If two angles are complementary of each other, then each angle is:
(*a*) an acute angle (*b*) a right angle
(*c*) an obtuse angle (*d*) a supplementary angle

4. The value of *z* (in degrees), in the given figure, is:
(*a*) 180°
(*b*) 216°
(*c*) 240°
(*d*) 40°

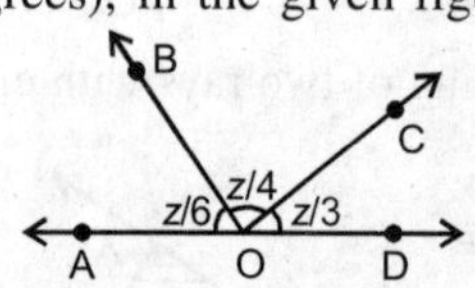

5. Which one of the following determines a plane?
(*a*) A line and a point on it (*b*) Two points
(*c*) Three non-collinear points (*d*) None of these

6. Which of the following statements is false?
(*a*) A line segment can be produced to any desired length
(*b*) Through a given point, only one straight line can be drawn

(*c*) Through two given points, it is possible to draw one and only one straight line

(*d*) Two straight lines can intersect in only one point

7. If AB and CD are two parallel lines and EF is a transversal which cuts. AB at P and CD at Q, then ∠APQ and ∠PQC are called as:

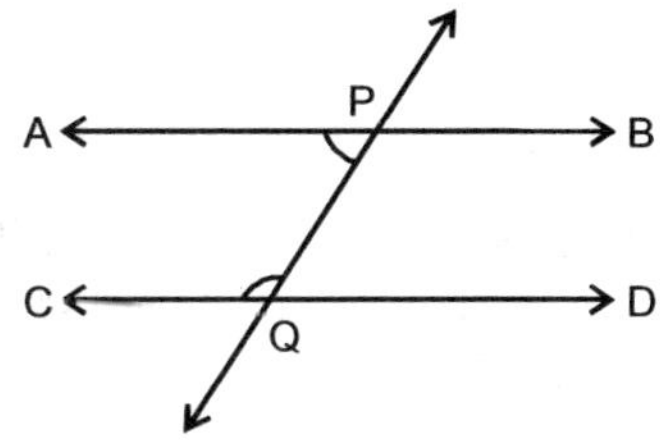

(*a*) adjacent angles
(*b*) alternate angles
(*c*) corresponding angles
(*d*) None of these

8. Number of pairs of vertical angles formed, when two lines intersect is/are:

(*a*) one pair (*b*) two pairs (*c*) four pairs (*d*) None of these

9. In figure determine the value of y:

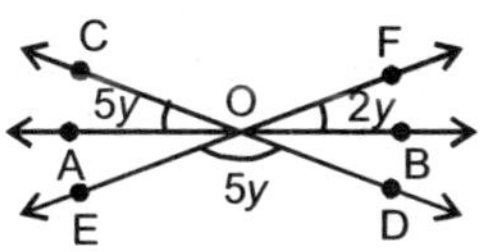

(*a*) 25° (*b*) 35° (*c*) 15° (*d*) 40°

10. In figure, the value of x which would make ABC a line:

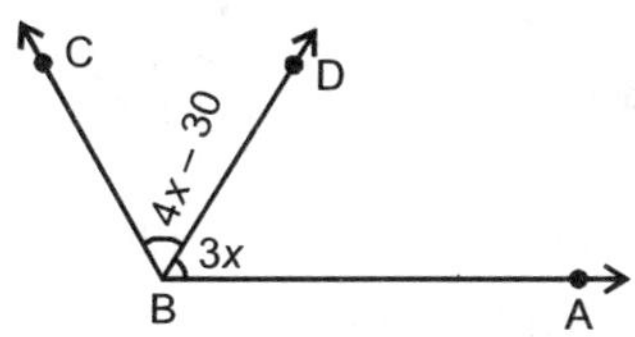

(*a*) 40° (*b*) 35° (*c*) 45° (*d*) 30°

11. If P and Q are points on the opposite sides of a straight line AB. If O is a point on AB, such that ∠AOP = ∠BOQ, then when one of the following is correct?

(*a*) ∠AOQ < ∠BOP (*b*) ∠AOQ > ∠BOP
(*c*) ∠AOP = 180° – ∠AOQ (*d*) ∠AOP = 90° – ∠AOQ

12. In the given figure. If PQ ∥ RS ∠QPT = 115° and ∠PTR = 20°, then ∠SRT is equal to:

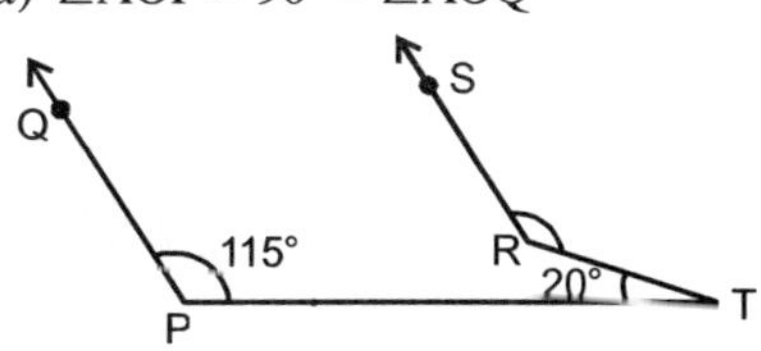

(*a*) 155° (*b*) 150°
(*c*) 135° (*d*) 95°

13. Two parallel lines are cut by a transversal then which of the following are true?

I. Pair of alternate interior angles are congruent.
II. Pair of corresponding angles are congruent.
III. Pair of interior angles on the same side of the transversal are supplementary.

(*a*) I, II, III are true (*b*) I, III are true
(*c*) I, II are true (*d*) II, III are true

14. AB and CD are two parallel lines. PQ cuts AB and CD at E and F respectively. EL is the bisector of ∠FEB. If ∠LEB = 35; then ∠CFQ will be:
(*a*) 130° (*b*) 85° (*c*) 70° (*d*) 95°

15. AB and CD are two parallel lines. The points B and C are joined such that ∠ABC = 65°. A line CE is drawn making angle of 35° with the line CB, EF is drawn parallel to AB, as show in figure then ∠CEF is equal to:

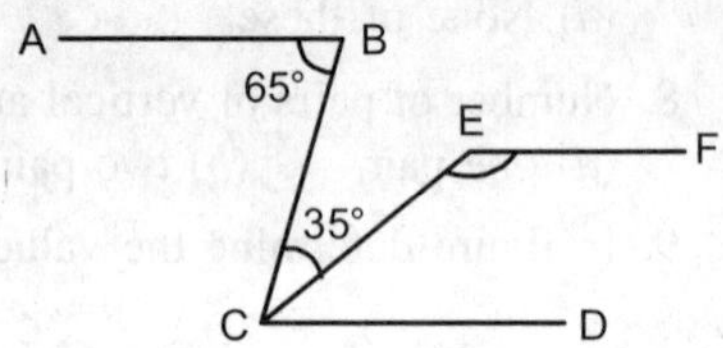

(*a*) 160° (*b*) 155° (*c*) 150° (*d*) 145°

16. In the figure below, RT is drawn parallel to the line SQ. The value of x is:

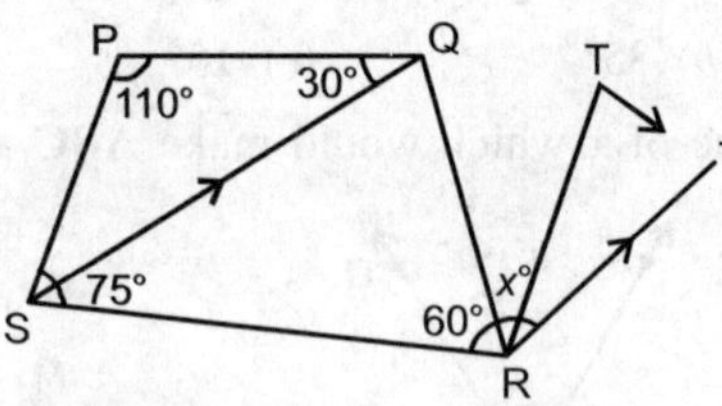

(*a*) 85° (*b*) 45° (*c*) 120° (*d*) 75°

17. AB is a straight line and O is a point on AB. If one draws a line OC not coinciding with OA or OB, then the ∠AOC and ∠BOC are:
(*a*) Equal (*b*) Complementary
(*c*) Supplementary (*d*) Together equal to 130°

18. In the given figure if EC ∥ AB, ∠ECD = 70°, ∠BDO = 20°, then ∠OBD is equal to:

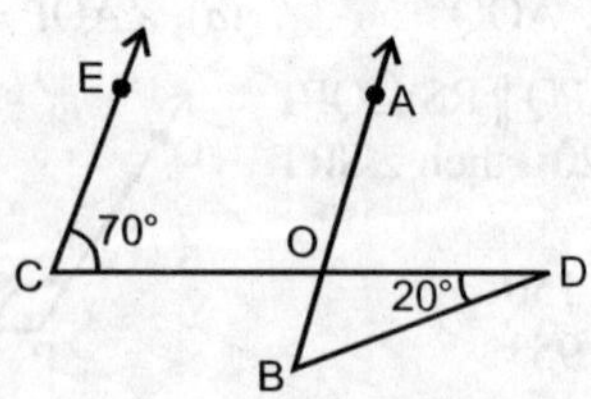

(*a*) 70° (*b*) 60° (*c*) 50° (*d*) 20°

19. Two parallel lines AB and CD are intersected by a transversal line EF at M and N respectively. The lines MP and NP are the bisectors of the interior angles BMN and DNM on the same side of the transversal. Then ∠MPN is equal to:

(*a*) 90° (*b*) 45° (*c*) 135° (*d*) 60°

20. AB and CD are parallel straight lines of lengths 5 cm and 4 cm respectively. AD and BC intersect at a point O such that AO = 10 cm, then OD equals:

(*a*) 7 cm (*b*) 8 cm (*c*) 5 cm (*d*) 6 cm

21. In the given figure if PQ || SR the relation between $\angle a$ and $\angle b$ is:

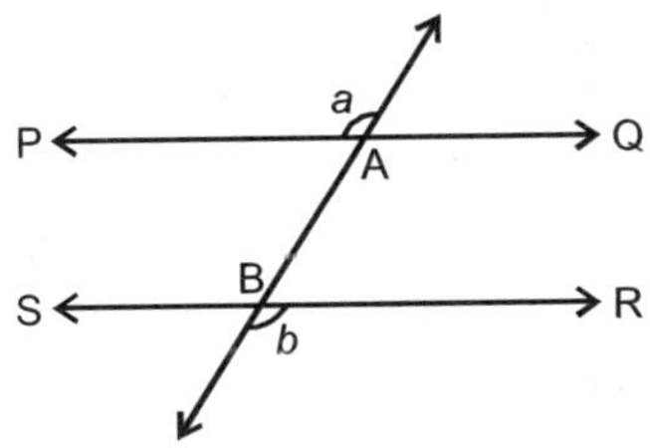

(*a*) $\angle a \neq \angle b$ (*b*) $\angle a < \angle b$ (*c*) $\angle a = \angle b$ (*d*) $\angle a > \angle b$

22. A set of concurrent lines contain:

(*a*) an indefinite number of common points

(*b*) a common line

(*c*) exactly two common points

(*d*) a unique common points

ANSWERS

1	2	3	4	5	6	7	8	9	10
(*c*)	(*a*)	(*a*)	(*c*)	(*c*)	(*b*)	(*d*)	(*b*)	(*c*)	(*d*)
11	**12**	**13**	**14**	**15**	**16**	**17**	**18**	**19**	**20**
(*c*)	(*c*)	(*a*)	(*c*)	(*c*)	(*a*)	(*c*)	(*c*)	(*a*)	(*b*)
21	**22**								
(*c*)	(*d*)								

SOME SELECTED EXPLANATORY ANSWERS

1. $x = z$ (Vertically opposite angles)

So $x = 45° \Rightarrow z = 45°$

also $y + x = 180°$

$y = 180° - 45°,\ y = 135°$

also $y = u \Rightarrow u = 135°$

So 135°, 45°, 135° is answer.

4. Here $\frac{z}{6}+\frac{z}{4}+\frac{z}{3} = 180°$

$$\frac{2z + 3z + 4z}{12} = 180°$$

$$\frac{9z}{12} = 180°$$

$$z = \frac{180 \times 12}{9} = 240°$$

5. Three non-collinear points

6. Since an infinite number of straight lines can be drawn to pass through a given point. Hence (*b*) is false statement.

7. ∠APQ and ∠PQC are interior angles on the same side of transversal.

9. Here as OA, OB are opposite rays.
∠AOC + ∠COF + ∠FOB = 180°
$5y + 5y + 2y = 180°$
$12y = 180° \Rightarrow y = 15°$

10. Here if ABC is a straight line
then ∠ABD + ∠DBC = 180°
$4x - 30° + 3x = 180°$
$7x = 180° + 30°$
$7x = 210° \Rightarrow x = 30°$

11. Here, as given
∠AOP = ∠BOQ
POQ is a straight line.
So ∠AOP + ∠AOQ = 180°
∠AOP = 180° – ∠AOQ

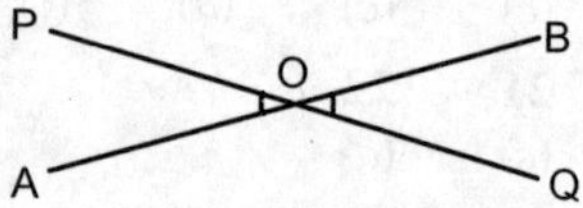

12. Here ∠QPL + ∠PLR = 180°
∠PLR = 180° – ∠QPL
= 180° – 115° = 65°
∠RLP = ∠LRT + ∠RTL
∠LRT = ∠RLP – ∠RTL
= 65° – 20° = 45°
∠SRT + ∠LRT = 180°
∠SRT = 180° – ∠LRT
= 180° – 45° = 135°
∠SRT = 135°

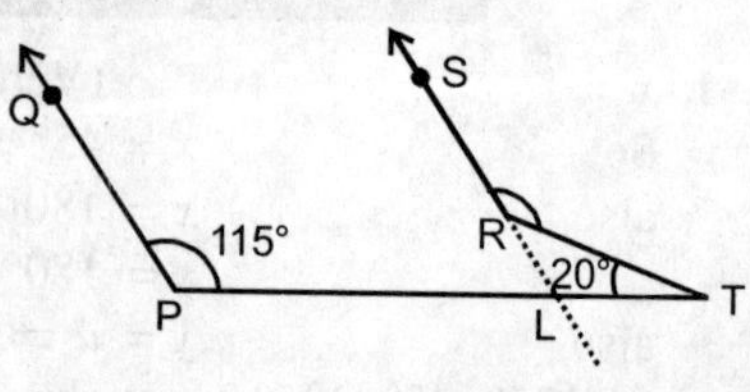

13. All the three statements are true regarding the condition.

14. $\angle LEB = 35°$
$\angle FEB = 2 \times \angle LEB = 70°$
$\angle CFQ = \angle FEB$ (alternate angles)
$\angle CFQ = 70°$

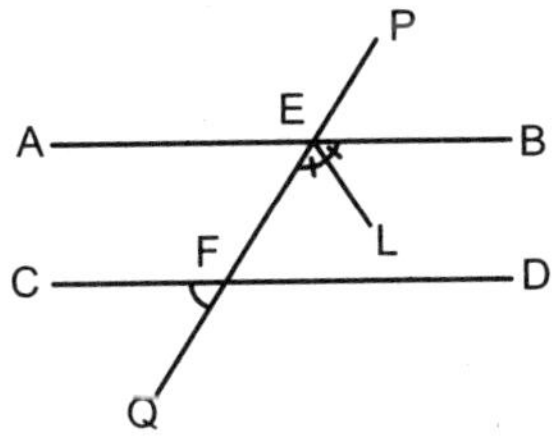

15. $\angle ABC = \angle BCD$ as $AB \parallel CD$
$\angle BCD = 65°$
$\angle ECD = 65° - \angle BCE = 65° - 35° = 30°$
$\angle CEF + \angle ECD = 180°$
$\angle CEF = 180° - 30° = 150°.$

16. Here $\angle PSQ = 180° - (110° + 30°)$
$\angle PSQ = 40°$
$\angle QSR = 75° - 40° = 35°$
$\angle QSR + \angle SRT = 180°$ [$SQ \parallel RT$]
$35° + 60° + x = 180°$
$x = 180° - 95°$
$x = 85°.$

17. Points A, O, B are collinear so
$\angle AOC + \angle BOC = 180°$
Hence are supplementary.

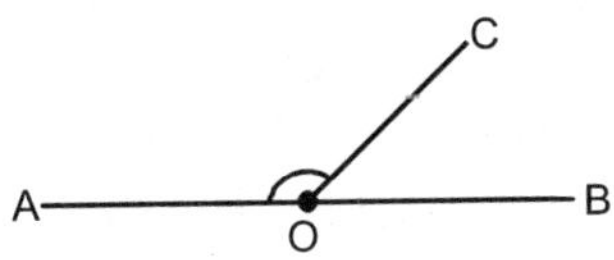

18. $\angle AOD = \angle ECO \Rightarrow \angle AOD = 70°$
So $\angle BOD = 110°$
Hence in ΔBOD
$\angle OBD + \angle BOD + \angle ODB = 180°$
$\angle OBD = 180° - (110° + 20°)$
$\angle OBD = 50°.$

19. As $\angle BMN + \angle DNM = 180°$
$\angle PMN + \angle PNM = 90°$
$\angle MPN = 180° - (\angle PMN + \angle PNM)$
$= 180° - (90°)$
$\Rightarrow \angle MPN = 90°.$

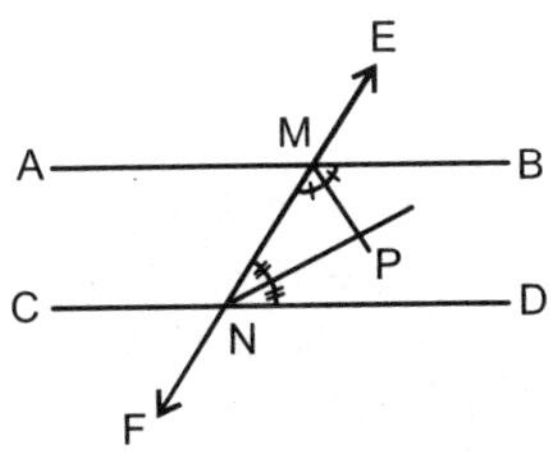

20. Here as $AB \parallel CD$

So $\dfrac{AB}{CD} = \dfrac{AO}{OD}$

$\dfrac{5}{4} = \dfrac{10}{OD} \Rightarrow OD = \dfrac{4 \times 10}{5} = 8$ cm.

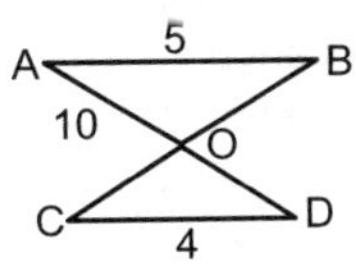

TRIANGLES

A plane (closed) figure bounded by three line segments is called a triangle. Triangles are denoted by Δ.

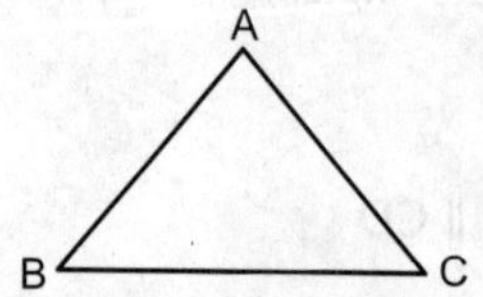

A ΔABC has:

- three vertices, namely A, B and C
- three sides, AB, BC and AC.
- three angles, namely ∠A, ∠B and ∠C.

A triangle has six parts—three sides and three angles.

Types of Triangles on the Basis of Angles

(a) Right-angled Triangle: A triangle in which one of the angles measures 90° is called a right-angled triangle. The side opposite to the right angle is called its hypotenuse and the remaining two sides are called as perpendicular and base depending upon conditions.

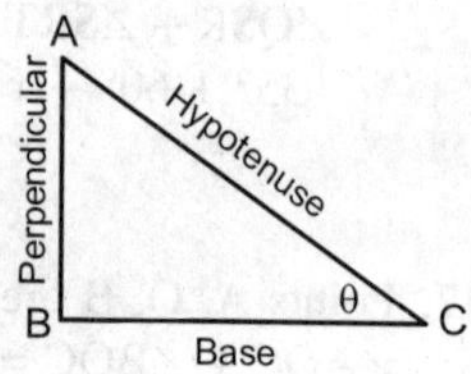

Here ΔABC has ∠B = 90° and AC is hypotenuse.

(b) Acute-angled Triangle: A triangle in which every angle measures more than 0° and is less than 90° is called an acute-angled triangle.

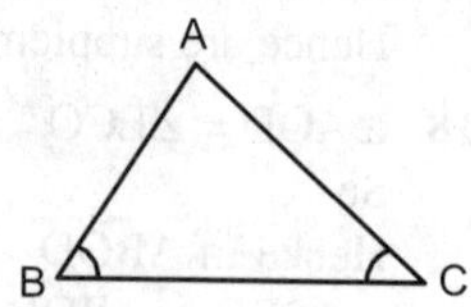

Here ΔABC is an acute-angled triangle.

(c) Obtuse-angled Triangle: A triangle in which one of the angles measures more than 90° but less than 180° is called an obtuse-angled triangle.

Here, ΔABC is an obtuse-angled and ∠ABC is the obtuse angle.

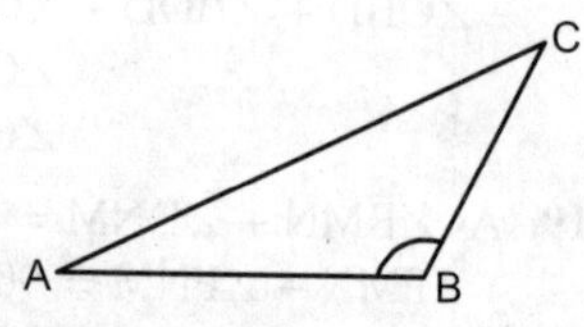

Types of Triangles on the Basis of Sides

(A) Scalene Triangle: A triangle in which all the sides are of different lengths is called a scalene triangle. ΔABC is a scalene triangle as AB ≠ BC ≠ AC.

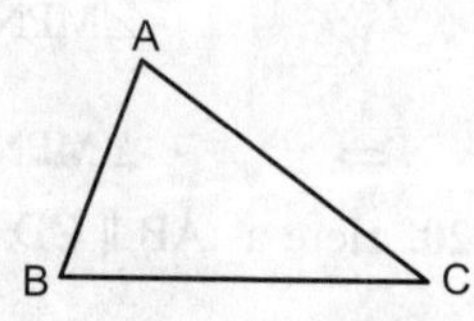

(B) Isosceles Triangle: A triangle in which two sides are equal is called an isosceles triangle. Here ΔABC is an isosceles triangle as AB = AC.

- Angles opposite to equal sides are equal *i.e.*, ∠B = ∠C

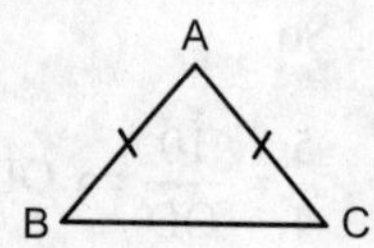

(C) Equilateral Triangle: A triangle having all sides equal is called an equilateral triangle. Here in ΔABC, AB = BC = AC.

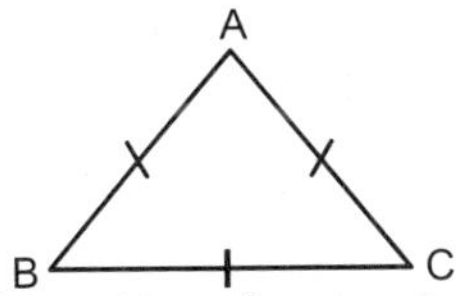

- All angles are equal and each is of measure 60°.

Perimeter of a Triangle : The sum of the lengths of three sides of a triangle is called its perimeter.

So in ΔABC, perimeter

= AB + BC + AC.

Some Terminologies Related to a Triangle

Altitudes: The altitude of a triangle is a line segment perpendicularly drawn from vertex to the side opposite to it. The side on which the perpendicular is being drawn is called its base.

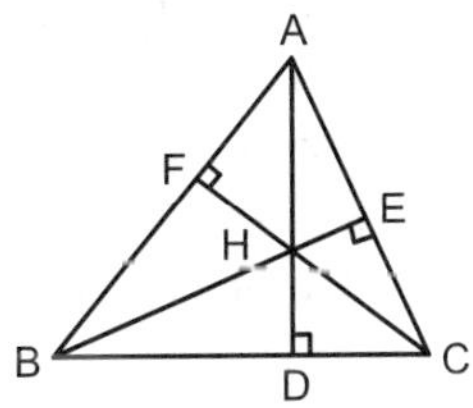

Here AD, BE and PC are altitudes drawn on BC, AC and AB respectively.

- Altitudes of a triangle are concurrent.
- The point of intersection of all the three altitudes of a triangle is called its ortho-centre.

Medians: A line segment joining the mid-point of the side with the opposite vertex.

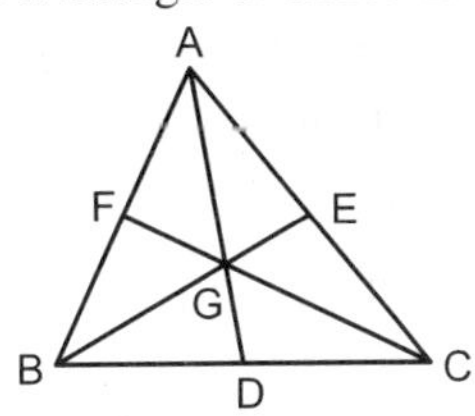

Here AD, BE and CP are medians.

- The medians of a triangle are concurrent.
- The point of intersection of all the three medians is called its **centroid**.
- Centroid is denoted by G.

In-centre of a Triangle: The point of intersection of all the three angle bisectors of a triangle is called its in-centre.

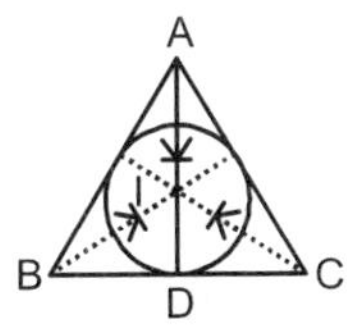

The circle with centre I and radius ID is called incircle and radius is called as inradius denoted by 'r',

Circumcentre of a Triangle: The point of intersection of the perpendicular bisectors of the sides of a triangle is called its circumcentre.

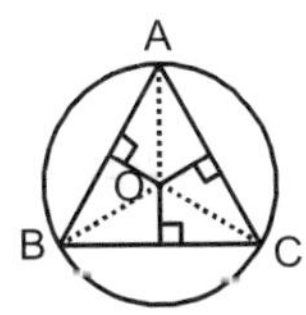

Circle through O as centre and radius OA = OB = OC passing through A, B, C is called circumcircle. Radius of circumcircle is called circumradius denoted by R.

Some Useful Results on Triangles

- The sum of the angles of a triangle is 180°.

- If a side of a triangle is produced, then the exterior angle so formed is equal to the sum of the two interior opposite angles.
- An exterior angle of a triangle is greater than either of the interior opposite angles.
- The internal bisector of one base angle and the external bisector of the other is equal to one half of the vertical angle.

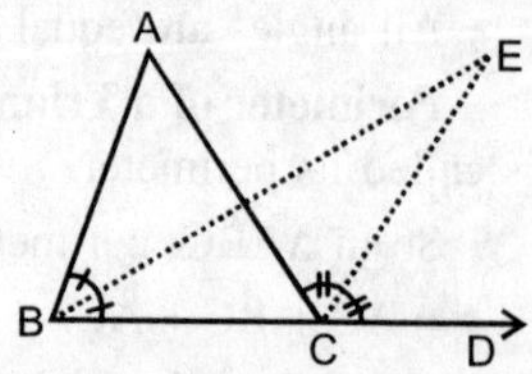

Here $\angle E = \frac{1}{2}\angle A$

- The side BC of ΔABC is produced to D. The bisector of $\angle A$ meets BC in L. Then $\angle ABC + \angle ACD = 2\ \angle ALC$.

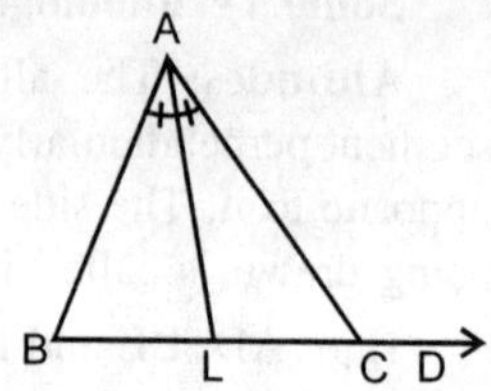

- In a ΔABC the bisector of $\angle B$ and $\angle C$ intersect each other at a point O.

$\angle BOC = 90 + \frac{1}{2}\angle A$

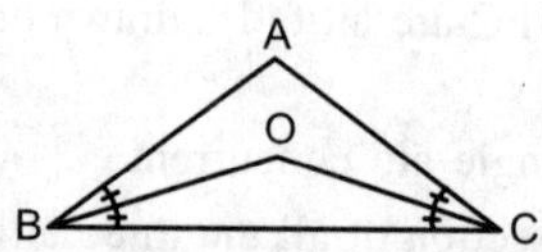

- In a ΔABC, the side AB and AC are produced to P and Q respectively. The bisectors of $\angle PBC$ and $\angle QCB$ intersect at a point O.

Then $\angle BOC = 90° - \frac{1}{2}\angle A$

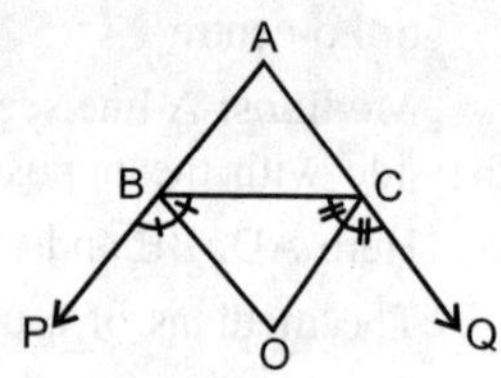

- In ΔABC, $\angle B > \angle C$. If AM is the bisector of $\angle BAC$ and $AN \perp BC$, then

$\angle MAN = \frac{1}{2}\angle B - \angle C$

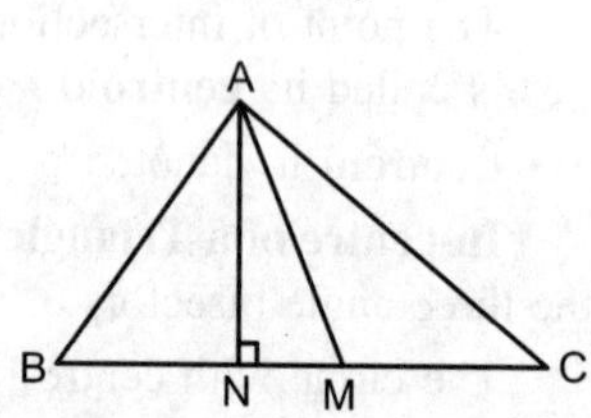

- The bisectors of the base angles of a triangle can never enclose a right angle.

Here OB and OC are the bisectors of $\angle B$ and $\angle C$.

But $\angle BOC \neq 90°$.

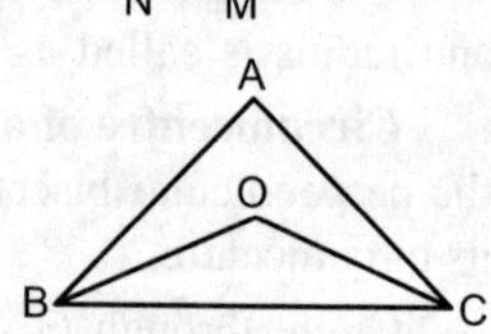

- In figure $\angle ADC = \alpha + \beta + \gamma$

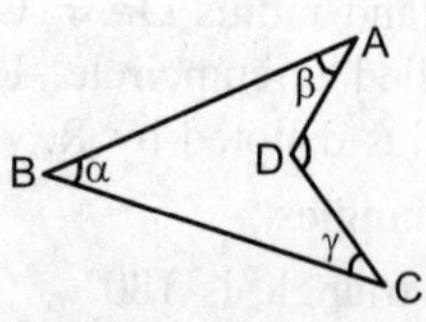

- If the three sides of a triangle be produced in order then the sum of all the exterior angles so formed is 360°.

  So $\angle DAB + \angle EBC + \angle ACF = 360°$

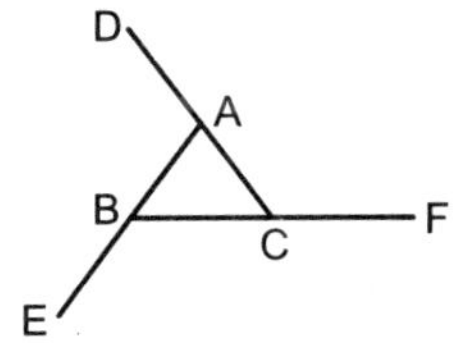

- The sum of any two sides of a triangle is greater than its third side.

  Here in ΔABC

  $AB + AC > BC$

  $AB + BC > AC$

  $BC + AC > AB.$

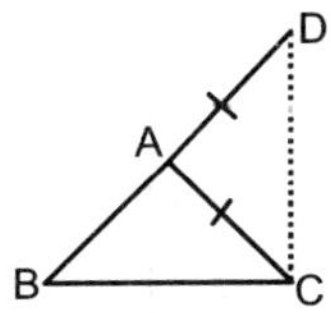

- The difference between any two sides of a triangle is less than its third side.

  Here in ΔABC,

  $AC - AB < BC$

  $BC - AC < AB.$

  $BC - AB < AC.$

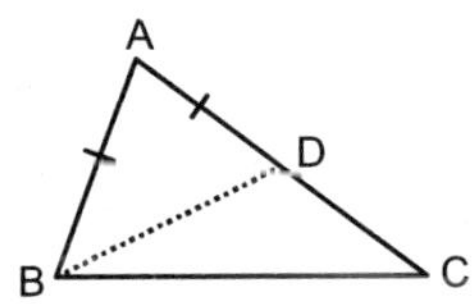

- If the bisector of the vertical angle of a triangle bisects the base, then that triangle is isosceles.
- If the altitude from one vertex of a triangle bisects the opposite side, then the triangle is isosceles.
- The perpendiculars drawn from the vertices of equal angles of an isosceles triangle to the opposite sides are equal.
- Medians of equilateral triangle are equal.
- If D is the mid-point of the hypotenuse AC of a right-angled ΔABC.

  Then $BD = \frac{1}{2} AC$

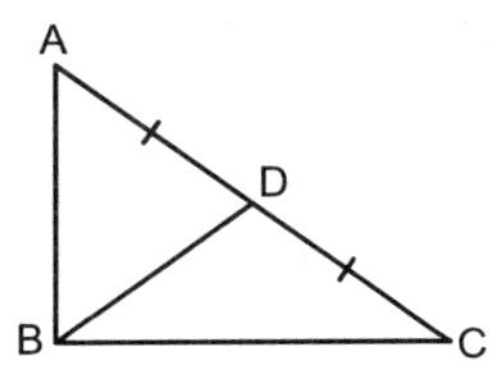

- The sum of any two sides of a triangle is greater than twice the median drawn to the third side.
- Perimeter of a triangle is greater than the sum of its three medians.

  So, $AB + BC + AC > AD + BE + CF$

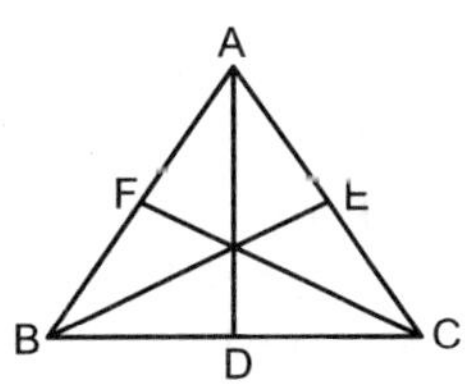

- In a ΔABC, $\angle B = 90°$, an obtuse angle or an acute angle accordingly

$AC^2 = AB^2 + BC^2$ if $\angle B = 90°$

$AC^2 > AB^2 + BC^2$ if $\angle B > 90°$

$AC^2 < AB^2 + BC^2$ if $\angle B < 90°$

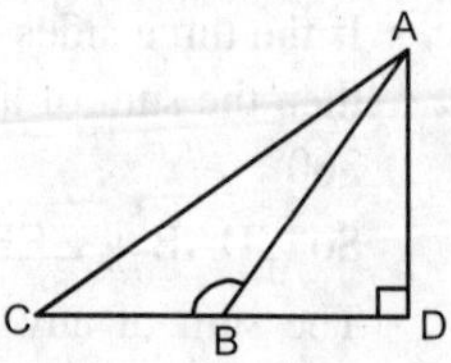

- In a ΔABC, $\angle B$ is obtuse, then
  $AC^2 = AB^2 + BC^2 + 2BC\ BD$
- In ΔABC if $\angle B$ is acute then $AB^2 = BC^2 + AC^2 - 2BC.\ CD$ and $AD \perp BC$.

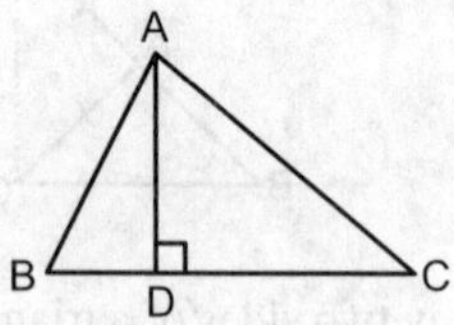

Congruent Triangles: Two triangles are said to be congruent if both are exactly of same size *i.e.*, all angles and sides are equal to corresponding angles and sides of other.

- Every triangle is congruent to itself $\Delta ABC \cong \Delta ABC$
- If $\Delta ABC \cong \Delta DEF$, then $\Delta DEF \cong \Delta ABC$
- If $\Delta ABC \cong \Delta DEF$ and $\Delta DEF \cong \Delta PQR$
  then $\Delta ABC \cong \Delta PQR$

Sufficient Conditions for Congruence of Two Triangles

Theorem 1: If two triangles have two sides and the included angle of the one are equal to the corresponding sides and the included angle of the other. (SAS)

Theorem 2: If two angles and the included side of one triangle are equal to the corresponding two angles and the included side of the other triangle. (ASA)

Theorem 3: If three sides of one triangle are respectively equal to the three sides of the other. (SSS)

Theorem 4 : If the hypotenuse and other side of one triangle are respectively equal to the hypotenuse and the corresponding side of the other triangle. (RHS)

Some other Relations in a Triangle

- Angles opposite to two equal sides of a triangle are equal.
- If two angles of a triangle are equal then the sides opposite to them are also equal.
- If two sides of a triangle are unequal the longer side has greater angle opposite to it.
- In a triangle, the greater angle has the longer side opposite to it.

Congruent Figures: The geometrical figures having the same shape and size are known as congruent figures.

Congruent figures are just like photostat copies, which are alike in every respect.

Similar Figures: Geometric figures having the same shape but different sizes are known as similar figures.

- The congruent figures are always similar but two similar figures need not be congruent, *e.g.*, Any two circles are similar. Any two rectangles are similar.

Similar Triangles: Two triangles are said to be similar to each other if

- their corresponding sides are proportional.
- their corresponding angles are equal.

EXERCISE

1. If ABC and DEF are similar triangles in which $\angle A = 47°$ and $\angle E = 83°$, then $\angle C$ is:

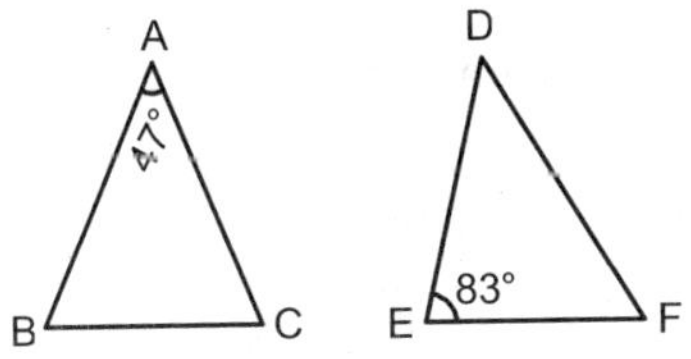

(*a*) 50° (*b*) 70° (*c*) 60° (*d*) 80°

2. In the adjoining figure if $m\ \angle ABC = m\ \angle ACE$, then ΔABC is:

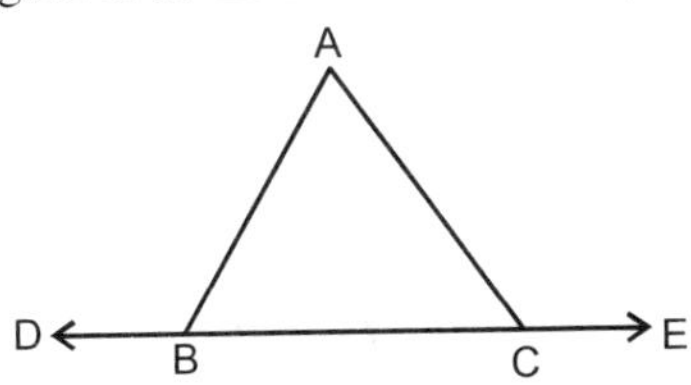

(*a*) right-angled (*b*) isosceles (*c*) equilateral (*d*) obtuse-angled

3. In triangle PQR length of the side QR is less than twice the length of the side PQ by 2 cm. Length of the side PR exceeds the length of the side PQ by 10 cm. The perimeter is 40 cm. The length of the smallest side of the triangle PQR is :

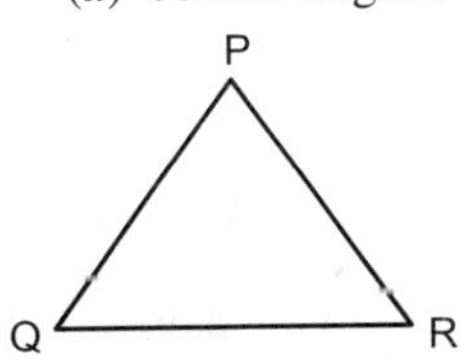

(*a*) 6 cm (*b*) 8 cm (*c*) 7 cm (*d*) 10 cm

4. In the adjoining figure which of the following statements is true?

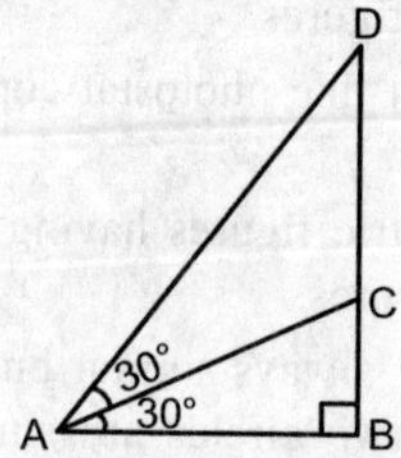

(*a*) AB = BD (*b*) AC = CD (*c*) BC = CD (*d*) AD < CD

5. In a ΔABC, $\angle A = 90°$, AL is drawn perpendicular to BC. Then $\angle BAL$ is equal to:

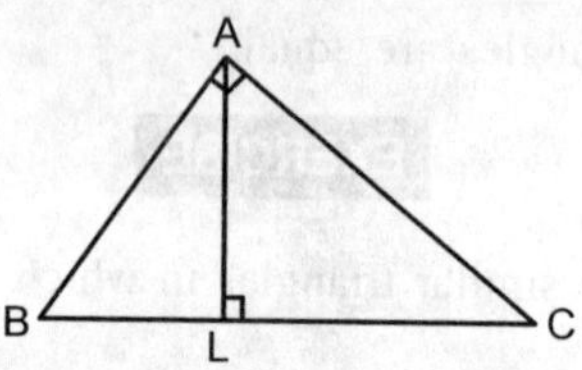

(*a*) $\angle ALC$ (*b*) $\angle ACB$ (*c*) $\angle BAC$ (*d*) $\angle B - \angle BAL$

6. OB and OC are respectively the bisectors of $\angle ABC$ and $\angle ACB$. Then $\angle BOC$ is equal to:

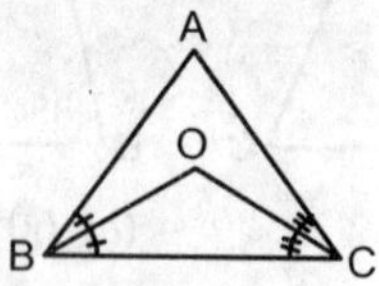

(*a*) $90° - \frac{1}{2}\angle A$ (*b*) $90° + \angle A$ (*c*) $90° + \frac{1}{2}\angle A$ (*d*) $180° - \frac{1}{2}\angle A$

7. In ΔPQR, PS is the bisector of $\angle P$ and $PT \perp QR$, then $\angle TPS$ is equal to:

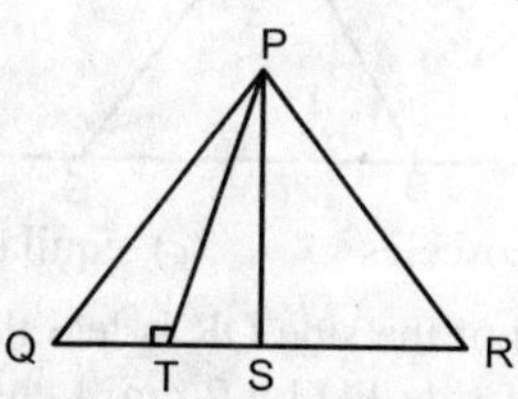

(*a*) $\angle Q + \angle R$ (*b*) $90° + \frac{1}{2}\angle Q$ (*c*) $90° - \frac{1}{2}\angle R$ (*d*) $\frac{1}{2}(\angle Q - \angle R)$

8. In the adjoining figure, sides AB and AC of a ΔABC are produced to P and Q respectively. The bisectors of $\angle PBC$ and $\angle QCB$ intersect at O. Then $\angle BOC$ is equal to:

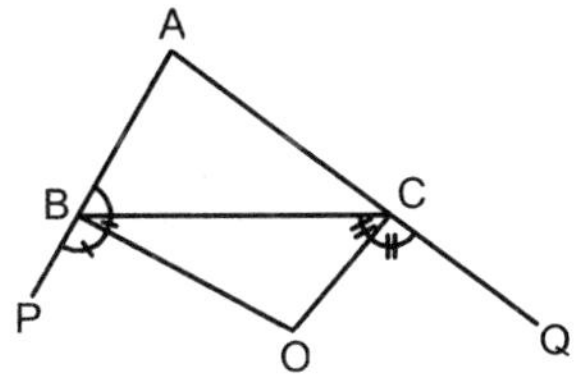

(*a*) $90° - \frac{1}{2}\angle BAC$ (*b*) $\frac{1}{2}(\angle PBC + \angle QCB)$

(*c*) $90° + \frac{1}{2}\angle BAC$ (*d*) None of these

9. The sides BC, CA and AB, of a ΔABC are produced in order, forming exterior angles $\angle ACD$, $\angle BAE$, and $\angle CBF$, then

$\angle ACD + \angle BAE + \angle CBF$ is equal to:

(*a*) 540° (*b*) 360° (*c*) 180° (*d*) None of these

10. The point of intersection of the altitudes of a triangle is called its:

(*a*) incentre (*b*) excentre (*c*) orthocentre (*d*) centroid

11. If $\angle A = \angle CED$ and $\Delta CAB \sim \Delta CED$ then the value of x is:

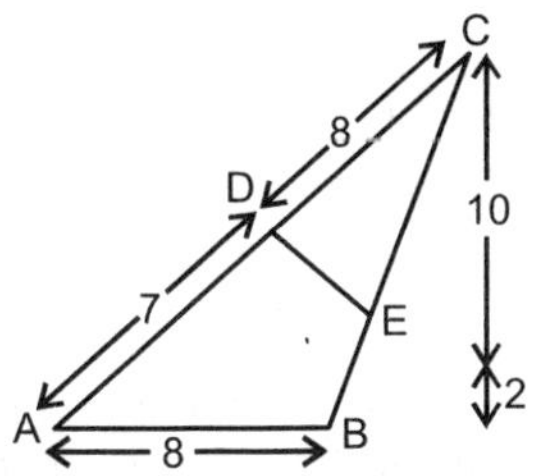

(*a*) 4 cm (*b*) 5 cm (*c*) 6 cm (*d*) 7 cm

12. In the adjoining figure AB, EF and CD are parallel lines. Given that EF = 5 cm, GC = 10 cm and DC = 18 cm, then EF is equal to:

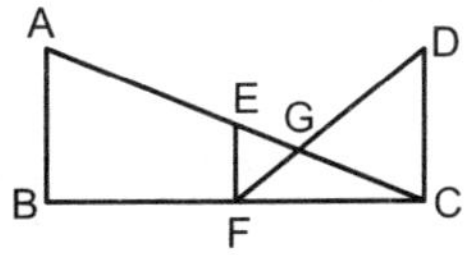

(*a*) 11 cm (*b*) 5 cm (*c*) 6 cm (*d*) 9 cm

13. If ABCD is a rhombus, then

$AB^2 + BC^2 + CD^2 + AD^2$ is equal to

(*a*) $AD^2 + BC^2$ (*b*) $AO^2 + OC^2$ (*c*) $AC^2 + BD^2$ (*d*) $2(AO^2 + OB^2)$

14. A point O in the interior of a rectangle is joined with each of the vertices A, B, C and D, then:

(*a*) $OB^2 + OD^2 = OC^2 + OA^2$ (*b*) $AO^2 - OD^2 = OC^2 - OA^2$

(*c*) $AO^2 + OD^2 = BO^2 + OC^2$ (*d*) $AO^2 + OB^2 = AC^2 - BD^2$

15. If AD, BE, CF are the medians of a ΔABC then the correct relation between the sum of the squares of sides to the sum of the squares of median is:

(*a*) $2(AB^2 + BC^2 + AC^2) = 3(AD^2 + BE^2 + CF^2)$

(*b*) $4(AB^2 + BC^2 + AC^2) = 3(AD^2 + BE^2 + CF^2)$

(*c*) $3(AB^2 + BC^2 + AC^2) = 4(AD^2 + BE^2 + CF^2)$

(*d*) None of these

16. Match the following:

1. Incentre
2. Circumcentre
3. Centroid
4. Orthocentre

(A) The point of intersection of all the three altitudes of a triangle.

(B) The point of intersection of all the three medians of any triangle.

(C) The point of intersection of all the three angle bisectors of a triangle.

(D) The point of intersection of the perpendicular bisectors of the sides of a triangle.

The correct match is:

	A	B	C	D
(*a*)	1	2	3	4
(*b*)	4	3	1	2
(*c*)	4	3	2	1
(*d*)	1	3	4	2

17. In an equilateral triangle, incentre, circumcentre and orthocentre are:

(*a*) collinear (*b*) concyclic (*c*) concurrent (*d*) None of these

18. Match list-I with list-II:

List-I

A. The sum of exterior angles of a triangle equals

B. Each angle of an equilateral triangle, equals

C. Each acute angle of an isosceles right angled triangle equals

D. A parallelogram is a rectangle if one of its angles equals

List-II

1. 90° 2. 180° 3. 360° 4. 60° 5. 45°

	A	B	C	D
(*a*)	2	4	5	1
(*b*)	2	5	4	1
(*c*)	3	4	5	1
(*d*)	3	5	4	1

19. Consider the following statements :
Two right angled triangles are congruent if
I. the hypotenuse of one triangle is equal to the hypotenuse of the other.
II. a side of one triangle is equal to the corresponding side of the other triangle.
III. sides of the triangles are equal
IV. an angle of the triangle are equal
Of these statements, the correct ones are combinations of:
(*a*) 1 and II (*b*) II and III (*c*) I and III (*d*) IV only

20. In the given figure, $\angle A = 80°$, $\angle B = 60°$, $\angle C = 2x$ and $\angle BDC = y°$. BD and CD bisect angles B and C respectively. The values of x and y respectively are:

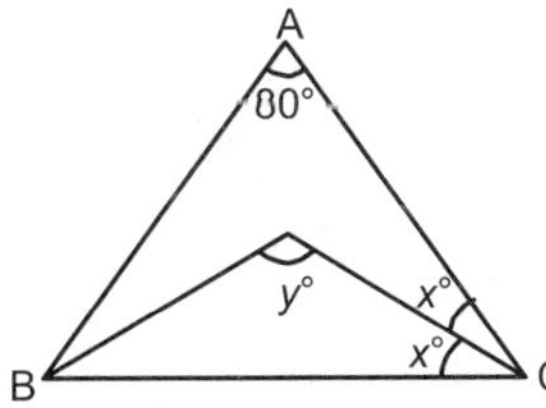

(*a*) 15° and 70° (*b*) 10° and 160° (*c*) 20° and 130° (*d*) 20° and 125°

21. If in the given figure $\sin 52° = \cos 2\alpha = x$, then $\cos 2\beta$ is equal to:

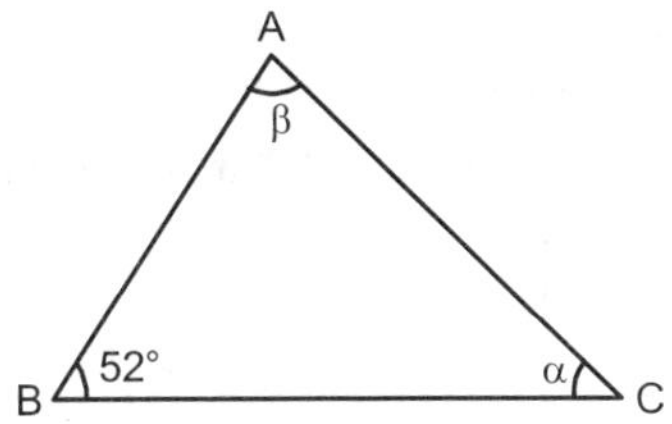

(*a*) $2x$ (*b*) x (*c*) x^2 (*d*) $-x$

22. Consider the following statements:
I. Every equilateral triangle is necessarily an isosceles triangle.
II. Every right-angled triangle is necessarily an isosceles triangle.
III. A triangle in which one of the medians is perpendicular to the side it meets, is necessarily an isosceles triangle.
The correct statements are:
(*a*) I and II (*b*) II and III (*c*) I and III (*d*) I, II and III

23. Consider the following statements:
I. If three sides of a triangle are equal to three sides of another triangle, then the triangles are congruent.

II. If three angles of a triangle are respectively, equal to three angles of another triangle, then the two triangles are congruent.

Of these statements:

(*a*) I and II both are true (*b*) I is true and II is false
(*c*) I is false and II is true (*d*) None of these

24. In an equilateral triangle ABC, the side BC is trisected at D. Then the correct relation is :

(*a*) $9\ AD^2 = 7\ AB^2$ (*b*) $8\ AD^2 = 9\ AB^2$
(*c*) $7\ AD^2 = 9\ AB^2$ (*d*) None of these

25. In the given figure ABC is a non-isosceles right-angled triangle, ∠B being a right-angled. EF and BG are perpendiculars on the hypotenuse AC, then ∠CEF is equal to:

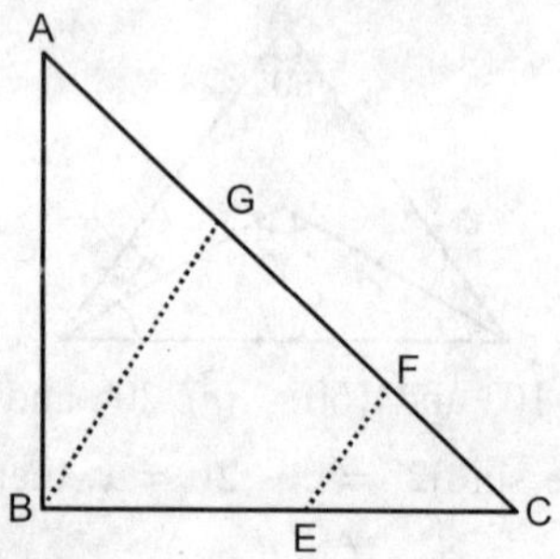

(*a*) ∠EFC (*b*) ∠BAG (*c*) ∠ECF (*d*) ∠ABG

26. In the adjoining figure PA, QB and RC are each perpendicular to AC, then:

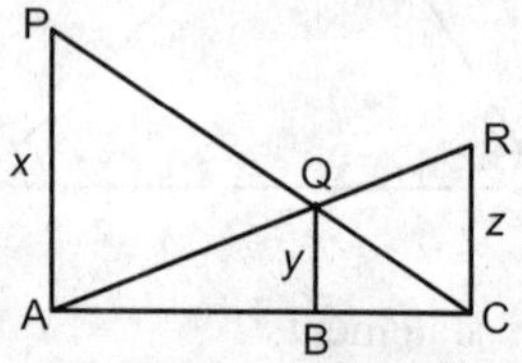

(*a*) $\frac{1}{x}+\frac{1}{y}=\frac{1}{z}$ (*b*) $\frac{1}{x}-\frac{1}{y}=\frac{1}{z}$ (*c*) $\frac{1}{x}+\frac{1}{y}=\frac{2}{z}$ (*d*) $x + z = y$

27. In the adjoining figure ΔADE, and ΔABC are similar, if AC : BC = 3 : 2, then the ratio $\frac{DE}{AE}$ is:

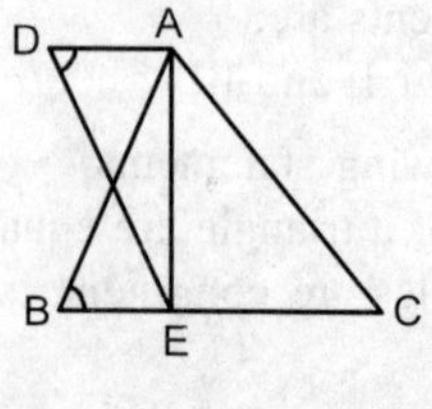

(*a*) 3 : 2 (*b*) 2 : 3 (*c*) 1 : 3 (*d*) 1 : 2

28. The ratio of the area of the equilateral triangle de scribed on the side of a square to the area of the equilateral triangle described on its diagonal is:

(*a*) 1 : 3 (*b*) $\sqrt{3} : 4$ (*c*) 1 : 2 (*d*) 1 : 4

29. In the adjoining figure ABCD is a square. F is the midpoint of AB, BE is one-third of BC. If the area of the ΔFBE is 108 sq. cm. Then the length of AC is :

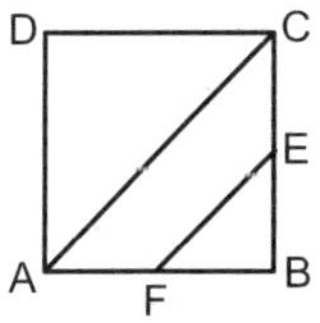

(*a*) $36\sqrt{3}$ cm (*b*) $35\sqrt{2}$ cm

(*c*) $12\sqrt{3}$ cm (*d*) $36\sqrt{2}$ cm

30. In a quadrilateral ABCD, $\angle B = 90°$, and $AD^2 = AB^2 + BC^2 + CD^2$. Then ΔADC is :

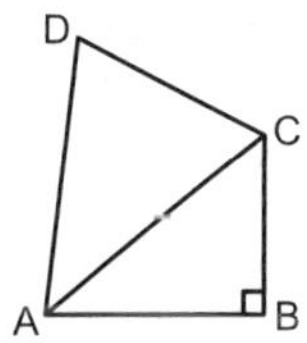

(*a*) equilateral triangle (*b*) isosceles

(*c*) right angled triangle (*d*) None of these

31. In ΔABC, AD ⊥ BC, then :

(*a*) $AB^2 - BD^2 = AC^2 - CD^2$ (*b*) $AB^2 + BD^2 = AC^2 - CD^2$

(*c*) $AB^2 + BD^2 = AC^2 + CD^2$ (*d*) $AB^2 + AC^2 = BD^2 + DC^2$

32. ΔABC is right-angle at C and *p* is the length of the perpendicular from C to AB. If BC = *a*, AC = *b*, AB = *c* then:

(*a*) $\frac{a}{b} = \frac{p}{c}$ (*b*) $pc = ab$ (*c*) $\frac{1}{a} + \frac{1}{b} = \frac{1}{ab}$ (*d*) None of these

33. In an equilateral triangle with side *a* the altitude of the triangle is:

(*a*) $\frac{a\sqrt{3}}{2}$ (*b*) $\frac{\sqrt{3}}{4}a$ (*c*) $\frac{4}{\sqrt{3}}a$ (*d*) $\frac{\sqrt{3}}{2a}$

ANSWERS

1	2	3	4	5	6	7	8	9	10
(*a*)	(*b*)	(*b*)	(*a*)	(*b*)	(*c*)	(*d*)	(*a*)	(*b*)	(*c*)
11	**12**	**13**	**14**	**15**	**16**	**17**	**18**	**19**	**20**
(*c*)	(*d*)	(*c*)	(*a*)	(*c*)	(*b*)	(*c*)	(*c*)	(*a*)	(*c*)
21	**22**	**23**	**24**	**25**	**26**	**27**	**28**	**29**	**30**
(*d*)	(*c*)	(*b*)	(*a*)	(*b*)	(*a*)	(*b*)	(*c*)	(*d*)	(*c*)
31	**32**	**33**							
(*a*)	(*b*)	(*a*)							

SOME SELECTED EXPLANATORY ANSWERS

1. Since $\Delta ABC \sim \Delta DEF$

$\therefore \angle B = \angle E = 83°$

Hence, in ΔABC, $\angle C = 180° - (\angle A + \angle B)$

$\Rightarrow \angle C = 180° - (47 + 83)° = 50°$.

2. Since $\angle ABD = \angle ACE$

$\therefore 180° - \angle ABC = 180° - \angle ACB$

$\Rightarrow \angle ABC = \angle ACB$

Hence, ΔABC is isosceles triangle.

4. Sides opposite to equal angles are equal. Here, $\angle ADB = \angle BAD = 60°$

So, AB = BD.

5. $\angle BAL + \angle B + 90° = 180°$

$\Rightarrow \angle BAL + \angle B = 90°$

$\Rightarrow \angle BAL = 90° - \angle B$ ...(*i*)

Now in ΔABC, $\angle ACB + \angle B + \angle A = 180°$

$\Rightarrow \angle ACB + \angle B = 180° - 90°$

$\Rightarrow \angle ACB + \angle B = 90°$

$\Rightarrow \angle ACB = 90° - \angle B$ ...(*ii*)

From (*i*) and (*ii*) $\angle BAL = \angle ACB$

6. In ΔBOC,

$\angle 1 + \angle 2 + \angle BOC = 180°$

$\angle A + \angle B + \angle C = 180°$

$$\frac{1}{2}\angle A + \frac{1}{2}\angle B + \frac{1}{2}\angle C = 90°$$

$$\Rightarrow \frac{1}{2}(\angle A) + \angle 1 + \angle 2 = 90°$$

$$\Rightarrow \angle 1 + \angle 2 = 90° - \frac{1}{2}\angle A$$

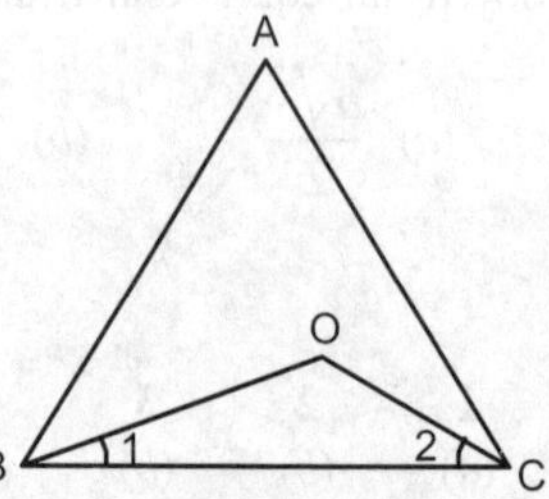

Put $\angle 1 + \angle 2$ in (*i*)

$$\angle BOC = 180° - \left(90° - \frac{1}{2}\angle A\right) = 90° + \frac{1}{2}\angle A.$$

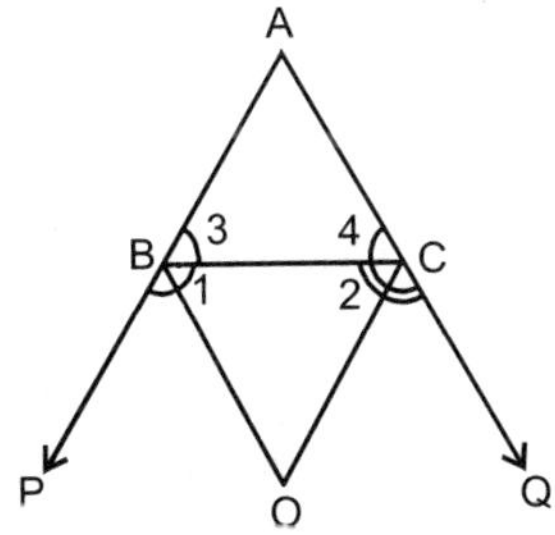

8. $\angle 1 = 90° - \frac{1}{2}\angle 3$

$\angle 2 = 90° - \frac{1}{2}\angle 4$

Now in ΔBOC

$\angle 1 + \angle 2 + \angle BOC = 180°$

$\angle BOC = 180° - (\angle 2 + \angle 1)$

$= 180° - \left[90° - \frac{1}{2}\angle 4 + 90° - \frac{1}{2}\angle 3\right]$

$\Rightarrow \angle BOC = \frac{1}{2}(\angle 3 + \angle 4)$

$\Rightarrow \angle BOC = \frac{1}{2}(180° - \angle A)$

$\angle A + \angle 3 + \angle 4 = 180°$

$\Rightarrow \angle BOC = 90° - \frac{1}{2}\ \angle A.$

9. By exterior angle theorem, we have

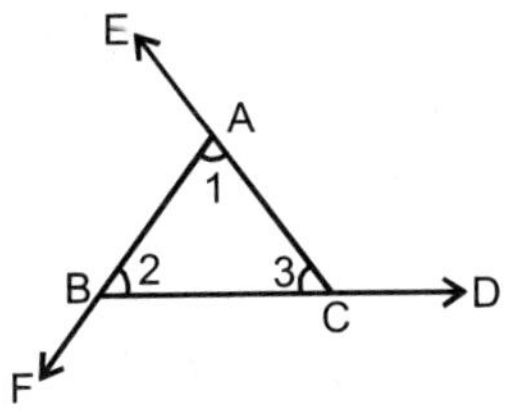

$\angle ACD = \angle 1 + \angle 2$

$\angle BAE = \angle 2 + \angle 3$

$\angle CBF = \angle 3 + \angle 1$

$= \angle ACD + \angle BAE + \angle CBF$

$= \angle 1 + \angle 2 + \angle 2 + \angle 3 + \angle 3 + \angle 1$

$= 2(\angle 1 + \angle 2 + \angle 3) = 2\ (180°) = 360°.$

10. Clearly orthocentre.

11. As $\Delta CAB \sim \Delta CED$

$\therefore \frac{CA}{CD} = \frac{CE}{DE} = \frac{CB}{CD}$

So, $\frac{AB}{DE} = \frac{CB}{CD}$

$\therefore \quad \frac{9}{x} = \frac{10+2}{8} \qquad \therefore\ x = \frac{8 \times 9}{12} = 6$ cm.

12. In ΔGEF and ΔGCD, we have

$\angle EFG = \angle GDC$, (Alternate angles)

$\angle EGF = \angle CGD$ (Vertically opposite angles)

$\Delta GEF \sim \Delta GCD$

$$\therefore \frac{GE}{CG} = \frac{EF}{CD} \Rightarrow \frac{5}{10} = \frac{EF}{18} \Rightarrow EF = \frac{5 \times 18}{10} = 9 \text{ cm}$$

14. Draw a line OE parallel to AB.

Apply Pythagoras theorem to triangles AOE, ΔDOE, ΔFOC and ΔOFB,

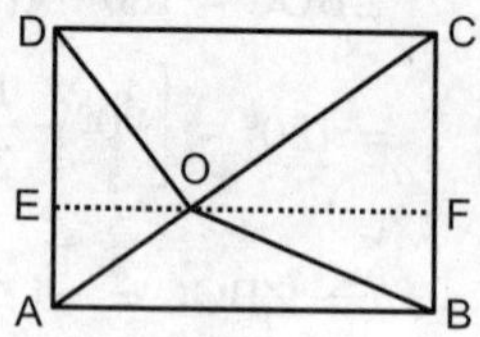

$OA^2 = OE^2 + EA^2$

$OD^2 = OE^2 + DE^2$

$OC^2 = OF^2 + FC^2$

$OB^2 = OF^2 + FB^2$

Adding and equating we get,

$OB^2 + OD^2 = OC^2 + OA^2$

15. Let G be the centroid of ΔABC.

In ΔABC

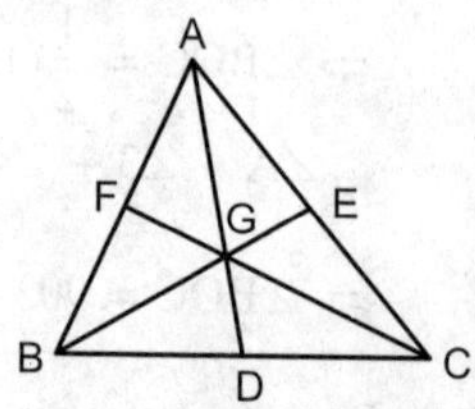

[The sum of the squares of any two sides is equal to twice the square of half of the third side together with the square of the median bisecting the third side]

$$\therefore AB^2 + AC^2 = 2AD^2 + 2\left(\frac{1}{2}BC\right)^2 \quad \text{...}(i)$$

$$\Rightarrow AB^2 + AC^2 = 2AD^2 + \frac{1}{2}BC^2$$

$$BC^2 + AB^2 = 2BE^2 + \frac{1}{2}AC^2 \quad \text{....}(ii)$$

$$BC^2 + AC^2 = 2CF^2 + \frac{1}{2}AB^2 \quad \text{...}(iii)$$

Adding (*i*), (*ii*) and (*iii*), we get

$2(AB^2 + BC^2 + AC^2)$

$$= 2(AD^2 + BE^2 + CF^2) + \frac{1}{2}(AB^2 + BC^2 + AC^2)$$

$\therefore 3(AB^2 + BC^2 + AC^2) = 4(AD^2 + BE^2 + CF^2)$

16. Clearly (*b*) is correct.

17. Clearly (*c*) is true.

19. Two right-triangles are congruent if the hypotenuse of one triangle is equal to the hypotenuse of the other, and a side of one triangle is equal to the corresponding side of the other triangle. Clearly it is RMS axiom.

20. $\angle A + \angle B + \angle C = 180°$

$\angle C = 180° - (\angle A + \angle B) = 180 - (80 + 60)$

$\angle C = 40°$ $\qquad$ [$\angle C = 2x$]

$\Rightarrow 2x = 40 \Rightarrow x = 20°$

$y = 180° - \left(\frac{1}{2}\angle B + x\right)$ [ΔBDC]

$= 180° - \left(\frac{1}{2} \times 60° + 20°\right) = 180° - (30° + 20°) = 130°$

So $x = 20°$ and $y = 130°$

21. As given that $\sin 52° = \cos 2\alpha = x$.

$\therefore \cos (90° - 52°) = \cos 2\alpha = x$

$\Rightarrow \cos 38° = \cos 2\alpha = x$

$\Rightarrow 2\alpha = 38° \Rightarrow \alpha = \frac{38}{2} = 19°$

$\therefore \beta - 180° - (52° + 19°)$

$\beta = 109°$

$\therefore \cos 2\beta = \cos 2 \times (109°)$

$= \cos 218° = \cos (180 + 38°) = - \cos 38°$

$\Rightarrow \cos 2\beta = -x$.

24. Let ABC be an equilateral triangle and let D be a point on BC. Here,

$BD = \frac{1}{3} BC$ (given)

In ΔAEB and ΔAEC. Draw $AE \perp BC$

$\therefore AB = AC$, $AE = AE$ and $\angle AEB = \angle AEC$ (90° each)

$\therefore \Delta AEB \equiv \Delta AEC$. So $BE = EC$

$\therefore DB = \frac{1}{3}BC, DC = \frac{2}{3}BC, EC = \frac{1}{2}BC$

$\therefore$ In ΔADC, $AD^2 = AC^2 + DC^2 - 2DC \times EC$

$= AC^2 + \left(\frac{2}{3}BC\right)^2 - 2 \times \frac{2}{3}BC \times \frac{1}{2}BC$

$= AB^2 + \frac{4}{9}AB^2 - \frac{2}{3}AB^2$

But as AC = BC = AB

$\therefore AD^2 = \frac{7}{9}AB^2 \Rightarrow 9AD^2 = AB^2$

25. As in ΔBGC

EF $\parallel$ BG

$\therefore \angle CEF = \angle CBG$ (corresponding angles)

$\angle CBG = 90° - \angle ABG$

$= 90° - \angle ECF$ ($\angle ABG = \angle ECF$)

$= 90° - (90° - \angle BAG)$

$\Rightarrow \angle CBG = \angle BAG$

$\therefore \angle CEF = \angle BAG$

26. Here in ΔBCQ and ΔACP

$\angle QBC = \angle PAC$ [Each = 90°]

$\Rightarrow \angle QCB = \angle PCA$ $\therefore \Delta BCQ \sim \Delta ACP$

$$\frac{BQ}{AP} = \frac{BC}{AC} \Rightarrow \frac{z}{y} = \frac{BC}{AC} \quad ...(i)$$

Similarly in ΔABQ and ΔACR

$\Delta ABQ \sim \Delta ACR$

$$\therefore \frac{BQ}{CR} = \frac{AB}{AC} \Rightarrow \frac{z}{y} = \frac{AC - BC}{AC}$$

$$\Rightarrow \frac{z}{y} = 1 - \frac{BC}{AC} = 1 - \frac{z}{x} \text{ from } (i)$$

$$\therefore \frac{z}{x} + \frac{z}{y} = 1 \Rightarrow \frac{1}{x} + \frac{1}{y} = \frac{1}{z}$$

27. As $\Delta ADE \sim \Delta ABC$

$$\text{So, } \frac{AD}{AB} = \frac{DE}{BC} = \frac{AE}{AC}$$

$$\frac{DE}{AE} = \frac{BC}{AC} = \frac{2}{3}$$

Hence, DE : AE = 2 : 3.

28. Here $AC^2 = 2AB^2$

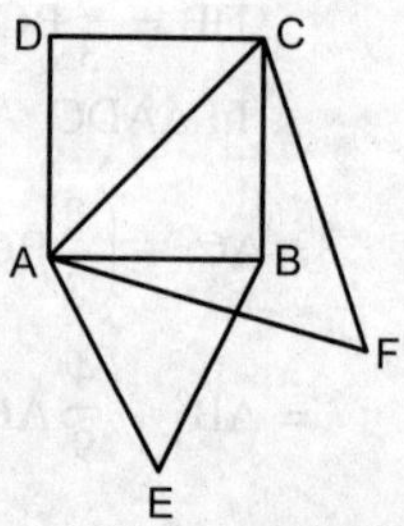

As ΔABE and ΔABC are equiangular so $\Delta ABE \sim \Delta ABC$

[The ratio of the areas of two similar triangles is equal to the ratio of their corresponding sides]

$$\frac{\text{area of }(\Delta ABE)}{\text{area of }(\Delta ACF)} = \frac{AB^2}{AC^2} = \frac{AB^2}{2AB^2} = \frac{1}{2}$$

29. Area of $\Delta FBE = 108 \text{ cm}^2$

Let each side be $6x$.

$\therefore\ BE = \frac{1}{3}BC = \frac{1}{3} \times 6x = 2x$

$BF = \frac{1}{2}AB = \frac{1}{2} \times 6x = 3x$

Area of $\Delta FBE = \frac{1}{2}3x \times 2x = 3x^2$

$\therefore\ 3x^2 = 108$

$\therefore\ x^2 = 36$

$\Rightarrow\ x = 6$ cm.

$\therefore\ AC^2 = AB^2 + BC^2 = 2AB^2$ [AB = 36]

$= 2(36)^2$

$\Rightarrow AC = 36\sqrt{2}$ cm.

30. Here, $AD^2 = AB^2 + BC^2 + CD^2$

$AD^2 = AC^2 + DC^2$

$\therefore\ \Delta ACD$ is a right-angled triangle.

31. Here in AADC

$AB^2 = AD^2 + BD^2$ ...(*i*)

In right-angled ΔACD, we have

$AC^2 = AD^2 + CD^2$ ...(*ii*)

By (*i*) – (*ii*)

$AB^2 - AC^2 = BD^2 - CD^2$

$\Rightarrow AB^2 - BD^2 = AC^2 - CD^2$

33. Here in ΔADC

$AD^2 = AC^2 + DC^2$

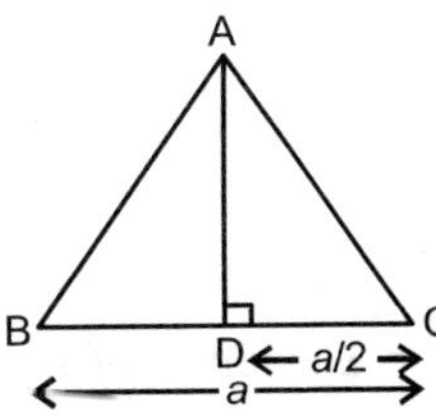

$\Rightarrow AD^2 = AC^2 - DC^2 = a^2 - \frac{a^2}{4}$

$\Rightarrow AD^2 = \frac{4a^2 - a^2}{4} = \frac{3a^2}{4} \Rightarrow AD = \frac{\sqrt{3}a}{2}$

QUADRILATERALS

A plane, closed figure bounded by four line segments is called quadrilateral. There are different types of quadrilaterals so called trapezium, parallelogram, rhombus, rectangle, square.

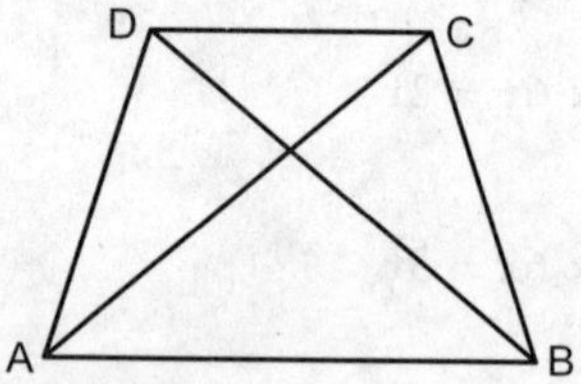

- Sum of all the angles of a quadrilateral is 360°.
- Here ABCD is a quadrilateral. ($\angle A$, $\angle B$); ($\angle B$, $\angle C$); ($\angle C$, $\angle D$); ($\angle D$, $\angle A$) are four pairs of consecutive angles of quadrilateral ABCD.
- AC and BD are diagonals.
- (AB, BC); (BC, CD); (CD, DA) and (DA, AB) are four pairs of adjacent sides.

Various types of quadrilaterals

(A) Parallelogram: A quadrilateral in which opposite sides are equal and parallel then it is a parallelogram, written as || gm,

e.g., square, rectangle, rhombus.

Properties of Parallelogram

(*a*) Opposite sides are equal.

(*b*) Opposite angles are equal.

(*c*) The two diagonals bisect each other.

(*d*) Diagonal are equal in case of square and rectangle but not in rhombus.

Square: A parallelogram in which all sides are equal and are parallel. Here angle between the adjacent sides is 90°.

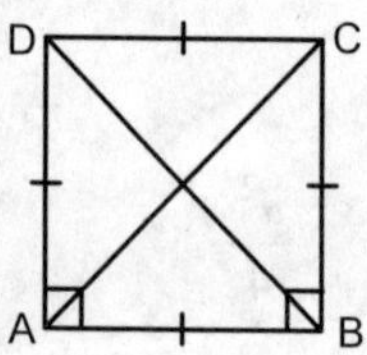

- Diagonals of square are equal.
  AC = BD
- Diagonals bisects the angle
- Diagonals are perpendicular to each other.

Rectangle:

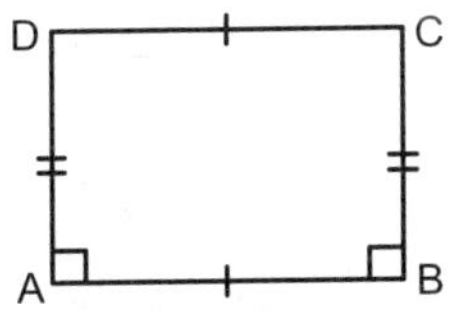

The parallelogram in which only opposite side are equal and parallel, angle between adjacent sides is 90°.

Rhombus :

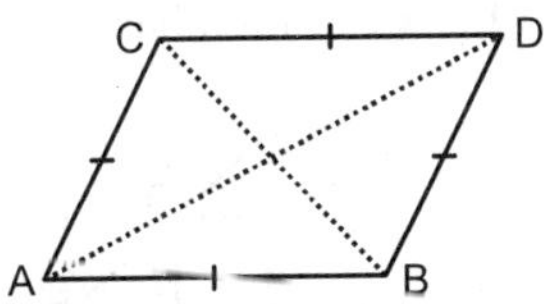

A parallelogram in which all sides are equal is called a rhombus.

- Diagonals bisect each other at 90°
- Diagonals are not equal
- Sum of square of sides is equal to sum of the square of diagonal, *i.e.*

$AB^2 + BC^2 + CD^2 + DA^2 = AC^2 + BD^2$

Kite:

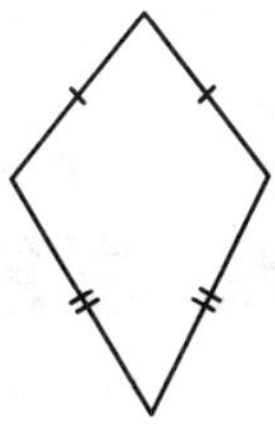

A quadrilateral in which two pairs of adjacent sides are equal is known as kite.

Trapezium:

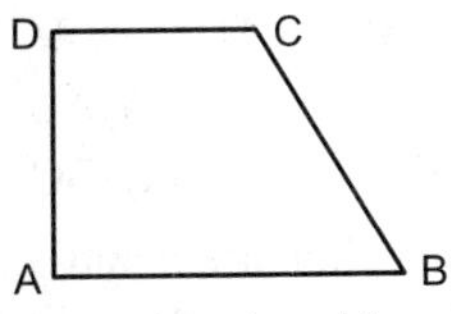

A quadrilateral in which two opposite sides are parallel and two opposite sides are not parallel. It is called a trapezium.

Here AB | | DC

Some facts about to remember

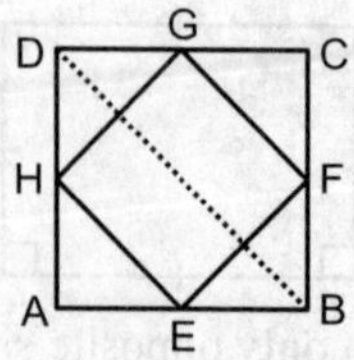

- The quadrilateral formed by joining the mid-points of the consecutive sides of a rectangle is a rhombus. Here E, F, G, H are mid-points of AB, BC, CD, DA respectively, then EFGH is a rhombus.

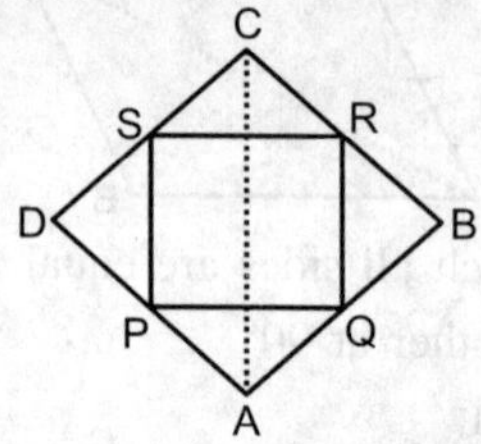

- The quadrilateral formed by joining the mid-point of the consecutive sides of a rhombus is a rectangle. Here PQRS will be a rectangle.
- The quadrilateral formed by joining the mid-points of the sides of a square, is also a square.
- The figure formed by joining the mid-points of the pairs of consecutive sides of a quadrilateral is a parallelogram.

EXERCISE

1. A point O in the interior of a rectangle ABCD is joined with each of the vertices A, B, C and D. Then:
(*a*) OB + OD = OC + OA (*b*) $OB^2 + OA^2 = OC^2 + OD^2$
(*c*) OB . OD = OC . OA (*d*) $OB^2 + OD^2 = OC^2 + OA^2$
2. In a trapezium ABCD, if AB || CD, then $AC^2 + BD^2$ is equal to:
(*a*) $BC^2 + AD^2 + 2AB \cdot CD$ (*b*) $AB^2 + CD^2 + 2AD \cdot BC$
(*c*) $AB^2 + CD^2 + 2AB \cdot CD$ (*d*) $BC^2 + AD^2 + 2BC \cdot AD$
3. The parallel sides of a trapezium are *p* and *q* respectively. The line joining the mid-points of its non-parallel sides will be:
(*a*) $\sqrt{pq}$ (*b*) $\frac{2pq}{p+q}$ (*c*) $\frac{(p+q)}{2}$ (*d*) $\frac{1}{2}(p-q)$

4. ABCD is a trapezium in which AB || CD and AB = 2 CD. Its diagonals intersect each other at O, then the ratio of the areas of the triangles AOB and COD is :

(*a*) 1 : 2 (*b*) 2 : 1 (*c*) 4 : 1 (*d*) 1 : 4

5. In the figure, ABCD is a parallelogram with AD = *a* units, DC = 2*a* units and DE : EC = 1 : 2. CEFG is a rectangle with FE = 3 AE. What is the ratio of the areas of the parallelogram and the rectangle?

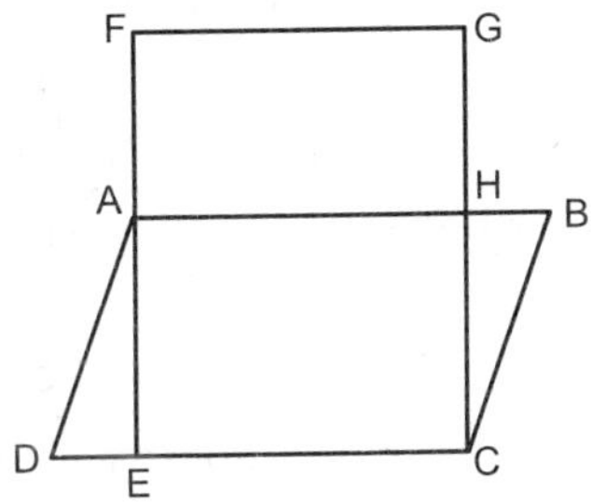

(*a*) 1 : 1 (*b*) 1 : 2 (*c*) $\frac{a^2}{5} : 1$ (*d*) 2 : 1

6. In the figure, AB || PQ, AC || PR and BC || QR, then AP is:

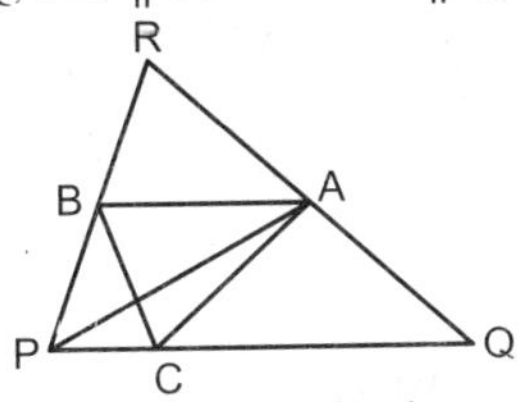

(*a*) perpendicular to QR (*b*) the angle bisector of ∠QPR

(*c*) a median of ∠PQR (*c*) None of these

7. "P" is the point in the plane of a rhombus ABCD are such that "P" is equidistant from the sides of ABCD. How many points?

(*a*) 4 (*b*) 2 (*c*) 1 (*d*) 0

8. If ABCD is a rectangle, E, P are the mid-points of BC and AD respectively and G is any point on EF, then ΔGAB equals:

(*a*) $\frac{1}{6}$ (rectangle ABCD) (*b*) $\frac{1}{4}$ (rectangle ABCD)

(*c*) $\frac{1}{3}$ (rectangle ABCD) (*d*) $\frac{1}{2}$ (rectangle ABCD)

9. If area of a parallelogram with sides *p* and *q* is R and that of a rectangle with sides *p* and *q* is S, then :

(*a*) R > S (*b*) R < S (*c*) R = S (*d*) None of these

10. If a square and a rhombus stand on the same base, then the ratio of the areas of the square and the rhombus is:

(*a*) equal to $\frac{1}{4}$ (*b*) equal to $\frac{1}{2}$ (*c*) equal to 1 (*d*) greater than 1

11. The sides BA and DC of quadrilateral ABCD are produced as shown in figure. Then which of the following statements is correct?

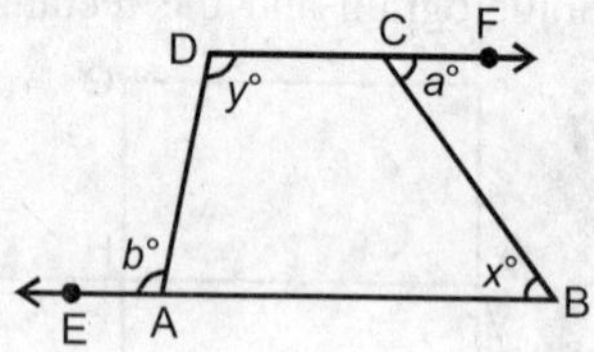

(*a*) $2x° + y° = a° + b°$ (*b*) $x° + \frac{1}{2}y° = \frac{a° + b°}{2}$

(*c*) $x° + y° = a° + b°$ (*d*) $x° + a° = y° + b°$

12. In the quadrilateral ABCD, the line segments bisecting ∠C and ∠D meet at E. Then the correct statement is:

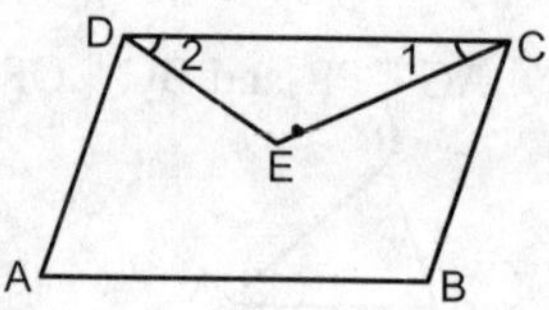

(*a*) ∠A + ∠B = ∠CED (*b*) ∠A + ∠B = 2∠CED

(*c*) ∠A + ∠B = 3∠CED (*d*) None of these

13. If ABCD is a quadrilateral whose diagonals AC and BD intersect at O, then:

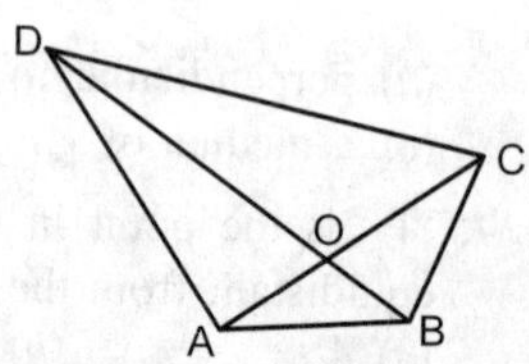

(*a*) (AB + BC + CD + DA) < (AC + BD)

(*b*) (AB + BC + CD + DA) > 2(AC + BD)

(*c*) (AB + BC + CD + DA) > (AC + BD)

(*d*) AB + BC + CD + DA = 2(AC + BD)

14. In the adjoining figure, ABCD is a quadrilateral in which AB is the longest side and CD is the shortest side, then:

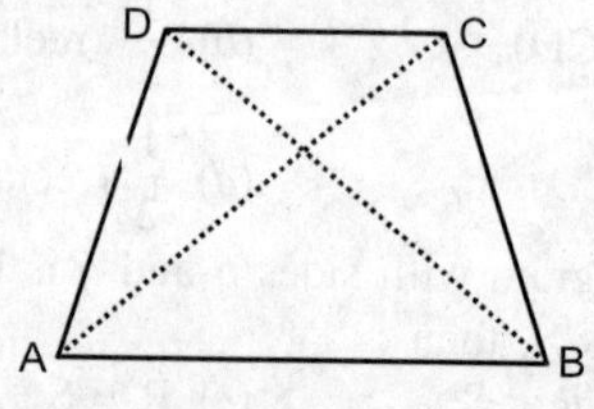

(*a*) $\angle C > \angle A$ and $\angle D > \angle B$ (*b*) $\angle C > \angle A$ and $\angle B > \angle D$
(*c*) $\angle C < \angle A$ and $\angle D < \angle B$ (*d*) $\angle C < \angle A$ and $\angle D = \angle B$

15. In the given figure, PQRS is a square and $\angle ABC = 90°$. If AQ = BR = SC, then consider the following statements:

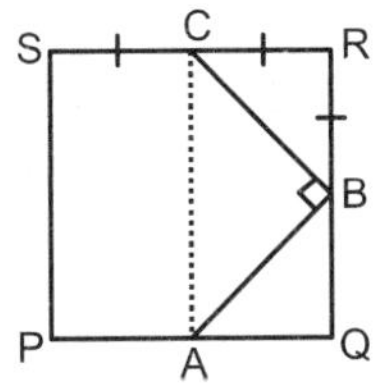

I. QB = RC
II. AB = BC
III. $\angle BAG = 45°$
IV. AC = PS

(*a*) Only I and IV are correct (*b*) I, II and III are correct
(*c*) II, III and IV are correct (*d*) All are correct

16. In the given figure, ABCD is a square. A line segment DX cuts the side BC at X and the diagonal AC at O such that $\angle COD = 105°$ and $\angle OXC = x$. The value of x is:

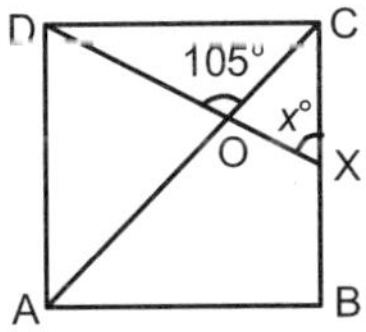

(*a*) 40° (*b*) 60° (*c*) 80° (*d*) 85°

ANSWERS

1	2	3	4	5	6	7	8	9	10
(*d*)	(*a*)	(*c*)	(*c*)	(*b*)	(*b*)	(*c*)	(*b*)	(*b*)	(*c*)
11	**12**	**13**	**14**	**15**	**16**				
(*c*)	(*b*)	(*c*)	(*a*)	(*d*)	(*b*)				

SOME SELECTED EXPLANATORY ANSWERS

1. Draw EF || AB

In right angled ΔEOA and ΔOCF

$OA^2 = OE^2 + AE^2$ and $OC^2 = OF^2 + CF^2$

$\therefore OA^2 + OC^2 = OE^2 + AE^2 + OF^2 + CF^2$ ...(*i*)

In right angled ΔDEO and ΔOBF

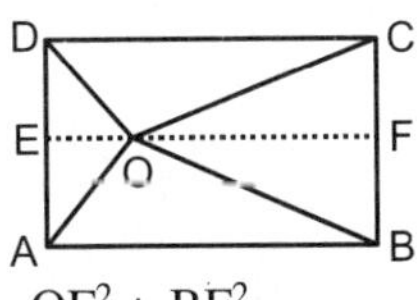

$OD^2 = OE^2 + DE^2$, $OB^2 = OF^2 + BF^2$

$\Rightarrow OD^2 + OB^2 = OE^2 + OF^2 + DE^2 + BF^2$ ...(*ii*)

As FB = EA and DE = CF
Here from (*i*) and (*ii*)
$OA^2 + OC^2 = OD^2 + OB^2$

3. Here as ABCD is trapezium

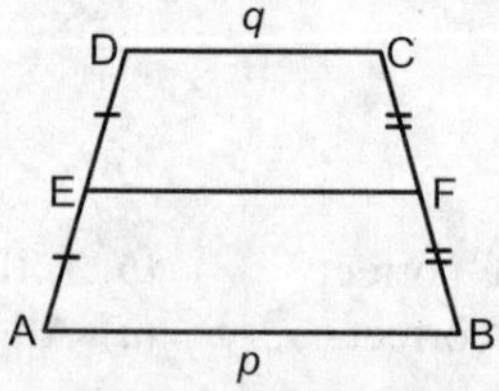

So, $EF = \frac{1}{2}(AB + DC)$

$\Rightarrow EF = \frac{1}{2}(p + q)$

$\{AB = p,\ DC = q\}$

4. Let PQ be the perpendicular distance between the two parallel sides AB and CD.

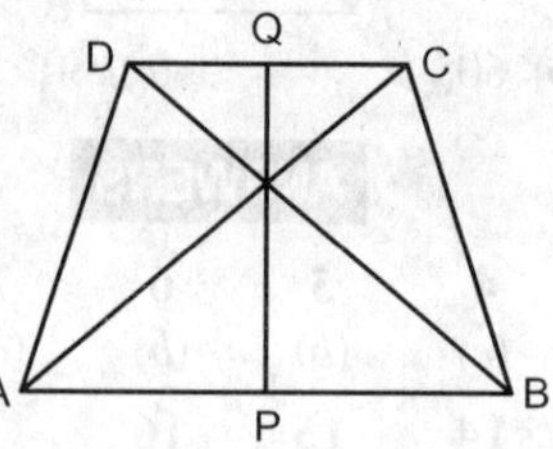

So, $\frac{\text{area of } \Delta AOB}{\text{area of } \Delta COD} = \frac{\frac{1}{2} AB \times OP}{\frac{1}{2} CD \times OQ}$ [OP = 2OQ]

$= \frac{2CD \times 2OQ}{CD \times OQ} = \frac{4}{1}.$

5. Area of parallelogram ABCD
= 2 (area ΔADE) + (area of ∥ gm AECH)

$= 2 \times \frac{1}{2} DE \times AE + AE \times EC$

$= DE \times AE + AE \times EC$

$= AE \times DC$ $\left[\frac{DE}{EC} = \frac{1}{2} = \frac{FE}{3} \times \frac{3EC}{2} \Rightarrow \frac{DE + EC}{EC} = \frac{3}{2} \right.$

$$= \frac{FE \times EC}{2} \Rightarrow \frac{DC}{EC} = \frac{3}{2}\Big]$$

$$= \frac{\text{Area of rectangle EFGC}}{2}$$

Required ratio = 1 : 2

8. AB || EF || CD. So ABEF is a rectangle

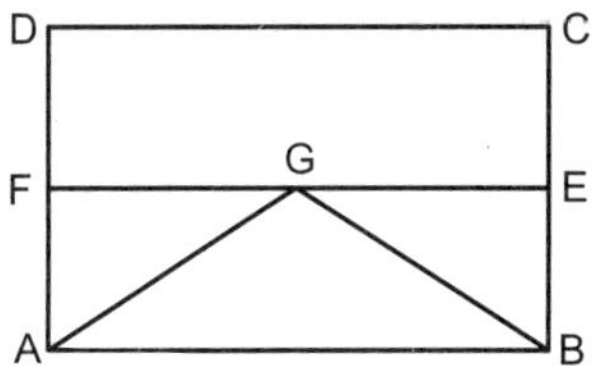

$$\therefore \Delta AGB = \frac{1}{2} \text{ (area of rectangle ABEF)}$$

$$= \frac{1}{2} \times \left(\frac{1}{2} \text{ area of rectangle ABCD}\right)$$

$$= \frac{1}{4} \text{ (area of rectangle ABCD)}$$

9. Let h be the height of the parallelogram. Then, clearly, $h < q$

So, $R = p \times h < p \times q = S$

So, R < S

11. As $\angle A + b° = 180°$

$\Rightarrow \angle A = 180° - b$

Also $\angle C + a° = 180°$ (linear pair)

$\Rightarrow \angle C = 180° - a°$

But $\angle A + \angle B + \angle C + \angle D = 360°$

$\Rightarrow (180° - b°) + x + (180° - a°) + y° = 360°$

$\Rightarrow x° + y° = a° + b°$

13. In ΔABC, ΔACD, ΔBCD and ΔABD

AB + BC > AC

CD + DA > AC

BC + CD > BD

DA + AB > BD

Adding above inequalities

2(AB + BC + CD + DA) > 2 (AC + BD)

⇒ AB + BC + CD + DA > (AC + BD)

14. Join AC and BD.
As AB > AC ⇒ ∠ACB > ∠BAC
Also AD > DC ⇒ ∠ACD > ∠CAD
∴ ∠ACB + ∠ACD > ∠BAC + ∠CAD
= ∠C > ∠A, similarly ∠D > ∠B

16. ∠OCX = 45°
∠COD + ∠COX = 180°
⇒ ∠COX = 180° – ∠COD = 180° – 105° = 75°
In ΔOCX
∠OCX + ∠COX + ∠OXC = 180°
⇒ 45° + 75° + ∠OXC = 180°
⇒ ∠OXC = 180° – 120° = 60° ⇒ ∠x = 60°

POLYGONS

A polygon is a closed, plane figure bounded by 'n' straight lines ($n \geq 3$). Each of the n line segment forming the polygon is called its sides.

A polygon may be a triangle, quadrilateral, pentagon etc. Polygons are classified according to the number of sides as given below:

Number of sides	Name
3	Triangle
4	Quadrilateral
5	Pentagon
6	Hexagon
7	Heptagon
8	Octagon
9	Nonagon
10	Decagon

Regular Polygon: A polygon is called a regular polygon if all its sides are equal and all angles are equal.

Convex Polygon:

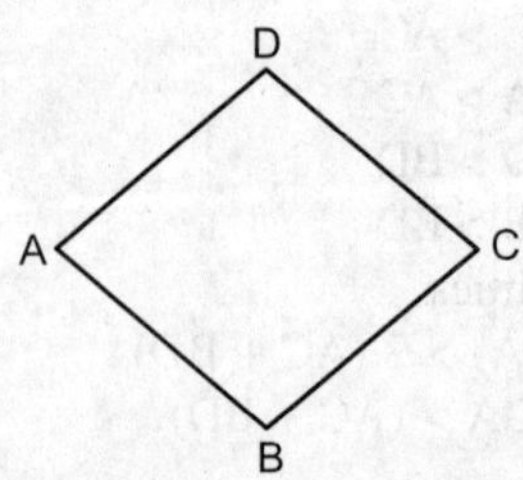

A polygon is said to be a convex polygon, if each side of the polygon, the line containing that side has all the other vertices on the same side of it.

- None of its interior angle is more than 180°.

Concave Polygon:

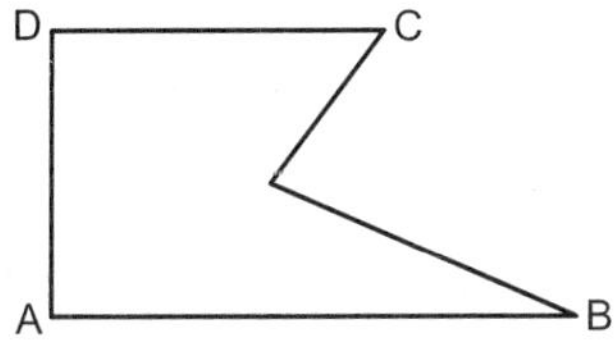

A polygon in which at least one of the interior angle is more than 180°. Then the polygon is said to be a concave polygon.

IMPORTANT RESULTS

- If there is a polygon of n sides ($n \geq 3$) then we can cut it into $(n - 2)$ triangles with common vertex. Then sum of the interior angles of a polygon of n sides is $(n - 2) \times 180°$ or $(2n - 4) \times 90°$.
- Each exterior angle of a regular polygon of n sides is $\left(\frac{360}{n}\right)^\circ$.
- Each interior angle of a regular polygon of n sides is $\frac{(n-2) \times 180°}{n}$ or interior angle = 180° – (exterior angle).
- The sum of all the exterior angle formed by producing the sides of a convex polygon in the same order is equal to 360°.
- Number of diagonals of a polygon of n sides is $\frac{n(n-1)}{n} - n$.

EXERCISE

1. The sum of all exterior angles of a convex polygon of n sides is:

(*a*) 4 right angle (*b*) $\frac{2}{n}$ right angle

(*c*) $(2n - 4)$ right angle (*d*) $\frac{2}{n}$ right angle

2. The measure of each angle of a regular hexagon is :

(*a*) 90° (*b*) 120° (*c*) 105° (*d*) 135°

3. Each interior angle of a regular polygon is 150°. The number of sides of the polygon is:
(*a*) 4 (*b*) 8 (*c*) 12 (*d*) 16

4. How many diagonals are there in a octagon?
(*a*) 8 (*b*) 16 (*c*) 18 (*d*) 20

5. A polygon has 35 diagonals, The number of sides of the polygon is:
(*a*) 4 (*b*) 6 (*c*) 8 (*d*) 10

6. If one of the interior angles of a regular polygon is found to be $\frac{9}{8}$ times of one of the interior angles of a regular hexagon, then the number of sides of the polygon is:
(*a*) 8 (*b*) 14 (*c*) 12 (*d*) 10

7. The angles of a hexagon are $x°$, $(x - 5)°$, $(x - 5)°$, $(2x - 5)°$, $(2x - 5)$ and $(2x - 20)°$ then the value of x is:
(*a*) 60° (*b*) 80° (*c*) 90° (*d*) 45°

8. Four angles of a 8-sided figure are each 154°. If the remaining four angles are equal then the measure of each angle:
(*a*) 100° (*b*) 110° (*c*) 116° (*d*) 120°

9. The angles of a quadrilateral are in the ratio 3 : 4 : 5 : 6, the largest angle is:
(*a*) 120° (*b*) 130° (*c*) 110° (*d*) 80°

10. The angles of a pentagon are in the ratio 1 : 2 : 3 : 5 : 9, the largest angle is:
(*a*) 81° (*b*) 135° (*c*) 243° (*d*) 249°

11. The exterior angle of a regular polygon is one third of its interior angle. The number of sides of polygon is :
(*a*) 2 (*b*) 4 (*c*) 6 (*d*) 8

12. The ratio between the number of sides of two regular polygon is 1 : 2 and the ratio between their interior angles 2 : 3. The number of sides of these polygons are respectively:
(*a*) 4, 8 (*b*) 5, 9 (*c*) 4, 10 (*d*) 6, 8

13. The ratio between the number of sides of two polygon is 2 : 1 and the ratio between their interior angle is 4 : 3. The number of sides of these polygons are respectively:
(*a*) 8, 4 (*b*) 10, 5 (*c*) 12, 6 (*d*) 14, 7

14. The ratio of an interior angle to the exterior angle of a regular polygon is 5 : 1. The number of sides of polygon is:
(*a*) 10 (*b*) 11 (*c*) 12 (*d*) 14

15. The difference between the interior and exterior angles of a regular polygon is 60°. The number of sides in the polygon is:
(*a*) 4 (*b*) 5 (*c*) 6 (*d*) 8

ANSWERS

1	2	3	4	5	6	7	8	9	10
(*a*)	(*b*)	(*c*)	(*d*)	(*d*)	(*a*)	(*b*)	(*c*)	(*a*)	(*c*)
11	**12**	**13**	**14**	**15**					
(*d*)	(*a*)	(*b*)	(*c*)	(*c*)					

SOME SELECTED EXPLANATORY ANSWERS

1. Clearly sum of all exterior angles of a convex polygon of n sides = 4 right angles.

2. Here $n = 6$

Sum of interior angles of a hexagon

$= (6 - 2) \times 180° = 4 \times 180° = 720° = 45°$

Number of angles = 6

$\therefore$ Each angle $= \dfrac{720°}{6} = 120°.$

3. Each interior angle $= \dfrac{(n-2)\times 180°}{n}$

$$\therefore \quad \frac{(n-2)\times 180°}{n} = 150°$$
$$(n - 2)\ 180 = n \times 150$$
$$30n = 360$$
$$n = \frac{360}{30} \qquad n = 12$$

4. Number of diagonals of a polygon of n sides

$$= \frac{n(n-1)}{2} - n = \frac{8(8-1)}{2} - 8 = 20$$

5. Let number of sides be n

$$\frac{n(n-1)}{n} - n = 35 \qquad \frac{n^2 - n - 2n}{2} = 35$$

$\Rightarrow n^2 - 3n - 70 = 0$

$\Rightarrow n^2 - 10n + 7n - 70 = 0$

$(n - 10)(n + 7) = 0$

$\Rightarrow n = 10$ and $n \neq -7$

7. Sum of interior angles of a hexagon = 720°

$\therefore x^{o} + (x-5)^{\circ} + (x-5)^{\circ}\ (2x-5)^{\circ} + (2x-5)^{\circ} + (2x+20)^{o} = 720^{o}$

$$9x = 720^{\circ}$$

$$x = \frac{720^{\circ}}{9} = 80^{\circ}$$

8. Let measure of each angle be x then, measure of all angles = 1080°

$\therefore 4 \times 154^{\circ} + 4x = 1080^{\circ}$

$$4x = 1080^{\circ} - 616^{\circ} = 464^{\circ}$$

$$x = \frac{464^{\circ}}{4^{\circ}} = 116^{\circ}$$

9. Let angles be $3x$, $4x$, $5x$, $6x$

$\therefore 3x + 4x + 5x + 6x = 360^{\circ}$

$$18x = 360^{\circ}$$

$$x = \frac{360^{\circ}}{18^{\circ}} = 20^{\circ}$$

$\therefore$ Largest angle = $20 \times 6 = 120^{\circ}$

10. Sum of all angles of a pentagon

$= (n-2) \times 180 = (5-2) \times 180^{\circ} = 3 \times 180 = 540^{\circ}$

Let the angle be x, $2x$, $3x$, $5x$ and $9x$

$\therefore \quad x + 2x + 3x + 5x + 9x = 540^{\circ}$

$$20x = 540$$

$\Rightarrow \quad x = 27^{\circ}$

$\therefore$ Largest angle = $9x = 9 \times 27^{\circ} = 243^{\circ}$

11. Let number of sides be n.

Each exterior angle of regular polygon of n sides = $\frac{360^{\circ}}{n}$

Each interior angle = $\frac{(n-2)\,180^{\circ}}{n}$

So, $\frac{360}{n} = \frac{1}{3}\left[\frac{(n-2) \times 180}{n}\right]$

$\Rightarrow \quad \frac{360}{n} = \frac{(n-2)60}{n} \Rightarrow 360 = (n-2)\ 60$

$\Rightarrow 6 = n - 2 \Rightarrow n = 8.$

15. Here interior angle – exterior angle = 60°

$$\frac{(n-2)\times 180}{n} - \frac{360}{n} = 60$$

$$\frac{1}{n}[(n-2)\times 180 - 360] = 60$$

$$\frac{1}{n}[180n - 360 - 360] = 60$$

$$\frac{1}{n}[180n - 720] = 60$$

$$180n - 720 = 60n$$

$$120n = 720$$

$$n = \frac{720}{120} = 6.$$

CIRCLES

DEFINITIONS

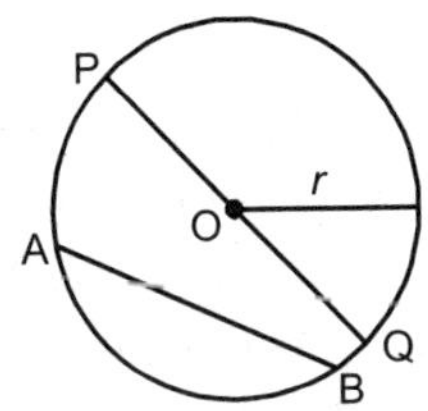

Circle: As circle is a set of points which lie in a plane and at a constant distance from a fixed point in the plane.

Here the fixed point 'O' is called the **centre** of the circle and the constant distance is called **radius** of circle denoted by '*r*'.

Chord: A line segment whose end points belong to the circle is a chord. So here AB is the chord.

Diameter: The chord which passes through the centre of a circle is called a diameter of the circle. Here PQ is the diameter.

Diameter is the longest chord.

Diameter = 2 × radius.

Diameter divides a circle into two equal parts. Each part is called a **Semi-circle.**

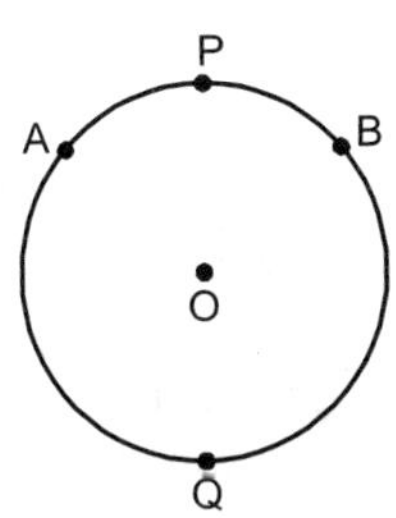

Arc: Any part of a circle is called an arc of the circle. Here AB is an arc of circle and written as AB.

If arc is less than semicircle it is called a **minor arc,** otherwise it is called as **major arc.**

APB is minor arc and AQB is major arc.

Segment: The area enclosed by an arc and its corresponding chord is called a segment of the circle.

A segment is minor if its arc is minor.

A segment is major if its arc is major.

Sector: The area enclosed by any two radii and the arc determined by the end points of the radii is called a sector of the circle.

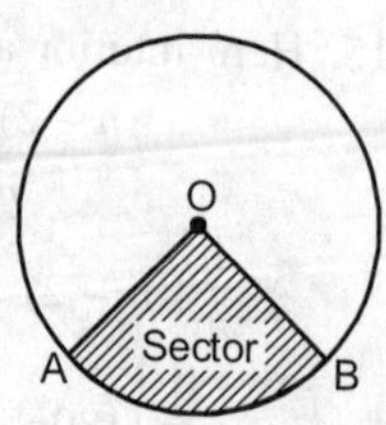

Circumference: It is the distance travelled if you will go once around a circle.

Circumference = $2\pi r$

Concentric circles: In a plane two or more circles are called concentric if they have a common centre.

- Infinite number of circles can be drawn with same centre.

SOME RESULTS ON CIRCLES

Theorem 1. If two arcs of a circle arc congruent then the corresponding chords are equal.

Theorem 2. The perpendicular from the centre of a circle to a chord bisects the chord.

So here OD $\perp$ AB then

AD = DB

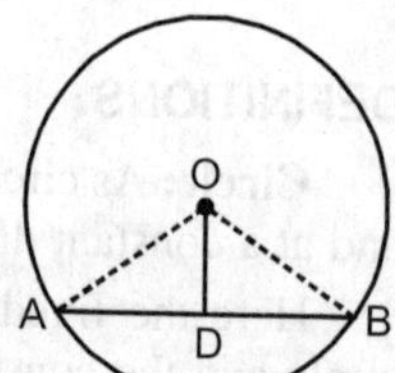

Theorem 3. The line joining the centre to the mid-point of a chord is perpendicular to the chord.

Here if AD = DB then $\angle$ADO = $\angle$ODB = 90°

Theorem 4. The perpendicular bisectors of two chords of a circle intersect at its centre.

Here AB, CD are the chords and l, m are perpendicular bisector of AB and CD. So l and m meet at 'O'.

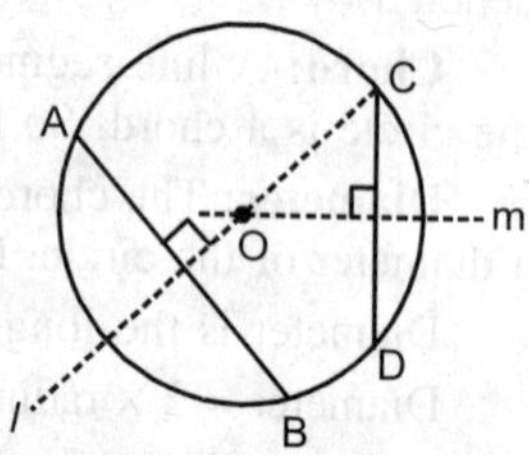

Theorem 5. There is one and only one circle passing through three non-collinear points.

- An infinite number of circles can be drawn to pass through a single point.
- An infinite number of circles can be drawn to pass through two given points.
- A unique circle can be drawn to pass through three given non-collinear points.

Theorem 6. Equal chords of congruent circles are equidistant from the corresponding centres.

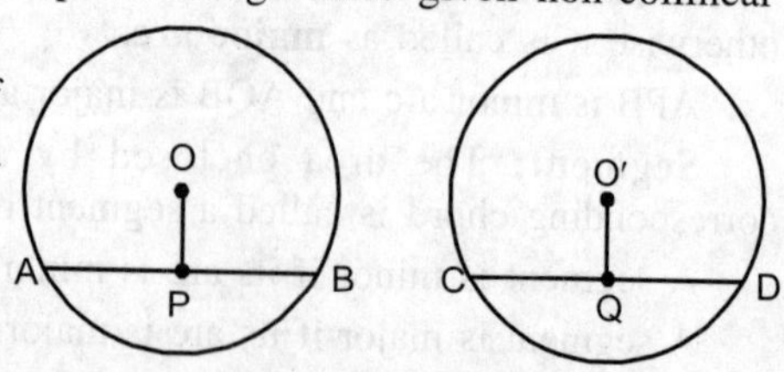

Here it AB = CD then OP = O′Q

Theorem 7. Chords which are equidistant from the corresponding centres are equal.

So in above figure if OP = O′Q then AB = CD.

Theorem 8. Equal chords of a circle are equidistant from the centre.

Here if AB and CD are equal chords of circle, then OP = OQ. (conversely) if OP = OQ then also AB = CD

i.e., chords at equal distance for the centre are equal.

Theorem 9. Of any two chords of a circle, the greater chord is nearer to the centre.

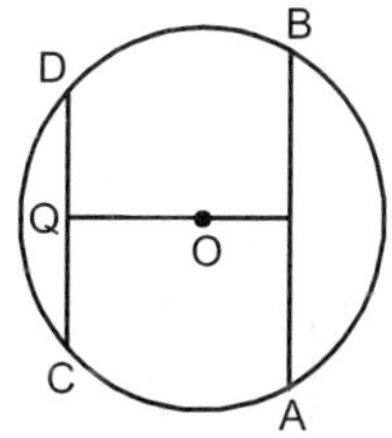

Here if OQ > OP then AB > CD, where AB and CD are chords.

Theorem 10. The angle subtended by an arc of a circle at the centre is double the angle subtended by it at any point on the circumference of circle. Here three case arises.

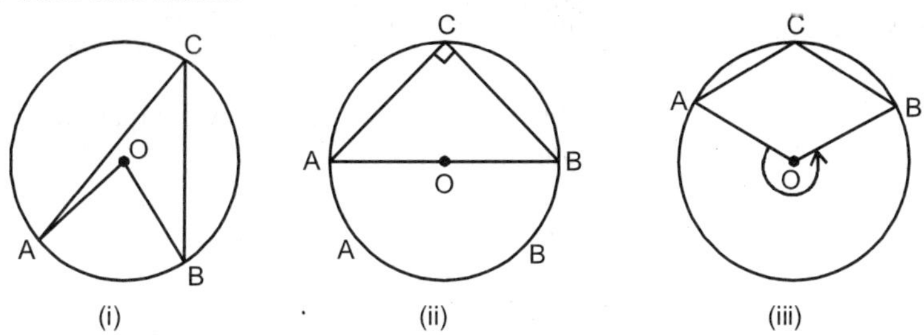

Here in all the three cases ∠AOB = 2 ∠ACB

Theorem 11. The angle in a semi-circle is a right angle.

Theorem 12. Angle in the same segment of the circle are equal.

Here ∠ACB = ∠ADB

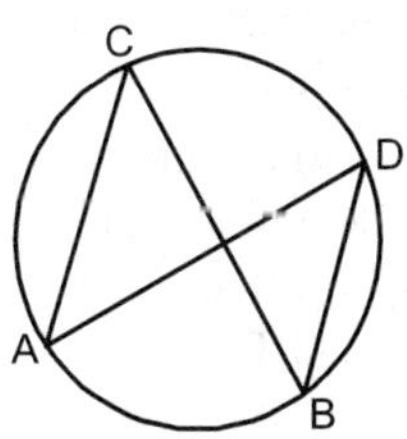

Theorem 13. If two chords, AB and CD of a circle intersect inside or outside the circle when produced at a point P.

Then, AP × PB = DP × PC

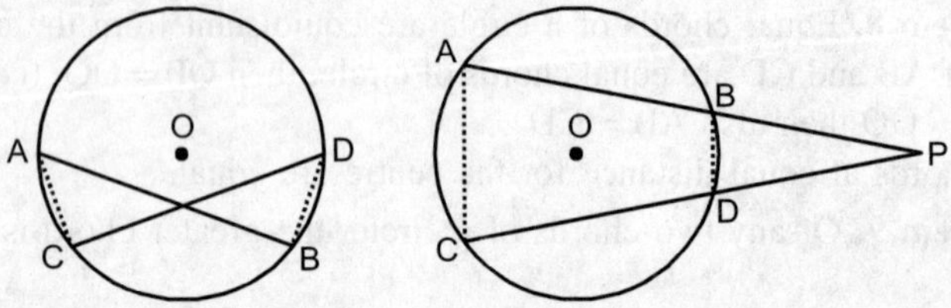

CYCLIC QUADRILATERAL

A quadrilateral whose vertices lie on a circle is called a cyclic quadrilateral.

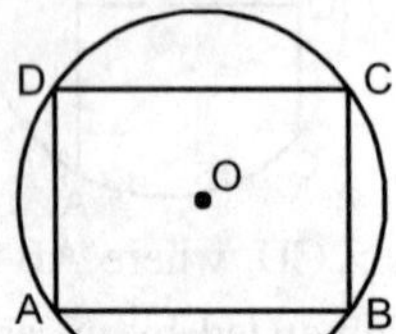

- ∠A, ∠B, ∠C and ∠D are interior angles.
- ∠A and ∠C are opposite angles also ∠B and ∠D.
- ∠A + ∠C = 180° = ∠B + ∠D.
- The exterior angle, formed by producing a side of a cyclic quadrilateral is equal to the interior opposite angles.

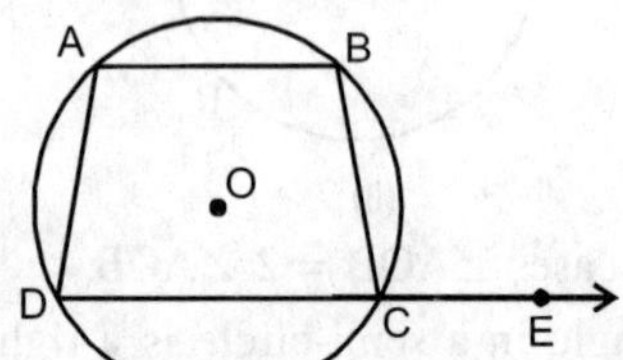

Here ∠BAD = ∠BCE

Secant: A line which intersects a circle in two distinct points is called a secant of the circle. Here PAB is secant.

Tangent: A line meeting a circle only in one point is called a tangent to the circle. And the point where tangent meets is called point of contact. Here PT is a tangent and T is point of contact.

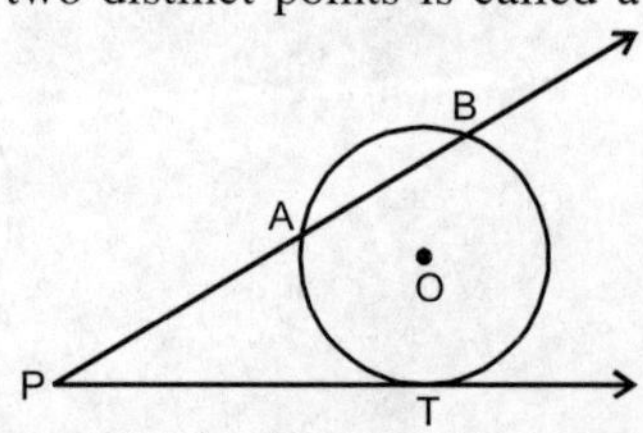

EXERCISE

1. In a circle with centre O, AOC is a diameter of the circle, BD is a chord and OB and CD are joined. If ∠AOB = 130° then ∠BDC = ?

(*a*) 30° (*b*) 25° (*c*) 50° (*d*) 60°

2. Inscribed ∠ACB intercepts AB of circle with centre O. If the bisector of ∠ACB meets arc AB in M then:

(*a*) *m*AM > *m*MB (*a*) *m*AM < *m*MB

(*c*) *m*AM = *m*MB (*d*) None of these

3. ΔABC is inscribed in a circle ∠P, ∠Q and ∠R are angles inscribed in the arcs cut off by sides BC, AC and AB respectively. Then ∠P + ∠Q + ∠R is equal to:

(*a*) 180° (*b*) 360° (*c*) 240° (*d*) None of these

4. CD is a direct common tangent to two circles intersecting each other at A and B. Then ∠CAD + ∠CBD is equal to

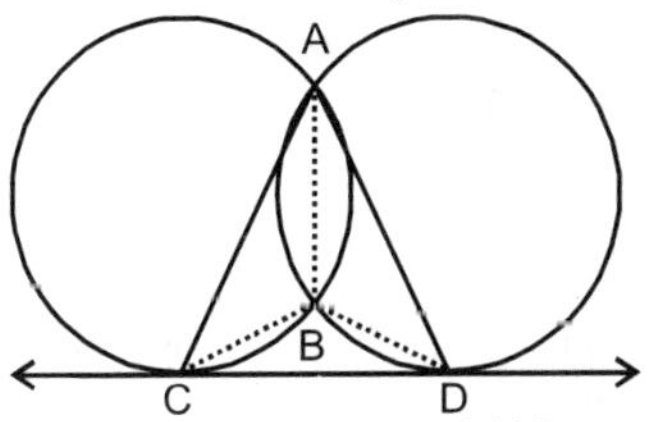

(*a*) 180° (*b*) 90° (*c*) 360° (*d*) 120°

5. A circle has two equal chords and radius *r*, then the line joining the mid-points of the chords is:

(*a*) straight line (*b*) equal to radius

(*c*) less than radius (*d*) greater than radius

6. P and Q are the centres of two circles whose radii are 12 cm and 5 cm respectively. The direct common tangents to the circles meet PQ at O, Then O divides PQ :

(*a*) externally in the ratio 12 : 5 (*a*) externally in the ratio 5 : 12

(*c*) internally in the ratio 12 : 5 (*d*) internally in the ratio 5 : 12

7. Incentre of a triangle lies in the interior of:

(*a*) an equilateral triangle only (*b*) an isosceles triangle only

(*c*) right triangle only (*d*) any triangle

8. Match List-I with List-II and select the correct answers using the codes given below the lists:

List-I (Relative position of two circles)

A. Non-intersecting and one is inside the other

B. Non-intersecting and one is not inside the other
C. Intersecting

List-II (Number of common tangents)

1. Zero 2. Two 3. Three 4. Four

Codes:

	A	B	C
(*a*)	3	1	2
(*b*)	1	4	3
(*c*)	3	2	4
(*d*)	1	4	2

9. In the adjoining figure AB = 10 cm, PB = 4 cm, PD = 8 cm; the measure of PC is :

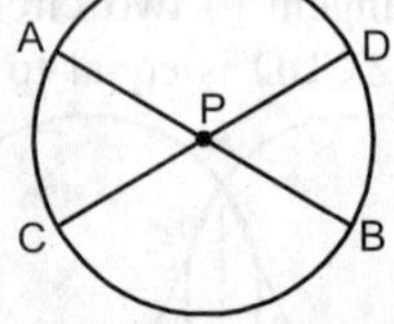

(*a*) 3 cm (*b*) 8 cm (*c*) 6 cm (*d*) 5 cm

10. $\angle LTP = 38°$, the measure of the reflex angle TOL is:

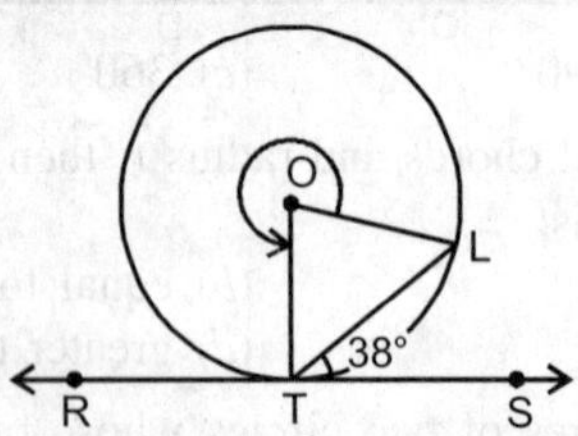

(*a*) 76° (*b*) 294° (*c*) 274° (*d*) 284°

11. AB and CD are equal chords of a circle whose centre is O. When produced these chords meet at E. Then :
(*a*) EB = ED (*b*) EA = EC (*c*) EA = ED (*d*) both (*a*) and (*b*)

12. In a circle of radius 17 cm, two parallel chords are drawn on opposite side of a diameter. The distance between the chords is 23 cm. If the length of one chord is 16 cm, then the length of the other is :
(*a*) 34 cm (*b*) 15 cm (*c*) 23 cm (*d*) 30 cm

13. It is not possible to draw a circle having its centre on a fixed straight line *l* and passing through two points A and B not on *l* if:
(*a*) *l* is parallel to $\overline{AB}$

(*b*) l is the perpendicular bisector of $\overline{AB}$

(*c*) l is perpendicular to $\overline{AB}$ but does not bisect it

(*d*) l is not perpendicular to $\overline{AB}$ but bisects it

14. If AB is a chord of a circle, P and Q are the two points on the circle different from A and B, then:

(*a*) The angles subtended at P and Q by AB are always equal

(*b*) The sum of the angles subtended by AB at P and Q is always equal to two right angles

(*c*) The angles subtended by AB at P and Q are either equal or supplementary

(*d*) The sum of the angles subtended at P and Q is to four right angles

15. In the adjoining figure, POQ is the diameter of the circle, R and S are any two points on the circles. Then:

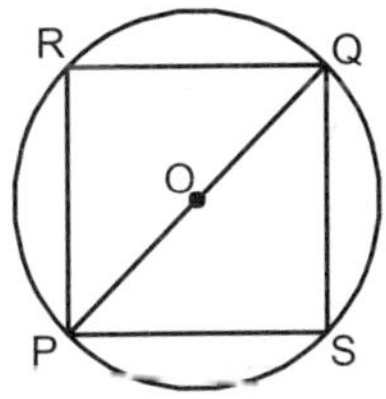

(*a*) $\angle PRQ > \angle PSQ$ (*b*) $\angle PRQ < \angle PSQ$

(*c*) $\angle PRQ = \angle PSQ$ (*d*) $\angle PRQ = \frac{1}{2} \angle PSQ$

16. If the four sides of a quadrilateral ABCD are tangential to a circle, then:

(*a*) AC + AD = BD + CD (*b*) AB + CD = BC + AD

(*c*) AB + CD = AC + BC (*d*) AC + AD = BC + BD

17. If O is the centre of the circle, the value of '*x*' in the adjoining figure is:

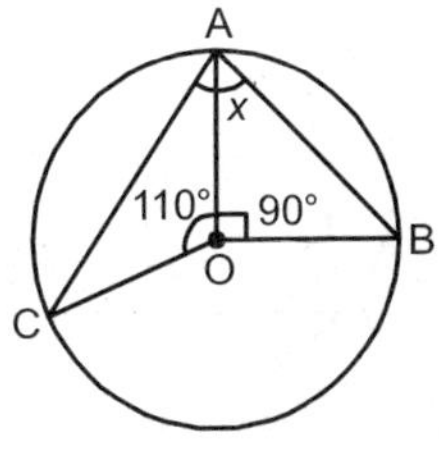

(*a*) 80° (*b*) 70° (*c*) 60° (*d*) 50°

18. In the adjoining figure, ΔABC is an isosceles triangle, with AB = AC and $\angle ABC = 50°$. Then $\angle BDC$ is:

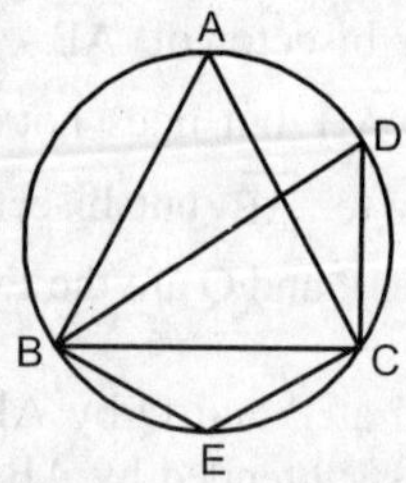

(*a*) 110° (*b*) 90° (*c*) 80° (*d*) 70°

19. Any cyclic parallelogram is a:
(*a*) rhombus (*b*) trapezium (*c*) quadrilateral (*d*) rectangle

20. The quadrilateral formed by angle bisectors of a cyclic quadrilateral ABCD is a
(*a*) rhombus (*b*) parallelogram
(*c*) cyclic quadrilateral (*d*) trapezium

21. In the adjoining figure A, B, C, D are the concyclic points. The value of '*x*' is :

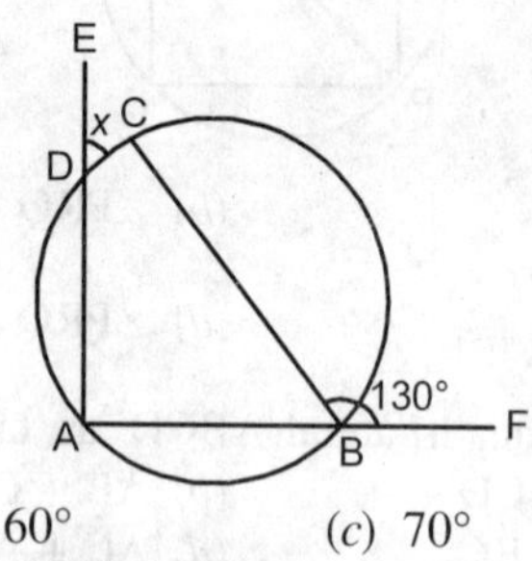

(*a*) 50° (*b*) 60° (*c*) 70° (*d*) 90°

22. If O is the centre of the circle, then '*x*' is

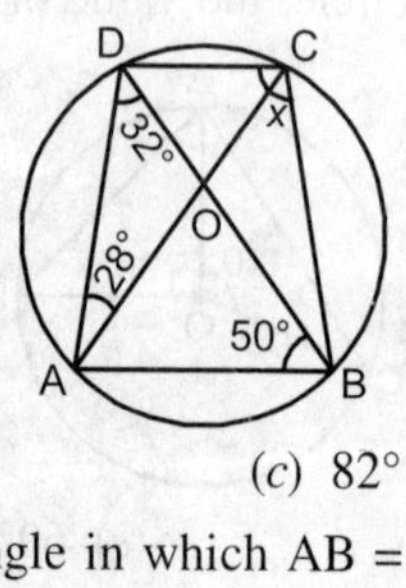

(*a*) 72° (*b*) 62° (*c*) 82° (*d*) 52°

23. ABC is an isosceles triangle in which AB = AC. If D and E are the mid-points of AB and AC respectively. The point B, C, D, E are :

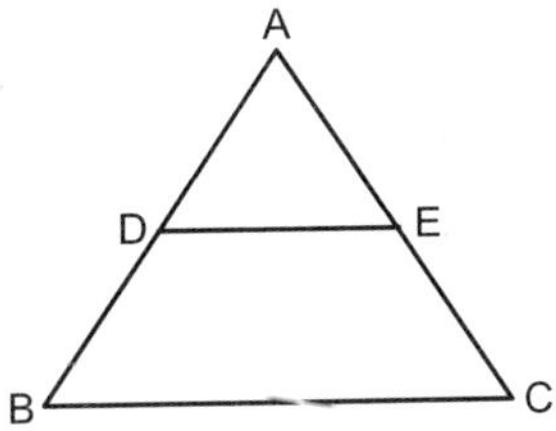

(*a*) collinear (*b*) non-collinear (*c*) concyclic (*d*) None of these

24. Two circles touch each other internally. Their radii are 2 cm and 3 cm. The biggest chord of the outer circle which is outside the inner circle is of length:

(*a*) $2\sqrt{2}$ cm (*b*) $3\sqrt{2}$ cm (*c*) $2\sqrt{3}$ cm (*d*) $4\sqrt{2}$ cm

25. If two circles are such that the centre of one lies on the circumference of the other then the ratio of the common chord of the two circles to the radius of any one of the circles is:

(*a*) 2 : 1 (*b*) $\sqrt{3} : 1$ (*c*) $\sqrt{5} : 1$ (*d*) 4 : 1

26. If one angle of a cyclic trapezium is triple of the other, then the greater one measures :

(*a*) 90° (*b*) 105° (*c*) 120° (*d*) 135°

27. A circle of radius r has been inscribed in a triangle of area Δ. If the semi-perimeter of the triangle be S, then the correct relation is :

(*a*) $2r = \frac{\Delta}{S}$ (*b*) $r = \frac{\Delta}{S}$ (*c*) $r = \frac{S}{\Delta}$ (*d*) $2S = \Delta r$

28. In a cyclic quadrilateral ABCD, if $\angle B - \angle D = 60°$ then the measure of the smaller of the two is:

(*a*) 60° (*b*) 40° (*c*) 38° (*d*) 30°

29. The incircle of a ΔABC touches the sides AB, BC and AC at the points P, Q, R respectively, then which of the following statements is/are correct:

I. AP + BQ + CR = PB + QC + RA

II. AP + BQ + CR = $\frac{1}{2}$(perimeter of ΔABC)

III. AP + BQ + CR = 3 (AB + BC + CA)

(*a*) I, II and III (*b*) only I

(*c*) II and III only (*d*) I and II

30. In the given figure, ABCD is a cyclic quadrilateral. AE is drawn parallel to CD and BA is produced. If $\angle ABC = 92°$ and $\angle FAE = 20°$, then $\angle BCD$ is equal to:

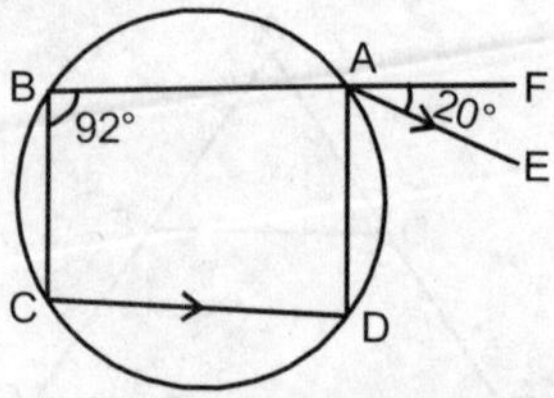

(*a*) 88° (*b*) 98° (*c*) 108° (*d*) 72°

ANSWERS

1	2	3	4	5	6	7	8	9	10
(*b*)	(*c*)	(*b*)	(*a*)	(*a*)	(*a*)	(*d*)	(*d*)	(*a*)	(*d*)
11	**12**	**13**	**14**	**15**	**16**	**17**	**18**	**19**	**20**
(*d*)	(*d*)	(*c*)	(*c*)	(*c*)	(*b*)	(*a*)	(*c*)	(*d*)	(*c*)
21	**22**	**23**	**24**	**25**	**26**	**27**	**28**	**29**	**30**
(*a*)	(*c*)	(*c*)	(*d*)	(*b*)	(*d*)	(*b*)	(*a*)	(*d*)	(*c*)

SOME SELECTED EXPLANATORY ANSWERS

1.

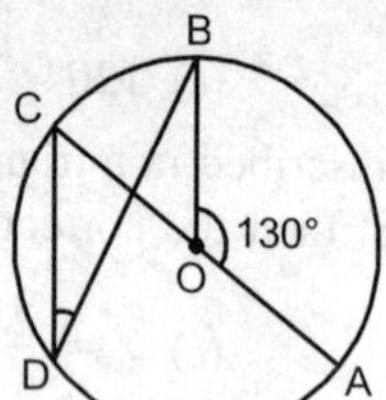

$$\angle AOB = 130°$$

$$\Rightarrow \quad \angle BOC = 180° - \angle AOB = 50°$$

$$\angle BDC = \frac{1}{2}\angle BOC = \frac{1}{2} \times 50° = 25°$$

2.

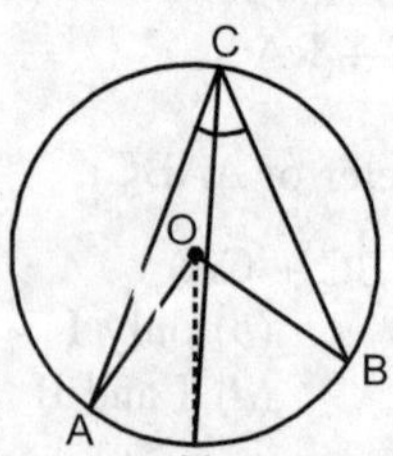

$$m\text{AM} = \angle AOM = 2\angle ACM$$

$$mMB = \angle MOB = 2\angle MCB$$

but $\angle ACM = \angle MCB \Rightarrow mAM = mMB$

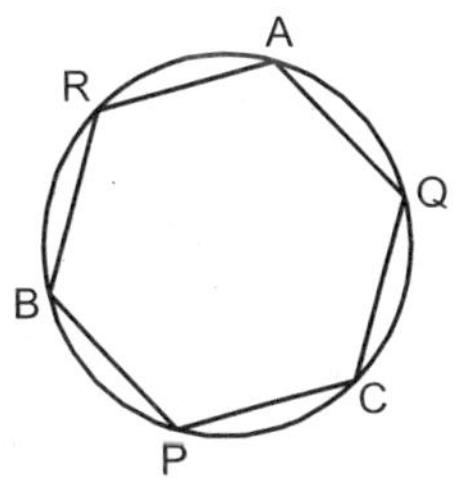

3. $\angle R + \angle ACB = 180°$

$\angle P + \angle BAC = 180°$

$\angle Q + \angle ABC = 180°$

$\angle P + \angle Q + \angle R + \angle BAC + \angle ABC + \angle ACB = 540$

$\angle P + \angle Q + \angle R = 540° - 180°$

$\angle P + \angle Q + \angle R = 360°$

4. Here $\angle CAB = \angle BCD$ (angles in alternate segments) and $\angle DAB = \angle CDB$ (angles in alternate segments)

$\angle CAD = \angle CAB + \angle DAB = \angle BCD + \angle CDB$

$\Rightarrow \angle CAD + \angle CBD = \angle BCD + \angle CDB + \angle CBD = 180°$ (angles of a Δ)

5. As line joining the mid-points of the chords can be greater than radius or less than radius.

7. Incentre is the centre of the circle, so it always lies inside the triangle.

9. $AP \times PB = PC \times PD$

$\Rightarrow \quad 6 \times 4 = 8 \times PC$

$\Rightarrow \quad PC = \dfrac{24}{8} = 3$ cm

11.

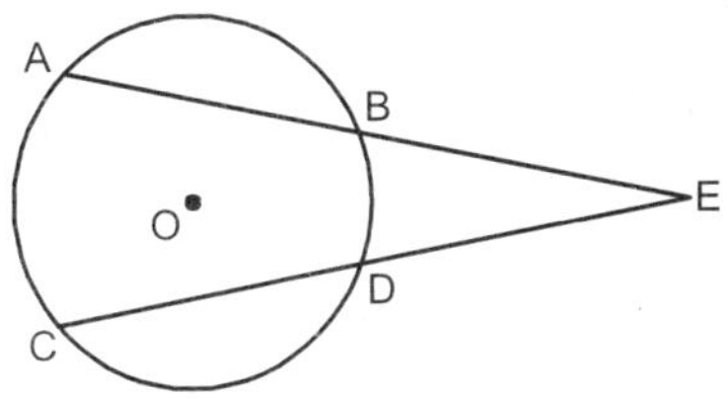

Clearly AE = EC and as AB = CD ⇒ EB = ED

15. $\angle PRQ = \angle PSQ = 90°$ (each angle in semi-circle)

16. As the tangents to a circle from a point outside it are equal,

So,

AP = AS, PB = BQ,

QC = RC, DR = DS

Now, (AP + PB) + (DR + RC) = (AS + DS) + (BQ + CQ)

⇒ AB + CD = AD + BC

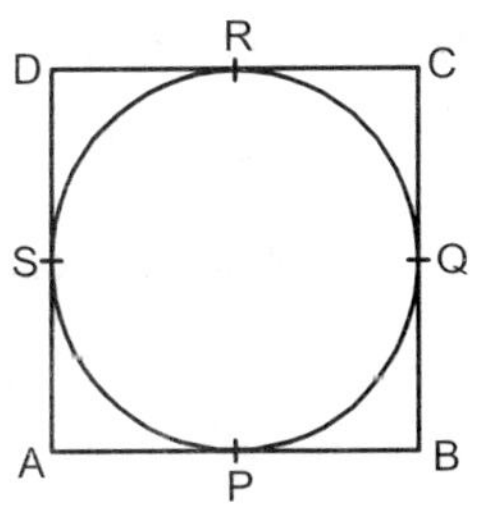

17. $\angle COB = 360° - (110° + 90°) = 160°$

$\therefore \quad x = \angle CAB$

$= \frac{1}{2}\angle COB = \frac{1}{2} \times 160° = 80°$

18. As, $\quad AB = AC$

$\Rightarrow \quad \angle ACB = \angle ABC = 50°$

$\therefore \quad \angle BAC = 180° - (50 + 50) = 80°$

$\therefore \quad \angle BDC = \angle BAC = 80°$ (angles in the same segment)

19. Here, ABCD is a cyclic parallelogram.

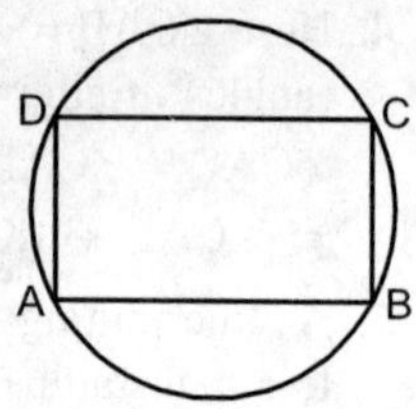

$\therefore \quad \angle B + \angle D = 180°$

also $\angle B = \angle D \Rightarrow \angle B = \angle D = 90°$

But a parallelogram one of whose angles is 90° is a rectangle.

21. $\quad \angle CBF = \angle CDA$

$\Rightarrow \quad \angle CDA = 130°$

$\angle CDA + x = 180°$ (linear pair)

$\Rightarrow \quad x = 180° - 130°$

$\Rightarrow \quad x = 50°$

22. $\quad \angle ACB = \angle ADB = 32°$

$\angle ACD = \angle ABD = 50°$

$\therefore \quad x = \angle BCD$

$= \angle ACB + \angle ACD = 82°$

23. As DE || BC, so $\angle ADE = \angle ABC$

Also, $\quad \angle ABC = \angle ACB$

$\therefore \quad \angle ADE = \angle ACB \qquad (\quad AB = AC)$

$\therefore \quad \angle ADE + \angle EDB = 180°$

$\Rightarrow \quad \angle ACB + \angle EDB = 180°$

Hence, B, C, D and E are concyclic.

24. Here, OA = 10 cm, OB = 3 cm

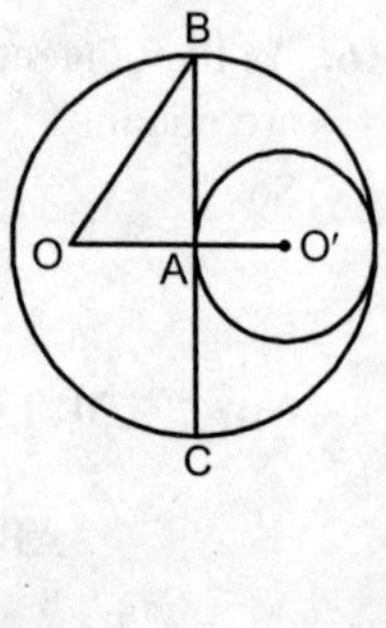

$\therefore \quad AB = \sqrt{3^2 - 1^2} = \sqrt{8}$ cm

$\therefore$ Required length $= BC = 2AB$

$= 2\sqrt{8}$ cm $= 4\sqrt{2}$ cm.

25. Here let O, O′ be the centres of the circle. As the centre of each lies on the circumference of the other, the two circles will have the same radius. Let it be r.

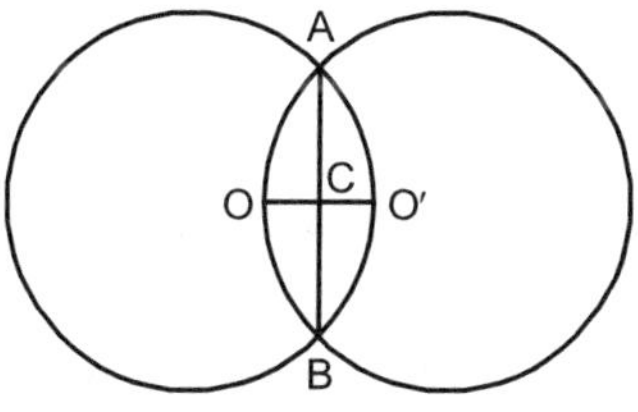

$$\therefore \quad OC = O'C = \frac{r}{2}$$

$$\therefore \quad AC = \sqrt{OA^2 - OC^2}$$

$$= \sqrt{r^2 - \frac{r^2}{4}} = \frac{\sqrt{3}}{2}r$$

$$AB = \sqrt{3}\,r$$

Hence $\dfrac{\text{Common chord}}{\text{Radius}} = \sqrt{3}\,r : r = \sqrt{3} : 1$

27. Let OD ⊥ BC, OE ⊥ AC, OF ⊥ AB, then

Δ = area (ΔOBC) + area (ΔCOA) + area (ΔAOB)

$$= \frac{1}{2}BC \times OD + \frac{1}{2}AC \times OE + \frac{1}{2}AB \times OF$$

$$= r \cdot \frac{1}{2}(BC + AC + AB) \quad (\;\; OD = OF = OE = r)$$

$$= r \cdot \frac{1}{2} \times 2s$$

$$\Delta = rs \Rightarrow r = \frac{\Delta}{S}$$

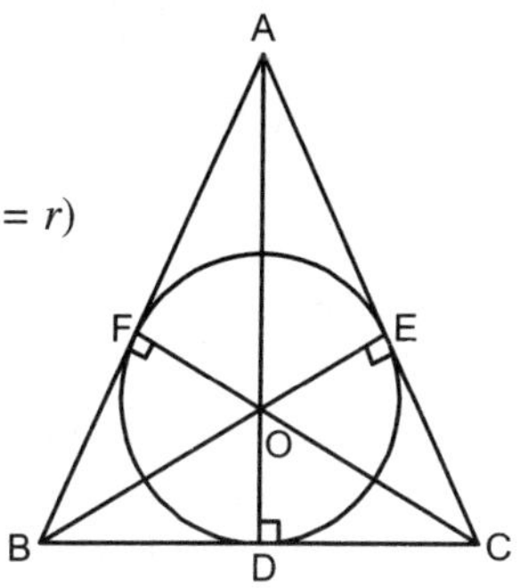

28. As $\angle B + \angle D = 180°$ and

$\angle B - \angle D = 60° \;\Rightarrow\; \angle B = 120°$ and $\angle D = 60°$

30. $\angle B + \angle D = 180°$

$\Rightarrow \;\angle D = 180 - \angle B = 180° - 92° = 88°$

$$\angle DAE = \angle D = 88°$$

$$\angle FAD = 88° + 20° = 108°$$

$$\angle BCD = \angle FAD = 108°$$

$$\Rightarrow \quad \angle BCD = 108°$$

~~~~~~
~~~~~~

25. AREA AND PERIMETER

I. Results on Triangles :

1. Sum of the angles of a triangle is 180°.
2. The sum of any two sides of a triangle is greater than the third side.
3. **Pythagoras Theorem:** In a right-angled triangle,
   $$(\text{Hypotenuse})^2 = (\text{Base})^2 + (\text{Height})^2.$$
4. The line joining the mid-point of a side of a triangle to the opposite vertex is called the ***median.***
5. The point where the three medians of a triangle meet, is called ***centroid.*** *The* centroid divides each of the medians in the ratio 2 : 1.
6. In an isosceles triangle, the altitude from the vertex bisects the base.
7. The median of a triangle divides it into two triangles of the same area.
8. The area of the triangle formed by joining the mid-points of the sides of a given triangle is one-fourth of the area of the given triangle.

II. Results on Quadrilaterals:

1. The diagonals of a parallelogram bisect each other.
2. Each diagonal of a parallelogram divides it into two triangles of the same area.
3. The diagonals of a rectangle are equal and bisect each other.
4. The diagonals of a square are equal and bisect each other at right angles.
5. The diagonals of a rhombus bisect each other at right angles.
6. A parallelogram and a rectangle on the same base and between the same parallels are equal in area.
7. Of all the parallelogram of given sides, the parallelogram which is a rectangle has the greatest area.

IMPORTANT FORMULAE

I. 1. Area of a rectangle = (Length × Breadth).

$$\therefore \quad \text{Length} = \left(\frac{\text{Area}}{\text{Breadth}}\right) \text{ and Breadth} = \left(\frac{\text{Area}}{\text{Length}}\right)$$

2. Perimeter of a rectangle = 2 (Length + Breadth).

II. Area of a square = $(\text{side})^2 = \frac{1}{2} (\text{diagonal})^2$.

III. Area of 4 walls of a room = 2 (Length + Breadth) × Height.

IV. 1. Area of a triangle = $\frac{1}{2}$ × Base × Height.

2. Area of a triangle = $\sqrt{s(s-a)(s-b)(s-c)}$, where a, b, c are the sides of the triangle and $s = \frac{1}{2}(a + b + c)$.

3. Area of an equilateral triangle = $\frac{\sqrt{3}}{4} \times (\text{side})^2$.

4. Radius of incircle of an equilateral triangle of side $a = \frac{a}{2\sqrt{3}}$.

5. Radius of circumcircle of an equilateral triangle of side $a = \frac{a}{\sqrt{3}}$.

6. Radius of incircle of a triangle of area Δ and semi-perimeter $s = \frac{\Delta}{s}$.

V. 1. Area of a parallelogram = (Base × Height).

2. Area of a rhombus = $\frac{1}{2}$ × (Product of diagonals).

3. Area of a trapezium = $\frac{1}{2}$ × (sum of parallel sides) × distance between them.

VI. 1. Area of a circle = πR^2, where R is the radius.

2. Circumference of a circle = $2\pi R$.

3. Length of an arc = $\frac{2\pi R\theta}{360}$, where θ is the central angle.

4. Area of a sector = $\frac{1}{2}(\text{arc} \times R) = \frac{\pi R^2 \theta}{360}$.

VII. 1. Area of a semi-circle = $\frac{\pi R^2}{2}$

2. Circumference of a semi-circle = πR.

SOLVED EXAMPLE

1. If the diagonal of a rectangle is 17 cm long and its perimeter is 46 cm, find the area of the rectangle.

Sol. Let length = x and breadth = y. Then,

$2(x + y) = 46$ or $x + y = 23$ and $x^2 + y^2 = (17)^2 = 289$.

Now, $(x + y)^2 = (23)^2 \Leftrightarrow (x^2 + y^2) + 2xy = 529$

$\Leftrightarrow 289 + 2xy = 529 \Leftrightarrow xy = 120$.

$\therefore$ Area $= xy' = 120$ cm^2.

2. A rectangular grassy plot 110 m by 65 m has a gravel path 2.5 m wide all round it on the inside. Find the cost of gravelling the path at 80 paise per sq. metre.

Sol. Area of the plot = (110×65) m^2 = 7150 m^2.

Area of the plot excluding the path = $[(110 - 5) \times (65 - 5)]$ m^2 = 6300 m^2

$\therefore$ Area of the path = $(7150 - 6300)$ m^2 = 850 m^2

Cost of gravelling the path = ₹ $\left(850 \times \frac{80}{100}\right)$ = ₹ 680.

3. A room 5 m 55 cm long and 3 m 74 cm broad is to be paved with square tiles. Find the least number of square tiles required to cover the floor.

Sol. Area of the room = (544×374) cm^2

Size of largest square tile = H.C.F. of 544 cm and 374 cm = 34 cm

Area of 1 tile = (34×34) cm^2.

$\therefore$ Number of tiles required = $\left(\frac{544 \times 374}{34 \times 34}\right) = 176$.

4. The base of a triangular field is three times its altitude. If the cost of cultivating the field at ₹ 24.68 per hectare be ₹ 333.18, find its base and height.

Sol. Area of the field = $\frac{\text{Total cost}}{\text{Rate}} = \left(\frac{333.18}{24.68}\right)$ hectares = 13.5 hectares

$= (13.5 \times 10000)$ m^2 = 135000 m^2.

Let altitude = x metres and base = $3x$ metres.

Then, $\frac{1}{2} \times 3x \times x = 135000 \Leftrightarrow x^2 = 90000 \Leftrightarrow x = 300$.

$\therefore$ Base = 900 m and Altitude = 300 m.

5. The difference between two parallel sides, of a trapezium is 4 cm. The perpendicular distance between them is 19 cm. If the area of the trapezium is 475 cm^2, find the lengths of the parallel sides.

Sol. Let the two parallel sides of the trapezium be a cm and b cm.

Then, $a - b = 4$ ...(*i*)

And $\frac{1}{2} \times (a + b) \times 19 = 475$

$$\Rightarrow \quad (a + b) = \left(\frac{475 \times 2}{19}\right) \Leftrightarrow a + b = 50 \quad \text{...}(ii)$$

Solving (*i*) and (*ii*), we get : $a = 27$, $b = 23$.

So, the two parallel sides are 27 cm and 23 cm.

6. Find the length of a rope by which a cow must be tethered in order that it may be able to graze an area of 9856 sq. metres.

Sol. Clearly, the cow will graze a circular field of area 9856 sq. metres and radius equal to the length of the rope.

Let the length of the rope be R metres.

Then, $\pi R^2 = 9856 \Leftrightarrow R^2 = \left(9856 \times \frac{7}{22}\right) = 3136 \Leftrightarrow R = 56.$

$\therefore$ Length of the rope = 56 m.

EXERCISE

1. What will be the area (in square metres) of 1.5 metre wide garden developed around all the four sides of a rectangular field having area equal to 300 square metres and breadth equal to three-fourth of the length?

(*a*) 96 (*b*) 105
(*c*) 114 (*d*) Cannot be determined

2. The ratio of length and breadth of a rectangular plot is 8 : 5 respectively. If the breadth is 60 metre less than the length, what is the perimeter of the rectangular plot?

(*a*) 260 metres (*b*) 1600 metres (*c*) 500 metres (*d*) None of these

3. Find the number of bricks each of dimensions 25 cm × 12.5 cm × 7.5 cm to make a wall of dimensions 5 m × 3 × 20 m.

(*a*) 1200 (*b*) 1350 (*c*) 128000 (*d*) 1400

4. The measure of each of two opposite angles of a rhombus is 60° and the measure of one of its sides is 10 cm. The length of its smaller diagonal is:

(*a*) 10 cm (*b*) $10\sqrt{3}$ cm (*c*) $10\sqrt{2}$ cm (*d*) $\frac{5}{2}\sqrt{2}$ cm

5. The area of the shaded region in the figure given below is

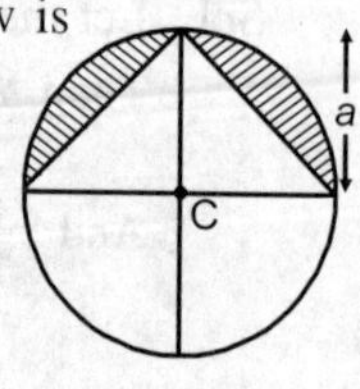

(*a*) $\frac{a^2}{2}\left(\frac{\pi}{2}-1\right)$ sq. units (*b*) $a^2 (\pi - 1)$ sq. units

(*c*) $a^2\left(\frac{\pi}{2}-1\right)$ sq. units (*d*) $\frac{a^2}{2}(\pi - 1)$ sq. units

6. The perimeter of the floor of a room is 18 m. What is the area of the walls of the room, if the height of the room is 3 m?

(*a*) 21 m^2 (*b*) 42 m^2 (*c*) 54 m^2 (*d*) 108 m^2

7. What would be the cost of building a 7 metres wide garden around a circular field with diameter equal to 280 metres if the cost per sq, metre for building the garden is ₹ 21?

(*a*) ₹ 1,56,242 (*b*) ₹ 2,48,521 (*c*) ₹ 1,11,624 (*d*) None of these

8. In an isosceles triangle, the measure of each of equal sides is 10 cm and the angle between them is 45°, the area of the triangle is

(*a*) 25 cm^2 (*b*) $\frac{25}{2}\sqrt{2}$ cm^2 (*c*) $25\sqrt{2}$ cm^2 (*d*) $25\sqrt{3}$ cm^2

9. The length of a rectangle, which is 25 cms. is equal to the length of a square and the area of the rectangle is 125 cms. less than the area of the square. What is the breadth of the rectangle?

(*a*) 15 cms. (*b*) 20 cms. (*c*) 12 cms. (*d*) 15 cms.

10. What is the area of a circle with the circumference of 88 cms. ?

(*a*) 618 sq.cms. (*b*) 516 sq. cms. (*c*) 600 sq. cms. (*d*) None of these

11. The radius of a circle is 20% more than the height of a right angled triangle. The base of triangle is 36 cm. If the area of triangle and circle be equal, what will be the area of circle?

(*a*) 72 cm^2 (*b*) 144 cm^2 (*c*) 216 cm^2 (*d*) 128 cm^2

12. The area of a square of side 8 cm is equal to a rectangle. Which of the following statement/s is/are definitely true about the rectangle?

(*a*) The length of rectangle is 16 times its breadth

(*b*) The length of rectangle is 32 times its breadth

(*c*) The breadth of rectangle is $\frac{1}{6}$ of its length

(*d*) The breadth of rectangle is $\frac{1}{9}$ of its length

13. What will be the area of a circle whose perimeter is 88 cms?

(*a*) 576 cm^2 (*b*) 616 cm^2

(*c*) 636 cm^2 (*d*) Cannot be determined

14. The areas of a square and a rectangle are equal. The length of the rectangle is greater than the length of a side of the square by 5 cm and the breadth is less than the length of the side of the square by 3 cm. The perimeter of the rectangle is:
(*a*) 17 cm (*b*) 26 cm (*c*) 30 cm (*d*) 34 cm

15. What is the area of a circle of diameter of 28 cm?
(*a*) 2464 sq. cm (*b*) 616 sq. cm (*c*) 88 sq. cm. (*d*) 176 sq. cm

16. The area of a rectangle with 10 cm length is equal to the area of a circle. Find the circumference of the circle.
(*a*) 36 cm (*b*) 34 cm
(*d*) 26 cm (*d*) Cannot be determined

17. What would be the diagonal of a square whose area is 25 sq. cm?
(*a*) 7 (*b*) $\sqrt{60}$ (*c*) 9 (*d*) None of these

18. The ratio between length and breadth of a rectangular plot is 5 : 3 respectively and its perimeter is 48 metres. What will be its area in sq. metres?
(*a*) 120 (*b*) 116 (*c*) 115 (*d*) None of these

19. What will be the area of a circle whose circumference is 132 cm?
(*a*) 693 cm^2 (*b*) 264 cm^2 (*c*) 5227 cm^2 (*d*) None of these

20. What will be the cost of gardening 1 metres broad boundary around a rectangular plot having perimeter of 340 metres at the rate of ₹ 10 per square metre?
(*a*) ₹ 3,400 (*b*) ₹ 1,700
(*c*) ₹ 3,440 (*d*) Cannot be determined

21. What will be the area of a semi-circle of 14 metres diameter?
(*a*) 154 sq. metres (*b*) 77 sq. metres
(*c*) 308 sq. metres (*d*) 22 sq. metres

22. In the figure, if $\angle BAT = 65°$, find $\angle BDA$.

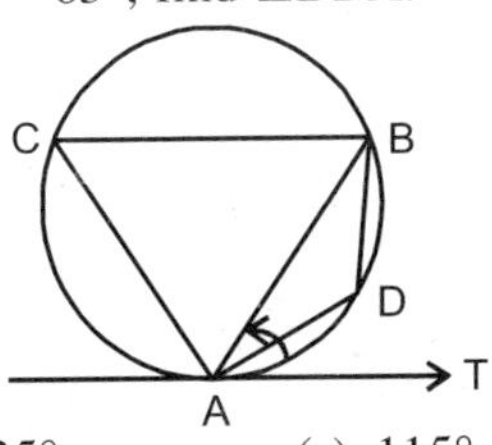

(*a*) 65° (*b*) 125° (*c*) 115° (*d*) 85°

23. A wire, when bent in the form of a square encloses an area of 484 sq. cm. What will be the enclosed area when the same wire is bent into the form of a circle? $\left(\text{Take } \pi = \frac{22}{7}\right)$
(*a*) 462 sq. cm (*b*) 539 sq.cm (*c*) 616 sq.cm (*d*) 693 sq.cm

24. What is the cost of flooring the rectangular hall?

I. Length and the breadth of hall are in the respective ratio of 3 : 2

II. Length of the hall is 48 metres and cost of flooring is $s. 850 per square metres.

III. Perimeter of the hall is 160 metres and cost of flooring is ₹ 850 per square metres.

Which of the above statement (s) is/are necessary to answer the question?

(*a*) Only I and II (*b*) Only I and III
(*c*) Only III (*d*) Any two of the three

25. The area of the circle 'C' is 9π What is the area of PQRS?

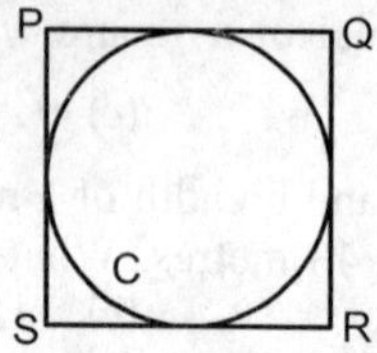

(*a*) 24 (*b*) 30 (*c*) 36 (*d*) 81

26. Cost of fencing a rectangular garden at ₹ 5 per metre is ₹ 2505. The length of the garden is one and half times its breadth, then the breadth of the garden is closer to:

(*a*) 100 m (*b*) 150 m (*c*) 200 m (*d*) 250 m

27. A wire is bent in the form of a circle of 56 cm radius. It is opened and bent to form a square. The side of the square will be

(*a*) 16 cm (*b*) 44 cm (*c*) 56 cm (*d*) 88 cm

28. In the circle given below, AB is a diameter, ∠BOD = 15° & ∠EOA = 85°, then ∠ECA = ?

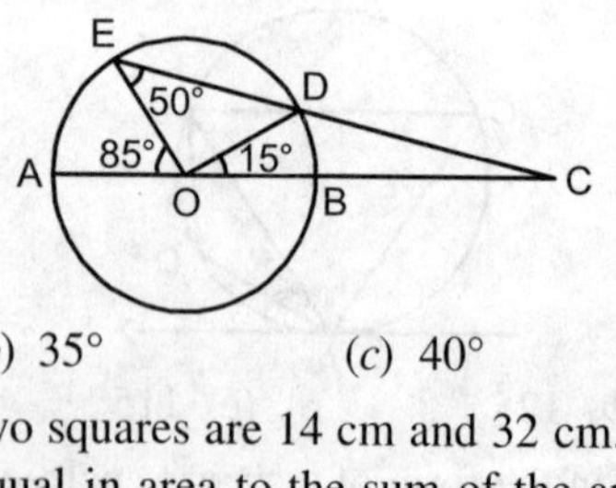

(*a*) 20° (*b*) 35° (*c*) 40° (*d*) 45°

29. The perimeter of two squares are 14 cm and 32 cm. The perimeter (in cm) of a third square equal in area to the sum of the areas of these squares is

(*a*) 45 (*b*) 40 (*c*) 32 (*d*) 48

30. The length of a rectangular garden is 12 metres and its breadth is 5 metres. Find the length of the diagonal of a square garden having the same area as that of the rectangular garden (*a*) $2\sqrt{30}$ m (*b*) $\sqrt{13}$ m (*c*) 13 m (*d*) $8\sqrt{15}$ m

31. The base of a triangle is 15 cm and height is 12 cm. The height of another triangle of double the area having the base 20 cm is

(*a*) 9 cm (*b*) 18 cm (*c*) 8 cm (*d*) 12.5 cm

32. The diagonals of a rhombus are 32 cm and 24 cm respectively. The perimeters of the rhombus is:

(*a*) 80 cm (*b*) 72 cm (*c*) 68 cm (*d*) 64 cm

33. A rectangle has width '*a*' and length '*n*'. If the width is decreased by 20% and the length is increased by 10%, then what is the new area?

(*a*) 0.88 *ab* (*b*) 0.92 *ab* (*c*) 1.1 *ab* (*d*) 1.04 *ab*

34. The length and the breadth of a rectangular field are increased by 15% and 10% respectively. What will be the effect on its area?

(*a*) 25% increase (*b*) 22.5% increase

(*c*) 26.5% increase (*d*) Cannot be determined

35. What will be the effect on the area of an isosceles triangle if all the sides are doubled in length?

(*a*) Increase to four times the area of original triangle

(*b*) Increase to two times the area of original triangle

(*c*) Increase by 150%

(*d*) Increase by 200%

36. What is the cost of painting the two adjacent walls of a hall which has no windows or doors?

I. The area of the hall is 24 sq. metres.

II. The breadth, length and the height of the hall are in the ratio of 4 : 6 : 5 respectively.

III. Area of one wall is 30 square metres.

Which of the above statement (s) is/are necessary to answer the question?

(*a*) Only I (*b*) Only II (*c*) Only II (*d*) Data inadequate

37. The area of a circle is 154 cm^2. Its radius is $\left[\text{Use } \pi = \frac{22}{7}\right]$

(*a*) 149 cm (*b*) π cm (*c*) 7 cm (*d*) 122 cm

38. The ratio of breadth and length of a rectangular field is 2 : 3. If the cost of the wall is ₹ 260 per metre, and its area is 1350 sq. metres, then find the cost to build the wall?

(*a*) ₹ 31,200 (*b*) ₹ 39,000 (*c*) ₹ 37,700 (*d*) Data inadequate

39. The area of a rectangle is 110 cm^2. If each of its sides is decreased by 4 cm, then the area is 42 cm^2. What is the width of the rectangle?
(*a*) 6 cm (*b*) 11 cm
(*c*) 10 cm (*d*) Can't be determined

40. The length and breadth of the floor of a room are 20 feet and 10 feet respectively. Square tiles of 2 feet length of three different colours are to be laid on the floor. Black tiles are laid in the first row on all sides. If white titles are laid in the one-third of the remaining and blue tiles in the rest, how many blue tiles will be there?
(*a*) 16 (*b*) 32 (*c*) 48 (*d*) 24

41. If the area of a circle is 1386 sq.cm, then find its radius.
(*a*) 132 cm (*b*) 66 cm (*c*) 88 cm (*d*) None of these

42. If the area of a triangle is 1176 cm^2 and base: corresponding altitude is 3 : 4, then the altitude of the triangle is
(*a*) 42 cm (*b*) 52 cm (*c*) 54 cm (*d*) 56 cm

43. If the circumference and area of a circle are numerically equal, then the diameter is equal to
(*a*) area of the circle (*b*) $\frac{\pi}{2}$
(*c*) 2π (*d*) 4

44. 2 metres broad pathway is to be constructed around a rectangular plot. The area of the plot is 96 m^2. The cost of construction is ₹ 50/m^2. Then find the total cost of construction.
(*a*) ₹ 4800 (*b*) ₹ 4000 (*c*) ₹ 2400 (*d*) Data inadequate

45. The area of the ring between two concentric circles, whose circumferences are 88 cm and 132 cm, is
(*a*) 780 cm (*b*) 770 cm (*c*) 715 cm (*d*) 660 cm

46. The perimeters of a square and a circular field are the same. If the area of the circular field is 3850 sq metres, what is the area (in m^2) of the square?
(*a*) 4225 (*b*) 3025 (*c*) 2500 (*d*) 2025

47. The area of a right angled triangle is two-third of the area of a rectangle. The base of the triangle is 80 per cent of the breadth of the rectangle. If the perimeter of the rectangle is 200 cm, what is the height of the triangle?
(*a*) 20 cm (*b*) 30 cm (*c*) 15 cm (*d*) Data inadequate

48. When the length of a rectangular plot is increased by four times, its perimeter becomes 480 metres and the area becomes 12800 square metres. What was its original length (in metre)?
(*a*) 160 (*b*) 40 (*c*) 20 (*d*) None of these

49. The diameter of a toy wheel is 14 cm. What is the distance travelled by it in 15 revolutions?
(*a*) 880 cm (*b*) 660 cm (*c*) 600 cm (*d*) 560 cm

ANSWERS

1	2	3	4	5	6	7	8	9	10
(*c*)	(*d*)	(*c*)	(*a*)	(*c*)	(*c*)	(*d*)	(*c*)	(*b*)	(*d*)
11	**12**	**13**	**14**	**15**	**16**	**17**	**18**	**19**	**20**
(*a*)	(*a*)	(*b*)	(*d*)	(*b*)	(*d*)	(*d*)	(*d*)	(*d*)	(*a*)
21	**22**	**23**	**24**	**25**	**26**	**27**	**28**	**29**	**30**
(*b*)	(*c*)	(*c*)	(*d*)	(*c*)	(*a*)	(*d*)	(*b*)	(*b*)	(*a*)
31	**32**	**33**	**34**	**35**	**36**	**37**	**38**	**39**	**40**
(*b*)	(*a*)	(*a*)	(*c*)	(*a*)	(*d*)	(*c*)	(*b*)	(*c*)	(*a*)
41	**42**	**43**	**44**	**45**	**46**	**47**	**48**	**49**	
(*d*)	(*d*)	(*d*)	(*d*)	(*b*)	(*b*)	(*d*)	(*c*)	(*b*)	

SOME SELECTED EXPLANATORY ANSWERS

2. Let the length and breadth of the rectangular plot be $8x$ and $5x$ metres respectively.

According to the question,

$$8x - 5x = 60$$

$$\Rightarrow \quad 3x = 60$$

$$\therefore \quad x = \frac{60}{3} = 20$$

Perimeter of the plot $= 2(8x + 5x) = 26x$ metre
$= 26 \times 20 = 520$ metre

3. Number of bricks

$$= \frac{\text{Volume of wall}}{\text{Volume of a brick}} = \frac{500 \times 300 \times 2000}{25 \times 12.5 \times 7.5} = 128000.$$

4. Let AB = BC = CD = DA = 10 cm

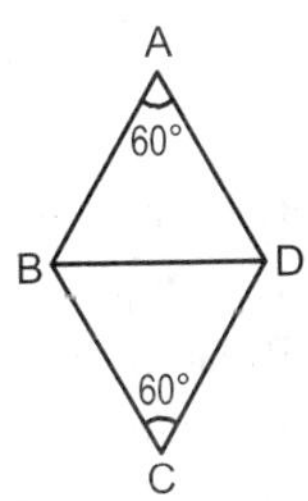

$$\angle BAD = \angle BCD = 60°$$

$$\therefore \quad \angle ABC = \angle ADC = 120°$$

$$\therefore \quad \angle CBD = \angle CDB = 60°$$

$$\therefore \quad BD = 10 \text{ cm}$$

6. Area of four walls of a room

$= 2$ (length + breadth) $\times$ height

$=$ Perimeter of floor $\times$ height $= 18 \times 3 = 54$ m^2.

7. Radius of the field = 140 m

Width of garden = 7 m

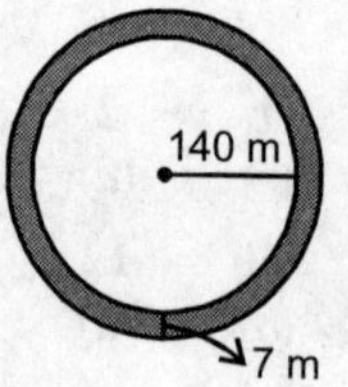

$\therefore$ Area of garden $= \pi\ (147^2 - 140^2)$

$= \frac{22}{7}\ (147 + 140)\ (147 - 140) = 22 \times 287 = 6314$ m^2

Required cost = ₹ (21×6314) = ₹ 132594.

8. AB = AC = 10 cm

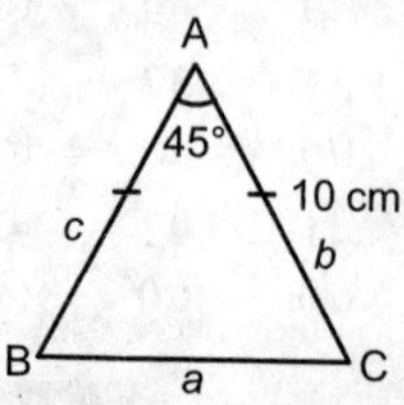

$\therefore$ Area $= \frac{1}{2}\ bc \sin A$

$= \frac{1}{2} \times 10 \times 10 \sin 45°$

$= \frac{50}{\sqrt{2}} = \frac{50 \times \sqrt{2}}{\sqrt{2} \times \sqrt{2}} = 25\sqrt{2}$ cm^2

9. Area of square = $(\text{Side})^2 = (25)^2 = 625$ sq. cms

Afea of rectangle = 625 – 125 = 500 sq. cms

$\therefore$ Breadth of rectangle $= \frac{500}{25} = 20$ cms

10. Circumference of circle $= 2\pi r = 88$ cm

$\therefore r = \frac{88 \times 7}{2 \times 22} = 14$ cm

$\therefore$ Area of circle $= \frac{22}{7} \times 14 \times 14 = 616$ sq.cm

13. Let the radius of circle be r cms

$\therefore \quad 2\pi r = 88$

$\Rightarrow \quad r = \frac{88 \times 7}{2 \times 22} = 14$ cms.

$\therefore \quad$ Area $= \pi r^2 = \frac{22}{7} \times 14 \times 14 = 616$ cm^2

14. Let the side of square be x cm.

$\therefore$ Length of rectangle $= (x + 5)$ cm

Breadth of rectangle $= (x - 3)$ cm

As given,

$(x + 5)(x - 3) = x^2 \Rightarrow x^2 + 5x - 3x - 15 = x^2$

$\Rightarrow 2x = 15$

$\therefore$ Perimeter of rectangle $= 2(x + 5 + x - 3) = 2(2x + 2)$

$= 2(15 + 2) = 34$ cm

15. Radius of circle = 14 cm

$\therefore$ Area $= \pi r^2 = \frac{22}{7} \times 14 \times 14 = 616$ sq cm.

16. To find out the area of a rectangle we should know both the length and width of the rectangle.

17. Diagonal of square $= \sqrt{\text{Area}} = \sqrt{25} = 5$ cm.

18. Perimeter = 2 (Length + Breadth)

$48 = 2(5x + 3x)$

$\therefore x = \frac{48}{16} = 3$

$\therefore$ Area $= (5 \times 3) \times (3 \times 3) = 15 \times 9 = 135 \text{ m}^2$.

20. Total area of rectangular plot to be gardened

$= 340 \times 1 = 340$ sq.m.

$\therefore$ Total cost $= 340 \times 10 =$ ₹ 3400.

21. Diameter of the circle = 14 m.

$\therefore$ Radius = 7 m

Area of semi-circle $= \frac{\pi r^2}{2} = \frac{22}{7 \times 2} \times 7 \times 7 = 77$ sq. metres

22.

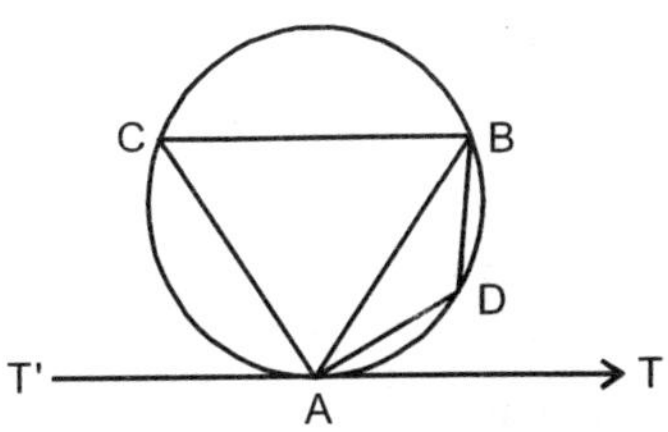

Theorem: If a line touches a circle and from the point of contact a chord is drawn, the angles which this chord makes with the given line are equal resepectively to the angles formed in the corresponding alternate segments.

i.e. $\angle BAT = \angle BCA = 65°$.

Now, we know that the sum of the opposite angles of a cyclic quadrilateral is 180°.

$\angle BDA + \angle BCA = 180°$

$\angle BDA = 180° - 65° = 115°$

26. Perimeter of the rectangular garden

$= \text{Length of fence} = \dfrac{2505}{5} = 501 \text{ m.}$

Now, let the breadth be x m, then length $= \dfrac{3}{2}x$ m.

$\therefore\ 2\left(\dfrac{3x}{2} + x\right) = 501$

$\Rightarrow 3x + 2x = 501$

$\Rightarrow x = \dfrac{501}{2} = 100.2 \text{ m} \approx 100 \text{ m.}$

27. Perimeter of square = Circumference of circle

$\therefore$ 4 (side) = 2π (radius)

$\text{side} = \dfrac{1}{4}\left[2 \times \dfrac{22}{7} \times 56\right] = 88 \text{ cm}$

28. Perimeter of square = Circumference of circle

$\angle EOD = 180° - (15° + 85°) = 180° - 100° = 80°$

$\therefore \angle ODC = 80° + 50° = 130°$

$\therefore \angle ECA = 180° - 130° - 15° = 35°.$

30. Area of the rectangular garden = $12 \times 5 = 60 \text{ m}^2$ = Area of the square garden

$\therefore$ Side of the square garden = $\sqrt{60} \text{ m}^2$

$\therefore$ Diagonal of the square garden = $\sqrt{2} \times \text{side}$

$= \sqrt{2} \times \sqrt{60} = \sqrt{120} = \sqrt{4 \times 30} = 2\sqrt{30} \text{ m}$

31. Area of the first triangle $= \dfrac{1}{2} \times \text{base} \times \text{height}$

$= \dfrac{1}{5} \times 15 \times 12 = 90 \text{ cm}^2$

According to the question

Area of the another (second) triangle

$= 2 \times 90 = 180 \text{ cm}^2$

∴ Area of the new triangle

$$180 \text{ cm}^2 = \frac{1}{2} \times 20 \times \text{height}$$

$$\therefore \text{Height} = \frac{180 \times 2}{20} = 18 \text{ cm.}$$

33. $\% \text{ change in area} = \left(x + y + \dfrac{xy}{100}\right)\%$

$$= \left(10 - 20 + \frac{(10)(-20)}{100}\right)\% = (-10 - 2)\% = -12\%$$

∴ New area = $ab - 0.12ab = 0.88ab$.

35. If the sides of any 2-dimensional figure (*i.e.* triangle, rectangle, square, circle, rhombus) are increased by $x\%$, then its area is increased

by $\left(2x + \dfrac{x^2}{100}\right)\%$

In this question, sides are doubled. It means increase is 100%

$$\therefore \text{Increase in area} = \left[2 \times 100 + \frac{100 \times 100}{100}\right]\% = 300\%$$

We can also say that area will increase to four times the area of original triangle.

36. Since the rate of cost of painting has not been given in any of the above statements, the answer cannot be found.

37. Area of the circle = π (radius)^2

$$\therefore \text{Radius} = \sqrt{\frac{\text{Area}}{\pi}} = \sqrt{154 \times \frac{7}{22}}$$

$$\sqrt{7 \times 7} = 7\text{cm.}$$

41. $\text{Radius of the circle} = \sqrt{\left(\dfrac{\text{Area}}{\pi}\right)} = \sqrt{\left(\dfrac{1386}{\frac{22}{7}}\right)}$

$$= \sqrt{\left(\frac{1386 \times 7}{22}\right)} = \sqrt{441} = \sqrt{21 \times 21} = 21 \text{ cm.}$$

42. Let the base and altitude be $3x$ and $4x$ respectively.

$\therefore$ According to the question,

$$\frac{1}{2} \times \text{base} \times \text{altitude} = 1176 \text{ cm}^2$$

or, $\frac{1}{2} \times 3x \times 4x = 1176$

or, $x^2 = \frac{1176}{6}$

or, $x^2 = 196$

or, $x = \sqrt{196} = 14$ cm

$\therefore$ Altitude of a triangle $= 4x = 4 \times 14$ cm $= 56$ cm.

43. For a circle of diameter D,

$$\text{Area} = \frac{\pi D^2}{4} \text{ and}$$

Circumference $= \pi D$

Now, according to the question,

$$\frac{\pi D^2}{4} = \pi D$$

or, $D = \frac{\pi D \times 4}{\pi D}$

$\therefore$ $D = 4$

44. Area of the path $= (x + 4)(y + 4) - xy$

$= xy + 4(x + y) + 16 - xy$

$= 4(x + y) + 16$

Since the value of $(x + y)$ or perimeter is not given, the question cannot be answered.

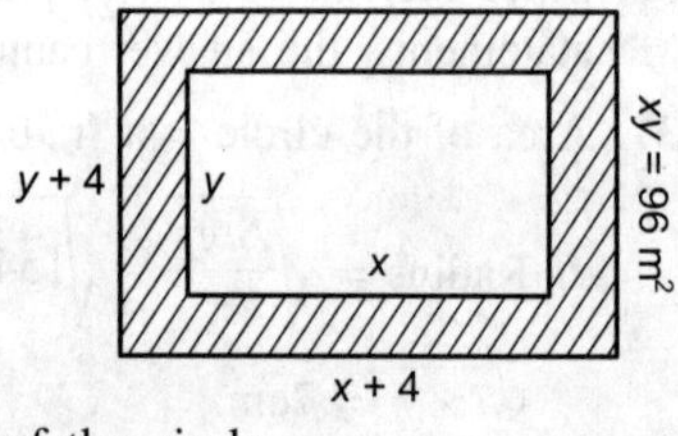

46. Let S : Side of the square and r : radius of the circle.

Given : Perimeter of the square = Perimeter of the circle

or, $4S = 2\pi r$

or, $\frac{S}{r} = \frac{\pi}{2}$

$$\frac{\text{Area of the square}}{\text{Area of the circle}} = \frac{S^2}{\pi r^2} = \frac{1}{\pi}\left(\frac{\pi}{2}\right)^2 = \frac{\pi}{4}$$

$\therefore$ Area of the square $= \frac{\pi}{4}$ (Area of the circle)

$$= \frac{\pi}{4} \times 3850 \text{ m}^2 = \frac{22}{7 \times 4} \times 3850 \text{ m}^2 = 3025 \text{ m}^2$$

48. Let the original length be x metre and breadth y metre.

According to the question,

New length $= 4x$

So, Perimeter $= 2\,(L + B)$

or, $480 = 2(4x + y)$

or, $4x + y = \frac{480}{2} = 240$ ...(*i*)

and Area $= L \times B$

or, $12800 = 4x \times y$

or, $xy = 3200$ ...(*ii*)

From equations (*i*) and (*ii*) $x = 40, 20$

So, length may be either 40 or 20.

49. Circumference of the wheel $= \pi D$

$$= \frac{22}{7} \times 14 = 44 \text{ cm.}$$

$\therefore$ Total distance travelled by the wheel in 15 revolutions

$= 15 \times 44$ cm $= 660$ cm.

~~~~~~
~~~~~~

26. VOLUME AND SURFACE AREA

IMPORTANT FORMULAE

I. CUBOID

Let length = l, breadth = b and height = h units. Then,

1. ***Volume*** = $(l \times b \times h)$ cubic units.
2. ***Surface area*** = $2\,(lb + bh + lh)$ sq. units.
3. ***Diagonal*** = $\sqrt{l^2 + b^2 + h^2}$ units.

II. CUBE

Let each edge of a cube be of length a. Then,

1. ***Volume*** = a^3 cubic units.
2. ***Surface area*** = $6a^2$ sq. units.
3. ***Diagonal*** = $\sqrt{3}\,a$ units.

III. CYLINDER

Let radius of base = r and Height (or length) = h. Then,

1. ***Volume*** = $(\pi r^2 h)$ cubic units.
2. ***Curved surface area*** = $(2\pi rh)$ sq. units.
3. ***Total surface area*** = $(2\pi rh + 2\pi r^2)$ sq. units
   = $2\pi r\,(h + r)$ sq. units.

IV. CONE

Let radius of base = r and Height = h. Then,

1. ***Slant height,*** $l = \sqrt{h^2 + r^2}$ units.
2. ***Volume*** = $\left(\frac{1}{3}\pi r^2 h\right)$ cubic units.
3. ***Curved surface area*** = (πrl) sq. units.
4. ***Total surface area*** = $(\pi rl + \pi r^2)$ sq. units.

V. SPHERE

Let the radius of the sphere be r. Then,

1. ***Volume*** = $\left(\frac{4}{3}\pi r^3\right)$ cubic units.
2. ***Surface area*** = $(4\pi r^2)$ sq. units.

VI. HEMISPHERE

Let the radius of a hemisphere be r. Then,

1. ***Volume*** $= \left(\frac{2}{3}\pi r^3\right)$ cubic units.
2. ***Curved surface area*** $= (2\pi r^2)$ sq. units.
3. ***Total surface area*** $= (3\pi r^2)$ sq. units.

Remember : 1 litre = 1000 cm^3.

SOLVED EXAMPLE

1. Find the volume and surface area of a cuboid 16 m long, 14 m broad and 7 m high.

Sol. Volume $= (16 \times 14 \times 7)\ m^3 = 1568\ m^3$

Surface area $= [2\,(16 \times 14 + 14 \times 7 + 16 \times 7)]\ cm^2$

$= (2 \times 434)\ cm^2 = 868\ cm^2$.

2. The surface area of a cube is 1734 sq. cm. Find its volume.

Sol. Let the edge of the cube be a. Then,

$6a^2 = 1734 \Rightarrow a^2 = 289 \Rightarrow a = 17$ cm

$\therefore$ Volume $= a^3 = (17)^3\ cm^3 = 4913\ cm^3$.

3. A cube of edge 15 cm is immersed completely in a rectangular vessel containing water. If the dimensions of the base of vessel are 20 cm × 15 cm, find the rise in water level.

Sol. Increase in volume = Volume of the cube $= (15 \times 15 \times 15)\ cm^3$

$\therefore$ Rise in water level $= \left(\frac{\text{Volume}}{\text{Area}}\right) = \left(\frac{15 \times 15 \times 15}{20 \times 15}\right)$ cm = 11.25 cm.

4. Two cubes have their volumes in the ratio 1 : 27. Find the ratio of their surface areas.

Sol. Let their edges be a and b. Then,

$$\frac{a^3}{b^3} = \frac{1}{27} \text{ or } \left(\frac{a}{b}\right)^3 = \left(\frac{1}{3}\right)^3 \text{ or } \frac{a}{b} = \frac{1}{3}.$$

$\therefore$ Ratio of their surface areas $= \frac{6a^2}{6b^2} = \frac{a^2}{b^2} = \left(\frac{a}{b}\right)^2 = \frac{1}{9}$, *i.e.,* 1 : 9.

EXERCISE

1. The radius of the base and height of a metallic solid cylinder are r cm and 6 cm respectively. It is melted and recast into a solid cone of the same radius of base. The height of the cone is:
(*a*) 54 cm (*b*) 27 cm (*c*) 18 cm (*d*) 9 cm

2. The volumes of a sphere and a right circular cylinder having the same radius are equal. The ratio of the diameter of the sphere to the height of the cylinder is
(*a*) 3 : 2 (*b*) 2 : 3 (*c*) 1 : 2 (*d*) 2 : 1

3. A hemisphere and a cone have equal bases. If their heights are also equal, the ratio of their curved surfaces will be:
(*a*) $1 : \sqrt{2}$ (*b*) $\sqrt{2} : 1$ (*c*) 1 : 2 (*d*) 2 : 1

4. A solid metallic spherical ball of diameter 6 cm is melted and recasted into a cone with diameter of the base as 12 cm. The height of the cone is
(*a*) 6 cm (*b*) 2 cm (*c*) 4 cm (*d*) 3 cm

5. If the radius of a sphere is increased by 2 cm, its surface area increases by 352 cm^2. The radius of the sphere before increase was $\left[\text{Take } \pi = \frac{22}{7}\right]$
(*a*) 3 cm (*b*) 4 cm (*c*) 5 cm (*d*) 6 cm

6. A circular cylindrical iron piece of radius 14 cm & height 20 cm is moulded into a solid cone with the same radius of the base. What is the height of the cone?
(*a*) 36 cm (*b*) 40 cm (*c*) 60 cm (*d*) 48 cm

7. The base radii of two cylinders are in the ratio 2 : 3 and their heights are in the ratio 5 : 3. The ratio of their volumes is
(*a*) 27 : 20 (*b*) 20 : 27 (*c*) 9 : 4 (*d*) 4 : 9

8. A hemispherical bowl of internal radius 9 cm contains a liquid. This liquid is to be filled into cylindrical shaped small bottles of diameter 3 cm and height 4 cm. How many bottles will be needed to empty the bowl?
(*a*) 54 cm (*b*) 63 cm (*c*) 27 cm (*d*) 72 cm

9. Three solid metallic spheres of diameters 6 cm, 8 cm and 10 cm are melted and recast into a new solid sphere. The diameter of the new sphere is
(*a*) 4 cm (*b*) 6 cm (*c*) 8 cm (*d*) 12 cm

10. The slant height of a conical mountain is 2.5 km and the area of its base is 1.54 km^2. Taking $\pi = \frac{22}{7}$, the height of the mountain is

(*a*) 2.2 km (*b*) 2.4 km (*c*) 3 km (*d*) 3.11 km

11. A hemisphere and a cone have equal bases. If their heights are also equal, the ratio of their curved surfaces will be

(*a*) $1 : \sqrt{2}$ (*b*) $\sqrt{2} : 1$ (*c*) 1 : 2 (*d*) 2 : 1

12. A right circular cylindrical tank has the storage capacity of 38808 ml. If the radius of the base of the cylinder is three fourth of the height, what is the diameter of the base?

(*a*) 28 cms (*b*) 56 cms (*c*) 21 cms (*d*) 42 cms

13. In a triangle, two sides of 12 cm and 5 cm are at right angle. If the triangle is revolved along 12 cm side, the curved surface of the cone so formed will be

(*a*) 156 π cm^2 (*b*) 78 π cm^2 (*c*) 65 π cm^2 (*d*) 130 π cm^2

14. A well 3.5 m and of 2 m diameter has been dug out. What is the cost of plastering the inner surface of the well at the rate of ₹ 0.75 per sq. m?

(*a*) ₹ 15.50 (*b*) ₹ 16.50 (*c*) ₹ 17.50 (*d*) ₹ 18.00

15. A hollow sphere of internal and external diameters 4 cm and 8 cm respectively is melted into a cone of base diameter 8 cm. The height of the cone is

(*a*) 12 cm (*b*) 18 cm (*c*) 14 cm (*d*) 15 cm

16. A circular cylindrical iron piece of radius 14 cm and height 20 cm is moulded into a solid cone with the same radius of the base. What is the height of the cone?

(*a*) 36 cm (*b*) 40 cm (*c*) 60 cm (*d*) None of these

17. If whole surface area of a sphere is 100π, then its radius will be

(*a*) 4.5 (*b*) 7 (*c*) 5 (*d*) 54

18. The radius of the cylinder is half of its height and area of the inner part is 616 sq. metres approximately. How many litres of milk can it contain?

(*a*) 1.4 (*b*) 1.5 (*c*) 1.9 (*d*) 2.2

19. The surface of water in a swimming pool is a rectangle 32 m long and 9.5 m wide and the depth of water increases uniformly from 1.5 m at one end to 4.5 m at the other end. What is the volume of water in the pool?

(*a*) 912 m^3 (*b*) 729 m^3 (*c*) 840 m^3 (*d*) None of these

20. In the figure given below, POQ and ROS are diameters of a circle with center O and radius 14 cm. Find the area of the shaded region. $\left(\text{Use } \pi = \frac{22}{7}\right)$.

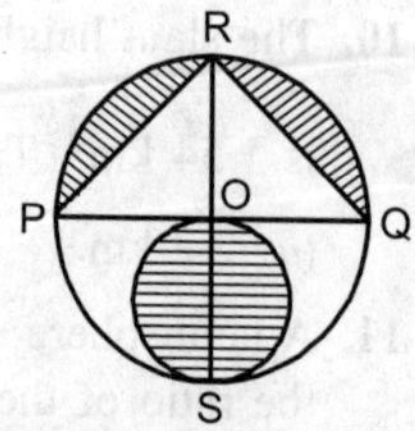

(*a*) 240 cm² (*b*) 257 cm²
(*c*) 266 cm² (*d*) None of these

21. The volume of a cone, whose height (*h*) is twice the radius (*r*) of its base, is

(*a*) $\frac{2}{3}\pi r^3$ (*b*) $2\frac{1}{3}\pi r^2 h$ (*c*) $13\pi r^2 h$ (*d*) $\frac{1}{3}\pi r^3$

22. The volumes of two spheres are in the ratio 8 : 27. The ratio of their surface area is

(*a*) 4 : 9 (*b*) 2 : 3 (*c*) 4 : 5 (*d*) 5 : 6

ANSWERS

1	2	3	4	5	6	7	8	9	10
(*c*)	(*a*)	(*b*)	(*d*)	(*d*)	(*c*)	(*b*)	(*a*)	(*d*)	(*b*)
11	**12**	**13**	**14**	**15**	**16**	**17**	**18**	**19**	**20**
(*b*)	(*d*)	(*c*)	(*b*)	(*c*)	(*c*)	(*c*)	(*d*)	(*a*)	(*c*)
21	**22**								
(*b*)	(*d*)								

SOME SELECTED EXPLANATORY ANSWERS

1. Volume of the cylinder = $\pi r^2 \times h$

$= \pi r^2 \times 6 = 6\pi r^2$ cm³

Let the height of the cone be h cm

$\therefore$ Volume of the cone = $\frac{1}{3}\pi r^2 h$

According to the question,

Volume of the cone = Volume of the cylinder

$\Rightarrow \frac{1}{3}\pi r^2 h = 6\pi r^2 \Rightarrow h = 18$ cm.

2. Volume of sphere = $\frac{4}{3}\pi r^3$

Volume of cylinder = $\pi r^2 h$

As given,

$$\pi r^2 h = \frac{4}{3}\pi r^3 \Rightarrow h = \frac{4}{3}r$$

$$\Rightarrow \frac{h}{r} = \frac{4}{3} \Rightarrow \frac{h}{2r} = \frac{4}{3 \times 2} = \frac{2}{3}$$

$$\Rightarrow \frac{d}{h} = \frac{3}{2}, \text{ where } d = 2r.$$

3. Curved surface of hemisphere = $2\pi r^2$

Height of cone = Height of hemisphere = r

Curved surface of cone = $\pi rl = \pi r\sqrt{r^2 + r^2} = \sqrt{2}\pi r^2$

$\therefore$ Ratio of curved surfaces = $2\pi r^2 : \sqrt{2}\pi r^2 = \sqrt{2} : 1$

5. Let the original radius be r cm.

According to the question,

$4\pi(r + 2)^2 - 4\pi r^2 = 352$

or, $4\pi\,(r^2 + 4r + 4 - r^2) = 352$

or, $4r + 4 = \frac{352}{4\pi} = \frac{352 \times 7}{4 \times 22}$

or, $4r + 4 = 28$

or, $r = \frac{24}{4} = 6$ cm

6. Volume of circular cylindrical iron piece = $\pi r^2 h$

$= \frac{22}{7} \times 14 \times 14 \times 26 = 44 \times 14 \times 20 \text{ cm}^3$

When it is moulded into a solid cone, the volume remains same:

Let the required height be h cm.

$$\therefore \quad \frac{1}{3} \times \pi \times 14 \times 14 \times h = 44 \times 14 \times 20$$

$$\Rightarrow h = \frac{44 \times 14 \times 20 \times 3 \times 7}{14 \times 14 \times 22} = 60 \text{ cm.}$$

7. Let the radii of two cylinders are r_1, r_2 and lengths of the cylinders are h_1, h_2 respectively.

According to the question $\frac{r_1}{r_2} = \frac{2}{3}$ and $\frac{h_1}{h_2} = \frac{5}{3}$

$\therefore$ Ratio of their volumes = $\pi r_1^2 h_1 : \pi r_2^2 h_2 = r_1^2 h_1 : r_2^2 h_2$

$= (2)^2 \times 5 : (3)^2 \times 3 = 4 \times 5 : 9 \times 3 = 20 : 27$

9. According to the question, three solid metallic spheres are melted and recast into a new solid sphere. It means that the volume of new solid sphere will be equal to the sum of volumes of three solid spheres.

$\therefore$ Volume of new solid sphere

$$= \frac{4}{3}\pi\left(\frac{6}{2}\right)^3 + \frac{4}{3}\pi\left(\frac{8}{2}\right)^3 + \frac{4}{3}\pi\left(\frac{10}{2}\right)^3$$

or, $\frac{4}{3}\pi r^3 = \frac{4}{3}\pi\left[(3)^3 + (4)^3 + (5)^3\right]$

or, $r^3 = 27 + 64 + 125$

or, $r^3 = 216$

or, $r^3 = (6)^3$

or, $r = 6$ cm

$\therefore$ Diameter of the new sphere = $2 \times 6 = 12$ cm.

10. Area of the base of mountain = πr^2

$1.54 \text{ km}^2 = \frac{22}{7} r^2$

$\Rightarrow \frac{1.54 \times 7}{22} = r^2$

$\Rightarrow 0.49 = r^2$

$\therefore r = 0.7$ km

Slant height = 2.5 km

$\therefore$ Height of the mountain = $\sqrt{(2.5)^2 - (0.7)^2}$

$= \sqrt{6.25 - 0.49} = \sqrt{5.76} = 24$ km.

14. Area of the curved inner surface = 2π (radius) (depth)

$= 2 \times \frac{22}{7} \times \left(\frac{2}{2}\right) \times (3.5) = 22 \text{ m}^2$

$\therefore$ Total cost = ₹ 0.75 × 22 = ₹ 16.50.

15. Volume of the cone = Volume of the spherical shell

$\frac{1}{3}\pi r^2 h = \frac{4}{3}\pi\left[R_o^3 - R_i^3\right]$

$h = \frac{4\left[R_o^3 - R_i^3\right]}{r^2} = 4\frac{\left[4^3 - 2^3\right]}{4^2} = 14$ cm.

16. Volume of the cone = Volume of the circular cylinder

$$\frac{1}{3}\pi r^2 h = \pi r^2 H$$

or, $h = 3H = 3 \times 20 = 60$ cm

17. Area of sphere = 4π (Radius)^2

$$\therefore \text{ Radius} = \sqrt{\frac{\text{Area}}{4\pi}} = \sqrt{\frac{100\pi}{4\pi}} = \sqrt{25} = 5$$

18. Volume of cylinder = $\pi r^2 h$

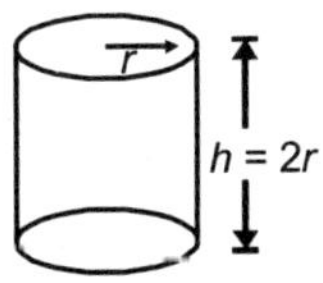

Given: $h = 2r$

$V = \pi r^2 \times (2^r) = 2\pi r^3 = 4\pi r^2$

$4\pi r^2 = 616$

or, $r^2 = 49$

or, $r = 7$

$\therefore$ $V = 2\pi\,(7)^3 = 2156 \text{ cm}^3 = 2.156$ litres ≈ 2.2 litres.

21. Given: $h = 2r$

$$\text{Volume of cone} = \frac{1}{3}\pi r^2 h = \frac{1}{3}\pi r^2 \times (2r) = \frac{2}{3}\pi r^3$$

22. $A^3 \propto V^2$

Ratio of surface areas = (Ratio of volumes)$^{2/3}$

$$= \left(\frac{8}{27}\right)^{\frac{2}{3}} = \left(\frac{2}{3}\right)^2 = \frac{4}{9} = 4 : 9.$$

~~~~~~
~~~~~~

SECTION-II

DATA ANALYSIS

27. STATISTICS

MEAN, MEDIAN, MODE AND RANGE

The mean, median and mode are three different ways of describing the average.

- To find the mean, add up all the numbers and divide by the number of numbers.
- To find the median, place all the numbers in order and select the middle number. If there are two values in the middle then the median is the mean of those two numbers.
- The *mode* is the number which appears most often.
- The *range* gives an idea of how the data are spread out and is the difference between the smallest and largest values.

MEASURES OF CENTRAL TENDENCY

Average or Central Value: One single value that describes the characteristic of the entire mass of unwieldy data is called the Central Value or an Average.

Types of Averages: The following are the important types of averages:

1. Arithmetic mean:
   (*i*) Simple and (*ii*) Weighted
2. Median
3. Mode
4. Geometric mean
5. Harmonic mean

1. ARITHMETIC MEAN

(a) Calculation of Arithmetic Mean – Individual Observations

$$\bar{X} = \frac{X_1 + X_2 + X_3 + ... + X_N}{N} = \frac{\Sigma X}{N}$$

where, $\bar{X}$ = Arithmetic mean

ΣX = Sum of all the values of the variables X *i.e.* $X_1, X_2, X_3, ..., X_N$

N = Number of observations.

The arithmetic mean can be calculated by using arbitrary origin. In this method, assume a mean. Then, take deviation of items from the assumed mean and denote these deviations by *d*.

Hence, $d = X - A$

where, A = Assumed mean

$$\bar{X} = A + \frac{\Sigma d}{N}$$

(b) Calculation of Arithmetic Mean – Discrete Series

The formula for computing mean is

$$\bar{X} = \frac{\Sigma fX}{N}$$

where f = frequency
X = the variable in question
N = total number of observations i.e. Σf.

By appling shortcut method,

$$\bar{X} = A + \frac{\Sigma fd}{N}$$

where A = Assumed mean
$d = X - A$
N = total number of observations, *i.e.* Σf

(*c*) Calculation of Arithmetic Mean – Continuous Series

$$\bar{X} = \frac{\Sigma fm}{N}$$

where, m = mid-point of various classes
f = the frequency of each class
N = the total frequency.

By applying shortcut method

$$\bar{X} = A + \frac{\Sigma fd}{N}$$

where, A = assumed
d = deviations of mid-points from assumed mean *i.e.* $(m - A)$;
N = total number of observations

Step Deviation method

$$\bar{X} = A + \frac{\Sigma fd}{N} \times i$$

where A = assumed mean
f = frequency
$$d = \frac{(m - A)}{i}$$
N = total frequency
i = class interval.

Correcting Incorrect Values

To find out the correct mean, in case where certain wrong values are taken while calculating mean, follow the given process. From ΣX deduct wrong items and add correct items and then divide the corrected ΣX by the number of observations. The result so obtained will give the value of correct mean.

Combined Average

In case where we have the arithmetic mean and number of items of two or more than two related groups, we can compute combined average of these groups by applying the following formula:

$$\bar{X}_{12} = \frac{N_1\bar{X}_1 + N_2\bar{X}_2}{N_1 + N_2}$$

where,

$\bar{X}_{12}$ = Combined mean of the two groups.

$\bar{X}_1$ = Arithmetic mean of first group.

$\bar{X}_2$ = Arithmetic mean of second group.

N_1 = Number of items in the first group.

N_2 = Number of items in the second group.

Weighted Arithmetic Mean

$$\bar{X}_W = \frac{\Sigma WX}{\Sigma W}$$

where,

$\bar{X}_W$ = represents the arithmetic mean

W = Weights

X = the variable

2. MEDIAN

The median by definition is the value of the distribution.

Calculation of Median–Individual Observations

$$\text{Median} = \text{Size of } \frac{N+1}{2} \text{ th item.}$$

Before applying the formula, arrange the data in ascending or descending order of magnitude.

Computation of Median–Discreate Series

Steps

(1) Arrange the data in ascending or descending order of magnitude

(2) Find out cumulative frequencies

(3) Apply the formula : Median = Size of $\frac{N+1}{2}$ th item

(4) Now look at the cumulative frequency column and find that total which is either equal to $\frac{N+1}{2}$ or next higher than that and determine the value of the variable corresponding to this which will give the value of median.

Calculation of Median–Continuous Series

Steps

(1) Determine the particular class in which the value of median links. Use $\frac{N}{2}$ as the rank of median.

(2) Apply the formula of interpolation

$$Md = L + \frac{N/2 - c.f.}{f} \times i$$

where,

L = Lower limit of the median class, i.e., the class *in* which the middle item of the distribution lies.

cf = cumulative frequency of the class preceding the median class or sum of the frequencies of all classes lower than the median class

f = simple frequency of the median class

i = the class interval of the median class.

Calculation of Median when Class Intervals are Unequal

Where the class intervals are unequal the frequencies need not be adjusted to make the class intervals equal and the same formula for interpolation can be applied as discussed above.

Computation of Quartiles, Deciles, Percentiles etc.

Quartiles, deciles, percentiles etc. are computed in the same manner as median.

While calculating these values in individual and discrete series we add one to N whereas in continuous series we do not add one.

Individual and Discrete Series

$$Q_1 = \text{Size of } \frac{N+1}{4} \text{ th item}$$

$$Q_3 = \text{Size of } 3\left(\frac{N+1}{4}\right)\text{th item}$$

$$Q_4 = \text{Size of } 4\left(\frac{N+1}{10}\right)\text{th item}$$

$$Q_{60} = \text{Size of } 60\left(\frac{N+1}{100}\right)\text{th item}$$

Continuous Series

$$Q_1 = \text{Size of } \frac{N}{4}\text{th item}$$

$$Q_3 = \text{Size of } 3\left(\frac{N}{4}\right)\text{th item}$$

$$D_4 = \text{Size of } 4\left(\frac{N}{10}\right)\text{th item}$$

$$P_{60} = \text{Size of } 60\left(\frac{N+1}{100}\right)\text{th item}$$

3. MODE

The mode is often said to be that value which occurs most frequently.

In the words of Alva M. Tuttle, it is the value which has the greatest density in its immediate neighbourhood.

Calculation of Mode – Individual Observations

For determining mode count the number of times the various values repeat themselves and the value which occurs the maximum number of times is the modal value.

Calculation of Mode – Discrete Series

In discrete series mode can be determined by looking to that value of the variable around which the items are most heavily concentrated.

Calculation of Mode – Continuous Series

$$M_o = L + \frac{\Delta_1}{\Delta_1 + \Delta_2} \times i$$

where, L = Lower limit of the modal class

Δ_1 = the difference between the frequency of the modal class and the frequency of the pre-modal class, i.e. preceding class (ignoring signs).

Δ_2 = the difference between the frequency of the modal class and the frequency of the post modal class, i.e., succeeding class (ignoring signs)

i = the size of the class interval of the modal class.

We can also say,

$$M_0 = L + \frac{f_1 - f_0}{2f_1 - f_0 - f_2} \times i$$

where f_1 = frequency of the modal class

f_0 = frequency of the class preceding the modal class

f_2 = frequency of the class succeeding the modal class.

Where mode is ill defined, its value may be ascertained by the following formula based upon the relationship between mean, median and mode.

Mode = 3M*d* – 2 Mean

4. GEOMETRIC MEAN

Geometric mean is defined as the *n*th root of the product of N item of series.

$$GM = \sqrt[n]{(X_1) \times (X_2) \times (X_3) \times ... X_n}$$

where X_1, X_2, X_3 etc. refer to various items of the series.

In Individual observation, $GM = \text{Antilog}\left(\frac{\Sigma \log X}{N}\right)$

In discrete series $GM = \text{Antilog}\left(\frac{\Sigma f \log X}{N}\right)$

In continuous series $GM = \text{Antilog}\left(\frac{\Sigma f \log m}{N}\right)$

5. HARMONIC MEAN

It is defined as the reciprocal of the arithmetic mean of the reciprocal of the individual observations.

$$HM = \frac{N}{\left(\frac{1}{X_1} + \frac{1}{X_2} + \frac{1}{X_3} + ... + \frac{1}{X_n}\right)}$$

Calculation of Harmonic Mean

In Individual observation

$$HM = \frac{N}{\left(\frac{1}{X_1} + \frac{1}{X_2} + \frac{1}{X_3} + ... + \frac{1}{X_n}\right)}$$

In discrete series

$$\text{HM} = \frac{\text{N}}{\Sigma\left(f \times \frac{1}{\text{X}}\right)}$$

In continuous series

$$\text{HM} = \frac{\text{N}}{\Sigma\left(f \times \frac{1}{m}\right)}$$

where m = mid-points

MEASURES OF VARIATION

A measure of dispersion is designed to state the extent to which the individual measures, differ on an average from the mean.

The following are the important methods of studying variation:

1. Range
2. Inter-quartile Range and the Quartile Deviation
3. Mean Deviation
4. Standard Deviation

1. Range

It is defined as the difference between the value of the smallest item and the value of the largest item included in the distribution.

$$\text{Range} = \text{L} - \text{S}$$

Where, L = Largest value, S = Smallest value

$$\text{Coefficient of range} = \frac{\text{L} - \text{S}}{\text{L} + \text{S}}$$

2. Inter-quartile Range and the Quartile Deviation

Inter-quartile range represents the difference between the third quartile and the first quartile.

$$\text{Inter-quartile range} = Q_3 - Q_1$$

$$\text{Quartile Deviation or Q.D.} = \frac{Q_3 - Q_1}{2}$$

$$\text{Co-efficient of Q.D.} = \frac{Q_3 - Q_1}{Q_3 + Q_1}$$

3. Mean Deviation

It is the average difference between the items in a distribution and the median or mean of that series.

Computation of Mean Deviation

Individual Observations

$$\text{E.D.} = \frac{\Sigma|D|}{N}$$

$$\text{Co-efficient of M.D.} = \frac{\text{M.D.}}{\text{Median}}$$

Discrete Series

$$\text{M.D.} = \frac{\Sigma f|D|}{N}$$

Continuous Series

$$\text{M.D.} = \frac{\Sigma f|D|}{N}$$

In this case, obtain mid-points of the various classes and take the deviations of these mid-points from median.

4. Standard Deviation

The Standard deviation measures the absolute dispersion or variability of a distribution.

Standard deviation is also known as root-mean square deviation.

Calculation of Standard Deviation – Individual Observation

(1) Deviation taken from Actual Mean

$$\sigma = \sqrt{\frac{\Sigma x^2}{N}}$$

where $x = (X - \bar{X})$ and N = number of observations

(2) Deviations taken from Assumed Mean

$$\sigma = \sqrt{\frac{\Sigma d^2}{N} - \left(\frac{\Sigma d}{N}\right)^2}$$

Where $d = X - A$

Calculation of Standard Deviation – Discrete Series

(1) Actual Mean Method

$$\sigma = \sqrt{\frac{fx^2}{N}}$$

where $x = (X - \bar{X})$

(2) Assumed Mean Method

$$\sigma = \sqrt{\frac{\Sigma fd^2}{N} - \left(\frac{\Sigma fd}{N}\right)^2}$$

where $d = X - A$

(3) Step Deviation Method

$$\sigma = \sqrt{\frac{\Sigma fd^2}{N} - \left(\frac{\Sigma fd}{N}\right)^2} \times i$$

$$d = \frac{(X - A)}{i} \text{ and } i = \text{class interval}$$

SOLVED EXAMPLE

1. Find

(*a*) the mean (*b*) the median

(*c*) the mode (*d*) the range of this set of data

5, 6, 2, 4, 7, 8, 3, 5, 6, 6

Sol. (*a*) The mean is

$$\frac{5+6+2+4+7+8+3+5+6+6}{10} = \frac{52}{10} = 5.2$$

(*b*) To find the median, place all the numbers in order.

2, 3, 4, 5, 5, 6, 6, 6, 7, 8

As there are two middle numbers in this example, 5 and 6.

$$\text{Median} = \frac{5+6}{2} = \frac{11}{2} = 5.5$$

(*c*) From the list in (*b*) it is easy to see that 6 appears more than any other number, so mode = 6

(*d*) The range is the difference between the smallest and largest numbers, in this case 2 and 8. So the range is

$$8 - 2 = 6$$

2. Five people play golf and at one hole their scores are

3, 4, 4, 5, 7

For these scores, find

(*a*) the mean (*b*) the median (*c*) the mode (*d*) the range

Sol. (*a*) The mean is $\frac{3+4+4+5+7}{5} = \frac{23}{5} = 4.6$

(*b*) The numbers are already in order and the middle number is 4.

So, Median = 4

(*c*) The score 4 occurs most often, so, mode = 4

(*d*) The range is the difference between the smallest and largest numbers, in this case 3 and 7, so
range = 7 – 3 = 4.

3. A football team keep records of the numbers of goals it scores per match during a season.

No. of Goals	Frequency
0	8
1	10
2	12
3	3
4	5
5	2

Find the mean numbers of goals per match.

Sol.

No. of Goals	Frequency	No. of Goals × Frequency
0	8	$0 \times 8 = 0$
1	10	$1 \times 10 = 10$
2	12	$2 \times 12 = 24$
3	3	$3 \times 3 = 9$
4	5	$4 \times 5 = 20$
5	2	$5 \times 2 = 10$
Totals	**40**	**73**
	(Total matches)	**(Total goals)**

The table above can be used, with a third column added. The mean can now be calculated.

$$\text{Mean} = \frac{73}{40} = 1.825 \text{ goals per match.}$$

4. The bar chart shows how many cars were sold by a salesman over a period of time.

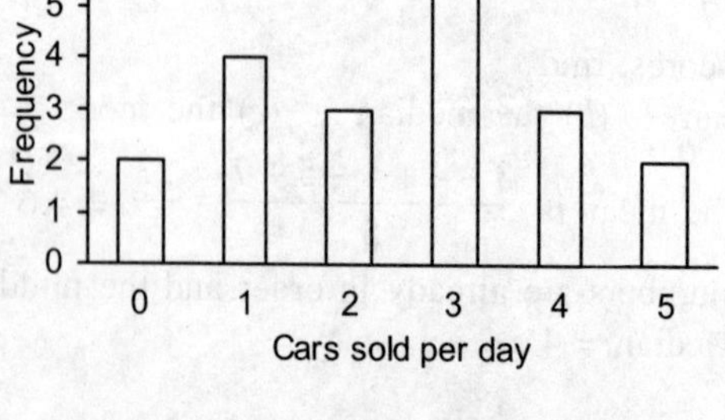

Sol. The data can be transferred to a table and a third column included as shown.

Cars sold daily	Frequency	Car sold × Frequency
0	2	$0 \times 2 = 0$
1	4	$1 \times 4 = 4$
2	3	$2 \times 3 = 6$
3	6	$3 \times 6 = 18$
4	3	$4 \times 3 = 12$
5	2	$5 \times 2 = 10$
Totals	**20**	**50**

(Total days) **(Total number of cars sold)**

Mean $= \dfrac{50}{20} = 2.5$ cars sold per day

5. The age of children in a primary school were recorded in the table below.

Age	5 – 6	7 – 8	9 – 10
Frequency	29	40	38

(a) Estimate the mean.

(b) Find the class interval that contains the median value.

(c) Find the modal age.

Sol. (a) To estimate the mean, we must use the mid-point of each interval; so, for example for '5 – 6', which really means
$5 \leq$ are < 7
the mid-point is taken as 6.

Age Group	Mid-point	Frequency	Mid-point × Frequency
5 – 6	6	29	$6 \times 29 = 174$
7 – 8	8	40	$8 \times 40 = 320$
9 – 10	10	38	$10 \times 38 = 380$
	Totals	**107**	**874**

Mean $= \dfrac{874}{107} = 8.2$ (to 1 decimal place)

(*a*) The median is given by the 54th value which lies within the age group 7 – 8, since 29 + 40 is greater than 54 so this interval must contain the median.

(*b*) The modal age is the 7 – 8 age group because there are more children in this age group than in any other.

6. The mean of a simple of 6 numbers is 3.2. An extra value of 3.9 is included in the sample. Wha is the mean?

Sol. Total of original numbers = 6 × 3.2 = 19.2

New total = 19.2 + 3.9 = 23.1

$$\text{New mean} = \frac{23.1}{7} = 3.3$$

7. The mean number of a set of 5 numbers is 12.7. What extra number must be added to bring to mean up to 13.1?

Sol. Total of original numbers = 5 × 12.7 = 63.5

Total of the new numbers = 6 × 13.1 = 78.6

Difference = 78.6 – 63.5 = 15.1

Therefore, the extra number is 15.1

EXERCISE

1. Find the mean, median, mode and range of each set of numbers below.

(*a*) 3, 4, 7, 3, 5, 2, 6, 10

(*b*) 8, 10, 12, 14, 7, 16, 5, 7, 9, 11

(*c*) 17, 18, 16, 17, 17, 14, 22, 15, 16, 17, 14, 12

(*d*) 108, 99, 112, 111, 108

(*e*) 64, 66, 65, 61, 67, 61, 57

(*f*) 21, 30, 22, 16, 24, 28, 16, 17

2. Twenty children were asked their shoe sizes. The results are given below.

$$8,\ 6,\ 7,\ 6,\ 5,\ 4\frac{1}{2},\ 4\frac{1}{2},\ 6\frac{1}{2},\ 4\frac{1}{2},\ 10$$

$$7,\ 5,\ 5\frac{1}{2},\ 8,\ 9,\ 7,\ 5,\ 6,\ 8\frac{1}{2},\ 6$$

For this data, find

(*a*) the mean (*b*) the median (*c*) the mode (*d*) the range

3. Eight people work in a shop, they are paid hourly rates of ₹ 2, ₹ 15, ₹ 5, ₹ 4, ₹ 3, ₹ 4, ₹ 3, ₹ 3.

(*a*) Find

(*i*) the mean (*ii*) the median (*iii*) the mode

(*b*) Which average would you use if you wanted to claim that the staff were:

(*i*) well paid (*ii*) badly paid?

(*c*) What is the range?

4. Two people work in a factory making parts for cars. The table shows how many complete parts they make in one week.

Worker	Mon	Tue	Wed	Thu	Fri
Satish	20	21	22	20	21
Anuj	30	15	12	36	28

(*a*) Find the mean and range for Satish and Anuj.
(*b*) Who is most consistent?
(*c*) Who makes the most parts in a week?

5. A garage owner records the number of cars which visit his garage on 10 days. The numbers are:
204, 310, 279, 314, 257, 302, 232, 261, 308, 217
(*a*) Find the mean number of cars per day.
(*b*) The owner hopes that the mean will increase if he includes the number of cars on the next day. If 252 cars use the garage on the next day, will the mean increase or decrease?

6. The children in a class state how many children there are in their family. The numbers they state are given below.
1, 2, 1, 3, 2, 1, 2, 4, 2, 2, 1, 3, 1, 2,
2, 2, 1, 1, 7, 3, 1, 2, 1, 2, 2, 1, 2, 3
(*a*) Find the mean, median and mode for this data.
(*b*) Which is the most sensible average to use in this case?

7. The mean number of people visiting Jitendra each day over a five-day period is 8. If 10 people visit Jitendra the next day, what happens to the mean?

8. The table shows the maximum and minimum temperatures recorded in six cities one day last year.

City	Maximum	Minimum
Bangalore	22°C	12°C
Shimla	22°C	–3°C
Kashmir	18°C	–9°C
Agra	27°C	8°C
Nainital	13°C	–15°C
Cochin	28°C	13°C

(*a*) Work out the range of temperature for Agra.
(*b*) Which city in the table had the lowest temperature?
(*c*) Work out the difference between the maximum temperature and the minimum temperature for Kashmir?

9. Pupils in Year 8 are arranged in eleven classes. The class sizes are 23, 24, 24, 26, 27, 28, 30, 24, 29, 24, 27

(*a*) What is the modal class size?

(*b*) Calculate the mean class size.

The range of the class sizes for Year 9 is 3.

(*c*) What does this tell you about the class sizes in Year 9 compared with those in Year 8?

10. A school has to select one pupil to take part in a General Knowledge Quiz.

Kavita and Pratima took part in six trial quizzes. The following lists show their scores.

Kavita	28	24	21	27	24	26
Pratima	33	19	16	32	34	18

Kavita had a mean score of 25 with a range of 7.

(*a*) Calculate Pratima's mean score and range.

(*b*) Which pupil would you choose to represent the school? Explain the reason for your choice, referring to the mean scores and ranges.

11. A survey of 100 households asked how many cars there were in each household. The results are given below.

No. of Cars	0	1	2	3	4
Frequency	5	70	21	3	1

Calculate the mean number of cars per household.

12. The survey of question 1 also asked how many TV sets there were in each household. The results are given below.

No. of TV Sets	Frequency
0	2
1	30
2	52
3	8
4	5
5	3

Calculate the mean number of TV sets per household.

13. A manager keeps a record of the number of calls she makes each day on her mobile phone.

Number of calls per day	0	1	2	3	4	5	6	7	8
Frequency	3	4	7	8	12	10	14	3	1

Calculate the mean number of calls per household.

14. A cricket team keeps a record of the number of runs scored in each over.

Number of calls per day	0	1	2	3	4	5	6	7	8
Frequency	3	2	1	6	5	4	2	1	1

(a) Calculate the mean number of runs per over.
(b) How many runs would the team expect to score in a 40-over match?

15. A door to door salesman keeps a record of the number of homes he visits each day.

Home visited	0 – 9	10 – 19	20 – 29	30 – 39	40 – 49
Frequency	3	8	24	60	21

(a) Estimate the mean number of homes visited.
(b) Find the class interval that contains the median value.
(c) What is the modal class?

~~~~~~

ANSWER KEY

1.

	Mean	Median	Mode	Range
(a)	4.5	4.5	3	8
(b)	9.9	9.5	7	11
(c)	16.25	16.5	17	10
(d)	107.6	108	108	13
(e)	63	64	61	10
(f)	21.75	21.5	16	14

2. (a) 6.45 (b) 6 (c) 6 (d) $5\frac{1}{2}$

3. (a) (i) 4.875 (ii) 3.5 (iii) 3 (b) (i) 5 (ii) 3 (c) 13

4. (a)

	Mean	Range
Satish	20.8	2
Anuj	24.2	21

(b) Satish is most consistant.
(c) Anuj makes most parts in the week.

5. (a) 268.4 (b) Mean will decrease

6. (a) 2.035 (mean), 2 (median), 2 (mode) (b) 2 is most sensible average.

7. 8.33 the mean will increase

8. (a) 35°C (b) Nainital lead the lowest temperature. (c) 27°C

9. (a) 24 (b) 26 (c) Increases

10. (a) Mean = 25.33, Range = 18
(b) Pratima will represent the school because she has higher mean values.

11. 1.25 **12.** 1.93 **13.** 4.08 **14.** (a) 3.42 (b) 139

15. (a) 30.61 (b) 30-39 (c) 30-39
~~~~~~

28. DATA ANALYSIS

TABLES AND GRAPHS

Introduction: Data analysis is an important aspect of almost every competitive examination today. Usually, a table or a bar diagram or a pie-chart or a sub-divided bar diagram or a graph is given and candidates are asked questions that test their ability to analyse the data given in those forms.

In order to solve such questions quickly, you should try to have the following things in mind:

(*i*) First have a cursory glance at the given diagram. Try to digest quickly what the diagram represents. **Take special care of units** because in some examinations two lines in a single graph have been found to be in different units. If you find anything striking, or odd, make a note of it somewhere alongside the answer book.

(*ii*) If you are doing a table always make sure what the sum of all entries in one row represents and what the sum of all entries in a column represents. A good example of such a question is Q 1 of Ex 1 below. In this question you are asked to find out the year in which the disbursement of loans of all the banks (it means the sum of all entries in one column, remember) is the least compared to the average disbursement of loans over the years. If you are reading this question like any other student you will immediately start calculating the average disbursement of loans over the years. But as a student of our Quicker Mathematics you should always think before you act. The year in which disbursement was minimum will remain so whatever be the quantity you compare with. Hence to answer this question you should simply find out the year in which the disbursement of loans was the least.

(*iii*) Questions having diagrams give you the facility of having an idea of diagram. If a candidate starts using his pen and begins calculating, he will only be wasting his time. **Never use your pen for a question which your eyes can solve.**

SOLVED EXAMPLE

Ex. 1. Study the following table carefully and answer the questions given below:

Loan disbursed by 5 banks
(Rupees in Crores)
Years

Banks	1982	1983	1984	1985	1986
A	18	23	45	30	70
B	27	33	18	41	37
C	29	29	22	17	11
D	31	16	28	32	43
E	13	19	27	34	42
Total	118	120	140	154	203

1. In which year was the disbursement of loans of all the banks put together least compared to the average disbursement of loans over the years?
(*a*) 1982 (*b*) 1983 (*c*) 1984 (*d*) 1985

2. What was the percentage increase of disbursement of loans of all banks together from 1984 to 1985?
(*a*) 110 (*b*) 14 (*c*) $90\frac{10}{11}$ (*d*) 10

3. In which year was the total disbursement of loans of banks A & B exactly equal to the total disbursement of banks D and E?
(*a*) 1983 (*b*) 1986 (*c*) 1982 (*d*) None of these

4. In which of the following banks did the disbursement of loans continuously increase over the years?
(*a*) A (*b*) B (*c*) C (*d*) E

5. If the minimum target in the preceding years was 20% of the total disbursement of loans, how many banks reached the target in 1983?
(*a*) 1 (*b*) 3 (*c*) 2 (*d*) 4

Sol. 1. (*a*) For explanation, refer to the dicussion above.

2. (*d*) All banks together means sum of columns. Thus we have to find out the percentage increase in 140 to 154. You should be able to do the remaining mentally.

3. (*d*) [**Note:** No shortcut. Calculation is needed for all the cases.]

4. (*d*) [**Note:** Only a visual glance is needed.]

5. (*c*) [B and C achieved the target. Target was 20% of 118 + 23.6].

Ex. 2. Study the following graph carefully and answer the following questions.

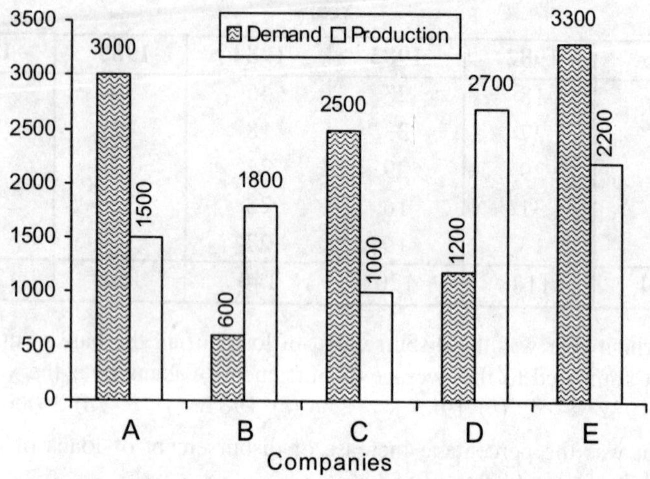

1. What is the ratio of companies having more demand than production to those having more production than demand?
   (*a*) 2 : 3 (*b*) 4 : 1 (*c*) 2 : 2 (*d*) 3 : 2
2. What is the difference between average demand and average production of the five companies taken together?
   (*a*) 1400 (*b*) 400 (*c*) 280 (*d*) 138
3. The production of company D is approximately how many times of the production of the company A?
   (*a*) 1.8 (*b*) 1.5 (*c*) 2.5 (*d*) 1.11
4. The demand for company 'B' is approximately what per cent of the demand for company 'C'?
   (*a*) 4 (*b*) 24 (*c*) 20 (*d*) 60
5. If company 'A' desires to meet the demand by purchasing surplus T.V. sets from a single company, which one of the following companies can meet the need adequately?
   (*a*) B (*b*) C (*c*) D (*d*) None of these

Sol. 1. (*d*) A simple inspection is enough to tell that.

2. (*c*) Average demand

$$= \frac{1}{5}(3000 + 600 + 2500 + 1200 + 3300) = 2120.$$

Average production

$= \frac{1}{5}(1500 + 1800 + 1000 + 2700 + 2200) = 1840.$

∴ Difference between average demand and average production
= (2120 – 1840) = 280.
So, answer (c) is correct.

3. (*a*) Let k (1500) = 2700 or $k = \frac{2700}{1500} = 1.8.$

So, answer (*a*) is correct.

4. (*b*) Let x% of (demand for C) = (demand for B).

i.e., $\frac{x}{100} \times 2500 = 600$ or $x = \left(\frac{600 \times 100}{2500}\right) = 24\%.$

∴ Answer (*b*) is correct.

5. (*c*) See the explanation in the introductory discussion.

Ex. 3. The following graph shows the no. of workers of different categories A, B, C, D, E, F, G and H of a factory for the two different years.

Total no. of workers in 1997 = 1900 In 1998 = 1800

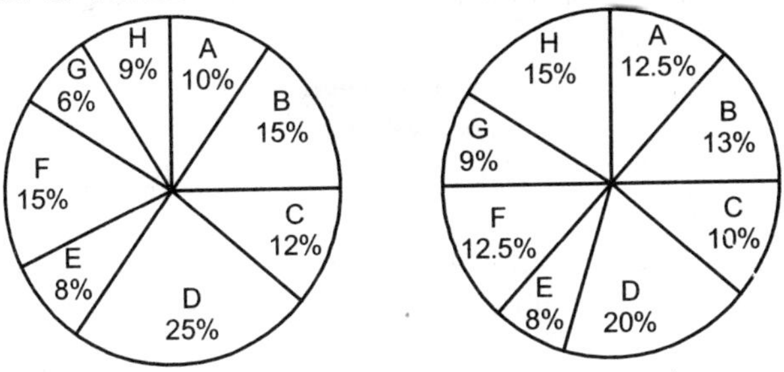

1. What is the total no. of increased workers for the categories in which the no. of workers has been increased?

2. Find the percentage decrease in the no. of workers for the categories D and F taken together?

3. Which categories have shown the decrease in the no. of workers from 1997 to 1998?

4. Find the maximum possible difference of the no. of workers of any two categories taken together for one year and any two for the other year.

5. What is the difference between the no. of workers of the category F for the two years and the angular values of the same category for the two years?

Sol.

	1997	1998
A →	(10% of 1900 =) 190	(12.5% of 1800 =) 225
B →	285	234
C →	228	180
D →	475	360
E →	152	144
F →	285	225
G →	114	162
H →	171	270

1. The no. of workers has been increased in the category A (from 190 to 225 = 35), G (from 114 to 162 = 48) and H (from 171 to 270 = 99).

   ∴ Total no. of increased workers = 35 + 48 + 99 = 182.
2. Reqd. percentage decrease

   $$= \frac{(475 - 360) + (285 - 225)}{475 + 285} \times 100\% = \frac{175}{760} \times 100\% = 23\%$$
3. Reqd. categories are B, C, D, E and F.
5. The difference between the no. of workers of the category F for the two years = 285 – 225 = 60.

EXERCISE

Directions (Q. 1-5): *Study the following graph carefully and answer the questions given below:*

Value of imports and exports by a company over the years.

Value of imports (in ₹ cr)

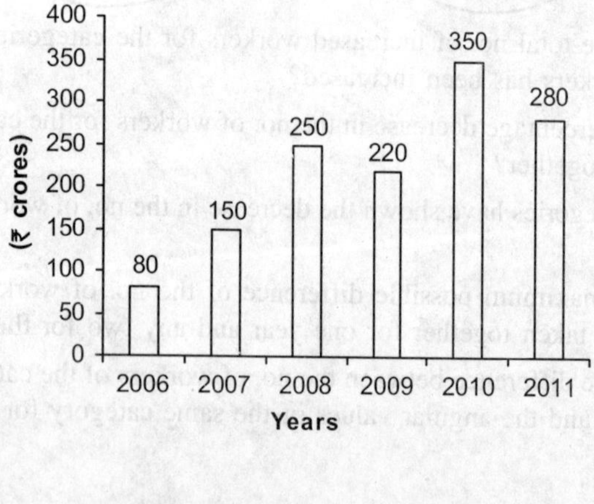

Value of exports (in ₹ cr)

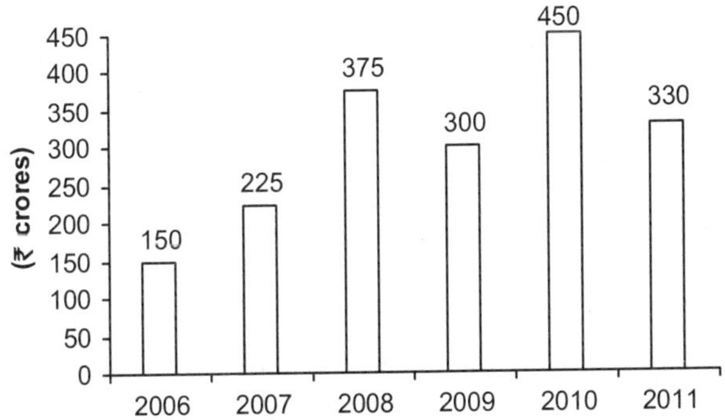

1. The value of exports in 2010 was what percentage of the average value of imports in the years 2008, 2009 and 2011?
(*a*) 200 (*b*) 100 (*c*) 300 (*d*) None of these

2. The value of exports in 2008 was exactly what percentage of the value of imports in the same years?
(*a*) 125 (*b*) 160 (*c*) 200 (*d*) None of these

3. What was the approximate difference between the value of average exports and the value of average imports of the given years?
(*a*) ₹ 85 cr (*b*) ₹ 100 cr (*c*) ₹ 75 cr (*d*) ₹ 90 cr

4. In which of the following years was the difference between the value of exports and the value of imports exactly ₹ 100 cr?
(*a*) 2007 (*b*) 2010 (*c*) 2009 (*d*) 2011

5. What was the percentage increase in the value of exports from 2009 to 2010?
(*a*) 150 (*b*) 100 (*c*) 75 (*d*) 50

Directions (Q. 6-10): *Study the following table carefully and answer the questions given below:*

Production of main crops in India (in million tonnes)

Crops	2005-06	2006-07	2007-08	2008-09	2009-10	2010-11
Pulses	20.5	22.4	24.6	23.5	27.8	28.2
Oilseeds	32.4	34.6	40.8	42.4	46.8	52.4
Rice	80.5	86.4	88.2	92.6	94.2	90.8
Sugercane	140.8	150.2	152.2	160.3	156.4	172.5
Wheat	130.2	138.4	146.8	141.6	152.2	158.4
Coarse grain	45.6	52.8	60.4	62.4	58.2	62.8
Sum	**450**	**484.8**	**513.2**	**522.8**	**535.6**	**565.1**

6. Production of sugarcane in 2007-08 was approximately what percentage of the production of rice in 2006-07?
(*a*) 50 (*b*) 75 (*c*) 150 (*d*) 175

7. Production of what type of crop was going to increase in each year in the given years?
(*a*) Rice (*b*) Pulse (*c*) Sugarcane (*d*) Oilseeds

8. What was the average production of pulse in the given years?
(*a*) 26.8 million tonnes (*b*) 20.5 million tonnes
(*c*) 24.5 million tonnes (*d*) 22.5 million tonnes

9. Production of oilseeds was what percentage of the total crops produced in the year 2005-06?
(*a*) 7.2 (*b*) 8.4 (*c*) 2.7 (*d*) 6.4

10. In which of the following years the total production of oilseeds in the years 2008-09, 2009-10, and 2010-11 was equal to the production of wheat?
(*a*) 2007-08 (*b*) 2008-09 (*c*) 2010-11 (*d*) 2006-07

Directions (Q. 11-15): *Study the following graphs carefully and answer the questions given below it.*

Marks obtained by two students in six subjects in an examination
Maximum marks in Physics, Chemistry and English are 200.
Maximum marks in History, Geography and Hindi are 150.

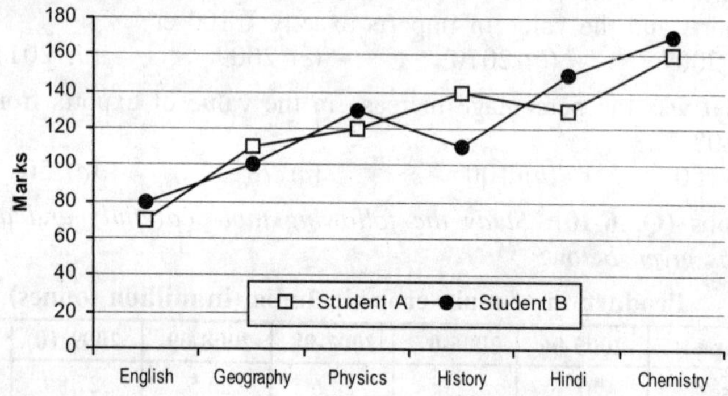

11. Marks obtained by student B in Hindi was what percentage of the marks obtained by student B in physics?
(*a*) 25 (*b*) 150 (*c*) 125 (*d*) None of these

12. **Approximately** what was the average percentage of marks obtained by A in all the subjects?
(*a*) 75 (*b*) 60 (*c*) 80 (*d*) 70

13. **Approximately** what was the average marks obtained by B in Geography, History and Hindi?

(*a*) 120 (*b*) 80 (*c*) 140 (*d*) 110

14. In how many subjects did student B obtain more than 70 percentage of marks?

(*a*) 1 (*b*) 2 (*c*) 3 (*d*) 4

15. What was the difference in percentage of marks between A and B in History?

(*a*) 30 (*b*) 25 (*c*) 40 (*d*) 20

Directions (Q. 16-20): *Study the following graph carefully and answer the questions that follow.*

Production of steel by different companies in three consecutive years (in lakh tonnes)

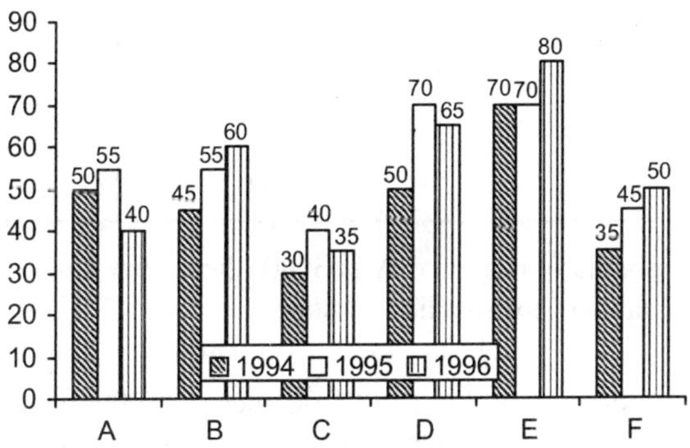

16. What is the difference between average production of the six companies in 1995 and average production of the same companies in 1994?

(*a*) 7,05,000 tonnes (*b*) 7,50,000 tonnes
(*c*) 75,000 tonnes (*d*) None of these

17. What is the percentage decline in production by company C from 1995 to 1996?

(*a*) 5% (*b*) 20% (*c*) 15% (*d*) 12.50%

18. Which of the following companies recorded the minimum percentage growth from 1994 to 1995?

(*a*) A (*b*) B (*c*) C (*d*) D

19. Production of company 'C' in 1995 and production of company 'F' in 1994 together is what per cent of production of B in 1996?

(*a*) 80% (*b*) 75% (*c*) 133% (*d*) None of these

20. In which of the following pairs of companies the difference between average production for the three years is maximum?
(*a*) E and F (*b*) D and C (*c*) E and C (*d*) A and E

Directions (Q. 21-25): *Study the following table and answer the following questions carefully.*

Following table shows the percentage population of six states below poverty line and the proportion of male and female

State	Percentage population below poverty line	Proportion of male and female	
		Below poverty line M : F	Above poverty line M : F
A	12	3 : 2	4 : 3
B	15	5 : 7	3 : 4
C	25	4 : 5	2 : 3
D	26	1 : 2	5 : 6
E	10	6 : 5	3 : 2
F	32	2 : 3	4 : 5

21. The total population of state A is 3000, then what is the approximate no. of females above poverty line in state A?
(*a*) 1200 (*b*) 2112 (*c*) 1800 (*d*) 1950

22. If the total population of C and D together is 18000, then what is the total no. of females below poverty line in the above stated states?
(*a*) 5000 (*b*) 5500 (*c*) 4800 (*d*) Data inadequate

23. If the population of males below poverty line in state A is 3000 and that in state E is 6000, then what is the ratio of the total population of state A and E?
(*a*) 3 : 4 (*b*) 4 : 5 (*c*) 1 : 2 (*d*) None of these

24. If the population of males below poverty line in state B is 500 then what is the total population of the state?
(*a*) 14400 (*b*) 6000 (*c*) 8000 (*d*) 7600

25. If in state E population of females above poverty line is 19800 then what is the population of males below poverty line in that state?
(*a*) 5500 (*b*) 3000 (*c*) 2970 (*d*) None of these

Directions (Q. 26-30): *Read the following table carefully and answer the questions given below.*

Highest marks and average marks obtained by students in subjects over the years
The maximum marks in each subject is 100.

	Subjects									
	English		Hindi		Maths		Science		History	
	High	Avg	High	Avg	High	Avg	High	Avg	High	Avg
1992	85	62	75	52	98	65	88	72	72	46
1993	80	70	80	53	94	60	89	70	65	55
1994	82	65	77	54	85	62	95	64	66	58
1995	71	56	84	64	92	68	97	68	68	49
1996	75	52	82	66	91	64	92	75	70	58
1997	82	66	81	57	89	66	98	72	74	62

26. What was the grand average marks of the five subjects in 1996?
(*a*) 63 (*b*) 64 (*c*) 65 (*d*) 68

27. The difference in the average marks in History between 1994 and 1995 was exactly equal to the difference in the highest marks in Hindi between which of the following pairs of years?
(*a*) 1992 and 1995 (*b*) 1993 and 1995
(*c*) 1992 and 1996 (*d*) 1993 and 1997

28. What was the approximate percentage increase in average marks in History from 1992 and 1993?
(*a*) 20 (*b*) 25 (*c*) 24 (*d*) 16

29. The average highest marks in English in 1992, 1993 and 1996 was exactly equal to the highest marks in Hindi in which of the following years?
(*a*) 1996 (*b*) 1997 (*c*) 1994 (*d*) 1993

30. The difference between the highest marks and the average marks in Hindi was maximum in which of the following years?
(*a*) 1994 (*b*) 1997 (*c*) 1995 (*d*) 1993

Directions (Q. 31-35): *Study the following chart to answer the question given given below:*

Village	% population below poverty line
A	45
B	52
C	38
D	58
E	46
F	49
G	51

Proportion of population of seven villages in 1995

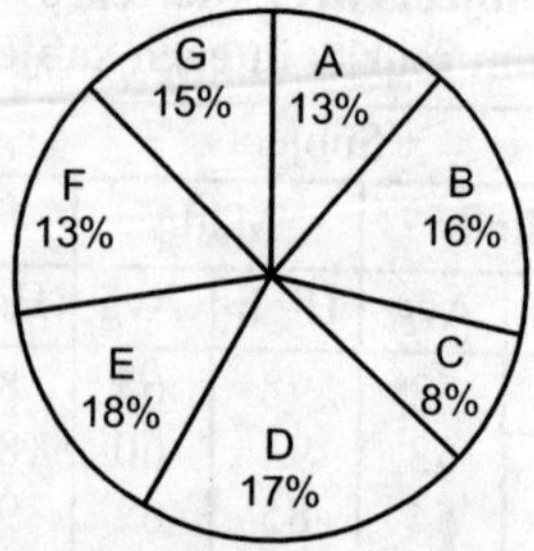

31. In 1996, the population of villages A as well as B is increased by 10% from the year 1995. If the population of village A in 1995 was 5000 and the percentage of population below poverty line in 1996 remains same as in 1995, find approximately the population of village B below poverty line in 2010.

(*a*) 4000 (*b*) 4500 (*c*) 2500 (*d*) 3500

32. If in 1997 the population of village D is increased by 10% and the population of village G is reduced by 5% from 1995 and the population of village G in 1995 was 9000, what is the total population of village D and G in 1997?

(*a*) 19770 (*b*) 19200 (*c*) 18770 (*d*) 19870

33. If in 1995 the total population of the seven villages together was 55,000 approximately, what will be population of village F in that year below poverty line?

(*a*) 3000 (*b*) 2500 (*c*) 4000 (*d*) 3500

34. If the population of village C below poverty line in 1995 was 1520, what was the population of village F in 1995?

(*a*) 4000 (*b*) 6000 (*c*) 6500 (*d*) 4800

35. The population of village C is 2000 in 1995. What will be the ratio of population of village C below poverty line to that of the village E below poverty line in that year?

(*a*) 207 : 76 (*b*) 76 : 207

(*c*) 152 : 207 (*d*) Data inadequate

Directions (Q. 36-42): *Study the given graphs and table and answer the following questions given below.*

The total population of the different states in 1993 is 25 lakhs

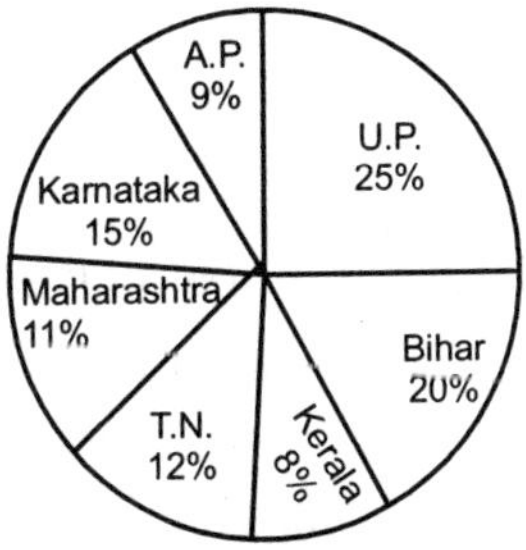

Sex-and-literacywise population ratio

States	Sex	Literacy
	M — F	Literate — Illiterate
U.P.	5 : 3	2 : 7
Bihar	3 : 1	1 : 4
A.P.	2 : 3	2 : 1
Karnataka	3 : 5	3 : 2
Maharashtra	3 : 4	5 : 1
Tamil Nadu	3 : 2	7 : 2
Kerala	3 : 4	9 : 4

M = Male, F = Female.

36. Approximately what is the total number of literate people in Maharashtra and Karnataka together?
(*a*) 4.5 lakh (*b*) 6.5 lakh (*c*) 3 lakh (*d*) 3.5 lakh

37. Approximately what will be the percentage of total male in UP, Maharashtra and Kerala of the total population of the given states?
(*a*) 20% (*b*) 18% (*c*) 28% (*d*) 25%

38. If in ther year 1993 there was an increase of 10% population of U.P. and 12% of Bihar compared to the previous year, then what was the ratio of the population of UP to Bihar in year 1992?
(*a*) 50 : 40 (*b*) 40 : 50 (*c*) 48 : 55 (*d*) None of these

39. What was the approximate percentage of women of Andhra Pradesh to the women of Tamil Nadu?
(*a*) 90% (*b*) 110% (*c*) 120% (*d*) 85%

40. What is the ratio of the number of females in Tamil Nadu to the number of females in Kerala?

(*a*) 1 : 2 (*b*) 1 : 1 (*c*) 2 : 1 (*d*) None of these

41. In Tamil Nadu if 70% of the females are literate and 75% of the males are literate, what is the total number of illiterates in the state?

(*a*) 75,000 (*b*) 85,000 (*c*) 71,000 (*d*) 81,000

42. What is the ratio of literates in Andhara Pradesh to the literates in Bihar?

(*a*) 2 : 5 (*b*) 3 : 5 (*c*) 3 : 2 (*d*) 2 : 3

Directions (Q. 43-47): *Study the following table carefully and answer the questions given below it:*

Statewise and Disciplinewise Number of Candidates Appeared (App.) and Qualified (Qual.) at a Competitive Examination)

State	A.P.		U.P.		Kerala	
Discipline	App.	Qual.	App.	Qual.	App.	Qual.
Arts	5420	1840	4980	1690	2450	845
Commerce	8795	2985	6565	2545	3500	2040
Science	6925	2760	8750	3540	4250	2500
Engg.	1080	490	2500	1050	1200	450
Agri.	840	850	1085	455	700	200
Total	23060	8425	23880	9280	12100	6035

Orissa		M.P.		W.B.		Total	
App.	Qual.	App.	Qual.	App.	Qual.	App.	Qual.
3450	1200	7500	2000	4800	1500	28600	9075
4800	2200	8400	2400	7600	2700	39660	14870
4500	1950	6850	3000	8500	3200	39775	16950
1850	850	2500	750	3400	1400	12530	4990
450	150	1500	475	1200	500	5775	2130
15050	6350	26750	8625	25500	9300	126340	48015

43. For which of the following discipline the proportion of qualifying candidates to the appeared candidates from U.P. State is the lowest?

(*a*) Arts (*b*) Commerce (*c*) Science (*d*) Engineering

44. For which of the pair of States, the qualifying percentage from Agriculture discipline is exactly the same?

(*a*) A.P. & U.P. (*b*) A.P. & West Bengal

(*c*) U.P. & West Bengal (*d*) Kerala & Orissa

45. For which of the following states the percentage of candidates qualified to appeared is the minimum for commerce discipline?
(*a*) AP (*b*) UP (*c*) Kerala (*d*) MP

46. Approximately what is the ratio between total qualifying percentage of UP and that of MP?
(*a*) 15 : 16 (*b*) 13 : 14 (*c*) 14 : 13 (*d*) 19 : 16

47. The qualifying percentage for which of the following states is the lowest for Science discipline?
(*a*) AP (*b*) UP (*c*) West Bengal (*d*) Kerala

ANSWERS

1	2	3	4	5	6	7	8	9	10
(*d*)	(*d*)	(*a*)	(*b*)	(*d*)	(*d*)	(*d*)	(*c*)	(*a*)	(*b*)
11	**12**	**13**	**14**	**15**	**16**	**17**	**18**	**19**	**20**
(*d*)	(*e*)	(*a*)	(*c*)	(*d*)	(*d*)	(*d*)	(*a*)	(*d*)	(*c*)
21	**22**	**23**	**24**	**25**	**26**	**27**	**28**	**29**	**30**
(*a*)	(*d*)	(*d*)	(*c*)	(*a*)	(*a*)	(*a*)	(*a*)	(*d*)	(*d*)
31	**32**	**33**	**34**	**35**	**36**	**37**	**38**	**39**	**40**
(*d*)	(*a*)	(*d*)	(*c*)	(*b*)	(*a*)	(*d*)	(*d*)	(*b*)	(*d*)
41	**42**	**43**	**44**	**45**	**46**	**47**			
(*d*)	(*c*)	(*a*)	(*b*)	(*d*)	(*d*)	(*c*)			

SOME SELECTED EXPLANATORY ANSWERS

1. Average value of imports in the years 2008, 2009 and 2011

$$= \frac{250 + 220 + 280}{3} = ₹\ 250 \text{ cr}$$

$$\therefore \text{ Required percentage } = \frac{450}{250} \times 100 = 180\%$$

2. Required percentage $= \dfrac{375}{250} \times 100 = 150\%$

3. Average import $= \dfrac{80 + 150 + 250 + 220 + 350 + 280}{6}$

$$= \frac{1330}{6} \approx 222 \text{ cr}$$

$$\text{Average export} = \frac{150 + 225 + 375 + 300 + 450 + 330}{6} = 305 \text{ cr}$$

$\therefore$ Required difference = 83 cr $\approx$ 85 cr.

5. Required percentage increase = $\frac{450 - 300}{300} \times 100 = \frac{150}{300} \times 100 = 50\%$.

6. Required per cent increase = $\frac{152.2}{86.4} \times 100 \approx 175\%$

8. Average production of pulse

$$= \frac{20.5 + 22.4 + 24.6 + 23.5 + 27.8 + 28.2}{6} = \frac{147.0}{6}$$

= 24.5 million tonnes

9. Required percentage = $\frac{32.4}{450} \times 100 = 7.5\%$

10. Total production of oilseeds in the given yrs
= 42.4 + 46.8 + 52.4 = 141.6
Which is equal to the production of wheat in 2008-09

11. Required percentage = $\frac{150}{130} \times 100 = 115.38\%$

12. % marks in Eng = $\frac{70}{200} \times 100 = 35$

% marks in Geo = $\frac{110}{150} \times 100 \approx 73$

% marks in Phy = $\frac{120}{200} \times 100 = 60$

% marks in His = $\frac{140}{150} \times 100 = 93$

% marks in Hin = $\frac{120}{150} \times 100 = 80$

% marks in Che = $\frac{160}{200} \times 100 = 80$

$\therefore$ Average % marks = $\frac{421}{6} \approx 70$

13. Marks obtained by B in Geography, History and Hindi
$= 100 + 110 + 150 = 360$

$\therefore$ average $= \dfrac{360}{3} = 120$

14. Percentage of marks obtained by student B

English	Geography	Physics	History	Hindi	Chemistry
40	66.6	65	73.33	100	85

15. Required difference $= \dfrac{140 - 110}{150} \times 100 = \dfrac{30}{150} \times 100 = 20\%$

16. Required difference $= \dfrac{335 - 280}{6} = 916666$ tonnes

17. Percentage decline $= \dfrac{40 - 35}{40} \times 100 = 12.50\%$

18. It is clear from the graph. But see the table which shows the percentage growth of six companies from 1994 to 1995.

A	B	C	D	F
10%	22.22%	33.33%	40%	28.57%

19. Required percentage $= \dfrac{40 + 35}{60} \times 100 = 125\%$

20. It is clear that the highest average production is in E and lowest average production is in C. So, the maximum difference would be in E & C.

21. No. of females above poverty line in state A

$= 3000 \times (100 - 12)\% \times \dfrac{3}{7} \approx 1200$

22. Since we cannot find the population of states C and D separately, we can't find the required value.

23. Population of state A below poverty line $= 3000 \times \dfrac{5}{3} = 5000$

$\therefore$ Total population of state A $= \dfrac{5000}{12} \times 100$

and the population of state E below poverty line $= 6000 \times \frac{11}{6} = 11000$

$\therefore$ Total population of state E $= \frac{11000}{10} \times 100$

$\therefore$ Required ratio $= \frac{5}{12} \times \frac{10}{11} = \frac{25}{66}$.

24. Total population of state B $= 500\left(\frac{5}{12}\right)\left(\frac{100}{15}\right) = 8000.$

25. Population of state E $= 19800\left(\frac{5}{2}\right)\left(\frac{100}{100-10}\right) = 55000$

$\therefore$ Population of males below poverty line $= 55000\left(\frac{10}{100}\right)\left(\frac{6}{11}\right) = 3000.$

26. Average $= \frac{52+66+64+75+58}{5} = \frac{315}{5} = 63.$

27. The difference is 9.

28. Percentage increase $= \frac{55-46}{46} \times 100 \approx 20\%$

29. Average highest marks $= \frac{85+80+75}{3} = \frac{240}{3} = 80.$

31. Population of village B in 1995 $= 5000 \times \frac{16}{13} \approx 6150$

Population of B in 1996 $\approx 6150 \times \frac{110}{100} = 6750$

Pop. below poverty line = 52% of 6750 ≈ 3500

32. Population of village D in 1995 $= 9{,}000 \times \frac{17}{15} = 10{,}220$

Population of village D in 1997 $= 10{,}200 \times \frac{110}{100} = 11{,}220$

Population of village G in 1997 $= 9{,}000 \times \frac{95}{100} = 8{,}550$

$\therefore$ Total population of villages D and G in 1997

$= 11{,}220 + 8{,}550 = 19{,}770$

33. Population of village F below poverty line

$$= 55000 \times \frac{13}{100} \times \frac{49}{100} \approx 3500$$

34. Population of village F in 1995

$$= 1520 \times \frac{100}{38} \times \frac{13}{8} = 6500$$

35. Population of village C below poverty line $= 2000 \times \frac{38}{100} = 760$

Population of village E below poverty line

$$= \frac{2000}{8} \times 18 \times \left(\frac{46}{100}\right) = 2070$$

$\therefore$ Required ratio $= \frac{760}{2070} = 76 : 207.$

36. Total no. of literate people in Maharashtra and Karnataka

$$= \left[\frac{5}{6} \times 11\% + \frac{3}{5} \times 15\%\right] \text{ of 25 lakh}$$

$$= \left[\frac{55}{6} + 9\right] \text{ of } \frac{25}{100} \text{ lakh} = \frac{109}{6} \times \frac{25}{100} \approx 4.50 \text{ lakh}$$

37. Required percentage $= \left[25\% \text{ of } \frac{5}{8} + 11\% \text{ of } \frac{3}{7} + 8\% \text{ of } \frac{3}{7}\right] \times 100$

$$= \frac{125}{8} + \frac{33}{7} + \frac{24}{7} \approx 25\%$$

38. Required ratio $= \dfrac{\frac{100}{110} \times 25\% \text{ of 25 lakh}}{\frac{100}{112} \times 20\% \text{ of 25 lakh}}$

$$= \frac{112 \times 25}{110 \times 20} = \frac{14}{11} = 14 : 11$$

39. Required percentage $= \dfrac{\frac{3}{5} \text{ of } 9\% \text{ of 25 lakh}}{\frac{2}{5} \text{ of } 12\% \text{ of 25 lakh}} \times 100$

$$= \frac{3 \times 9}{2 \times 12} \times 100 = \frac{9 \times 100}{8} = 9 \times 12.5 \approx 110(\%)$$

40. Required ratio = $\dfrac{\frac{2}{5} \text{ of } 12\% \text{ of } 25 \text{ lakh}}{\frac{4}{7} \text{ of } 8\% \text{ of } 25 \text{ lakh}}$

$$= \frac{\frac{2}{5} \times 12}{\frac{4}{7} \times 8} = \frac{2 \times 12 \times 7}{5 \times 4 \times 8} = \frac{3 \times 7}{5 \times 4} = \frac{21}{20}$$

41. The total no. of illiterates in Tamil Nadu = (100 – 70 =) 30% of females + (100 – 75 =) 25% of males in the state

$= \left(\frac{30}{100} \times \frac{2}{5} + \frac{25}{100} \times \frac{3}{5}\right)$ of 12% of 25 lakh

$= (6 \times 2 + 5 \times 3 =) \frac{27}{100} \times \frac{12}{100} \times 2500000$

$= 27 \times 12 \times 250 = 81{,}000$

42. Required ratio = $\dfrac{\frac{2}{3} \text{ of } 9\% \text{ of } 25 \text{ lakh}}{\frac{1}{5} \text{ of } 20\% \text{ of } 25 \text{ lakh}} = \dfrac{\frac{2}{3} \times 9}{\frac{1}{5} \times 20} = \dfrac{2 \times 3}{4} = 3 : 2.$

43. UP (Qua/App)

Arts	Commerce	Science	Engg.	Agr.
0.33	0.38	0.40	0.42	0.41

Quicker Approach: $\dfrac{\text{Qual.}}{\text{App.}}$ should be the least.

$\Rightarrow \dfrac{\text{App.}}{\text{Qual.}}$ should be the maximum.

Now, for Arts, if we divide (4980 ≈) 5000 by (1690 ≈) 1700 we find the value of quotient near about 3. But in other cases the quotient is just more than 2. So, our answer is Arts.

45. Percentage of students qualified in commerce

A.P.	U.P.	Kerala	Orissa	M.P.
33.9	38.7	58.2	45.8	28.5

Quicker Approach: Follow the same as in Soln. 43. Only for MP

$\frac{\text{App.}}{\text{Qual.}} = 3.5$ (more than 3). In other cases $\frac{\text{App.}}{\text{Qual.}} < 3$.

46. Qualifying percentage of UP = $\frac{9280}{23880} \times 100 = 38.86$

Qualifying percentage of MP = $\frac{8625}{26750} \times 100 = 32.24$

Ratio = 38 : 32 = 19 : 16

47. Qualifying percentage for Science

A.P.	U.P.	W.B.	Kerala
39.8	40.4	37.6	58.8

Quicker Approach: Follow the same as in Soln. 43 & 45.

~~~~~~
~~~~~~

29. TRIGONOMETRY

MEASUREMENT OF ANGLES

INTRODUCTION: Measurement of Angles: Trigonometry means the science of measuring triangles. Given some of the sides and angles of a triangles, trigonometry helps us to calculate the remaining sides and angles.

You will be happy to know that the study of trigonometry was first started in **India.** Elements of the subjects can be found even in **Rigveda**. The **Greeks** had also started a study of trigonometry but their approach was so clumsy that when the Indian approach became known, it was immediately adopted throughout the world.

ANGLES: An angle is considered as the figure obtained by rotating a given ray about its end-point. The original ray is called the initial side and the ray into which the initial side rotates is called terminal side.

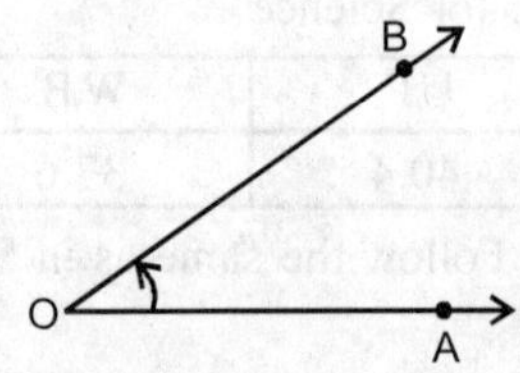

In fig. OA is **initial side** and OB is the **terminal side** of $\angle AOB$.

Sense of an Angle: The sense of an angle is derived from the direction of rotation of the initial side into the terminal side.

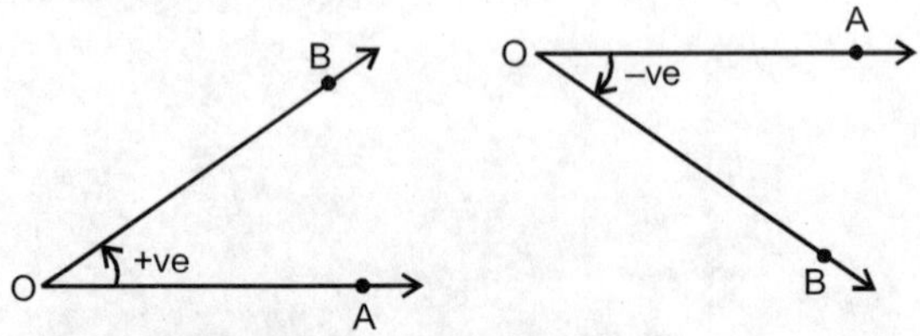

If the direction is **anti-clockwise** then the sense is said to be **positive** and if this direction is **clockwise** then the sense is **negative.**

Measure of an Angle: The measure of an angle is the amount of rotation required to get the terminal side from the initial side.

Divide the circumference of the circle into 360 equal parts, called **degrees.** The number of degrees on the circumference between the initial and terminal sides of the angle is its degree measure.

Mainly there are three systems for measuring angles.

(*a*) **Sexagesimal System (English System):** In this system, angle is measured in degrees.

1 right angle = $90°$, $1° = 60'$ and $1' = 60''$

(*b*) **Centesimal System (French System) :** In this system, angle is measured in grades.

1 right angle = 100^g, $1^g = 100'$, $1' = 100''$

(*c*) **Circular Measure:** In this system, angle is measured in radians.

The angle subtended at the centre of a circle by an arc of length equal to its radius is 1 radian, written as 1^c.

Comparing all the above three measuring systems we have $\pi^c = 180° = 200^g$ = 2 right angle.

SOME USEFUL TERMS: Quadrants: Let XOX′ and YOY′ be two lines at right angles in the plane of paper. These two perpendicular lines divide the plane of the paper into four equal parts. These four parts are known as four quadrants and lines XOX′ and YOY′ are known as *x*-axis and *y*-axis respectively.

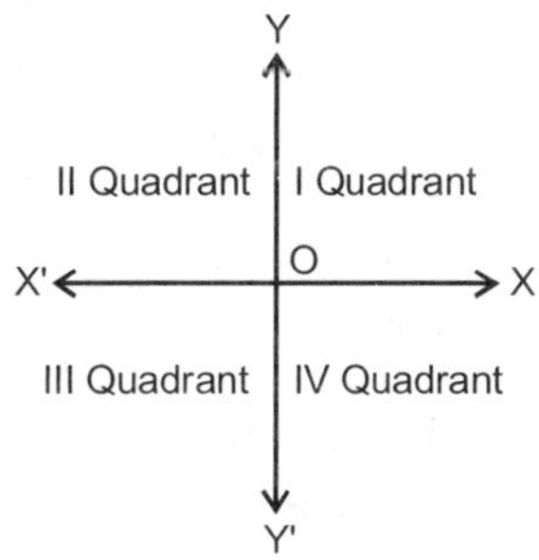

The parts XOY, YOX′, X′OY′ and Y′OX are known as 1st, 2nd, 3rd and 4th quadrant respectively.

Angle in a Quadrant: An angle is said to be in a particular quadrant, if the terminal side of the angle in standard position lies in that quadrant.

Triangle of Reference: If from any point P on the terminal side of an angle in standard position a perpendicular PQ is drawn on x-axis, then the right angled triangle OPQ thus formed is called the triangle of reference of ∠XOP.

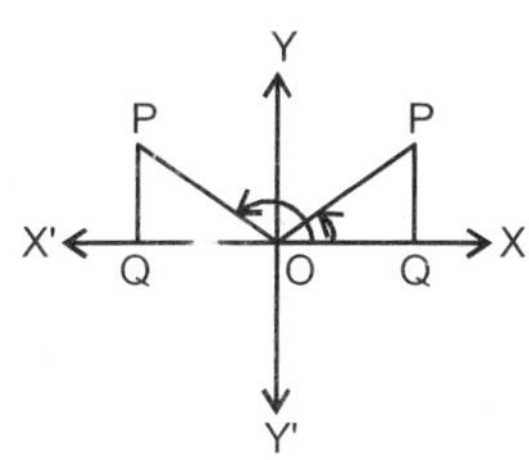

SOME BASIC FORMULAE

1. Relation between Angles, Radius and Arc length: If '*l*' is the length of a circle of radius *r*. If this are subtends an angle θ radians at the centre of the circle then

$$l = r\theta \Rightarrow \theta = \frac{l}{r}$$

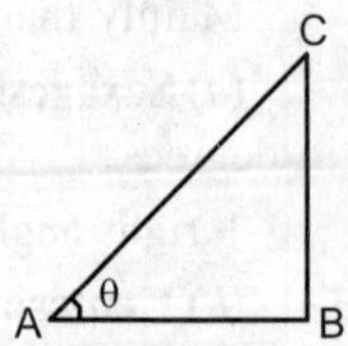

2. Trigonometric Ratios: If we consider a ΔABC right angled at B then the side opposite to $\angle B$ *i.e.,* AC is called hypotenuse and if AB is chosen an initial line then AB is called as base and BC will be perpendicular.

So the trigonometric ratios can be represented as

$$\sin\theta = \frac{\text{Perpendicular}}{\text{Hypotenuse}} = \frac{BC}{AC}$$

$$\cos\theta = \frac{\text{Base}}{\text{Hypotenuse}} = \frac{AB}{AC}$$

$$\tan\theta = \frac{\text{Perpendicular}}{\text{Base}} = \frac{BC}{AB}$$

$$\text{cosec}\,\theta = \frac{\text{Hypotenuse}}{\text{Perpendicular}} = \frac{AC}{BC} = \frac{1}{\sin\theta}$$

$$\sec\theta = \frac{\text{Hypotenuse}}{\text{Base}} = \frac{AC}{AB} = \frac{1}{\cos\theta},$$

$$\cot\theta = \frac{\text{Base}}{\text{Perpendicular}} = \frac{AB}{BC} = \frac{\cos\theta}{\sin\theta} = \frac{1}{\tan\theta}$$

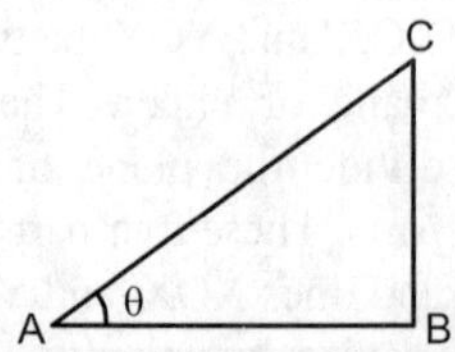

Indentities

(1) $\sin^2\theta + \cos^2\theta = 1$ (2) $1 + \tan^2\theta = \sec^2\theta$

(3) $1 + \cot^2\theta = \text{cosec}^2\theta$

Note: $\sin^2 A + \cos^2 B$ can not be equal to 1 because the angles are different.

Relation Among T. Ratios

	sin θ	**cos θ**	**tan θ**	**cot θ**	**sec θ**	**cosec θ**
sin θ	$\sin\theta$	$\sqrt{1-\cos^2\theta}$	$\frac{\tan\theta}{\sqrt{1+\tan^2\theta}}$	$\frac{1}{\sqrt{1+\cot^2\theta}}$	$\frac{\sqrt{\sec^2\theta-1}}{\sec\theta}$	$\frac{1}{\text{cosec}\,\theta}$
cos θ	$\sqrt{1-\sin^2\theta}$	$\cos\theta$	$\frac{1}{\sqrt{1+\tan^2\theta}}$	$\frac{\cot\theta}{\sqrt{1+\cot^2\theta}}$	$\frac{1}{\sec\theta}$	$\frac{\sqrt{\text{cosec}^2\theta-1}}{\text{cosec}\,\theta}$
tan θ	$\frac{\sin\theta}{\sqrt{1-\sin^2\theta}}$	$\frac{\sqrt{1-\cos^2\theta}}{\cos\theta}$	$\tan\theta$	$\frac{1}{\cos\theta}$	$\frac{1}{\sqrt{\sec^2\theta-1}}$	$\frac{1}{\sqrt{\text{cosec}^2\theta-1}}$
cot θ	$\frac{\sqrt{1-\sin^2\theta}}{\sin\theta}$	$\frac{\cos\theta}{\sqrt{1-\cos^2\theta}}$	$\frac{1}{\tan\theta}$	$\cot\theta$	$\frac{1}{\sqrt{\sec^2\theta-1}}$	$\sqrt{\text{cosec}^2\theta-1}$
sec θ	$\frac{1}{\sqrt{1-\sin^2\theta}}$	$\frac{1}{\cos\theta}$	$\sqrt{1+\tan^2\theta}$	$\frac{\sqrt{1+\cot^2\theta}}{\cot\theta}$	$\sec\theta$	$\frac{\text{cosec}\,\theta}{\sqrt{\text{cosec}^2\theta-1}}$
cosec θ	$\frac{1}{\sin\theta}$	$\frac{1}{\sqrt{1-\cos^2\theta}}$	$\frac{\sqrt{1+\tan^2\theta}}{\tan\theta}$	$\sqrt{1+\cot^2\theta}$	$\frac{\sec\theta}{\sqrt{\sec^2\theta-1}}$	$\text{cosec}\,\theta$

Sign of Trigonometric Ratios

Quadrant	sin θ	cos θ	tan θ	cot θ	sec θ	cosec θ
I	+	+	+	+	+	+
II	+	–	–	–	–	+
III	–	–	+	+	–	–
IV	–	+		–	+	–

TRIGONOMETRIC RATIOS OF ALLIED ANGLES

Two angles are said to be allied when their sum or difference is either zero or a multiple of 90°.

The angles like $-\theta$, $90° + \theta$, $180° \pm \theta$, $360° \pm \theta$ etc. are angles allied to the angle θ if θ is measured in degrees.

Trigonometric ratios of (–θ) in terms of θ:

$$\sin(-\theta) = -\sin\theta$$
$$\cos(-\theta) = \cos\theta$$
$$\tan(-\theta) = -\tan\theta$$
$$\cot(-\theta) = -\cot\theta$$
$$\sec(-\theta) = \sec\theta$$
$$\text{cosec}(-\theta) = -\text{cosec}\,\theta$$

- If θ is –ve when only cos and sec are positive as –θ lies in IV Quadrant.
- For 90° – θ all T-ratios are positive as 90° – θ lies in 1st quadrant.

Trigonometric ratios of (90° + θ) in terms of θ

$$\sin(90° + \theta) = +\cos\theta$$
$$\cos(90° + \theta) = -\sin\theta$$
$$\tan(90° + \theta) = -\cot\theta$$
$$\cot(90° + \theta) = -\tan\theta$$
$$\sec(90° + \theta) = -\text{cosec}\,\theta$$
$$\text{cosec}(90° + \theta) = +\sec\theta$$

- As (90° + θ) lies in IInd quadrant so only sin (90° + θ) and cosec (90° + θ) are positive
- sin↔cos, tan↔cot, sec↔cosec

Trigonometric ratios of (180° – θ) in terms of θ

$$\sin(180° - \theta) = +\sin\theta$$

$$\cos(180° - \theta) = -\cos\theta$$
$$\tan(180° - \theta) = -\tan\theta$$
$$\cot(180° - \theta) = -\cot\theta$$
$$\sec(180° - \theta) = -\sec\theta$$
$$\text{cosec}(180° - \theta) = +\text{cosec}\,\theta$$

- As $(180° - \theta)$ lies in IInd quadrant so only $\sin(180° + \theta)$ and cosec $(180° + \theta)$ are +ve.
- In $(180° - \theta)$ T-ratio does not changes.

Trigonometric ratios of (180° – θ) in terms of θ

$$\sin(180° + \theta) = -\sin\theta$$
$$\cos(180° + \theta) = -\cos\theta$$
$$\tan(180° + \theta) = +\tan\theta$$
$$\cot(180° + \theta) = +\cot\theta$$
$$\sec(180° + \theta) = -\sec\theta$$
$$\text{cosec}(180° + \theta) = -\text{cosec}\,\theta$$

- As $(180° + \theta)$ lies in IIIrd quadrants so only $\tan(180° + \theta)$ and $\cot(180° + \theta)$ are +ve.
- T-ratio remain same as $\sin(180° + \theta) = -\sin\theta$

Trigonometric ratios of (270° – θ) in terms of θ

$$\sin(270° - \theta) = -\cos\theta$$
$$\cos(270° - \theta) = -\sin\theta$$
$$\tan(270° - \theta) = \cot\theta$$
$$\cot(270° - \theta) = +\tan\theta$$
$$\sec(270° - \theta) = -\text{cosec}\,\theta$$
$$\text{cosec}(270° - \theta) = -\sec\theta$$

- As $(270° - \theta)$ lies in IIIrd quadrant so only $\tan(270° - \theta)$ and $\cot(270° - \theta)$ are +ve.
- sin↔cos, tan↔cot, sec↔cosec

Trigonometric ratios of (270° + θ) in terms of θ

$$\sin(270° + \theta) = -\cos\theta$$
$$\cos(270° + \theta) = +\sin\theta$$
$$\tan(270° + \theta) = -\cot\theta$$
$$\cot(270° + \theta) = -\tan\theta$$
$$\sec(270° + \theta) = +\text{cosec}\,\theta$$
$$\text{cosec}(270° + \theta) = -\sec\theta$$

- As $(270° + \theta)$ lies in IVth quadrant so only $\cos(270° + \theta)$ and $\sec(270° + \theta)$ are positive.
- sin↔cos, tan↔cot, sec↔cosec

Trigonometric ratios of (360° – θ) in terms of θ

$$\sin(360° - \theta) = -\sin\theta$$
$$\cos(360° - \theta) = +\cos\theta$$
$$\tan(360° - \theta) = -\tan\theta$$
$$\cot(360° - \theta) = -\cot\theta$$
$$\sec(360° - \theta) = +\sec\theta$$
$$\text{cosec}(360° - \theta) = -\text{cosec}\,\theta$$

- As $(360° - \theta)$ lies in IVth quadrant so only $\cos(360° - \theta)$ and $\sec(360° - \theta)$ are positive.
- T-ratio does not changes.

Trigonometric ratios of (360° + θ) in terms of θ

$$\sin(360° + \theta) = \sin\theta$$
$$\cos(360° + \theta) = \cos\theta$$
$$\tan(360° + \theta) = \tan\theta$$
$$\cot(360° + \theta) = \cot\theta$$
$$\sec(360° + \theta) = \sec\theta$$
$$\text{cosec}(360° + \theta) = \text{cosec}\,\theta$$

- As $(360° + \theta)$ lies in Ist quadrant so all are +ve.
- T-ratio does not changes.

HEIGHT & DISTANCE

Trigonometry helps us in finding heights of objects and distances between the points without actually measuring them.

Angle of Elevation: Let PQ be a tower (pillar/shell/minar/pole) etc. standing on a level ground and the observer is standing at any point R on the level ground, is viewing at P.

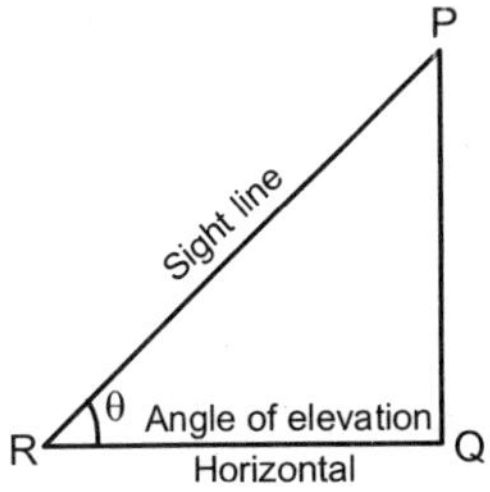

The angle, which the line RP makes with the horizontal line RQ is called angle of elevation. So, ∠PRQ is angle of elevation.

Angle of Depression: If observer is at Q and is viewing an object R on the ground, then angle between PQ and QR is the angle of depression. So, ∠PQR is angle of depression.

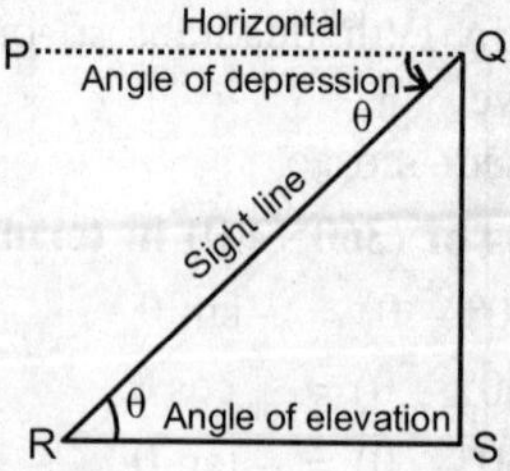

Note

- Numerically angle of elevation is equal to the angle of depression.
- The angle of elevation and the angle of depression both are measured with the horizontal.

SHORT CUT FORMULAE

1. If 'h' is height of building and the observer is x units away from base then.

   $h = x \tan \theta$ and $x = h \cot \theta$

2 If '$DC = h$' be the height of a building and θ_1 and θ_2, are elevations measured at B and A respectively along the same straight line which are x units apart then

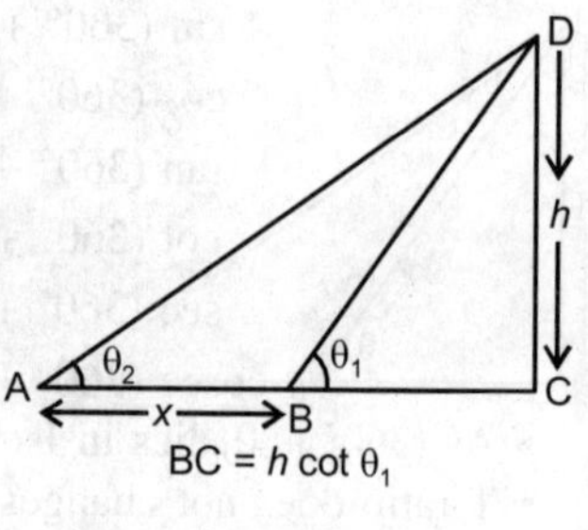

$$h = \frac{x}{\cot \theta_2 - \cot \theta_1}$$

- Here if θ_1 and θ_2 are complementary then $\theta_1 + \theta_2 = 90°$

EXERCISE

1. If $\tan A = 1$ and $\tan B = \sqrt{3}$, then $\cos A \cdot \cos B$ and $\sin A \cdot \sin B$ is equal to

(*a*) $\frac{1+\sqrt{3}}{2\sqrt{2}}$ (*b*) $\frac{1-\sqrt{3}}{2\sqrt{2}}$ (*c*) $\frac{2\sqrt{2}}{3}$ (*d*) 1

2. If $\tan \theta + \frac{1}{\tan \theta} = 2$ then the value of $\tan^2\theta + \frac{1}{\tan^2 \theta}$ is equal to

(*a*) 6 (*b*) 4 (*c*) 2 (*d*) 3

3. If $\sec \theta = \frac{13}{5}$, then $\frac{2\sin\theta - 3\cos\theta}{4\sin\theta - 9\cos\theta}$ is equal to (*a*) $\frac{1}{3}$ (*b*) –3 (*c*) 3 (*d*) 2

4. If $\sqrt{3}\ \tan 2\theta - 3 = 0$, then the angle θ is

(*a*) 30° (*b*) 60° (*c*) 90° (*d*) None of these

5. If $\tan (A - B) = \frac{1}{\sqrt{3}}$ and $\tan (A + B) = \sqrt{3}$, then the values of A and B are

(*a*) 45°, 15° (*b*) 40°, 20° (*c*) 30°, 60° (*d*) None of these

6. If $\sec \alpha = \frac{5}{4}$, then $\frac{\tan \alpha}{1 + \tan^2 \alpha}$ is equal to

(*a*) $\frac{9}{25}$ (*b*) $\frac{12}{25}$ (*c*) $\frac{3}{4}$ (*d*) $\frac{1}{25}$

7. If $3 \tan \theta = 4$, then $\sqrt{\frac{1 - \sin \theta}{1 + \sin \theta}}$ is equal to

(*a*) $\frac{1}{2}$ (*b*) $\frac{2}{3}$ (*c*) $\frac{1}{3}$ (*d*) None of these

8. If $\tan \theta = \frac{12}{13}$, then $\frac{2 \sin \theta \cos \theta}{\cos^2 \theta - \sin^2 \theta}$ is equal to

(*a*) $\frac{123}{25}$ (*b*) $\frac{312}{25}$ (*c*) $\frac{231}{25}$ (*d*) $\frac{192}{25}$

9. Given that $16 \cot \theta = 12$, then $\frac{\sin \theta + \cos \theta}{\sin \theta - \cos \theta}$ is equal to

(*a*) 7 (*b*) –7 (*c*) $\frac{1}{7}$ (*d*) $\frac{2}{7}$

10. The value of x, if $x \cot^2 45° - \sec^2 60° + \sin^2 30° = \frac{1}{8}$ is

(*a*) 31 (*b*) 32 (*c*) $\frac{31}{8}$ (*d*) None of these

11. If $\sqrt{2}\ \sin (60° - \theta) = 1$ then, the value of θ is

(*a*) 20° (*b*) 30° (*c*) 15° (*d*) None of these

12. The value of $\dfrac{\cos(90° + A)\sec(360° - A)\tan(180° - A)}{\sec(A - 720°)\sin(540° + A)\cot(A - 90°)}$ is

(*a*) 0 (*b*) 1 (*c*) ∞ (*d*) None of these

13. If 3 sec A – 2 cos B = $\sqrt{3}$ and $\angle$B = 30°, then the value of cos (A – B) is

(*a*) 1 (*b*) 2 (*c*) 3 (*d*) 0

14. ABC is a right angled triangle, right angled at C. If $\angle$A = 60° and AB = 40 unit, then the length of AC is

(*a*) 30 (*b*) 20 (*c*) 40 (*d*) None of these

15. If $\sin\theta = \dfrac{5}{13}$ then the values of tan θ and sec θ respectively are

(*a*) $\dfrac{5}{12}$ and $\dfrac{13}{12}$ (*b*) $\dfrac{5}{12}$ and $\dfrac{11}{13}$ (*c*) $\dfrac{5}{12}$ and $\dfrac{14}{19}$ (*d*) $\dfrac{11}{12}$ and $\dfrac{5}{13}$

16. A rhombus of side 10 cm has two angles of 60° each. Then, the length of diagonals are

(*a*) $10\sqrt{3}$, 10 cm (*b*) $10\sqrt{2}$, 10 cm
(*c*) 5, 10 cm (*d*) None of these

17. If $\sin\theta = -\dfrac{12}{13}$ and $\pi < \theta < \dfrac{3\pi}{2}$ then the value of sec θ is

(*a*) $\dfrac{13}{5}$ (*b*) $-\dfrac{13}{5}$ (*c*) $-\dfrac{12}{13}$ (*d*) None of these

18. In a rectangle ABCD, AB = 15 cm, $\angle$BAC = 60°, then the length of side BC is

(*a*) $15\sqrt{2}$ cm (*b*) 15 cm (*c*) $15\sqrt{5}$ cm (*d*) $15\sqrt{3}$ cm

19. The altitude AD of a ΔABC in which $\angle$A is obtuse, is 10 cm. If BD = 10 cm and CD = $10\sqrt{3}$ cm, then $\angle$A is

(*a*) 60° (*b*) 30° (3) 105° (*d*) None of these

20. The value of $\dfrac{\tan^2 60° + 4\sin^2 45° + 3\sec^2 30° + 5\cos^2 90°}{\text{cosec}\,30° + \sec 60° - \cot^2 30°}$

(*a*) 5 (*b*) 3 (*c*) 9 (*d*) 2

21. If cos 2x = cos 60° cos 30° + sin 60° sin 30°, then the value of x is

(*a*) 15° (*b*) 40° (*c*) 30° (*d*) None of these

22. If $\tan\theta + \sin\theta = m$ and $\tan\theta - \sin\theta = n$, then $m^2 - n^2$ is equal to

(*a*) $4\sqrt{mn}$ (*b*) $\sqrt{mn}$ (*c*) $2\sqrt{mn}$ (*d*) None of these

23. There is a small island in the middle of a 100 m wide river. There is a tall tree on the island. Points P and Q are points directly opposite to each other on the two banks and in line with the tree. If the angles of elevation of the top of the tree at P and Q are 30° and 45°, then the height of tree is:

(*a*) $50(\sqrt{3}-1)$ m (*b*) $50\sqrt{3}$ m

(*c*) $50(\sqrt{3}+1)$ m (*d*) $\frac{100}{\sqrt{3}-1}$ m

24. At a point P on the ground, the angle of elevation of the top of a 10 m tall building and of a helicopter hovering some distance over the top of the building are 30° and 60° respectively. Then, the height of the helicopter above the ground is

(*a*) $\frac{10}{\sqrt{3}}$ m (*b*) $10\sqrt{3}$ m (*c*) $\frac{20}{\sqrt{3}}$ m (*d*) 30 m

25. A person of height 2 m wants to get a fruit which is on a pole of height $\left(\frac{10}{3}\right)$m. If he stands at a distance of $\left(\frac{4}{\sqrt{3}}\right)$m from the foot of the pole, then the angle at which he should throw the stone, so that it hits the fruit is

(*a*) 60° (*b*) 45° (*c*) 90° (*d*) 30°

26. A straight highway leads to the foot of a 50 m tall tower. From the top of the tower the angles of depression of two cars on the highway are 30° and 60°. What is the distance between the two cars?

(*a*) $\frac{100}{\sqrt{3}}$ m (*b*) $100\sqrt{3}$ m (*c*) 86.50 m (*d*) None of these

27. From the top of a pillar of height 20 m the angles of elevation and depression of the top and bottom of another pillar are 30° and 45° respectively. The height of the second pillar (in metre) is:

(*a*) $\frac{20}{\sqrt{3}}(\sqrt{3}-1)$m (*b*) $\frac{20}{\sqrt{3}}(\sqrt{3}+1)$m

(*c*) $20\sqrt{3}$ m (*d*) $\frac{20}{\sqrt{3}}$ m

28. The angle of elevation of a cloud at a height h above the level of water in a lake is α and the angle of the depression of its image in the lake is β. Then, the height of the cloud above the surface of the lake is

(a) $h \cot \beta$ (b) $h(\cot \alpha + \cot \beta)$

(c) $h \cot \alpha$ (d) $h\left(\dfrac{\cot\alpha + \cot\beta}{\cot\alpha - \cot\beta}\right)$

29. At the foot of a mountain the elevation of its summit is 45°; after ascending 1000 m towards the mountain up a slope of 30° inclination, the elevation is found to be 60°. Find the height of the mountain:

(a) $\dfrac{\sqrt{3}+1}{2}$ km (b) $\dfrac{\sqrt{3}-1}{2}$ km (c) $\dfrac{\sqrt{3}}{2}$ km (d) $\dfrac{1}{\sqrt{3}}$ km

30. If the angles of a tower from two points distant a and b $(b > a)$ from its foot and in the same straight line from it are 60° and 30°, then the height of the tower is:

(a) $\sqrt{a-b}$ (b) $\sqrt{b-a}$ (c) $\sqrt{ab}$ (d) $\sqrt{\dfrac{a}{b}}$

31. The angles of depression of two ships from the top of the light house are 45° and 30° towards east. If the ships are 100 m apart, then the height of the light house is :

(a) $50(\sqrt{3}-1)$ m (b) $50(\sqrt{3}+1)$ m

(c) $50(\sqrt{3})$ m (d) $\dfrac{50}{\sqrt{3}-1}$ m

32. A balloon of radius r makes an angle α at the eye of an observer and the angle of elevation of its centre is β. The height of its centre from the ground level is given by:

(a) $r \sin \beta \operatorname{cosec} \dfrac{\alpha}{2}$ (b) $r \operatorname{cosec} \dfrac{\alpha}{2} \sin \alpha$

(c) $r \operatorname{cosec} \alpha \sin \beta$ (d) None of these

33. The angle of elevation 'θ' of the top of a light house at a point 'A' on the ground is such that $\tan \theta = \dfrac{5}{12}$. When the point is moved 240 m towards the light house, the angle of elevation becomes ϕ such that $\tan \phi = \dfrac{3}{4}$. Then the height of light house is :

(a) 225 m (b) 200 m (c) 215 m (d) 235 m

ANSWERS

1	2	3	4	5	6	7	8	9	10
(*b*)	(*c*)	(*c*)	(*a*)	(*a*)	(*b*)	(*c*)	(*b*)	(*a*)	(*c*)
11	**12**	**13**	**14**	**15**	**16**	**17**	**18**	**19**	**20**
(*c*)	(*b*)	(*a*)	(*b*)	(*a*)	(*a*)	(*b*)	(*d*)	(*c*)	(*c*)
21	**22**	**23**	**24**	**25**	**26**	**27**	**28**	**29**	**30**
(*a*)	(*a*)	(*a*)	(*d*)	(*d*)	(*a*)	(*b*)	(*d*)	(*a*)	(*c*)
31	**32**	**33**							
(*b*)	(*a*)	(*a*)							

SOME SELECTED EXPLANATORY ANSWERS

2. $\tan 0 + \frac{1}{\tan\theta} = 2$

Squaring on both sides,

$$\tan^2\theta + \frac{1}{\tan^2\theta} + 2\cdot\tan\theta\cdot\frac{1}{\tan\theta} = 4$$

$$\Rightarrow \tan 2\theta + \frac{1}{\tan^2\theta} = 4 - 2 = 2.$$

4. $\sqrt{3}\tan 2\theta - 3 = 0$

$\Rightarrow \sqrt{3}\tan 2\theta = 3$

$\Rightarrow \tan 2\theta = \sqrt{3} = \tan 60°$

$\Rightarrow 2\theta = 60°$

$\Rightarrow \theta = 30°$

5. $\tan(A - B) = \frac{1}{\sqrt{3}}$

$\Rightarrow \tan(A - B) = \tan 30°$

$\Rightarrow A - B = 30°$ ...(*i*)

$\tan(A + B) = \sqrt{3} = \tan 60°$

$\Rightarrow A + B = 60°$ ...(*ii*)

On solving Eqs. (*i*) and (*ii*), we get

$A = 45°$ and $B = 15°$.

6. $\therefore \sec\alpha = \dfrac{5}{4}$ $\quad\therefore \tan\alpha = \sqrt{\sec^2\alpha - 1}$

$$= \sqrt{\frac{25}{16} - 1} = \sqrt{\frac{25-16}{16}} = \sqrt{\frac{9}{16}} = \frac{3}{4}$$

Now, $\dfrac{\tan\alpha}{1+\tan^2\alpha} = \dfrac{3/4}{1+(3/4)^2} = \dfrac{3/4}{1+9/16} = \dfrac{3/4}{25/16} = \dfrac{12}{15}$.

7. $3\tan\theta = 4 \Rightarrow \tan\theta = \dfrac{4}{3}$

$$\sqrt{\frac{1-\sin\theta}{1+\sin\theta}} = \sqrt{\frac{1-\sin\theta}{1+\sin\theta} \times \frac{1-\sin\theta}{1-\sin\theta}} = \frac{1-\sin\theta}{\cos\theta} = \sec\theta - \tan\theta$$

$$= \sqrt{1+\tan^2\theta} - \tan\theta = \sqrt{1+\left(\frac{4}{3}\right)^2} - \frac{4}{3}$$

$$= \sqrt{1+\left(\frac{16}{9}\right)} - \frac{4}{3} = \frac{5}{3} - \frac{4}{3} = \frac{1}{3}$$

8. $\tan\theta = \dfrac{12}{13}$

$$\therefore \frac{2\sin\theta\cdot\cos\theta}{\cos^2\theta - \sin^2\theta} = \frac{2\tan\theta}{1-\tan^2\theta} = \frac{2\times\frac{12}{13}}{1-\frac{144}{169}} = 2\times\frac{12}{13}\times\frac{169}{25} = \frac{312}{25}.$$

9. $16\cot\theta = 12 \Rightarrow \cot\theta = \dfrac{12}{16} = \dfrac{3}{4}$

$$\therefore \frac{\sin\theta+\cos\theta}{\sin\theta-\cos\theta} = \frac{\frac{\sin\theta}{\sin\theta}+\frac{\cos\theta}{\sin\theta}}{\frac{\sin\theta}{\sin\theta}-\frac{\cos\theta}{\sin\theta}} = \frac{1+\cot\theta}{1-\cot\theta} - \frac{1+\frac{3}{4}}{1-\frac{3}{4}} = \frac{\frac{7}{4}}{\frac{1}{4}} = 7.$$

10. $x\cot^2 45° - \sec^2 60° + \sin^2 30° = \dfrac{1}{8}$

$$\Rightarrow x - (2)^2 + \left(\frac{1}{2}\right)^2 = \frac{1}{8} \Rightarrow x - 4 + \frac{1}{4} = \frac{1}{8}$$

$$\Rightarrow x = \frac{1}{8} - \frac{1}{4} + 4 \Rightarrow x = \frac{1-2+32}{8} = \frac{31}{8}.$$

11. $\sqrt{2}\sin(60^\circ - \theta) = 1$

$\Rightarrow \sin(60^\circ - \theta) = \dfrac{1}{\sqrt{2}} \Rightarrow \sin(60^\circ - \theta) = \sin 45^\circ$

$\Rightarrow 60^\circ - \theta = 45^\circ \Rightarrow \theta = 15^\circ.$

12. $\dfrac{\cos(90^\circ + A)\sec(360^\circ - A)\tan(180^\circ - A)}{\sec(A - 720^\circ)\sin(540^\circ + A)\cot(A - 90^\circ)}$

$= \dfrac{(-\sin A)\sec A[-\tan(A)]}{\sec(720^\circ - A)\sin(360^\circ + 180^\circ + A)[-\cot(90^\circ - A)]}$

$= \dfrac{\sin A \sec A \tan A}{\sec A(-\sin A)(-\tan A)} = \dfrac{\sin A \sec A \tan A}{\sin A \sec A \tan A} = 1$

14. $\dfrac{AC}{AB} = \cos 60^\circ$

$AC = AB\cos 60^\circ = 40 \times \dfrac{1}{2} = 20$ unit.

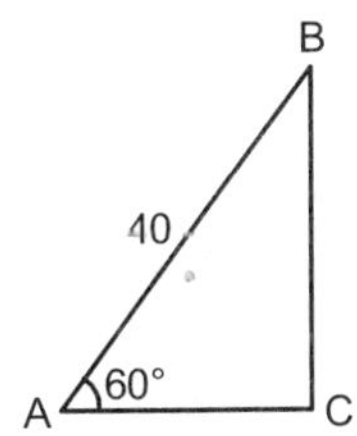

15. $\sin\theta = \dfrac{5}{13}$, $\tan\theta = \dfrac{\sin\theta}{\sqrt{1 - \sin^2\theta}}$

$= \dfrac{\frac{5}{13}}{\sqrt{1 - \frac{25}{169}}} = \dfrac{\frac{5}{13}}{\sqrt{\frac{144}{169}}} = \dfrac{5}{13} \times \dfrac{13}{12} - \dfrac{5}{12}$

and $\sec\theta = \sqrt{1 + \tan^2\theta} = \sqrt{1 + \left(\dfrac{5}{12}\right)^2} = \sqrt{\dfrac{144 + 25}{144}} = \sqrt{\dfrac{169}{144}} = \dfrac{13}{12}$

17. $\sin\theta = -\dfrac{12}{13}$ and $\pi < \theta < \dfrac{3\pi}{2}$

$\sec\theta = -\dfrac{1}{\sqrt{1 - \sin^2\theta}} = -\dfrac{1}{\sqrt{1 - \left(\dfrac{12}{13}\right)^2}} = -\dfrac{1}{\sqrt{\dfrac{25}{169}}}$

$\sec\theta = -\dfrac{13}{5}$

19. $\angle BAD = \angle ABD = 45^\circ$

$\therefore AD = BD$

In ΔADC,

$\tan\angle CAD = \dfrac{CD}{AD}$

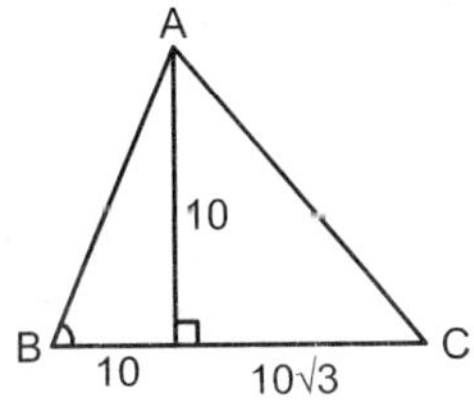

$$\tan \angle CAD = \frac{10\sqrt{3}}{10} = \sqrt{3}$$

$\tan \angle CAD = \tan 60°$
$\Rightarrow \angle CAD = 60°$
But $\angle A = \angle BAD + \angle CAD = 45° + 60° = 105°$

20. $$\frac{\tan^2 60° + 4\sin^2 45° + 3\sec^2 30° + 5\cos^2 90°}{\operatorname{cosec} 30° + \sec 60° - \cot^2 30°}$$

$$= \frac{(\sqrt{3})^2 + 4\left(\frac{1}{\sqrt{2}}\right)^2 + 3\left(\frac{2}{\sqrt{3}}\right)^2 + 5(0)}{2 + 2 - (\sqrt{3})^2} = \frac{3 + 2 + 4 + 0}{1} = 9.$$

21. $\cos 2x = \cos 60° \cos 30° + \sin 60° \sin 30°$

$$\Rightarrow \cos 2x = \frac{1}{2} \times \frac{\sqrt{3}}{2} + \frac{\sqrt{3}}{2} \times \frac{1}{2}$$

$$\Rightarrow \cos 2x = \frac{\sqrt{3}}{4} + \frac{\sqrt{3}}{4} = \frac{\sqrt{3}}{2}$$

$\Rightarrow \cos 2x = \cos 30°$
$\Rightarrow 2x = 30° \Rightarrow x = 15°.$

24. Let RQ be the height of building, then RQ = 10 m, S be the position of helicopter. Then

In ΔPQR,

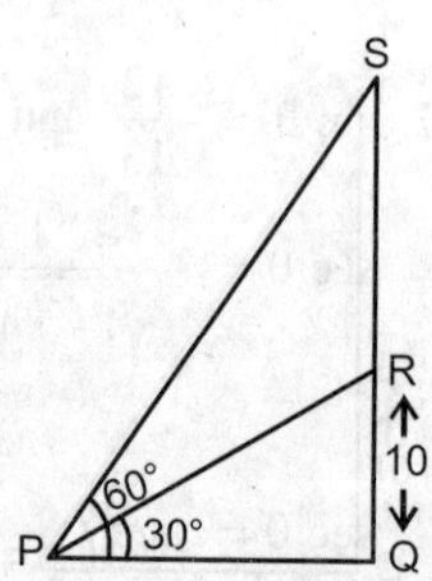

$$\frac{RQ}{PQ} = \tan 30°$$

$$\Rightarrow \quad PQ = \frac{RQ}{\tan 30°} = 10\sqrt{3}$$

$\therefore$ In ΔSPQ, $\tan 60° = \dfrac{SQ}{PQ}$

$$\Rightarrow \frac{SQ}{PQ} = \sqrt{3} \Rightarrow SQ = PQ \times \sqrt{3}$$

$$= 10\sqrt{3} \times \sqrt{3} = 30 \text{ m}$$

25. BE = CD = height of man = 2 m

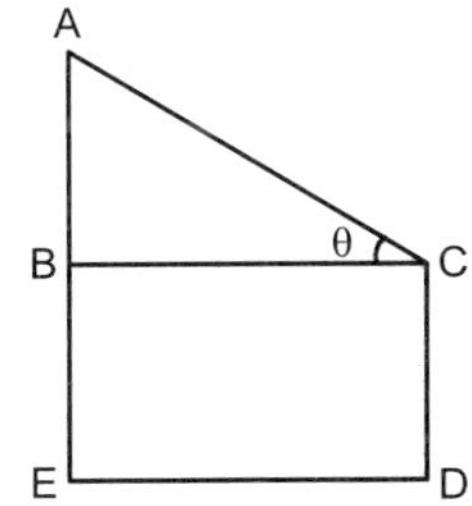

$$\tan\theta = \frac{AB}{BC} = \frac{\frac{10}{3} - 2}{\frac{4}{\sqrt{3}}} = \frac{4}{3} \times \frac{\sqrt{3}}{4} = \frac{1}{\sqrt{3}}$$

$= \tan 30° \Rightarrow \theta = 30°$

27. Let AB and CD are pillars

Let DE = h

From ΔADE, tan 30°

$$= \frac{h}{AE} = \frac{1}{\sqrt{3}}$$

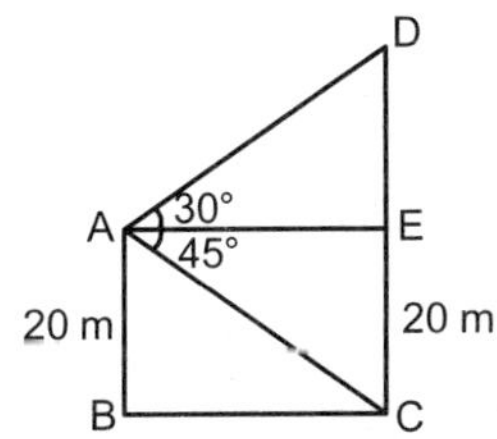

$$\Rightarrow \qquad AE = h\sqrt{3} \qquad ...(i)$$

From ΔACE, $\qquad \tan 45° = \frac{20}{AE} \Rightarrow AE = 20$

From equation (i),

$$20 = h\sqrt{3}$$

$$\Rightarrow \qquad h = \frac{20}{\sqrt{3}} \text{ m}$$

$$\therefore \qquad \text{Required height} = 20 + \frac{20}{\sqrt{3}} = \frac{20}{\sqrt{3}}(\sqrt{3}+1) \text{ m}.$$

29. Suppose P be the summit of the mountain and Q be the foot. Here BN and BM are perpendiculars from B to PQ and AQ respectively.

Here $\qquad AB = 100 \text{ m} = 1 \text{ km}$

$\angle MAB = 30°, \angle MAP = 45°,$

$\angle NBP = 60°, \angle BAP = 15°$

$\angle APB = 15°$

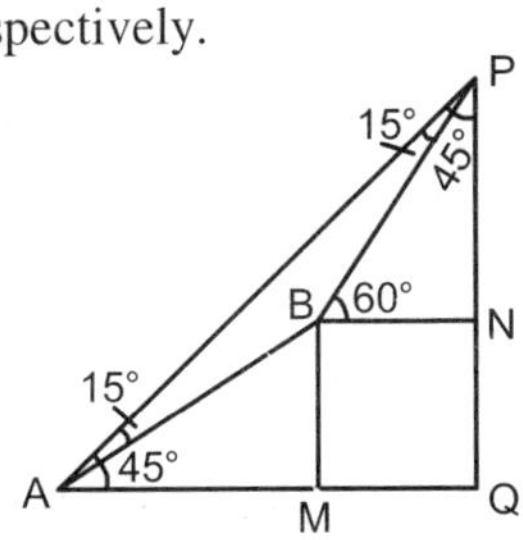

∴ ΔABP is isosceles and AP = BP

But $\qquad AB = 1 \text{ km} = PB$

In ΔPBN, $\qquad PN = BP \sin 60°$

In ΔABM, $\qquad BM = AB \sin 30°$

$$PQ = PN + NQ = PN + BM$$

$$= BP \sin 60° + AB \sin 30°$$

$$= 1\frac{\sqrt{3}}{2} + 1.\frac{1}{2} = \frac{\sqrt{3}+1}{2}$$

∴ Height of the mountain is $\frac{\sqrt{3}+1}{2}$ km.

30. Let AB be the tower such that

CB = a and BD = b

In ΔABC

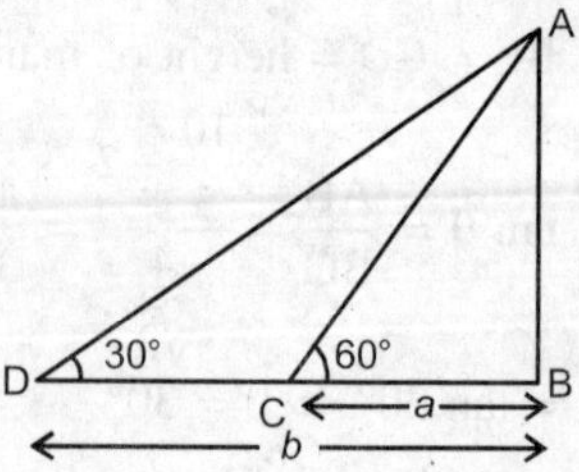

$$\tan 60° = \frac{AB}{BC} = \frac{AB}{a}$$

$$\Rightarrow \quad AB = a\sqrt{3} \qquad ...(i)$$

In ΔABD,

$$\tan 30° = \frac{AB}{BD}$$

$$\Rightarrow \quad \frac{1}{\sqrt{3}} = \frac{AB}{b} \qquad ...(ii)$$

From equations (i) and (ii)

$$(AB)^2 = ab$$

$$AB = \sqrt{ab}$$

32. Let O be the position of the man's eye and C be the centre of the balloon

In ΔCOA

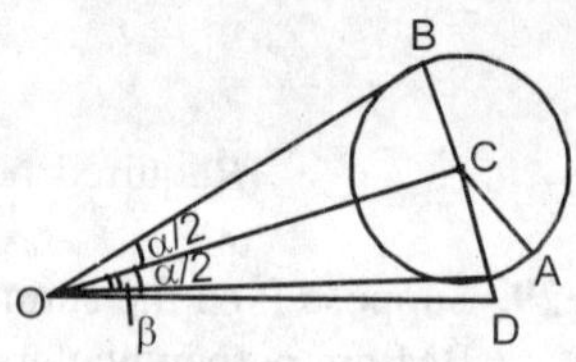

$$\angle BOC = \angle COA = \frac{\alpha}{2}$$

Here $\quad CA = BC = r$

In right angled ΔCOD

$$\sin \beta = \frac{CD}{OC}$$

$$\therefore \quad CD = OC \sin \beta \qquad ...(i)$$

In right angled ΔCOA, we have

$$\sin \beta = \frac{CA}{OC} \qquad \therefore OC = \frac{r}{\sin \frac{\alpha}{2}} = r \operatorname{cosec} \frac{\alpha}{2}$$

∴ So (i) become

$$CD = r \operatorname{cosec} \frac{\alpha}{2} \sin \beta$$

∴ Height of centre of the balloon is

$r \sin \beta \operatorname{cosec} \frac{\alpha}{2}$.

~~~~~~
~~~~~~

30. ALGEBRA

Algebraic Expression: A combination of one or more terms including letters in addition to numbers and symbols along with the signs of mathematical operations is termed as an *algebraic expression.* In an algebraic expression a letter always represents for a number. Therefore, we can add, subtract, multiply, divide and perform other mathematical operations on letters too.

For example, $x + x = 2x$; x^2 means x times x and so on.

Often we have to deal with quantities that have unknown numerical values. For instance, Ram's age is three times Mohan's age. If Mohan's age is taken as x and Ram's age as y, then x and y are unknown numbers. But we are given that the value of y is three times the value of x

$\therefore \quad y = 3x$

Some examples of algebraic expressions are

$x + 4y$, $x^2 + 4$, $x^3 + 2y^2 + 3xy$, $x^2 + y^2 + 2x(y + 5)$ etc.

When letters or numbers are written together without any sign or symbol in between them, it is automatically assumed in such cases that a multiplication sign exists between them. For instance, $4x$ means 4 times x and $8xy$ means 8 times x times y. $6xy$ together is called a term. Different terms are usually separated by an arithmetical operation symbol (+, –, × or ÷).

For example, $2x + 3xy - 4y^2$ is an algebraic expression containing three terms viz; $2x$, $3xy$ and $4y^2$ and they are combined by arithmetic signs + and – respectively.

An algebraic expression consisting of only one term is called a *monomial.*

An algebraic expression containing two terms is called a *binomial.*

In general, an algebraic expression which has more than one term is called *a polynomial.*

The letters in an algebraic expression are called *variables* or *unknowns.*

When a term consists of variables and a number expressed as their product, the number is called the *coefficient* of the variable.

For example, in the expression $5x^2 + 2xy + 6$,

5 is the coefficient of x^2 and 2 is the coefficient of xy.

Simplification of Algebraic Expressions

We must know how to identify expressions which are equal, simplify a given expression and write its equivalent expression. It is very helpful when we are solving problems which give complex algebraic expressions.

Expressions not Containing Parentheses:

(*i*) Perform divisions or multiplications before performing additions or subtractions. For example, $8x + 10x \div 2$.

First divide $10x$ by 2 which gives $5x$. then add this $5x$ to $8x$ which gives $13x$.

An alternative way of writing this expression is

$$8x + 10x \div 2 = 8x + \frac{10x}{2}$$

If we first add $8x$ and $10\,x$ ($= 18x$) and then divide the sum by 2, it gives $9x$ which is wrong.

$$\therefore \quad 8x + 10x \div 2 \neq \frac{8x + 10x}{2}$$

Similarly, $10y - 4y \times 2 = 10y - 8y = 2y$

(*ii*) The sequence in which terms are added or subtracted in an expression is immaterial as all give the same result:

$$5x + 3y - 9 + 2x = 5x + 2x + 3y - 9 = 3y + 2x - 9 + 5x$$

(*iii*) The sequence in which numbers and letters in a term are multiplied is immaterial for the result obtained in each case is the same.

$$7xy = 7yx = yx \times 7 = 7 \times x \times y$$

$$2x^2y = 2yx^2 = x^2y \times 2 = 2 \times x \times x \times y.$$

(*iv*) If terms contain roots or powers of variables or numbers, they may be simplified applying the taws of indices or exponents.

$$5xy^2(xy)^3 = 5xy^2.x^3y^3$$
$$= 5x^{(1+3)}.y^{(2+3)} = 5x^4y^5$$
$$6xy(2x^2y)^2 = 3 \times 2xy.\ 2^2.\ x^{(2\times 2)}.y^2$$
$$= 3 \times 2^{(1+2)}.\ x^{(1+4)}.\ y^{(1+2)}$$
$$= 3 \times 2^3x^5y^3 = 24x^5y^3$$

(*v*) **Combine terms which are alike or similar**

Terms are said to be similar or alike when they contain same variables raised to same powers.

In combining like terms, we simply add or subtract the coefficients of like terms and the result is the coefficient of that term in the simplified expression.

$$10x^2 - 6x^2 + 3x^2 + 9y^2 - 2y^2 + 5xy - 3xy - 7 + 14 - 4$$

In the above example, for easier understanding, we separate the groups of like terms and then perform operations as discussed above.

$$10x^2 - 6x^2 + 3x^2 = (10 - 6 + 3)x^2 = 7x^2$$
$$9y^2 - 2y^2 = (9 - 2)y^2 = 7y^2$$
$$5xy - 3xy = (5 - 3)xy = 2xy$$
$$(-7 + 14 - 4) = 3$$

So, the given expression is equal to $7x^2 + 7y^2 + 2xy + 3$

(*vi*) Algebraic expressions which involve division or contain factors can be simplified applying the laws of indices and using the methods applicable to fractions.

Note: Division by x^n is equivalent to multiplication by x^{-n}

$$6x^5 \div 3x^2 = \frac{6x^5}{3x^2} = \frac{6}{3}x^{5-2} = 2x^3$$

Factorisation of Algebraic Expressions

We have seen that the product of two or more algebraic expressions is also an algebraic expression. Therefore, the expressions whose multiplication yields the given product expression are called its factors. For instance,

$$(2a + b)(2a - b) = 4a^2 - b^2.$$

Therefore, $(2a + b)$ and $(2a - b)$ are factors of $(4a^2 - b^2)$.

Factorising algebraic expressions are very helpful in solving quadratic equations and division of algebraic expressions.

In factorisation, first of all we look for any monomial factor that appears in every term of the given expression and if there is any, we take it out as a common factor.

(*i*) $5a + 5b = 5(a + b)$

(*ii*) $4a + 3ab = a(4 + 3b)$

(*iii*) $12ab^2 + 8a^2b = 4ab\ (3b + 2a)$

In the above examples, 5, a and $4ab$ all are monomial factors.

Next we look for linear factors, quadratic factors and so on. Linear expression is one in which variables are raised only to their first power.

For example, $(a + 2)$, $5a$, $(a - b)$ etc.

Quadratic expression is one in which sum of the powers of the variables in any of its term is maximum 2.

For example, $(a^2 + 5)$, $(a^2 + 4b)$, $(5 + ab)$, $(a^2 + 2ab + 3b^2)$ etc.

Some standard formulae of algebra prove to be very helpful in factorisation and hence need to be remembered.

For example, $a^2 + 2ab + b^2 = (a + b)^2$

$$a^2 - 2ab + b^2 = (a - b)^2$$

$$a^2 - b^2 = (a + b)(a - b)$$

Thus, the difference of two squares can always be factorised as

$$\mathbf{a^2 - b^2 = (a + b)(a - b).}$$

In case an expression contains squared as well as linear terms, we adopt the following procedure:

$x^2 + bx + c$ will have factors of the form $(x + p)(x + q)$.

$$(x + p)(x + q) = x^2 + (p + q)x + pq.$$

On comparing with the given expression we can write

$p + q - b$ (coefficient of the linear term)

and $pq = c$ (numerical term) numbers

Therefore, we look for a pair of numbers p and q such that their sum is equal to b and their product is equal to c.

Quadratic Equations: If an equation contains at least one such term, the sum of powers of whose variables is maximum 2, it is termed as *Quadratic Equation.* Here we will consider only simple standard quadratic equation with one variable. The terms of such an equation contain squares of one variable and linear terms. A quadratic equation usually has two different solutions but sometimes it may have only one solution or even no real solution.

For example,

$$x^2 + 5x + 4 = 0$$

$$3x^2 + 2x + 5 = 2x^2 - 7x$$

$$x + 5 = a^2 + 1$$

are all quadratic equations.

The most common standard quadratic equation is represented by

$$ax^2 + bx + c = 0$$

Its solutions are given by

$$x = \frac{-b \pm \sqrt{b^2 - 4ac}}{2a}$$

or, $$x_1 = \frac{-b + \sqrt{b^2 - 4ac}}{2a}$$

and $$x_2 = \frac{-b - \sqrt{b^2 - 4ac}}{2a}$$

Notes: (*i*) If ($b^2 - 4ac$) *is negative,* the quadratic equation has *no real solutions* because the square roots of a negative quantity are not real numbers.

(*ii*) If $b^2 - 4ac = 0$, the two solutions of the quadratic equation are *equal* and is a *real number* equal to $\left(\frac{-b}{2a}\right)$.

(*iii*) If $b^2 - 4ac$ is a *positive number,* the quadratic equation has *two real solutions* but they are *unequal.*

SOLVED EXAMPLE

1. Simplify:

$$6x^2 - 2x^2 - 5\sqrt{x} + \sqrt{9x} + 3xy - \sqrt{4x^2y^2} + x^2.$$

Sol. $\sqrt{9x} = \sqrt{9} \cdot \sqrt{x} = 3\sqrt{x}$

$$\sqrt{4x^2y^2} = \sqrt{4}\sqrt{(xy)^2} = 2xy$$

(For simplicity, we have taken only the positive value of the square root).

The given expression can now be written as

$$6x^2 - 2x^2 + x^2 - 5\sqrt{x} + 3\sqrt{x} + 3xy - 2xy$$

or, $(6 - 2 + 1)x^2 + (-5 + 3)\sqrt{x} + (3 - 2)xy$

or, $5x^2 - 2\sqrt{x} + xy$.

2. Find $(a + 2b)(3a + 4)(2b + 6) = ?$

Sol. $(a + 2b)(3a + 4)(2b + 6)$

$= [a(3a + 4) + 2b(3a + 4)](2b + 6)$

$= [3a^2 + 4a + 6ab + 8b](2b + 6)$

$= 2b(3a^2 + 4a + 6ab + 8b) + 6\,(3a^2 + 4a + 6ab + 8b)$

$= 6a^2b + 8ab + 12ab^2 + 16b^2 + 18a^2 + 24a + 36ab + 48b$

Combining the like terms

$= 18a^2 + 16b^2 + 6a^2b + 12ab^2 + 44ab + 24a + 48b.$

3. Find the factors of the expression $x^2 + 7x + 12$.

Sol. Given expression is $x^2 + 7x + 12$

$$p + q = 7$$

$$pq = 12$$

Possible combinations of 12 are (1, 12), (2, 6) and (3, 4). Out of these only (3, 4) satisfy the condition $p + q = 7$.

$\therefore \quad x^2 + 7x + 12 = (x + 3)(x + 4).$

4. Factorise : $x^2 - 15x + 36$.

Sol. Let the factors of $x^2 - 15x + 36$ be $(x + p)$ and $(x + q)$.

$$(x + p)(x + q) = x^2 + (p + q)\,x + pq$$

One comparing we get,

$$p + q = -15$$
$$pq = 36$$

The combination of (p, q) which satisfy the above two conditions simultaneously is $(-12, -3)$.

$$x^2 - 15x + 36 = (x - 12)(x - 3).$$

5. Solve: $2x^2 + 9x = -4$.

Sol.
$$2x^2 + 9x = -4$$
$$2x^2 + 9x + 4 = 0$$
$$2x^2 + x + 8x + 4 = 0$$
$$x(2x + 1) + 4(2x + 1) = 0$$
$$(2x + 1)(x + 4) = 0$$

Then, $2x + 1 = 0$ or $x + 4 = 0$

$\therefore \quad x = -\frac{1}{2}$ or $x = -4$.

6. Solve: $2x^2 + 4x + 5 = 0$ for x.

Sol. Given : $2x^2 + 4x + 5 = 0$

The factors are not easily visible in this equation. So, we use the quadratic formula.

Here,
$$a = 2,\ b = 4,\ c = 5$$
$$b^2 - 4ac = 4^2 - 4 \times 2 \times 5 = 16 - 40 = -24$$

Since $(b^2 - 4ac)$ is negative, its square root can't be a real number. Hence, the equation does not have any real solution.

7. $2x + 3y = 18$ and $2x - y = 2$, then $x + y = ?$

Sol.
$$2x + 3y = 18 \qquad ...(i)$$
$$2x - y = 2$$
$$\Rightarrow \quad 7y = 2x - 2 \qquad ...(ii)$$

Putting the value of y in (i)

$$2x + 3(2x - 2) = 18$$

$$2x + 6x - 6 = 18$$
$$8x = 24$$
$$x = 3 \quad \text{then} \quad y = 4$$
$$\therefore \quad x + y = 7.$$

8. If $3y + 2x = 47$ and $11x = 7y$ then what is the value of $y - x$?

Sol. Given $\quad 3y + 2x = 47 \quad$ ...(*i*)

$$7y - 11x = 0 \quad \text{...(ii)}$$

From equation (*ii*), $x = \frac{7}{11}y$

$\therefore$ Equation (*i*) reduces to

$$3y + 2 \times \frac{7}{11}y = 47$$

or, $\quad \frac{33y + 14y}{11} = 47 \quad$ or, $y = \frac{11 \times 47}{47} = 11$

From equation (*ii*), $x = \frac{7 \times 11}{11} = 7$

$\therefore$ Required difference $= y - x = 11 - 7 = 4.$

9. If $\frac{2a + b}{a + 4b} = 3$, then find the value of $\frac{a + b}{a + 2b}$.

Sol. $\frac{2a + b}{a + 4b} = 3$ (Given)

or, $2a + b = 3a + 12b$

or, $3a - 2a = b - 12b$

or, $a = -11b$

Then, $\frac{a + b}{a + 2b} = \frac{-11b + b}{-11b + 2b} = \frac{-10b}{-9b} = \frac{10}{9}$.

10. Find values of x and y for equations $x + 3y = 15$ and $5x - 2y = 7$.

Sol. $x + 3y = 15$

$\therefore \quad x = 15 - 3y$

Put this value of x in the second equation $5x - 2y = 7$

$$5(15 - 3y) \quad 2y - 7$$
$$75 - 15y - 2y = 7$$
$$75 - 17y = 7 \Rightarrow 17y = 68$$

$$y = 4$$
$$x = 15 - 3y \Rightarrow x = 15 - 3 \times 4$$
$$x = 15 - 12 \Rightarrow x = 3$$

The values of x and y are 3 and 4 respectively.

11. If $\sqrt{1 + \frac{x}{144}} = \frac{13}{12}$ then x equals to:

Sol. $\sqrt{1 + \frac{x}{144}} = \frac{13}{12}$; $1 + \frac{x}{144} = \left(\frac{13}{12}\right)^2$

$$1 + \frac{x}{144} = \frac{169}{144}; \quad \frac{x}{144} = \frac{169}{144} - 1$$

$$\frac{x}{144} = \frac{169 - 144}{144}; \quad \frac{x}{144} = \frac{25}{144}$$

$x = 25.$

12. If $\sqrt{b} = 4a$, then $\frac{a^2}{b} = ?$

Sol. $\sqrt{b} = 4a \Rightarrow b = (4a)^2 \Rightarrow b = 16a^2$

$$\frac{a^2}{b} = \frac{1}{16}.$$

13. If $\frac{x^2 - 1}{x + 1} = 4$, $x = ?$

Sol. $\frac{x^2 - 1}{x + 1} = 4$

or, $\frac{(x + 1)(x - 1)}{x + 1} = 4$

or, $x - 1 = 4$

or, $x = 5.$

EXERCISE

1. If $x + \frac{1}{2x} = 2$, find the value of $8x^3 + \frac{1}{x^3}$.

(*a*) 48 (*b*) 88 (*c*) 40 (*d*) 44

2. If $x = 2 - 2^{1/3} + 2^{2/3}$, then the value of $x^3 - 6x^2 + 18x + 18$ is

(*a*) 22 (*b*) 33 (*c*) 40 (*d*) 45

3. If $x + \frac{1}{x} = 2$ and x is real, then the value of $x^{17} + \frac{1}{x^{19}}$ is

(*a*) 1 (*b*) 0 (*c*) 2 (*d*) –2

4. If $x^2 + y^2 - 4x - 4y + 8 = 0$, then the value of $x - y$ is

(*a*) 4 (*b*) –4 (*c*) 0 (*d*) 8

5. If $a^3 - b^3 - c^3$ $3abc = 0$, the n

(*a*) $a = b = c$ (*b*) $a + b + c = 0$ (*c*) $a + c = b$ (*d*) $a = b + c$

6. If $2x + \frac{1}{3x} = 5$, find the value of $\frac{5x}{6x^2 + 20x + 1}$.

(*a*) $\frac{1}{4}$ (*b*) $\frac{1}{6}$ (*c*) $\frac{1}{5}$ (*d*) $\frac{1}{7}$

7. If for two real constants a and b, the expression $ax^3 + 3x^2 - 8x + b$ is exactly divisible by $(x + 2)$ and $(x - 2)$, then

(*a*) $a = 2, b = 12$ (*b*) $a = 12, b = 2$

(*c*) $a = 2, b = -12$ (*d*) $a = -2, b = 12$

8. If $x^2 - 3x + 1 = 0$, then the value of $x^3 + \frac{1}{x^3}$ is

(*a*) 9 (*b*) 18 (*c*) 27 (*d*) 1

9. If $x^2 + y^2 + 2x + 1 = 0$, then the value of $x^{31} + y^{35}$ is

(*a*) –1 (*b*) 0 (*c*) 1 (*d*) 2

10. The lines $2x + y = 5$ and $x + 2y = 4$ intersect at the point:

(*a*) (1, 2) (*b*) (2, 1) (*c*) $\left(\frac{5}{2}, 0\right)$ (*d*) (0, 2)

11. The value of the expression $x^4 - 17x^3 + 17x^2 - 17x + 17$ at $x = 16$ is

(*a*) 0 (*b*) 1 (*c*) 2 (*d*) 3

12. If $x - \frac{1}{x} = 5$, then $x^2 + \frac{1}{x^2}$ is:

(*a*) 5 (*b*) 25 (*c*) 27 (*d*) 23

13. If $(2^x)(2^y) = 8$ and $(9^x)(3^y) = 81$, then (x, y) is:

(*a*) (1, 2) (*b*) (2, 1) (*c*) (1, 1) (*d*) (2, 2)

14. If $x = 3 + 2\sqrt{2}$, then the value of $\left(\sqrt{x} - \frac{1}{\sqrt{x}}\right)$ is :

(*a*) 1 (*b*) 2 (*c*) $2\sqrt{2}$ (*d*) $3\sqrt{3}$

15. If $a = 23$ and $b = -29$ then the value of $25a^2 + 40ab + 16b^2$ is:

(*a*) 1 (*b*) –1 (*c*) 0 (*d*) 2

16. If $\frac{a}{3} = \frac{b}{2}$, then value of $\frac{2a + 3b}{3a - 2b}$ is

(*a*) $\frac{12}{5}$ (*b*) $\frac{5}{12}$ (*c*) 1 (*d*) $\frac{12}{7}$

17. The average of x numbers is y and average of y numbers is x. Then the average of all the numbers taken together is

(*a*) $\frac{x + y}{2xy}$ (*b*) $\frac{2xy}{x + y}$ (*c*) $\frac{x^2 + y^2}{x + y}$ (*d*) $\frac{xy}{x + y}$

18. If $x + \frac{1}{4x} = \frac{3}{2}$, find the value of $8x^3 + \frac{1}{8x^3}$.

(*a*) 18 (*b*) 36 (*c*) 24 (*d*) 16

19. If $x = \frac{4ab}{a + b}$ $(a \neq b)$, the value of $\frac{x + 2a}{x - 2a} + \frac{x + 2b}{x - 2b}$ is

(*a*) a (*b*) b (*c*) $2ab$ (*d*) 2

20. If $x = b + c - 2a$, $y = c + a - 2b$, $z = a + b - 2c$, then the value of $x^2 + y^2 - z^2 + 2xy$ is

(*a*) 0 (*b*) $a + b + c$ (*c*) $a - b + c$ (*d*) $a + b - c$

21. If $(a - 1)^2 + (b + 2)^2 + (c + 1)^2 = 0$, then the value of $2a - 3b + 7c$ is

(*a*) 12 (*b*) 3 (*c*) –11 (*d*) 1

22. $(y - z)^3 + (z - x)^3 + (x - y)^3$ is equal to

(*a*) $3(y - z)(z + x)(y - x)$ (*b*) $(x - y)(y + z)(x - z)$

(*c*) $3(y - z)(z - x)(x - y)$ (*d*) $(y - z)(z - x)(x - y)$

23. If the sum of $\frac{a}{b}$ and its reciprocal is 1 and $a \neq 0$, $b \neq 0$, then the value of $a^3 + b^3$ is

(*a*) 2 (*b*) –1 (*c*) 0 (*d*) 1

24. If $x^2 + y^2 + \frac{1}{x^2} + \frac{1}{y^2} = 4$, then the value of $x^2 + y^2$ is

(*a*) 2 (*b*) 4 (*c*) 8 (*d*) 16

25. If $x^2 = y + z$, $y^2 = z + x$, $z^2 = x + y$, then the value of $\frac{1}{x+1} + \frac{1}{y+1} + \frac{1}{z+1}$ is

(*a*) –1 (*b*) 1 (*c*) 2 (*d*) 4

26. If $x + \frac{1}{x} = \sqrt{3}$ then the value of $x^{18} + x^{12} + x^6 + 1$ is

(*a*) 0 (*b*) 1 (*c*) 2 (*d*) 3

27. If $a^2 + b^2 = 2$ and $c^2 + d^2 = 1$, then the value of $(ad - bc)^2 + (ac + bd)^2$ is

(*a*) $\frac{4}{9}$ (*b*) $\frac{1}{2}$ (*c*) 1 (*d*) 2

28. If $\frac{5x-3}{x} + \frac{5y-3}{y} + \frac{5z-3}{z} = 0$, value of $\frac{1}{x} + \frac{1}{y} + \frac{1}{z}$ is

(*a*) 5 (*b*) 10 (*c*) 15 (*d*) 3

29. If $x^4 + \frac{1}{x^4} = 119$ and $x > 1$, then the value of $x^3 - \frac{1}{x^3}$ is

(*a*) 54 (*b*) 18 (*c*) 72 (*d*) 36

30. If $x - y = \frac{x+y}{7} = \frac{xy}{4}$, the numerical value of xy is

(*a*) $\frac{4}{3}$ (*b*) $\frac{3}{4}$ (*c*) $\frac{1}{4}$ (*d*) $\frac{1}{3}$

31. If $(x + y - z)^2 + (y + z - x)^2 + (z + x - y)^2 = 0$, then the value of $x + y - z$ is

(*a*) $\sqrt{3}$ (*b*) $3\sqrt{3}$ (*c*) 3 (*d*) 0

32. If $x + y + z = 0$, then $\frac{x^2}{yz} + \frac{y^2}{zx} + \frac{z^2}{xy} = ?$

(*a*) $(xyz)^2$ (*b*) $x^2 + y^2 + z^2$ (*c*) 9 (*d*) 3

33. If $x^2 + 2 = 2x$, then the value of $x^4 - x^3 + x^2 + 2$ is

(*a*) 0 (*b*) 1 (*c*) –1 (*d*) $\sqrt{2}$

34. If $2^x = 3^y = 6^{-z}$ then $\left(\frac{1}{x}+\frac{1}{y}+\frac{1}{z}\right)$ is equal to

(a) 0 (b) 1 (c) $\frac{3}{2}$ (d) $-\frac{1}{2}$

35. If $\frac{1}{x+y} = \frac{1}{x} + \frac{1}{y} (x \neq 0, \ y \neq 0, x \neq y)$ then, the value of $x^3 - y^3$ is

(a) 0 (b) 1 (c) −1 (d) 2

36. For real a, b, c if $a^2 + b^2 + c^2 = ab + bc + ca$, then value of $\frac{a+c}{b}$ is

(a) 1 (b) 2 (c) 3 (d) 0

37. If $x = a(b - c)$, $y = b(c - a)$ and $z = c(a - b)$, then $\left(\frac{x}{a}\right)^3 + \left(\frac{y}{b}\right)^3 + \left(\frac{z}{c}\right)^3 =$

(a) $\frac{xyz}{3abc}$ (b) $3\ xyzabc$ (c) $\frac{3xyz}{abc}$ (d) $\frac{xyz}{abc}$

38. Minimum value of $x^2 + \frac{1}{x^2+1} - 3$ is :

(a) 0 (b) −1 (c) −3 (d) −2

39. If $3x + \frac{1}{2x} = 5$, then the value of $8x^3 + \frac{1}{27x^3}$ is :

(a) $118\frac{1}{2}$ (b) $30\frac{10}{27}$ (c) 0 (d) 1

40. If the average of x and $\frac{1}{x}$ $(x \neq 0)$ is M, then the average of x^2 and $\frac{1}{x^2}$ is:

(a) $1 - M^2$ (b) $1 - 2M$ (c) $2M^2 - 1$ (d) $2M^2 + 1$

41. If a, b, c are real and $a^2 + b^2 + c^2 = 2(a - b - c) - 3$, then the value of $2a - 3b + 4c$ is:

(a) −1 (b) 0 (c) 1 (d) 2

42. If $(a - 3)^2 + (b - 4)^2 + (c - 9)^2 = 0$, then the value of $\sqrt{a+b+c}$ is:

(a) −4 (b) 4 (c) ±4 (d) ±2

43. If $x + y = z$, then the expression $x^3 + y^3 - z^3 + 3xyz$ will be equal to:

(a) 0 (b) $3xyz$ (c) $-3xyz$ (d) z^3

44. If the square root of x is the cube root of y, then the relation between x and y is:

(*a*) $x^3 = y^2$ (*b*) $x^2 = y^3$ (*c*) $x = y$ (*d*) $x^6 = y^5$

45. If $2^{x+3} = 32$, then the value of 3^{x+1} is equal to

(*a*) 27 (*b*) 81 (*c*) 72 (*d*) 9

46. If $x + \frac{1}{x} = 2, x \neq 0$ then value of $x^2 + \frac{1}{x^3}$ is equal to

(*a*) 1 (*b*) 2 (*c*) 3 (*d*) 4

47. If $\frac{a}{b} + \frac{b}{a} = 1, a \neq 0, b \neq 0$ the value of $a^3 + b^3$ is

(*a*) 0 (*b*) 1 (*c*) –1 (*d*) 2

48. If $a^2 + b^2 + c^2 + 3 = 2(a + b + c)$ then the value of $(a + b + c)$ is

(*a*) 2 (*b*) 3 (*c*) 4 (*d*) 5

49. The line passing through the points (–2, 8) and (5, 7)

(*a*) cuts y-axis only (*b*) cuts both the axes

(*c*) does not cut any axes (*d*) cut x-axis only

50. If x varies inversely as $(y^2 - 1)$ and is equal to 24 when $y = 10$, then the value of x when $y = 5$ is

(*a*) 99 (*b*) 12 (*c*) 24 (*d*) 100

51. If $m + \frac{1}{m-2} = 4$, find the value of $(m-2)^2 + \frac{1}{(m-2)^2}$.

(*a*) –2 (*b*) 0 (*c*) 2 (*d*) 4

52. If $a^2 = b + c$, $b^2 = c + a$ and $c^2 = a + b$, then the value of

$\frac{1}{1+a} + \frac{1}{1+b} + \frac{1}{1+c}$ is

(*a*) abc (*b*) $a^2b^2c^2$ (*c*) 1 (*d*) 0

53. The equation of this graph is

(*a*) $y = x$ (*b*) $y = 3x$

(*c*) $y = -x$ (*d*) $y = -3x$

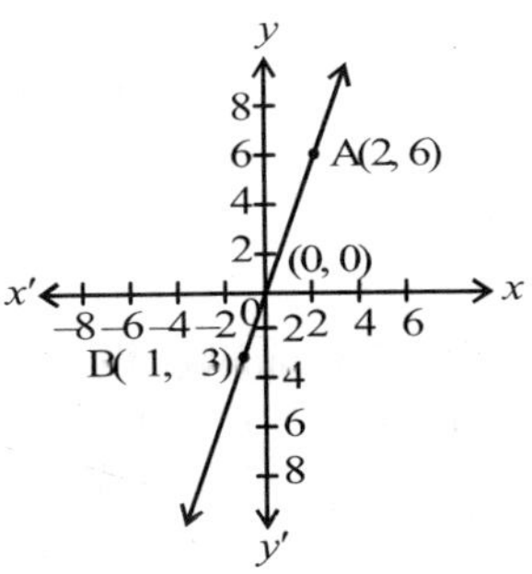

54. If $a^2 + b^2 + 2b + 4a + 5 = 0$, then the value of $\frac{a-b}{a+b}$ is:

(a) 3 (b) –3 (c) $\frac{1}{3}$ (d) $-\frac{1}{3}$

55. If $a = 2.361$, $b = 3.263$ and $c = 5.624$, then the value of $a^3 + b^3 - c^3 + 3abc$ is

(a) 35.621 (b) 0 (c) 19.277 (d) 1

56. If $x + y = a$ and $xy = b^2$, then the value of $x^3 - x^2y - xy^2 + y^3$ in terms of a and b is:

(a) $(a^2 + 4b^2)a$ (b) $a^3 - 3b^2$ (c) $a^3 - 4b^2a$ (d) $a^3 + 3b^2$

57. If $(3a + 1)^2 + (b - 1)^2 + (2c - 3)^2 = 0$, then the value of $(3a + b + 2c)$ is equal to:

(a) 3 (b) –1 (c) 2 (d) 5

58. If $xy(x + y) = 1$, then the value of $\frac{1}{x^3y^3} - x^3 - y^3$ is:

(a) 0 (b) 1 (c) 3 (d) –2

59. If $\frac{x}{2x^2 + 5x + 2} = \frac{1}{6}$, value of $\left(x + \frac{1}{x}\right)$ is:

(a) 2 (b) $\frac{1}{2}$ (c) $-\frac{1}{2}$ (d) –2

60. The shaded region represents

(a) $y \geq x$ (b) $y \leq -x$
(c) $y \leq x$ (d) $y \geq -x$

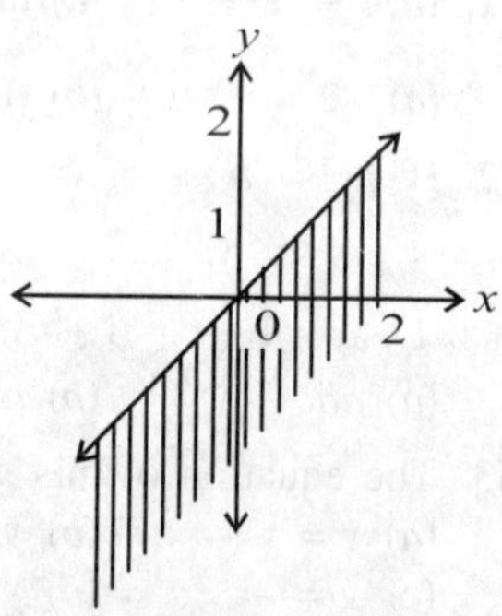

61. If $\frac{2x - y}{x + 2y} = \frac{1}{2}$, then value of $\frac{3x - y}{3x + y}$ is:

(a) $\frac{1}{5}$ (b) $\frac{3}{5}$ (c) $\frac{4}{5}$ (d) 1

62. In a two digit number the digit in the unit's place is more than twice the digit in ten's place by 1. If the digits in the unit's place and the ten's place are interchanged, the difference between the newly formed number and the original number is less than the original number by 1. what is the original number?

(*a*) 52 (*b*) 73 (*c*) 25 (*d*) 37

63. One fifth of a number is equal to $\frac{5}{8}$th of another number. If 35 is added to the first number it becomes four times of the second number. Find the second number.

(*a*) 125 (*b*) 70 (*c*) 40 (*d*) 25

64. For which of the following values of x the inequality $x^2 - 3x + 2 > 2x - 4$ gets satisfied?

(*a*) $2 < x < 3$ (*b*) $x > 3$ or $x < 2$ (*c*) $x \geq 3$ (*d*) $x \leq 2$

65. The sum of four numbers is 64. If you add 3 to the first number, 3 is subtracted from the second number, the third is multiplied by 3 and the fourth is divided by 3, then all the results are equal. What is the difference between the largest and the smallest of the original numbers?

(*a*) 32 (*b*) 27 (*c*) 21 (*d*) None of these

66. If $2x + 3y = 34$ and $\frac{x+y}{y} = \frac{13}{8}$, then $5y + 7x = ?$

(*a*) 82 (*b*) 75 (*c*) 178 (*d*) 185

67. Out of three numbers, the first is twice the second and is half of the third. If the average of the three numbers is 56, then difference of first and third numbers is

(*a*) 12 (*b*) 20 (*c*) 24 (*d*) 48

68. If $2x + 3y + z = 55$; $x + z - y = 4$ and $y - x + z = 12$, then what is the value of y?

(*a*) 7 (*b*) 8 (*c*) 12 (*d*) None of these

ANSWERS

1	2	3	4	5	6	7	8	9	10
(*c*)	(*c*)	(*c*)	(*c*)	(*d*)	(*d*)	(*c*)	(*b*)	(*a*)	(*b*)
11	**12**	**13**	**14**	**15**	**16**	**17**	**18**	**19**	**20**
(*b*)	(*c*)	(*a*)	(*b*)	(*a*)	(*a*)	(*b*)	(*a*)	(*d*)	(*a*)
21	**22**	**23**	**24**	**25**	**26**	**27**	**28**	**29**	**30**
(*d*)	(*c*)	(*c*)	(*a*)	(*b*)	(*a*)	(*d*)	(*a*)	(*d*)	(*a*)
31	**32**	**33**	**34**	**35**	**36**	**37**	**38**	**39**	**40**
(*d*)	(*d*)	(*a*)	(*a*)	(*a*)	(*b*)	(*c*)	(*d*)	(*b*)	(*c*)

41	42	43	44	45	46	47	48	49	50
(c)	(c)	(a)	(a)	(a)	(b)	(a)	(b)	(b)	(a)
51	**52**	**53**	**54**	**55**	**56**	**57**	**58**	**59**	**60**
(c)	(c)	(b)	(c)	(b)	(c)	(a)	(c)	(b)	(c)
61	**62**	**63**	**64**	**65**	**66**	**67**	**68**		
(b)	(d)	(c)	(b)	(a)	(b)	(d)	(d)		

SOME SELECTED EXPLANATORY ANSWERS

1. $x + \frac{1}{2x} = 2 \Rightarrow 2x + \frac{2}{2x} = 4 \Rightarrow 2x + \frac{1}{x} = 4$

On cubing

$$8x^3 + \frac{1}{x^3} + 3.2x.\frac{1}{x}\left(2x + \frac{1}{x}\right) = 64$$

$$\Rightarrow 8x^3 + \frac{1}{x^3} + 6 \times 4 = 64$$

$$\Rightarrow 8x^3 + \frac{1}{x^3} = 64 - 24 = 40.$$

3. $x + \frac{1}{x} = 2 \Rightarrow x^2 - 2x + 1 = 0 \Rightarrow (x-1)^2 = 0 \Rightarrow x = 1$

$$\therefore \; x^{17} + \frac{1}{x^{19}} = 1 + 1 = 2.$$

4. $x^2 + y^2 - 4x - 4y + 8 = 0$

$\Rightarrow x^2 - 4x + 4 + y^2 - 4y + 4 = 0$

$\Rightarrow (x-2)^2 + (y-2)^2 = 0 \Rightarrow x = 2$ and $y = 2$

$\therefore x - y = 2 - 2 = 0.$

5. $a^3 + b^3 + c^3 - 3abc = 0$, if $a + b + c = 0$

$\therefore a^3 - b^3 - c^3 - 3\,abc = 0$

$\Rightarrow a - b - c = 0 \Rightarrow a = b + c.$

7. $P(x) = ax^3 + 3x^2 - 8x + b$

$\therefore P(-2) = -8a + 12 + 16 + b = 0$

$\Rightarrow \quad -8a + b + 28 = 0 \quad ...(i)$

$\Rightarrow \quad P(2) = 8a + 12 - 16 + b = 2$

$\Rightarrow \quad 8a + b - 4 = 0$ ...(ii)

By equations (i) + (ii)

$$2b + 24 = 0$$

$$\Rightarrow \quad b = -\frac{24}{2} = -12$$

From equation (i),

$$-8a - 12 + 28 = 0$$

$$\Rightarrow \quad -8a = -16$$

$$\Rightarrow \quad a = 2.$$

8. $x^2 - 3x + 1 = 0$

$$\Rightarrow \quad x^2 + 1 = 3x$$

$$\Rightarrow \quad x + \frac{1}{x} = 3$$

$$\therefore \quad x^3 + \frac{1}{x^3} = \left(x + \frac{1}{x}\right)^3 - 3x \cdot \frac{1}{x}\left(x + \frac{1}{x}\right)$$

$$= 27 - 3 \times 3 = 18$$

9. $x^2 + y^2 + 2x + 1 = 0$

$$\Rightarrow \quad x^2 + 2x + 1 + y^2 = 0$$

$$\Rightarrow \quad (x + 1)^2 + y^2 = 0$$

$\Rightarrow x + 1 = 0 \Rightarrow x = -1$ and $y = 0$

$\therefore \quad x^{31} + y^{35} = -1.$

11. $x^4 - 17x^3 + 17x^2 - 17x + 17 = x^4 - 16x^3 + 16x^2 - 16x - x^3 + x^2 - x + 17$

When $x = 16$,

Expression $= 16^4 - 16^4 + 16^3 - 16^2 - 16^3 + 16^2 - 16 + 17 = 1.$

12. $x - \frac{1}{x} = 5$

On squaring both sides,

$$x^2 + \frac{1}{x^2} - 2 = 25 \Rightarrow x^2 + \frac{1}{x^2} = 27.$$

13. $2^x . 2^y = 8 \Rightarrow 2^{x+y} = 2^3$

$\Rightarrow \quad x + y = 3$ ...(i)

$$9^x . 3^y = 3^4$$

$$\Rightarrow \quad 3^{2x} . 3^y = 3^4$$

$\Rightarrow \quad 2x + y = 4$ ...(*ii*)

By equations (*ii*) – (*i*), $x = 1$

From equation (*i*), $1 + y = 3$

$\Rightarrow \quad y = 2.$

14. $x = 3 + 2\sqrt{2}$

$$\therefore \quad \frac{1}{x} = \frac{1}{3+2\sqrt{2}} = \frac{1}{3+2\sqrt{2}} \times \frac{3-2\sqrt{2}}{3-2\sqrt{2}}$$

$$= \frac{3-2\sqrt{2}}{9-8} = 3 - 2\sqrt{2}$$

$$\therefore \quad \left(\sqrt{x} - \frac{1}{\sqrt{x}}\right)^2 = x + \frac{1}{x} - 2$$

$$= 3 + 2\sqrt{2} + 3 - 2\sqrt{2} - 2 = 4$$

$$\therefore \quad \sqrt{x} - \frac{1}{\sqrt{x}} = 2.$$

15. $25a^2 + 40ab + 16b^2$

$$= (5a + 4b)^2 = (5 \times 23 - 29 \times 4)^2$$

$$= (115 - 116)^2 = 1$$

16. $\frac{a}{3} = \frac{b}{2} \Rightarrow \frac{a}{b} = \frac{3}{2}$

$$\therefore \quad \frac{2a + 3b}{3a - 2b} = \frac{2 \times \frac{a}{b} + 3}{3 \times \frac{a}{b} - 2}$$

$$= \frac{2 \times \frac{3}{2} + 3}{3 \times \frac{3}{2} - 2} = \frac{6}{\frac{9-4}{2}} = \frac{12}{5}.$$

17. Sum of x numbers = xy

Sum of y numbers = xy

$$\therefore \text{ Required average} = \frac{xy + xy}{x + y} = \frac{2xy}{x + y}.$$

18. $x + \frac{1}{4x} = \frac{3}{2} \Rightarrow 2x + \frac{1}{2x} = 3$

Cubing both sides, $8x^3 + \dfrac{1}{8x^3} + 3 \times 2x \times \dfrac{1}{2x}$

$$\left(2x + \frac{1}{2x}\right) = 27$$

$$\Rightarrow \quad 8x^3 + \frac{1}{8x^3} + 3 \times 3 = 27$$

$$\Rightarrow \quad 8x^3 + \frac{1}{8x^3} = 27 - 9 = 18.$$

19. $x = \dfrac{4ab}{a+b} \Rightarrow \dfrac{x}{2a} = \dfrac{2b}{a+b}$

By componendo and dividendo,

$$\frac{x+2a}{x-2a} - \frac{2b+a+b}{2b-a-b} = \frac{3b+a}{b-a}$$

Again,
$$\frac{x}{2b} = \frac{2a}{a+b}$$

$$\Rightarrow \quad \frac{x+2b}{x-2b} = \frac{2a+a+b}{2a-a-b} = \frac{3a+b}{a-b}$$

$$\therefore \quad \frac{x+2a}{x-2a} + \frac{x+2b}{x-2b} = \frac{3b+a}{b-a} + \frac{3a+b}{a-b}$$

$$= \frac{3b+a-3a-b}{b-a} = \frac{2b-2a}{b-a} = \frac{2(b-a)}{b-a} = 2.$$

20.
$$x^2 + y^2 - z^2 + 2xy = x^2 + y^2 + 2xy - z^2$$
$$= (x+y)^2 - z^2 = (x+y+z)(x+y-z)$$
$$= (b + c - 2a + c + a - 2b + a + b - 2c)(x + y - z)$$
$$= 0.$$

24. $x^2 + y^2 + \dfrac{1}{x^2} + \dfrac{1}{y^2} - 4 = 0$

$$\Rightarrow \quad x^2 + \frac{1}{x^2} - 2 + y^2 + \frac{1}{y^2} - 2 = 0$$

$$\Rightarrow \quad \left(x - \frac{1}{x}\right)^2 + \left(y - \frac{1}{y}\right)^2 = 0$$

$$\Rightarrow x - \frac{1}{x} = 0 \Rightarrow x^2 - 1 = 0 \Rightarrow x = 1$$

Similarly, $y = 1$

$\therefore \quad x^2 + y^2 = 1 + 1 = 2.$

25. $x^2 = y + z$

$\Rightarrow \quad x^2 + x = x + y + z$

$\Rightarrow \quad x(x + 1) = x + y + z \quad$ ...(*i*)

Similarly, $y(y + 1) = x + y + z \quad$ ...(*ii*)

and, $z(z + 1) = x + y + z \quad$ ...(*iii*)

$$\therefore \quad \frac{1}{x+1} + \frac{1}{y+1} + \frac{1}{z+1} = \frac{x}{x+y+z} + \frac{y}{x+y+z} + \frac{z}{x+y+z}$$

$$= \frac{x+y+z}{x+y+z} = 1$$

26. $x + \frac{1}{x} = \sqrt{3}$

Cubing both sides,

$$x^3 + \frac{1}{x^3} + 3\left(x + \frac{1}{x}\right) = (\sqrt{3})^3$$

$$\Rightarrow \quad x^3 + \frac{1}{x^3} + 3\sqrt{3} = 3\sqrt{3}$$

$$\Rightarrow \quad x^3 + \frac{1}{x^3} = 0$$

Now, $x^{18} + x^{12} + x^6 + 1 = x^{12}(x^6 + 1) + 1(x^6 + 1)$

$$= (x^{12} + 1)(x^6 + 1)$$

$$= (x^{12} + 1) \cdot x^3\left(x^3 + \frac{1}{x^3}\right) = 0.$$

27. $(ad - bc)^2 + (ac + bd)^2 = a^2d^2 + b^2c^2 - 2abcd + a^2c^2 + b^2d^2 - 2abcd$

$$= a^2d^2 + b^2c^2 + a^2c^2 + b^2d^2$$

$$= a^2d^2 + b^2d^2 + b^2c^2 + a^2c^2$$

$$= d^2(a^2 + b^2) + c^2(b^2 + a^2)$$

$$= (a^2 + b^2)(c^2 + d^2) = 2 \times 1 = 2$$

28. $\frac{5x - 3}{x} + \frac{5x - 3}{y} + \frac{5z - 3}{z} = 0$

$$\Rightarrow \quad \frac{5x}{x} - \frac{3}{x} + \frac{5y}{y} - \frac{3}{y} + \frac{5z}{z} - \frac{3}{z} = 0$$

$$\Rightarrow \frac{3}{x}+\frac{3}{y}+\frac{3}{z}=15 \Rightarrow \frac{1}{x}+\frac{1}{y}+\frac{1}{z}=\frac{15}{3}=5.$$

30. $x - y = \dfrac{x+y}{7} = \dfrac{xy}{4} = k$

$\Rightarrow \quad x - y = k$

$\quad\quad x + y = 7k$

$\therefore \quad (x+y)^2 - (x-y)^2 = 49k^2 - k^2$

$\Rightarrow \quad 4xy = 48\ k^2$

$\Rightarrow \quad 16k = 48\ k^2$

$\Rightarrow \quad k = \dfrac{1}{3}$

$\therefore \quad xy = 4k = 4 \times \dfrac{1}{3} = \dfrac{4}{3}.$

31. $(x + y - z)^2 + (y + z - x)^2 + (z + x - y)^2 = 0$

$\Rightarrow (x + y - z) = 0$

32. $\dfrac{x^2}{yz}+\dfrac{y^2}{zx}+\dfrac{z^2}{xy} = \dfrac{x^3+y^3+z^3}{xyz} = \dfrac{3xyz}{xyz} = 3$

35. $\dfrac{1}{x+y} = \dfrac{1}{x}+\dfrac{1}{y} = \dfrac{y+x}{xy}$

$\Rightarrow (x + y)^2 = xy$

$\Rightarrow x^2 + 2xy + y^2 = xy$

$\Rightarrow x^2 + xy + y^2 = 0$

$\therefore x^3 - y^3 = (x - y)(x^2 + xy + y^2) = 0$

36. $a^2 + b^2 + c^2 = ab + bc + ca$

$\Rightarrow 2a^2 + 2b^2 + 2c^2 = 2ab + 2bc + 2ca$

$\Rightarrow a^2 - 2ab + b^2 + b^2 - 2bc + c^2 + c^2 - 2ac + a^2 = 0$

$\Rightarrow (a - b)^2 + (b - c)^2 + (c - a)^2 = 0$

$\Rightarrow a - b = 0 \Rightarrow a = b$

$\quad b - c = 0 \Rightarrow b = c$

$\quad c - a = 0 \Rightarrow c = a$

$\Rightarrow a = b = c$

$\therefore \quad \dfrac{a+c}{b} = \dfrac{a+a}{a} = 2$

37. $\frac{x}{a} = b - c; \frac{y}{b} = c - a; \frac{z}{c} = a - b$

Again, $b - c + c - a + a - b = 0$

$\therefore \left(\frac{x}{a}\right)^3 + \left(\frac{y}{b}\right)^3 + \left(\frac{z}{c}\right)^3$

$= (b - c)^3 + (c - a)^3 + (a - b)^3 = 3(b - c)(c - a)(a - b) = \frac{3xyz}{abc}$

38. $x^2 \geq 0$

$\therefore$ Minimum value $= 0 + \frac{1}{1} - 3 = -2.$

40. $\frac{x + \frac{1}{x}}{2} = M$

$\Rightarrow \quad x + \frac{1}{x} = 2M$

Required average $= \frac{x^2 + \frac{1}{x^2}}{2} = \frac{\left(x + \frac{1}{x}\right)^2 - 2}{2}$

$= \frac{4M^2 - 2}{2} = 2M^2 - 1.$

41. $a^2 + b^2 + c^2 = 2a - 2b - 2c - 3$

$\Rightarrow a^2 - 2a + b^2 + 2b + c^2 + 2c + 1 + 1 + 1 = 0$

$\Rightarrow (a^2 - 2a + 1) + (b^2 + 2b + 1) + (c^2 + 2c + 1) = 0$

$\Rightarrow (a - 1)^2 + (b + 1)^2 + (c + 1)^2 = 0$

$\Rightarrow a - 1 = 0 \Rightarrow a = 1$

$\Rightarrow b + 1 = 0 \Rightarrow b = -1$

and $c + 1 = 0 \Rightarrow c = -1$

$\therefore 2a - 3b + 4c = 2 + 3 - 4 = 1$

42. $(a - 3)^2 + (b - 4)^2 + (c - 9)^2 = 0$

$\Rightarrow a - 3 = 0 \Rightarrow a = 3$

$b - 4 = 0 \Rightarrow b = 4$

and $c - 9 = 0$

$\Rightarrow c = 9$

$\therefore \sqrt{a + b + c} = \sqrt{3 + 4 + 9} = \sqrt{16} = \pm 4$

43. $x + y = z \Rightarrow x + y + (-z) = 0$

$\therefore\ x^3 + y^3 - z^3 + 3xyz = x^3 + y^3 + (-z)^3 - 3x.y\ (-z) = 0$

45. $2^{x+3} = 32 = 2^5$

$\Rightarrow x + 3 = 5$

$\Rightarrow x = 5 - 3 = 2$

$\therefore\ 3^{x+1} = 3^3 = 27$

46. $x + \dfrac{1}{x} = 2$

$\Rightarrow x^2 + 1 = 2x$

$\Rightarrow x^2 - 2x + 1 = 0$

$\Rightarrow (x - 1)^2 = 0$

$\Rightarrow x = 1$

$\therefore\ x^2 + \dfrac{1}{x^3} = 1 + 1 - 2.$

47. $\dfrac{a}{b} + \dfrac{b}{a} = 1$

$\Rightarrow \dfrac{a^2 + b^2}{ab} = 1$

$\Rightarrow a^2 + b^2 = ab$

$\Rightarrow a^2 + b^2 - ab = 0$

$\therefore\ a^3 + b^3 = (a + b)(a^2 - ab + b^2) = 0$

48. $a^2 + b^2 + c^2 + 3 = 2a + 2b + 2c$

$\Rightarrow a^2 - 2a + 1 + b^2 - 2b + 1 + c^2 - 2c + 1 = 0$

$\Rightarrow (a - 1)^2 + (b - 1)^2 + (c - 1)^2 = 0$

$\Rightarrow a - 1 = 0 \Rightarrow a = 1;\ b - 1 = 0 \Rightarrow b = 1$

and, $c - 1 = 0 \Rightarrow c = 1$

$\therefore\ a + b + c = 3$

50. $x \propto \dfrac{1}{y^2 - 1}$

$\Rightarrow\ x = \dfrac{k}{y^2 - 1}$

Where k is a constant.

When $y = 10$, $x = 24$, then

$$\therefore\ 24 = \frac{k}{10^2 - 1} \Rightarrow 24 = \frac{k}{99} \Rightarrow k = 24 \times 99$$

When $y = 5$, then $x = \frac{k}{y^2 - 1} = \frac{24 \times 99}{5^2 - 1} = \frac{24 \times 99}{24} = 99.$

51. $m + \frac{1}{m - 2} = 4$

$$\Rightarrow (m - 2) + \frac{1}{m + 2} = 4 - 2 = 2$$

On squaring both sides,

$$(m - 2)^2 + \frac{1}{(m - 2)^2} + 2(m - 2)\left(\frac{1}{m - 2}\right) = 4$$

$$\Rightarrow (m - 2)^2 + \frac{1}{(m - 2)^2} = 4 - 2 = 2.$$

53. $y = 3x$

when, $x = 2$, $y = 6$

when, $x = -1$, $y = -3$.

54. $a^2 + b^2 + 2b + 4a + 5 = 0$

$\Rightarrow a^2 + 4a + b^2 + 2b + 5 = 0$

$\Rightarrow a^2 + 4a + 4 + b^2 + 2b + 1 = 0$

$\Rightarrow (a + 2)^2 + (b + 1)^2 = 0$

It is possible only when

$a + 2 = 0 \Rightarrow a = -2$ and, $b + 1 = 0 \Rightarrow b = -1$

$$\therefore\ \frac{a - b}{a + b} = \frac{-2 + 1}{-2 - 1} = \frac{-1}{-3} = \frac{1}{3}$$

55. $a + b + (-c) = 2.361 + 3.263 - 5.624 = 0$

$\therefore\ a^3 + b^3 + (-)^3 - 3ab\,(-c) = 0$

56. $x^3 - x^2y - xy^2 + y^3 = x^3 + y^3 - x^2y - xy^2$

$= (x + y)^3 - 3xy\,(x + y) - xy(x + y)$

$= (x + y)^3 - 4xy\,(x + y) = a^3 - 4b^2a.$

57. $(3a + 1)^2 + (b - 1)^2 + (2c - 3)^2 = 0$

$\Rightarrow 3a + 1 = 0 \quad \Rightarrow 3a = -1$

$\quad b - 1 = 0 \quad \Rightarrow b = 1$

$2c - 3 = 0 \quad \Rightarrow 2c = 3$

$\therefore \; 3a + b + 2c = -1 + 1 + 3 = 3$

59. $\dfrac{x}{2x^2 + 5x + 2} = \dfrac{1}{6}$

$\Rightarrow 2x^2 + 5x + 2 = 6x$

$\Rightarrow 2x^2 + 2 = 6x - 5x = x$

$\Rightarrow x^2 + 1 = \dfrac{x}{2}$

On dividing by x,

$\Rightarrow \; x + \dfrac{1}{x} = \dfrac{1}{2}$

60. When $x = 1$, $y = -1$, $-1 < 1$ when $x = 1$, $y = 1$

61. $\dfrac{2x - y}{x + 2y} = \dfrac{1}{2}$

$\Rightarrow 4x - 2y = x + 2y \Rightarrow 3x = 4y \Rightarrow \dfrac{x}{y} = \dfrac{4}{3}$

$$\therefore \quad \frac{3x \quad y}{3x + y} = \frac{y\left(3\frac{x}{y} - 1\right)}{y\left(3\frac{x}{y} + 1\right)} = \frac{3 \times \frac{4}{3} - 1}{3 \times \frac{4}{3} + 1} = \frac{4 - 1}{4 + 1} = \frac{3}{5}$$

62. Let the original number be $xy \Leftrightarrow 10x + y$

According to the question,

$$y = 2x + 1$$

and $\quad (10y + x) - (10x + y) = (10x + y) - 1$

or, $\quad 19x - 8y = 1$

or, $\quad 19x - 8(2x + 1) = 1 \qquad$ (Putting $y = 2x + 1$)

or, $\quad 3x = 9$

or, $\quad x = 3$

and $\quad y = 2x + 1 = 7$

$\therefore$ The original number = 37 **Ans.**

63. Let the two numbers be x and y respectively

According to the question,

$$\frac{x}{y} = \frac{5}{8}y$$

or, $x = \frac{25}{8}y$ ...(i)

Again, $\frac{25}{8}y + 35 = 4y$

or, $4y - \frac{25}{8}y = 35$

or, $32y - 25y = 35 \times 8$

or, $7y = 35 \times 8$

or, $y = 40.$

66. $\frac{x + y}{y} = \frac{13}{8}$

or, $8x + 8y = 13y$

or, $8x - 5y = 0$ ...(i)

also, $2x + 3y = 34$

or, $8x + 12y = 34 \times 4 = 136$ ...(ii)

Subtract equation (i) from equation (ii):

$17y = 136$

or, $y = \frac{136}{17} = 8$

Substitute it in equation (i) : $8x - (5 \times 8) = 0 \Rightarrow x = 5$

$\therefore\ 5y + 7x = (5 \times 8) + (7 \times 5) = 40 + 35 = 75.$

68. $2x + 3 + z = 55$ ... (i)

$x + z - y = 4$ ...(ii)

$y - x + z = 12$ ...(iii)

From equations (ii) and (iii)

$2z = 16 \Rightarrow z = 8$

From equation (ii), $x + 8 - y = 4$

or, $x = 4 - 8 + y = y - 4$

Putting this value in equation (i) we get

$2(y - 4) + 3y + 8 = 55$

or, $2y - 8 + 3y + 8 = 55$

or, $5y = 55 \Rightarrow y = 11.$

~~~~~~
~~~~~~

31. LOGARITHMS

IMPORTANT FACTS AND FORMULAE

I. Logarithm : If a is a positive real number, other than 1 and $a^m = x$, then we write : $m = \log_a x$ and we say that the value of log x to the base a is m.

Example:

(*i*) $10^3 = 1000 \Rightarrow \log_{10} 1000 = 3$ (*ii*) $3^4 = 81 \Rightarrow \log_3 81 = 4$

(*iii*) $2^{-3} = \frac{1}{8} \Rightarrow \log_2 \frac{1}{8} = -3$ (*iv*) $(.1)^2 = .01 \Rightarrow \log_{(.1)} .01 = 2.$

II. Properties of Logarithms :

1. $\log_a (xy) = \log_a x + \log_a y$
2. $\log_a \left(\frac{x}{y}\right) = \log_a x - \log_a y$
3. $\log_x x = 1$
4. $\log_a 1 = 0$
5. $\log_a (x^p) = p (\log_a x)$
6. $\log_a x = \frac{1}{\log_x a}$
7. $\log_a x = \frac{\log_b x}{\log_b a} = \frac{\log x}{\log a}.$

Remember: When base is not mentioned, it is taken as 10.

III. Common Logarithms: Logarithms to the base 10 are known as common logarithms.

IV. The logarithm of a number contains two parts, namely *characteristic* and *mantissa.*

Characteristic: The integral part of the logarithm of a number is called its ***characteristic.***

Case I : When the number is greater than 1.

In this case, the characteristic is one less than the number of digits in the left of the decimal point in the given number.

Case *II : When the number is less than 1.*

In this case, the characteristic is one more than the number of zeros between the decimal point and the first significant digit of the number and it is negative.

Instead of –1, –2, etc. we write, $\bar{1}$ (one bar), $\bar{2}$ (two bar), etc.

Example :

Number	*Characteristic*	*Number*	*Characteristic*
348.25	2	0.6173	$\bar{1}$
46.583	1	0.03125	$\bar{2}$
9.2193	0	0.00125	$\bar{3}$

Mantissa: The decimal part of the logarithm of a number is known is its ***mantissa.*** For mantissa, we look through log table.

SOLVED EXAMPLE

1. Evaluate: (*i*) $\log_3 27$ (*ii*) $\log_7\left(\frac{1}{343}\right)$ (*iii*) $\log_{100}(0.01)$

Sol. (*i*) Let $\log_3 27 = n$.

Then, $3^n = 27 = 3^3$ or $n = 3$. $\therefore \log_3 27 = 3$.

(*ii*) Let $\log_7\left(\frac{1}{343}\right) = n$

Then, $7^n = \frac{1}{343} = \frac{1}{7^3} = 7^{-3}$ or $n = -3$. $\therefore \log_7\left(\frac{1}{343}\right) = -3$.

(*iii*) Let $\log_{100}(0.01) = n$.

Then, $(100)^n = 0.01 = \frac{1}{100} = (100)^{-1}$ or $n = -1$

$\therefore \log_{100}(0.01) = -1$.

2. Simplify: $\left[\frac{1}{\log_{xy}(xyz)} + \frac{1}{\log_{yz}(xyz)} + \frac{1}{\log_{zx}(xyz)}\right]$

Sol. Given expression $= \log_{xyz}(xy) + \log_{xyz}(yz) + \log_{xyz}(zx)$

$= \log_{xyz}(xy \times yz \times zx) = \log_{xyz}(xyz)^2$

$= 2\log_{xyz}(xyz) = 2 \times 1 = 2$. $\left[\because \log_a x = \frac{1}{\log_x a}\right]$

3. If log 2 = 0.30103, find the number of digits in 2^{56}.

Sol. $\log(2^{56}) = 56 \log 2 = (56 \times 0.30103) = 16.85768$.

Its characteristic is 16. Hence, the number of digits in 2^{56} is 17.

EXERCISE

1. The value of $\log_2 16$ is:

(a) $\frac{1}{8}$ (b) 4 (c) 8 (d) 16

2. If $\log_x 4 = 0.4$, then the value of x is:

(a) 1 (b) 4 (c) 16 (d) 32

3. If $\log_x y = 100$ and $\log_2 x = 10$, then the value of y is:

(a) 2^{10} (b) 2^{100} (c) 2^{1000} (d) 2^{10000}

4. $\frac{\log\sqrt{8}}{\log 8}$ is equal to:

(a) $\frac{1}{\sqrt{8}}$ (b) $\frac{1}{4}$ (c) $\frac{1}{2}$ (d) $\frac{1}{8}$

5. Which of the following statements is not correct?

(a) $\log_{10} 10 = 1$ (b) $\log (2 + 3) = \log (2 \times 3)$

(c) $\log_{10} 1 = 0$ (d) $\log (1 + 2 + 3) = \log 1 + \log 2 + \log 3$

6. If $a^x = b^y$, then:

(a) $\log\frac{a}{b} = \frac{x}{y}$ (b) $\frac{\log a}{\log b} = \frac{x}{y}$ (c) $\frac{\log a}{\log b} = \frac{y}{x}$ (d) None of these

7. $2 \log_{10} 5 + \log_{10} 8 - \frac{1}{2} \log_{10} 4 = ?$

(a) 2 (b) 4 (c) $2 + 2 \log_{10} 2$ (d) $4 - 4 \log_{10} 2$

8. If $\log_a (ab) = x$, then $\log_b (ab)$ is :

(a) $\frac{1}{x}$ (b) $\frac{x}{x+1}$ (c) $\frac{x}{1-x}$ (d) $\frac{x}{x-1}$

9. If $\log 2 = x$, $\log 3 = y$ and $\log 7 = z$, then the value of $\log (4.\sqrt[3]{63})$ is:

(a) $2x + \frac{2}{3}y - \frac{1}{3}z$ (b) $2x + \frac{2}{3}y + \frac{1}{3}z$

(c) $2x - \frac{2}{3}y + \frac{1}{3}z$ (d) $-2x + \frac{2}{3}y + \frac{1}{3}z$

10. If $\log_{12} 27 = a$, then $\log_6 16$ is:

(a) $\frac{3-a}{4(3+a)}$ (b) $\frac{3+a}{4(3-a)}$ (c) $\frac{4(3+a)}{(3-a)}$ (d) $\frac{4(3-a)}{(3+a)}$

11. If $\log_{10} 2 = 0.3010$, the value of $\log_{10} 80$ is:
(*a*) 1.6020 (*b*) 1.9030 (*c*) 3.9030 (*d*) None of these

12. If $\log (0.57) = \bar{1}.756$, then the value of $\log 57 + \log (0.57)^3 + \log \sqrt{0.57}$ is:
(*a*) 0.902 (*b*) $\bar{2}.146$ (*c*) 1.902 (*d*) $\bar{1}.146$

13. If $\log_{10} 2 = 0.3010$, then $\log_2 10$ is equal to :
(*a*) $\frac{699}{301}$ (*b*) $\frac{1000}{301}$ (*c*) 0.3010 (*d*) 0.6990

14. If $\log 2 = 0.3010$ and $\log 3 = 0.4771$, the value of $\log_5 512$ is:
(*a*) 2.870 (*b*) 2.967 (*c*) 3.876 (*d*) 3.912

15. If $\log_{10} 5 + \log_{10} (5x + 1) = \log_{10} (x + 5) + 1$, then x is equal to:
(*a*) 1 (*b*) 3 (*c*) 5 (*d*) 10

16. If $\log_{10} 7 = a$, then $\log_{10}\left(\frac{1}{70}\right)$ is equal to:
(*a*) $-(1 + a)$ (*b*) $(1 + a)^{-1}$ (*c*) $\frac{a}{10}$ (*d*) $\frac{1}{10a}$

17. If $a = b^x$, $b = c^y$ and $c = a^z$, then the value of xyz is equal to:
(*a*) −1 (*b*) 0 (*c*) 1 (*d*) *abc*

18. If $\log_{10} 2 = 0.3010$, the value of $\log_{10} 5$ is:
(*a*) 0.3241 (*b*) 0.6911 (*c*) 0.6990 (*d*) 0.7525

19. If $\log 27 = 1.431$, then the value of $\log 9$ is:
(*a*) 0.934 (*b*) 0.945 (*c*) 0.954 (*d*) 0.958

20. If $\log 2 = 0.30103$, the number of digits in 2^{64} is :
(*a*) 18 (*b*) 19 (*c*) 20 (*d*) 21

ANSWERS

1	2	3	4	5	6	7	8	9	10
(*b*)	(*d*)	(*c*)	(*c*)	(*b*)	(*c*)	(*a*)	(*d*)	(*b*)	(*d*)
11	**12**	**13**	**14**	**15**	**16**	**17**	**18**	**19**	**20**
(*b*)	(*a*)	(*b*)	(*c*)	(*b*)	(*a*)	(*c*)	(*c*)	(*c*)	(*c*)

SOME SELECTED EXPLANATORY ANSWERS

1. Let $\log_2 16 = n$. Then, $2^n = 16 = 2^4 \Rightarrow n = 4$.

$\therefore \log_2 16 = n$.

2. $\log_x 4 = 0.4 \Leftrightarrow \log_x 4 = \frac{4}{10} = \frac{2}{5} \Leftrightarrow x^{2/5} = 4 \Leftrightarrow x = 4^{5/2} = (2^2)^{5/2}$

$$\Leftrightarrow x = 2^{\left(2\times\frac{5}{2}\right)} = 2^5 \Leftrightarrow x = 32.$$

3. $\log_2 x = 10 \Rightarrow x = 2^{10}$

$\therefore \log_x y = 100 \Rightarrow y = x^{100} = (2^{10})^{100} \Rightarrow y = 2^{1000}$.

4. $\frac{\log\sqrt{8}}{\log 8} = \frac{\log(8)^{1/2}}{\log 8} = \frac{\frac{1}{2}\log 8}{\log 8} = \frac{1}{2}$.

6. $a^x = b^y \Rightarrow \log a^x = \log b^y \Rightarrow x \log a = y \log b \Rightarrow \frac{\log a}{\log b} = \frac{y}{x}$.

7. $2\log_{10} 5 + \log_{10} 8 - \frac{1}{2}\log_{10} 4 = \log_{10}(5^2) + \log_{10} 8 - \log_{10}(4^{1/2})$

$$= \log_{10} 25 + \log_{10} 8 - \log_{10} 2 = \log_{10}\left(\frac{25\times 8}{2}\right) = \log_{10} 100 = 2.$$

9. $\log(4.\sqrt[3]{63}) = \log 4 + \log(\sqrt[3]{63}) = \log 4 + \log (63)^{1/3}$

$= \log (2^2) + \log (7 \times 3^2)^{1/3}$

$= 2\log 2 + \frac{1}{3}\log 7 + \frac{2}{3}\log 3 = 2x + \frac{1}{3}z + \frac{2}{3}y.$

11. $\log_{10} 80 = \log_{10}(8 \times 10) = \log_{10} 8 + \log_{10} 10$

$= \log_{10}(2^3) + 1 = 3\log_{10} 2 + 1$

$= (3 \times 0.3010) + 1 = 1.9030.$

13. $\log_2 10 = \frac{1}{\log_{10} 2} = \frac{1}{0.3010} = \frac{10000}{3010} = \frac{1000}{301}$.

16. $\log_{10}\left(\frac{1}{70}\right) = \log_{10} 1 - \log_{10} 70 = -\log_{10} (7 \times 10)$

$= -(\log_{10} 7 + \log_{10} 10) = -(a + 1).$

18. $\log_{10} 5 = \log_{10}\left(\frac{10}{2}\right) = \log_{10} 10 - \log_{10} 2 = 1 - \log_{10} 2$

$= (1 - 0.3010) = 0.6990.$

19. $\log 27 = 1.431 \Rightarrow \log (3^3) = 1.431 \Rightarrow 3 \log 3 = 1.431$

$\Rightarrow \log 3 = 0.477$

$\therefore \log 9 = \log (3^2) = 2 \log 3 = (2 \times 0.477) = 0.954.$

20. $\log (2^{64}) = 64 \times \log 2 = (64 \times 0.30103) = 19.26592.$

Its characteristic is 19. Hence, the number of digits in 2^{64} is 20.

~~~~~~
~~~~~~